From the Red To the Rio Grande

A History of the Free Will Baptists in Texas

1876 - 2014

Thurmon Murphy

Copyright 2017
By
Thurmon Murphy

ISBN 978-1-940609-83-6
Soft cover

All rights reserved
No part of this book may be reproduced or transmitted in any form or by any means, electronic or mechanical, including photocopying, recording, or by any information storage and retrieval system, without permission in writing from the copyright owner.
This book was printed in the United States of America.
To order additional copies of this book contact:

Thurmon Murphy
5037 Lindale Drive
Wichita Falls, Texas 76310-2544

FWB Publications
Columbus, Ohio

FWB

Preface

In June of 2013, at the ninety-ninth annual session of the Texas State Association of Free Will Baptists, I was asked to write a history of the Free Will Baptist work in Texas for the one hundredth session of the association, which was coming up in 2014. The committee which asked me to do the writing was expecting a small booklet of sixteen to eighteen pages, and they were expecting it by June of 2014. They didn't get what they were expecting, though I did provide them with a preview booklet of what was to come. On my own I decided to write a book on the history of the work in Texas, rather than a booklet, one that would give a more complete story than anyone had a right to expect. I did this because the history of the Free Will Baptist work in Texas needed to be preserved, and the story would be exciting. I felt rather strongly about this and also believed that no one else would write such a story. I laid aside temporarily the writing projects on which I was already working, such as the book on feet washing.

The Texas State Association provided no funding for the project. For one thing there was no money with which to fund such a project. Therefore, because this has been a labor of love for me, I have spent three and a half years traveling the state of Texas, interviewing people, photographing churches and old church sites, gathering rare photographs, minutes, and other documents and, of course, countless days in my office doing the actual writing. I have on three occasions visited the Free Will Baptist Historical Collection at Welch College in Nashville, Tennessee, once spending three days there photocopying fifteen hundred pages of historical material. I owe a huge debt of gratitude to librarian Carol Reid, and her clerks. They have often e-mailed additional photocopies to me and met every request for information I made of them. Dr. Robert E. Picirilli, who voluntarily catalogues all of the historical material in the historical collection, has been invaluable with his assistance. He is a denominational treasure. I have visited with and consulted numerous times with librarian Nancy Draper at Randall University in Moore, Oklahoma. I owe a debt of gratitude to her for helping me find information and for e-mailing copies of various documents to me. Gregory McCarthy, pastor of a Free Will Baptist Church in Indianapolis, Indiana, a history buff himself, has been very helpful in supplying me with copies of many old documents, especially copies of *The Morning Star,* a weekly newspaper of the Randall Movement of Free Will Baptists. He put me on to the fact that the earliest Free Will Baptist churches in Texas were black churches, something which I had already come to suspect.

Bates College in Lewiston, Maine, a former Free Will Baptist school, has been helpful in enabling me to locate information. I wish I had had the funds to visit the historical collection of the American Baptist Convention, the old Northern Baptist Convention with which Free Will Baptists merged in 1910-1911. Their historical materials have been moved to Atlanta, Georgia.

I want to thank three additional people who have also been of special help to me. Mary Kathryn Inbody, a retired librarian in Edmond, Oklahoma, has been especially helpful in assisting me in some important research, doing the initial proofreading for me, and providing some editorial suggestions. Dr. Teressa Voltz, a member of the Texas State Board of Christian Education, has done an excellent job of doing the final proofreading of the manuscript. Then, there is Lacy Dedear Murphy, of Georgetown, Texas, who has served as the editor of the book. The work and encouragement of these three ladies have been invaluable to me.

Then, of course, there is my family, especially my wife Karen, who have sacrificed so I could do the work and take the time necessary to complete this project.

As has been characteristic of me for fifty years, I have not used the title Reverend with the names of ministers. I hope no one is offended. "Reverend" does appear in copies of written reports where it was used by the authors of the reports.

I have purposely tried to do very little editorializing, except in the last chapter where I try to evaluate the Free Will Baptist work in Texas and take a look at what the future possibly holds for us. Some things needed to be said which no one else was going to say, at least in print.

Unfortunately, some of the people from whom I tried to gather biographical information did not supply it, even after several appeals, and, therefore, do not have profiles in the book.

Some of the material in this book will be distasteful. Some would suggest that such information should have been omitted from the book because it is offensive to them. It is offensive to me. This material is included because it is part of the history of Texas Free Will Baptists. Some will object to the inclusion of the chapter on women preachers from Texas. This, too, is part of our history and is therefore included.

I have donated the photographs, minutes, and other documents collected for this book to the Free Will Baptist Historical Collection at Welch College for the sake of future researchers. I encourage district clerks and the clerk of the state association to mail copies of all minutes and other important documents to the collection annually. Church clerks or pastors should also send important documents to the collection. What is fresh today will be history tomorrow. It is deeply regrettable that entire boxes of old minutes of some churches and associations have been thrown away. Thus, much of our history has been forever lost to us.

It is my hope that you will enjoy reading the history of the Free Will Baptists in Texas. Hopefully, this book will help you understand and appreciate your denominational heritage. Perhaps it will help you see where there needs to be a change of direction. The book should serve as a valuable reference tool to some of you. It has been my pleasure to do this for you.

Table of Contents

Chapter 1	The Beginnings: 1870 to 1914	Page 1
Chapter 2	The State Association (1915) to the National Association (1935)	Page 31
Chapter 3	1936 to 1950	Page 71
Chapter 4	1951 to 1975	Page 115
Chapter 5	1976 to 1990	Page 133
Chapter 6	1991 to 2000	Page 159
Chapter 7	2001 to 2014	Page 171
Chapter 8	Character Profiles	Page 183
Chapter 9	Notable Churches	Page 281
Chapter 10	Texas Home Missions	Page 321
Chapter 11	Missionaries from Texas	Page 343
Chapter 12	Women's Work, Woman's Auxiliary, Texas Women Active for Christ	Page 377
Chapter 13	Texas' Women Preachers	Page 389
Chapter 14	An Evaluation and Outlook	Page 407
Addendum 1	Closed Churches in Texas	Page 431
Addendum 2	Denominational Distinctives	Page 439
Addendum 3	Free Baptists, Freewill Baptists, Free Will Baptists	Page 441
Addendum 4	The Free Will Baptist Logo	Page 447

Chapter One

The Early Beginnings
1870 to 1914

For the sake of those less familiar with the history of Free Will Baptists in America we must give a little background. Free Will Baptists in America are the result of two different groups. The earlier group resulted from the work of Paul Palmer who started a Free Will Baptist church in North Carolina in 1727. This group is generally referred to as the Palmer Movement. The second group was started by Benjamin Randall in New Durham, New Hampshire, in 1780, often referred to as the Randall Movement.[1] The Free Will Baptist work in Texas began as the result of missionaries sent to Texas by the General Conference of Free Will Baptists[2], the Randall Movement, beginning in 1870. During the formative years of the work in Texas many of the state leaders were men from the North who were trained in Free Will Baptist schools. In addition to Stewart there were men such as Z. B. Dally, S. L. Morris, and J. J. Tatum, to name a few. Shortly after Stewart arrived in East Texas, Free Will Baptist ministers began migrating into Texas from the South and planting churches. The Randall movement influenced Texas Free Will Baptists in many ways, but perhaps the greatest was in giving us the *Free Will Baptist Treatise*. Two additional things should be noted: one is that the denomination went by the name Free Baptists; and secondly, those churches did not practice feet washing until, one by one they began to adopt the practice sometime around the middle of the Twentieth Century.

It is often said that Texas is like a whole other country. In fact, Texas was a country, a sovereign nation, a republic, for ten years, from March 2, 1836 to February 19, 1845, when Texas joined the Union as a state. Texas is big, diverse, unique. Texas is known all over the world, envied by many, and scorned by some. It is a vast land of legendary adventures, climactic battles, and world famous leaders. Who doesn't know the names of Stephen F. Austin, Sam Houston, William Barrett Travis, Jim Bowie, David Crockett, Lyndon Baines Johnson, Audie Murphy, and George Bush, both of them? Texas is a land of history, both good and bad. It has made its imprint on the world. And, yes, Texas is a land of myths; think of Pecos Bill.

Into this vast land, Texas, from the Native American word *tejas*, meaning "friendly," came pioneer settlers from the United States, Europe and Asia. Sadly, slaves were forcefully brought from the slave states and from Africa. Among the peoples coming here in search of new land, freedom, and opportunity, were farmers, ranchers, oil men, business men, explorers, soldiers of fortune, adventurers, entrepreneurs, and more. Along with them came a different sort of men, men

---

[1] William F. Davidson, *Free Will Baptists in America 1727-1984* (Randall House Publications, Nashville, Tennessee, 1985) page 367.
[2] The General Conference was the broadest body of Free Will Baptists at the time, similar to our current National Association. "Broadest" is the correct word here, rather than "highest." A district association is a broader body than a local church, not a higher body; a state association is a broader body than a district association, not a higher body; and the National Association is a broader body than a state association, not a higher body.

who were not looking for fortune, land, buffalo hides, oil, or fame. They were looking for souls. They came here to preach the gospel of Jesus Christ, to win followers to him, and to build churches. They were Baptists, Methodists, Presbyterians, Lutherans, and a lesser known group -- Free Will Baptists.

In order to give ourselves a little perspective we should look at the growing population of Texas at the time of the beginning of the Free Will Baptist work here. The first federal census was taken in Texas in 1850 and it listed the population of the state at 212,592, not counting Native Americans. By 1860 the population had tripled to 604,215 as settlers poured into the state. Settlement slowed down considerably from 1860 to 1870 because of the Civil War. The 1870 population, when the first church was planted in Lancaster, was 818,579. After 1870 the population exploded to 1,591,749 by 1880; 2,235,527 by 1890; and 3,048,710 by 1900. Adding more perspective is the fact that the population of Dallas was 3,000 (an estimation) in 1870; 10,358 in 1880; 38,067 in 1890; and 42,638 in 1900.

It is a little difficult to pinpoint just when the earliest Free Will Baptists came to Texas, or their exact identity. We will have to rely on the identified names and information available. All of them were important and their names and accomplishments should never be forgotten, nor what they did. They lit the spark that became a flame. Once that initial spark was lit there was an explosion of Free Will Baptists in Texas, as we will soon see.

Damon Dodd, in *The Free Will Baptist Story,* says, "Free Will Baptist work had been started in Texas by Elder J. T. Eason. One of the earliest and most widely known Free Will Baptist preachers of Texas was Elder Charles Stetson, better known as the 'cowboy' preacher. He published a paper known as the 'Free Will Baptist Banner.' "[3] Unfortunately Dodd did not tell us more and he did not footnote his source. The names of Elders Eason and Stetson do not appear in any of the minutes now available to us. It is highly probably that these were black churches, of which we will learn shortly.

It is not generally known that the earliest Free Will Baptist work in Texas was an effort to reach black people. This was a missionary effort of the Randall movement of Free Will Baptists of New England. The St. Paul Free Will Baptist Church was started in Lancaster, Texas, in 1870, six years before the first white Free Will Baptist church was founded in East Texas. Soon there were numerous other black Free Will Baptist churches, enough to organize two quarterly meetings. In 1891 these two quarterly meetings formed the Northern Texas Yearly Meeting, following the organizational model of the Randall Movement. This yearly meeting is described later in this chapter.

The August 13, 1873 *The Morning Star*[4] contained a letter written by a white minister working in Texas. His name and place of residence were omitted by the *Morning Star* for what the paper called "obvious reasons." Part of his letter, though not flattering to Texans, is given here:

> I am in Texas and getting along as well as could be expected. The society is dull, and the people seem to have a form of religion, but they are so prejudiced against the colored people and Yankees, that they can have but a little of the love of Christ in their hearts. War and bitterness seem to fill their hearts.[5] In some localities they have burned down the school houses built for the colored people, and do all they can to prevent their having any

---

[3] Damon C. Dodd, *The Free Will Baptist Story* [hereafter called *The Free Will Baptist Story*](Executive Department of the National Association of Free Will Baptists, Nashville, Tennessee, 1956) page 60.
[4] *The Morning Star,* a weekly newspaper, was the official publication of the Randall Movement.
[5] The Civil War had ended only eight years earlier.

school. If a Yankee preaches he must look out for himself, or he will have trouble.... I think that I shall organize two Freewill Baptist churches soon. I find also many colored people that want to be organized into a church. They like the Freewill doctrine because it is the teaching of the Bible. There are some of the Close Communionists that are coming over. There are some colored preachers that want to become Freewill Baptists, but they have been ordained in the close faith. We are very much in want of some copies of the Treatise and Register, which I will send for as soon as I get some money.

As noted above the Free Will Baptist work came about as a result of both Palmer and the Randall movements. These two influences gave birth to much of the diversity among Free Will Baptists, including Texas Free Will Baptists. That diversity was seen in that, for the most part, ministers from the northern movement were better educated than their counterparts in the south, due to the large number of schools they had and the fact that ministers were expected to be trained for the ministry. Additionally, they came from an area of the country where Free Will Baptists generally had larger church buildings to accommodate larger congregations and they were usually constructed in much better locations.

The Texas Association of Free Will Baptists, 1878

The available records indicate that Angus McAllister Stewart, generally known as A. M. Stewart, a missionary from the Randall Movement, started the white Free Will Baptist work in East Texas. He first organized the Liberty Free Will Baptist Church in the town of Clayton,[6] Panola County, in 1876, long celebrated as the first (white) Free Will Baptist church in the state of Texas. The population of Panola County was 10,119 in 1870. Reaching beyond the immediate vicinity of Clayton, Stewart gathered and organized a church in Beckville (which later disbanded), along with the Good Hope and Union Springs churches in Rusk County. Extending the work still further he organized the Lone Star church in the Lone Star community, and the Rape's Chapel church, both in Cherokee County. Several of the churches planted by Stewart continue in existence well into the Twenty-first Century.

James (Jim) Pierce Lunsford,[7] a Civil War veteran, came to Texas from Alabama by wagon train in 1876 and settled in Cherokee County. Later he moved to Rusk County where he started the Old Prospect church in 1887. Later, when they met in the Mount Union school house, the name of the church was changed to Mount Union Free Will Baptist Church. Lunsford also organized a church in Mt. Pleasant. Mount Union continues its ministry even now.

Very soon there was a need for the churches to form a quarterly meeting. The quarterly meeting was an organization which Benjamin Randall, the founder of the northern movement of Free Will Baptists, wisely put in place in the late 1800's. The quarterly meetings provided a sense of identity to the churches, enabled the pastors and church members opportunity for fellowship with like-minded people, provided a means of helping weaker churches in need, and made it possible for the churches to accomplish together what one church could not do alone. History has shown that churches which exist alone in isolation from other churches tend to die off sooner than

---

[6] Clayton, Texas, located at the junction of State Highway 315 and Farm Road 1970, sixteen miles southwest of Carthage in southwestern Panola County, was first settled around 1845.

[7] Much of the information about James Pierce Lunsford was supplied by Mary A. Wharton of Nacogdoches, Texas, via telephone conversation and a personal letter received on January 17, 2014. She also supplied the photograph of Pastor Lunsford. The copy of the photograph had to be made through the glass cover of the picture frame because the photo itself was too brittle to remove from the frame.

they would otherwise. Randall knew that the quarterly meetings, what we now call district associations, quarterly conferences in some areas, were necessary for cohesiveness, strength, and identity as a movement. In 1878 the Texas churches organized the Texas Freewill Baptist Association, often simply called the Texas Association. In 1954 it changed its name to the East Texas District Association of Free Will Baptist Churches

When missionary A. M. Stewart moved from East Texas to the Bryan area and began planting churches in Central Texas those churches also became members of the Texas Association. This affiliation of churches in East Texas and Central Texas in the same association continued well into the Twentieth Century. They also participated together in the ministry of the East Texas Youth Camp for many years.

The Free Will Baptist Association, 1880

The 1880 edition of the *Freewill Baptist Register,* a book published every three years and which listed all the statistics for the denomination, listed two associations in Texas. One of them was the Texas Freewill Baptist Association, which became the East Texas District Association mentioned above. The other one was called The Freewill Baptist Association. Here is what is stated about it: "The Freewill Baptist Association in Texas held its annual meeting at Cross Roads Church, Harrison Co., and the minutes give the names of 33 ministers, but the number of churches and members is not reported." At this writing we have no further information on this association. It is highly likely that this was an association of black churches.

Perhaps not related to either of the associations listed above, there is a report in the March 17, 1880, issue of *The Morning Star* which is of interest: "Rev. J. A. Halloway reports that he is holding meetings on the Texas frontier, and has already organized three churches—the Grayham, the Pleasant Hill and the North Bend, with an aggregate membership of 80 persons. The Grayham church was organized four years ago, and has sent out one licensed minister."

Northern Texas Yearly Meeting, 1891

Benjamin Randall, the founder of the Free Will Baptist movement in the North in 1780 wisely established the quarterly meeting system for the fledgling denomination. Two or more quarterly meetings were organized into yearly meetings which, in turn, formed the General Conference, the broadest body of Free Will Baptists, similar to our own National Association. Several yearly meetings were organized in Texas, reflecting the Randall model.

One of these yearly meetings was the Northern Texas Yearly Meeting, which consisted of two quarterly meetings. As noted above the first church to have been started was the St. Paul Freewill Baptist Church in Lancaster, which was founded in 1870.[8] This church continues to serve Lancaster to this day and is the longest existing Free Will Baptist church in the state. Soon other churches were started in the Dallas area and, as a result, the Northwest Texas Quarterly Meeting[9] was organized in 1883. The number of churches continued to grow and as a result another quarterly meeting was organized, the Dallas Quarterly Meeting. The two quarterly meetings formed the Northern Texas Yearly Meeting in 1891. Again, these churches were the result of the missionary efforts of the Randall Movement of Free Will Baptists.

---

[8] From "St. Paul Freewill Baptist Church, 1870 - 1985," a short history of the church, page 3.
[9] It was called the Western District Quarterly Meeting from 1892 to 1998, when the name reverted back to Northwest Texas Quarterly Meeting.

The Northwest Texas Quarterly Meeting consisted of at least the following churches up until 1911: Arlington, Carrolton, Ebenezer, Mt. Olive 1, Mt. Olive 2, Mt. Pilgrim (in McKinney), Randall (in Dallas, corner of Cochrane and Hall Streets), St. Paul (in Lancaster), Goodwill (in Ferris), Bethel Chapel, Lilly Hill, Potter Creek, Spring Hill, Elizabeth Chapel, Walnut Spring, St. James, Chapel Hill, and Bethlehem.

The Dallas Quarterly Meeting was composed of the following churches: Mt. Carrol, Mt. Zion, New Zion, Randall, St. Matthew, St. Paul, Mt. Pilgrim, Mt. Pleasant, Friendship, Miller's Chapel, and Taylor's Chapel.

It seems that another quarterly meeting was soon organized, the East Texas Quarterly Meeting, not to be confused with the East Texas District Association. Churches in this quarterly meeting were Cedar Springs, Lilly Hill, Longview Blossom, Spencer's Chapel, and Spring Hill. It may be that some of the churches at one time or another changed quarterly meetings. The churches in these quarterly meetings were black churches[10] and they were never members of the broader Free Will Baptist work in Texas. Yet they were and still are Free Will Baptists. They were the result of the missionary efforts of the Randall movement and used the *Free Will Baptist Treatise*. The Randall movement had been very active in reaching America's black people from early on, had vigorously fought slavery, and had founded Storer College in 1867 at Harper's Ferry, West Virginia, specifically for black people. Whether the white Free Will Baptists of Texas should have reached out to embrace them is a matter of discussion. Texas, being one of the Confederate states, had very strong feelings about black people and those feelings were shared by many white Free Will Baptists. After more than a hundred years, with changes in the culture, attitudes, and laws, it is hard to judge them. Would we reach out to them now in an effort to embrace them and include them in the larger Free Will Baptist work? This question is worthy of discussion for the simple fact that the black Free Will Baptist work is still alive and well in Texas.

These black Free Will Baptist churches belong to the Northern Texas Yearly Meeting which, along with other yearly meetings, belong to the United American Free Will Baptist Association.[11]

Western Texas Yearly Meeting

The Western Texas Yearly Meeting consisted of two quarterly meetings. One of them was the Western Texas Quarterly Meeting. We have no minutes of either of these quarterly meetings. Statistics for them, however, are given in the *Freewill Baptist Register* for the years 1898 to 1908. The following churches were members during all or part of that time: Bee Rock, Charity Hill, Delmar, Easley's Chapel, Jones Chapel, Liberty, Macedonia, Mt. Olive, New Salem, Salt Springs, Shady Grove, Energy, and Elm Grove. The Register does not give the locations of the churches, but it does give the post offices of the pastors. The pastors, who did not always live in the same community as their churches, resided in Temple, Gustine, Cisco, Comanche, Highland, Carbon, Belton, Floydada, Deleon, Acton, and Dublin. The Easley's Chapel, Salt Springs, and New Salem churches were listed as members of the West Texas Association in 1910 (see below).

---

[10] I am indebted to Free Will Baptist pastor Gregory K. McCarty, of Indianapolis, Indiana, for calling my attention to this and supplying me with copies of the *Freewill Baptist Register* in which they are listed. The *Register* was published every three years (the General Conference met every three years) and contained the statistics for the Free Will Baptist denomination.

[11] The United American Free Will Baptist Association consists of 1800 Free Will Baptist churches worldwide and it owns and operates United American Free Will Baptist Bible College in Kinston, North Carolina.

The other quarterly meeting was the Cypress Ridge Quarterly Meeting. We have no minutes of this quarterly meeting, either. However, we find the statistics for it in the *Freewill Baptist Register,* along with those of the Western Texas Quarterly Meeting. Churches which were members of the Cypress Ridge Quarterly Meeting included the following: Cedar Spring, Longview Blossom, Lily Hill, Mt. Zion, Pleasant Hill #1, Pleasant Hill # 2, Potter's Creek, Spring Hill, St. James, and Spencer's Chapel. The mailing addresses for the pastors were all in Longview and Marshall.

The Denton Creek Association, 1889

The Denton Creek Association was initially composed of four churches northwest of Dallas.[12] They were the Bethel, Big Springs, Corinth, and DeSoto churches. These are the same four churches which are listed in the 1894 *Freewill Baptist Register.* Big Springs should not be confused with the city of Big Spring, located on I-20, east of Midland in West Texas. One of the ministers in the association was J. W. Johnson, who was born on August 4, 1845, and passed away on July 24, 1899. He is buried in the King Cemetery, Henderson County, Texas. An inscription on his tombstone reads "Co K3 Texas Cav C.S.A."[13] This indicates that he served in the Texas Cavalry during the Civil War on the side of the Confederate States of America. The total membership in the association in 1888 was 143. However, the association had grown considerably by 1893. The January 21, 1893 issue of the *Morning Star* stated that there were fifteen churches in the association, with a total membership of 500, twenty-three ordained ministers, and one licensed minister. The 1894 *Freewill Baptist Register* listed the following ministers as members of the association: L. W. Miller,[14] J. W. Johnson, F. T. Eason, F. L. Phillips, and H. Bryant. The late Oklahoma pastor Bob Ketchum had several minutes of the Denton Creek Association, but these were lost to us after his death. The Denton Creek Association was not listed in the Free Will Baptist Register after 1894.

---

[12] *Free Baptist Cyclopaedia*, page 642.
[13] Alton E. Loveless, *Handbook of Historical Free Will Baptist Burial Places* (Free Will Baptist Publications, Columbus, Ohio, 2013) page 402.
[14] L. W. Miller started the New Hope Free Will Baptist Church, out of Weatherford, Texas, circa 1894, according to an article in the January, 1941, *Free Will Baptist Gem*.

Undated photo of a Southeast Texas quarterly meeting

The Southeast Texas Association, 1889

I have copies of the minutes of three annual sessions of the Southeast Texas Free Will Baptist Association, 1941, 1942, and 1958. The 1941 and 1942 minutes state that they are of the 53rd and 54th annual sessions, respectively. That would mean that the first annual session would have been in 1889.

The 1941 minutes list four churches in the Southeast Texas Association: Bonami, Friendship, Cairo Springs, and China Grove. The State of Churches committee reported that "regular monthly services are held at each church by T. W. Smith." At the time Brother Smith seems to have been the only preacher in the association, serving all four churches. The report of the Ministerial Character committee seems to confirm this by stating "We, your Committee on Ministers, find our minister doing all he can in the work of Christ."[15] The situation was similar the following year, 1942, which prompted Mrs. T. W. Smith to make "a good talk on the Scarcity of Ministers."[16] Her husband, T. W. Smith gave most of the committee reports. That year the association could not send a delegate to the state association, but they did send a letter of explanation and one dollar along with the letter. The Articles of Faith for 1941 and 42 list two ordinances, baptism and the Lord's Supper.

The third session of which we have minutes convened October 10-12, 1958, with the Bonami Free Will Baptist Church near Bonami, Texas. The minutes list only two ministers, one ordained and one licensed: R. E. (Bob) Sheffield, of Newton, Texas, who was ordained, and L. G. Sweat, of Kirbyville, Texas, who was licensed. The State of Churches report states, "We have only two churches in working order. We have one pastor and one assistant pastor." The Obituary Report, however, lists three deceased members of the China Grove Free Will Baptist Church. The Finance Committee report stated, "Cairo Springs Church is community owned and valued at $2000.00. Bonami is owned by Free Will Baptist (sic) and valued at $5800.00."

---

[15] Minutes of the 53rd Annual Session of the Southeast Texas Free Will Baptist Association, 1941, page 2.
[16] Minutes of the 54th Annual Session of the Southeast Texas Free Will Baptist Association, 1942, page 3.

The partial list of ministers in the minutes of the 1928 Texas State Association meeting gives the names of two ministers from Kirbyville: J. T. Lee and A. W. West. The minutes of the 1930 session of the Texas (East Texas) Association of Free Will Baptists mentions two ministers from the Southeast Texas Association: F. Whitaker and J. W. Doster. The minutes of the 1947 Texas State Association indicate that the Southeast Texas Association represented by letter and three delegates. The statistical table mentioned that the association had four churches, and the directory lists one pastor, Alvin Young, of Kirbyville, Texas.

One interesting item is that, even though the association's Articles of Faith do not list feet washing, one of the resolutions passed was: "We resolve that we stress the Ordinances of the Lord's Supper and Washing of the Saints' Feet, to each other; that we may bring all into these services."

Bonami is sixty miles north of Beaumont in east central Jasper County. An online site says, "While there is no town center today an abandoned sawmill and the Freewill Baptist Church are reminders of the once vital town." Ned Graham remembers preaching at the church and he also remembers that there was a family by the name of Ford in the church. The minutes mention several Fords: Thelma, Howard, Mary Francis, and Barbara.

Kirbyville is on Trout Creek, U.S. Highway 96, eighteen miles south of Jasper in east central Jasper County.

There is a China Grove, Texas, located twelve miles east of San Antonio and fourteen miles west of La Vernia on Highway 87 in Bexar County. This may or may not be the China Grove where the above referenced China Grove Free Will Baptist Church was located.

The West Texas Association, 1891

I have one copy of the minutes of the West Texas Association. The minutes are of the nineteenth annual session which convened at the Easley's Chapel Free Will Baptist Church in Comanche County, Texas, September 2-3, 1910. That would mean that the first annual session would have been held in 1891. The moderator was A. J. Barnett, Carbon, Texas, R. F. D. No. 2, and the clerk was S. P. Easley, Comanche, Texas, R. F. D. No. 4. The association was composed of three churches:
- Salt Springs Church, located six miles each of Comanche,
- Easley's Chapel at Vandyke, Texas, which would later move south and become Easley's Chapel at Gartman's View, and the
- Liberty Hill Church, the location of which is unknown to me.

The annual report shows the following amounts paid to the pastors for their year's work in the ministry: Salt Springs, $111.16; Liberty Hill, $5.50, and Easley's Chapel, $28.45. In addition, Liberty Hill had given $10.00 to missions.

Ministers on the "Ministerial Roll" were: J. C. Creamer, Sister M. J. Creamer, R. B. Easley, A. J. Barnett, T. A. Strain, J. C. Harvey, and J. C. Withers. However, Miss Lizzie Lawless was listed as the pastor of Easley's Chapel. Miss Lawless had been licensed in 1909 at Cross, Texas, and would be ordained in 1911 at North Zulch. This is the Miss Lizzie which became Mrs. Hiram M. McAdams on April 19, 1911, and went on to become the well-known Free Will Baptist evangelist Lizzie McAdams.

Among the several resolutions passed was this one: "Realizing the importance of Christian education and the necessity of a closer fellowship relation of our people, we heartily endorse the

Free Will Baptist News and recommend that it be read by every Free Will Baptist family." The Free Will Baptist News was published in Bryan, Texas, by S. L. Morris.

An interesting article in the constitution was: "We believe it is appointedly against the laws of Christ to make His church a legislative body; we therefore refuse to correspond with other denominations in their legislative bodies."

The minutes of the 1910 meeting contain the following covenant, which is of interest partly because it is different than our present church covenant:

Covenant

1. We believe that the unions of Christians in a visible church is sanctioned by the teachings of Christ and the practice of His apostles and that it is adopted to promote piety and increase Christian influence. We do now heartily enter into covenant before God and with each other.
2. We will constantly strive to maintain true piety in our own hearts, keep ourselves in vital communion with God and commend religion to others, not only in words, but by means of a devout spirit and holy example, always careful of each other's reputation and usefulness.
3. We will watch over each other in a spirit of true charity, seeking to share each other's burdens, assist the needy, strengthen the weak, encourage the despondent, sympathize with the sorrowful, reprove the erring, win back the straying to duty, maintain wholesome discipline and receive Christian admonition in meekness, keep the unity of the spirit in the bond of peace, and cheerfully submit to such regulations as the majority may approve. We will contribute according to our ability for pastorial (sic) support, maintain secret and family prayer, and aid by our presence and otherwise in sustaining public and social worship.
4. We will give an active and consistent support to the great causes that aim to promote religion; we will refuse all sanction to those worldly amusements that tends to lessen piety in ourselves or weaken christian (sic) influence over others so that religion be not reproached on our account. May He who has promised His help, enable us to keep His covenant, and grant us grace to be faithful in all things until He has gathered us unto Himself and crown us with final victory. Amen.

Another item in the 1910 minutes of the West Texas Association which catches our attention is called "Rules of Ordination." They appear to be questions to be asked of those who are candidates for ordination to the gospel ministry. The questions are given, and then the answers. The questions, answers, as well as what isn't asked, say a lot about the association. For your edification, they are:

Do you believe in total depravity of the human heart? Answer -- No.
Do you believe that infants are saved while in a state of innocence, as Adam was before he transgressed? Answer -- I do.
Do you believe in free and full salvation to all who will accept it on gospel terms? -- I do.
Do you believe that communion and footwashing are gospel ordinances of Christ and are to be practiced until His coming? Answer -- I do.
Do you believe that the burial of a believer in Christ in water, after he has been baptism (sic) into Christ by the Holy Ghost, is the only gospel baptism? Answer -- I do.
Will you solemnly pledge yourself to preach and practice the same, God being your helper? -- I will by the help of God.
Do you believe none will be saved but those who persevere in holiness to the end? Answer -- I do.

There is no mention in these 1910 minutes of the merger with the Northern Baptists which occurred in 1910-11. There is, however, a reference that R. B. Easley was elected as a delegate to the Southwestern Convention, mentioned below.

The West Fork District Association, circa 1892

It is difficult to establish firmly the date of the organization of the West Fork District Association. According to several reports was organized in 1889. The earliest minutes we have, such as the 1901 minutes, state that the 1901 session was the tenth annual session, which, if true, would indicate that the association was organized in 1892. However, later minutes would give a different date. For instance, the 1934 minutes indicate that the 1934 meeting was the 45th annual session. If true, the West Fork was organized in 1890. Subsequent minutes concur with that date. J. A. Ford, brother of the founder of the New Salem Free Will Baptist Church in Decatur, wrote in an article in *The Morning Star*[17] that the West Fork was organized in 1890. So far we cannot establish with certainty exactly when the West Fork was organized.

Two of the ministers who were instrumental in organizing the West Fork Association were Josephus Wesley Ford and his brother, J. A. Ford. Some of the earliest churches in the association were the Rock Hill Church in Reno, Parker County, which may have been the same as the Walnut Creek Church; Union Grove, located at Briar in Parker County, which may have been the same as the Union Grove Church; the Glendale Church, located in Sunset, Montague County; the Macedonia Church, located in Boonesville, Wise County; and Mount Olive, located in Willow Point, Jack County. New Salem in Decatur, Wise County, was organized in 1893 and joined the West Fork. Three additional churches joined the West Fork in 1901: Bluff Spring, Azle, Parker County; Catlett Creek, ten miles east of Decatur, Wise County; and New Hope, out of Weatherford, Parker County. L. W. Miller organized the New Hope church in 1891 but the church didn't join until ten years later. The Gartman's View Church, out of Comanche, was previously a member of the old West Texas Association but joined the West Fork when the West Texas Association folded. In his 1891 diary J. A. Ford mentioned that he had organized a church in the Huff Schoolhouse. The name of the church and its location are unknown.[18]

The tabernacle, now in a pasture, is all that is left of the New Hope Free Will Baptist Church in Parker County, out of Weatherford, Texas.

The *Freewill Baptist Register* for the year 1909 listed the following churches as members of the West Fork: Rock Hill, New Hope, Blewin Chapel, New Salem, Bethel, Bluff Spring, Shiloh, Weatherford, Woodlawn, and Harmony. Since the *Register* did not list the communities in which the churches served, we do not know where some of these churches were located.

---

[17] *The Morning Star*, 1901
[18] Thanks to Ronald Womack, deacon at New Salem, who is a relative of J. W. and J. A. Ford.

The West Fork, even though all of the original churches eventually closed, went on to become one of the stronger associations in Texas. Though in serious decline in recent years it continues to be an active association in the Texas State Association.

The Central Brazos Association, 1892

Another association of Free Will Baptist churches began to form in Johnson County, south of Fort Worth, sometime prior to 1890, when new churches were planted there. We have located one copy of the minutes of the Central Brazos Association, which met with the Post Oak Church in Johnson County, Texas, on August 6-10, 1913. The 1913 session was the twenty-second annual session, which means that the first session would have been in 1892. The Free Will Baptist merger with the Northern Baptists occurred in 1910-11, so these churches were not lost to us in the merger, and this session was only two years after the merger.

Ten churches are listed as member churches of the association:

- Post Oak
- Union Grove
- Eldorado
- Odom Chapel
- Alvarado
- Mt. View
- Ham
- Fall Creek
- Ft. Spunkey
- Oak Grove

There were also ten pastors listed by name, two of which were out of fellowship with the association, though the minutes do not state which ones. The dollar figure is the amount of salary the pastors had received for the year from their churches. The pastors listed, along with their post offices, were:

- J. E. Raney,[19] Granbury, $223.45
- T. J. Fenn, Alvarado, $1.00
- M. I. Sanford, Alvarado
- J. S. Dillard, Milford
- W. T. Clement, Alvarado
- J. H. Haney, Kemp, $ 12.50
- R. A. Roberts, Egan, $103.65
- S. P. Morris, Burleson
- S. M. Carter, Granbury
- W. H. Davidson, Fort Worth

Tidbits of information from the minutes include the following. The moderator was J. E. Raney, of Granbury, Texas, and the clerk was R. A. Roberts, of Egan, Texas. The session began on Wednesday evening and concluded on Sunday evening, with preaching Sunday morning and Sunday night, which likely meant that the other churches in the association did not have services that Sunday. This was normal procedure for many associations in the early twentieth century.

The association adopted the following resolution: "Resolved it is the sense of this body that our people should be awakened on the subject of giving systematically to the support of mission (*sic*) and pastors. Pastors should know definitely what they are to receive when practicable."

The biblical title "elder" was used of all the pastors, rather than Reverend. Elders R. A. Roberts and J. E. Raney, who had served as delegates to the Southwestern Convention the previous year, reported on that convention. Three elders were elected to be delegates to the next Southwestern Convention: R. A. Roberts, J. E. Raney, and W. T. Clement.

The minutes of the Friday evening business session, prior to the preaching at 8:30, state: "Letter read from Elder G. L. Rogers which shows he has gone into heresy. Motion to withdraw

---

[19] J. E. Raney was known as "The Walking Bible" because of his knowledge of the Scriptures, according to Rev. Clarence J. Hearron.

from Elder G. L. Rogers and request him to send in his credentials. Committee to receive G.L. Rogers credentials: R. A. Roberts, J.H. Mitchell, W. T. Clement."

The Eldorado church, the location for the 1914 session of the association, was mentioned as being located in Tarrant County, one and a half miles northeast of Retta, which lies between Burleson and Mansfield.

The closing line of the minute's states, "General handshaking ended one of the most pleasant sessions of the association."

The Northeast Texas Association, 1897

I have one copy of the minutes of the Northeast Texas Association of Freewill Baptists. They are of the twenty-first annual session, held October 26-28, 1917, at the Friendship Free Will Baptist Church in Bowie County, Texas. This being the twenty-first annual session would mean that the first annual session would have been in 1897, if there had been no interruptions. This association meeting occurred only six years after the merger of a majority of Free Will Baptist churches with the Northern Baptist Convention in 1910-11. In 1917 there were four churches which comprised the association: Friendship, Union Hill, Pleasant Grove, and Cedar Grove.

As was normal for associational meetings in those days the session started on Friday night and continued through Sunday morning. This was possible in part because the churches which composed the association did not have services every Sunday, often following a first Sunday-third Sunday or a second Sunday-fourth Sunday schedule. If a month had a fifth Sunday there might be special services or no services.

Several items of business in this session catch our attention. The first one is that on Saturday morning the preaching service was dispensed with so they could conduct a full slate of business. The Free Will Baptist associations and churches which did not participate in the merger of 1910-11 were beginning to pull together and reorganize. This is reflected in the business conducted that Saturday morning in 1917 by the Northeast Texas Association. W. B. Rhea presented the body with scriptural references for the Article of Faith which were being considered for adoption. The Articles of Faith were adopted and inserted into the minutes.

Then there was a motion to adopt the new *Treatise*, published by the Cooperative General Association. The Cooperative General Association had been formed in 1916 in Pattonsburg, Missouri, and they published the first *Treatise* since the merger in 1910-11, mentioned above. That *Treatise* was printed by the New Morning Star Print, Tecumseh, Oklahoma. The Cooperative General Association was the broadest body of Free Will Baptists west of the Mississippi River. Free Will Baptists in the East were uniting together in the General Conference of Free Will Baptists. It would be these two groups which would come together in 1935 to form the National Association of Free Will Baptists. The 1916 *Treatise* is almost identical to the one adopted in 1935, as is the church covenant. Only two ministers submitted reports of their work for the year. They are as follows:

F. BLACKWELL -- Pastored two churches; held two revivals meetings with good results; received nine members; baptized four, and four by letter; married five couples.

B. RHEA -- One more year has passed and gone, and I am still preaching for my Lord. I found Cedar Grove Church in bad condition. I commenced gathering the Church together in February, 1917, and caused the Church to come to life again. We now have twenty-five members. I have baptized two; married six couples, and received $7.00.

The church letter from Cedar Grove to the association reported that they had paid the pastor, W. B. Rhea, 50¢ for the year.

The ten members of the Executive Committee were all from the towns of: Dalby Springs, in Bowie County; Avery, in Red River County; and DeKalb, in Bowie County. Local historians say that De Kalb was named by David Crockett in 1835 when he passed through on his way to the Alamo.

An article about the Northeast Texas Association in the May, 1918, issue of *The New Morning Star* indicates that the association, meeting with the Friendship Church in Bowie County, March 29-30, 1918, observed the Lord's Supper and Feet Washing. The practice of observing the Lord's Supper and Feet Washing at association meetings was not uncommon in earlier years.

The Northeast Texas Association

The minutes of the 1886 General Conference of Free Will Baptists, which met in Marion, Ohio, mention that the following yearly meeting or associations were admitted to membership in the General Conference: South Carolina, West Missouri, Bon Eagle (Miss), Northeast Texas, Northwest Missouri, Pleasant Hill (Mo.), Cedar Creek (Tenn.), Chattahoochee (Ga.), Cape Fear (N. C.), and Mississippi. This does not seem to be the same Northeast Texas association mentioned above. For one thing this Northeast Texas Association was admitted into the General Conference in 1886, while the minutes I have of the other Northeast Texas Association indicate that it was formed in 1897, eleven years later, and reported to the First Oklahoma Association. Secondly, the letter to the General Conference at which this Northeast Texas Association was admitted says, "We meet with great opposition here, because of our free doctrines, and our color. We are determined to live and enjoy our freedom. We ask admission to your body." It seems highly likely, therefore, that there were two Northeast Texas associations, this latter one composed of black people. There were a number of yearly meetings or associations in the General Conference of Free Will Baptists which were composed of black people, many of them former slaves. The letter to the General Conference from West Missouri states, for instance, "When we were bought and sold as property you were our friends, and we can trust you now." The Bon Eagle, Mississippi, letter states, "Your remembrance of us when we were enslaved draws our hearts towards you, and we ask to be received as a member of your body."

This association of black churches never affiliated with the white Free Will Baptist work in Texas. Perhaps we should say that the white Free Will Baptist churches never affiliated with the black Free Will Baptist churches in Texas. There was a lot of racial prejudice on the part of many of the white Free Will Baptist pastors, as we will see later.

The Southwestern Freewill Baptist General Convention, 1901

In the late 1800's Free Will Baptists began to form regional associations, each encompassing several states, for the same reasons churches had formed what we now call district associations: fellowship, cooperation in various enterprises, mutual encouragement, etc.[20] Some states had formed state associations. Ohio, West Virginia, and Kentucky had formed a "Tri-State Association." In 1881 some churches, chiefly in Minnesota and Iowa, met in Wykoff, Minnesota, and formed the Northwestern Free Will Baptist Association. The name was later changed to the

---

[20] From an e-mail from Dr. Robert Picirilli dated July 16, 2014.

Western Association of Free Baptists.[21] Similarly, in East Tennessee, Western North Carolina, and Southwest Virginia they formed a "Mountain Association."

In 1901 the Free Will Baptists in Texas, Oklahoma, and Missouri formed the Southwestern Freewill Baptist General Convention, usually referred to simply as the Southwestern Convention.[22] It was described as an intermediate body between the yearly meeting or association and the Free Will Baptist General Conference. The convention came to include parts of Arkansas and Louisiana. Texas was very active in this regional association for as long as it existed. The convention often met in Texas. It met in Coppell in November of 1908[23] and in Weatherford in 1909. In 1909 T. C. Ferguson and his wife, Myrtle, accepted a position with the Southwestern Convention as traveling evangelists, with both of them preaching. They often spent their summers in Texas holding evangelistic meetings. In 1909 the convention purchased a large tent which was used by the Fergusons for their meetings. In 1909 he wrote, "I found the Free Baptist cause in Texas in a very prosperous condition. Quite a large number of new churches have been organized the past year." He also stated that within the convention, which covered a large area, there lived ten thousand Free Baptists. This may have been an "evangelistic count." We have a photograph and good information about the 1909 meeting in Weatherford. Henry M. Ford wrote an article about the convention and it was published in the December 16, 1909 issue of *The Morning Star*. Excerpts of it are provided here because of the valuable information the report contained:

> There was a considerable delegation, besides visitors, and seven out of the thirteen associations composing this convention, three in Oklahoma and ten in Texas, were represented....The singing was lively, the preaching biblical and enthusiastic. One brother, during his sermon, quoted accurately, without a break, more than 100 passages of Scripture, and gave chapter and verse off-hand. This was certainly as rare as it was remarkable. There is a strong tendency toward doctrinal preaching, with a free use of Scripture. In their preaching they always start out to prove something from the Bible, and draw from Scripture, combining and weaving together texts in a most unique and remarkable manner. These preachers were rural like our fathers, and have not had the advantages of scholastic training, but they are vigorous and original....
>
> The younger ministers are feverish for school, and expressed its conviction that the convention could well afford to assist financially one or two of its young men annually while pursuing studies in some school....
>
> A very interesting part of the program was the examination and ordination of Mrs. T. C. Ferguson, a woman gifted with a sweet spirit, womanly ways, an earnest message and a rare way of telling it....
>
> Here in this southwestern country lies an immeasurable territory, affording a boundless opportunity for ingathering and up building. Here people are gospel hungry, the message reaches anxious listeners always, revivals are natural and successful without great effort. There is not that fruitless, disheartening result so characteristic of the North. Crowds eagerly hang on the message and when the invitation comes some are ready to decide.
>
> I was somewhat surprised and not prepared to find that in all the six days and nights in which the services were crowded, with scores of people unable to get in and crowding

---

[21] *Free Baptist Cyclopaedia* [hereafter *Cyclopaedia*], editors John T. Ward and Gideon A. Burgess (Free Baptist Cyclopaedia Co., 1989), page 686. The copy of the Free Baptist Cyclopaedia which I have was given to Rev. M. L. Sutton by Rev. J. L. (Luther) Payne, whose name appears all over the minutes of Free Will Baptists in Texas. Brother Sutton gave it to me.

[22] It was usually referred to in print as the Southwestern Free Baptist Convention, as in *The Morning Star* of January 28, 1909, page 13.

[23] *The Morning Star*, January 28 1909, page 13.

around outside the tent, there was not the first indication of disorder: all were reverent and when the meeting was over people quietly dispersed and went home....

These brethren were not ready to consider Union. Denominational lines are rigidly drawn and differences rather then likes are emphasized, but the tolerant spirit is growing and sweetening, yet they are not ready to accept or favor anything looking toward cooperation or affiliation with any people who do not have "Free Will Baptists" written upon their banner. The brethren are preparing for a great forward movement the coming year; they have already caught the larger vision of the Kingdom of God for this southwestern country.

Southwestern Convention of Freewill Baptists, Weatherford, Texas, fall of 1909

People we can identify: on the back row, extreme left, is T. C. Ferguson. His wife, Myrtle Henderson Ferguson, stands directly in front of him. Their daughter, Jewel, is the little girl dressed in black standing in front of Mrs. Ferguson. From the extreme right, the second man from the right, the man holding the folder, is S. L. Morris, editor of The Free Baptist News, later called The Free Will Baptist News. Also in that row, the sixth person from the right is James Milton Walker. Dr. Ford, of Hillsdale College in Michigan, stands at about the middle of the tent, back row. Written on the tent is "Freewill Baptist Meeting."

An article in *The Morning Star* informs us that the convention passed strong resolutions for the need of an educated ministry and expressed its conviction that the convention could well afford to financially assist one or two of the young men who were preparing for the ministry.[24]

There are three minutes in the Free Will Baptist Historical Collection at Welch College of the Southwestern Freewill Baptist General Convention, the minutes of the 1912, 1914, and 1915 conventions. The 1912 minutes are of the twelfth annual session, meaning that this convention was formed around 1901, as stated above. This was several years before the merger of 1910-11 and it continued until around the time of the formation of the Co-operative General Association, which we will discuss below. According to William F. Davidson the Southwestern Convention

---

[24] *The Morning Star,* December 16, 1909, page 12.

was admitted to the General Conference of Free Will Baptists of New England in 1907.[25] Davidson states that a small remnant of the Southwestern Convention remained to establish later Free Will Baptist works in the area, but that the convention did not remain with the denomination and, therefore did not have claim to space in his book. When the Texas State Association of Free Will Baptists was formed in 1915, they sent a delegate to the Southwestern Convention as will be noted below.

There is an article and a photograph in *The Morning Star*, dated January 26, 1911, which is included here because of its historical content relative to Texas. Free Will Baptists had voted to merge with the Northern Baptists in 1910. The merger was consummated later in 1911. The article, written by Frederick L. Wiley, reads:

> Special interest in our brethren of the Southwest was awakened by correspondence in the effort to collect ministerial-record statistics for our late General Conference. This interest was intensified by acquaintance with Rev. T. C. Ferguson, who came to General Conference as a representative of the Southwestern Convention of Freewill Baptists, and has grown with subsequent correspondence.
>
> The Southwestern Convention is an intermediate body between the Yearly Meeting or Association and General Conference. It covers portions of Texas, Arkansas, Oklahoma, Louisiana and Missouri. According to recent reports it has a constituency of about 36,000. But a majority of Southwestern Yearly Meetings have joined neither the Convention nor General Conference.
>
> The Convention has within its limits a large number of well located "church houses," but for evangelistic work, and the convening of its annual assemblies, it owns and sustains a large, movable sanctuary, or tabernacle. A good view of the tabernacle is given in the accompanying picture. The photograph from which the picture was made was taken in connection with the session of the Convention convened at Weatherford, Texas, in the fall of 1909.
>
> Weatherford is a beautiful city of about 10,000 inhabitants, but it manages to get along with neither a saloon nor several other places of public resort that are likely to disgrace a city of that size. It wouldn't be strange if the presence of many vigorous Free Baptists and the publication of "The Free Baptist News" in the city were factors promotive of its high plant of civic righteousness.
>
> The convention delegates and others are represented in the groups in front of the tabernacle. The evidences that they belong to the commonwealth of Israel make one feel like passing around and shaking hands with each of them. Our instructions enable us to locate only a few.
>
> At the left, the first in the second row from the top, is Evangelist Ferguson. Directly in front of him stands his wife. In front of her, the little girl in black, is their daughter Jewel. Dr. Ford, of Hillsdale, stands at about the middle of the tabernacle. Whatever the success of others in locating him, probably he can find himself. If he doesn't it will be the first time he was ever known to fail of finding himself when occasion required. That large, good looking man standing next to the one at the extreme right, is Rev. S. L. Morris, President of the Convention Home Mission Board and editor of "The Free Baptist News."
>
> The pleased look on the face of Editor Morris may be an expression of his satisfaction with the general trend of convention happenings. Possibly that, and possibly more. Evangelist Ferguson has just promised to secure seventy-five new subscribers for the "News." Knowing his man, he expects Mr. Ferguson to make good. That's enough to

---

[25] William F. Davidson, *The Free Will Baptists in History,* (Randall House Publications, Nashville, Tennessee, 2001) page 261.

bring a smile to the face of any editor. But the mouse in the sanctum corner--if it could talk--might tell how that smile broadened, when, a few months later, Editor Morris ordered his mailing clerk the hundred and three new subscriptions reported by Evangelist Ferguson.

Rev. T. C. Ferguson and his wife, Rev. Myrtle Henderson Ferguson, have been traveling evangelists of the Southwestern Convention for the last three years. He is a ready, off-hand speaker, and the Lord's message falls from his lips with convincing and persuasive power. He has preached the gospel in twelve states of the Union, in parts of Canada and Old Mexico.

Mrs. Ferguson travels with her husband and takes her turn at preaching in the big tabernacle. She is an accomplished musician, and some of the most effective hymns in connection with their evangelistic work are both of her composition and singing. Even their little five-year-old daughter Jewel, has recently sung before the great tabernacle congregations, with melting effect, hymns adapted to her age.

The record of facts in connection with the evangelistic and constructive work which God is accomplishing through the agency of the Ferguson family reads like romance. By moving about among the states covered by the Southwestern Convention, they find climate condition congenial for work the year around. Of the yearly average of nearly a thousand professed conversions, after counting out about two hundred who join churches of other denominations, and a considerable number who unwisely choose the liberty of "the mountains, will and bare" to the shelter of any fold, there are enough to greatly strengthen existing Free Baptist churches and organize several new ones.

As an aftermath of evangelistic work, many church edifices have been built and several young men and young women have been helped into the ministry.

As with the tabernacle of ancient story, so--by adapted benediction--it may be said of this modern sanctuary: "Then the cloud covered the tent of the congregation, and the glory of the Lord filled the tabernacle."

"Lord, thy church is still thy dwelling.
　Still is precious in thy sight,
Judah's temple far excelling,
　Beaming with the Gospel's light."

The minutes of the 1912 session of the Southwestern Convention are chock full of information relative to Texas. One of the things of particular interest is the list of licensed and ordained ministers from Texas who were members of the convention. They are listed here for two reasons. First, so we can see how many ministers there were from Texas who were members of the convention at the time and, secondly, to see where the ministers were located, possibly giving us information about where Free Will Baptist churches existed in 1912. First are listed the licensed ministers, nineteen in all.

N. W. Stout, Garner, Texas
C. B. Thompson, Carrolton, Texas
J. D. Adams, Carrolton, Texas
G. W. Thompson, Coppell, Texas
Cliff Fain, Nolansville, Texas
James Gartman, Youngsport, Texas
Daniel Desirens, Tama, Texas
J. A. Rice, Layton, Texas
L. D. Jones, Francis, Texas

W. A. Rogers, Bradley, Texas
Mrs. Cora Mann, Henderson, Texas
A. Rolins, Henderson, Texas
C. Phelips (Phillips?), Henderson, Texas
T. W. Smith, Henderson, Texas
J. R. Conley, Elderville, Texas
H. L. Byrd, Garrison, Texas
Mrs. M. J. Creamer, Comanche, Texas

Then, the list of ordained ministers from Texas, ninety-four in all, is more than we might have expected. Please take note of where they lived.

I. G. Swearingen, Warren, Texas
E. N. Waldrip, Votaw, Texas
J. T. Lee, Kirbyville, Texas
J. C. Caraway, Silsbee, Texas
T. J. McBride, Wills Point, Texas
J. C. Havens, Wills Point, Texas
G. N. Chastain, Cash, Texas
J. L. Tatum, Bryan, Texas
W. M. Higgins, Graham, Texas
J. B. Hoosier, Vera, Texas
J. A. Edmoson, Olney, Texas
C. Purcelley, Loving, Texas
D. R. Jimerson, Henderson, Texas
D. J. Dollar, Henderson, Texas
A. M. Swindell, Hallsville, Texas
E. S. Jimerson, Henderson, Texas
J. C. Creamer, Comanche, Texas
A. J. Barnett, Corbon, Texas
J. H. Raney, Ham, Texas
M. I. Sanford, Alvarado, Texas
W. T. Clement, Alvarado, Texas
S. M. Carter, Granbury, Texas
J. E. Graham, Elgia, Texas (Eliga?)
J. W. Desirens, Tama, Texas
L. F. Fitzgerald, Tama, Texas
Z. T. Fuller, Belton, Texas
J. E. Jones, Loreno, Texas (Lorena?)
Watton Graham, Ballinger, Texas
J. L. Payne, Zulch, Texas
J. W. Dowell, Normangee, Texas
E. E. Dowell, Normangee, Texas
J. L. Bounds, Piedmont, Texas
Henry Hunter, Millican, Texas
S. L. Morris, Weatherford, Texas
J. A. Montgomery, Weatherford, Texas
James M. Walker, Weatherford, Texas
Mrs. Verda Walker, Weatherford, Texas
J. B. Holmes, Weatherford, Texas
J. T. Trotter, Newark, Texas
L. W. Pace, Springtown, Texas
John Shipley, New Castle, Texas
J. Cole, Garner, Texas
J. A. Ford, Paradise, Texas
T. J. Easton, Saint Joe, Texas
R. E. Helms, Chico, Texas
T. C. Ferguson, Weatherford, Texas
J. M. Smith, Dozier, Texas

A. D. Lindsey, Sartago, Texas
B. F. Sistruck, Kirbyville, Texas
William Denman, Buna, Texas
A. E. Dewson, Rosenville, Texas
A. J. Birdwell, Wills Point, Texas
I. W. Smith, Cash, Texas
J. T. Lynch, Cash, Texas
J. J. Tatum, Bryan, Texas
. W. Shultes, Elbert, Texas
T. E. Glase, Haskell, Texas
A. M. Griffin, Weinert, Texas
B. D. Badgett, Vera, Texas
A. M. Stewart, Carthage, Texas
H. C. Dunn, Henderson, Texas
A. J. Smith, Dirgin, Texas
R. B. Easley, Comanche, Texas
T. A. Strain, Cisco, Texas
J. E. Raney, Granbury, Texas
R. A. Roberts, Egan, Texas
S. P. Morris, Burleson, Texas
J. S. Dillard, Italy, Texas
W. H. Davidson, Fort Worth, Texas
J. C. Hodges, Bruceville, Texas
L. D. Farrer, Chilton, Texas
J. F. Leatherwood, Killeen, Texas
E. G. Pirtle, Salado, Texas
H. M. Graham, Ballinger, Texas
J. F. Scott, Ringgold, Texas
J. L. Thomas, Iola, Texas
D. C. Hargrove, Iola, Texas
A. L. Carter, Piedmont, Texas
J. O. Riggs, College, Texas
John Orr, Kerrville, Texas
R. V. Whitaker, Weatherford, Texas
T. H. Newsom, Springtown, Texas
G. C. Morris, Weatherford, Texas
J. A. Martin, Weatherford, Texas
L. W. Miller, Dicey, Texas
J. H. Barton, Springtown, Texas
W. E. Dearmore, Boyd, Texas
E. L. Hill, Garner, Texas
N. B. Stanley, Bluegrove, Texas
J. T. Jones, Alvord, Texas
C. C. Skipper, Chico, Texas
Mrs. Lizzie McAdams, Weatherford, Texas
Mrs. Myrtle Ferguson, Weatherford, Texas
W. G. Wetsel, Comanche, Texas

That is a total of one hundred twelve Free Will Baptist preachers from Texas who were members of the Southwestern Convention in 1912. At present we have no idea how many of the towns listed above, where Free Will Baptist preachers lived, had Free Will Baptist churches. As observed above the pastors did not always live in the communities where their churches were located.

The merger with the Northern Baptists was very much on the minds of the delegates to the Southwestern Convention at their 1912 session. The minute's record that on Thursday morning there was a motion to ask Dr. A. W. Anthony a question regarding the union with the Baptists of the North. Dr. Anthony and his wife Gertrude were present from Lexington, Maine. He was a corresponding messenger from the General Conference. Then on Friday morning a motion called for Rev. T. C. Ferguson to spend thirty minutes talking about the union with "the Baptists of the north." The convention still had a relationship with the Randall movement which had merged with the Northern Baptists. They elected Dr. I. W. Yandell, E. S. Jimerson, W. E. Dearmore, C. C. Wheeler, and J. J. Tatum to serve as delegates to the General Conference, which would meet at Ocean Park, Maine, in 1913.

Here we must digress a moment to answer the question as to why the General Conference of Free Will Baptists still existed, when they had merged with the Northern Baptists in 1910-11. Here I must rely upon Dr. Picirilli again. He points out that it was necessary for the General Conference of Free Will Baptists, the Randall Movement, to continue to exist as a legal entity, and have regular meetings, in order to handle all the legal and financial matters that were involved. It took a number of years for this to be done, all assets transferred over, all obligations to be fulfilled, etc. One example is that many wills were made out to the General Conference and all this had to be resolved. Was there some sentimental value? Perhaps. It was a "paper" organization, but a small group continued to meet as the General Conference and carry out some of the programs to which the conference had been committed for some time.

Another item of interest in the 1912 minutes is the names of the district associations in Texas which belonged to it at the time. They were the West Fork, Central Texas, Central Brazos, Woodlawn, Southeast Texas, Denton Creek, Northwest Brazos, West Texas, and Texas.

The 1913 session of the Southwestern Convention met at the Free Will Baptist Church in Alvarado, Texas, November 18-23. I have not been able yet to find the name of that church and minutes of the meeting are not available.

The 1914 convention, the fourteenth annual session, met at the Free Will Baptist Church in North Zulch, Texas, November 17-22. Nine associations in Texas are listed as member associations in the Southwestern Convention: Texas, West Fork, Central Brazos, Northwest Brazos, Central Texas, West Texas, Sabine River, Woodlawn, and Southeast Texas. It is interesting that all of the general officers elected at the 1914 session were from Texas, even though the convention included associations in Oklahoma and Missouri. They also elected a nine member home missions board, seven of whom were from Texas, two from Oklahoma, and none from Missouri.

Thirty year old Lizzie McAdams preached on Thursday evening of the convention. The Committee on the State of the Denomination reported "We find that more new churches have been organized than any year possibly....and we are advancing faster than ever before in number, having more increase, or as much as any year in our history."

The report of the Committee on Education includes an interesting paragraph about Free Will Baptist schools. Remember that the merger of the northern movement of Free Will Baptists with the Northern Baptists had occurred in 1910-11. The Southwestern Convention was still aligned with the Free Will Baptists and still supported the schools in that movement. Here is the paragraph:

> We believe in a distinctively Christian education such as is given in academies and colleges with the patronage and direction of the church. We appreciate the services of our fathers in founding such institutions. We approve and commend as our own, Hillsdale College, Mich; Bates College, Lewiston, Maine; Rio Grande College, Rio Grande, Ohio; Keuga College, Keuga, N. Y.; Storer College, Harper's Ferry, W. Va; and other F. B. Institutions of learning.

The Committee on Doctrine also has an interesting paragraph in their report. It is about Free Will Baptist distinctives. As was often the case in the 1800's and early 1900's it did not mention feet washing. Here is part of the paragraph.

> We, your committee on Doctrine, beg leave to submit the following report: We are glad to say that we find throughout the bounds of the Southwestern Convention of Freewill Baptists that our people are still holding fast the Faith and Doctrine delivered to our forefathers. We still have on our banner, Freedom of the Will, Free Communion, Free Grace and a Believer's baptism by immersion in Water.

For the past one hundred years Free Will Baptists have not been particularly well known for our ministry in meeting social needs. The Southwestern Convention operated a city missions rescue mission, located at 1123 North Main Street in Fort Worth. It was under the direction of G. C. and Annie Morris. Their 1914 report is given below. From it we learn something of the efforts of Free Will Baptists to minister in this needy field. Here is the report.

> We, Your city missionaries in Fort Worth, Texas, beg leave to submit the following as our report of work done in 1914. We have held 212 meetings, 111 converted and reclaimed, organized one church with the help of Revs. H. M. and Lizzie McAdams, held 47 Sunday schools, have saved 5 girls from the white slave traffic, have helped in the Home 125 persons, served 4600 meals, given out 5003 pieces of clothing, helped 23 needy families, married 27 couples, baptized 10, contracted with the U. S. Emigrant Prospector to care for the Government white slave cases, arranged for the County to maintain a temporary detention home for the Juvenile Court and have visited the jails 14 times to try to lead the lost souls to Christ. -- G. C. and Annie Morris.

The convention gave them a glowing commendation as follows:

> We desire to call attention to the Fort Worth Mission work done by Brother and Sister G. C. Morris in our name. The nature and character of the work for good done by these people of God deserves the highest words of commendation and hearty, loyal interest and support of all. They have worked hard, denied themselves many comforts, and sacrificed much to save those needy ones coming under their care. We would recommend that this work be continued if possible, and their services secured, if it can be done.

The Woodlawn Association, 1901

The Woodlawn Association of Free Will Baptist churches was centered south of Waco and east of the the Bruceville-Eddy-Troy area of what is now the I-35 corridor. The Free Will Baptist churches, most of them rural, organized into the Woodlawn Association in 1901 and continued to exist for several decades. The last remaining church, the First Free Will Baptist Church in Waco, eventually became a part of the West Fork District Association.

Two copies of the minutes of the Woodlawn Association are available: the 36th annual session, which met at the First Free Will Baptist Church in Waco, on October 9-10, 1936, and the 40th session which met August 1-3, 1940, also at the First Free Will Baptist Church in Waco. These being the thirty-sixth and the fortieth sessions, respectively, would mean that the first session would have been held in 1901.

The minutes of the Southwestern Convention of Freewill Baptists in 1914 list the following ministers as members of the convention: John E. Graham, Killeen, Texas; L. D. Farrer, Chilton, Texas; J. C. Hodges, Bruceville, Texas; J. F. Leatherwood, Killeen, Texas; Z. T. Fuller, Belton, Texas; J. W. Deserens, Killeen, Texas; J. E. Jones, Eddy, Texas; E. G. Pirtle, Salado, Texas; C. W. Fain, Belton, Texas; and W. T. Hardy, Chilton, Texas.

According to these two minutes, the Woodlawn Association consisted of the following churches at the time:

- First Free Will Baptist Church, Waco, pastored by J. L. Bounds
- Liberty Free Will Baptist Church, Dott, pastored by Allie Ferguson
- Long Branch Free Will Baptist Church, Eddy, pastored by John E. Graham; I. E. Vaughn was also a member
- Eliga Free Will Baptist Church, Eliga, pastored by J. E. Vaughn
- Woodlawn Free Will Baptist Church, Cego, on FM 1550, about eight miles east of I-35 at Eddy, in Falls County
- Long Prairie Free Will Baptist Church, Long Prairie

The 1936 session opened with "a God-inspiring sermon" delivered by Mrs. Lizzie McAdams. Miss Lucille Gardner was elected association missionary. The "Enrollment of Ministers" in 1936 named: I. E. Vaughan, Eddy, Texas; Lizzie McAdams, Midway, Texas; H. M. McAdams, Midway, Texas, and Milton Graham, Killeen, Texas. The roll of ministers in 1940 named: J. E. Graham, Killeen; J. L. Bounds, Waco; Allie Ferguson, Dott; and J. E. Vaughn, Eddy. Tiff Covington was there as a correspondent representing the West Fork District Association.

It seems that the First Church in Waco was an every Sunday church while the others met only once or twice a month for preaching, though some of them had Sunday school every Sunday. A couple of the church letters will give us an insight to the strength and condition of the churches.

Long Branch Church

1940 - To the Woodlawn Association of Free Will Baptist Church (sic) while convened with the First Free Will Baptist Church at Waco, Texas, Aug. 1, 1940: We send delegates, our beloved Brethren and Sisters, Bro. Adolphus Conaway, Sister Lula Philips, Clara Sewett and Pearl Mauen, whom we pray you to receive to sit with you in your delegation. State of Religion poor; members received none; baptized none; dismissed two; died two; total membership 50; prayer meeting good, but small attendance; Sunday School very poor; average number of pupils 10 or 12; officers 2; teachers 2. Paid pastor $45.40; Home Mission $19.13; Foreign Mission

none; for building and repairs none; lettered out 2 for education $.70; amount enclosed for Minutes [does not state].
Rev. John E. Graham, Mod.
Pearl Maricle, C.C.

Liberty Free Will Baptist Church

We, the Church of God, known as Free Will Baptist, worshipping as Liberty Church, Dott, Texas. To the Woodlawn Association when convened with Waco Church. We send as our delegates: Sister Leola Martin, Sister Pauline Maricle and Bro. Layton Maricle, whom we pray you receive them in your honorable body. New members received 8, baptized 5; prayer meeting good; Sunday School good; paid pastor $100.00; Evangelistic work $30.00; property $800.00.

Eliga Free Will Baptist Church

1936 - We, the church of God, known as Free Will Baptist, worshipping at Eliga, met in conference and elected the following delegates to the Woodlawn Association when convened with the Waco Church: Bro. Carl Patterson, Sister Alvie Webb, Bro. and Sister T. L. Shafer, Brother and Sister O. E. Morris, and Sister Mary Graham. We pray that you receive them in the name of the Lord to your honorable body. We have no Sunday School or prayer meetings. Paid Rev. I. E. Vaughan $25.00 for holding meeting, also Bro. Elbert Vaughan $10.00. Support for Pastor, $10.00, Home Mission, $50.00, Association Minutes, $3.00, Clerk fee, 50¢.
Milton Graham, Church Clerk
Route 3, Box 112, Killeen, Texas

A big issue of the time is referenced in the Temperance Committee Report at the 1940 session:

> We, your committee on Temperance, beg to submit the following: We feel that the Eighteen Amendment [which ended Prohibition] should never have been repealed, but since it has we can and do urge that we abstain from the use of all intoxicating beverages, and that we be temperate in all things, and May God help us to make this one of our chief aims in life.
>
> James H. Maricle
Leroy Conaway
Rev. Tiff Covington

The Articles of Faith in the 1936 and 1940 minutes of the Woodlawn Association are the articles adopted in 1935 at the first session of the National Association of Free Will Baptists. The 1935 annual session of the Woodlawn Association met in October, while the first National Association met in November, a month later. The 1936 meeting of the Woodlawn Association, therefore, was the first annual session to meet after the formation of the National Association, yet the National isn't mentioned in the 1936 minutes. The Church Covenant in the 1936 Woodlawn Association minutes is not the same covenant adopted by the 1935 National Association; it is an earlier one.

All of the churches which comprised the Woodlawn Association eventually closed. A number of names from those days are still remembered by older Free Will Baptists of our own day as many of them ended up in the First Free Will Baptist Church in Waco: W. H. Calvary, Sr.,

Leroy Conaway, Sister Leroy Conaway, B. L. Conaway, Adolphus Conaway, James H. Maricle, Pauline Maricle, Pearl Maricle, Layton Maricle, James H. Rancher, and others. The best known Woodlawn Association pastors from these two sets of minutes would most likely be J. L. Bounds and Allie Ferguson. Tiff Covington, from the West Fork District Association, visited the Woodlawn Association in 1940 as a corresponding delegate and served on a couple of committees.

Tiff Covington pastored the Liberty Free Will Baptist Church in Dott, driving down from Buffalo Springs on weekends when preaching services were conducted. John A. Brooks, however, lived in the community of Dott while he pastored there.

A letter published in *The New Morning Star* in 1918 gives us a little insight into the state of the Woodlawn Association. The letter states in part: "Our churches in the part of the country seem to be on the drag. The people are divided on different questions. Oh! if the preachers would preach salvation instead of preaching about what Adam done, we would have a different world. The Sunday Schools are on the drag also, yet our people say they love the Sunday school work. I say, let a man prove his faith by his works.

The May 1, 1918, issue of *The New Morning Star* contains the following report of the church in Alvarado, Texas:

> ALVARADO -- Dear readers of the New Morning Star: I will write a few lines from this part of the field. Our churches in this part of the country seem to be on the drag. The people are divided on different questions. Oh! If the preachers would preach salvation instead of preaching about what Adam done, we would have a different world.
>
> The Sunday schools are on the drag also, yet our people say they love the Sunday school work. I say, let a man prove his faith by his works.
>
> Our next Quarterly Meeting will convent with the Bradley Church on Friday night before the fifth Sunday in June. The subject for discussion will be as follows:
>
> Is It Right for Women to Preach the Gospel? Pray for us down here in Johnson County.
>
> E. C. Lewis

The Liberty Free Will Baptist Church in the Dott Community of McClennan Country, south of Waco. Pastor John A. Brooks is pictured at the lower right, sitting. Standing next to Pastor Brooks is Ellis Calvery, father of Wesley Calvery, later a missionary to Japan. The young boy standing front row center, with his hands by his side, is Milburn Crosby. The young lady standing halfway between Ellis Calvery and Milburn Crosby, with her head cocked to one side, is Glendene Martin, sister of Billie Martin Crosby Bankhead. The young girl standing next to Pastor Brooks is Jeanette Crosby.

An Ugly Letter in The Morning Star, 1902

The following letter was printed in *The Morning Star* in the summer of 1902. It is so bad that we hesitate to reproduce it here. However, it is part of our history, as ugly as it is. The letter was written by R. V. Whitaker, pastor of the Rockhill Free Baptist Church in Azle, Texas. You may want to skip to the next section of this chapter, but here it is for those who wish to read it:

> Dear Editor, You are making against the MORNING STAR in Texas by your continual ridicule of the South on the nigger question. There are many places in Texas where they won't let a nigger stay long enough to get his breakfast, especially while the white man's union prevails. If editors of Northern journals want to stop nigger lynching let them remove their crimes. No matter what you say or think, this is the way and the only way. I do not approve of mob law, but as long as the people of the South continue to love home and mother, wife and sister, so long will they do away with the black brutes in human form by going the nearest way to the end of a rope. Having been a reader of THE STAR for three years I think we need more religion and less nigger equality.

The editor of *The Morning Star* responded thusly:

> We do not doubt that "more religion" would be a good thing for all of us, North and South, whatever might be the effect of less Negro equality. We have tried to read this letter in a candid spirit. It is always desirable to get the view-point of the person from whom you seem to differ, in order to judge him fairly. We admire love of "home and mother, wife and sister," wherever it appears, and we wish success to all who would truly hold these institutions and relations. We condemn the crimes that are usually alleged in these cases of Negro lynching as strongly as anyone can, and we believe in removing these crimes, to adopt the idea of our correspondent, but we do not believe in the lynching. We believe rather in the appeal to law, and the trial and punishment of the criminals in a lawful manner and by the proper authorities. This applies to white sand blacks alike.
>
> We would like to ask our correspondent if he does not think that the mob spirit in a community is in danger of going to such excess that it may eventually endanger all order and make all of the relations of life insecure in that community? We do not "ridicule" the South. In our judgment the case is too serious for ridicule. The national reputation as well as the national security is seriously imperiled by forms of lawless killing that every civilized nation condemns. We would not let criminals to unpunished, but we would let both the crime by determined and the punishment be inflicted lawfully, whether the accused be white or black. What does our correspondent think of the following sentiments, uttered by a Southerner — a citizen of Georgia — in the July *Atlantic*: -
>
>> The white man who wrongs a black man and the white mob that lynches a negro have by that act and to that extent become criminals in the eyes of the law — and should be dealt with unsparingly as such. It should no longer be a notable thing, to be chronicled in the news columns and elicit editorial comment, that several white men should be punished for the brutal murder of one inoffensive Negro. It should be the rule. And as for lynching, — let all the officers of the law, with all the powers of the law, defend the rights and life of every prisoner. Surely we who can revel in the burning of a fellow human being, and a section, some of whose prominent men can soberly defend such a bloody proceeding, ought not to have any over-sensitive scruples at the shedding of a little additional blood, and that, too, of criminals caught in the very act of crime. So let our marshals have instructions, failure to obey which shall result in criminal prosecution, to protect at any cost the accused who come into their care.[26]

Central Texas District Association, 1906

A. M. Stewart moved his family from East Texas to Bryan where he continued his church planting ministry in Central Texas as a mission endeavor of the Randall Movement of Free Will Baptists.[27] There were a number of other pioneer ministers involved in the establishment of churches in Central Texas including the highly regarded W. T. Woods and J. J. Tatum, along with T. A. Searcy, S. T. Thomas, and others. The first Free Will Baptist church established in the Central Texas area was the Bright Light Church, which was organized in 1893 in the Harvey Community, near Bryan. This was followed by the establishment of the Bryan Free Will Baptist Church in 1894, which would eventually be known as the First Free Will Baptist Church of Bryan.

---

[26] *The Morning Star*, July 10, 1902.
[27] *A 63 Year History of the First Free Will Baptist Church, Bryan, Texas*; Editorial Committee: Mrs. Lillie Belle Gilpin Kinne, Mrs. Elizabeth Holmes Wykes, Miss Mildred Cloud, and Rev. Charles L. Sapp (the Scribe Shop, 1957) page v.

T. H. Adams worked together with A. M. Stewart in the establishment of a number of churches in Brazos and Grimes counties. They organized the Evergreen Church in 1895, in Keith, and the Christian Home Church in the Kurten Community in 1896. The Blue Lake Church in the Piedmont Community was established in 1899. These new churches in and around the Brazos County area were initially members of the Texas Association of Freewill Baptists in East Texas. However, because of the explosion of Free Will Baptist churches in the area, the "Central Texas Free Baptist Association" was organized in 1906. Churches continued to be planted, such as the North Zulch Church, in 1907. The Cross Free Will Baptist Church in Iola became an important church in this growing movement of Free Will Baptist churches. At first the Central Texas Association, functioning like a yearly meeting, consisted of two quarterly meetings: The Plainview Quarterly Meeting and the Brazos County Quarterly Meeting. There were fourteen churches in the association. In time the association ceased to function as two quarterly meetings.

The Central Texas District Association continued to grow and eventually extended into the Corpus Christi area. In time the association divided once again into two quarterly meetings, each meeting three times a year, with the annual meeting being a joint session of the two quarterly meetings. The churches in the Corpus Christi area, mostly because of the distance, eventually formed their own association called the Mission District Association. One by one the churches in the Mission District closed until the Mission District Association ceased to be.

The Central District continues to be a very strong association, partly because of the number of new churches which have been planted within its borders in recent years and the continuing strength of some of the older churches. The new churches have been established because of two influences. One of them has been the work of the State Home Missions Board. The other has been the church planting work of Pastor Bobby Ferguson and the First Free Will Baptist Church of Houston. When the property of the First Church was paid in full the church, under Pastor Ferguson's influence, turned its attention to planting other churches in the greater Houston area.

The Northwest Brazos District Association, 1910

The Northwest Brazos District Association was organized in 1910, consisting of a number of churches which had previously been established. However, it did not petition the state association for membership until November 6, 1929. There were at one time seventeen churches in the Northwest Brazos. The association was spread out from North Central Texas to the Permian Basin in West Texas, including the First Church in Odessa; to the Texas Panhandle, including churches in Amarillo and Pampa, and even into New Mexico, including the First Church in Hobbs. Two of the older churches were the First Free Will Baptist Church in Vernon and the First Free Will Baptist Church in Crowell.

There isn't an abundance of materials available on the Northwest Brazos. The Free Will Baptist Historical Collection at Welch College has a half dozen copies of old minutes, but the collection at Hillsdale Free Will Baptist College has none. Edith Gill, clerk of the association for many years, had several boxes of associational minutes but after her death on May 13, 2013, her collection was thrown away.

Bits and pieces of information can be gleaned from the minutes about the founding of some of the churches. The First Free Will Baptist Church in Vernon was founded by A. J. Edmondson. The Oakdale Church in Amarillo was founded by William Troy Harp. The Faith Free Will Baptist Church in Shallowater was founded by Jackie Farmer. The First Free Will Baptist Church in Pampa was founded by L. C. Lynch. One couple which needs to be mentioned here is Bob and

Edith Gill who labored for many years in the Northwest Brazos. Brother Gill was pastor of the First Oakdale Free Will Baptist Church in Amarillo and Edith served as clerk of the association. The name First Oakdale came about as a result of a merger between the First Church and the Oakdale Church.

From various minutes we can list some of the member churches of the association, though not all. The following is a list of churches which we know to have been in the Northwest Brazos.

First Free Will Baptist Church, Amarillo	North Amarillo Free Will Baptist Church
Oakdale Free Will Baptist Church, Amarillo	First Free Will Baptist Church, Vernon
First Free Will Baptist Church, Crowell	First Free Will Baptist Church, Memphis
First Free Will Baptist Church, Pampa	Faith Free Will Baptist Church, Shallowater
First Free Will Baptist Church, Midland	First Free Will Baptist Church, Odessa
First Free Will Baptist Church, Hobbs, NM	Salt Creek Free Will Baptist Church[28]
Goodcreek Free Will Baptist Church[29]	Friendship Free Will Baptist Church, Benjamin
Free Will Baptist Church, Seagraves	Second Free Will Baptist Church, Amarillo
Free Will Baptist Church, Sayre, OK	Artesia Free Will Baptist Church, Artesia, NM
First Free Will Baptist Church, Andrews	First Free Will Baptist Church, Lamesa
First Free Will Baptist Church, Kermit	Free Will Baptist Church, Levelland
Midland Fellowship Church, Midland	

The Northwest Brazos District Association continued to have a church covenant which was different than the one adopted at the organizational meeting of the National Association in 1935. It is reproduced here.

CHURCH COVENANT

Having given ourselves to God, through Jesus Christ, and adopted the foregoing practices as our confession of faith, we now give ourselves to one another by the will of God and agree to the following Church Covenant:

1. We solemnly covenant before God that we will strive, by His assisting grace, to exemplify our profession by a corresponding practice. We covenant and agree as members of the church and as Christians to watch over each other in love for the mutual upbuilding of the unity of the spirit in the bond of peace, to be careful of each other's reputation, to confess our faults one to another, to strengthen the feeble and kindly admonish the erring, and to labor together for the upbuilding of the church, and denomination and the salvation of sinners.

2. We promise that we will faithfully and constantly maintain family prayer and religiously instruct those under our care.

3. We covenant and agree to use our influence to sustain the regular public worship of God, contributing according to our ability and circumstances for the support of the ministry and other church expenses among us that we will be benevolent to the needy, and especially to the poor of our church.

---

[28] Apparently located in Cottle County, south of Paducah.
[29] Information about this church came from Mrs. Viola Harp, widow of Troy Harp, who wasn't sure if Goodcreek was the location or just part of the name of the church.

4. We promise that as far as we are able we will attend upon public worship and the social meetings of the church and regularly report ourselves at monthly conferences, and that we will walk in all the ordinances of the Lord's House.

5. And we covenant and agree that we will abstain from all vain amusements and simply conformities to the world, that we will not traffic in the use, nor furnish to others, intoxicating beverages, and that we will sustain the benevolent enterprises of our denomination as missions, education, Sabbath schools, moral reform, and all others that tend to the glory of God and the welfare of men. And may the God of Peace sanctify us Holy, preserve us blameless until the coming of the Lord Jesus Christ that we may join the glorified around the throne of God in ascribing blessings, honor, glory and power to Him that sitteth on the throne and the lamb forever. Amen.[30]

The Northwest Brazos District Association, after showing such good promise early on, grew weaker and weaker until, near the end, there were only two churches remaining: Faith church in Shallower and Oakdale First in Amarillo. When Oakdale First closed, the association ceased to exist. The Faith church currently is a member of the new West Texas Association.

The Merger with the Northern Baptists

For several decades the northern movement of Free Will Baptists, the Randall Movement, had been working to promote the unity of the Church. They saw the division of the Church into many denominations as detrimental to the kingdom of God and sought to bring about as much unity in the body of Christ as possible. In this effort they merged with several smaller denominations of like faith, absorbing them into the denomination. Near the end of the nineteenth century Free Will Baptists began to look to larger groups, even groups which differed significantly from them in doctrine and practice, to continue the merging of various denominations into one group, intending to bring about more unity to the Church. At least that seems to have been the primary motivation. This merging into one movement resulted in the merger of the Randall Movement of Free Will Baptists with the larger Northern Baptist Convention in 1910-11. The vote was taken in 1910 and the merger was consummated in 1911. In essence, the Northern Baptist Convention absorbed the smaller General Conference of Free Will Baptists, though some Free Will Baptists in the South, including most of Texas, did not participate in the merger. There was a scattered remnant left, mostly in tatters.

Texas Free Will Baptists should be aware of what Free Will Baptists lost in the merger with the Northern Baptists. The late Dr. Jack L. Williams, in a paper written in 1994 at the request of the Commission for Theological Integrity of the National Association of Free Will Baptists, and read at the 1994 Bible Conference at Free Will Baptist Bible College, listed the major losses. To be thorough we will show here what Dr. Williams listed:
1. Number of members lost
    - There are conflicting numbers ranging from 45,000 to 100,000. The number was probably closer to 60,000.
    - The 1908 *Free Baptist Register* and *Yearbook* lists 68 yearly meetings and associations, 1,292 churches, and 87,015 members.
    - The 1911 *Free Baptist Register* and *Yearbook* (year the merger consummated) reports over 100,000 members.
2. Number of colleges lost

---

[30] Minutes of the Northwest Brazos District Association, 1949, page 10.

- Three schools of "Academic Grade": New Hampton Literary Institution, Maine Central Institute, and Manning Bible School
- Six Colleges
    - Bates College, Lewiston, Maine
    - Hillsdale College, Hillsdale, Michigan
    - Keuga College, Keuga, New York
    - Parker
    - Rio Grande College, Rio Grande, Ohio
    - Storer College, Harper's Ferry, West Virginia, a school for blacks
- Two Theological Seminaries: Cobb Divinity School at Bates and the Theological Department at Hillsdale
- Along with the physical property the following were also lost: trained faculty, several hundreds of students, libraries carefully built over the years, and the future.

3. Number of churches lost: The title of the lecture was "The Day We Lost 600 Churches." It could easily have been, "The Day We Lost 1,000 Churches," because if the Northern Baptist Convention had not absorbed the 1,292 churches reported in 1908, they either died, joined other groups or remained independent. Not many joined the southern Free Will Baptist movement. Let's suppose for argument's sake that the numbers were: 60,000 members and 600 churches lost. What would that mean in 1994? That would be like losing every church and every member in Oklahoma, Arkansas, and Tennessee. What would that do to our national work?

4. Transfer of money and property
    - To American Baptist Home Missions Society: $130,298.10 -- cash, mortgages, bonds, stocks (according to Alfred Williams Anthony in his 1913 report, "Getting Together")

    - To American Baptist Foreign Missions Society: $66,569.05 -- cash, stocks, etc., plus everything on all mission fields, including India, Barbados and Africa. By 1900, the Bengal-Orissa field in India had 17 missionaries in the field, 8 on furlough, and 63 native assistants; the visible results of their work in India at that time were one yearly meeting, two quarterly meetings and 18 churches; they had 45 ministers and a membership of 1,487, and 4,365 Sunday school pupils, and 4,437 pupils in day school. Their yearly meeting in India had a theological school with $10,000 endowment funds; they also had a high school with 196 students. They had a permanent fund of $82,033.48 on hand. They also had a mission in the Barbados; there were four churches, four ministers and 316 members. They also had a small mission in Africa.

5. Merged *The Morning Star* with *The Watchman* and ceased publication after 75 years of weekly publishing[31]

This merger affected Texas both directly and indirectly. It affected Texas directly in that some of the Free Will Baptist churches in Texas participated in the merger and were absorbed into the Northern Baptist Convention. We cannot identify those churches because of the lack of available records and minutes. We do know that most of the Free Will Baptist churches and associations in Texas did not participate in the merger. As to why they didn't participate Dr. Picirilli speculates, "Perhaps it was as simple as the fact that they were not in an area where there were 'Northern Baptists' to join in with."[32] The West Fork, the Texas Association, West Texas, Central Brazos, Southeast Texas, Northwest Brazos, and Central Texas remained alive and active, though small and weak, and there was no state association to bind them together. Additionally, there was no national organization which connected the various states and regional associations.

---

[31] Dr. Jack L. Williams, "The Day We Lost 600 Churches," March 9, 1994, Free Will Baptist Historical Collection, Welch College, Nashville, Tennessee, pages 2-3.
[32] In an e-mail from Dr. Picirilli, dated July 16, 2014

At the 1930 session of the Texas State Association of Free Will Baptists, one report stated: "...Texas has lost heavily in membership, churches, and associations as compared to reports of fifteen and twenty years ago."[33] In that session they severed any connection or relationship with the Northern Baptist Convention whom they blamed, in part, for the losses. The report did not state how many Texas churches and associations were directly lost in the merger.

Indirectly, Texas was affected by the loss of all the Free Will Baptist colleges and seminaries. The entire foreign missions program, including the properties in India, the home missions program, and the denomination's publishing house, which produced an abundance of books and Sunday school literature, were all lost. The loss of the educational institutions had an adverse effect on the quality of the ministry. An untrained ministry became the norm in Texas, as well as most other states. Now, well into the Twenty-First Century, Texas has not recovered from this loss. Some local church properties were lost, too, by churches not participating in the merger. Damon Dodds said, "Supreme court decisions in Nebraska, Kansas, Illinois, and Texas gave the local church property to the merged groups, leaving Free Will Baptists destitute and homeless."[34] Without checking the minutes of the Northern Baptist Convention, now the American Baptist Convention, and perhaps court records, we cannot identify those churches.

Sabine River Association

The minutes of the fourteenth annual session of the Southwestern Convention of Freewill Baptists twice mention a Sabine River Association. Their 1913 report indicates that 35 people had joined the association.[35] Additionally, the minutes list the following ministers as members: L. R. Hollis, Commerce, Texas; A. J. Birdwell, Wills Point, Texas; J. C. Haven, Wills Point, Texas; C. B. Wright, Quinlan, Texas; G. V. Christian, Cash, Texas; T. J. Lynch, Cash, Texas; and N. Linsey, Quinlan, Texas. Nothing else is known about the Sabine River Association and it seems that it did not affiliate with the the Texas State Association when it formed in 1915 or thereafter.

Four Quarterly Meetings

The minutes of the 1914 session of the Southwestern Convention mention four quarterly meetings which are otherwise unknown. They are reported as having financially supported a Free Will Baptist rescue mission in Fort Worth. The four quarterly meetings were the Parker County Quarterly Meeting, the Wise County Quarterly Meeting, Willow Quarterly Meeting, and the Willow Hole Quarterly Meeting.[36] Is it possible that we know these four quarterly meetings by different names?

In 1914 there was an urgent need for a broader organization, a state association, to bind the district associations together to strengthen, coordinate, unify, and give a greater sense of identity to the the Free Will Baptist work in Texas. We will see that in the next chapter.

---

[33] Minutes of the 1930 session of the Texas State Convention of Free Will Baptists, page 10.
[34] *The Free Will Baptist Story,* page 111. Much of the information about these early efforts come from Dodd's book.
[35] Minutes of the fourteenth annual session of the Southwestern Freewill Baptist Convention, 1914, pages 34, 36.
[36] Minutes of the Fourteenth Annual Session of the Southwestern Convention of Freewill Baptists, 1914, page 12.

Chapter Two

The Formation of the Texas State Association to the Formation of the National Association

1915 to 1935

The rapid, explosive growth of the Free Will Baptist work in Texas from 1870 to 1910 soon led to the need for a broader organization, a state association. Additionally, the losses incurred by the merger of Free Will Baptists with the Northern Baptists in 1910-11 necessitated the creation of an umbrella organization, which could bring the district associations together in unity, give leadership to the overall work, and coordinate the efforts of the various associations. Fortunately, there were men with the leadership ability and vision to bring about such an organization. Among those who stepped up to take on the task were such men as E. L. Hill, W. E. Dearmore, T. H. Newsom, E. S. Jameson, C. C. Wheeler, J. J. Tatum, R. A. Roberts, and S. L. Morris. Morris, who lived in Weatherford, about thirty miles west of Fort Worth, was the editor and publisher of a Free Will Baptist newspaper, the *Freewill Baptist News*. In his paper Morris announced a meeting for the purpose of organizing a statewide body. The announcement called for pastors and delegates to meet at Bradley,[37] Texas, on October 8-9, 1915. The *News* went out to the churches and pastors of Texas and beyond. We have not been able to find the name of that church, which was simply called the Bradley Church in the minutes.

With a dozen local associations in existence we would expect a large and enthusiastic participation from them at the convention. This seems not to have been the case. The minutes of that meeting do not list the associations represented. However, it would appear that enthusiasm for such a meeting, as important as it was, was minimal. The Credentials Committee reported at the second annual session in 1917 that the following three local associations were represented: the Texas Association, Central Brazos, and Central Texas. Three associations. Noticeably absent were the West Fork, Southeast Texas, Northwest Brazos, Woodlawn, West Texas, and the Denton Creek Associations — along with the black associations.

The First Annual Session of the Texas State Association

At that first annual session in 1915 E. L. Hill was elected moderator and W. E. Dearmore was elected clerk. A committee consisting of J. J. Tatum, W. E. Dearmore, and C. C. Wheeler,

---

[37] Bradley, Texas, was located sixteen miles northeast of Cleburne in extreme northeastern Johnson County. In 1900 the local school had eighty-seven pupils and one teacher. In the 1930's the community reported a population of twenty-five, with one business. The community was abandoned in the 1940's.
www.tshaonline.org/handbook/online/articles/hv90, accessed January 29, 2014.

Early Texas Free Will Baptist pastors
Front row seated, left to right: J. L. Payne, unknown, J. J. Tatum. Back row standing, left to right: unknown, John Swanwick, Charles C. Wheeler, J. H. Dowell.

was appointed to write a proposed constitution and by-laws. C. E. Lewis was elected as a delegate to the Southwestern Convention. No committees or boards had been at work for the association during the previous year and so there are no reports of the work in the minutes. The minutes simply report who preached, who was elected, and the formation of the association, resulting in very brief minutes.

Since that 1915 session was the organizational meeting, and was the first annual session, we show here the entire minutes of the meeting. They were handwritten, though in a beautiful hand by W. E. Dearmore, and somewhat faded. As best we can make them out, with spelling and punctuation as in the original, with words sometimes left out, they are as follows:

October 8th, 1915

The meeting of the Bradley Meeting was called through the *Freewill Baptist News* on the above date. By vote W. E. Dearmore preached the introductory sermon. Text Acts 9:6. Bro. Bob Roberts was elected to temporary chairman and W. E. Dearmore temporary clerk.

On motion the moderator a pulpit committee Rev. Lemons, Rev. Dearmore and Deacon Lewis were appointed. Motion prevailed that we adjourn to meet Saturday morning, October 9th, 1915.

Saturday Morning

Song by choir "Higher Ground." Prayer by brother Roberts. The house was called to order by temporary chairman with the temporary clerk at his desk. Rev. E. L. Hill was elected permanent moderator of the meeting. Rev. W. E. Dearmore was elected permanent clerk.

The call in the *Freewill Baptist News* was read and discussed. Motion carried that we enter into business. Motion prevailed that the moderator proceed with the organization, an amendment was offered that we petition the Southwestern Convention for membership - amendment lost motion carried.

Motion with 2nd that above Motion with the amendment be rescinded, and that the above motion with the amendment be voted on. Carried. Motion prevailed that each delegate and minister present be entitled to a seat. Motion carried that the Mass Meeting be adjourned and the organization of the State association be affected. By motion the preaching service dispensed with and business session continued. By motion the Moderator appointed a committee to draft By-Laws and Constitution. Rev. J. J. Tatum, Rev. W. E. Dearmore and Rev. C. C. Wheeler were appointed. Motion prevailed that the body meet annually and the time should be Thursday night before the first Sunday in December of each year - embracing Sunday.

Motion Carried that this organization be called The State Association of Freewill Baptist.[38] By vote the Moderator appointed a program committee to arrange a program for the next meeting, also to select place of meeting. The association to send delegates to the Southwestern convention of Free Baptist, C. E. Lewis was elected as a delegate.

Motion carried that the secretary W. E. Dearmore be made treasurer of the assn.

Motion that churches be urged to take offerings to pay delegates fare to the Convention.

By vote the moderator appointed Rev. Lemons, Rev. T. H. Newsom and Rev. E. S. Jameson to act as a board until next session.

A vote of thanks was extended to the Bradley Church and people of the Community. Motion prevailed that the clerk transcribe the minutes and send them to the *Freewill Baptist News* for publication.

Rev. E. L. Hill, Moderator, Garner, Tex
Rev. W. E. Dearmore, Sec., Boyd, Texas

P. S. The minutes were tendered as directed to the editor of *The Freewill Baptist News* and he refused to print them - Sec.[39]

No meeting was convened in 1916 due to illness in the community where the state association was to be held. The second annual session convened in January of 1917, and then the third annual session was held in December of 1917, making 1917 the only year in which two annual sessions of the Texas State Association occurred.

---

[38] This was not the first time that the "s" was left off the plural word Baptists, and it would certainly not be the last.

[39] There is no explanation given as to why Rev. S. L. Morris, who had announced the meeting in his paper, refused to print the minutes.

Second Annual Session - 1917

The second annual session was then held, January 10-13, 1917. The meeting was held at the Unity Free Will Baptist Church in Azle, Texas. The minutes of that meeting are here presented in full because of the historical information contained therein and to give an idea of what the association was like, with all officers, and committees having had a year to work. They are transcribed as written.

On account of illness in the community in which the state association of Freewill Baptist was to have met in December 1916 the meeting was postponed until Jan. 10th, 1917. On this date the delegates and ministers assembled with the Unity Freewill Baptist Church at Azle, Tex. They were called to order by Chairman Rev. E. L. Hill. Rev. E. S. Jamerson preached the opening sermon - Text "What must I do to work the works of him that sent me." After divine service a program was offered by the committee which was received and adopted with necessary changes. Motion carried that the association adjourn to meet again Thursday morning.

Thursday Morning Session

The association was called together by song. Prayer by Bro. C. Davis.

By vote of the body Revs. E. S. Jamerson, T. H. Newsom and J. E. Raney were appointed as a Committee on Credentials - and after some deliberations made the following report which was adopted: We submit the following as Credentials Committee. We find three associations having duly elected delegates and recommend the seating named delegates and ministers from these associations: Texas Freewill Baptist Association - T. D. Ross, Miss Minnie Jimmerson, Rev. A. R. Harper, Rev. Mrs. A. R. Harper, and Rev. E. S. Jamerson. Central Brazos - T. Brown, Rev. J. E. Raney. Central Texas Freewill Baptist association - E. F. Trant, James Tobias, Rev. L. L. Payne, Rev. J. W. Cook, Rev. T. H. Newsom, Rev. J. J. Tatum, Rev. C. C. Wheeler, and Rev. Fred Comber.

A suggestive Constitution was read an article at a time, save article 8, which was referred to the for consideration. Motion carried that the Constitution Committee be empowered to change any wording in order to make clear the meaning of any clause.

We grant our Colporters[40] and Sunday School missionaries, Bro. and Sister Dally the full privileges of the house. We recommend that all our Corresponding Messengers the respective associations represented be seated with privileges of this body, and through them hereby extend a hearty invitation to these afore said associations to become members of this State Association - Viz: Bro. J. W. Deseres of the Woodlawn Ass'n, and Rev. E. L. Hill of the West Fork association Opportunity to membership to the association. Rev. E. L. Hill expressed a desire as an individual to become a member and was heartily received.

At this time the president addressed the association. We are very sorry that we cannot give our readers the address.

Rev. Z. B. Dally reported beside the books, Bible and tracts distributed he and Sister Dally organized five Sunday Schools and furnished literature to a number of other schools.

Reports from standing committees were called for. None being ready to report. This part of the program was deferred.

---

[40] A colporter was a person who travelled to sell or publicize Bibles, religious tracts, or books.

An interesting discussion was led by Miss Jimmerson, "The Sunday School's place in the church and community." Also "Our relations to the American Baptist Publications Society" was led by Z. B. Dally.

Business meeting adjourned until 9 o'clock Friday morning. Rev. E. S. Jameson occupied the pulpit at 7:30 p.m. Text Gal. 6:2.

Friday morning - Devotional service was conducted by Bro. Bert Rogers reading John 15th chapter. Prayer by E. E. Hill.

The chairman appointed as a committee on resolutions, Rev. E. L. Hill, Rev. J. W. Deseres and Miss Minnie Jimmerson. On Nominations: Rev. E. S. Jameson, Rev. J. H. Dowell and Miss Ruby Lawless. On obituaries: Rev. J. J. Tatum, J. P. Gilpin and C. T. Rogers.

A page is apparently missing here. Then, on the next page:

...E. S. Jameson which was unanimously adopted: We recommend that the State association ask for at least one dollar from every member for missions, to be divided according to General Conf. Two-fifths Foreign, two-fifths home and one-fifth for education.

The preaching hour was dismissed and part of the time given to discussion of the paper, *Free Will Baptist Sentinel*.

At 11:30, Rev. E. L. Hill preached to the congregation. Text Heb. 11:35.

Friday afternoon. This session was opened by Rev. G. W. Robertson reading Psalms 19, and a prayer by Rev. W. N. Crenshaw. At this time the Sentinel as a layperson sees it, was discussed by J. P. Gilpin and others. The association was then given over to the Woman's Missionary Work, with the president, Miss Minnie Jimmerson, in charge. The 6th chapter of Ephesians and prayer was offered by Mrs. Willie Payne.

The State society re-elected all officers to fill their respective places for the ensuing year. A splendid was then rendered as follows: Lecture by Mrs. Z. B. Dally, "World Wide Missions." Recitation by Miss Ruby Lawless, "Pray, Give, or Go." Paper by Mrs. J. L. Payne, "The Value of Literature in Missions." Song by Rev. and Mrs. Z. B. Dally. Recitation by Miss Evie Gilpin, "A Little Pilgrim or Jesus Paid the Fare." Curios from India were exhibited and discussed by Mrs. Z. B. Dally. A missionary offering was taken at this time, which amounted to $5.85.

Miss Minnie Jimmerson and Mrs. J. L. Payne were appointed as a committee to solicit donations as a sinking fund for the *Free Will Baptist Sentinel*.

They succeeded in raising in cash and pledges during the association $150.50. The association adjourned until 9 o'clock Saturday morning.

Preaching at 7:30 by Dr. Wilson Mills, Omaha, Neb. Text John 8:31-32.

Saturday Morning -- Rev. W. N. Crenshaw opened the morning session by reading a portion of the 119th Psalm. Prayer by Rev. J. H. Dowell.

The Nominating Committee reported, and on motion the nominees named were elected by one vote of the association. Miss Minnie Jimmerson gave a verbal report of her work with the Young People's Societies during the year. By rising vote the association extended its appreciation and thanks for her faithful and sacrificial work. Rev. E. S. Jameson made the following motion which met with a second and carried unanimously: That we extend a vote of thanks to our brethren Z. B. Dally and wife, C. C. Wheeler, J. E. Raney and J. L. Payne for their efficient work on the *Sentinel*.

The committee on constitution and by-laws reported and read notice of change of article 9 of the Constitution, said notice having been given at the previous annual session. The amendment shall read: That all meetings subsequent to 1918 shall be held from

Tuesday evening until Friday evening, inclusive, instead of from Wednesday evening until Sunday evening. This amendment was adopted.

Rev. E. S. Jameson made following motion which carried: That the executive committee of the State Association become the mission board of the state work and that all funds collected from the field on the recommendation of this body be forwarded to State Treas. T. D. Ross, Clayton, Texas.

Committee on State of Denomination made the following report: This is the first time in the history of this State Association this committee has made its annual report. A review of the past year reveals to us several very gratifying facts. The spiritual interest in our denomination in the state has been well sustained, as the result of an intelligent (not legible). Many revivals have been enjoyed. Many souls saved. Most of our churches have pastors who are faithful, God fearing men.

No period, nor people, in the history of the state has presented so many strong testimonies on the part of ministry and membership of a genuine loyalty to the principle, doctrines and usages, held and observed by the fathers, and taught as they believe in the word of God, as the last year by those belonging to the association.

Some have knocked at our door for admission and their reception makes an encouraging addition to our number.

Our benevolent work has gone forward with some success. Our missionary Mrs. Ida Holder's salary has been paid with a balance in the treasury. The interest in foreign missions is growing among our churches. The home field has been cultivated with pleasing results. Many open doors are before us today, which a year ago we knew little or nothing of.

Several of our young preachers see the need of more efficient leaders and are now in school better preparing themselves for their life's work. May God speed the day when they may return to us, more efficient to preach the Word.

Our Sunday Schools are in much better condition than in the past.

Our young people's labor has produced better results.

Our ministry and churches yet maintain a radical and aggressive temperance activity. We trust they will continue until Texas is "dry" and tobacco "cut out."

We recognize with gladness that our ministry and churches such a system of public instruction as will give every citizen of this republic a protestant Christian education.

We are gratified to find our people kindly, but firmly, declaring loyalty to our distinctive principles - freedom of the will, full salvation, immersion of all regenerated and forgiven persons and freedom of the communion table of all who love and serve our Lord Jesus Christ.

We believe there is a demand in Texas for the proclamation and propagation of these sentiments. Therefore there is abundant reason for the maintenance of our denominational identity, and the vigorous prosecution of the works the Master has called us to perform. In this regard permit us a word of warning. We would warn people to use care and good judgement, not permitting themselves to be led astray by designing persons, periodicals, or organizations which, by their representatives may even seem to seek to disturb our Free Baptist relation.

We congratulate the committee on the establishing and publication of the *Free Will Baptist Sentinel*, for through this publication we have been enabled to keep in touch with each other, and our work has continued to prosper although unscrupulous persons have sought to tear down and destroy.

The praise is not unto us. The blessing of God, faithful to his promises that has attended the labors of the denomination 137 years has laid the foundation for another 137 years of denominational existence and we trust a much longer measure of unselfish Christian effort.

On the publication of a paper devoted to state work in Texas we find the *Sentinel*, under the present editor, has been of such value to our churches that we hope it may under his management be able to speak to us for a long time.

We would urge that this association take definite action to establish the *Sentinel* so that it may become a permanent organ of the state association.

We find that many of our churches have no system of financing the work of the church,[41] which hinders the church in its efficiency. While we are confident that the bible system is the best of all ways, and everywhere, when properly used, yet, until its adoption can be secured, inferior are better than none at all. Therefore it is the appropriate and imperative duty of each pastor to see that the churches, of which he has the oversight, contribute regularly to the support of our various benevolent institutions, as upon them depends the successful prosecution of the enterprise, strengthening our present churches, and extending our cause to new regions, in putting an evangelist in the field and giving him a hearty and substantial support. It seems to your committee that there are now in our churches in this state, a sufficient number of persons, who would pay on average of one dollar each. This year if the importance of this effort was brought before them. Therefore, be it resolved: That we endeavor to raise an evangelist fund of not less than $1000.

Rev. Fred Comber (dec.)
Rev. J. L. Payne
T. D. Ross

An invitation to the Association by the Bryan church, through Rev. J. J. Tatum to attend the dedication of their new church building, Sunday at 11 a.m., also the service at 3 o'clock p.m. and at night.

The association went into the election of officers. Rev. Z. B. Dally, Weatherford, Tex. was elected Moderator. Rev. C. C. Wheeler North Zulch Texas assistant Moderator. J. L. Payne, North Zulch, Texas, Clerk and Rev. J. P. Brown (not legible) Tex. assistant Clerk. On motion Revs. A. R. Harper, J. J. Tatum and J. E. Raney elected as a committee on Committees.

Association voted that Rev. Fred Comber preach at 11 o'clock.

Business session adjourned until time stated on the program Thursday afternoon.

Thursday Afternoon

Prayer by Rev. E. S. Jamerson. Reading of proposed By-Laws which were adopted item by item and then adopted as a whole.

The time of the annual meeting was deferred until a later time during this session.

A motion carried that all resolutions be presented in writing.

All visiting brethren and Sisters were to a seat in the association and to enjoy all the privileges of visitors. The Nominating Committee made the following report which was adopted: On Sunday School S T. Spears, James Tobias, and Miss Minnie Jimmerson. On temperance - T. H. Newsom, W. T. Watson and E. F. Trant. On Education Fred

---

[41] Free Will Baptists had not yet adopted tithing as a means of supporting the church. Tithing had not been taught by the churches in Europe nor in the churches in the American colonies. The 1916 edition of the *Treatise* contained no statement about tithing or any other method of supporting the local church or the broader work of the church, except a brief statement in the church covenant: "...nor fail to pay according to our ability for the support of the church, of its poor, and all its benevolent work." The concept of tithing would be introduced later to Free Will Baptists as other denominations began to adopt it and demonstrate its potential as a means of supporting their churches and denominational work. Additionally, the Cooperative Program would be adopted by Southern Baptists on May 13, 1925, and much later by Free Will Baptists.

Comber, E. L. Hill and Mrs. A. R. Harper. On Missions C. C. Wheeler, Z. B. Dally and L. W. Miller. On By-Laws & Constitution - T. H. Newsom, J. L. Payne and J. C. Hodges. On Publication Mrs. Z. B. Dally, T. D. Ross and J. C. Hodges. On Young Peoples' Work Mrs. Ina G. Stout, C. C. Wheeler and J. P. Brown. Woman's Missionary Society - Mrs. A. R. Harper, Mrs. Ina G. Stout, Miss Minnie Jimmerson, and Mrs. Z. B. Dally. On Program - Mrs. T. D. Ross, E. S. Jimmerson and H. W. Watson. On Nominations - C. C. Wheeler, T. D. Ross, and J. E. Raney. On request (not legible)

By vote of body the motion to the By-Laws as a whole with Article 6 and 9 of the Constitution was referred back to the joint committee. Rev. Fred Comber offered the following resolution which was adopted: Revolved, that our clerk be instructed to report the proceedings of this association to the county paper The Standard of Chicago and the New Morning Star of Weatherford, Texas.

A motion carried that this association in 1917 on the night of Oct. 31st (Wednesday) and include Sunday Nov. 4th. By vote the report of the joint committee on By-Laws and Constitution be made a special order for tomorrow (Friday) morning. The program was then resumed.

On motion Bro. Tatum was given 15 minutes time in which to discuss Rev. R. B. Easley's subject "Why a State Association?" also the subjects given Bro. Raney and Jamerson by many that were present.

Minutes of the previous meeting were read and adopted with necessary corrections.
Round table discussion of the subject of "Social Service" led by Mrs. Stout.
On motion the association adjourned until time stated on program.

Friday Morning Session Jan 12, 1917

Friday morning the association was called together by Moderator at time stated on program. A quorum not being present the meeting adjourned subject to call of chair. Later: meeting called to order. Prayer by Rev. L. W. Miller. Minutes of previous session were read and adopted.

Joint committee on Constitution and By-Laws reported and on motion the two articles of the Constitution referred back to the committee with two additional articles were adopted. The Constitution was then unanimously adopted as a whole. Articles 8 and 11 of the By-Laws were adopted, then By-Laws were adopted as a whole.

Rev. Fred Comber offering the following resolution which was referred to the Sunday School Com.

Revolved, That we recommend the election of Rev. and Mrs. Z. B. Dally Texas Freewill Baptist State association Sunday School and Young People missionaries with full power to visit the Sunday Schools and Young People's Societies with a view of strengthening and the bringing also of better conditions by up to date Sunday School Methods. Also to organize Sunday Schools and Young People's Societies in the churches of our connection.

Committee of Education made report, also Com. on Sunday School.

Rev. Fred Comber offered the following resolution which was adopted: Resolved, That the clerk be instructed to purchase a record book to keep the transactions of the business of this associations, and collection be taken at this time to purchase same. Should there be any over than what is needed, the amount to be applied to the clerk's salary. Amount of collection $4.45.

The minutes of last year's meeting were read and adopted the clerk being instructed to make necessary corrections also to send Bro. Dearmore a letter of appreciation for service.

Rev. Z. B. Dally read a splendid paper on "Preparation for Life's Work." A vote of thanks and appreciation was extended to Bro. Dally for the paper and it was recommended that the paper be printed in booklet form for the benefit of the churches.

Committee reported that Bro. J. E. Raney would preach at 11 o'clock. On motion the association (illegible) for divine service.

Friday Afternoon Session

The afternoon session was opened by Mrs A. R. Harper reading the 1st and 2nd Psalms. Prayer by Miss Minnie Jimmerson (not legible) Song by Rev. and Mrs. Dally "God Is Calling." Reading - "Who Will Stand for Little Willie?" by Miss Minnie Jimmerson. Reading - "Twins" by Mrs. Z. B. Dally.

A letter from our missionary President - Mrs. Lucy P. Durgin was read by Mrs. A. R. Harper. A missionary offering was taken which amounted to $8.65. An address was given by Mrs. Ina Stout of Champlain Min on "Responsibility." At this time a state organization was affected with Miss Minnie Jimmerson of Henderson, Tex., Pres. Miss Jettie Duke Carthage, Tex, Secretary. Mrs. Matt Holmes, Bryan Texas Treasurer. Mrs. Z. B. Dally Weatherford, Texas Helper Agent.

A local organization of the Unity Church was also affected at this session.

On motion the report on committees was made a special order for 9:30 Saturday morning.

On Friday evening Rev. J. C. Hodges from the Woodlawn gave an address who was followed with an address by Rev. Dr. Williams, President of the Westminster College Tehaucana, Tx.[42]

Saturday Morning Session

Prayer by assistant moderator Rev. C. C. Wheeler. Minutes of previous session were read, necessary corrections made, and adopted. Time was given for hearing reports from several committees. See reports.

Rev. C. C. Wheeler, North Zulch Texas was elected Denom. Secretary of Young People's Work.

By vote of the association the minutes were to be published. Business was suspended and Rev. Williams addressed the association.

Com. announced that Rev. Comber was to preach at 11 o'clock. Meeting adjourned for preaching service.

Saturday Afternoon Session

Prayer by J. L. Payne. Minutes of morning session were read and approved.

Committee on By-Laws and Constitution gave notice of change of Article 9 of the Constitution.

A bill was presented by the Wallace Printing Co. Bryan, Texas, for $1.75 for printing programs. Association received same and voted to take offering to pay bill - offering $2.00.

On motion the Executive Committee was instructed to take the matter of publishing a paper under serious consideration and push the matter to a successful termination. After discussion prayer was offered by Moderator - The motion carried.

---

[42] From 1869 to 1902 Tehuacana, a town in Limestone County, was also home to Trinity University.

The following resolution on Evangelism was offered by Rev. Comber and adopted by the association: "Resolved. That we as an association heartily endorse any action our Executive Committee may deem fit to take in putting an evangelist or evangelists in the field in the great State of Texas, and we obligate ourselves financially and morally to support them in anything they may undertake to accomplish then carried out."

Minutes were read and approved.

On motion the association closed business session with prayer by Rev. J. E. Raney.

Rev. J. E. Raney, Grandbury Tx Moderator
Rev. J. L. Payne North Zulch Tx Clerk

Reports of Committees

We your committee on nominations recommend the election of the following to serve as standing committees for one Year together with three members of the Executive Committee: Executive Com. J. E. Raney, J. J. Tatum, and (illegible). Sunday School (illegible). Temperance - Fred Comber, J. P. Brown and E. C. Lewis. Ladies Missionary Work - Mrs. J. J. Tatum, Mrs. Mattie Duke and Mrs. A. R. Harper. State of Denomination - J. J. Tatum, T. H. Newsom and J. W. Cook. State of Our Country - Fred Comber, T. D. Ross and J. L. Payne. Social Service - A. R. Harper, E. S. Jameson, and James Tobias. By-Laws and Constitution - A. R. Harper, E. F. Trant, and H. W. Watson. Finance - J. E. Raney, H. W. Watson and T. H. Newsom.
Com.   C. Wheeler
T. D. Ross
J. E. Raney
Publications

We your Committee on Publication beg leave to submit the following: (1st) Realizing the broadening influence of the *Christian Newspaper*, we recommend to our people the reading of our denominational papers, and knowing that we cannot be interested in missions unless we know something about the needs of the field and the work being done, we urge that our people subscribe for and read the *Missionary Helper*.
(2nd) We recommend the New Morning Star so far as its publication may be congenial with our work. (3rd) We urge the use of our own literature in our Sunday School. (4th) Realizing the great need of a State paper of our own to get our work before the people, we recommend that our leaders take steps to found such a paper as soon as may be possible. (5) We recommend that the proceeding of our different meetings be more widely advertised in both secular and religious papers.
Com.   Mrs. Z. B. Dally, T. D. Ross, C. Hodges

Sunday School

We your Committee on Sunday School beg leave to submit the following. We find on investigation that several of our churches are without Sunday Schools and realizing the need of Sunday School in every church and realizing the need of God's Word being taught for the spiritual uplift of the rising generation, we recommend that the pastors cooperate with the Sunday School Evangelists and try to have a Sunday School organized in each their own churches. We further recommend that as far as possible we use our own literature.
Com.   S. T. Spear
James Tobias
Minnie Jimmerson

Temperance

Whereas we as a denomination stand unitedly opposed to the liquor traffic because of it iniquitous character and its pernicious influence upon our entire civilization: Therefore be it resolved that we now petition the State Legislature of Texas now in session to grant submission to the voters of Texas at the next regular election that no compromise be made with the liquor interests and that a copy of this petition signed by the president and Secretary be sent immediately to the State legislature at Austin through our representatives.
(2nd) Whereas we recognize the deleterious effects of tobacco, in its various forms upon physical, moral, social, and spiritual nature of mankind: Therefore be it resolved the urge an incessant warfare against the manufacture and sale of same.
Com.   T. H. Newsom
H. W. Watson
E. F. Trant

Education

Resolved: We seek out those of our young men who are entering the ministry and urge them to attend one of the following educational institutions: Hillsdale, Bates, Keika Park, N. Y. or any other recognized of our denomination. Should the opportunity not afford itself to attend any of these institutions recommended we urge the taking of a correspondence course furnished by Bates Correspondence School of Lewiston, Maine. We also recommend the above schools as worthy of patronage of those not aspirants to the ministry.
Com.   Fred Comber
Mrs. A. R. Harper
E. L. Hill

Missions

We your Committee on Missions submit the following: We find quite an interest now being taken in the home field. Some associations have taken steps toward putting a regular associational missionary in the field on salary which steps we heartily commend and would heartily recommend that each of our associations would work to that end -- to care for their run down church and build up the waste places by systematical giving -- this we feel could be accomplished.

We find that during the time we have taken upon ourselves the salary of Mrs. Holder there is a deficiency of something near $400.00. Be it therefore resolved that the Secretary asked to ascertain a correct report from the National Society and mail statement to each church and request the strenuous effort be put forth at once to meet this deficiency. Be it further resolved that our pastors be requested to inform themselves and preach at least twice each year during the year on Missions and that regular offerings be taken during the year for both the work at home and abroad.
Com. C. C. Wheeler
Z. B. Dally
W. Miller

Young People's Work

We find that few of our churches have organized societies, and recognizing the great need of training our young people for service, be it therefore resolved that during this year strenuous effort be put forth by our pastors and all concerned to organize in their churches Christian Endeavor Societies for the purpose of training our young furthering the kingdom of God. and further we would recommend that each society have one or more delegates in the State Convention to be held in Houston Texas sometime during the month of June. also that each society should be requested to send one or more delegates to our next State association for the purpose of organizing an auxiliary to our State association and that our program committee be asked to give the place on the program for this work and that this association elect one person who shall act in the capacity of Young People's Secretary until a state organization be perfected.
Com.   Mrs. Ina Stout
C. C. Wheeler

Notify Proposed Amendment of article 9 of the Constitution

We your committee recommend article 9 of the Constitution be so amended that all meetings be held from the 1st Tuesday evening until Friday evening inclusive instead of Wednesday evening until Sunday evening as provided in the Constitution.
Com.   T. H. Newsom
J. L. Payne
Resolution of Thanks

We the delegates and visitors of the Texas Freewill Baptist association submit the following resolution: Resolved. That we extend our sincere thanks and appreciation to Rev. Z. B. Dally for his courteous, faithful, efficient and (illegible) pastor for his Christian friendliness and faithfulness in looking after the wants of the delegates and visitors. To the friends and members of the church for the kindness with which opened their homes and hearts to delegates and visitors and to the choir and organist for the splendid music furnished during the sessions of this association.
Com.   Fred Comber
J. J. Tatum

And so the Texas State Association of Free Will Baptists was in place and getting to the the task at hand. It is clear that they had a vision for the future and saw the needs for all aspects of the work: missions, education, youth, publications, etc. One thing that is easily noticeable in the early minutes is the prominence of women's involvement in the work of the state association. There were lots of them and they served in almost every capacity. They preached, brought devotions, presented special programs, served on boards and committees, and helped conduct business. The one position to which they did not attain was the office of moderator.

The new organ of the state association, the *Freewill Baptist Sentinel,* was prominent in the discussions during the first 1917 state meeting. *The Freewill Baptist News,* which had announced the 1915 and first 1917 state meetings, had been purchased by the Co-operative General Association (see below), renamed *The New Morning Star*, and was being moved to Tecumseh, Oklahoma, the location of the new Free Will Baptist School, Tecumseh College, which was to open in the fall of 1917. The *Sentinel* was edited by Z. B. Dally, of Weatherford, Texas, one of the most active of the leaders in the new Texas State Association.

Several items of interest should be noted in the minutes of the second annual session of the Texas State Association. One, the association recommended that young ministers attend the colleges which had been lost in the merger of 1910-11, such as Hillsdale College in Michigan and Bates College in Lewiston, Maine. Those two colleges continue as prominent schools of higher education today. Two, the Free Will Baptist women of Texas were organized into an auxiliary organization called Ladies Missionary Work or Woman's Missionary Work. The women's work has been one of the most successful aspects of the Free Will Baptist work in Texas and continues today as the Texas Women Active for Christ.

The Co-operative General Association, 1916

As noted above some groups survived the merger for various and sundry reasons, choosing not to participate in it. The Missouri State Association, and smaller groups in Oklahoma, Texas, Arkansas, Kentucky, West Virginia, Ohio, Alabama, North Carolina, Nebraska, Kansas, Illinois, and Tennessee, to name a few, did not go along with the merger. At this point we will narrow our focus to Free Will Baptists in the West for a moment.

There arose a desire and need to have a broader organization than the Southwestern Convention in the West. Enter John H. Wolfe.[43] Wolfe, along with several others, such as Hirem and Lizzie McAdams of Texas, T. C. Ferguson, of Missouri, and G. S. Lattimer, of the Northwest Missouri Yearly Meeting, had opposed the merger with the Northern Baptists. John H. Wolfe, his wife, Delia Wolfe, herself a minister, and G. S. Lattimer, while in conversation one day, raised the question "Why can't we have a Conference of Free Will Baptists of the West?"[44] The three of them planned it and the following fall met with the Missouri State Association and laid the proposal before them. The plan Wolfe presented to the Missouri State Association contained four grand and sweeping proposals:
1. That they, along with other bodies, organize a co-operative association
2. That the new association start a denominational paper jointly with other bodies
3. That they start a college
4. That they, along with other like bodies, start a Biblical Correspondence School[45]

The Missouri State Association approved these proposals and set about to make them a reality. They voted to hold a meeting near Pattonsburg, Missouri, in December of 1916 for the purpose of organizing a co-operative association. They also voted to accept an offer from S. L. Morris, of Weatherford, Texas, to sell them the *Freewill Baptist News* plant for $350.00 and to ask Brother Morris to continue as editor and publisher until after the meeting in Pattonsburg. They voted to change the name of the paper from the *Freewill Baptist News* to *The New Morning Star*.[46] That name was undoubtedly chosen because Free Will Baptists had long had a paper called *The Morning Star* which had been lost in the merger of 1910-11.

The planned meeting to organize a co-operative association was held December 27-31, 1916, at the Philadelphia Church near Pattonsburg, Missouri. Delegates from nine different bodies in Kansas, Nebraska, Missouri, and Texas met and organized the desired broader body and named it the "Co-operative General Association of Freewill Baptists." Wolfe was elected president. The

---
[43] *Little Known Chapters in Free Will Baptist History*, by Dr. Robert E. Picirilli (Randall House Publications, Nashville, Tennessee, 2015), pages 181-244, hereafter *Little Known Chapters*.
[44] *Little Known Chapters*, page 203.
[45] *Little Known Chapters*, page 204.
[46] Rev. W. A. Hearron, the father of Rev. Clarence J. Hearron, became the editor of the *New Morning Star* in 1922.

Texas delegate was R. A. Roberts, representing the Central Brazos Association. S. L. Morris, Z. B. Dally and his wife, all of Weatherford, and J. J. Tatum[47] of Bryan were welcomed as visitors. They adopted the *Freewill Baptist Treatise* as revised at Harper's Ferry, West Virginia, in 1899, and to establish a denominational school with John H. Wolfe as its president. That school, Tecumseh College, located at Tecumseh, Oklahoma, opened in the fall of 1917.[48] The grand plans laid out by the Wolfes and Lattimer were coming to fruition. In 1917 and 1918 the Co-operative General Association grew to include bodies in Oklahoma, Texas (Central Brazos and West Fork associations only), Kentucky, West Virginia, Illinois, Michigan, Tennessee, and Ohio. Free Will Baptists in the West were well on their way to becoming an established denomination once again. With continued growth the Co-operative General Association could have become a national association.

With the organization of the Co-operative General Association, the Southwestern Convention ceased to exist, giving way to the larger and broader association.

The General Conference of Free Will Baptists, 1921

There were efforts to bring into the Co-operative General Association the various associations in the Southeast, but this effort failed because of the issue of feet washing. The associations in the West wanted to leave it an open question, leaving the question up to each individual and each local church, but the associations in Tennessee and North Carolina wanted it as an ordinance. This one thing kept the Co-operative General Association from becoming a national body, a national association. As a result the associations in the East formed the General Conference of Free Will Baptists in 1921 at a meeting at the Cofer's Chapel Free Will Baptist Church in Nashville, Tennessee. Tennessee left the Co-operative General Association and joined the General Conference of Free Will Baptists. The General Conference consisted of associations in North Carolina, South Carolina, Virginia, Florida, Georgia, Alabama, Mississippi, and Tennessee. This brought Free Will Baptists together into two regional organizations, the Co-operative General Association in the West and the General Conference in the East. These broader associations served to bring the scattered remnants together into organizations which would enable them to have a Free Will Baptist identity, to draw strength from each other, encourage one other, and to provide some mechanism by which they could work together, pooling their efforts, talents, and monies, to accomplish together what they could not do alone. No church alone could build a college or seminary, send out foreign missionaries, or have an aggressive home missions program. No church alone could own and operate a youth camp. By working together, however, they could do an unlimited number of things. Those are the same reasons we have district and state associations, and a national association today. It was the two groups, one from the West and one from the East, which met in 1935 and formed the National Association of Free Will Baptists. Later in this chapter we will focus on Texas' involvement in the formation of the National Association of Free Will Baptists.

The General Conference united the Free Will Baptist churches in the East. There is no evidence of participation of Texas associations until 1930. In '30 and '31 the Texas State Convention sent a "corresponding delegate," layman J. L. Edge of Bryan. In 1933 the Texas State Convention joined the General Conference. Dr. Robert E. Picirilli says, "Of course, I assume that all the associations that were part of the Texas State Convention were therefore (by virtue of their

---

[47] Zally and Tatum, influential Texas preachers were publishing a paper called the *Freewill Baptist Sentinel*.
[48] Tecumseh College continued to exist until 1927 when it was burned in a fire. It was never rebuilt.

membership in it) also "officially" tied in to the General Conference).[49] The Free Will Baptist work, spread across much of the country, was making progress toward being a national denomination again, and Texas was a part of that effort. In fact, Texas was a big part of it, as we shall soon see.

Meanwhile Back at the Ranch

Having focused briefly on the development of two broader associations which extended far beyond the borders of Texas, we now return our attention to the work in Texas itself, focusing on the Texas State Association.

Third Annual Session - 1917
The minutes of the third annual session, which would have been held in December of 1917, have not been located, to date.

Fourth Annual Session - 1918

The fourth annual session of the Texas State Association of Free Will Baptists was held at the Clayton Free Will Baptist Church in Clayton, Texas, starting on Tuesday evening, November 12, 1918. The opening sermon was preached by J. J. Tatum. On Wednesday morning the devotional service was led by J. B. Dally due to the fact that President C. C. Wheeler[50] was absent "having gone home." J. J. Tatum was chosen temporary chairman and T. D. Ross assistant clerk. The following people were appointed to serve as the Committee on Committees: J. B. Dally, Miss Minnie Jimmerson, and A. W. West.

Letters were read from the following associations: Southeast Texas, Central Texas, and the Texas Association, which would later be renamed the East Texas District Association. The Texas Association (East Texas) recommended that the state association take steps in helping Bro. J. W. Wheeler obtain an education. The matter was referred to the Committee on Requests. A special committee which had previously been appointed in 1917 to purchase a car for the state secretary reported that they had, indeed, purchased a car for him and that the cost of the purchase was $350.00. $225.00 had been paid in cash for the car, leaving a balance on a note of $125.00.

Z. B. Dally preached on Wednesday evening, using the text Matthew 17:4. On Thursday morning the editor of *The Sentinel* gave a report, which was referred to the Executive Committee. The report is not in the minutes. On Thursday morning at 11:00 o'clock Mr. H. L. McKnight, of the A.M. Extension Department, "gave the association a very interesting and helpful address which was appreciated by all present." Part of the afternoon session was given over to the Women's Missionary Society which "had a very interesting program. The particulars of the program are not in the minutes because it "appeared in *The Sentinel* some time ago." The association adopted a recommendation that the State Secretary take the lead and work in conjunction with the various

---

[49] From an e-mail from Dr. Picirilli dated June 27, 2014.
[50] Rev. C. C. Wheeler pastored the Bryan Free Will Baptist twice, 1913-15 and again in 1917-18. He was born on January 28, 1886, in Limestone County, Texas, and received his theological training at Westminster College in Tehuacana, Texas. In addition to the Bryan church he also pastored North Zulch, Kurten, Cross, Bright Light, and Keith. He also pastored two churches in Nebraska, at Geneva and Sutton. This information comes from *A 63 Year History of First Free Will Baptist Church, Bryan, Texas*, by Walter J. Coulter, 1957, page 23.

associations in the evangelistic campaign for the following year, and that his salary be increased by $200.00.

Fifth Annual Session - 1919

The fifth annual session of the Texas State Association of "Free Baptists" met with the Bryan Church in Bryan, Texas, Tuesday evening, November 18 through Friday evening, November 21, 1919. The meeting was called to order by the President, J. J. Tatum. T. H. Newsom of Azle, Texas, preached the opening sermon. His text was Hebrews 12:1. On Wednesday morning, after the devotional services, the business session was postponed until the afternoon so a series of prayers could be offered to God that He would bless the association. Part of the afternoon was devoted to the Woman's Missionary work, with Mrs. Kirby Chapman as chairman. The Pulpit Supply Committee reported that J. L. Lee of Kirbyville, Texas, would preach the evening sermon.

The report of the treasurer was given. The association voted that a letter be sent by the clerk requesting an itemized statement of the receipts, disbursements, and balance. A motion was then passed that no monies be paid out by the treasurer for any purpose except upon a written order from the clerk, signed by the president (moderator).

J. J. Tatum read a report of his work as president for the year, and his work as state secretary. A verbal report was given by J. J. Tatum and J. Swanwick on the state association car. A motion was adopted that the matter of the disposal of the state car be referred to the Executive Committee, who would report to the body.

The association voted that they ask for a charter under the laws of Texas. The clerk was assigned responsibility for this. The Executive Committee recommended that the state association pay the Central Texas Association the amount they paid for the car and that the car be returned to its original use in the state work. They also recommended that J. J. Tatum be paid $83.33 for his work as the state secretary.

Z. B. Dally reported on his work as editor of *The Sentinel*, and offered his resignation. The association voted to receive his resignation and to express their thanks to Brother and Sister Dally for their faithfulness and untiring efforts in getting out the paper. The association voted to take the *Free Baptist Treatise* off the hands of Brother Dally, who kept them in stock to sell to those who wanted to purchase a copy, and pay him $4.00 for the 39 copies he had. A Mr. Chism gave "a splendid address on Sunday school work."

The following committee was appointed to serve with the state secretary in procuring a state evangelist and arranging for meetings: J. L. Edge, Central Texas Association, Bryan, Texas; J. E. Raney, West Texas Association, Granbury, Texas; T. E. Fain, Woodlawn Association, Killeen, Texas; E. S. Jameson, Texas Association (East Texas), Tatum, Texas; J. T, Ratcliff, Southeast Texas Association, Beach Grove[51]; Ira Johnson, Mount Zion,[52] Glendale, Texas. The state secretary was instructed to get the cooperation of the association near DeKalb, Texas.[53]

The Woman's Missionary Society re-elected all officers except Mrs. Kirby Chapman, president, and Mrs. C. C. Wheeler, vice-president. A motion passed that the Evangelistic Committee cooperate with E. S. Jamerson in the Conservation Campaign Drive. The association

---

[51] There is no information whether Beech Grove was the name of a church or a community.
[52] Mount Zion must have been the name of a church.
[53] This would be the Northeast Texas Association. DeKalb is in Bowie County, Texas.

also voted that the minutes of the session be published in the paper.[54] A motion referred the matter of selecting an editor for the paper to the Publications Board.

The association voted that the 1920 session be held with the West Fork District Association, beginning on Tuesday night before the first Sunday in November and close with the Friday night service. At the Friday evening service the Honorable W. C. Davis addressed the association. There is no information about who he was or what his addressed concerned.

Sixth Annual Session - 1920

Minutes of the sixth annual session of the Texas State Association have not been located. The minutes of the 1919 session, as noted above, state that the meeting was to be held with the West Fork District Association, starting on Tuesday before the first Sunday in November, 1920.

Seventh Annual Session - 1921

Minutes of the seventh annual session of the Texas State Association are not available. We do, however, have the minutes of the Executive Committee which met in Bryan, Texas, on February 26, 1921. They are as follows:

Minutes of Executive Committee held at Bryan, Texas, February 26, 1921

Persuant to call the Executive Committee of the State Conference of Freewill Baptist met in Bryan, Texas, Feb. 26, 1921, with President Rev. J. E. Raney, Grandbury, Texas; Rev. E. Jameson, Tatum, Texas; Rev. C. B. Thompson and J. L. Payne, Bryan, Tex. present. After reading Scripture lesson prayer was offered by Rev. C. B. Thompson.

The president stated the object of this meeting was to discuss and devise plans for our denominational paper - *The Sun*, and plan for a special Soul winning and membership Campaign, also push the consecration Campaign, and devise way for collecting pledges already due.

The committee [voted] that a report of this meeting be sent to the Treasurer and that he be requested to furnish a quarterly report of money received and expended. By vote the committee adjourned to meet again at 1 o'clock p.m.

The committee [was called] together at 1 o'clock by the president. Prayer was offered by J. L. Payne.

The committee was advised that all money [sent] as Subscription to *The Sun* be sent to the treasurer, T. D. Ross, Clayton, Texas, and in case money is sent to the editor he receipt treas. for same in order that proper record might be kept.

The committee voted that the manager of the Consecration Campaign Drive take steps immediate to collect pledges due and to take new pledge, also to collect all subscriptions to *The Sun* in arears at the same time putting forth a greater effort for new subscribers.

State Manager E. S. Jameson named the following as associational managers for the Consecration Campaign Drive: J. W. Diserens, Woodlawn; J. H. Dowell,

---

[54] Evidently *The Sentinel* was meant.

Central Texas; J. T. Lee, South East Texas; E. L. Hill, West Fork; J. E. Raney, general man[ager].

The committee offered the following recommendations: That we put on a special campaign aside from our summer revivals for decisions for Christ and membership to the church beginning the first of May and continuing to the close of the conference year and we urge each pastor and each member of the churches to join in this campaign.

The committee granted the clerk all power of authority to secure charter for State Conference.

President of State Conference, J. E. Raney, Granbury, Texas, was made manager of the Membership Campaign.

On motion with second the committee adjourned subject to call of president.

J. E. Raney, Pres.
J. L. Payne, Clk.

We have one copy of the program for the meeting and it is reproduced here because the program itself is instructive. Notice how much emphasis the session placed on teaching on doctrines and practices of Free Will Baptists.

PROGRAM

Texas Free Baptist Conference
Comanche, October 28-31, 1921

TUESDAY, 7:30 P. M. - Sermon
        9:00 a.m.   Devotional and Business
       10:00 a.m.   Announcement of Standing Committees and Appointment of Session
                              Committees
                            Welcome Address by Pastor Rev. J. C. Hodges
                            Response by Mrs. C. B. Thompson
       11:00 a.m.   Sermon
        2:00 p.m.   Devotional. Reports of committees by Chairmen:
                            Executive, W. D. Phillips; Missions, Mrs. Wainwright;
                            Sunday School, E. S. Jameson; Social Service, C. B. Thompson;
                            State of Denomination, J. J. Tatum
        3:00 p.m.   Address: Value of Christian Centers," J. B. Brown
        3:30 p.m.   "The Enterprise of the Church," J. S. Dillard
        4:00 p.m.   "Enlistment for Life," J. L. Bounds
        7:30 p.m.   "Man, His Origin and His Destiny," J. C. Hodges
        8:00 p.m.   Sermon

THURSDAY
        9:00 a.m.   Devotional. Business and Reports of Committees by
                            Chairmen: Education, W. E. Youngblood; Evangelism, J. P. Brown;
                            Temperance,   J. W. Diserens

	10:00 a.m.	Address, "The Seat of Authority in Religion," R. B. Easley
	10:30 a.m.	"The Value of an Annual Assembly for Training Workers," Ira Harper
	11:00 a.m.	Sermon
	2:00 p.m.	Devotional. Business and Reports of C. E. Trustee C. B. Thompson and Field Secretary J. J. Tatum
	3:00 p.m.	Address, "The Deepening of the Spiritual Life of our Churches," J. E. Raney
	3:30 p.m.	Address, "The Joys of the Ministry."
	4:00 p.m.	"Perils and Possibilities of Present Day Pastors," J. H. Dowell
	7:30 p.m.	"Ready for Action at Daybreak," C. B. Thompson
	8:00 p.m.	Sermon

FRIDAY

	9:00 a.m.	Devotional. Business and Reports of Officers and Committees
	10:00 a.m.	Address, "Challenging God's Men," D. G. Berkman
	10:30 a.m.	Trusteeship, Diserens; Stewardship, J. E. Graham
	11:00 a.m.	Sermon
	2:00 p.m.	"Stewardship of Time," John Swanwick
	2:30 p.m.	"Stewardship of Property," B. A. Wainwright
	3:00 p.m.	"Tithing," E. S. Jameson[55]
	7:30 p.m.	Young Peoples' Meeting
	8:00 p.m.	Sermon
	2:00 to 3:00 p.m.	- Women's Missionary Meeting in charge of Mrs. Jeff Easley

Eighth Annual Session - 1922

The eighth annual session of the Texas State Association was held at the Bryan Free Will Baptist Church,[56] Bryan, Texas, from October 31 to November 3, 1922. Vice-president J. E Raney called the meeting to order in the absence of the president. The opening sermon was preached by J. W. Handy of Alvarado, Texas. The president, J. J. Tatum, of Bryan, was present for the Wednesday morning session. Letters were read from the Southeast Texas Association. J. S. Dillard, of Waxahachie, Texas, preached on Wednesday morning.

The Committee on the Southwestern Convention[57] made its report which was adopted and the committee retained. Their report, signed by C. B. Thompson and J. C. Hodges, was:

> We have been gathering all the information we could and have visited other sections. We are led to believe that the time is not here for the reorganization of the S.W Convention. But we feel sure it is not far in the future when the convention will begin activities. We would recommend that this committee be continued.

The State Missions report was read and adopted, which refers to Miss Elsie Barnard as "our missionary to India." Half of her salary, $400.00 per year, was supposed to be paid by Texas

---

[55] It is interesting that the issues of tithing and stewardship were presented. This was new territory.
[56] The church wasn't called the First Free Will Baptist Church until years later.
[57] The Southwestern Convention of Free Will Baptists had ceased meeting after about 1915.

Free Will Baptists and the other $400.00 by New England Free Will Baptists.[58]   Historical Secretary E. S. Jamerson gave a verbal report on his work. There is written account of his report. The Honorable Lee J. Roundtree addressed the convention on "The Church's Part in Law Enforcement." Afterward, D. G. Berkman preached.

A letter from the Woodlawn Association was read, along with a petitionary letter from Easley's Chapel, and the church received. C. B. Thompson, of Bryan, presented a bill for printing the programs, $3.25, and the bill was paid from the treasury. A letter of greeting from Brother and Sister Stout of Champlin,[59] Minnesota, was read and the clerk was instructed to reply. The letter from the Central Texas Association was read. The Executive Committee recommended that, due to the war, and the resulting depressed financial conditions, the Consecration Campaign be discontinued. Strong resolutions were passed condemning the use of tobacco and liquor, and commending the country for passing Prohibition.[60]

The following officers were elected: President, J. C. Hodges; Vice-president, J. J. Tatum; Secretary, J. L. Payne; Treasurer, J. L. Payne; State Field Secretary, J. J. Tatum; Statistical Secretary, J. P. Brown; and C. E. Trustee, J. J. Tatum. The editor of *The Sun*[61] gave his report, which was received. J. E. Graham, of Killeen, Texas, preached. A motion was passed that one day of the convention be set aside as a day of study. A committee, composed of J. E. Raney, E. S. Jamerson, and C. B. Thompson, was appointed to arrange for the day. The business was adjourned for the presentation of the Woman's Missionary Society program. The convention then, as a body, visited the A&M College.

Outgoing President J. J. Tatum, after an appropriate address, presented the President-elect, J. C. Hodges, a gavel and block from a tree which grew in the yard of the first white Free Baptist church organized in Texas, the Liberty Free Will Baptist Church organized by A. M. Stewart. The convention voted that the churches observed Foreign Missions Day during the months of May and October, and Home Missions Day during March and September. J. C. Hodges addressed the convention on "The Divinity of Christ Manifest in all That He Made."

On Friday morning, as recommended by the Executive Committee, the association adopted the following goals:

That we teach our young the observance of the national holiday in a more reverent way

That each church win at least five persons to Christ

That each official member of the church become a leader in public prayer

That each district association establish at least one new church during the year

That each district association have at least seventy-five percent with Evergreen Sunday schools, and fifty percent with live young people's societies

That *The Sun* be in every Free Will Baptist home in the state

---

[58] The minutes refer to a "New England district," and also states "New England has always been the stronghold of FWB, and Texas is the latest of the F. W .B. to take up the work." Were Texas Free Will Baptists continuing to work in cooperation with at least some Free Will Baptist in New England after the merger of 1910-11?
[59] Champlin is a northern suburb of Minneapolis, Minnesota. The population was 23,089 in the 1910 census.
[60] The Prohibition Era was from 1920 to 1933.
[61] This is the first mention of *The Sun*, a paper published under the auspices of the state association and edited by E. S. Jamerson.

That we have at least one rally during the year in each association under the direction of the field secretary.

E. S. Jamerson delivered the morning sermon at 11:00 o'clock. In the afternoon session a resolution was adopted that arrangements be made for a denominational encampment. E. S. Jamerson was selected to plan and arrange for this encampment. John Swanwick, Clyde Goen, and C. B. Thompson were appointed to audit the association's books for the 1921-22 fiscal year. J. E. Raney preached the evening sermon. After the sermons there was some additional business conducted. The association voted to send a letter of greeting to Miss Minnie Jimmerson who was graduated from, and became a member of the faculty of, the Baptist Missionary Training School, Chicago, Illinois. The needs of *The Sun* were presented by E. S. Jamerson and financial aid was given in the amount of $103.00 by individuals. The association voted to pay him what was due him and retain him as editor for another year. Jamerson reported that he had received in subscriptions for *The Sun* $129.25, and had received a donation from C. B. Thompson in the amount of $25.00.

It is noteworthy that Mrs. A. M. Stewart was listed as a member of the Publications Committee. You will remember that she was the widow of the man who started the first white Free Will Baptist Church in Texas.

Ninth Annual Session - 1923

The ninth annual session of the Texas State Association of Free Will Baptists met in 1923, but there are no minutes of this meeting available currently.

Tenth Annual Session - 1924

The tenth annual session of the Texas State Association of Free Will Baptists met at the Easley's Chapel Free Will Baptist Church, Comanche, Comanche County, Texas, October 28-30, 1924. J. E. Graham preached the opening sermon, using Matthew 24:7 as his text. The president and clerk were both absent and J. W. Hanly was elected president *pro tem* and T. H. Newsom was elected temporary clerk.

On Wednesday morning the following officers were elected: president, C. B. Thompson; vice-president, J. W. Diserens; secretary-treasurer, T. H. Newsom; field secretary, J. J. Tatum; statistical secretary, J. W. Collins; historical secretary, E. S. Jameson; executive committee, J. P. Brown, C. B. Thompson, and J. W. Diserens. Letters from the following four associations were read and adopted: Central Texas, West Fork, Woodlawn, Texas (East Texas) and Easley's Chapel Church. There was a motion passed that an ordaining council consisting of J. C. Hodges, R. B. Beasley,[62] and some member of Easley's Chapel be appointed for the purpose of ordaining M. Gaines.

The Wednesday afternoon session consisted of reports by the Nominating Committee, Social Services Committee, Sunday School Committee, and the State of the Denomination Committee. C. B. Thompson preached a sermon on the subject "Enlistment for Life."

The Wednesday evening session was opened by a song service led by J. W. Diserens. C. B. Thompson preached the evening message: "The Spirit's Leadership."

On Thursday morning Joe Lemons brought a devotion from Psalm 23. A motion passed that an expense of $3.25 be acknowledged and paid. What it was for isn't stated. The secretary

---

[62] R. B. Easley is probably meant.

(clerk) noted that there was a motion that a committee on the laymen's movement, with E. S. Jamerson as chairman, report at the afternoon session. The reports of the Committee on Evangelism and the Temperance Committee were given and approved. E. S. Jameson gave an address on "The Value of an Annual Assembly for Training Workers." J. J. Tatum and J. P. Brown gave an address on "The Seat of Authority in Religion." E. S. Jameson then gave a second address: "Tithing."[63]

On Thursday afternoon John A. Brooks brought a devotion, using 2 Corinthians 1. The report of the Committee on the Laymen's Movement was read and approved. The committee consisted of E. S. Jameson, J. L. Edge, W. K. O'Brien, J. W. Collins, and A. D. Taylor. The report of the C. E. Trustee, C. B. Thompson, was read and approved. The report of the Field Secretary, J. J. Tatum, regarding the work in the field, was "very encouraging." J. J. Tatum also gave a report as delegate to the Northern Baptist Convention[64] was read and approved. Two addressed were then presented: "The Joys of the Ministry" by J. A. Brooks, and "Perils and Possibilities of Present Day Pastors" by J. H. Dowell

On Thursday evening another address was given, this one entitled "Ready for Action at Daybreak" was delivered by C. B. Thompson. The evening sermon was preached by J. P. Brown.

The Friday morning session started with a devotion by J. W. Handy. The Resolutions Committee report was read and adopted. A letter of greeting from the Texas Association was read and approved. J. W. Bounds was chosen to deliver the introductory sermon at the 1925 state meeting. There was a motion that a historical secretary be selected from each association to collect data for the upcoming Semi-Centennial. The report of the Committee on the Disposition of the Ford car used by the field secretary was read and approved. There was a motion that the secretary be permitted to make all necessary changes when preparing the minutes for the press. Three committees then read their reports, all which were adopted: Sunday School, Statistical Secretary, and Resolutions. C. B. Thompson brought a devotion.

Only two reports are written in the minutes available because part of the second report and then all the rest are missing. What remains is interesting and are included here.

Report of State Woman's Missionary Society

We your S. W. M. Society met Friday afternoon, October 31, with Mrs. Jeff Easley presiding.

After prayer by Mrs. C. B. Thompson we moved into the election of officers for the coming year, as follows: President, Mrs. C. B. Thompson; Vice-President, Mrs. Jeff Easley; Secretary-Treasurer, Mrs. Mark Detrick; and Corresponding Secretary, Mrs. George Smith. Adjourned to meet at Bryan, October 30, 1925. Mrs. C. B. Thompson, President

Sunday School

We your committee on Sunday School beg leave to submit the following report: We find our denomination becoming more interested in Sunday school

---

[63] This is perhaps the first occurrence of the word tithing I have seen in any Texas Free Will Baptist minutes or other documents.

[64] Most Free Will Baptists had merged with the Northern Baptist Convention in 1910-11. Most of the Texas Free Will Baptist churches had not.

work. The Texas Association has eleven schools well organized and equipped and doing a concrete work. By this we mean they are encouraging their pupils to do real practical things.

Central Texas reports nine schools all doing good work. These schools are getting on a higher plane each year.

Woodlawn Association comes nearest the 100% basis with S. S. organization than any other association, having a Sunday school in almost every church.

West Fork has some good live schools but we are unable to get statistics. We have no report on S. S. from other associations.

We submit the following recommendations..................

Eleventh Annual Session - 1925

We have found no minutes of the 1925 meeting of the state meeting. We do have a little information about it, however, gleaned from two sources. The minutes of the 1924 meeting announced that the meeting would be in Bryan, Texas, October 27-30, 1925. J. W. Bounds was scheduled to deliver the introductory sermon (according to the 1924 minutes).

The second source is the minutes of the Executive Committee, which met on October 30, 1925, probably just after the conclusion of the state meeting. Those minutes are brief and reproduced here in their entirety.

Minutes of Executive Committee held at Bryan, Texas, October 30, 1925.

The Executive Committee of the Texas State Conference of Free-Will Baptists meet in regular session at Bryan, Texas, Oct. 30, 1925.
8:00 a.m. Motion that a committee be appointed to formulate plans for publishing of a paper for the State Conference. Committee appointed as follows: Will Phillips, C. B. Thompson, J. C. Hodges, J. J. Tatum, and T. H. Newsom.

Motion that an indebtedness of $224.00 due John Swanwick be acknowledged and liquidated.

Motion to raise funds to defray expenses of a delegate to the Northern Baptist Convention to convene in May at Washington D. C. Plans formulated and approved by convention.

Adjourned subject to call of chair.

E. S. Jameson, Pres., T. H. Newsom, Clerk

Twelfth Annual Session - 1926, no minutes available

Thirteenth Annual Session - 1927, no minutes available

Fourteenth Annual Session - 1928

The Fourteenth Annual Session of the Texas Free Will Baptist Convention met at the Woodlawn Free Will Baptist Church in McClellan County, near Bruceville, Tuesday through

Friday, August 28-31, 1928. The president (moderator) was Mr. J. L. Edge of Bryan, Texas. M. L. Hollis, pastor of the church in Bryan preached the introductory sermon. Hollis made his fame in Mississippi and Alabama as a church planter. The minutes do not mention which associations represented. C. B. Thompson preached on Wednesday evening on the subject "The Challenge of Evangelism" and then preached again on Thursday evening on "The More Abundant Life." The meeting date of the convention was changed from the last Tuesday of August to the first Tuesday of November. M. L. Sutton preached on Thursday at 11:00 o'clock.

The Executive Committee reported that they had met in the Bryan office of President J. L. Edge and had "discussed the work of the Free Baptist in the State from every angle." The committee consisted of President J. L. Edge, C. B. Thompson, J. L. Bounds, Clyde Goen, and Noah Cole. Field Secretary J. J. Tatum gave the committee a report on his work.

Grace Goen, wife of Clyde F. Goen, read a paper on "The Importance of Women's Work in the State," which elicited a vote of thanks from the body for such a valuable paper. Her paper is included elsewhere in this book. The body voted to meet at the church in Fort Worth, on its new date, Tuesday though Friday, November 5-8, 1929. C. B. Thompson was to preach the introductory sermon.

Fifteenth Annual Session - 1929

The fifteenth annual session of the Texas State Convention of Free Will Baptists was held with the First Free Will Baptist Church of Fort Worth, pastored by M. L. Sutton. Wednesday through Saturday, November 5-8, 1929. The president (moderator) was Mr. J. L. Edge of Bryan, Texas. The clerk was T. D Ross of Clayton, Texas. C. B. Thompson preached on Wednesday evening. He also delivered an address on "Stewardship." T. H. Newsom delivered what the clerk described as "a very able address" on the subject of Christian Leadership. R. L. Cotnam preached on the subject "The Signs of the Times." Cotnam, substituting for J. A. Edmonson, also delivered an address on "The Needed Awakening," delivered a lecture on "Roman Catholicism," and introduced a plan whereby the convention could take care of their retired ministers. J. J. Tatum also preached but his subject is not given.

Two district associations petitioned the state association for membership and were accepted. They were the Northwest Brazos[65] and the Mt. Zion associations. I have no further information about the Mt. Zion association, what area it covered, which churches composed it, how long it lasted, etc. Other business included a vote to pay J. J. Tatum the indebtedness owed to him for his work as State Secretary and the adoption of a plan to raise $1,500.00 for home missions.

Several committees or boards carried out much of the work of the convention during the year. They included the Executive Board, Foreign Missions, Home Missions, Sunday Schools, Social Service, Education, Evangelism, Temperance and Law Enforcement, Resolutions, Young People's Work, Women's Work, State of the Denomination, and Laymen's Work.

W. D. Phillips, a deacon of the New Salem Church in Decatur, J. C. Hodges, T. H. Newsom, J. J. Tatum, M. L. Sutton, and R. L. Cotnam were elected as delegates to the Cooperative General Association of Free Will Baptists, the broadest Free Will Baptist organization in the West. President J. L. Edge and his wife were elected as delegates to the Eastern General Association, the broadest organization of Free Will Baptists in the East, meeting in Vernon, Alabama, June 11-12, 1930. This connection with the Eastern General Association resulted in the Texas State

---

[65] The Northwest Brazos Association, organized in 1910, only now joins the State Association.

Association being affiliated with the Eastern General Association rather than the Cooperative General Association of the West.

A Sunday School Convention, 1932, Weatherford, Texas. The only people we can identify in this group are M. L. Sutton, on the front row, fourth from the left; and Mrs. Clara Sutton, standing in the back row, to the very left.

Board and committee reports in 1929 were very instructive and we will note some of the information in them here. The directory of ministers listed forty-nine ministers and observes that it was not a complete list. The Temperance and Law Enforcement Committee mentioned that there were ten thousand Free Will Baptists in Texas. The report, written by President J. L. Edge, entioned that there was a strong push nationally to repeal Prohibition. Prohibition ended in 1933. The Home Missions Report is included in the chapter of this book on Home Missions. The Committee on Sunday Schools reported that almost all the churches had Sunday schools and that the total enrollment in Texas was 840.

April 3, 1932: Pastor M. L. Sutton's Sunday school class, First Free Will Baptist Church, Fort Worth, Texas. Pastor Sutton is front row left, hat and Bible in hands.

Sunday, June 28th, 1931: Baptismal service conducted by Pastor M. L. Sutton, who is standing in the Trinity River, far left, with his hands folded across his chest. In the 1930's it was not unusual for a church to have a baptismal service in which dozens of converts were baptized, especially following a revival meeting.

The report of the Foreign Missions Committee is of special interest and is reproduced here in full:

> Our chief Foreign Mission field is in India, and is known as the Bengal-Orissa Mission. It was first occupied by the Free Will Baptist Foreign Missions Society[66] in the year 1836. It lies on the eastern side of India and on the Bay of Bengal. Its most southern station is Chandbali, about two hundred miles southwest of Calcutta, the most northern station is Bimpore, about eighty miles west of Calcutta.
>
> It embraces the two districts of Midnapore Balasore. From the time Eli Noyes entered the field in 1836 until this good day there has never been more heroic effort nor greater on any field of activity. A few names among the many will be sufficient to any well informed Free Will Baptist to cause a halt to silently thank God we have been privileged to be associated with them in their ministry to humanity---Phillips Bacheler, Coombs, Buckholder, Butts, Coldren, Stiles, Miner, Lougher, Barnes, Keenan.

---

[66] The Foreign Missions Society was the missionary arm of the General Conference of Free Will Baptists, the Randall movement of Free Will Baptists. Even though the merger of 1911 had taken place, with the General Conference being absorbed by the Northern Baptists, Free Will Baptists in Texas and elsewhere continued for a while to support the foreign missions effort in India. This would soon cease. The National Association of Free Will Baptists was formed in 1935, with a foreign missions board. Miss Laura Belle Barnard was the first missionary sent to the field, and she was sent to India.

But those most endeared as perhaps Murphy,[67] Griffin, Collett, Oxreder, Coe, and Holder. Some of these faithful laborers have visited our churches and homes. Since the return of Mrs. Holder, as the committee sees it, we have become careless and indifferent to those representing us so faithfully on our mission field. Therefore, be it

Resolved, That we, as a denomination, have reasons for devout gratitude to God for that call of His providence and His servants which led us into the Foreign Mission field; since eternity alone will reveal how much good may have been accomplished through our missionary efforts.

We further recommend that the waning interest be awakened and greater activitivities [surely they meant activities] be put forth in this field of opportunities.

We further recommend that our pastors be urged to preach at least one sermon per year on the subject of Foreign Missions and that collections be taken for this work. The month of May being designated for this collection.

Mrs. M. L. Hollis
Mrs. Jack R. Bullard

The 1929 minutes of the Texas State Convention of Free Will Baptists have proven to be a gold mine of important information. We will include here the Report on the State of the Denomination because it is historically pertinent. Why? It shows us something of the effect of the merger of 1911 and the more or less final break Texas made with the merged group in 1929. The report was adopted, with an amendment to refer to the churches for ratification. Here it is:

We, your Committee on Denomination, beg leave to report as follows: From a study of reports we find that our denomination in Texas has lost heavily in membership, churches, and associations as compared with reports of fifteen and twenty years ago. But while this is true as regards our work in Texas, we are much encouraged to note that decided gains have been made in many of our Southern States. While we shall not attempt to give all of the reasons for this decline of interest and progress in Texas, we shall offer some of the reasons that we believe to be the cause of this result.

First, the lack of co-operation on our part with our Free Will Baptist brethren in the South. One of the reasons we have been unable to give and receive full and complete co-operation with these, our brethren, is because of the relationship we have sustained toward another organization not of our own faith and order, namely: The Northern Baptist Convention. This peculiar relationship has existed by reason of the Basis of Union affected several years ago between the General Conference of Free Will Baptists and the Northern Baptist Convention. We understood in the organization of this Texas State Convention at our first meeting at Bradley Junction, that we were to sustain our connection with the General Conference of Free Will Baptists so long, and only so long as it remained a General Conference of Free Will Baptists. As a result of the union between the General Conference of Free Will Baptists and the Northern Baptist Convention, the former has long since ceased to be a General Conference of Free Will Baptists, but has been so completely merged with the Northern Baptist Convention as to entirely lose its identity as a General Conference of Free Will Baptists. As whereas the Northern Baptist Convention has become completely honey-combed with Darwinian Evolution and modern forms of

---

[67] This undoubtedly refers to Dr. Howard Randall Murphy, who had left the Free Will Baptist Church in Cheyenne, Wyoming, to go to medical school and then to India as a medical missionary. Dr. Murphy, who saw my picture in the Free Will Baptist Bible College Bulletin, wrote to me when I was a student at the Bible College and sent a thousand dollars to the college library. He told me he was named after Benjamin Randall. He also sent me a copy of his unpublished autobiography. He passed away in a nursing home in Concordia, Kansas. We were not related.

infidelity. Therefore we recommend that we hereby declare, and publish to the world, that we, The Texas State Conference of Free Will Baptists, refuse to longer recognize any connection or relationship, other than Christian fellowship, with the Northern Baptist Convention.
T. H. Newsom
J. A. Edmonson

Sixteenth Annual Session - 1930

The 1930 session was held in Central Texas, at North Zulch, Madison County, beginning on Tuesday night the 4th day of November, 1930. Minutes of the meeting are not available

Seventeenth Annual Session - 1931, no minutes available

Eighteenth Annual Session - 1932, no minutes available

In the early 1930's there were regional training sessions for Sunday school and Free Will Baptist League teachers and workers. Pictured below is the third semi-annual Sunday School and League Convention which met at the First Free Will Baptist Church of Weatherford, Texas, in 1932. These were organized and promoted by Pastor M. L. Sutton of the Trinity Free Will Baptist Church in Fort Worth. Workers from East Texas often attended these training session. Free Will Baptist League was later changed to Church Training Service (CTS).

One of the really remarkable ministries which was occurring in Texas in the early 1930's was the ministry of Pastor M. L. Sutton. He pastored the First Free Will Baptist Church in Fort Worth and then founded the Trinity Free Will Baptist Church, also in Fort Worth. The photographs below show something of the scope and size of his ministry.

Another Sunday School and League Convention at the Trinity Free Will Baptist Church in Fort Worth, circa 1934. Seated on the front row, left to right: M. L. Sutton, Moselle Franks, Clarence Hearron, A. L. "Doc" Baber, Jack Turrentine, unknown woman, Juanita Hearron, Bobby McLain.

Nineteenth Annual Session - 1933, no minutes available

Twentieth Annual Session - 1934

The twentieth annual session of the Texas State Association met at the First Free Will Baptist Church of Waco, Texas, October 30 through November 2, 1934. The Tuesday evening session was opened with singing led by E. C. Morris[68] and a devotion given by Sister Gus Smith. The opening sermon was delivered by C. B. Thompson.

The Wednesday morning session was open with singing led by E. C. Morris. Allie Ferguson brought a devotion. I. J. Blackwelder[69] led in prayer. The President's message was given by E. C. Morris. J. L. Bounds led in prayer. After a ten minute recess the service resumed with I. J. Blackwelder leading a song. E. J. Vaughn preached "The Hand of the Lord Was Upon Me," using Ezekiel 37:1-11 as his text.

The Wednesday afternoon session featured song leading by J. W, Diserens and a devotion by Mrs. Bell Hodges. A duet was sung by J. W. Diserens and Milton Graham. A letter requesting admission into the association was read from the First Free Will Baptist Church of Scurry County, Texas. The request was granted and the delegates seated. An address, "The Possibilities and Responsibilities of Texas Free Will Baptists," was given by M. L. Sutton of Fort Worth. Two additional addresses were given: "Free Will Baptist Trumpet" by Chas. B. Weir, and "Our Free Will Baptist Gem" by C. J. Turrentine. Allie Ferguson dismissed the service in prayer.

The Wednesday evening session opened with I. J. Blackwelder leading singing. The devotion was given by Brother J. W. Knight and prayer was led by J. W. Moore of Scurry County. After a testimony service prayer was led by Fleming McDuffie. A quartet composed of M. L. Sutton, E. C. Morris, Allie Ferguson, and Charles B. Weir, sang "He Is Coming Again." I. J. Blackwelder preached a sermon entitled "Jesus Only," using Matthew 17:8 as his text. Fleming McDuffie dismissed the service in prayer.

The Thursday morning session opened with singing led by E. C. Morris, devotion by Fleming McDuffie, and prayer by E. J. Vaughn. There was a motion made and passed that the title of the ministers of the state of Texas be known as "Reverend." The committees for the state meeting were appointed. A motion was passed that a committee of five be appointed to revise the Constitution and By-Laws. The committee appointed consisted of T. H. Newsom, M. L. Sutton, C. B. Thompson, J. C. Hodges, and J. L. Bounds. I. J. Blackwelder delivered an address entitled "The Necessity of Denominational Cooperation." A sermon entitled "Why Should the Work Cease," using Nehemiah 6:1-7 as his text, was delivered by M. L. Sutton.

The Thursday afternoon session opened with congregational singing led by I. J. Blackwelder. James H. Maricle gave a devotion and led in a testimonial service. The following committee reports were read and adopted: Committee on Committees, Extension Worker, and

---

[68] E. C. Morris pastored the First Free Will Baptist Church of Bryan, Texas, from 1929 to 1932.
[69] Isaac Joshua Blackwelder (1896-1980) was just getting started in a long and distinguished ministry. He was licensed to preach in 1925 and then ordained in 1926. He pastored the First Free Will Baptist Church in Bryan, Texas, from 1932 to 1935. He was very well educated, a talented song writer, wrote *The Bible Teacher* for years, pastored successfully in Texas, Florida, North Carolina, Georgia, Tennessee, and South Carolina, and served as an editor for the Free Will Baptist Press in Ayden, North Carolina. He was one of the great denominational leaders in his time. He was one of the committee members selected by the Cooperative General Association in Denison, Texas, in 1934, to make further plans for the merger with the General Conference to form the National Association of Free Will Baptists in 1935. He was the first secretary-treasurer of foreign missions for the newly formed National Association. It was my privilege to hear him preach one time.

Home Missions. A motion passed that the Program Committee make space on the program of the next session for the Auxiliaries.

The Thursday evening service opened with I. J. Blackwelder leading the singing. A motion was made and adopted that the Plainview Church Letter be received and the delegates seated, with the necessary changes made. A motion was made and passed that the 1935 session of the association meet at the New Hope Free Will Baptist Church in Rusk County, north of Henderson. Tiff Covington was elected to preach the opening sermon of that session. A motion was made that 1000 copies of the minutes be printed.[70]

It was announced that the next General Conference[71] was to convene at Greenville, North Carolina, on Tuesday night after the second Sunday in June, 1935. The following delegates were elected to represent Texas at that meeting: M. L. Sutton, and J. L. Bounds. Alternates elected were Allie Ferguson and C. J. Turrentine. The evening sermon was delivered by J. L. Bounds, using the text: "And who then is willing to consecrate his service this day to the Lord" (1 Chronicles 29:5).

The Friday morning session featured I. J. Blackwelder again leading singing. The devotion was brought by Lee Crosby. A letter of greeting was read from the Cedar Valley Independent Baptist Church of Dallas, Texas. A motion was passed that the association extend an invitation to F. P. Dailey to attend the 1935 session. The reports of the Religious Education Committee and the Resolutions Committee were read and adopted. The following officers were elected:

President   J. L. Edge,[72] Bryan, Texas
Vice-President   M. L. Sutton, Fort Worth, Texas
Secretary-Treasurer C. J. Turrentine, Fort Worth, Texas

Charles B. Weir, of Fort Worth, and J. L. Bounds, of North Zulch, were appointed (or elected) to the Executive Committee. The following officers were elected to the ladies' work: President, Sister Ines Morris; Vice-President, Sister W. G. Reynolds. Elected to the Young People's Work were: President, I. J. Blackwelder; Vice-President, Sister Delores Vance. There was a motion, which passed, that the officers of the state body be nominated from the floor and elected by majority vote. The motion that the revised Constitution and By-Laws be adopted was passed.

The body voted that the job of statistician be given to the clerk. The moderator appealed to all Free Will Baptists of Texas to give the clerk their backing as statistician. Evidently 1934 was no different than today as far as trouble collecting statistical data from the churches.

The body voted to discontinue the office of Church Extension Worker and give that task to the Executive Committee, and that each church in the association contribute not less than one dollar per month to the Church Extension Fund. These funds were to be spent at the discretion of the Executive Committee for church extension work in Texas.

Apparently there were some outstanding debts. The body voted that the clerk pay old debts first, then notify all churches of their part of the indebtedness. There was a song and a fond farewell to Pastor and Mrs. E. C. Morris who were leaving the state, apparently leaving the Bryan Church for their native North Carolina.

---

[70] This number is indicative of the growth of the association in that the previous number printed was 300.

[71] At this time the broadest bodies of Free Will Baptists were the Cooperative General Conference, consisting of associations in the West, and the General Conference, consisting of association in the East. The on going movement to bring these two bodies together to form a national association was nearing its climax.

[72] J. L. Edge, a layman and businessman, was one of the most prominent and beloved citizens of Bryan, Texas. He and his wife donated the funding for the construction of the First Free Will Baptist Church in Bryan. A front page article, with a picture of Mr. and Mrs. Edge, was published in *The Bryan Eagle*.

The *New Morning Star,* the newspaper published by the Southwestern Convention of Freewill Baptists since 1916 ceased publication at some point during the year.

Twenty-First Annual Session - 1935

The twenty-first annual session of the Texas State Association of Free Will Baptists was held at the New Hope Free Will Baptist Church, Rusk County, Henderson, Texas, October 29 through 31, 1935. The Tuesday evening song service was led by Marvin Sheffield. Clyde Goen, of Bryan, gave a devotion. J. L. Bounds led the opening prayer. The introductory sermon was delivered by C. J. Turrentine, using 1 Corinthians 3:1-19 as his text. The service was closed in prayer by E. Sterl Phinney, pastor of the First Free Will Baptist Church in Bryan.

The Wednesday morning session was called to order by President J. L. Edge. Mrs. Lizzie McAdams led the opening prayer. E. Sterl Phinney brought a devotion and led in prayer. President J. L. Edge delivered the President's message. J. L. Bounds, pastor of the host church, gave a welcome address. The Constitution and By-Laws approved at the 1934 session were read, along with the amendments. This constitution was not printed in the minutes and is not available.

The following delegates were seated (as we can best make out the names):

    Bright Light, Bryan, Texas: K. Kelly, Miss Ivy Goen
    Christian Home, Kurten, Texas: not discernible
    Edge Church, Edge, Texas: Emmett Holland
    Evergreen Church, Keith, Texas: J. W. Rice, Top Bean
    Friendship, Southeast Texas Convention: Marvin Sheffield, Luther   Fairchild
    Grace Free Will Baptist Church, Weatherford: Florence Withers, Mr. and Mrs.
        Henry Measures
    New Hope Church, Henderson: Lee Poole, A. E. Stokes
    Plainview, North Zulch: Mrs. Dessie Cameron, Dallas Guinn
    First Church, Waco: Mrs. A. Sullins, Tom Holcome
    Woodlawn Association: Lucie Gardner, Aisha Marie Howell, A. Sullins,
        Ellis Calvery
    First Church, Fort Worth: H. Killough, Rev. J. C. Hodges
    Bryan Church, Bryan: Mrs. J. L. Edge, T. A. Cloud

Following the song service, C. B. Thompson delivered a sermon entitled "That Great Salvation," using Hebrews 2:1-3 as his text. The service was dismissed in prayer by J. A. Smith.

The Wednesday afternoon session opened by singing led by Marvin Sheffield and a devotion by T. A. Cloud. J. C. Hodges led in prayer. A Resolution Committee was appointed consisting of the following: E. Sterl Phinney, Mrs. W. B. Duke, and Mrs. T. A. Cloud. The reading of the church letters, showing the work of the various churches, indicated that they "were in very good condition." Mrs. W. G. Reynolds reported verbally on the Ladies Work. A motion carried that the Free Will Baptist State Association (Home Missions Com.) take over the back debt of the First Free Will Baptist Church in Waco until it was paid, and that they continue to help this and other such churches as they may be in such need. C. J. Turrentine tendered his resignation as the Secretary-Treasurer of the state association. Thomas A. Cloud was elected to take his place. The service was dismissed in prayer by Clyde Goen.

The Wednesday evening service was opened by singing led by Marvin Sheffield and prayer by Lizzie McAdams. The devotion consisted of a chalk talk given by Lura Lee Moore. Her subject was "I'll Go Where You Want Me to Go." A memorial service was conducted by J. L. Bounds for Pastor Jimmerson (Uncle Dock) and Sister Minnie Jimmerson. He used John 14:1-14 as a scripture text. C. J. Hodges and C. B. Thompson led in prayer. K. V. Shutes[73] preached on the subject "Digging Again the Wells of Our Fathers," using Genesis 26:16-23 as his text. Lizzie McAdams led the body in prayer. The service was then dismissed in prayer by Egbert Jimmerson.

The Thursday morning session opened with congregational singing led by Ira Harper, a devotion by J. A. Smith, and prayer by J. C. Hodges. Lizzie McAdams was elected as President of the state "Ladies mission work," and Sister W. G. Reynolds was elected Vice-President. Sister B. A. Grant was elected Secretary-Treasurer. K. V. Shutes delivered an address on "Denominational Cooperation." The morning sermon was delivered by Lizzie McAdams, using "Blessed is the man that heareth me, watching daily at my gates, waiting at the posts of my doors" (Proverbs 8:34) as her text. Ira Harper led in the closing prayer.

The Thursday afternoon session was open by singing led by Clyde F. Goen, a devotion by J. C. Hodges, and prayer by C. J. Turrentine. The report of the Resolutions Committee was read and adopted. The report was as follows:

> *Resolved,* that the Texas State Convention of Free Will Baptists elect a Home and Foreign Mission Secretary who is to work in cooperation with the Executive Committee and through whom all state, home, and foreign mission funds are to be disbursed, as designated by the committee.   Rev. E. Sterl Phinney was elected.
>
> *Resolved,* that each pastor and preacher in the state convention push the work of our church as has been planned by the conference.
>
> *Resolved,* that the chairmen of all committees and all executives work at their task twelve months a year rather than just a few days before [the] convention meets.
>
> *Resolved,* that the Texas State Convention of Free Will Baptists elect an Education Secretary whose duty shall be to collect funds for our Free Will Baptist College, and to further the cause of Christian education in Texas.   C. F. Goen was elected.
>
> *Resolved,* that the Texas State Convention of Free Will Baptists extend its vote of thanks to the members of New Hope Church, to Brother Harper's churches, and to Brother Thompson's churches for their kind hospitality in entertaining the state convention.
> Rev. E. Sterl Phinney
> Mrs. T. A. Cloud

An "inspirational address" was given by E. S. Jimmerson. He then led in a hand shake and time of consecration. The following officers were elected:
President: J. L. Edge, Bryan, Texas
Vice-President: Rev. C. B. Thompson, Bryan, Texas
Secretary-Treasurer: Thomas A. Cloud, Bryan, Texas

---

[73]K. V. Shutes (1905-1962) was one of the denominational leaders in the movement to bring together Free Will Baptists nationally into one organization, the National Association of Free Will Baptists. In 1934 her served on the General Conference Committee, along with J. L. Welch, for whom Welch College is named, E. C. Morris, and I. J. Blackwelder, mentioned above. For many years he directed the Superannuation Board, now called The Retirement Board. In 1935 he would have been the pastor of the First Free Will Baptist Church in Denison, Texas.

J. L. Bounds and K. V. Shutes were appointed to the Executive Committee. The body voted to meet in 1936 at the Bryan Free Will Baptist Church, Bryan, Texas. The service was dismissed in prayer by E. Sterl Phinney.

The Thursday night service was opened by singing led by Clyde F. Goen. C. J. Turrentine sang a solo, "I'll Not Have to Cross Jordan Alone." B. A. Grant brought a devotion. Ira Harper led in prayer. Clyde F. Goen then sang a solo, "Pearly White City." The evening sermon, "The True Church," was delivered by E. Sterl Phinney, using 1 Thessalonians and Psalm 6-10 as his scripture. The service was closed in prayer by Brother H. H. Killough.

The Friday morning session was opened by congregational singing led by B. A. Grant. Mrs. W. G. Reynolds brought a devotion on John 3, "The New Birth." J. L. Bounds led in prayer. An oral report on young people's work was given by Miss Clara Young, Florence (illegible) and Lura Lee Moore. Sister Billie Hodges gave a devotion. J. H. Measures delivered a sermon, reading Genesis 22:1-19 and using verse 8 as his text. The service was closed in prayer by B. A. Grant.

The Friday afternoon session opened with Ira Harper leading the singing. The Constitution and By-Laws were adopted, "with changes." That is all the information we are given about the constitution. C. J. Turrentine and Lizzie McAdams were elected Field Evangelists, without salary. A motion to amend Article 13 of the constitution was adopted. The amendment read: "The deacons shall be seated as delegates with right to vote as do ministers." The service was dismissed by J. L. Bounds.

For the sake of better preserving the names of the era, listed here are the committees appointed to serve for the 1935-1936 year:

Foreign Missions:	Mrs. W. G. Reynolds
	Mrs. H. S. Edge
	Mrs. P. K. Trant
Home Missions:	E. Sterl Phinney
	N. C. Cole
	Emmett Holland
Sunday School	T. W. Smith
	Miss Clara Young
	Mrs. Gus Smith
Education	J. L. Bounds
	Clyde F. Goen
	C. B. Thompson
Evangelism	K. V. Shutes
	H. Killough
Temperance	C. J. Turrentine
	Lizzie McAdams
	Mrs. T. A. Cloud
	Mrs. J. L. Edge
Young People's Work	Miss Lucile Gardner
	Miss Alisha Marie Howell
	Miss Hollie Watkins

Woman's Work	Mrs. J. C. Hodges
	Mrs. W. T. Benton
	Mrs. F. Ferguson
Denomination	J. C. Hodges
	T. H. Newsom
	J. L. Bounds
Laymen's Work	E. J. Jimmerson
	W. B. Duke
Credentials	Walter Watson
	Ira Harper
	A. Sullins
	J. W. Knight
Resolutions	B. A. Grant
	C. J. Turrentine
	C. B. Thompson
Obituary	E. R. Jimmerson
	T. H. Newsom
	Kovey Windsor (unclear)
Program	T. A. Cloud
	E. Sterl Phinney
	C. B. Thompson

Committee on Committes
A. Mullens
C. F. Goen
B. A. Grant

Free Will Baptists, and perhaps especially Texas Free Will Baptists, are notoriously negligent in providing church statistics, such as membership and attendance numbers. Therefore, it is difficult to state with any degree of accuracy at all what the numerical strength of the work in the state was during the years from 1915 to 1935. Generally speaking, however, this was a period of growth and advancement for the Free Will Baptist work in Texas.

Even though some churches died, and along with them some district associations, there were new churches planted and at least one new association formed, the Mt. Zion Association, which was accepted into the state association in 1929. Unfortunately, the minutes only state that they were admitted, without telling us which churches comprised it, and it was not long lived and then came the National Convention.

The Formation of the National Association of Free Will Baptists

Efforts to bring together the scattered remnants of the merger with the Northern Baptists continued unabated following the formation in the West of the Co-operative General Association in 1916 and in the East the General Conference of Free Will Baptists in 1921, mentioned above. Though the unity of the denomination into one national organization would take time, key leaders from a number of states began to work together to bring about just such an organization. Texas was a key player in this effort under the personal leadership of such people as Hiram and Lizzie McAdams, C. B. Thompson, Clyde Goen, J. L. Bounds, M. L. Sutton, J. L. Edge, E. C. Morris, and others.

In 1924 delegates from the Co-operative General Association and the General Conference began to visit the other, and by 1930 such visiting was a regular occurrence. It was in 1930 that the Texas State Convention sent Mr. and Mrs. J. L. Edge of Bryan as representatives to the General Conference, which met that year in Vernon, Alabama. The 1931 session of the General Conference was held at the Horse Branch Free Will Baptist Church in Turbeville, South Carolina. President of the Texas State Convention, J. L. Edge, and his pastor, E. C. Morris, were there from Texas. Mister Edge invited the General Conference to convene at his home church, the First Free Will Baptist Church of Bryan, in 1932. The invitation was accepted. In November of 1931 M. L.

1935 Treatise Revision Committee, National Association of Free Will Baptists
Left to right: J. C. Griffin, C. B. Thompson of Texas, Ralph Staten, E. B. Joyner, E. E. Morris, Winford Davis, W. B. Davenport, M. L. Morse, Millard F. Van Hoose.

Sutton, J. L. Bounds, E. C. Morris, and Mrs. Morris, attended the Cooperative General Association, meeting at Purdy, Missouri. As the condition of the divided denomination was discussed, the men from Texas suggested that the Cooperative General Association send delegates to the General Conference which was to meet the next year in Bryan, Texas. The suggestion was accepted and the appointed delegates attended and requested that a delegation of observers to meet with the Cooperative General Association at their next session.[74]

People in both groups soon recognized the need for educational institutions, a foreign missions program, and other denominational agencies. Delegates began to meet for exploratory talks on the possibility of a union of the Co-operative General Association and the General Conference. Committee members from the two groups worked hard and in 1933 recommended to the General Conference the merging of the Co-operative General Association and the General Conference into one body. E. C. Morris, pastor of the First Free Will Baptist Church of Bryan, and one of the Texas state leaders, is said to be the author of the first formal proposals for merger discussion between the Cooperative Association and the General Conference. He led the State Convention of Texas into a formal relationship with the Eastern General Conference in 1933.[75] The General Conference in 1933, meeting in Nashville, Tennessee, agreed to send a committee to Denison, Texas, to the next regular meeting of the Co-operative General Association. The committee representing the East was composed of J. L. Welch, E. C. Morris, I. J. Blackwelder, and K. V. Shutes. Blackwelder and Shutes both pastored in Texas at some point in their ministries, as did E. C. Morris. The Co-operative General Association met at the First Free Will Baptist Church of Denison, Texas, November 6-9, 1934. The committee representing the Co-operative General Association working toward unity was composed of J. L. Waltman, Noel Turner, Bert F. Rogers, F. S. Van Hoose, and Self Jones. The two committees gave their report on November 8, 1934, as follows:

> The committees representing the General Conference and the Cooperative General Association met in a joint session during the sitting of the Cooperative General Association, Denison, Texas, November 8, 1934, and continued the work of uniting the above named bodies as follows:
> 1) In addition to the terms agreed upon in Nashville, Tennessee, on June 15, 1933, we, the committees representing the Cooperative General Association and the General Conference, agree to unite the above named bodies into one national body to be known as the National Association of Free Will Baptists, with the understanding that the two bodies thus united continue to operate under their present organization without becoming in any way responsible for each other's present obligations, and with the understanding that neither of the two shall in any way have jurisdiction over the other, but at the same time they are to continue their work as part of the national body.
> 2) That the National Association of Free Will Baptists meet in its first session in the East Nashville church, Nashville, Tennessee, on Tuesday night after the first Sunday in November 1935.
> 3) That Rev. J. L. Welch act as temporary moderator and Rev. Winford Davis as assistant moderator of the first session of this national body.
> 4) That the moderator and assistant moderator act as a program committee for the first session.

---

[74] Some of this information came from a letter written by E. C. Morris to the writers of "The History Corner" in *Contact Magazine*, dated December 28, 1971. The letter is in the Historical Collection at Welch College.

[75] Dr. Kevin Hester, "Heritage from the Past, Horizons for the future: Free Will Baptists in America," a paper presented at the Texas State Association meeting, 2014.

The basis of agreement was to be the Articles of Faith of the 1901 *Free Will Baptist Treatise* and the Church Covenant of the 1901 and 1916 *Treatise*. There was nothing to do now except wait for the scheduled 1935 meeting, to be held in November. Finally, the time for the meeting in Nashville arrived, November 5, 1935. Due to the fact that the East Nashville church was undergoing a change in pastors, the meeting place was changed to the Cofer's Chapel Free Will Baptist Church, also in Nashville. Ministers and delegates from all over began arriving. The copy of the minutes of that meeting from which I am working has a hand written note that states that twelve states were represented, fifteen different associations, 27 ministers, and 33 delegates. In addition, there were about sixty other ministers present and a host of visitors. Delegates from Texas made their presence known as they played key roles in the meeting. The official delegates from Texas were Clyde F. Goen and E. Steryl Phinney, representing the Texas State Convention, and J. L. Bounds, and C. B. Thompson, representing the Central Texas District Association. E. Sterl Phinney, who had recently become pastor of the First Free Will Baptist Church of Bryan, Texas, was placed on the Committee on Constitution and By-Laws.

The ministers who were present at Cofer's Chapel Free Will Baptist Church in Nashville, Tennessee, in 1935, when the National Association of Free Will Baptists was formed. The three women preachers at the right are: Lizzie McAdams of Texas, Sadie Fincher of Oklahoma, and Tommie Franklin of Texas.

The committee that could make or break the National Association was the Treatise Revision Committee. C. B. Thompson was appointed to that committee. This committee was so important that a special photograph of it was taken and sold.

Clyde Goen, a layman in the Bright Light Free Will Baptist Church in the Harvey Community, out of Bryan, Texas, was elected to the Executive Committee.

On Thursday morning, November 7, at approximately 10:15 a.m., the report of the Treatise Revision Committee was given. This was the crucial moment and the wording of the *Treatise* could divide the delegates and destroy the National Association before it was born, because differences in belief and practices existed among them. Lizzie McAdams, who had worked long and hard for the formation of the National, stood and moved that the report of the Treatise Revision Committee be accepted without a public reading. This was a bold and daring gamble, if we may call it that. Her motion was immediately seconded and the vote was overwhelmingly unanimous. The National Association of Free Will Baptists had been formed.

Free Will Baptists had come together, united for a common cause. The *Treatise* was later read and it turned out to be virtually the same as the *Treatise* adopted by the 1916 Co-operative General Association. The final service of the convocation was held that afternoon. Several sermons had been preached during the meeting, from Tuesday evening through Thursday morning, by Winford Davis of Missouri, S. H. Stryon of North Carolina, Thomas H. Willey of North Carolina, later of Cuba fame, and Millard S. Van Hoose of Kentucky. C. B. Thompson, of Bryan,

Texas, preached on Thursday afternoon before the association was dismissed amid great rejoicing. A professionally made photograph of the entire delegation was taken and orders for copies of it taken. In the picture (below), on the far right, were three women preachers. One of them was Sadie Fincher of Oklahoma. The other two were Lizzie McAdams and Miss Tommie Franklin, both Texans.

National Meetings in Texas

Texans would continue to play key roles in the National Association of Free Will Baptists, serving in many capacities on key boards and committees, and often preaching at the conventions.
July 26, 2014: Pastor Tom Quinones, center, Friendship Free Will Baptist Church, Fort Worth, shows Impact Fort Worth volunteers where their ministry assignments will be.

The second session of the National Association met in Nashville, Tennessee, in 1938, at the East Nashville Free Will Baptist Church, where it had been scheduled to meet in 1935.

The third session of the National Association met at the First Free Will Baptist Church of Bryan, Texas, July 11-14, 1939. The entire delegation could be seated in the church.

The National Association has continued to meet in Texas over the years, meeting at the Fort Worth Convention Center four times: in 1972, 1982, 1996, and again in 2014. Convention centers became the venue of necessity due to the remarkable growth of the denomination over the years. The total registration of the 1972 convention was 3,172; the 1982 convention, 5,318 (attendees may have been counted more than once if they registered for multiple parts of the convention); the 1996 convention, 6,771; and the 2014 contention, 4,320, with attendees counted only once, even if they registered for multiple parts of the convention.

Chapter 3

Growth and Expansion
1936 to 1950

Twenty-Second Annual Session - 1936

The twenty-second annual session of the Texas State Association of Free Will Baptists met at the First Free Will Baptist Church, Bryan, Texas, October 27-29, 1936. The introductory sermon on Tuesday night was preached by M. L. Sutton. "I am set for the defense of the gospel" (Philippians 1:17) was his text.

The State Association was called to order on Wednesday morning by the President, J. L. Edge. The President then named the following as the Credentials Committee: M. L. Sutton, Mrs. C. B. Thompson, and Mrs. C. B. Moehlman. As was the usual practice, the association recessed for half an hour while the committee met to make a list of the delegates. There were four district associations which reported with delegates: Central Texas Association, East Texas Association,[76] Woodlawn Association, and the West Fork Association. The following fourteen churches represented with delegates: Bright Light, Bryan First, Christian Home, Fort Worth First, Fort Worth Trinity, Edge, Plainview, Evergreen, New Hope, Mt. Olive, North Zulch, Pine Prairie, and First Waco. It seems the State Sunday School and League Convention was entitled to delegates, too, for they named four.

Mabel Willey gave a "lecture" on scriptures found in Isaiah 59. This was during the preaching hour at 11:00 o'clock on Wednesday. Though not called a preacher, she could preach with the best of them. In the afternoon session C. J. Turrentine stated that he had many copies of the *Free Will Baptist Treatise* and desired to place a copy in every home at only 25¢ per copy. The Committee on Committes was appointed and then the report of home and foreign missions was given and adopted. The Committee on Education report was read by C. F. Goen and adopted. Mrs. W. G. Reynolds volunteered the services of the two mission circles in helping organize and assist any church that had no organization of ladies work.

On Wednesday night host Pastor E. Sterl Phinney and his wife rendered a special song in music, and then Mrs. Phinney led a song by the choir and congregation, "I Am Bound for the Promised Land." M. L. Sutton sang a solo. J. L. Bounds preached the evening sermon, entitled "The Coming Jesus," using John 14:1-14 as his text.

The Thursday morning business session was scheduled to begin with a report by the Committee on Sunday Schools. However, they failed to report. This led to a recommendation from M. L. Sutton of the Trinity Free Will Baptist Church in Fort Worth, that the Bible only be

---

[76] This designation seems a little strange because the East Texas District Association was called the Texas Association until 1954. Perhaps in practice it may have already come to be called the East Texas District.

used as a textbook in teaching and that the Six Point Record System be used in all Sunday schools. The clerk records, "However, the convention went on record as endorsing the use of all Sunday school literature and helps of the Free Will Baptist denomination."

The reports of the Committees on Evangelism, Temperance, Young People's Work, and Laymen's Work were all given and adopted. During the eleven o'clock worship hour C. B. Thompson preached a sermon, using "Without a vision the people perish" (Proverbs 18:29) as his text. In the afternoon the report of the Committee on Resolutions was presented and adopted. The report isn't in the minutes. The report on Women's Work was given and adopted. The Committee on Committees named the committee members who were to serve for the following year.

The association voted unanimously to meet at the Trinity Free Will Baptist Church in Fort Worth, Texas, for the twenty-third annual session, starting on November 2, 1937. Officers elected were:

        President: Clyde F. Goen
        Vice-President: J. L. Bounds
        Secretary of Missions: E. Sterl Phinney
        Secretary of Education: Clyde F. Goen

A motion passed unanimously that the Texas State Association of Free Will Baptists send a tithe of net receipts to the National Association of Free Will Baptists.

The report of the Committee on [the State of the] Denomination was read and adopted. Two new members were elected to the Executive Board: E. F. Trant and H. H. Killough. On motion of Sterl Phinney it was voted that a committee be framed and present to next state association meeting a plan for funds for retirement of superannuated ministers. The committee consisted of T. A. Cloud, Jack Bullard, and Noah Cole.

Clyde F. Goen was elected delegate to the Eastern Association[77] at --

E. Sterl Phinney, pastor of the host church, the First Free Will Baptist Church in Bryan, moved that "the name of our State Convention be changed to Texas State Association to conform to the general name throughout the general association." The motion carried and thereafter the state association has been called the "Texas State Association of Free Will Baptists" rather than the "Texas State Convention."

Tiff Covington was chosen to preach the opening sermon at the 1937 meeting in Fort Worth, Texas.
J. L. Edge, President
Thomas A. Cloud, Secretary-Treasurer

(Addenda)
Churches were instructed to send a letter of greeting and names of delegates rather than a statistical report which is to be furnished by District Associations.   [Initialed] T.A.C.

Twenty-Third Annual Session - November 2-4, 1937

The twenty-third annual session of the Texas State Association met November 2 through 4 at the Trinity Free Will Baptist Church in Fort Worth, Texas. J. E. Dearmore, clerk of the first Texas state meeting, but then of Oklahoma, led the opening prayer. President Clyde F. Goen called

---

[77] The National Association had been formed in November, 1935, and was to meet every three years, but agreed that the Cooperative General Association of the West and the General Conference of the East continue to meet separately and conduct their own business. This arrangement lasted only until 1938 when the National realized it needed to meet every year.

the meeting to order and then called for more songs. Another prayer was led by T. H. Newsom of Springtown, Texas. The introductory sermon was preached by Tommy[78] Smith of Henderson, Texas.

The Wednesday morning session began by congregational singing led by E. A. O'Donnell of Oklahoma, and then prayer by M. M McKee, also of Oklahoma. Host pastor, M. L. Sutton, gave the welcome address, followed by a response given by B. A. Grant of Jacksonville, Texas. Tiff Covington of Buffalo Springs delivered the morning sermon, using the text Psalm 118:22-23.

The afternoon session began with a devotion brought by A. F. Ferguson. The Credentials Committee reported the following associations and churches represented with delegates present:

Associations

West Fork Association: A. M. Ferguson, Edith Brooks, J. H. McIntire, R. L. White, W. D. Phillips, Mrs. H. H. Killough, C. B. Weir, H. Woods, G. W. Taylor

Friendship Association: Ruby Thrasher, Ella Wharton

Texas Association: A. E. Shutes, Gus Smith, F. W. Dollar, J. O. Roberts, J. L. Ross, Mrs. B. A. Grant, T. T. Megasson (unclear)

Central Texas Association: Mrs. O. L. Moore, Mrs. C. F. Hodges, J. L. Edge, Mrs. T. A. Cloud, Miss Geraldine Gilpin

Woodhaven Association: Mrs. W. T. Smith

Fellowship Association: Monroe Parker, Mrs. S. H. Hicks

Churches

Bright Light Church: Miss Ivy Goen

New Salem Church: J. W. Taylor

New Hope Church (Parker County): Mrs. R. L. White

New Hope Church (Henderson Country): Mrs. E. A. Stokes, Mrs. Gus Smith

First Church (Fort Worth): C. J. Turrentine, Mrs. J. C. Hodges

Trinity Church (Fort Worth): Mrs. Maud Weir, A. L. Gardner

Buffalo Springs Church: J. E. Ford, L. J. White

First Church (Bryan): Mrs. Charles Moehlman, Mrs. W. G. Reynolds

Plainview: Dallas Grimes

Christian Home: Mrs. Jas. Lang

First Church (Waco): Mrs. A. Sullins, Mrs. Lula Gresham

There was a motion to seat visiting members from churches who had no delegates, but the motion was defeated. Visiting members were instructed to meet and appoint a delegate from their ranks. This was done and three more churches were permitted to seat delegates. A petitionary letter was read from the Friendship Association asking for admittance to the state association. Its letter was unanimously accepted and their delegates seated, followed by a general fellowship and hand shaking, which would seem to indicate the state association was glad to receive the new district association. We do not know where this association was located or the names of any of the churches which composed it. It seems to have been short lived.

Two other associations listed, the Woodhaven and the Fellowship, are also otherwise unknown to us. The Fellowship Association listed here is not the same as the Fellowship Association which was organized in 1956 in the Fort Worth area. Both of these were short lived, too.

---

[78] Tommy was usually spelled Tommie in the minutes. It is Tommie on her gravestone.

The rest of the afternoon consisted of reports by the various standing committees. Some things of note are: J. R. Davidson[79] was a member of the Foreign Missions Committee, Clyde F. Goen was elected as secretary-treasurer, J. W. Workington was elected state reporter, and Mrs. W. G. Reynolds and Lizzie McAdams reported on the "Women's Work."

The Wednesday evening service featured a devotion by J. E. Dearmore of Oklahoma and "a rousing testimonial meeting," followed by a sermon by J. R. Davidson. Clerk Thomas A. Cloud noted that J. R. Davidson "preached a great sermon from 2nd chapter of Romans, subject 'There is no difference.'"

The Thursday morning session consisted largely of more reports and the election of officers. J. L. Bounds, pastor of the First Free Will Baptist Church in Waco, was elected president. The association voted to have the next session at the First Free Will Baptist Church in Waco, in 1938. For some reason the report of the Temperance Committee, which isn't available, was read and then tabled. M. M. McKee preached from Matthew 7:13-14 on "The Two Ways." He illustrated his sermon with a chart.

The Thursday afternoon session featured congregational singing led by J. L. Bounds, prayer by Mrs. Lizzie McAdams, and a devotion by Mrs. Lula Gresham (?). Mrs. M. L. Sutton exhibited an especially made quilt depicting many gospel and devotional messages to be auctioned later. Mrs. Lizzie McAdams reported the following officers elected to serve the Woman's Auxiliary[80] for one year: President, Mrs. M. L. Sutton; Vice-President, Mrs. W. G. Reynolds; Secretary-Treasurer, Mrs. C. B. Moehlman. M. L. Sutton then offered to print a leaflet of information for guidance of Women's Work, which offer was gladly accepted. The congregation stood as prayer was offered for guidance in establishing a new church in Huntsville, Texas. The report of the Temperance Committee was re-read and after considerable discussion was adopted as read.

M. L. Sutton reported that at the noon hour an organization was formed composed of the ministers of the Free Will Baptist denomination in Texas, said organization to meet at least once a year in a school of instruction in doctrine and discipline as taught by the Free Will Baptists. The first meeting was to be held with the First Free Will Baptist Church of Fort Worth for a one week session in March 1938. The organization was heartily endorsed by the whole body in session.

The state association endorsed a plan to create a loan fund for our worthy young people and elected an educational board to handle the funds. J. L. Edge, John Swanwick, and M. L. McAdams were elected.

In the Thursday evening session J. C. Turrentine made a motion that the body send delegates and $10.00 membership fee to the Eastern Association of Free Will Baptists, meeting at Smithville, Mississippi, June 1938, and also send a corresponding messenger to the Western Association. The motion carried 23 to 9. J. R. Davidson was elected as the delegate to the Eastern Association and M. L. Sutton was elected as the corresponding messenger to the Western Association.[81] The evening sermon was delivered by J. K. Workenton. He preached from Pilate's quote: "What Is Truth?"

---

[79] J. R. Davidson pastored the First Free Will Baptist Church in Bryan, 1937-1942, and was one of the best known denominational leaders at the time. Davidson Hall at Free Will Baptist Bible College, the college's first building, was named for him. He served as moderator of the National Association of Free Will Baptists.

[80] This is the first time in the state minutes that the women's work has been called the Woman's Auxiliary.

[81] The two associations had come together in 1935 and formed the National Association of Free Will Baptists. However, they voted that the Eastern and Western Associations continue meeting and conducting their own business. The National Association initially voted that the new organization meet every three years, but by 1938 they saw the need for the National to meet every year, and it has thereafter.

Twenty-Fourth Annual Session - 1938

The twenty-fourth annual session of the Texas State Association of Free Will Baptists met with the First Free Will Baptist Church of Waco, Texas, November 1-4, 1938. The Tuesday evening congregational singing was led by host pastor J. L. Bounds, followed by a devotion brought be Miss Lucile Gardner, using the text 2 Timothy 2:1-26. The introductory sermon was delivered by E. J. Vaughan of North Zulch, Texas. Using the third chapter of Revelation, he preached on the subject, "The Victorious Church."

The Wednesday morning session began with singing led by Allie Ferguson and a devotion by Mattie Garvin, using James 1:1-27 as her text. "An inspiring praise service" ensued in which practically everyone present participated. W. V. McVail preached the morning sermon, using the text Luke 15:8. His subject was "When We Reach Home."

The delegates were seated in the afternoon session. The Credentials Committee reported the following district associations and local churches represented:

Woodlawn Association: Mrs. Alvin Sodey, R. L. White, Grady Calvery
Central Texas Association: Mesdames [plural for madam] C. Moehlman, C. F. Goen,
    L. J. Lawliss, W. M. Stewart, R. C. Wiggs; Misses Fletta Woods, Ivy Goen;
messers J. L. Edge. L. J. Lawliss, Pat Rice
West Fork Association: Mrs. McPhail, Mrs. McPhelly, Mrs. Weir, Mrs. Redenores,
    Mrs. J. K. Markenton, Jesse Ferguson, Edith Brooks, Mrs. K. Hemphill,
    C. C. Lamb, G. W. Taylor
First Church (Bryan): Mrs. T. A. Cloud, Mrs. Floy Life
Bright Light: no letter, 1 delegate (not named)
Plainview: Will Lawson, Aston Pegues
Christian Home: Mrs. H. H. Holligan, Mrs. Joey Lnag
North Zulch: no letter
Evergreen: Mr. and Mrs. R. T. Trant
New Hope (Parker County): Mrs. Turrentine, Jeff Hemphill
Pine Grove: no letter, one delegate (not named)
Trinity: Charles B. Weir, Mrs. Clara Sutton
Woodlawn: Dennis Taylor, Frances Wiley
Pine Prairie: no letter
First Church (Waco): W. C. Scarborough, Jewell Sorley
Fellowship: P. H. Graves, Mrs. Mattie Garvin
Buncombe: P. Hesmanes, T. M. Hays
New Hope (Rusk Country): Mrs. G. W. Smith, Mrs. Mattie Garvin
First Church (Denison): Herbert Lamb, Mrs. E. Dalton
Dott: Mrs. O. M. Martin, Mrs. Leroy Conaway
Pleasant Mound: Ola Moore, Miss Lucile Cozart
First Church (Fort Worth): no letter
Long Branch Church: Mrs. A. Conaway, Cecil Phillips

J. R. Davidson gave a verbal report of his visit to the Eastern Association of Free Will Baptists. A motion prevailed dismissing the committee on student funds, returning all funds collected to the donors after paying all necessary expenses. A vote of thanks was given for the committee. T. H. Newsom was elected President for the next year and J. L. Bounds was elected Vice-President. The following were elected to serve as delegates to the second session of the

National Association of Free Will Baptists, which met November 15-18, 1938, at the East Nashville Free Will Baptist Church, Nashville, Tennessee: Aston Pegues and Mrs. D. Lawliss. The association authorized the secretary-treasurer to pay $25.00 on expenses.

On motion by J. R. Davidson a committee was chosen to revise the Constitution and By-Laws and present the proposed revisions at the next annual association. The committee appointed consisted of J. R. Davidson, Mrs. Charles Moehlman, and Earl Campbell. The secretary-treasurer was instructed to reimburse the Program Committee for expenses of printing the program for the current session and a vote of thanks was tendered M. L. Sutton for an offer to print next year's program *gratis*.

On Wednesday evening Dr. Scarborough introduced W. C. Scarborough, Jr., Wright Bounds, Miss Bernice Jones, Miss Dell Keith, and Vivian Sullens who presented a playlet "An Operation for Sin," which was well received. Miss Gladys Sparks then commented on the play, showing the importance of Bible study, prayer, and church attendance as against selfishness, stinginess, and indifference. "Her comments being one of the highlights of the association," stated clerk Thomas A. Cloud. A collection was taken for the Foreign Missions Fund, which totaled $14.26. J. K. Markenton then sang a solo: "Wayfaring Pilgrim." M. L. Sutton then preached a sermon, using 1 Corinthians 1:20-26 as his text, and his subject being "How Is It Then, Brethren, When Ye Come Together?" which was well received, according to the clerk.

The Thursday morning session consisted of committee reports, none of which were preserved for us. The sermon was preached by T. W. Smith, who used John 8:36 as his text. The sermon was entitled "Religious Freedom," and according to the clerk it was a "great" sermon.

The afternoon session featured an address by J. R. Davidson on the subject "The Church and Apostasy." After the address a motion was passed that a copy of the lecture be sent to *The Free Will Baptist*[82] for publication. Reports then followed from the following committees: Foreign Missions, Laymen's Work, Temperance, Sunday Schools, Resolutions, Evangelism, Obituary, "Ladies Auxiliary," and Education. J. R. Davidson was selected to preach the opening sermon at the next session of the state association, which was to meet October 31, 1939, at the First Free Will Baptist Church in Denison, Texas. A motion was made and carried that the next session extend "through the three days." This session ended at the close of the afternoon business, with no evening service.

Twenty-Fifth Annual Session - 1939

The National Association, July

Prior to the meeting of the Texas State Association in November, the third session of the National Association of Free Will Baptists met at the First Free Will Baptist Church of Bryan, Texas, July 11-14, 1939. The following eight state associations represented: Georgia, Kentucky, Missouri, North Carolina, Oklahoma, Tennessee, Texas, and Virginia. District associations from Alabama, Mississippi, and Ohio also represented. Damon Dodd reported that twenty-two states and district associations were represented by 52 delegates and 51 ministers.[83] The entire National Association met in the Bryan Church. It must have been packed, however, as one speaker referred to this "vast congregation."

---

[82] *The Free Will Baptist* was and is the state paper of the North Carolina State Convention, which was widely read prior to the split of the convention.
[83] Damon Dodd, *The Free Will Baptist Story*, page 126.

Melvin Bingham, of Tulsa, Oklahoma, preached at the opening service on Tuesday evening. His text was "And let the beauty of the LORD our God be upon us; and establish thou the work of our hands upon us; yea, the work of our hands establish thou it" (Psalm 90:17). Brother Bingham, speaking forcefully, with vivid illustrations and earnest admonition, related some of the work that the denomination should do and how it could meet with success.

There were several resignations from the various boards, including Lizzie McAdams from the Home Missions Board. C. B. Thompson was elected to the Foreign Missions Board to replace Mrs. J. R. Bennett, who had resigned.

On Thursday afternoon the business was suspended for a National Declamation Contest on stewardship.

Numerous Texans served as members of various boards. J. K. Warkentin, of Fort Worth, served on the Executive Committee; Clyde Goen, of the Harvey Community out of Bryan, and C. B. Thompson[84] on the Foreign Missions Board; J. K. Warkentin, of Fort Worth, on the Home Missions Board; Aston Pegues, of Normangee, on the Sunday School Board; R. C. Wiggs, of North Zulch, on the Free Will Baptist League Board; J. R. Davidson, of Bryan, on the Education Board; and Clyde Goen on the Superannuation Board.

The Foreign Missions Report is very interesting. The board approved the transfer of Thomas and Mabel Willey from Panama to Nicaragua, the Willey's having been forced out of Panama by an intolerant government. Their salary was to continue at $150.00 per month. The board approved that the salary of Miss Laura Bell Barnard, serving in India, be continued at $50.00 per month. The board approved a salary of $50.00 per month for Miss Bessie Yeley and that she be given $200.00 for her transportation to Venezuela. The total Foreign Missions budget for the coming year was $$3,950.00, with Texas' quota being $400.00.

The Education Board asked for and received authorization to establish and maintain a Bible College for the training of ministers and other Christian workers. The board, with $1,019.99 on hand, announced that with the support and backing of the denomination such a school would open by September 1 of 1940, and no later than January 1, of 1941. J. R. Davidson, pastor of the First Free Will Baptist Church in Bryan, was a primary proponent of establishing a Bible College for the denomination. He was such a force in this effort that the first building of Free Will Baptist Bible College, which opened in September of 1942, was named Davidson Hall. Clyde Goen gave such significant financial support to the college that the first building specifically built as a dormitory was named Goen Hall.

The Texas State Association, October 1939

The Twenty-fifth annual session of the Texas State Association of Free Will Baptists met with the First Free Will Baptist Church of Denison, Texas, starting on Tuesday evening, October 31, 1939. President T. H. Newsom introduced Miss Tommie Franklin who brought a devotion, using Psalm 103 as her text. T. W. Smith, of Clayton, Texas, preached the introductory sermon. The sermon, from the Book of Philippians, was entited "Suffering for Christ."

The Wednesday morning session, after proper preliminaries got down to business. The following associations and churches reported:

---

[84] C. B. Thomson was temporarily of Goldsboro, North Carolina.

Associations
- *Central Texas Association*: Mrs. R. C. Cloud, Mrs. Belle Casey, Mrs. C. H. Moehlman, Mrs. R. C. Wiggs, with $10.00 fees
- *West Fork Association*: Mrs. Maud Weir, Miss Lucile Cozart, W. D. Phillips, Mrs. J. K. Markenton, Mrs. J. A. (Edith) Brooks, A. J. Measures, C. T. Stubbs, Jim Collins, $4.00 cash, $9.00 vouched for
- *Texas Association*: Mrs. Gus Smith, $10.00
- *Woodlawn Association*: Lucile Gardner, Mrs. A. Sullins, Mrs. W. T. Holcomb, B. F. Connally and J. B. Williams, $5.00

Churches
- *Trinity Church, Fort Worth*: C. B. Weir, Mrs. Clara Sutton, $2.00
- *First Church, Waco*: Mrs. Lula Gresham, Mrs. Clara Smith, $2.00
- *Liberty Church, Dott*: Layton Maricle, Opal Calvery, $2.00
- *Pine Prairie Church, Huntsville*: no delegates, $1.00 cast, $1.00 vouched for
- *First Church, Bryan*: Mrs. T. A. Cloud, $2.00
- *North Zulch*: no delegates, $2.00
- *New Hope Church, Rusk County*: Mrs. Mattie Garvin, Joe Mark Whitten, $2.00
- *Plainview Church, Normangee*: no delegates, $2.00 vouched for
- *Bright Light*: no delegates, $2.00 vouched for
- *Evergreen, Iola*: no delegates, $2.00 vouched for
- *Edge Church, Edge*: no delegates, $2.00 vouched for
- *Christian Home Church, Kurten*: no delegates, $2.00 vouched for
- *New Hope Church, Parker County*: no delegates, $2.00 vouched for
- *Pleasant Mound, Buffalo Springs*: Mrs. Carrie Covington, $2.00
- *First Church, Denison*: Mrs. C. T. Stubbs, O. K. Busby, $2.00

Tiff Covington of Buffalo Springs, Texas, preached "a very spiritual sermon" from the 17th chapter of John, entitled "What Jesus Prayed For."

On Wednesday afternoon a draft of the revisions of the Constitution and By-Laws was presented. A motion carried that the Constitution and By-Laws be ratified or amended article by article. Later, a motion prevailed that action be postponed until Thursday morning. A mission's address was given by J. R. Davidson and a round table discussion on missions followed. Mrs. R. C. Wiggs presented a program and short business session covering the women's work. Mrs. Charles Moehlman read a report of their work by reading the minutes of their previous meeting, including reports of officers, and amounts collected and disbursed during the year, which showed quite a bit of activity.

At 6:30 p.m. a song and praise service was conducted by Tiff Covington, which lasted for thirty minutes. This included a quartet composed of four members of the Trice family. A quartet was also rendered by E. A. O'Donnell, M. L. Sutton, Bert Rogers, and Sally White. The evening service started at 8:00 o'clock with congregational singing, a devotion and another song by the Trice Quartet. The sermon was delivered by J. R. Davidson, entitled "The Mission of the Church." His text was Matthew 5:13. The service was dismissed by Tiff Covington.

The Thursday morning session was begun by singing led by E. A. O'Donnell, a devotion led by Leroy Conaway, of Eddy, Texas. Prayer was led by Paul Purcell. A short address was given by J. E. Dearmore on memory work of the Bible. At the close of his address the secretary-treasurer was instructed to advance $15.00 to Dearmore to enable him to publish a booklet on the subject of "Bible Memory."

At 9:40 a motion was made that the proposed Constitution and By-Laws be re-read and action taken. After reading and a few minor amendments had been offered the new Constitution and By-Laws was unanimously adopted. In the 11:00 o'clock worship service Bert Rogers "preached a fine sermon" from Job 8:7. His sermon was entitled "Increased Blessings."

On Thursday afternoon the business session included a motion that the state association purchase a copy of Parliamentary Rules and Order to be in the custody of the secretary. The motion lost. The following committees gave their reports: Treasurer of Foreign Missions, Foreign Missions, Denomination, Education, Evangelism, Women's Work, and Temperance. A collection for education was taken and $4.38 secured.

In the Thursday evening service the congregational singing was led by C. B. Weir and prayers were led by T. W. Smith and Miss Tommie Franklin. The following committees reported: Obituary, Committee on Committees, Laymen's Work, and Young People's Work. The Trice Quartet sang a special and J. L. Bounds preached a sermon from Revelation 22, entitled "The Coming Jesus." An offering for missions was received in the amount of $3.66.

On Friday morning the singing was led by B. A. Grant and the devotion was brought by Miss Lucile Gardner of Waco, Texas, quoting different parts of God's Word. At 9:30 M. L. Sutton submitted a resolution opposing war in any form and another opposing capital punishment. The resolutions passed and a request was made that copies be sent to our U. S. Senator and Governor. The following officers were elected for the following year:

President	M. L. Sutton
Vice-President	T. H. Newsom
Recording Secretary	Miss Lucile Gardner
Treasurer	Thomas A. Cloud
Publicity Director	R. C. Wiggs
Statistician	C. J. Turrentine
Parliamentarian	J. L. Bounds
Secretary-Treasurer of Foreign Missions	Clyde Goen

The association voted to delegate to the Executive Committee the responsibility of naming delegates to the National Association and the treasurer was authorized to pay the fees of the delegates. The 1939 state association meeting was held from October 31 through November 3, and the 3rd session of the National Association had already been held, July 11-14, 1939, at the First Free Will Baptist Church in Bryan, Texas. This, then, would have to refer to the 4th session of the National Association which was held in Paintsville, Kentucky, July 15-19, 1940. The association voted to allow time on the program of the 1940 state meeting for the "Ladies Work." R. C. Wiggs preached at the 11:00 o'clock worship hour.

Twenty-Sixth Annual Session - 1940

The twenty-sixth annual session of the Texas State Association of Free Will Baptists met with the Friendship Free Will Baptist Church, Clayton, Texas, October 29 through November 1, 1940. The Tuesday evening service began at 7:30 p.m. Mrs. Leroy Conaway, of the Dott Church, gave a devotion from Psalm 23 and John 14. Ruel Conner preached the introductory sermon, using Philippians as his Scripture.

The Wednesday morning session began at 9:30 a.m. with singing led by Charles B. Weir of Fort Worth, and a devotion by Mrs. Jessie Ferguson, reading Scripture from Matthew 14. The business began at 9:45. E. S. Jameson gave a short history of Free Will Baptist churches, stating that they were meeting in the first Free Will Baptist church to be organized in the state of Texas,

62 years ago. In the 11:15 worship service the sermon was given by E. J. Vaughan, who used Luke 11:2 as his text, and his subject being "Prayer."

The afternoon session began at 1:30 with congregational singing led by Charles B. Weir of Fort Worth, and a devotion by Mrs. Charles Moehlman of Bryan. The following associations and churches represented:

Associations

Texas Association: J. E. Tompkins, C. E. Custrow, H. D. Browning,
P. H. Graves, J. L. Ross, Ernie Weaver, E. T. Tipps, Mrs. Frank Birdwell, Ernest Hensley, J. H. Fitzgerald, T. T. Megason

West Fork Association: C. B. Weir, A. J. Measures, Ruel Conner, Cleve Stubbs,
J. W. Taylor, Mrs. Rena Benton, M. L. Sutton, J. K. Warkentin

Central Texas Association: Mrs. Anna Winsor, Mrs. T. A. Cloud,
Mrs. W. G. Reynolds, Miss Icy Goen

Southeast Texas Association: Dick Adams, Alvin Young

Victory Association: by letter M. T. Holley

Churches

Trinity Church, Fort Worth: Lena Mullins, Jessie Ferguson, $2.00

Pine Prairie, Huntsville: Mr. and Mrs. Hudspeth, $2.00

Liberty Church, Dott: Mrs. Leroy Conaway, Miss Eula Mae Martin, $2.00

North Zulch: no delegates, $2.00 vouched for by Aston Pegues

Pleasant Mound, Buffalo Springs: R. H. Cowley, $2.00

New Hope Church: Atlas Grant, Mrs. A. E. Stokes, $2.00

First Church, Bryan: Mrs. Charles Moehlman, Mrs. J. L. Edge, $2.00

Evergreen Church, Keith: no delegates, $2.00

First Church, Waco: Mr. and Mrs. Riley White, $2.00

First Church, Fort Worth: no delegates, $5.00

A petitionary letter from the Victory Association was read and their delegates seated. There is little information available about this new association, which seems to have been centered in the Lubbock area. M. T. Holley, of Lubbock, preached at the Wednesday evening service as we see below.

The amount of $4.61 due from last year, 1939, from the West Fork Association was turned in to the clerk. A motion was made and carried that the association visit the flower nursery in Carthage on Thursday afternoon at 3:00 o'clock. A vote of thanks was extended to Thomas A. Cloud for contributing the program for the 1940 association meeting. The names of those on various committees were read so they might have their reports ready the following day. T. A. Cloud gave the treasurer's report and a motion was made that $2.00 be taken up to clear the deficit in the treasury. $4.66 was collected. Invitations were extended from the Pleasant Mound Free Will Baptist Church in Buffalo Springs and from the Free Will Baptist Church in Bryan, for the 1941 session of the state association. The Bryan Church was chosen as the meeting place. Rev. Tiff Covington was chosen to preach the associational sermon at the 1941 session. A motion was made and carried that the associational sermon be preached at the 11:00 o'clock service of the first full day of the association. A motion was made and carried that the treasurer be authorized to pay the $10.00 fee for the National Association and that the moderator of the convention be authorized to appoint the delegates. The 1941 National Association convention met at the Drumright Free Will Baptist Church, Drumright, Oklahoma, July 13-18.

The Wednesday evening service contained a Young People's Hour led by Miss Lucile Gardner, of Waco. Helping her was Aston Pegues of North Zulch, who spoke on "The Family

Altar, A Help to Sunday Schools and Leagues." The evening sermon was then preached by M. T. Holley of Lubbock, Texas.

Business occupied the Thursday morning session as various reports were read and adopted: Temperance, Young People's Work, Women's Missions, and Denomination. The report on Sunday School was read, after which a motion to table the report until a further date was passed. The report on Home Missions was given and a motion was made that it be tabled until other recommended items were added. The Committee on Committees was appointed as follows: Rev. E. J. Jameson, Mrs. Charles Moehlman, and Mrs. Jessie Ferguson. The eleven o'clock worship hour featured a sermon preached by L. R. Ennis of Goldsboro, North Carolina. His sermon subject was "Seeing Jesus," using Hebrews 2:9 as his text. After the sermon Ennis[85] discussed plans of organizing a Free Will Baptist school in the near future as had been brought out at the 1940 National Association meeting in Paintsville, Kentucky. A collection was taken for the Education Fund and $30.00 was received.

The Thursday afternoon session began with a report of the Woman's Work. In the absence of the chairman, Mrs. R. C. Wiggs, Mrs. Charles Moelhman presided. The women and pastors were urged to increase "ladies auxiliary work" throughout the state. Tiff Covington made a recommendation that L. R. Ennis be invited to attend the Minister's Convention in March and bring about three courses per session to the ministers. A motion to that effect was made and carried. An amendment to the Home Missions report was read and adopted. A certificate was approved to be given to Hubert Ray Berry, approving his work in the organization of a church in Houston, Texas. The report of Home Missions was read and adopted. The amendment added to the Sunday School report regarding changing of ages was read and adopted. The Sunday School report was then adopted.

The Thursday evening worship service began with congregational singing led by C. B. Weir, and a devotion given by Miss Eula Mae Martin[86] of Dott. Her text was Romans 1:3. W. V. McPhail, Waco, preached the evening sermon.

The Friday morning business session opened with C. B. Weir leading the singing and Brother A. W. West giving a devotion. A motion was made and carried that Article 9 of the By-Laws be changed to read: "The following standing committees shall be appointed or elected: Temperance, Resolutions, Credentials, Obituary, and Program, and directors shall be elected for the following activities: Home Missions, Foreign Missions, Christian Education, Laymen's Work, Free Will Baptist League, Sunday School, and Ladies Auxiliary Work." Directors who were nominated and elected were:

    Home Missions J. L. Edge, Bryan
    Foreign Missions   J. R. Davidson, Bryan
    Young Peoples Work   Miss Lucile Gardner, Waco [apparently same as League]
    Christian Education   R. C. Wiggs, North Zulch
    Laymen's Work B. F. Payne, Carthage
    Sunday School Aston Pegues, North Zulch
    Ladies Auxiliary   Mr. Charles F. Moehlman, Bryan

---

[85] Rev. L. R. Ennis was very instrumental in getting Free Will Baptist Bible College started. The second building purchased by the new school, which opened in the fall of 1942, was named Ennis Hall. He served for two years as president of the school.

[86] Eula Mae Martin was the sister of Billie Jean Martin Crosby Bankhead.

Two more reports were given and adopted: Obituary and Evangelism. Then the following general officers were elected:

President	M. L. Sutton, Fort Worth
Vice-President	Tiff Covington, Buffalo Springs
Rec. Secretary	Miss Lucile Gardner, Waco
Treasurer	Mrs. Riley White, Waco
Publicity	Charles Weir, Fort Worth
Statistician	E. J. Jameson
Parliamentarian	J. R. Davidson, Bryan

M. L. Sutton made a short talk on orphanage work, encouraging Free Will Baptists to consider the organization of a Free Will Baptist orphanage in the state of Texas. The orphanage fund report was given and accepted. The contents of the report are not given. Brother and Sister T. W. Smith received a hearty endorsement of the State Association of Free Will Baptists for their orphanage[87] work and a motion was made and carried that they be given a certificate of endorsement signed by the president and secretary for their good work. Tiff Covington made a talk boosting the support of orphanage and the young people's work in the state of Texas.

We will interject here that there was considerable interest in establishing an orphanage in Texas at the time. In February of 1940 the Free Will Baptist Gem carried an article by Elder C. J. Turrentine, encouraging the possibility. In part the article stated:

> Almost three years ago, in a ministerial meeting, I presented to our ministers the need of a state orphanage for our Free Will Baptist people. At this time, there was only one dollar given by our sister Rev. Jessie Ferguson, a young mother of two wonderful children, and a minister's wife.
>
> From this time until our state association in November, there has been $57.00 raised among the ministry. God has laid it on my heart to build this institution, and with God's help and yours, this can be done. Do you know and keep your Church Covenant? Won't you, dear reader, help build this Christian Home for orphan children? We know you will help, and tell your friends.

M. L. Sutton preached during the morning worship hour, using Galatians 2:11-21 as his text. An offering for the orphanage fund was received and $11.01 was collected, making a grand total on hand of $114.38 in the orphanage fund. President M. L. Sutton appointed the following to serve as delegates to the National Association to be held July 13-18 in Drumright, Oklahoma: Brother C. B. Weir, Brother Gus Smith, Mrs. Gus Smith, Mrs. T. W. Smith, and Miss Anna Reed.

Twenty-Seventh Annual Session - 1941

The Twenty-seventh annual session of the Texas State Association met at the First Free Will Baptist Church, Bryan, Texas, October 28-30, 1941. The host pastor, J. R. Davidson led the congregational singing and the opening sermon was preached by T. W. Smith of Kirbyville, Texas. His Scripture was Proverbs 2:1-13 and Isaiah 2:5, and his theme was "Walking With God."

---

[87] The orphanage to which this refers would be the Free Will Baptist orphanage at Ringling, Oklahoma, which the Oklahoma State Association owned and operated for fourteen years. A picture of it is on page 23 of *Oklahoma State Association of Free Will Baptists, The First 100 years 1908-2008*, published by the Oklahoma State Association of Free Will Baptists in 2009. The orphanage is also mentioned on pages 117-119 of the same book.

The Wednesday morning business session was called to order by Tiff Covington, Buffalo Springs, Texas, who was vice-president. The secretary was absent and so T. A. Cloud was elected secretary *pro tem*. President M. L. Sutton was present for the report of the Credentials Committee. The following associations represented:

    Central Texas Association: Clyde Goen, Mrs. R. E. Conner, Emmett Holland, Mrs. Clarence Parker, J. W. Rice, $10.00
    Southeast Texas Association, T. W. Smith, $1.00
    West Fork Association: $10.00

Tiff Covington, of Buffalo Springs, preached in the morning worship hour, using the text Revelation 18:4, his subject being "God's Call." A handshake was extended to Covington for his work and pledging support to the principles he addressed. The service was dismissed in prayer by E. E. Morris of Ada, Oklahoma.

In the Wednesday afternoon business session T. W. Smith, treasurer, showed a balance on hand from 1939-40 of $112.38, with $45.62 collected during 1940-41 making a total of $158.00 on hand. A collection was taken in which $16.40 was added making a total of $174.40. The following reports were read and adopted: Resolution and Foreign Missions.

The Wednesday evening worship hour consisted of congregational singing and a testimony service in which almost everyone present participated. J. K. Workington, of Fort Worth, preached the evening sermon, "Today's Progress of Apostasy," using 2 Thessalonians 2:1-17 as his text.

The Thursday morning business session began with a song and devotion by John Newberry of Longview. With two committees absent, the president, M. L. Sutton appointed C. F. Goen to the Committee on Laymen's Work and Sylvia Brooks, Miss Tommie Franklin, and Miss Lucile Cozart as the Temperance Committee. Two committees then reported. First was the Education Committee, whose report was accepted. Second, the Committee on Sunday Schools report was given by M. L. Sutton who recommended that the report of the previous year be again endorsed. He also recommended that the Sunday School Standard adopted by the National Association be adopted. His report was adopted. E. E. Morris, of Ada, Oklahoma, preached in the morning worship service. Using Proverbs 28:18 as his text, he preached on "A Vision."

The Thursday afternoon business session was opened by congregational singing and a devotion brought by Miss Tommie Franklin of Henderson. Mrs. J. R. Davidson gave the report on the Ladies Auxiliary work.

The following directors were elected:

Home Missions	M. L. Sutton
Foreign Missions	Clyde F. Goen
Young People's Work	Mrs. Wendell Withers
Christian Education	Charles B. Weir
Laymen's Work	W. J. O'Brien
Sunday School	M. L. Sutton
Ladies Auxiliary	Mrs. J. R. Davidson
Orphanage	T. W. Smith

The following general officers of the Texas State Association were elected:

President	J. R. Davidson
Vice-President	J. L. Bounds
Recording Secretary	Thomas A. Cloud
Treasurer	Ruel Conner
Publicity	Miss Tommie Franklin
Statistician	John Newberry
Parliamentarian	M. L. Sutton

The association voted to authorize the president to appoint delegates to the National Association, which was to meet at the First Free Will Baptist Church, Columbus, Mississippi, July 12-17, 1942. The following delegates were appointed: Miss Nelma Moody, Navasota, Texas; Mr. and Mrs. C. B. Weir, Fort Worth; Mrs. Gus Smith, Henderson, and Mrs. C. H. Moehlman, Bryan. The clerk was authorized to print a thousand copies of the minutes and include the Constitution and By-Laws.

The clerk, Thomas A. Cloud, drew a box on the last page of his hand written minutes which contained the following:

IN MEMORY of
James L. Edge
who departed this life July 1941

A charter member of the
First Free Will Baptist Church of
Bryan, Texas

Twenty-Eighth Annual Session - 1942

The twenty-eighth annual session of the Texas State Association of Free Will Baptists convened with the Pleasant Mound Free Will Baptist Church at Buffalo Springs, Texas, October 27-30, 1942. The Tuesday evening service began at 8:00 o'clock. W. C. Covington led the singing and the opening prayer was led by J. O. Fort, the new pastor of the First Free Will Baptist Church in Bryan. Ruel E. Conner, of North Zulch, Texas, preached the evening message, entitled "The Power of the Holy Spirit," using eleven verses from the first chapter of Acts.

The Wednesday morning business session began at 10:30 a.m. with devotional services. The association president, J. R. Davidson, called the session to order.[88] Prayer was led by "Mother Covington."

---

[88] J. R. Davidson had accepted the position of pastor in Ashland City, Tennessee, and J. O. Fort had assumed the pastorate of the First Free Will Baptist Church in Bryan. It is not stated where Brother Davidson was living at the time of the state meeting in 1942 and why or how he was able to still serve as state moderator, or as they called it then, president.

The Credentials Committee report was read and the following associations and church reported:

Victory Association, Levelland: Albert Lester, Estelline, Texas; Alta Eaton, Paducah, Texas; $4.50

Southeast Texas Association, Kirbyville: no delegates, $10.00

Central Texas Association: C. F. Goen, Lizzie McAdams, Mrs. T. A. Cloud, Mrs. Lizzie Trant, $10.00

West Fork Association: Mrs. Belle Easley, J. A. Brooks, Sallie White, W. A. Reeder, J. H. Measurer, H. H. Killough, Anderson, C. B. Weir, Hugh Brewer, and James Laymon, $10.00

J. O. Fort delivered the message in the morning worship service. His text was First John chapter three and his subject was "Our Obligations As Sons and Children."

The Wednesday afternoon business session featured a number of congregational songs and specials. J. K. Workington sang "Beautiful Garden of Prayer," and a quartet composed of Lillian White, Miss Lora Cozart, Miss Mickey Covington [Tiff's daughter] and Mrs. R. E. Conner. It was voted that the regular order of business be suspended and miscellaneous items of business be taken up. A report from the Director of Orphanage showed a balance of $243.70. It should be observed that Texas did not have an orphanage. Whether these funds were being sent to the orphanage at Ringling, Oklahoma, isn't stated. The associational treasurer gave his report and stated a balance of $63.25. On motion by C. B. Thompson the Committee on Resolutions was instructed to send an appropriate message of sympathy to the families of J. C. Hodges and his wife and T. H. Newsom and wife. The clerk was to have a thousand copies of the minutes printed, which was to include the Constitution and By-Laws. The president named the following to serve as delegates to the National Association, scheduled to meet July 11-16, 1943, at the East Nashville Free Will Baptist Church, Nashville, Tennessee: Mrs. M. L. Sutton, Fort Worth; H. H. Killough, Fort Worth; Morris Walling, Dallas; Mrs. R. E. Conner, North Zulch, and Mrs. W. G. Reynolds, Bryan. The association voted unanimously to meet at the First Free Will Baptist Church in Dallas in 1943.

The Wednesday evening service opened with a rousing song service, led by J. R. Davidson and M. L. Sutton. C. B. Thompson preached the evening message entitled "Witnessing for Jesus," using Acts 10:8 as his text.

The Thursday morning business session opened with singing led by J. R. Davidson and prayer by Edith Brooks. The Obituary Committee reported. Miss Killough of Fort Worth was asked to act as reading clerk to assist the regular clerk. The reports of Sunday School and Home Missions were read and approved. Several ministers present reported as having engaged in Home Mission work during the past year, all of which was very encouraging. The Director of Foreign Missions was absent and no report was obtainable. The morning worship hour began at 11:45 with singing led by M. C. Covington and prayer by H. H. Killough. At noon the message of the morning was delivered by J. R. Davidson, of Ashland City, Tennessee. His sermon was on the subject "Our Debt to Grace," using Ephesians 2:1-10 as his text. At the close of the service a collection was taken for education. The amount was $24.30.

After lunch a special program by the young people was conducted by Miss Killough, chairman of League work, who made a very interesting talk on young people's part in worship, followed by a song by three junior leaguers. The report of the Temperance Committee was read and adopted. A motion prevailed that the body in session be instructed to write the county commissioners of Wichita County commending them for their stand taken in the enforcement of Prohibition in their county. The report of the Woman's Auxiliary was given in the form of a letter from Mrs. J. R. Davidson.

General officers for 1942-1943 were elected as follows:

President	M. L. Sutton, Fort Worth
Vice-President	C. B. Thompson, Fort Worth
Secretary	Thomas A. Cloud, Bryan
Treasurer	C. B. Weir, Fort Worth
Publicity Director	R. E. Conner, North Zulch
Statistician	H. H. Killough, Fort Worth
Orphanage	T. W. Smith, Kirbyville
Parliamentarian	Tiff Covington, Buffalo Springs

It is noteworthy that there seems to have been no representation from the Texas Association, which would later be called the East Texas District Association. The minutes contain no comment as to why.

~~~~~~~~

Free Will Baptist Bible College opened in September of 1942, with four students. One of those students, Damon Dodd, had been won to Christ through the evangelistic ministry of Lizzie McAdams. For a time he served as the campaign song leader. One of the other three students was his wife, Myrtle. The opening of the college brought to fruition the dreams and efforts of many Free Will Baptists, including many leaders from Texas. Though Texas had no students in that first class, young men and women from Texas soon began to attend in significant numbers. Many of them, both men and women, went on to become missionaries, pastors, pastor's wives, denominational leaders, and church workers in many capacities.

~~~~~~~~

Twenty-Ninth Annual Session - 1943

The twenty-ninth annual session of the Texas State Association of Free Will Baptists convened with the Easley Chapel at Gartman's View Free Will Baptist Church, near Comanche, Texas, November 2-4, 1943. Two things become apparent as we read the minutes of that session. First, the association had voted at the previous session to meet with the First Free Will Baptist Church in Dallas, but the meeting is being held at the Easley Chapel Church. Second, the clerk elected for the 1942-43 year was Thomas A. Cloud, but the clerk actually serving in 1943 is Charles B. Weir, who wrote with excellent penmanship.

The Tuesday evening session opened with singing led by J. O. Fort, of Bryan, and a prayer led by Tiff Covington. The introductory message was delivered by C. B. Thompson of Fort Worth. After the message the delegates were assigned to homes.

The Wednesday morning session began with singing led by Allie Ferguson, of Fort Worth, prayer by Ova Stalcup, of Denison, and a devotion presented by B. A. Grant, of Henderson. For the first time the moderator is referred to as "moderator" rather than president. M. L. Sutton served in that capacity. John A. Brooks, host pastor, welcomed the association. The following associations represented:

Friendship Association: Mrs. J. J. Graham

Central Texas Association: Mrs. Ruby Withers, Mrs. Charles Moehlman, Mrs. Wheeler, Tatum Trant, and L. M. Adams; $15.00

Texas Association: F. W. Doctor, E. D. Lunsford, Bill Berry, D. D. Stokes, R. Jimmerson, P. H. Graves, J. E. Tompkins, M. C. Bole, H. F. Lunsford, A. J. Williams, and W. H. Hays; $11.00

West Fork Association: Mrs. Belle Easley; Mrs. Clara Phillips, Mr. Jess Lamb, Mrs. Charles B. Weir, Mrs. Sylvia Burks, and Mrs. Eva Conner; $10.00

Southeast Texas Association: no delegates; $1.00

The report of the orphanage work was given by Director T. W. Smith, of Iola, Texas, and was accepted.

A five minutes recess was taken, after which moderator M. L. Sutton called the assembly together for worship. After congregational singing a special song was rendered by Mrs. Julie Brouer, and Miss Patricia Pyles, both of Denison. M. L. Sutton, of the Trinity Free Will Baptist Church in Fort Worth, "broke the bread of life" and spoke on the subject "Now the Just Shall Live by Faith." A "bountiful"lunch was served.

The Wednesday afternoon business session started with the election of the following general officers for the 1943-44 year:

Moderator	J. O. Fort, Bryan
Assistant Moderator	C. B. Thompson, Fort Worth
Recording Secretary	Charles B. Weir, Fort Worth
Treasurer	M. L. Sutton, Arlington
Publicity Director	M. L. Sutton, Arlington
Statistician	J. B. Lowering, North Zulch
Parliamentarian	Tiff Covington, Buffalo Springs

The report on Christian Education was given and received. A motion was made and carried that the association grant T. W. Smith the authority to place money on hand for orphanage work with a bonding company, and that the bonding fee be taken from funds on hand. By vote the business session was extended until 4:30 p.m.

The Wednesday evening worship service, though it contained some business items, opened with congregational singing led by Mrs. Julie Brouer and prayer by J. H. Measures. Julie Brouer and Miss Patricia Pyles sang a special duet. C. B. Thompson gave the report on Foreign Missions, which was accepted, with an amendment that the speaker's remarks be endorsed by the association. The message of the evening was brought by Robert B. Crawford, Executive Secretary of the National Association of Free Will Baptists, from Nashville, Tennessee.[89]

The Thursday morning session started with congregational singing led by Mrs. Julie Brouer and a prayer led by C. B. Thompson. M. L. Sutton sang "Pearly White City." Three reports were given and received: Committee on Committees, Superannuation, and Sunday School. The minutes do not mention a morning worship service.

The Thursday afternoon business session began with a lively song service. A quartet composed of M. L. Sutton, Allie Ferguson, Sister Belle Easley, and Sister Julie Brouer, sang a special song. They were accompanied at the piano by Sister Sadie White. Two reports were then given and received: the Obituary Committee report, by T. W. Smith, and the report of the Ladies' Auxiliary, by Mrs. C. B. Moehlman. The congregation sang the missionary theme song: "Tell Me the Old, Old Story." A special offering was taken for a school fund for the children of Thomas and Mabel Willey, missionaries to Cuba, Thomas, Jr. and Barbara. The amount received was $87.69.

The following reports were then given and accepted: Temperance, Resolutions, Home Missions, and Free Will Baptist League. A motion carried that the association elect ministers and

---

[89] Robert B. Crawford served as Executive Secretary of the National Association of Free Will Baptists from 1943 to 1947. He was the son of Pink Crawford. Two of his sisters, Essie Collins and Merle Dyer, and one brother attended the First Free Will Baptist Church of Northport, Alabama, when I pastored there from 1967 to 1972. He once preached for me.

laymen to serve on a Superannuation Board and that delegates from each district association elect [nominate] candidates for that purpose. A motion then carried that the state association sponsor a Texas page in *The Free Will Baptist*, a denominational paper, and that M. L. Sutton be made editor [of that page] with the authority to revise copies of reports for publication. The association then proceeded to elect the following members of the Superannuation Board:

    Clyde Goen   Central District Association
    E. S. Jameson   Texas District Association
    Charles B. Weir   West Fork District Association
    M. L. Holley   Friendship District Association
    Marion Sheffield   Southeast Texas District Association
    A. Sullins   Woodlawn District Association

The association voted that the next session of the Texas State Association be held at the First Free Will Baptist Church in Waco, and that Tiff Covington preach the introductory sermon. J. O. Fort read the names of the directors for the ensuing year:

    Director of Women's Work Mrs. C. H. Moehlman, Bryan
    Director of Foreign Missions C. B. Thompson, Fort Worth
    Director of Home Missions Tiff Covington, Buffalo Springs
    Director of Sunday School M. L. Sutton, Arlington
    Director of Orphanage T. W. Smith, Iola
    Director of FWB League Mrs. Julie Brouer, Denison

Motion carried that the association send delegates and pay their entry fee to the National Association of Free Will Baptists, which was scheduled to meet July 9-14, 1944, at the Flat River Free Will Baptist Church, Flat River, Missouri.

The following delegates were elected:
    Sister Belle Easley   West Fork Association
    Sister Ruby Withers   Central Texas Association
    Brother G. R. Parker   Texas Association
    Sister J. J. Graham   Friendship Association
    Brother Leroy Conaway   Woodlawn Association

A series of motions were then made and carried:
- that the delegates be authorized to name their own alternates to the National
- that the clerk have one thousand copies of the state minutes printed
- that the treasurer pay the clerk the usual amount for his services, $10.00
- that $40.00 be taken out of the treasury that was paid our for last year's representation to the National Association
- that J. O. Fort and C. B. Thompson be paid $5.00 each for their entry to the National Association
- that a bill of $3.50 be paid for the printing of the programs

Miscellaneous business was then dispensed with and "an old fashioned handshake was extended to all ministers present.

Thirtieth Annual Session - 1944

The Thirtieth annual session of the Texas State Association of Free Will Baptists convened at the First Free Will Baptist Church, Waco, Texas, October 31 through November 3, 1944.

Congregational singing was led by E. J. Vaughn of the church, who also brought the devotion. The introductory sermon was "ably delivered" by C. B. Thompson.

The Wednesday morning session began with singing led by J. O. Fort, prayer by B. A. Grant, a devotion by Mrs. Jessie Ferguson, and a prayer by J. O. Fort. M. L. Sutton sang a special. Then proceeded the "enrollment of ministers." J. O. Fort preached the moderator's message, "The King Judges," using Matthew 21:1-16, 23-32 as his text. The service was dismissed in prayer by J. L. Bounds.

The Wednesday afternoon session opened with singing led by J. O. Fort, and a devotion by T. W. Smith. The following reports were made and accepted: Christian Education, by J. B. Lovering; Credentials (partial), and Sunday School, by M. L. Sutton. A motion carried that the association institute a State Sunday School Convention to convene on Monday evening before the state association meeting. The body voted that the next session of the association meet at the Fellowship Church, Henderson, Texas, and that the introductory sermon be delivered by J. B. Lovering. A motion carried that we enter into a round table discussion of home missions. A motion carried that we elect a Home Missions Board and to invite all local associations to pool their resources and cooperate. A motion carried that the previous motion be tabled until Thursday afternoon.

A motion carried that Article 9 of the By-Laws be changed to read as follows: "Article 9. The following committees shall be appointed at each sitting of the association: Temperance, Resolutions, Program, Credentials, Obituary, and Committee on Committees; and the following directors shall be elected, Christian Education, Free Will Baptist League, Woman's Auxiliary, Orphanage, Laymen's Work, and Denominational Literature, Sunday Schools, and Foreign Missions. The body shall elect boards of five members each for Superannuation and Home Missions."

The Wednesday evening worship hour/business opened by singing led by E. J. Vaughn, prayer by M. L. Sutton, and a devotion by B. A. Grant, who spoke on Psalm 85:6: "Wilt thou not revive us again: that they people may rejoice in thee?" T. W. Smith led in prayer, followed by a quartet number, "In the Shadow of the Cross," sung by M. L. Sutton, Robert B. Crawford, J. R. Davidson, and Mrs. Della Lawlis, with Mrs. C. B. Thompson at the piano. A special duet was sung, "The Royal Telephone." Robert B. Crawford delivered the evening sermon from the text, Mark 10:17-22 "Come, take up the cross and follow me."

The Thursday morning business session began with J. O. Fort again leading singing. M. T. Holley brought a devotion and led in prayer. C. B. Thompson read a report on foreign mission work, which was adopted as read. J. R. Davidson gave a report on Free Will Baptist Bible College. M. L. Sutton sang "I Won't Have to Cross Jordan Alone." Clyde Goen led in prayer. Miss Tommie Rae Brooks, daughter of John A. Brooks, sang "Satisfied with Jesus." John A. Brooks broke the bread of life at the hour for the morning sermon. His subject was "A Good Soldier," and his text was 2 Timothy 2:4. The clerk noted, "The message was so ably delivered that a call from the floor was made that we have a song and the right hand of fellowship be extended to Brother Brooks." "Onward Christian Soldiers" was sung. Moderator J. O. Fort led in prayer.

The business of the association resumed in the afternoon with congregational singing led by J. O. Fort. In the absence of Miss Tommie Franklin, who was on the program for the devotion, the moderator read from Matthew 25:31-46. C. B. Thompson led in prayer. The following reports were then read and accepted: Orphanage Work, by T. W. Smith; and Women's Work, by Mrs. Charles Moehlman. Robert Crawford, Executive Secretary of the National Association of Free Will Baptists, made comments on the 50,000 Co-laborers Campaign of the National Woman's

Auxiliary. The following reports were made and adopted: Treasurer, Temperance, Obituary, and Resolutions. M. L. Sutton was elected moderator. The minutes of the 1944 state meeting end here.

Thirty-First Annual Session - 1945

Historical Note
World War II had ended with the surrender of Germany on May 7, 1945, at Allied headquarters in Reims, France, to take effect the following day, ending the European conflict of World War II, and the surrender of Japan on September 2, 1945, aboard the *USS Missouri*, anchored in Tokyo Bay, ending the war in the Pacific.

The thirty-first annual session of the Texas State Association of Free Will Baptists convened with the Fellowship Free Will Baptist Church, Henderson, Texas, October 30 through November 2, 1945. L. D. Hardy led the congregational singing as the Tuesday evening session began. L. A. Norris brought a devotion from Philippians 2:5. The introductory sermon was delivered by J. B. Lovering. His sermon "Deep Waters" was based on Luke 5:4.

The Wednesday morning session opened by singing led by Ira Harper and prayer by A. D. Marchant. Alvin F. Halbrook brought a devotion, using "For we are laborers together with God," (1 Corinthians 3:1-9). "Enrollment by ministers, deacons, delegates." Prayer by Egbert Jameson. Moderator M. L. Sutton read the By-Laws and then delivered the moderator's message, "We then as workers together with God" (2 Corinthians 6:1).

The Wednesday afternoon session began with singing and then a devotion by A. F. Ferguson, "Put on the whole armor of God" (Ephesians 6:10-20). C. B. Thompson led in prayer. The delegates were seated by the clerk does not mention which associations and churches represented. The right hand of fellowship was extended to the corresponding delegates: E. E. Morris, Ada, Oklahoma; Robert B. Crawford, Nashville, Tennessee; P. H. Kaufman; and L. A. Norris, Kirbyville, Texas. The report on Christian Education was given by J. B. Lovering. Robert B. Crawford, Executive Secretary of the National Association of Free Will Baptists, reported on Free Will Baptist Bible College, Nashville, Tennessee. C. B. Thompson was appointed parliamentarian *pro tempore*. E. E. Morris gave a report on orphanage work in the state of Oklahoma. A partial report of the Resolutions Committee was received. Item number one of the Resolutions Committee report was:

> Be it resolved that the Texas State Association cooperate with the Oklahoma Orphanage program, inasmuch as Texas has discontinued its Orphanage work and Oklahoma will take our children. Adopted.

A motion carried that Article 9 of the By-Laws be amended as follows:
1. That the word "orphanage" be stricken out where it appears in the article.
2. And that the last sentence be amended so as to read "The body shall elect boards of five members each for Superannuation, Home Missions, and Orphanage."

Benediction by Pete Kaufman.

The Wednesday evening session opened with a good song service and several quartet numbers. Mrs. Jessie Ferguson gave a devotion. A special prayer was held by M. L. Sutton for the service men of our armed forces who had not returned to their homes. Mrs. Belle Easley sang a solo, "What Boundless Love." E. E. Morris, of Ada, Oklahoma, delivered the evening sermon from Zechariah 13:1. At the close of the sermon a special offering was taken for the orphanage work in the state of Oklahoma. The offering, which included a $100.00 deposit with the Trinity Church, along with pledges and cash, totaled $328.52. A motion that Article 3 of the Constitution be amended so that the last sentence will read as follows: "Each association with a membership of 500 or less shall send its representatives and letter and a minimum of $10.00; each association with more than 500 members shall send an additional $5.00 for each additional 500 members or fractional part thereof, and that each church send a minimum of $5.00." Miss Tommie Franklin dismissed the service in prayer.

The Thursday morning session opened with singing led by E. J. Vaughn, and a devotion by R. E. Conner. Robert B. Crawford, Executive Secretary of the National Association, brought his report on finance. T. W. Smith gave the report of the Home Missions Board. J. O. Fort discussed the resolutions of the board. A partial report of the Credentials Committee was accepted and the right hand of fellowship extended to the delegates. The following men were elected to the Home Missions Board: T. W. Smith, 1946; C. F. Goen, 1946; Mr. B. F. Payne, 1947; Tiff Covington, 1947; and J. O. Fort, 1948. J. O. Fort delivered the morning sermon, from Isaiah 63:1-3, and the benediction was given by E. J. Jameson.

The Thursday afternoon session opened with a fine song service led by Ira Harper. Henry Measures gave a devotion. The Woman's Auxiliary report was given by Tommie Franklin, and accepted. The moderator recognized J. O. Fort so he could meet with the Credentials Committee. The final report of the Credentials Committee was read and accepted. A motion carried that the moderator be endowed with the authority to appoint a committee to investigate the disturbance in the Northwest Brazos Association.[90] The moderator appointed John A. Brooks, B. A. Grant, and J. O. Fort.

The Thursday evening service began at 6:15 with singing led by Ira Harper, and a devotion by J. B. Lovering. In the absence of the clerk, Alvin F. Halbrook was elected clerk *pro tempore*. A motion carried that Brothers B. F. Payne and J. F. Johnson be seated as delegates. A motion carried that the report of the Resolutions Committee be received and acted upon item by item. Three items were adopted but we aren't told what they were. A motion carried that the body elect the members of the Board on Orphanage, with two members to serve a term of one year; two members for a term of two years; and a fifth member for a term of three years, after which all members shall be elected for terms of three years. The following men were elected: T. W. Smith and John A. Brooks, one year terms; B. F. Payne and B. F. Grant, two year terms; Ira Harper, three year term. A motion carried that brothers who were serving on two boards be granted permission to resign from one board and members be elected in their stead. The benediction was led by M. L. Sutton.

The Thursday evening service opened with singing led by L. D. Hardy, and a devotion led by S. M. Zeigler. Robert B. Crawford preached the evening sermon, "The Vision for Service," using the Scripture Isaiah 6:1-8.

The Friday morning session convened at 9:00 a.m., with singing, a devotion by the moderator, and prayer by Mrs. Alvin F. Halbrook. The moderator appointed a Temperance

---

[90] There is no mention of the nature of this disturbance until the report of the investigating committee is given at the 1946 state meeting.

Committee consisting of R. B. Crawford, Mrs. Alvin F. Halbrook, and Mrs. H. Ray (Asa) Berry. The Obituary Committee report was given and accepted as was a partial report of the statistician. The following officers were elected:

Moderator	M. L. Sutton
Vice-Moderator	B. A. Grant
Clerk	Alvin F. Halbrook
Treasurer	C. B. Thompson
Publicity Director	Allie Ferguson
Statistician	J. B. Lovering
Parliamentarian	J. O. Fort
State Orphanage Board	Mrs. T. W. Smith, one year term
State Orphanage Board	J. H. Measures, two year term
Superannuation Board	Bert Rogers, one year
Superannuation Board	L. D. Norris, one year
Superannuation Board	Alvin F. Halbrook, two years
Superannuation Board	Miss Tommie Franklin, two years
Superannuation Board	C. B. Thompson, three years

A motion made and carried that the moderator be invested with the authority to appoint a committee to make arrangements to entertain the Texas State Association at its next session. He appointed Alvin F. Halbrook, T. W. Smith, and J. O. Fort. Mrs. Asa Berry closed the morning session in prayer.

The morning worship service opened with singing led by L. D. Hardy and prayer by A. P. Reece. The sermon was preached by L. D. Norris. His subject was: "The Future Challenge of a People Who Are Known as Free Will Baptists." The right hand of Christian greeting was given to Brother Norris. The moderator appointed a Committee on Committees, composed of Ira Harper, H. W. Hays, and A. J. Williams. The moderator, in behalf of the state association, extended thanks to the Texas Association for its splendid entertaining of the Texas State Association. A motion carried that the body give a rising vote of thanks to the Texas Association for so graciously entertaining the Texas State Association. T. W. Smith gave the benediction.

The Friday afternoon session began with singing led by L. D. Hardy. The moderator, M. L. Sutton, read Psalm 1 and then prayer was offered by Samuel Goldberg.

The moderator read the names of the State Directors, as follows:

Christian Education	A. D. Marchant
Woman's Auxiliary	Asa Berry
Denominational Literature	B. A. Grant
Free Will Baptist League	L. A. Norris
Sunday School	J. B. Lovering

The following Temperance Committee was elected: E. J. Vaughn, A. J. Fielding, and J. B. Lovering. The Obituary Committee elected consisted of: Asa Berry, Mrs. W. H. Hayes, Mrs. L. A. Norris, Mrs. Belle Easley, and Mrs. J. H. Measures. The Resolutions Committee elected was: E. S. Jameson, C. F. Goen, and S. M. Zeigler. The Credentials Committee was: J. H. Measures, P. H. Graves, and M. L. Sutton. The Program Committee was: T. W. Smith, J. O. Fort, A. F. Halbrook, and deacons of entertaining church. The body voted to accept the invitation of the Central Texas Association to have the Texas State Association meet there at its next sitting.

The report of the treasurer was given and accepted. A motion carried that $35.00 be allocated as fees to the National Association, $10.00 be given the clerk for the preparation of the manuscript of the minutes for printing, and the clerk use his own discretion as to the publishing house printing the minutes. An offering of $44.65 was received toward the cost of the minutes. The reports of the Temperance Committee and the State Superannuation Board were read and accepted.

The By-Laws of the Texas State Home Missions Board were read. A motion carried to accept the policy of the Home Mission Board as outlined in its report. The report of Foreign Missions was read and accepted. A motion carried that the body elect, upon the recommendation of the moderator, the five delegates to the National Association meeting at the Alabama Orphanage near Eldridge, Alabama, July 17-19, 1946,[91] and the district associations appoint one delegate each to the National Association. The following delegates were elected: Mrs. H. Ray [Asa] Berry, Mrs. Charles Moehlman, Mrs. J. A. Alford, Mr. E. E. Eagleton, Sr., and Mrs. M. L. Sutton. A Texas Association delegate was named: B. F. Payne. A motion carried to grant A. P. Reece ten minutes to lecture on the subject "Shall Catholicism Rule this Country?" After a motion to adjourn a hymn was sung, "God Be with You 'Till We Meet Again." Benediction.

Thirty-Second Annual Session - 1946

The thirty-second annual session of the Texas State Association of Free Will Baptists convened with the North Zulch Free Will Baptist Church, North Zulch, Texas, October 29 through November 1, 1946. Alvin F. Halbrook, clerk, called the meeting to order on Tuesday evening. John A Brooks was selected moderator *pro tempore* in the absence of the moderator, RM. L. Sutton, who arrived before the evening message. Singing was led by L. A. Norris, the prayer was by Robert B. Crawford, and the devotion by J. B. Lovering. The introductory sermon was delivered by John A. Brooks, using Hebrews 2:6 as his text. A. F. Ferguson gave the benediction.

The Wednesday morning session opened by singing led by L. A. Norris, prayer by A. F. Ferguson, and a devotion by Clarence Hearron.[92] Mr. and Mrs. James F. Miller[93] coming to Texas to assume work in Huntsville, Texas, were recognized and welcomed. The benediction was given by Robert B. Crawford. The eleven o'clock worship service began by singing and was followed by prayer by C. B. Thompson. The associational sermon was preached by C. B. Thompson on the subject,"Go Forward," using Exodus 14:15 as his text. The benediction was given by S. M. Zeigler.

The Wednesday afternoon session opened with congregation singing, and prayer offered by J. O. Fort. The devotion was conducted by Harry Cox; Scripture: Psalm 90:1-4; Text: Psalm 90:1.

---

[91] As it turned out the 1946 National Association convention met at the Central Avenue Free Will Baptist Church, Oklahoma City, Oklahoma, instead of at the Alabama Children's Home.

[92] This is the first mention of Clarence Hearron, but his name appears throughout the minutes of Texas, except for during the nine years he was employed by Hillsdale Free Will Baptist College in Moore, Oklahoma.

[93] James F. Miller was a leader in the Free Will Baptist denomination at the time and had been for many years. He was very instrumental in bringing the Free Will Baptists from both the East and the West together to form the National Association of Free Will Baptists. He was also instrumental in getting Free Will Baptist Bible College started. It was my privilege to hear him preach on one occasion.

The partial report of the Credentials Committee was read, accepted and the delegates seated. District associations and churches reporting were:

District Associations
  Central Texas, seven delegates, $15.00
  East Texas,[94] eleven delegates, $11.00
  West Fork, eleven delegates, $20.00
  Southeast Texas, one delegate, $10.00
  Northwest Brazos, one delegate, $5.00

Local Churches
  Evergreen, two delegates, $5.00
  Huntsville Church, two delegates, $5.00
  Liberty Church, Dott, two delegates, $5.00
  Bright Light, two delegates, $5.00
  Bryan Church, two delegates, $10.00
  Trinity Church, two delegates, $5.00
  North Zulch Church, two delegates, $5.00
  First Church, Dallas, two delegates, $5.00
  First Church, Waco, two delegates, $5.00
  Pleasant Mound, Buffalo Springs, two delegates, $5.00
  First Church, Houston, two delegates, $5.00
  First Church, Weatherford, one delegate, $5.00
  New Hope Church, two delegates, $5.00
  First Church, Fort Worth, by letter, $5.00
  First Church, Henderson,[95] two delegates, $5.00

The report of Free Will Baptist Bible College was given by Robert B. Crawford. A motion carried that the moderator appoint a person to conduct a round table discussion on Christian Education. Robert B. Crawford was appointed. M. L. Sutton and J. O. Fort entered into the discussion. J. B. Lovering gave the report of Sunday School.

The following officers were elected:

Moderator	M. L. Sutton
Assistant Moderator	C. B. Thompson
Clerk	Alvin F. Halbrook
Treasurer	Mrs. Alvin F. Halbrook
Publicity Director	A. F. Ferguson
Statistician	J. B. Lovering
Parliamentarian	J. O. Fort

The moderator appointed several people to fill vacancies on various committees. The final report of the Credentials Committee was read and adopted, as follows:

> In regards to the report of the church in Memphis, Texas, consisting of S. M. Zeigler and his followers, we find them out of order. We recommend, therefore

---

[94] The Texas Association didn't change its name to the East Texas District Association 1954, but is apparently already being thought of as the East Texas District because all of its churches were in East Texas.
[95] This appears to be the first mention of the First Free Will Baptist Church in Henderson.

that their report be rejected, and that the report of the Committee on Investigation be accepted, which follows:

Report of the Special Committee appointed by the Thirty-First Annual Session of the Texas State Association of Free Will Baptists to investigate the Church troubles at Memphis, Texas.

After due investigation and examination of the Memphis Church trouble we submit our findings as follows.
1. That the Northwest Brazos Association of Free Will Baptists has withdrawn fellowship from Reverend S. M. Zeigler and his congregation for the Memphis Church, and has demanded that Reverend Zeigler surrender his credentials to preach the Gospel as a Free Will Baptist minister.
2. That Reverend Zeigler and his congregation from the Memphis Church have violated the Usages and Practices of the Free Will Baptist Church as laid down in our *Treatise of the Faith and Practices of Free Will Baptists* in that they have excommunicated certain members from the Church without giving them due and legal trial.
3. That the Northwest Brazos Association of Free Will Baptists has recognized the excommunicated members as legally the Free Will Baptist Church of Memphis, Texas.

We therefore offer the following recommendation to the Thirty-Second Annual Session of the Texas State Association of Free Will Baptists:

That this State Association endorse and sustain the Actions of the Northwest Brazos Association as enumerated in this report.

Signed:
J. A. Brooks
J. O. Fort
B. A. Grant

The benediction was given by A. F. Ferguson.

The Wednesday evening worship service opened with singing led by the association song leader, L. A. Norris, prayer by Troy McDonald, and a devotion conducted by A. F. Ferguson. M. L. Sutton offered another prayer and there was more congregational singing. Robert B. Crawford rendered "I'd Rather Have Jesus" as a solo, who then preached the evening message, using Romans 1:16 as his text. During the invitation Alvin Young came forward and acknowledged his call to the ministry. J. O. Fort led a special prayer for Mr. Young. N. C. Cole and J. L. Brandon were elected to fill vacancies on the Home Mission Board. M. L. Sutton gave the benediction.

The Thursday morning session opened with congregational singing. A quarter number, "If We Never Meet Again," was rendered by Clarence Hearron, Mrs. Otis Simons, M. L. Sutton, and A. F. Ferguson. Prayer was offered by J. B. Lovering. A devotion was conducted by J. L. Payne, using various verses from Ephesians chapters four through six. Robert B. Crawford gave his report as the Executive Secretary of the National Association. The benediction was given by M. L. Sutton.

The eleven o'clock worship service began with congregational singing, followed by prayer led by Rev. James F. Miller, who then proceeded to preach the evening sermon. He used Ephesians 4:13-14 as his text. The benediction was given by Clarence J. Hearron.

The Thursday morning session opened with singing, prayer by M. T. Holley, who then conducted a devotion, using John 14:27 as his text. The following reports were then given and received: Home Missions, State Home Missionary, Foreign Missions, Woman's Auxiliary, Resolutions (partial), Obituary, and Free Will Baptist League. The benediction was given by Jessie Ferguson.

The Thursday evening worship service opened with congregational singing, prayer by J. A. Brooks, and the evening sermon preached by Ruel E. Conner. He used Luke 10:30-37 as his text. Two vacancies were filled on the Superannuation Board: L. A. Norris and John A. Brooks. The moderator, M. L. Sutton appointed various directors. The report of the Orphanage Board was given and the following were elected to the board: Tiff Covington, R. E. Conner, and Clara Sutton. The report of the Superannuation Board was given as follows:

MINUTES OF CALLED MEETING OF THE TEXAS STATE BOARD
OF SUPERANNUATION

June 28, 1946, Huntsville, Texas

The meeting was at the home of Rev. Miss Tommie Franklin, with the following members present: Rev. C. B. Thompson, Rev. Miss Tommie Franklin and Rev. Alvin F. Halbrook. Also present was Rev. J. O. Fort, Secretary-Treasurer of the National Board of Superannuation.

Among others items of business discussed were the decision of the board to begin payments to all eligible retired ministers.

Basis of payment for retired ministers:

Continual service for 30 years or more -- 100% participant; 21-30 years -- 75% participant; 10-20 years -- 50% participant; less than 10 years' service -- left to the discretion of the board.

Motion carried to set $10.00 as maximum pay for ministers who qualify.

Motion to adjourn.   -Rev. Alvin F. Halbrook, Secretary

A motion carried to adjourn until Friday morning at 9:30 a.m. The benediction was given by Verna Lucas.

The Friday morning service began with congregational singing, prayer by T. W. Smith, and a devotion which consisted of a responsive reading of Romans 8:1-14. The association voted to meet for the 1947 session at the Pleasant Mound Free Will Baptist Church, Buffalo Springs, Texas. A motion carried that the Executive Committee be charged with the revision of the Constitution and By-Laws, to be presented for approval to the 1947 session of the Texas State Association.

The reports of the Statistician and Committee on Committees were given. The report of the Resolutions Committee was read, as follows:

REPORT OF RESOLUTIONS COMMITTEE

1. Be it resolved that the Texas State Association of Free Will Baptists adopt a Unified Program of support of our State and National work to wit:

That each church take an offering once each month for this work and carry all proceeds to its District Quarterly Meeting to be distributed by the Clerk of the Quarterly Meeting to the different phases of our work on the following basis:
- 40% to Christian Education (Free Will Baptist Bible College, 3609 Richland Avenue, Nashville, Tenn.)
- 30% to Foreign Missions (Rev. Winford Davis, Monett, Missouri)
- 20% to Home Missions (Treasurer of State Home Missions Board)
- 10% to Superannuation (Treasurer of State Superannuation Board)

The State Home Missions Board shall send 25% of its allocation to the National Home Missions Board. The State Superannuation Board shall send 25% of its allocation to the National Superannuation Board. Adopted

2. Whereas the National Board of Education has launched an Expansion Program, asking for the amount of one hundred thousand dollars for building purposes: And said Board is asking the State of Texas to raise five thousand dollars by July, 1948 over and above regular contributions to the maintenance of the Bible College; there being a large amount of the above stated sum in the hands of the treasurer of the college:

Be it resolved that we accept the challenge by the following allocations: Central Texas Association, $3,000.00; West Fork Association, $2,000.00; East Texas Association $1,000.00; Southeast Texas Association $100.00; and Northwest Brazos Association $100.00. Adopted

J. B. Lovering

3. Be it resolved that this body extend a rising vote of thanks to this church, also to this association and all who have helped in caring for this association in such a fine way. Adopted

                C. B. Thompson
                C. F. Goen
                R. E. Conner

The above resolution created the "Unified Program" for the Texas State Association of Free Will Baptists. This program, though it did not originate in Texas, evolved into the Cooperative Program now used by many states in the National Association of Free Will Baptists, including Texas.

A motion carried to give a rising vote of thanks to the moderator, M. L. Sutton, for his efficient and tireless service. The following delegates, who had been recommended by their district associations, were named to the National Association: Mrs. Reuben Hays, Mrs. T. A. Blackwood as alternate; Mrs. B. F. Payne; Mrs. M. L. [Clara] Sutton, Mr. B. B. Trant; and Mrs. H. Ray [Asa] Berry. Nominated and elected as delegates to the National Association were: Mr. Jack Lucas, Mrs. P. K. Trant, Mrs. James F. Miller, Mrs. C. B. Thompson, and Mrs. B. F. Payne. The report of the Temperance Committee was read and adopted. The Home Missions report and the home missionary work of Miss Tommie Franklin in Huntsville, Texas, was given as follows:

REPORT OF STATE HOME MISSIONARIES

To the Texas State Association of Free Will Baptists I submit the following report:

After my ten months as your State Home Missionary I can truly say this it has been one of the happiest experiences of my ministry. God has set His seal of approval upon the work by blessing in such a marvelous way. I have visited most of the churches and it did my soul good to see the people hunger for the Word and so eager to learn of the work being done by the denomination. The presenting of our program to the churches often resulted in a real revival; a number of souls were saved and many consecrated their lives to God and His service as a result of the messages brought by your missionary.

I travelled approximately 14,000 miles, preached 198 sermons and raised $1,447.33, collected $1,703.00, salary, $1,350.00, expenses, $240.

I have organized 2 churches; Huntsville, and El Paso. Other groups are ready to go into the organization as soon as pastors are available. There is no doubt in my mind but that God is in the Home Mission program and for this reason I say we must continue the work. I do not think it will be practical to keep a man on the field to do organizational work, since there are no pastors to take charge of the work at this time, but I do think that someone should keep in touch with the field and organize churches when all things are ready, also keep the work before the people and solicit their support. It will greatly help our Home Mission program if we will use some of the money to aid our new churches.

I recommend that someone be placed in charge of the Home Mission work, working under the Home Mission board, and that he be paid by the board for the time necessary to do his work.

                Texas State Home Missionary
                Rev. C. B. Thompson

To the Texas State Association of F. W. B. which convened with the North Zulch Free Will Baptist Church, at North Zulch, Texas, October 29, November 1, 1946.

Greetings in Jesus Name:

Report of Home Missionary work in Huntsville, Texas, from April 26, 1946, to July 21, 1946.

Organization of a spiritual Sunday School with an average of 20. Conversions, 14. Distribution of several hundred tracts. House to house visitation very profitable. Covered a large portion of city. Cottage prayer meetings conducted, 62. 15 months' salary at $35.00, $425.00. Love offerings, $532.79. Paid $20.00 per month for apartment, $300.00. Tithed out of entire amount received.

Received a bountiful grocery shower sponsored by three auxiliaries; namely, North Zulch, Bryan and Bright Light. God bless our dear women for same.

The little group was organized into a F. W. B. Church with 18 charter members with three additions, making a total of 21 when Bro. Miller, our pastor, came to the field. Left with over $400.00 in our church treasury, a little over $2,000 in Building Fund. I can't give the exact amount since in moving I lost exact figures.
Submitted, Tommie Franklin

A motion carried that the treasurer be authorized to draw on the treasury to pay the state association dues to the National Association. A. F. Ferguson gave the report of the Publicity Director. The motion to adjourn carried. The congregation sang the first verse of "Onward Christian Soldiers." The benediction was given by J. O. Fort.

1946 Statistical Report

The statistical tables contain the following important and informative information:

Association	Number of Churches	Church Membership
East Texas	15	601
Central Texas	10	641
Southeast Texas	4	59
West Fork	13	1,094
Northwest Brazos	5	125

Thirty-Third Annual Session - 1947

The 1947 Texas State Association Meeting, Pleasant Mound Free Will Baptist Church, Buffalo Springs, Texas

The thirty-third annual session of the Texas State Association of Free Will Baptists convened with the Pleasant Mound Free Will Baptist Church at Buffalo Springs, Texas, October 28-30, 1947. The Tuesday evening session was opened with singing conducted by A. F. Ferguson of Weatherford, Texas. The opening invocation was by Henry Melvin of Nashville, Tennessee. The Credentials Committee was appointed as follows: John A. Brooks, R. E. Conner, and Clyde Goen.

The song service continued with singing, followed by a quarter number, "Hide Me Rock of Ages." Prayer was offered by H. M. McAdams. Opening remarks were given by the moderator, M. L. Sutton. The introductory sermon was delivered by T. W. Smith, reading 1 Corinthians 13, and preaching on the subject "Faith, Hope, Charity." A partial report of the Credentials Committee was read and the delegates seated. The benediction was given by the moderator, M. L. Sutton.

The Wednesday morning session opened with singing, followed by the invocation by Virgil Bradford. The moderator read Romans 8:1-14. The Committee on Committees was appointed as follows: T. W. Smith, chairman, H. M McAdams, and [unclear]. A report on Free Will Baptist Bible College was given by the school's business manager, Henry Melvin.[96] His report was accepted and a special prayer was offered for the Bible College by Lizzie McAdams. An offering in cash of $130.60 was given for the college. The Program Committee appointed the moderator to give the report of Sunday School, which was adopted. The report of the Committee on Committees was given and adopted. A partial report of the temporary Credentials Committee was given and adopted. Delegates were given the right hand of fellowship. The session was recessed until after the worship hour with the benediction given by M. L. Sutton.

The Wednesday morning worship service opened with singing and prayer offered by Clara Sutton. The devotion was given by Lelia Estes, reading Psalm 23. The morning sermon was given by B. A. Grant, using Acts 20:24 as his text. The offering of thanks or the noon meal was given by J. L. Payne.

The Wednesday afternoon session began with singing, which was followed by prayer offered by Mr. W. D. Phillips, a deacon of the New Salem Free Will Baptist Church in Decatur, Texas. The devotion was by Heber Johnson. He used Luke 4:1-18. A duet, "A Mansion for Me," was given by the two Johnson children, Sonny Ray and June. The treasurer's report was given and adopted. The following officers were elected:

    Moderator   M. L. Sutton
    Assistant Moderator   Clyde F. Goen
    Clerk   Alvin F. Halbrook
    Treasurer   Ida Frances Halbrook
    Publicity Director   A. F. Ferguson

The following boards were elected:

    Home Missions
        C. F. Goen, 1950
        Tiff Covington, 1950
        A. F. Ferguson, 1949

    Superannuation
        Alvin F. Halbrook, 1950
        B. A. Grant, 1950
        T. W. Smith, 1949
        Lizzie McAdams, 1948

---

[96] It was my privilege to hear Brother Melvin preach when he was pastor of the East Nashville Free Will Baptist Church years later. Brother Melvin served as Executive Secretary of the National Association in 1948 and was the father of Rev. Billy Melvin who served in that position for many years.

Orphanage
  J. H. Measures, 1950
  B. A. Grant, 1950

The financial report of the secretary-treasurer of the Home Mission Board was read and adopted. A motion carried that the next session of the Texas State Association convene with the Texas Association at the New Hope Free Will Baptist Church near Henderson, Texas, in 1948. The report of the Temperance Committee was read and adopted. A motion carried that the Publicity Director send a copy of the Temperance Committee report to the Governor[97] of the state of Texas, and to the President of the United States.[98] The report of the Resolutions Committee was read and adopted. The report of the Obituary Committee was then given, following by a standing silent prayer, which was followed by prayer led by W. V. McPhail. New ministers were given a hand of fellowship and a pledge of full support in their work in the state of Texas. The report of the League Director was given and accepted. The benediction was given by Virgil Bradford.

The Wednesday evening service opened with singing followed by a solo, "It's Read." The invocation was given by Mrs. V. B. Stone. "The Old Ship of Zion" was sung by a quartet. The congregation then sang "If We Never Meet Again," which was followed by another quartet number "Take a Look at the Cross." There was a solo number, "I'm Going Higher Some Day." Henry Melvin offered a prayer and then preached the evening message entitled "The Fundamentals of Christianity," using John 19:13-18 and 20:1-14 as his text. There was another solo number, "Why Should He Love Me So?" An invitation was given to every unsaved person to accept the Christ. A quartet number, "I Can Tell You the Time," was rendered. A handshake with Henry Melvin, B. A. Grant, and T. W. Smith, and with one another was enjoyed, accompanied with shouting. M. L. Sutton led the benediction.

The Thursday morning business session opened with singing and prayer by A. F. Ferguson. There was a solo number, "I Won't Have to Cross Jordan Alone." A devotion was conducted by Lizzie McAdams. She read 1 Corinthians 1:1-6. The report of the Director of Woman's Auxiliary was given and accepted. The directors for 1947-1948 were named. The report of the Director of Foreign Mission was read and adopted. Instead of the report of the Orphanage Board, Virgil Bradford, State Field Worker for the Oklahoma Free Will Baptist Children's Home, Ringling, Oklahoma, gave a report of the children's home, which was adopted. A motion carried that anyone wishing to give an offering to the children's home give it personally to Bradford. The offering was [illegible]. A motion carried to recess for ten minutes. The benediction was given by R. E. Conner.

The Thursday morning worship service opening with singing and prayer by the moderator, M. L. Sutton. The morning message was delivered by Alvin F. Halbrook. His subject was "The Man God Uses," using Ezekiel 22:30 as his text. Tiff Covington dismissed the service in prayer for lunch.

The Thursday afternoon session opened with singing and prayer by Claude Lamb. The devotion was by Luther Payne, reading Psalm 116. A special prayer for foreign missions and the children's home was led by Maggie Cox.[99] A brief report of the Superannuation Board was given by the moderator, M. L. Sutton, and adopted. A report of the Committee on Constitution and By-

---

[97] Beauford Halbert Jester, served 1947 to 1949, the only Texas governor to die in office.
[98] Harry S. Truman
[99] Maggie Cox was the mother of H. Z. Cox.

Laws was given by the moderator. A motion carried to elect a committee of five to rewrite the Constitution and By-Laws. The body elected Tiff Covington, M. L. Sutton, C. B. Weir, Alvin F. Halbrook, and John A. Brooks to the committee. A motion carried to authorize the making and printing of a statistical report blank for district association reporting to the state association. The job was given to the Statistician. A motion carried to elect and send, with expenses paid, a representative to serve on the Revision Committee of the *Faith and Practices of Free Will Baptists*. M. L. Sutton was elected to serve as the representative, and Tiff Covington was elected as the alternate. The first report of the Credentials Committee was read and adopted. The moderator appointed five delegates from Texas to serve as delegates to the National Association of Free Will Baptists scheduled to meet July, 1948, in Pocahontas, Arkansas. He appointed the following: Clara Sutton, Clyde F. Goen, Mrs. Reuben Hayes, Mrs. E. E. Adams, and Mrs Lonnie Scott. The state association assessed the district associations the following amounts to pay the expenses of M. L. Sutton as the representative to the meeting of the Treatise Revision Committee: West Fork Association, $50.00, Central Texas Association, $50.00, Texas Association, $25.00, Southeast Texas Association, $10.00, and the Northwest Brazos Association, $15.00.[100] The treasurer was assigned the responsibility of securing the money. A report of the 1947 session of the National Association was given. The association adjourned, with the benediction led by Mrs. Alvin F. Halbrook.

Thirty-Fourth Annual Session - 1948

The thirty-fourth annual session of the Texas State Association of Free Will Baptists convened with the New Hope Free Will Baptist Church, Henderson, Texas, November 1-4, 1948. The Tuesday evening session opened with singing and prayer. Moderator M. L. Sutton appointed the Committee on Committees which was composed of John A. Brooks, B. A. Grant, J .L. Bounds, and J. M. Goode. A. F. Ferguson, pastor of the First Free Will Baptist Church of Weatherford, Texas, preached the introductory sermon. His subject was "An Open Door," using Romans 3:8 as his text. A partial report of the Credentials Committee was given and the delegates were seated.

The Wednesday morning session began at 9:00 o'clock with singing and prayer. C. C. Lamb of Vernon, Texas, gave a devotion, reading Ephesians 6. The moderator appointed the Committee on Committees as follows: H. M. McAdams, chairman, J. E. Maricle, and M. T. Holley. The report of Free Will Baptist Bible College was given by Henry Melvin, business manager of the college. A motion carried that Texas pay her balance of the suggested quota on the Expansion Program for the Bible College, which is $250.83. A motion carried to receive an offering for the college at the eleven o'clock hour. The partial report of the Credentials Committee was accepted. The right hand of fellowship was given by the moderator to the delegates. The report of the National Association delegate was given by Mrs. J. L. Vance. A motion carried to give the Director of the Woman's Auxiliary more time to prepare her report for the minutes.

The Wednesday morning worship hour opened with singing and prayer, and a devotion by J. M. Goode of Laneville, Texas. The morning sermon was delivered by N. B. Barrow of Bryan,

---

[100] These amounts are somewhat of an indication of the relative financial strengths of the district associations at the time.

Texas,[101] who spoke from 1 Thessalonians 1:6-10. At the close of the message the moderator presented Alvin F. Halbrook as the only ex-student present from the Free Will Baptist Bible College. The association received in pledges to the college, cash contributions, and offering, the amount of $170.16. This amount plus other monies given and pledged earlier in the service brought the grand total to $298.16. The benediction was led by Henry Melvin.

The Wednesday afternoon session was opened with singing led by A. F. Ferguson. A duet was given by two small girls from the Southeast Texas District Association. Alvin Young, of Kirbyville, Texas, gave a devotion, using John 14:1-4. J. B. Lovett of Arkansas was welcomed as a visiting minister. A partial report of the Credentials Committee was read, received, and the delegates seated. The report of the treasurer was read and received. The report of the Orphanage Board was given by R. E. Conner. Rex Weatherman, superintendent of the Free Will Baptist Children's Home in Ringling, Oklahoma, gave a report of the home. The report of the Home Mission Board was given, which included a report by the secretary-treasurer, L. C. Cole, and a report of the Home Mission Field Worker, R. E. Conner. Tiff Covington, chairman of the Home Mission Board, spoke in regard to the home mission program. The body voted to convene with the Trinity Free Will Baptist Church in Fort Worth for the 1949 session of the Texas State Association. The report of the Obituary Committee was given and the congregation stood in a moment of silent prayer, then was led in audible prayer by A. F. Ferguson. The report of the Director of Free Will Baptist League was read and received. The report of the Director of Foreign Missions was given, including the reading of a letter from Mr. and Mrs. Maurice Roach of Durham, North Carolina. The afternoon session adjourned with prayer by M. L. Sutton.

The Wednesday evening service began with singing and then a prayer led by J. E. Marecle. M. L. Sutton sang "A Wayfaring Pilgrim" as a solo. Prayer was led by W. F. McDuffie, who also brought a devotion from Exodus 12:11, 22: 14:15. Henry Melvin then sang "Ship Ahoy." Henry Melvin then brought the evening message from Hebrews 1:1-3. At the close of the sermon an invitation was given those who wished to accept Christ. Three persons, two men and one woman, who had previously known the Lord, came back to Him. A motion carried to hear reports of the Directors of Laymen's Work and Denominational Literature. A report on Sunday School was given by M. L. Sutton. During the closing hymn the hand of Christian fellowship was given to N. B. Barrow and W. F. McDuffie. The benediction was led by Mrs. Tiff [Carrie D.] Covington.

The Thursday morning session opened at 9:00 o'clock by singing led by A. F. Ferguson and prayer by H. H. Howard. J. L. Bounds, of Houston, delivered the morning devotion, with Scripture from 1 John 1. The following board members were elected:

Home Missions Board	A. F. Ferguson, 1951
Superannuation Board	Lizzie McAdams, 1951
Orphanage Board	Clara Sutton, 1951

The following officers were then elected:

Moderator	N. B. Barrow
Assistant Moderator	M. L. Sutton
Clerk	Alvin F. Halbrook
Treasurer	R. E. Conner

---

[101] Bruce Barrow pastored the First Free Will Baptist Church of Bryan, Texas, 1948-1950. Born in North Carolina, he graduated from Moody Bible Institute, Chicago, Illinois, in 1933, and from the Northern Baptist Seminary, Chicago, in 1935. He served for two years as moderator of the National Association of Free Will Baptists.

Publicity Director	A. F. Ferguson
Statistician	Tiff Covington
Parliamentarian	N. C. Cole

The report of the Resolutions Committee was given and items 1, 3, and 4 were adopted, while item 2 was referred back to the committee. The report of the Director of Denominational Literature was given by B. A. Grant and received. Item number 2 of the Resolutions Committee report was then adopted. The moderator appointed a committee to revise the Constitution and By-Laws. Brother Sutton appointed Alvin F. Halbrook, M. L. Sutton, and Tiff Covington.

The morning worship hour began by singing, led by W. F. McDuffie. John A. Brooks, of Fort Worth, brought the morning sermon on the subject "A Busy Life," using Luke 2:40-49 as his text. After the sermon the hand of Christian fellowship was given to Pastor Brooks, who then dismissed the service in prayer.

The Thursday afternoon session opened with singing led by W. F. McDuffie and a devotion brought by Asa Berry of Houston. She spoke on "The Walk of the Believer," using Galatians 6. The Director of Foreign Missions, A. F. Ferguson, led a splendid prayer for foreign missionaries and the Children's Home. The report of the Publicity Director was given and received. A motion carried to have the reading of a letter from the First Free Will Baptist Church of Midland, Texas. A motion carried to receive the First Free Will Baptist Church of Midland into the Texas State Association. The report of the Superannuation Board was given and received. A motion carried to dispense with the office of Director of Laymen's Work. The names of the members of the Revision Committee of the Constitution and By-Laws were read. A prayer of consecration was offered for them by W. F. McDuffie. A charge was given them by incoming moderator, N. B. Barrow. The moderator appointed the following as delegates to the National Association, scheduled to meet July 12-14, 1949, in Columbus, Georgia. M. L. Sutton, the Texas state representative on the National Revision Committee on the *Treatise of the Faith and Practices of Free Will Baptists*, gave his report, which was accepted. A motion carried to expunge from the records the previous motion, and notify the National Association we are in harmony with the National Association on the *Treatise of the Faith and Practices of Free Will Baptists* as revised at Pocahontas, Arkansas, July 1948, with the exception of Section V, Article 2, under Government of the Church. A motion carried in regard to the matter of the Texas State Association purchasing an interest in the church paper owned by the Oklahoma State Association, *The Small Voice*, be placed in the hands of the Texas State Minister's Conference. The session closed with a hymn and Christian handshake.

Historical Note

The Seventh annual session of the National Sunday School Convention of Free Will Baptists was held August 16-18, 1949, at the First Free Will Baptist Church, in Bryan, Texas. The president of the convention was LaVerne Miley, who would later become Dr. Laverne Miley, Free Will Baptist medical missionary to Ivory Coast, Africa. M. L. Sutton, pastor of the Trinity Free Will Baptist Church in Fort Worth, was at the time a member of the National Sunday School Board. The Sunday School Convention met annually for inspiration and information for the betterment of Free Will Baptist Sunday schools. The convention was welcomed by Mayor Dansby of Bryan and attended by numerous leaders and future leaders of the Free Will Baptist denomination: Billy Melvin, Wesley Calvery, Damon C. Dodd, E. E. Morris, R. B. Crawford, J. O. Fort, T. G.

Hamilton, and Luther Gibson. Dr. Clarence H. Benson, prominent author of books on Christian Education, was one of the teachers at the convention. Noah Tuttle of East Texas was one of the speakers.

~~~~~~~~~~

Thirty-Fifth Annual Session - 1949

The thirty-fifth annual session of the Texas State Association of Free Will Baptists convened with the Trinity Free Will Baptist Church, Fort Worth, Texas, November 1-3, 1949. The session was called to order by the last moderator, M. L. Sutton. A Credentials Committee was appointed as follows: J. L. Foreman, Troy McDonald, and M. T. Holley. The song service was led by A. F. Ferguson and the opening prayer was offered by A. Sullins. Two special numbers in song were rendered. A. F. Ferguson was elected moderator, *pro tempore*. J. M. Goode was appointed to deliver the associational message. His subject was "The Fruits of Faith," reading from Hebrews 11:5-28. A partial report of the Credentials Committee was given, received, and the delegates seated. Prayer was offered by J. L. Bounds and the benediction by Henry Melvin.

The Wednesday morning session assembled at 9:00 o'clock with singing led by Lucille Cozart, and prayer by B. A. Grant. A. F. Ferguson gave a devotion, reading Matthew 7:7-12. The following Committee on Committees was appointed: John Gary, A. Sullins, and J. A. C. Hughes. Jessie Ferguson was elected clerk, *pro-tempore*. A motion carried that someone be appointed to give a report on the Woman's Auxiliary work since Mrs. Halbrook could not be present. Mrs. John Gary was appointed. Henry Melvin led a song. Harry Ritenour led in prayer. Henry Melvin gave a report on Free Will Baptist Bible College in Nashville, Tennessee. The report of the Committee on Committees was given and accepted. A partial report of the Credentials Committee was read. The body voted to meet with the Central Texas District Association for the 1950 session. The body was dismissed for recess by Paul Purcell.

The Wednesday morning worship hour began with singing led by Wesley Calvery, and prayer by Herbert Richards. A duet number, "I Remember Calvary," was rendered by Wesley and Ailene Calvery. Emma Eagleton gave the devotion, speaking on "Obedience." The morning message was brought by Tiff Covington, speaking on the subject, "The Cornerstone," based on Psalm 118:22-23.

The Wednesday afternoon session assembled with singing led by Wesley Calvery, and prayer led by Cleo Purcell.[102] A solo number, "Nor Silver, Nor Gold," was sung by Henry Melvin. Sybil Gilchrist brought a devotion, reading the 88th Psalm. The report of the Woman's Auxiliary was given by Mrs. John Gary. C. F. Goen gave a report on the National Association. Rex Weatherman, Superintendent of the Free Will Baptist Children's Home at Ringling, Oklahoma, gave a report on the children's home. An offering was received for the home. Tiff Covington gave a report on his church, the First Free Will Baptist Church of Bowie, Texas. He then led a special prayer for Home Missions. A prayer of thanks for the offering for the Children's Home was offered by J. M. Goode. The final report of the Credentials Committee was given and the delegates seated. A report of the treasurer of the State Board of Superannuation was given and received. The report of the League Director was given and received. The report of the Director of Foreign Missions was given and received. An appeal for funds for the foreign missions treasury from Winford Davis, treasurer of the National Foreign Missions Board, was read. Following the appeal, Wesley Calvery offered himself as a foreign missionary. A motion carried to receive an

---

[102] Read about Cleo Purcell in the chapter on Women Preachers in Texas.

offering for Foreign Missions, which amounted to $28.97. A prayer of blessing for the offering was led by Wesley Calvery. The benediction was led by Noah Tuttle.

The Wednesday evening worship service began with singing led by Jesse Hensarling and prayer by Asa Berry. Mrs. Noah Tuttle sang, "There's No Friend to Me Like Jesus." Frank Parham gave a devotion, using "A Tribute to Ministers." A quarter number, "I Remember the Time," was rendered by M. L. Sutton, Allie Ferguson, Tiff Covington, and Wesley Calvery. Alvin F. Halbrook led in prayer. John A. Brooks brought the evening message from Matthew 25:31-41 and James 4:14. His subject was "What Is Your Life?" At the close of the message the following business was transacted. The report of the Director of Denominational Literature was given and received. The report of the Revision Committee on Constitution and By-Laws was read. The benediction was led by M. L. Sutton.

The Thursday morning session opened with singing led by Wesley Calvery, and prayer by Harry Zirl Cox. Eva Mae Rogers gave a devotion, reading James 1. Wesley Calvery sang a solo, "Grace Greater Than Our Sin."

The following officers were elected:

Moderator	A. F. Ferguson
Assistant Moderator	N. Bruce Barrow
Clerk	Alvin F. Halbrook
Treasurer	R. E. Conner
Publicity Director	Noah Tuttle
Statistician	Wesley Calvery
Parliamentarian	H. Z. Cox

The report of the Resolutions Committee was given and received. The report of the Publicity Director was given and received. The report of the Revision Committee [Constitution and By-Laws?] was given and received unanimously. Board members were elected.

The Thursday morning worship hour began with singing led by Wesley Calvery and prayer by M. L. Sutton. A special song was rendered by the Cozart Sisters [Lucille, Lora, and Lillian]. Another special was rendered by Marcia Allen. Delegates to the National Association, which was to meet in Richmond, California, July 11-13, 1950, were elected, as follows: C. F. Goen, Mrs. T. A. Blackwood, Mrs. John Gary, and Jim Vance. Alternates elected were: Asa Berry, Lucille Cozart, Mrs. C. R. Maxwell, Clara Sutton, Earl Eagleton, Mrs. Gus Smith, and Mrs. W. W. Winters. A motion carried to empower the clerk to make out a report for the Obituary Committee. A motion carried to recommend H. E. Ritenour for his work and give this information to the proper authorities. The following amendment to the above motion carried: "That this body elect a committee to investigate Rev. H. E. Ritenour and if he is worthy and efficient, the Executive Committee be authorized to endorse his work." A motion carried that the Home Missions Board be authorized to examine Ritenour. The report of the Executive Committee was read and approved. A motion carried that the clerk be authorized to compile a report blank for district associations to report to the state association. A motion carried that the Sunday School report be received with the stipulation that each district association send in their reports to the state clerk in time for him to have it ready to go in the minutes, when the Executive Committee meets to approve same. A motion carried that the Program Committee be requested to set up a Sunday school program for the Wednesday night session of the state association. A motion carried to pay the clerk $25.00 for his services. The benediction was offered by A. F. Ferguson.

The Thursday afternoon session began with singing led by Clyde F. Goen and prayer by J. E. Maricle. The moderator read Philippians 2:1-11. A motion carried that the committees serving at this session be retained as standing committees for the year. A motion carried to approve the minutes and another motion carried to authorize the clerk to have the minutes printed. The motion to adjourn carried, followed by the benediction led by John Gary.

Thirty-Sixth Annual Session - 1950

The thirty-sixth annual session of the Texas State Association of Free Will Baptists convened with the Bryan Free Will Baptist Church, Bryan, Texas, October 31-November 2, 1950. Noah G. Tuttle was the moderator and Alvin Halbrook was the clerk.

The Tuesday evening session opened by singing led by Clyde F. Goen. A. F. Ferguson assumed charge of the service. W. S. Mooneyham led in prayer. W. F. McDuffie, of North Zulch, brought the introductory message from Isaiah 54:1-4. He used as a text, "Lengthen thy cords and strengthen thy stakes."

Clyde F. Goen opened the Wednesday morning session by leading the congregational singing. John A. Brooks led the invocation and A. A. Williams, of Compton, Texas, brought the morning devotion. W. S. Mooneyham, editor of *The Small Voice*, gave a report. The partial report of the Credentials Committee was accepted and the delegates seated. The following district associations and churches reported, with dues:

District Associations
Texas Association	$16.00	Central Texas Association	$15.00
West Fork Association	$20.00	Southeast Texas Association	$10.00
Northwest Brazos Association	$10.00		

Local Churches
First Church, Waco	$ 5.00	First Church, Fort Worth	$5.00
Trinity, Fort Worth	5.00	First Church, Bryan	5.00
Bright Light, Harvey	5.00	Southside, Comanche	5.00
Blue Lake, Piedmont	5.00	Huntsville	5.00
First Church, Weatherford	5.00	Bonnie View	5.00
First Church, Vernon	5.00	Good Hope	5.00
New Hope	5.00	Houston	5.00
Mt. Olive	5.00	Pleasant Mound, Buffalo Springs	5.00
North Zulch	5.00	First Church, Bowie	5.00

Henry Melvin gave his report on Free Will Baptist Bible College. The morning message was delivered by Noah Tuttle, reading Romans 11:30-12:3, and using as a subject "The Believer's Hope." The service was dismissed in prayer by Lizzie McAdams.

The Wednesday afternoon session began with singing led by Clyde F. Goen, a devotion by W. W. Winters, of Vernon, Texas, and prayer by M. L. Sutton. The afternoon business consisted almost entirely of the following reports: Foreign Missions, Sunday School, Home Missions, Superannuation, Free Will Baptist Children's Home, Ringling, Oklahoma, National Association, and Publicity.

The Wednesday evening service opened with singing led by W. S. Mooneyham, of Oklahoma. Clarence Hearron sang "Face to Face" as a solo, and prayer was led by Alec Maricle. Gladys Beane sang a solo, "It Pays to Serve Jesus." A quartet number, "It Is Well with My Soul," was rendered by M. L. Sutton, A. F. Ferguson, C. J. Hearron, and W. S. Mooneyham. The quartet then sang, "Under His Wings." The evening message was brought by Henry Melvin of Nashville, Tennessee.

The Thursday morning session was opened by singing led by Clarence Hearron and prayer by John Gary, followed by a devotion brought by E. J. Vaughn, reading Ephesians 4:1-14. A motion carried that the moderator appoint a minister to bring the eleven o'clock message. Brother Ferguson appointed W. S. Mooneyham. The following reports were then given: Free Will Baptist League, Treasurer, Statistician, Obituary, Orphanage, and Temperance. The following board members were elected:

Christian Education	Asa Berry
F.W.B. League	Troy L. McDonald
Woman's Auxiliary	Mrs. R. E. Conner
Sunday School	Mrs. Roy T. Trant
Foreign Missions	Gaston Clary
Home Missions	Mrs. C. F. Goen, N. G. Tuttle
Superannuation	A. F. Halbrook, Clarence J. Hearron
Orphanage	A. A. Williams, Herbert Richards

M. L. Sutton tendered his resignation from the Board of Christian Education and the Orphanage Board, which was accepted. Elected to take his place were:

Christian Education	W. F. McDuffie
Orphanage	John Gary

The following general officers were elected:

Moderator	Noah Tuttle, Henderson, Texas
Assistant Moderator	A. F. Ferguson, Weatherford, Texas
Clerk	Alvin F. Halbrook, Bryan, Texas
Treasurer	W. F. McDuffie, North Zulch, Texas
Publicity Director	Gaston Clary, Bryan, Texas
Statistician	Clarence J. Hearron, Waco, Texas
Parliamentarian	Herbert Richards, Brownwood, Texas

After a five minutes recess the worship service began with singing led by Clarence Hearron. W. S. Mooneyham delivered the morning message. His subject was "The Three Commissions," reading from Mark 16. Gaston Clary dismissed the service in prayer.

The Thursday afternoon session opened with Clarence Hearron again leading the singing. Prayer was by R. H. Rogers and the devotion was brought by M. L. Sutton, reading the 133rd Psalm. The report of the Resolutions Committee was read and acted upon item by item, as follows:

<u>Resolutions Committee</u>

Be it resolved that the State Boards be authorized to work with the State Director selected by the National Association for the particular phase of work of the boards. Adopted.

Be it resolved that the State Association place a Promotional Secretary on the field to promote all phases of our Denomination work. Vote not stated.

Be it resolved that all directors have privilege of voting in the State Association.

Revolved that the State Foreign Missions Board be dissolved and that the State Director be made responsible for promoting Foreign Missions in Texas. Tabled indefinitely.

Be it resolved that the body give a rising vote of thanks in appreciation for the splendid hospitality given us by the host church and churches of this Association. Adopted.

A motion was made and carried that all present session committee members be dismissed and that committees be appointed at the next session of the Texas State Association. Motion carried to accept the invitation of the Mt. Olive Church in the Texas District Association, to meet with them for the 1951 session. The following delegates were elected to serve as delegates to the next National Association, scheduled to meet July 10-12, 1951, in the auditorium at Free Will Baptist Bible College, Nashville, Tennessee: Clyde F. Goen, L. M. Adams, Mrs. C. R. Maxwell, James Lang, Clara Sutton, Ray T. Trant, Darnell Stone, Mrs. Marie Bassham, Mrs. W. W. Winters, and Mrs. Bob Sheffield. A motion to adjourn carried. The benediction was led by A. F. Halbrook.

For historical purposes we list here the directory of ministers given in the minutes of the 1950 state minutes, both ordained and licensed, and the church(es) they pastored or attended, if listed:

Central Texas District Association
    R. B. Crawford, Bryan; First Free Will Baptist Church, Bryan
    Alvin F. Halbrook, Bryan; Bright Light, Evergreen, Blue Lake
    W. F. McDuffie, North Zulch; North Zulch
    Gaston Clary, Bryan; Pine Prairie, Cross Free Will Baptist Church, Iola
    H. Ray Berry, Houston; First Houston
    Mrs. Lizzie McAdams, Huntsville; Huntsville Church
    H. M. McAdams, Hunstville
    Mrs. Lillie Kelley, Huntsville
    Miss Tommie Franklin, Huntsville
    J. L. Payne, Houston
    H. W. Hardy, Houston

Texas District Association   [became the East Texas District Association in the mid 50's]
    Troy Lee McDonald, Laneville
    J. M. Goode, Kilgore
    Noah Tuttle, Henderson
    B. A. Grant, McLeod, Texas
    E. J. Vaughn, Beckville
    Mrs. Amanda Kester, Arp[103]
    Williams, Laneville

West Fork District Association
    Alvie L. Hudson, Bowie; New Salem Free Will Baptist Church, Decatur
    A. F. Ferguson, Weatherford; First Free Will Baptist Church, Weatherford
    Mrs. A. F. [Jessie] Ferguson, Weatherford
    Jewel Brandon, Weatherford
    Tiff Covington, Bowie; First Free Will Baptist Church, Bowie
    J. E. Marecle, Lake View, Texas; First Church, Waco
    Clarence Hearron, Waco; Gartman's View, Comanche
    M. L. Sutton, Arlington; Trinity Church, Fort Worth
    A. J. Fielding, Dallas; Vonnie View Church [or Bonnie View?], Dallas
    T. W. Nelson, Dallas
    W. V. Kennedy, Dallas
    W. Herbert Richards, Brownwood; South Side, Comanche

---

[103] Arp, Texas, is in Smith County and is part of the Tyler Metropolitan Statistical Area.

R. J. Rogers, Comanche
John A. Brooks, Fort Worth; First Church, Fort Worth
H. C. St. John, Fort Worth
C. Jack Turrentine, Fort Worth
C. C. Parris, Fort Worth
Joe Haney, Fort Worth; Liberty Free Will Baptist Church, Dott, Texas
J. W. Fulce, Denison; First Church, Denison
W. H. Coonrod, Denison
Bob Sampson, Denison
M. R. Gaines, Comanche; First Church, Comanche
H. Z. Cox, Dallas; First Church, Dallas
L. J. Foreman, Dallas
J. W. Gutherie, Dallas
Allen Gibson, Farmer's Branch
Ruel E. Conner, Bellevue; Pleasant Mound, Buffalo Springs
H. E. Reid, Denton; First Church, Denton
A. D. McKay, Denton
C. B. Kirby, Denton

Southeast Texas District Association
    A. A. Young, Kirbyville
    Cecil Derrmon, Buma, Texas
    Bob Sheffield, Roganville, Texas
    Jim Blair, Roganville

Northwest Brazos District Association
    M. T. Holley, New Deal, Texas
    T. P. Curley, Tulsa, Oklahoma
    Lelia Estes, Memphis, Texas
    H. H. Houston, Paducah, Texas
    W. W. Winters, Vernon
    Rufus Nall, Benjamin, Texas
    J. R. Thurson, Memphis, Texas
    Clark Brown, Crowell
    Owen Washburn, Crowell
    W. D. Haston, Chalk, Texas
    Jim Rogers, Big Spring, Texas

The minutes of the 1950 National Association give the following statistical report for Texas: Sunday schools, 48; Sunday school enrollment, 1150; leagues, 16; league enrollment, 263; woman's auxiliaries, 15; active members, 200; churches, 50; parsonages, 6; members, 2,865; new members 276; members dismissed, 89; members deceased, 30; paid pastors, $26,325.28; paid evangelists, $2,705.89; paid out for buildings and repair, $12,509.67; paid out for incidentals, $3,769.49; paid out for benevolence, $34.00; to student loan, $534.26; paid out for unified program, $536.35; Christian education, $30.00; foreign missions, $205.00; home missions, $446.92; orphanage, $60.00; literature, $173.64; miscellaneous, $2,279.93; value of buildings and equipment, $145,000.00; value of parsonages, $22,000.00.

Tex-Homa Ministers' Conference

For a few short years there was an organization consisting of ministers from both Texas and Oklahoma, called the Tex-Homa Ministers' Conference. One copy of the minutes and program are available, and it is included here. Though it was not a district association, the program and minutes of the winter and spring meetings, 1950-51, are included below because of their historical significance.

Program and Minutes of the Tex-Homa Ministers' Conférence

Winter and Spring
1950-51

OFFICERS
W. S. Mooneyham..................President
H. E. Stairs....................Vice-President
A. F. Ferguson.......Secretary-Treasurer

Inspiration • Information • Fellowship

Program for TEX-HOMA MINISTERS' CONFERENCE
May 3-4, 1951
Keynote [theme]: "They ceased Not to...Preach"
Acts 5:42

Thursday Evening

7:45   Hymns and Prayer,   J. Reford Wilson, Oklahoma City
8:15   Keynote message: "The Pattern of the Preacher" - H. Z. Cox, Dallas, Tex.

Friday Morning

9:30   Devotion,   Rufus Nall, Benjamin, Tex.
9:45   Reading the minutes
       Appointment of Committees
       Receiving of new members
10:10 Report of Simultaneous Revivals for Central Region, Willard Day, Wewoka, Okla.
10:20 Review of Calendar of Summer Activities, H. E. Staires, Oilton, Okla.
10:30 Business Session
11:05 Hymns and Prayer
11:30 Sermon: "The Power of the Preacher," N. G. Tuttle, Henderson, Tex.
12:00 Lunch and fellowship
Friday Afternoon

1:30   Hymns and prayer
         Conference addresses on the theme: - "They Ceased Not to...Preach"
1:40   "Preaching through Vacation Bible School" - Mrs. Bessie Staires, Tulsa, Okla.
         "Preaching through Evangelism Programs" - A. F. Ferguson, Weatherford, Tex.
2:20   "Preaching through Public Relations" - R. B. Crawford, Bryan, Tex.
2:40   "Preaching through Your Personal Life" - E. E. Morris, Oklahoma City, Okla.
3:00   "Preaching from the Pulpit" - John H. West, Tulsa, Okla.
3:20   Miscellaneous business
3:30   Adjourn conference

MINUTES OF SESSION HELD
September 9-10, 1950

Thursday Night

The opening session of the Tex-homa Free Will Baptist Ministers' Conference was introduced with singing led by W. S. Mooneyham and prayer by Harry E. Staires. Following special music given by the Sulphur trio, the children of the Home gave several songs and choruses and Mary Alice Weatherman gave a solo, "I Heard the Voice of Jesus Say."

The keynote message was brought by M. L. Sutton, Ft. Worth, on the subject, "That Thou Mayest Know How to Evangelize." The theme of the conference was, "That Thou Mayest Know How," taken from 1 Timothy 3:15.

Benediction by W. F. McDuffie.

Friday Morning

Singing for the morning session was led by W. S. Mooneyham, with prayer by Hattie Newman. Weldon Wood led the devotional.

In the absence of the president, E. E. Morris was elected as chairman *pro-tem*. On motion to select a program committee for the next session, A. F. Ferguson, W. S. Mooneyham and Harry E. Staires were appointed.

Following the approval of the minutes of the last meeting, M. L. Sutton, F. A. McCage an M. T. Holley were appointed to the Business Committee.

An invitation was extended for new members, and the Credentials Board recommended the following for membership: Weldon Wood, F. A. McCage, W. F. McDuffie, M. T. Holley, B. R. Nall, Roy J. Waddle, Frank Wharton, Eugene Riddle and W. F. Lee.

A. F. Ferguson gave a statistical report of the work in Texas, and E. E. Morris reported orally on progress in Oklahoma. Motion carried that these reports be received.

A short recess was called to give ministers an opportunity to pay their dues. Following the recess, Haskell Evans, superintendent of the Ringling schools, brought the welcome address.

A trio composed of Mrs. LaVerda Mooneyham, Charlsie Mobly and Marilyn Gentry rendered two special songs: "Guide Me, O Thou Great Jehovah" and "Trusting Jesus." Another special song was given by Mrs. Rex Weatherman, Mary Alice Weatherman and A. F. Ferguson: "When the Savior Reached Down His Hand for Me."

Following the theme of the session, W. F. McDuffie, North Zulch, Texas, brought the morning message on "That Thou Mayest Know How to Enlist." His text was Matthew 4:19. Benediction by H. E. Staires.

Friday Afternoon

After the opening exercises, with prayer by R. E. Conner, conference addresses were given following the theme, "That the Pastor May Know How."

E. E. Morris led with an address on "That the Pastor May Know How to Organize His Church." Proper organization in the choir, Sunday school, League, Woman's Auxiliary and Brotherhood were emphasized.

F. A. McCage followed with the subject "To Utilize Training Programs." He emphasized the importance of using all types of training programs to build the churches, stressing the necessity for correct home training.

"To Vitalize Visitation" was brought by Noah Tuttle. "Every organization of the church must have a visiting program," he said. "Regular visitation schedules by the different auxiliaries pays off in the salvation of souls." Going after them with the message of God, highlighted his message.

W. S. Mooneyham followed with the subject, "To Publicize His Church." The church must use every media of advertising. Telephone brigades, word of mouth, parades, radio, street meetings and the newspaper were among those named. "Keep your church in the news -- make friends for your church," highlighted Mooneyham's message.

"To advice through counseling" was the subject used by H. Z. Cox. As a basis for his remarks he used 1 Thessalonians 1:3. The pastor must be able to counsel, to aid and assist at all times, he said. He must be an example to the flock, and seek to counsel with them and guide them in all circumstances of life.

After a motion to go into the election of officers, W. S. Mooneyham was elected president; H. E. Staires, vice president and A. F. Ferguson, secretary-treasurer. Elected to the Credential Board for a year were M. L. Sutton, Clay Richey and F. A. McCage.

Motion carried to receive report of the Business Committee. The recommendation of the report was to allow the paying of printing and mailing programs of this conference. The amount was $8.40.

Motion carried that the body give a rising vote of thanks to the Home, the ladies who prepared meals and the surrounding community for the royal entertainment of the conference.

H. Z. Cox was elected to bring the introductory message at the next session, with Noah Tuttle as alternate. Motion carried that the program of the next conference and the minutes of this one be printed together.

Conference adjourned.

MEMBERS

This list of members is included here because there is a wealth of historical information in this list. To those of you who find this list as interesting as reading a genealogy in the Bible, you may go ahead and skip it. The history buffs among us, however, will find several things of interest, such as where the ministers lived, especially those in Texas. Street addresses have been omitted here because of space. Another thing of interest is the number of women preachers who were members of the Tex-Homa Ministers' Conference. There are nine of them and their names are in italics.

Bell, J. E., Barnsdall, Okla.
Bookout, Mrs. Faye, Drumright, Okla.
Brooks, J. A., Ft. Worth, Texas
Conner, R. E., Bellevue, Texas
Coursey, A. A., Tulsa, Okla.
Covington, Tiff, Bowie, Texas
Cox, H. Z. Dallas, Texas
Crain, Mrs. Elda, Miami, Okla.
Day, W. C., Wewoka, Okla.
Dressler, Mrs. Ida, Bristow, Okla.
Elliston, John, Stillwater, Okla.
Estes, Mrs. J. B., Memphis, Texas
Ferguson, A. F., Weatherford, Texas
Ferguson, Mrs. Jessie, Weatherford, Texas
Fincher, Mrs. Sadie, Drumright, Okla.
Florence, I. L., Poteau, Okla.
Florence, Virgil, Tulsa, Okla.
Franklin, J. A., Drumright, Okla.
Gage, Howard, Pryor, Okla.
Guinn, E. J., Shawnee, Okla.
Harris, R. C., Buffalo Springs, Texas
Hood, C. C., Tulsa, Okla.
Holly, M. T., New Deal, Texas
Hudson, J. O., Norman, Okla.
Johnson, G. H., Drumright, Okla.
Lamb, C. C., Vernon, Texas
Lane, R. G., Sapulpa, Okla.
Lee, W. F., Lindsey, Okla.

Mayfield, Mrs. Leona, Tulsa, Okla.
McCage, F. A., Porterville, Calif.
McDuffie, W. F., North Zulch, Texas
McKenzie, C. C., Sasakwa, Okla.
Mooneyham, W. S., Sulphur, Okla.
Morris, E. E., Oklahoma City, Oka.
Nall, B. R., Benjamin, Texas
Newman, Mrs. Hattie, Jennings, Okla.
O'Donnell, Dennis, Cromwell, Okla.
O'Donnell, E. A., Ada, Okla.
Purcell, Mrs. Cleo, Bristow, Okla.
Richey, Clay, Blanchard, Okla.
Riddle, Eugene, Haskell, Okla.
Staires, H. E., Oilton, Okla.
Stepp, J. D., Haskell, Okla.
Sutton, M. L., Arlington, Texas
Tuttle, N. G., Henderson, Texas
Waddle, Roy J., Norman, Okla.
Weatherman, Rex, Ringling, Okla.
Wharton, Frank, Atoka, Okla.
Wilson, E. J., Bristow, Okla.
Wilson, J. Reford, Oklahoma City, Okla.
Wilson, W. E., Holdenville, Okla.
Winfrey, Gene, Tulsa, Okla.
Winters, W. W., Vernon, Texas
Wood, W. V. Shawnee, Okla.
Wood, Weldon, Ada, Okla.

Chapter 4

1951 to 1975

The 1950's are remembered as a special decade. World War II had ended and the American economy was booming following the war, though many of us were still living in poverty. The Cold War hovered over us and we lived with the reality of Communism spreading to new countries and we lived under the threat of nuclear attack by the Soviet Union. But in spite of those fears the 50's were in many respects our favorite decade. Those of us who lived through the Fabulous Fifties remember that decade with great fondness, because we tend to forget the bad things and remember the good.

The Free Will Baptist work in Texas continued to grow and expand, in spite of the fact that some churches died and whole associations ceased to exist. There were significant changes in demographics, particularly in the migration of people from the rural areas to the cities. This had a huge impact on many of our Free Will Baptist churches simply because, for the most part, we were a rural denomination, with few churches established in the cities to receive the Free Will Baptist migrants. Huge numbers were thus lost to us and some rural churches closed. The work, however, went on.

Thirty-Seventh Annual Session - 1951

The thirty-seventh annual session of the Texas State Association of Free Will Baptists convened with the Texas Association [East Texas], meeting at the Mt. Olive Free Will Baptist Church, Laneville, Texas, October 30 through November 1, 1951. Noah Tuttle was the moderator, but the clerk's name is not given. The names of the reporting district associations were not listed. Several people led the singing, but most of the congregational singing was led by W. S. Mooneyham, Executive Secretary of the National Association of Free Will Baptists. Miss Jane Perry (the clerk most likely meant Miss Jane Berry, daughter of H. Ray and Asa Berry) sang "The Pearly White City."

The sermons preached at the session were "Passion for Souls" by Huey Gower, "Reaching the Lost by Preaching from the Pulpit" by Robert Crawford, "Reaching the Lost Through the Ministry of Free Will Baptist Bible College" by Henry Melvin. Huey Gower and his family were introduced as newcomers to the association.

Ruel E. Conner of Buffalo Springs gave a report on his work as State Director of Home Missions. He informed the association that the quota assigned to Texas for giving to National Home Missions for the following year was $320.00.

Thirty-Eighth Annual Session - 1952

The Thirty-eighth annual session of the Texas State Association convened with the West Fork District Association at the Pleasant Mound Free Will Baptist Church, Buffalo Springs, October 28-30, 1952. The moderator was Noah Tuttle, and the song leader was Huey Gower. Mrs. Huey Gower served as clerk *pro-tem*. Five district associations represented with dues: Northwest Brazos, Central, Southeast Texas, [East] Texas, and the West Fork.

Two young men, future missionaries, spoke. Kenneth Eagleton brought a devotion and Wesley Calvery preached on Tuesday evening. The minutes say that Wesley and Aileen Calvery were future missionaries to India.[104] During those days the state association had two mission boards, a Foreign Missions Board and a Home Missions Board. The Divine Service Committee announced that Ola Mae Winters would bring the devotional on Wednesday evening.

A resolution was introduced to the effect that the association go on record as rejecting the New Revised Standard Version of the Bible as being authentic to the true Word of God. The resolution was tabled until the following year. A resolution which was adopted called for each minister in the state association to give an annual report on the merits of his life and work to the body and be granted a card of good standing.

The State League Board asked the state association to be relieved of the responsibility of sponsoring a state youth camp, recommended that youth camps be conducted by one or more districts, and that donors of monies for a state youth camp be contacted concerning what should be done with the funds which were being held by the State League Board.

Thirty-Ninth Annual Session - 1953

The thirty-ninth annual session of the Texas State Association convened with the Central Texas District Association at the Bryan Free Will Baptist Church, October 27-29, 1953. C. B. Thompson served as moderator and the clerk was Herbert Richards. The following district associations represented: Central Texas, Northwest Brazos, Southeast Texas, [East] Texas, and West Fork. Twenty-four churches represented by letter and dues. Seventy-nine ministers were listed in the directory, including five women preachers. Damon Dodd,[105] Director of the National Home Missions Department, was present and reported on the work of home missions, and preached "a soul stirring message."

The resolution which was tabled the previous year concerning the rejection of the Revised Standard Version of the Bible as being authentic to the true word of God was removed from the table and adopted. The resolution which had passed at the previous session calling for each minister to make a report to the state association on the merits of his life and work and designating the state body to issue cards of good standing, was rescinded and the matter relegated to the district associations. The body adopted a resolution calling for the state association programs to be planned, using a theme. This was a step of progress.

The National Home Missions Board had appointed C. B. Thompson as State Home Missions Director, subject to the approval of the state body. The suggested quota for 1953-1954 was $500.00. Both of these items were adopted.

---

[104] Kenneth Eagleton served in Brazil and the Calvery's, though they may have initially intended to go to India, served for many years in Japan.
[105] Damon Dodd later wrote *The Free Will Baptist Story*, one of the best history books on modern Free Will Baptists.

The Christian Education Board reported the names of five students attending Free Will Baptist Bible College from Texas: June Goode, Marvis Nell Anderson, Miss Jane Berry, Bobby Joe Davis, and Kenneth Eagleton. Every single one of these five students became prominent in Free Will Baptist work. June Goode (Wilkinson-Hersey), Marvis Anderson (Eagleton) and Ken Eagleton spent the better part of their lives as foreign missionaries. Jane Berry was a prominent pastor's wife, and Bobby Joe Davis has spent his life as a pastor in Texas. Among the delegates appointed to represent Texas at the National Association was Miss Jane Berry, who would later become Mrs. Dale Burden. The board also reported that two youth camps had been held in Texas: one in the West Fork at Camp Holland, near Weatherford, and the other was a joint effort between the Central Texas and the East Texas[106] districts at Piney Woods near Groveton.

Fortieth Annual Session - 1954

The fortieth annual session of the Texas State Association convened with the East Texas District Association, meeting at the Jameson Memorial Free Will Baptist Church in Henderson, [107]November 2-4, 1954. Gaston Clary served as moderator and the clerk was Herbert Richards. Five district associations reported: East Texas, West Fork, Southeast Texas, Northwest Brazos, and Central Texas. Twenty-six churches reported by letter and dues. W. S. Mooneyham, executive secretary of the National Association was present and gave a report on the Co-operative Plan. The theme of the association was "Advancing with Christ."

The Credentials Committee moved that a committee be appointed to investigate the legality of the East Texas Association in calling for the credentials of Noah Tuttle and Huey Gower. The motion failed to pass, however, but see the resolution below. It is interesting that Noah Tuttle was present and led the prayer blessing the noon meal and closing the morning service. Herbert Richards moved that the state association underwrite the salary and expenses of Wesley and Aileen Calvary. The motion carried.

The body voted to elect an executive secretary for Texas and to have the Executive Committee prepare the necessary changes to the constitution. Clinton E. Oliver was elected. Some very important resolutions were presented. The first resolution, which was adopted, was:

> Be it resolved to place the matter of the East Texas District's canceling the credentials of Noah Tuttle and Huey Gower in the hands of the ordained ministers and ordained deacons of the State Association. The legal aspects of the action of said district to be investigated and disposed of by the committee. This meeting to take place immediately after the regular session adjourns Wednesday afternoon.[108]

The ministers and deacons met as scheduled and discussed the matter given to them by the body concerning Tuttle and Gower. Their report was as follows:

Special Report of the Committee of Ordained Ministers and Deacons

---

[106] The Texas Association was already being called East Texas, even though the name change wouldn't officially occur until the following year.
[107] Name of Jameson Memorial would later be changed to the First Free Will Baptist Church of Henderson.
[108] 1954 Minutes of the state meeting, page 5. The charges originally brought against the two ministers, made by Alvin Halbrook, was speaking in tongues.

The purpose of the committee was to investigate the legality of the action of the East Texas Association in canceling the credentials of Noah Tuttle and Huey Gower.

The meeting was opened with prayer by Rev. C. B. Thompson. Rev. Everett Hellard acted as chairman. Both parties involved gave their evidence and a vote was called for.

A motion carried to table the matter as it stood indefinitely; the state body accepting the decision of the East Texas Association as it stood.

The disciplinary action taken by the East Texas District, which the state association allowed to stand, apparently resulted in the reconciliation of Huey Gower, for he is mentioned as being active in subsequent state meetings.

The second resolution, which was also adopted, called for the state association to adopt the Co-operative Plan of support as outlined by the National Association. This was an historic event in the history of the Free Will Baptist work in Texas.

The Report of the Statistician shows something of the condition of the Free Will Baptist work in Texas in 1954, at least in terms of numbers, and it is, therefore, included here.

Report of Statistician

Number of Associations	5
Number of Churches	54
Total Membership	4,500
Number Ordained Ministers	80
Number Licensed Ministers	10
Number Sunday Schools	54
Sunday School Enrollment	2,540
Number Leagues	12
League Enrollment	650
Number Woman's Auxiliaries	12
Amount Raised for All Purposes	$ 80,141.90
Total Value of Church Property	$ 181,761.00

Two historic events occurred at the 1954 Texas State Meeting in Henderson. The first was that Texas voted to hire an executive secretary. Clinton E. Oliver was elected to the position. The second was that the association voted to adopt the Cooperative Plan of Support being promoted by the National Association as a means of providing adequate funding for state and national ministries.

Forty-First Annual Session - 1955

The forty-first annual session of the Texas State Association met at the First Free Will Baptist Church, Houston, Texas, November 1-3, 1955. Minutes of that meeting are not available to us.

Forty-Second Annual Session - 1956

The forty-second annual session of the Texas State Association convened with the West Fork District Association, meeting at the First Free Will Baptist Church of Dallas, October 29-31, 1956. Everett Hellard was the moderator. The following seven district associations represented: West Fork, Central Texas, East Texas, Southeast Texas, Northwest Brazos, Fellowship, and Permian Basin.[109] Moderator Everett Hellard, in his opening remarks said some things which bear repeating here. He spoke of the importance of good business and good judgment in carrying on the work of the Lord and urged the group to endorse only those things which could be done. He also stressed the fact that the entire program depended on the local churches and pastors. The theme for the meeting was "The Field Is the World."

It is interesting that Huey Gower, whose credentials had been canceled by the East Texas District, an action upheld by the state association in 1954, was living in Huntsville, Texas, possibly as pastor, and served on the Superannuation Board of the state association as well as the Temperance Committee. His wife served as president of the state Woman's Auxiliary, was appointed to the Committee on Committees, and was clerk of the Central Texas District.

Homer Willis, promotional secretary-treasurer of the National Home Missions Board and W. S. Mooneyham, national executive secretary-treasurer of the National Association, and Raymond Riggs, promotional secretary-treasurer of the National Foreign Missions Board, were present. These were the big guns.

Everett Hellard was elected to the position of executive secretary-treasurer by acclamation. The Children's Home Board was charged with the responsibility of looking into the possibility of establishing a children's home in Texas.

Lonnie and Bernice Palmer, members of the Trinity Church in Fort Worth, surrendered to the call of the Lord to the mission field. They bowed at the altar while Raymond Riggs prayed a prayer of dedication and thanksgiving for them. They planned to enter Free Will Baptist Bible College in January of 1957. M. L. Sutton showed two films on missions during the meeting.

One item in the report of the Temperance Committee stated: "We further recommend that Christians be taught specifically against buying on the Lord's Day. Further, that we patronize stores which do not handle beer and other intoxicating beverages, even to the extent of fasting if necessary." The body voted to invite the National Association to meet in Texas in 1959, and that the convention be held in College Station. This did not come to fruition.

The Fellowship Association, 1956

Another Fellowship Association formed in 1956, this one in the Fort Worth area. There is only one set of minutes of it available to us, the minutes of the first annual session which was held September 4-6, 1956, in Weatherford. The Fellowship Association was formed by a group of Fort Worth area churches which had pulled out of the West Fork District Association. Those churches, as listed in the minutes of that first annual session were the Bethel Free Will Baptist Church of Fort Worth, First Free Will Baptist Church of Denton, First Free Will Baptist Church of Fort Worth, the Trinity Free Will Baptist Church of Fort Worth, the First Free Will Baptist Church of Weatherford, and the First Free Will Baptist Church of Irving.

---

[109] The Fellowship and the Permian Basin Associations were admitted to membership in 1958.

The ministers who were members of the association in 1956 were A. L. (Doc) Baber, James Bandy, M. F. Bennett, Jewel Brandon, Braxton Chaffin, A. H. Corrender, Billy Daniels, J. B. (Jake) Estes, Jr, Chester Hall, Clarence Hearron, Alfred Justice, Henry Measures, A. G. McLain, R. O. O'Dell, H. E. Reid, H. R. Sheets, M. L. Sutton, and C. J. Turrentine. Allie Ferguson and Tiff Covington represented as corresponding messengers from the West Fork District Association. Judging from the minutes of that first annual session, the fellowship between the Fellowship Association and the West Fork was excellent, at least between the ministers of the Fellowship Association and the two corresponding messengers from the West Fork.

Lonnie Palmer, who was a member of the Trinity Free Will Baptist Church, and who would spend most of his life as a Free Will Baptist missionary in Africa, was ordained by the Fellowship Association.

There was a rather rancorous meeting of the Fellowship Association in 1959. It was over the issue of woman preachers.[110] This occurred at a quarterly meeting which was held at the First Free Will Baptist Church of Denton, March 6-7, 1959. The issue had become a problem at one of the fellowship meetings of the association. The association had quarterly fellowship meetings and quarterly youth meetings in addition to the quarterly meetings. Jake Estes, pastor of the Philadelphia Free Will Baptist Church in Weatherford, was scheduled to preach at one of the fellowship meetings, held at the Rock of Ages Free Will Baptist Church in Fort Worth, but he brought an Assembly of God woman preacher who preached in his place. Afterwards some of the pastors who were disturbed about having women preachers recognized went to Clarence Hearron, who was the moderator, and said that something needed to be done. They asked him to write a resolution and asked him to include in it that churches which recognized women preachers would not be recognized by the association. Brother Hearron told them that he refused to include that in the resolution, that he would not do what they asked of him. The resolution he wrote simply stated that the association would not recognize women preachers.

Pastor M. L. Sutton published a church newsletter and in the issue prior to the quarterly meeting he announced, incorrectly, though he probably believed it to be true, that the forthcoming resolution contained the provision that churches which recognized women preachers would not be recognized by the association. This was something, remember, which Brother Hearron had expressly stated would not be included in the resolution. The newsletter was sent to every pastor in the Fellowship Association. It arrived in their homes on Thursday, the day before the quarterly meeting, setting the stage for misunderstandings and hot tempers. The delegates assembled on Friday evening, March 6, 1959, at the First Free Will Baptist Church in Denton. Some of the pastors were loaded for bear. The resolution was presented during the Friday evening service. This was when the fire hit the fan. The debate became hot, tempers flared, and blood pressures rose. Things got so out of order that moderator Clarence Hearron told them sternly that order would be kept even if he had to ask the assistant moderator to go get a policeman. After a while the vote was taken and the resolution, that the Fellowship Association would not recognize women preachers, passed. However, that was not the end of the matter.

On Saturday the issue came up again for debate when M. L. Sutton, pastor of the Trinity Church, and who had been absent on the previous evening, made a motion to rescind action on the motion to adopt the resolution which had been adopted the previous evening. The debate was on again. Brother Sutton was joined in favor of rescinding the resolution by Jack Turrentine and Jake Estes. Brother Sutton had worked for a while on the evangelistic team of Lizzie McAdams, as

---

[110] Information about this quarterly meeting came from an interview with Clarence J. Hearron, who was the moderator of the meeting, and from a written account of the meeting given to me by Brother Hearron.

song leader and counselor. The wife of Jake Estes was an ordained Free Will Baptist preacher. Leading the opposition to rescinding the resolution, to let it stand, were Owen Barger and James Bandy. Pastor McClain was silent on the issue, and Brother Corrender said it didn't matter to him, that he would go along with the majority.

When the vote on rescinding the resolution was taken it passed by one vote.[111]

The 1958 minutes of the Texas State Association state that there were eleven churches in the Fellowship Association at the time.[112] The Fellowship Association was still in existence in 1962, the last year it is mentioned in the state minutes. All of the churches seem to have been members of the West Fork by the time of the West Fork annual meeting in 1964. Eventually most of the churches in the Fellowship Association closed. When I asked Jack Bankhead why the association was ever formed in the first place, he said a lot of it had to do with jealousy among the preachers. It turned out to be a weak association and M. L. Sutton later said that it was a mistake to ever start it in the first place.

Forty-Third Annual Session - 1957

The forty-third annual session of the Texas State Association convened at the Westside Free Will Baptist Church, Midland, Texas, October 30 - November 1, 1957. Minutes of that meeting are not available to us.

Forty-Fourth Annual Session - 1958

The forty-fourth annual session of the Texas State Association convened with the Central Texas District, meeting at the First Free Will Baptist Church of Bryan, October 28-30, 1958. The theme was "To God Be the Glory." H. Z. Cox was the moderator and Mrs. C. B. Thompson was the clerk. The association gave her an honorarium of fifty dollars. Malcolm Fry was the host pastor. The following district associations represented: East Texas, Central Texas, West Fork, Southeast Texas, and Fellowship. The Northwest Brazos represented by letter only. The Midessa District Association petitioned the body for membership and was accepted. Twenty-eight churches represented by letter. W. S. Mooneyham, Executive Secretary of the National Association, preached on Tuesday night and again on Wednesday morning. Charles Thigpen, dean of Free Will Baptist Bible College, preached on Wednesday morning, on Wednesday evening, and on Thursday morning. On Wednesday afternoon Joy Jones, wife of Bill Jones, sang a solo, accompanied at the piano by Jane Burden, wife of Dale Burden.

Jane (Berry) Burden

On Wednesday evening Jane sang a solo, accompanied at the piano by Joy.

Asa Berry gave the report of the Christian Education Board, which included a report on youth camps. It was noted that the Fellowship Association held a youth camp at Camp Holland

---

[111] One of the votes was cast by a woman who was not a delegate and who didn't have a vote, but Brother Hearron let it slide because he had had enough of this issue.
[112] Minutes of the 1958 state meeting, page 28.

near Weatherford. Mrs. June Wilkerson urged the association to support Ken and Marvis Eagleton who had to leave for Brazil before they could visit all the churches, resulting in low funding for them. The statistician, Gaston Clary, reported that Texas had fifty-eight churches and one-hundred ten preachers, licensed and ordained.

~~~~~~~~

The Midessa District Association, organized in 1958, consisted of three churches at the time: the First Free Will Baptist Church and the Bible Free Will Baptist Church, both in Odessa, and the Westside Free Will Baptist Church in Midland. The Westside Church had previously been a member of the West Fork District Association. The Permian Basin Association had dissolved and those churches made their way into the Midessa. In 1973, when the association was at its strongest point, it consisted of the following nine churches:

First Free Will Baptist Church 1501 Portland, Abilene, Texas	Pastor: Robert Barlow
Bible Free Will Baptist Church 4700 Bryan Road, Odessa, Texas	Pastor: Lonnie Hall
First Free Will Baptist Church 1015 W. Campbell, Kermit, Texas	Pastor: James Reddick
Faith Free Will Baptist Church 409 S. E. Avenue C, Andrews, Texas	Pastor: James Qualls
First Free Will Baptist Church 2203 W. 7th Street, Odessa, Texas	Pastor: Thurmon Murphy
Westside Free Will Baptist Church 4031 W. Illinois, Midland, Texas	Pastor: Glen Hood
First Free Will Baptist Church 504 N.W. Avenue F, Seminole, Texas	Pastor: Ernie Hale
Lubbock Free Will Baptist Church 4424 35th Street, Lubbock, Texas	Pastor: Robert Thompson

The Constitution and By-Laws of the Midessa District Association of Free Will Baptist stated the geographical boundaries of the district thusly: "The geographical location of this Association, using Midland as the center, shall be: North to Lubbock, East to Sweetwater, Southeast to Sonora and San Angelo, South to Sheffield, Southwest to Fort Stockton, West to Pecos and Northwest to the New Mexico State line."[113] In September, 1972, the association voted to extend the boundaries to include Abilene.

---

[113] 1968-69 Midessa Association Minutes, ARTICLE VI, FINANCE, Section II.

The Midessa District Association gave excellent financial support to the State and National Associations. One of the reasons was that their Constitution and By-Laws stated, "Each church must support the plan endorsed by the National Association of Free Will Baptists. The present plan being the cooperative plan which is 10% of the gross income of each church." Supporting the Cooperative Plan was mandatory in the Midessa, even though there was no scriptural basis for making it so. In 1974, the words "is recommended" were substituted for the word "must," when the association realized that the Cooperative Plan was optional. The association continued its excellent support of the state and national ministries.

The Constitution and By-Laws contained one by-law which had serious legal implications concerning church properties. It stated:

> 12. In the event any church in this Association becomes unorthodox in the Free Will Baptist faith and practices, or inactive, said church shall become Associational property. In the event this District becomes unorthodox in the Free Will Baptist faith and practices, or inactive, all church and Associational properties shall become the property of the Texas State Association of Free Will Baptists.
> *Amendment to By-Law No. 12* -- If any church of this Association becomes unorthodox in the Free Will Baptist faith and practices, or go down until they cannot transact business because they are disorganized, it shall become the property of the Association and the Executive Board shall have power to execute legal papers for the property. In the Event the churches in this Association become unorthodox in the Free Will Baptist Faith and practices, or inactive, all church and Association property shall become property of the Texas State Association of Free Will Baptists.[114]

The minutes of the March 10, 1973, quarterly meeting contain this motion about which should be the authoritative Bible: "Motion carried that in our district meetings and in the preaching and teaching in our Sunday Schools, that the King James version of the Bible be recognized as the authoritative Bible." District associations sometimes passed such a motion not realizing they had no biblical authority to do so.

Forty-Fifth Annual Session - 1959

The forty-fifth annual session of the Texas State Association convened at the First Free Will Baptist Church, 3419 Michigan Avenue, Dallas, Texas, October 27-29, 1959. No minutes of the meeting are available to us, but we glean the following information from a copy of the program. H. Z. Cox was the moderator. Everett Hellard was the executive secretary. The names of the speakers for Tuesday evening and Wednesday morning aren't given. The Wednesday evening message was delivered by E. E. Zoellers and the Thursday morning sermon was by Bobby Ferguson.

Forty-Sixth Annual Session - 1960

Minutes of the forty-sixth annual session of the Texas State Association are not available to us.

---

[114] Midessa Association Minutes, 1968-69, BY-LAWS, italics in the original.

Forty-Seventh Annual Session - 1961

We have not been able to locate any minutes of the 1961 state meeting.

Forty-Eighth Annual Session - 1962

The forty-eighth annual session of the Texas State Association convened with the East Texas District Association, meeting at the Mt. Olive Free Will Baptist Church, Henderson, October 30 - November 1, 1962. Eugene E. Zoellers was the moderator and Mrs. Huey Gower was the clerk. The report of the Credentials Committee states that seven districts represented, but only five are named: Central Texas, Caprock, East Texas, West Fork, and Midessa. The letter from the Northwest Brazos was read, though no one was present from there. Twenty-nine churches represented. H. Z. Cox, pastor of the First Free Will Baptist Church of Dallas, was the part-time executive secretary. Eighty four ministers are named as members of the association.

A word about the Caprock Association is in order. 1962 is the first time we see the name of the Caprock Association in the state minutes. We do not know when it was admitted and we have no minutes of the association, none at all. A good guess might be 1961. The name Caprock would indicate that the association was located on top of or along the caprock, a fifty foot to one hundred foot escarpment which extends along the edge of the High Plains from the Texas Panhandle south to near Odessa, separating the High Plains from the rolling prairies. The Caprock Woman's Auxiliary joined the WNAC in 1965. We will see later that the state association was hosted by the Caprock Association in 1966, meeting at the First Free Will Baptist Church of Odessa. One or more churches in New Mexico were also members of the Caprock. The Caprock Association seems to have eventually given way to the Midessa Association.

Roy Thomas, of Denver, Colorado, brought the message on Tuesday evening. J. Reford Wilson, director of the National Foreign Missions Department, preached on Wednesday morning. Missionary Dave Franks (Brazil) preached on Wednesday evening.

The Resolutions Committee report stated an appeal to the churches to secure ten members per church for the 500 Club. Nothing is said about what the 500 Club was.

The body adopted a resolution calling for the state association to hire a full-time executive secretary and noted that East Texas had pledged to pay $50.00 per month towards his salary. After the Wednesday evening service there was a short business session for the purpose of discussing the full-time executive secretary. No decision was reached. On Friday the Executive Committee, along with the moderators of each district association, was charged with the responsibility of studying the evidence from each district for an executive secretary and to plan a budget for the following year.

Forty-Ninth Annual Session - 1963

The only records available currently on the 1963 state meeting come from the cover of the 1962 minutes and a copy of the program for the meeting. The forty-ninth annual session met at the First Free Will Baptist Church in Dallas, 3419 Michigan Avenue, October 29-31, 1963. The theme was "Reaching Forth." Wade Jernigan, of Oklahoma, preached on Tuesday evening, Charles Thigpen, from Free Will Baptist Bible College, preached on Wednesday morning and Wednesday evening, and missionary Kenneth Eagleton preached on Thursday morning.

Westside Free Will Baptist Church, Midland, at one time was one of the largest Free Will Baptist churches in Texas. It eventually closed, the property sold, and the proceeds given to the Texas State Mission Board.

Fiftieth Annual Session - 1964

The fiftieth annual session of the Texas State Association met at the Westside Free Will Baptist Church in Midland, October 27-29, 1964. The theme was "Looking Unto Jesus." Two events preceded the meeting: the Minister's and Deacons meeting and the Woman's Auxiliary meeting; both met at 1:30 on Tuesday afternoon. Kenneth Brandon was the moderator and the clerk was E. E. Zoellers. Six district associations reported, along with thirty-two churches. Twenty-six ministers and deacons registered.

The executive committee scheduled seven sermons for the meeting. Don Payne, president of Oklahoma Bible College, preached on Tuesday evening. There were again two sermons on Wednesday morning, one by Roger C. Reeds, Director of the National Sunday School Department, and C. B. Thompson. Sam Johnson, Director of the National Church Training Service Department, spoke on Wednesday evening, explaining the new Church Training Service literature. Odus Eubanks preached on Wednesday evening. There were two sermons on Thursday morning, one by Rashie Kennedy and one by Bill Jones, listed as a missionary to Africa. Leroy Cutler brought the closing message.

The body voted to change the meeting time for the state association to the Tuesday night before the first Sunday in August, running through Thursday noon. They also voted to change the constitution by substituting the words "Church Training Service" for League. Perhaps for the first time the state meeting was provided with a Digest of Reports; most reports are not included in the minutes and we are told to see them in the Digest, which we don't have.

The Resolution Committee report, however, is given, and it contains some historical information. The first resolution, which passed, called for the executive committee to enlarge the state newsletter into a state paper. Another extended an invitation for the National Association to convene in Houston in 1968, which did not eventuate.

Fifty-First Annual Session - 1965

The fifty-first annual session of the Texas State Association convened with the Central Texas District, meeting at the First Free Will Baptist Church of Bryan, July 27-29, 1965. Leroy Cutler was the host pastor. The moderator was Clarence J. Hearron and Eugene E. Zoellers was the clerk. The clerk did not indicate which associations and churches represented, just that they were seated. H. Z. Cox was the part-time executive secretary. Dr. L. C. Johnson, president of Free Will Baptist Bible College, preached in the Tuesday evening service. Lionel Cooksey preached on Wednesday morning, as did H. Z. Cox. On Wednesday afternoon C. F. Ferguson preached. Wesley Calvary preached on Wednesday evening. J. A. Hearron, of Oklahoma and E. K. Brandon preached on Thursday morning.

The Board of Christian Education reported that the state youth rally held C.T.S. competition in Sword Drill, Declamations, Essays, and Bible Bowl. Eleanor Cutler was appointed as State Church Training Service director. The home going of J. L. Payne was duly noted and a moment of prayer was observed. A rising vote of thanks was given to H. Z. Cox for his years of service as the executive secretary. Brother Cox pointed out that the year just ending had been the best year of giving in the history of the state association. Odus K. Eubanks was elected part-time executive secretary.

The body voted to change the way it selected the meeting place for the state meeting. They voted to have a revolving list, kept by the clerk, of each district association. At the top of the list would be the last association hosting it. New associations would be put at the bottom of the list. The association voted for the executive committee to compose a standard examination and procedure for the ordination of all ordained personnel to be recommended for use by all districts and churches. Apparently this never came to fruition. The state still had two mission boards, foreign missions and home missions. Harvey Henderson, of Atmore, Alabama, was introduced as new home missionary to Austin, under the National's Project 30 program.[115]

Fifty-Second Annual Session - 1966

The 52nd annual session of the Texas State Association of Free Will Baptists convened with the Caprock District Association, August 2-4, 1966, at the First Free Will Baptist Church of Odessa. The meeting was moderated by Kenneth Brandon and the clerk was R. J. Kennedy, Jr. The following six district associations represented: Caprock, Central, East Texas, Midessa, Northwest Brazos, and the West Fork. One hundred ninety-four people registered for the meeting. The theme was "Show My People."

---

[115] For a perspective on Project 30 see the Harvey Henderson profile in the chapter on Profiles.

The preaching was delivered on Tuesday evening by Kenneth Brandon. Osmundo Corrales spoke on Wednesday morning as did E. E. Zoellers. Lonnie Palmer preached on Wednesday evening.

The part-time executive secretary was Odus Eubanks, who published the state paper, *The Texas Challenge*. Among the items recommended by the executive secretary, and passed, were these:

First Free Will Baptist Church, Odessa

- That a committee be appointed to study the desirability of the state association establishing a permanent Radio-Television Commission
- That they invite the National Association to come to Texas in 1972
- That a committee be appointed to study the possibilities and requirements to acquire and operate a state youth camp
- That the executive secretary proceed to have the state association incorporated
- That the executive committee study the means and necessity of employing a full-time executive secretary.

He reported that the giving through the state office for the year had jumped to $16,151.96, more than $5,000.00 over any previous year. The statistical report showed that Texas had 6 district associations, 61 churches, 4 missions, and a church membership of 4,443. The State Home Missions Board became the Missions-Church Extension Board, and took on the responsibilities of the State Foreign Missions Board, which was eliminated.

A resolution was presented calling for delegates to the state association to arrange for their own lodging and meals, rather than the host church providing rooms for them in the homes of their members. This matter was referred to the executive committee. The body voted to take on the project of purchasing a light generator and a vehicle for Lonnie and Bernice Palmer, missionaries to Africa, the cost not to exceed $4,500.00.

Fifty-Third Annual Session - 1967

The fifty-third annual session convened with the East Texas District Association, meeting in Henderson, August 1-3, 1967. The theme was "Christ Is for Today." Don Ellis was the moderator and the clerk was R. J. Kennedy. Odus Eubanks was the part-time executive secretary. The following five district associations represented: Caprock, Central, East Texas, Midessa, and West Fork. Thirty-four churches represented. On Tuesday evening Dr. Robert Picirilli, of Free Will Baptist Bible College, brought the keynote message, "Christ Is for Today's Youth."

The report of the Christian Education Board indicated that the board had contributed $25.00 to each of the Texas CTS contestants who had competed at the National. One of those contestants was Miss Deleen Huston, who later, as Deleen Cousineau, would serve as a missionary in Côte d'Ivoire. She had been a member of the Bible Bowl team.

Executive secretary Odus Eubanks announced that he was leaving Texas to accept a position at "our Free Will Baptist Bible College in California."[116] On Wednesday morning Clarence Hearron, of Oklahoma Bible College, preached on "Christ for a Changing Society." Rashie Kennedy, Sr. was elected as the new part-time executive secretary.

The body voted to recommend to the National that ordained deacons be made standing delegates to the National Association. The National adopted this recommendation. The state body adopted a resolution calling for the state association to appoint a historical committee to collect, hold, and maintain historical records as a means of preserving the history of Texas Free Will Baptists. Apparently this was never done. They voted to designate one service as a youth service. The body voted to change their fiscal year to January 1 to December 31 of each year. Rashie Kennedy preached on Thursday morning on the subject "Christ Is for Today's Local Church."

Fifty-Fourth Annual Session - 1968

The Fifty-fourth annual session of the state association convened with the West Fork District Association, meeting at the First Free Will Baptist Church in Dallas, July 30-August 1, 1968. Host pastor H. Z. Cox was the moderator and Mrs. Jessie Ferguson was the clerk. Five district associations represented, presumably the Central, East Texas, Midessa, Northwest Brazos, and West Fork,[117] plus thirty-two churches and one mission. Tuesday evening was a youth service and it featured the participation of a great number of young people. Eugene Richards preached on the subject "Peanuts." An unusually large number of out of state dignitaries were present.

On Wednesday morning Bobby Ferguson preached on the subject "The Time Has Come for More Training of Laymen in Local Churches." On Wednesday afternoon attention was given to the controversy in the denomination over the state of the backslider. For more on this subject, see the chapter on the National Association. In the evening service moderator H. Z. Cox presented plaques to two men, one to Bob Harless as the outstanding layman of the year, and the other to Herbert Richards as the outstanding minister of the year. Bob Shockey, director of the National Missions Church-Extension Department preached on "The Time Has Come to Expand or Expire."

An interesting deletion from the constitution was adopted. From the article on representation the following was deleted: "And one delegate for each one hundred dollars given during the previous year to our denominational ministries through the cooperative plan of support." The delegates were polled as to what kind of minutes they wanted. The delegates preferred the less expensive minutes, and suggested an off-set printing.

The Caprock Association made a request to the Executive Committee to withdraw from the Texas State Association to form a new association in New Mexico, to be named The Land of Enchantment Association of Free Will Baptists. The Executive Committee reported that they had granted the request.

---

[116] This school became California Christian College and is still active as of this writing.
[117] Judging from the report of the Obituary Committee which listed these five.

The Thursday morning worship service featured a sermon by National Executive Secretary Rufus Coffee, entitled "The Time Has Come."

The Report of the General Board records ten recommendations to the board which were discussed and acted upon. One was that the state buy property in Austin suitable for the State Office and for living quarters for the Executive Secretary. This recommendation was defeated. Two recommendations, presented together here were that the state association urge and show good reason why each church should tithe as a minimum to the district of which it is a member and that the state association urge and show good reason why each district should give this tithe to the state work on a 50/50 basis as a minimum support. These items carried. Another recommendation was for the state association to check on the possibility of setting up a literature, book, and general sales business by mail or a walk-in store. This item carried. This did not come to fruition for several years, however.

The death of preacher Mrs. Verda Walker is noted in the Report of the Obituary Committee.

Fifty-Fifth Annual Session - 1969

The fifty-fifth annual session of the Texas State Association convened with the Central Texas District, meeting at the First Free Will Baptist Church of Houston, July 29-31, 1969. The moderator was Herbert Richards and the clerk was Mrs. Lela Clary. The theme seems to have been "What We Need to Do." The following five district associations: East Texas, Midessa, Central, West Fork, and Northwest Brazos, along with twenty-seven churches, represented. The Tuesday evening youth service was conducted by Thomas Marberry, who also brought the evening message. Dr. L. C. Johnson, president of Free Will Baptist Bible College, preached on Wednesday morning on the subject "What We Need in a Local Church."

On Wednesday afternoon there was a motion to hire a full-time executive secretary. After much discussion the motion was defeated. Plaques were presented to Eugene Richards as the minister of the year, and to Bill Johnson as layman of the year. Bill Jones preached on "What We Need to Do About the Great Commission." Bobby Ferguson was elected part-time executive secretary. Missionary Ken Eagleton preached on the subject "What We Need to Do About Christian Education."

The movement toward hiring a full-time executive secretary was continuing to build. A motion was made and passed authorizing the moderator to appoint persons from each district to promote a plan through which Texas might hire a full-time executive secretary the next year. The new moderator, Everett Hellard, appointed men from each of the associations to promote the plan.

Fifty-Sixth Annual Session - 1970

The fifty-sixth annual session of the Texas State Association convened with the Central Texas District, meeting at the Fellowship Free Will Baptist Church in Bryan, July 28-30, 1970. Everett Hellard was the moderator and Eugene Richards was the clerk. Five district associations (Central, Midessa, Northwest Brazos, East Texas, and West Fork), and twenty-seven churches represented.

Don Ellis was present promoting the Free Will Baptist Children's Home in Greenville, Tennessee.

The annual youth service was conducted on Tuesday evening. The sermon was delivered by Raymond Getz. On Wednesday morning Charles Hampton preached on "Is Our Teaching-

Preaching Ministry What It Ought to Be?" Raymond Lee was named layman of the year and James Sturgill minister of the year. Jim was pastor of the First Free Will Baptist Church in Seminole, Texas, and doing an outstanding job, especially in building attendance at a isolated outpost in West Texas. He would soon leave Texas for a long ministry as a Free Will Baptist missionary in Brazil. On Wednesday night Wesley Calvery preached. The Calvery Family, and John Yasyda, a Japanese student attending Oklahoma Bible College, sang "To Tell the Story," a song composed by Wesley Calvery, in both English and Japanese. On Thursday morning the sermon was delivered by Paul Myer.

The General Board recommended that the association accept the invitation from the Westside Church in Midland to host the 1971 state association meeting, provided that delegates and visitors be responsible for their own meals and lodging. This item was defeated. They also recommended that the position of executive secretary continue as was for the time being. This item passed. A resolution which proposed changing the time of the state meeting to June was defeated.

There were sixty-three churches, including two missions, in the state in 1970. The Central District had twenty churches and one mission; the West Fork had twenty-three; East Texas, eight; Midessa, five churches and one mission; and the Northwest Brazos had five churches. The Central and West Fork District Association were seemingly at their apex, their zenith, their highest point in numbers of churches, while the Midessa and Northwest Brazos were noticeably down.

Fifty-Seventh Annual Session - 1971

The fifty-seventh annual session of the state association convened with the Northwest Brazos District Association, meeting at the First Free Will Baptist Church of Amarillo, July 27-29, 1971. Five district associations (Midessa, West Fork, East Texas, Central, and the Northwest Brazos) and thirty-five churches represented. The Caprock Association is no longer listed, but the High Plains District Association petitioned the state for membership and was admitted. It was composed of two churches: The Oakdale First Free Will Baptist Church of Amarillo and the First Free Will Baptist Church of Pampa. The High Plains district folded about 1973. Allen Moore was the moderator and Eugene Richards was the clerk. Rufus Coffee, Executive Secretary of the National Association of Free Will Baptists, preached on Tuesday evening and again on Wednesday morning.

The minister of the year and the layman of the year were recognized, Glen Hood and Weldon Huston, respectively. Weldon Huston was the father of Deleen Huston Cousineau, missionary to Coté d'Ivoire, West Africa, and a deacon in the First Free Will Baptist Church of Odessa. Roy Thomas, with the National Missions Church-Extension Department, preached on Wednesday evening. Once again the General Board recommended that the time of the state meeting be moved to June and once again the recommendation was defeated. A motion to have the Executive Committee study and recommend a day change for the time of the state meeting passed. A motion passed authorizing the executive secretary to mail the National Association qualifications for ministers and deacons to each district association, with a recommendation that the district use them. On Thursday morning Mack Humbles preached from Mark 16:15.

Fifty-Eighth Annual Session - 1972

The fifty-eighth annual session of the Texas State Association of Free Will Baptists convened with the East Texas District Association, meeting at Henderson, Texas, July 25-27, 1972. Allen Moore was the moderator and Eugene Richards was the clerk. Bobby Ferguson was part-time executive secretary. The following district associations reported: West Fork, Central, East Texas, Midessa, High Plains, and Northwest Brazos. In addition, twenty churches represented. Paul Ketteman, representing Free Will Baptist Bible College, preached on "Our Motivation for Soul Winning." On Wednesday morning Malcolm Fry preached on "The Mechanics of Soul Winning." On Wednesday evening Don Robirds, of the Free Will Baptist Foreign Missions Department, preached from Isaiah 6:1-11.

A recommendation from the General Board that the time of the state meeting be changed "to Thursday before the second Sunday in June" was adopted. This meant that the state meetings would be held before the National Association convened in July, better allowing the state to make recommendations to the National. The Obituary Committee noted the passing of J. L. Bounds and his wife. It also noted the passing of Dr. and Mrs. H. M. Wingfield of Bryan, in a plane crash. Leroy Cutler, pastor of the First Free Will Baptist Church in Bryan, and his wife Eleanor adopted the Wingfield children.

The move toward a full-time executive secretary continued to grow. A motion was made and passed authorizing the Executive Committee to formulate a plan for putting a full-time executive secretary on the field by the next state meeting. The body voted to support the home mission church being started by the Midessa Association in Abilene. Bob Scott preached on Thursday morning from the Book of Nehemiah.

The office of executive secretary was very much on the minds of the delegates. They voted to raise the salary of part-time executive secretary Bobby Ferguson from fifty dollars a month to seventy five dollars. Very importantly, they voted to put into the hands of the Executive Committee the responsibility of formulating a plan for putting a full-time state executive secretary on the field by the next year's meeting.

Statistical tables in the minutes indicate the following number of churches in the district associations: East Texas, 8; Midessa, 7; Central, 20; West Fork, 23; and High Plains, 2. The Northwest Brazos was not included in the tables.

Significantly, the total expenditures of the Board of Christian Education for the year was $291.57.

Fifty-Ninth Annual Session - 1973

The fifty-ninth annual session of the Texas State Association of Free Will Baptists convened with the First Free Will Baptist Church of Dallas, pastored by H. Z. Cox. I have no minutes of that meeting, but I was there, having started pastoring the Grace Free Will Baptist Church in White Settlement, a suburb of Fort Worth, in October of 1972. The position of executive secretary was a prime focus of the meeting. The Executive Committee had settled on a layman from Bryan, Jim Williams, who had just graduated from Free Will Baptist Bible College, as their recommendation for the full-time position of executive secretary. To help them sell the idea to the state association they had invited two full-time executive secretaries from other states to preach at the meeting: Lonnie Davoult of Oklahoma and Fred Warner of Arkansas. The association voted to hire Jim Williams and put him on as the state's first full-time executive secretary. He established his office in his home church, the First Free Will Baptist Church of Bryan, in an upstairs room the church provided for him in the educational building. Jim faithfully travelled the state, visiting the churches, pastors, quarterly meetings, and other denominational events to promote the Free Will Baptist work in Texas. He edited *The Texas Challenge* and promoted every phase of the work.

Jim Williams

Though this was my first Texas state meeting, and I was a stranger to almost everyone there, the body elected me to a position on the Board of Christian Education. This was significant to me because before I left Alabama, a denominational leader told me not to go to Texas because they would never receive me or allow me to hold any position in the state. I found that to be a completely mistaken opinion. From then until I retired the state gave me all the work that I could do and I have always been appreciative.

Sixtieth Annual Session - 1974

No minutes of the 1974 state meeting are available to me.

Sixty-First Annual Session - 1975

No minutes of the 1975 state meeting are available to me.

Chapter 5
1976 to 1990

Charles Dickens opened his classic book, *A Tale of Two Cities*, with the famous words: "It was the best of times, it was the worst of times…." The fifteen years, 1976 to 1990, were years of contrast for the Free Will Baptist work in Texas. As is true of most any period of time there were both good and bad things happening. There was growth and there was decline; some churches closed as new churches were planted. There was a bright and hopeful outlook for the future, and there was despair and gloom on the horizon. There were successes and there were failures. The glass was half full and it was half empty. And there was conflict.

Sixty-Second Annual Session - 1976

I have not been able to locate any minutes of the 1976 state meeting.

Sixty-Third Annual Session - 1977

The sixty-third annual session of the state association met at the Christ's Free Will Baptist Church, 3126 Gollihar Road, Corpus Christi, pastored by Herbert Richards. Three things stand out about this state meeting. One of them was that the state's executive secretary, Jim Williams, had announced his resignation from his position with the state association in order to accept a position in Mexico with the Free Will Baptist National Home Missions Department. One of his tasks was to reopen the Institute of Gold in Monterrey. The state was genuinely sorry to see him go, but wished him well in his new work. To show their appreciation the association presented him with a new camera, with multiple lenses, for his mission work in Mexico. The second was that Allen Moore was recommended by the Executive Board to replace Jim Williams as the executive secretary of the Texas State Association. Clarence J. Hearron was nominated from the floor but Brother Moore was elected and hired.

The third thing was that the body, at the recommendation of the Credentials Committee, did not seat the Midessa District Association. The reason was that the Midessa had not taken any disciplinary action toward one of its pastors, Archie Joe "Dusty" Cooksey, who pastored the First Free Will Baptist Church in Abilene. Cooksey had publicly stated several errant theological positions while addressing the Midessa Association on at least two occasions. Among the things he had avowed were the following:[118]

- Adam and Eve did not exist, the biblical story of the fall was a mythical story attempting to explain how the world got into such a mess.

---

[118] All of the information given here about the so called inspiration debate is taken from carefully kept records and documents, not just from my memory. I have attempted to give a fair and accurate account of the controversy. It was an unpleasant part of Texas Free Will Baptist history, yet nevertheless a part of that history. Therefore it is included.

- Rather than crossing the Red Sea as described in the Bible, Moses led the children of Israel across a swampy marsh and when Pharaoh's army tried to follow, their chariots got stuck in the mud, thus ending their pursuit of the fleeing Israelites.
- Paul's advice and instructions to the Corinthian church in 1 Corinthians about marriage was wrong. Consequently, someone other than Paul, but using Paul's name, wrote 2 Corinthians to correct what Paul had said in 1 Corinthians.
- Numerous books of the Bible were not written by the men whom the Bible says wrote them; they were written under false names, a view called pseudonymity. He listed the books of 2 Corinthians, Ephesians, Colossians, 2 Thessalonians, 1 and 2 Timothy, and Titus as having been written by someone using a pseudonym (false name) and not by Paul.
- The original books of the Bible, the original autographs, contained historical and scientific errors, the errors not being the result of copyists or translators.
- The Bible is accurate and trustworthy on salvatory matters, that is, on the doctrine of salvation, and that is all that matters.
- Inspiration extends to the thoughts and ideas of the Bible writers, but not to the words and phrases they used to write down those thoughts and ideas.
- Cooksey stated, "I am not a fundamentalist. I am an existential presuppositionalist."

Dennis Haygood, pastor of the Westside Free Will Baptist Church in Midland, and I, while pastoring the First Free Will Baptist Church in Odessa, had conveyed to the Midessa Association in late 1976 and early 1977 that these views were not acceptable to Free Will Baptists because they denied the inspiration, inerrancy, and authority of Scripture. All of the other Midessa Association pastors had taken the position that as long as the Bible was accurate and trustworthy when it told us how to be saved, it didn't matter that it was in error when it spoke on matters of history, science, chronology, etc. Unfortunately, news of this conflict had spread across the entire denomination. Several state papers carried articles about it and letters of some of the principle participants were copied and disseminated far and wide.

A word would be appropriate here as to why Dennis Haygood and I did not bring charges against Brother Cooksey and a formal trial conducted. We were working under two presuppositions based on our understanding of the *Treatise*. The first was that *three* ministers were required to present the charges, not two. Dennis and I were the only two ministers in the Midessa Association who questioned Brother Cooksey's views on inspiration. All of the other ministers supported him, as did virtually all of the laypeople. Secondly, it was our belief that all of the ministers signing the charges had to be members of the *local* association of which the accused was a member, in this case the Midessa Association. Numerous pastors from outside Texas, from as far away as the Carolinas, volunteered to sign the charges against Dusty so we could have the required three, but we turned them all down because they were not members of the Midessa Association. Therefore, formal charges were never brought against Dusty and there was no trial. We took a lot of criticism from fellow ministers in the denomination for not preferring charges but we felt strongly that we were bound by the *Treatise*.

Prior to the state meeting, while hiking the Lost Mine Trail in the Big Bend National Park, state executive secretary Jim Williams had asked me to write a position paper on the subject of the inspiration and inerrancy of Scripture for the state association, stating what was generally considered to be the Free Will Baptist position on the subject. I wrote the position paper requested by our executive secretary and Brother Williams distributed copies of it to the delegates at the

1977 state meeting in Corpus Christi. Some pastors stated the opinion that the statement in the *Treatise* was sufficient and that no further clarification of it was necessary, preferring the "simplicity" of that statement and the wide diversity it seemed to allow. Here is that *Treatise* statement:

CHAPTER 1

The Holy Scriptures

> These are the Old and New Testaments; they were written by holy men, inspired by the Holy Spirit, and are God's revealed word to man. They are a sufficient and infallible rule and guide to salvation and all Christian worship and service.[119]

Some people have questioned the need for a further, clarifying statement on what Free Will Baptists believe about the inspiration of the Bible. The first Free Will Baptist *Treatise*, which was adopted at the first General Conference in 1831 at Wilton, Maine, did not have a chapter on the inspiration and inerrancy of Scripture. Evidently there was no need for one since pretty much everyone believed that the Bible, as God's word, was inspired and inerrant. It wasn't until 1869 that a chapter was added to the *Treatise*, stating the Free Will Baptist view of Scripture. That 1869 statement was identical to the first paragraph of the present *Treatise*.

The *Treatise* chapter on the Scriptures had remained the same since the original statement of 1869. However, changing times, new meanings of old words, and new winds of doctrine, resulting in many vastly different views on inspiration had brought about a need for clarification of exactly what Free Will Baptists believed. The statement in the *Treatise* no longer covered all the issues involved. Our views hadn't changed but the need to make clear what we believed, and how we differed from other groups, especially the views of liberalism and neo-orthodoxy, had changed. For instance, on November 19, 1977, at the Executive Committee meeting of the Midessa District Association in Big Spring, Lionel Cooksey asked his son Dusty, "Do you believe in the divine inspiration of the Bible?" Dusty answered the question with "Yes." That answer fully satisfied everyone present except Dennis Haygood and me. Honestly, no one at the meeting, except Dennis and me, had any theological training in the doctrine of the Scriptures. We wanted to question Dusty at some depth on his view of inspiration, especially in light of the things he had stated previously which indicated to us that he held an errant view of inspiration. We were not allowed to ask any questions. None at all.

Some questions cannot be answered with a simple yes or no answer. Let me illustrate. If I ask Joe Brown if he has stopped beating his wife, what does he say? If he says "Yes," then I conclude that he has been beating her but has stopped. If he answers "No," I conclude that he has been beating her and still does. Again, you cannot answer some questions with a yes or no answer. There has to be an explanation. Dusty did not have to give an explanation of his statement that he believed in the divine inspiration of the Bible. In today's theological world a simple yes answer to the question, "Do you believe in the divine inspiration of the Bible?" does not properly reveal a person's true beliefs about inspiration. Some theologians believe inspiration of the Bible means

---

[119] *A Treatise of the Faith and Practice of the Original Free Will Baptists*, Published by the Executive Committee of the National Association of Free Will Baptists, 1962.

only that the human author received inspiration to write, much the same way Willie Nelson receives inspiration to write a love song. A person could answer the question put to Dusty with a "Yes" and still be liberal, neo-orthodox, or "existential presuppositionalist."

At any rate I wrote the position paper on inspiration which Jim Williams had asked me to write. Jim presented it to the state association's General Board and they recommended it to the state body for adoption. The state body unanimously[120] adopted it, along with instructions that a copy of it be sent to the National Association. For the record, here is the position paper in its entirety, exactly as written, included because of its importance:

Position Paper on Inspiration

For 250 years (1727-1977) Free Will Baptists have existed in America as a fundamental, evangelical, Bible believing denomination. Many other denominations, which once stood where we have always stood, have folded their tents and moved one by one into the camp of theological liberalism or neo-orthodoxy. Because of the influence of German higher criticism on American ecclesiastical bodies there is a danger that we, too, may cast off our moorings and begin to slide into the wasteland of humanistic rationalism.

Errant contemporary theological trends have begun to touch our beloved denomination. Questions arise which cast aspersions on the inspiration, authority, and infallibility of the Scriptures. Plenary verbal inspiration is redefined and made to mean less than it has meant as historically defined by the Church. Verbal inspiration is, in fact, made to mean thought or concept inspiration.

To some, infallibility, or inerrancy, means only that the Scriptures are inerrant in matters of faith and practice but not in matters of science, history, and chronology.

Following the German school of higher criticism, some have adopted a position of pseudonymity which says that many of the books of the Bible were not written by the men to whom they are attributed by the Bible itself but by impostors. For example, it is said that Daniel did not write the Book of Daniel, Paul did not write some of the Pauline Epistles, and Peter did not write Second Peter.

It is time for Free Will Baptists to catch up with other denominations in building larger, more beautiful, more effective churches on the proverbial Main Street. But it is not time, and may it never be time, for Free Will Baptists to catch up with other denominations and ecclesiastical bodies by tearing up our Bibles and undermining its complete trustworthiness. We believe there is no evidence available today which is sufficient to question the position that has been held by Free Will Baptists for 250 years.

As Free Will Baptists we believe that the plenary and verbal inspiration of the Bible is a foundational, fundamental, cardinal doctrine. If the Bible is not fully inspired and trustworthy, then we have no sure foundation on which to build the other doctrines of the Christian faith. We could not be sure that we have the truth about Christ, salvation, morality, or man's destiny.

The doctrine of the infallibility of the Bible has proven to be a theological watershed. If church history has any lessons to teach us, it is the lesson that once a denomination departs from a belief in biblical infallibility, it opens the doors to disbelief about other essential doctrines of the faith. Once a denomination denies the infallibility of the Bible, or adopts a position of limited inerrancy, it will only be a matter of time until they also deny the inerrancy of the Bible on matters of faith and practice.

Thus it is appropriate for us in this sixty-third session of the Texas State Association of Free Will Baptists to declare where we stand as to God's Word - our infallible guide.

---

[120] When I say "unanimously" I mean that everyone who voted, voted to adopt. There were no dissenting votes.

Therefore, we affirm for all to know, that:

1. We believe in the plenary verbal inspiration of the Bible. By plenary we mean "full and complete," that all parts of the Bible are inspired, that inspiration extends to all subjects dealt with. By verbal we mean that inspiration extends to the very words of Scripture, not just the thoughts and ideas in the minds of the human authors of Scripture.

2. We believe in the complete infallibility and inerrancy of Scripture. We believe the Bible is inerrant in all that it intends to teach as truth or fact, in matters of cosmogony, geology, astronomy, anthropology, history, chronology, etc., as well as in matters of faith and practice.

3. We believe that the human authors of Scripture were the very men to whom the Bible itself attributes the individual books, We reject the theory which says that many of the books were written under a pseudonym.

4. We accept the Bible, the Word of God, as our final authority and dedicate ourselves to the proclamation of it in its entirety, trusting in God to empower it to fruition.

We urge the adoption of this position paper by the Texas State Association of Free Will Baptists on this date, June 10, 1977, that it be printed in its entirety and distributed to all churches in the state, that copies of it be sent to all Free Will Baptist state papers, and that a copy of it be sent to the National Association of Free Will Baptists.

As directed by the state body, a copy of the position paper was sent to the National Association, which met in July in Detroit, Michigan. The Executive Office passed the position paper along to the Resolutions Committee, who presented it to the national body as a resolution in the following form:

Inspiration and Inerrancy of Scripture

Whereas,
Free Will Baptists have existed in America for the past 250 years as a fundamental, Bible-believing denomination, free from doctrinal corruption; and

Whereas,
Many other denominations who once stood true have been corrupted from within because of the influence of "German Higher Criticism"; and

Whereas,
Current theological trends cast doubt on or deny the inspiration, infallibility, of and inerrancy of Scriptures, defining inspiration, even plenary verbal inspiration, to mean less than it has historically meant; and

Whereas,
The doctrine of the full inspiration, inerrancy and trustworthiness of the Scriptures is the foundation of all Bible truth; and

Whereas,
Our beloved denomination is not immune to this type of problem; therefore,

Be it resolved:

1. That we reaffirm out belief in the plenary verbal inspiration of the Bible. By plenary we mean "full and complete," that all parts of the Bible are inspired, that inspiration extends to all subjects dealt with. By verbal

we mean that inspiration extends to the very words of Scripture, not just to the thoughts and ideas in the minds of the human authors of Scripture.

2. That we reaffirm our belief in the complete infallibility and inerrancy of Scripture. We believe the Bible is inerrant in all that it intends to teach as truth or fact, in matters of cosmogony, geology, astronomy, anthropology, history, chronology, etc., as well as in matters of faith and practice.

3. That we reaffirm our belief that the human authors of Scripture were the very men to whom the Bible itself attributes the individual books. We reject the theory which says that many of the books were written under a pseudonym.

4. That we accept the Bible, the Word of God, as our final authority and dedicate ourselves to the proclamation of it in its entirety, trusting in God to empower it to fruition.

Submitted by Resolutions Committee
Hobart Ashby, Chairman
Robert Parker
Jack Forlines
Guy Owens
Floyd Wolfenbarger

The resolution was unanimously adopted by the national body. In effect the National Association, by adopting the above resolution on inspiration and inerrancy, which mirrored very closely the position paper I had written, and the Texas State Association had adopted, took the same position on the inspiration question that Dennis Haygood and I had taken.

In addition, the national body voted to have the General Board write a statement on the inspiration and inerrancy of the Bible to be presented the following year, with a recommendation that the statement be inserted in the *Treatise* as an Appendix. The inspiration debate continued through 1978 and 1979, see below.

Sixty-Fourth Annual Session - 1978

The 1978 Texas state meeting convened with the West Fork District Association, meeting at the Western Hills Free Will Baptist Church in Fort Worth. I have not located a copy of the minutes of that meeting.

The Inspiration Debate Continues - Kansas City

The inspiration debate was an even hotter topic the next year when the National Association met July 16-20, 1978, in Kansas City, Missouri. Arising quickly was the matter of seating the Texas delegation. The North Carolina State Association had written a letter to the National recommending that the Texas delegation not be seated. There was widespread sentiment with the North Carolina recommendation.

However, the General Board, which met prior to the Credentials Committee meeting, adopted the following statement about seating the Texas delegation:

> We considered the letter from the North Carolina State Association recommending that the Texas State delegates not be seated. We recommend that the Credentials Committee be instructed to consult with the Texas State Association concerning this matter, and that the Texas delegation be seated for this session. We further recommend that if this committee incur any expenses, that these expenses be paid from the convention funds. This committee is to report to the General Board at the 1979 meeting.[121]

There was considerable discussion on the floor of the National, with many speaking who were uninformed or misinformed. However, common sense prevailed and the Texas delegation was seated.

The Credentials Committee met with the Texas delegation and on Wednesday afternoon the Credentials Committee gave a report on their meeting with the Texas delegation. Their report was as follows:

> In keeping with our commission in Section V of the General Board report approved by this national assembly, we, the Credentials Committee, having consulted with a delegation from Texas, have determined that the grievance lodged against the Texas State Association that they acted improperly is unfounded. It is the consensus of this committee that the Texas Association acted within the bounds of their procedure to insure that the integrity of the doctrine of plenary verbal inspiration was maintained in its constituent associations[122]

The issue reflected in the above Credentials Committee report was the question of whether the Midessa District Association, and the Texas State Association, had acted improperly by not bringing charges against Dusty Cooksey. At the heart of the issue was the lingering question of whether *three ministers, all from the Midessa District Association*, were required for the signing of charges against Dusty Cooksey.

There was still some dissatisfaction over the question of whether three men, all from the local association, were required for the signing of charges against an erring minister. Professor Leroy Forlines asked for an official interpretation of the *Treatise* statement concerning this matter. The *Treatise* stated that charges against a minister should normally be brought to the association by a local church. However, it contains an exception, namely:

> "The only exception that should be made arises when an offense involves a fellow minister (as object or witness) in a situation unknown to the local church. In this case, charges should be preferred by three ministers jointly, with the local church fully appraised of the fact."[123]

In response to Forlines inquiry, a motion was made and seconded that we interpret this to mean that the three ministers referred to in the section can be any three ministers in good standing and they can be from anywhere within the denomination. There was considerable disagreement and discussion on this point and no clear explanation seemed available. The national body did not vote on the motion.

---

[121] *The 1979 Free Will Baptist Yearbook*, minutes of the 1978 National Association, page 85.
[122] *1979 Yearbook*, minutes of the 1978 National Association, page 10.
[123] *Treatise*, as revised in 1969,, The Practices of Free Will Baptists, Chapter 2, His Discipline, Part B.

Instead, a motion carried to refer the item to the Executive Committee to bring a report to the General Board in its 1979 session.

As a result, the General Board then recommended to the national body the adoption of the following statement and footnote and that they be inserted in the *Treatise* as an addition to Chapter 1, The Holy Scriptures:

> Since the Bible is the Word of God, it is without error in all matters upon which it speaks, whether history, geography, matters relating to science, or any other subject."
>
> FOOTNOTE: The last sentence of chapter 1, which was added in July 1979 does not represent any change or modification of thought in the doctrine of the Holy Scriptures as it has been historically believed by Free Will Baptists. In view of the fact that some, in the theological world, have claimed to believe that the Bible is an infallible rule of faith and practice, while at the same time professing to believe that the Bible contains errors which were a part of the original manuscripts, this statement was added to make the position already held by Free Will Baptists, unmistakably clear.[124]

This recommendation had to lie on the table until the following year, thus prolonging the inspiration debate ever further.

Furthermore, as commissioned by the body in 1977, the General Board presented a statement on the inspiration and inerrancy of Scripture, and recommended that it, too, be inserted in the *Treatise* as an Appendix. The statement presented by the General Board was as follows:

> Inspiration Statement
> Free Will Baptists believe in the plenary, verbal inspiration of the Bible. By *plenary* we mean "full and complete." We hold that all parts of the Bible are inspired and that inspiration extends to all its subjects. By *verbal* we mean that inspiration extends to the very words of the Scriptures, not just to the thoughts and ideas expressed by human authors. We believe the Scriptures are infallible and inerrant. The Bible is without error and trustworthy in all its teachings, including cosmogony, geology, astronomy, anthropology, history, chronology, etc., as well as in matters of faith and practice. Being the very word of God, it is God's final revelation and our absolute authority.[125]

The recommended appendix also had to lie on the table until the following national convention in 1979, which would meet in Charlotte, North Carolina.

Sixty-Fifth Annual Session - 1979

The sixty-fifth annual session of the Texas State Association convened with the Central Texas District Association, meeting at the Fellowship Free Will Baptist Church in Bryan, June 7-8, 1979. Earl Scroggins was the moderator and Billy Walker was the clerk. Six district associations represented: Northwest Brazos, West Fork, Midessa, Mission, East Texas, and Central Texas, along with fifty churches, which was an unusually large number of churches reporting. The clerk did not record what transpired on Wednesday evening and Thursday morning, though it was most likely the youth service and the CTS competition. The state meeting proper

---

[124] *1979 Yearbook*, page 87
[125] *1979 Yearbook*, Minutes of the 1978 National Association, page 86, italics theirs.

began on Thursday evening. Moderator Scroggins led a special prayer on behalf of the Clyde Gillentine family, whose daughter and unborn child were killed in an automobile accident on the way to the hospital. Roy Norie preached on the subject "Laboring for Jesus," using Titus 2:11-14 as his text. Ron McMillan presented the awards to the winners of the 1979 CTS competitive activities.

Verlin Pegues was elected to serve as the first state senator for the Master's Men from Texas. Mrs. Ava Hellard, president of the Woman's Auxiliary, called for prayer for the Free Will Baptist people in Wichita Falls who had suffered a great deal because of the April 10 tornado. She reported that Mike and Deleen Cousineau had spoken at the auxiliary meeting. Allen Moore was elected to serve a two year term as Texas' executive secretary. Keith Woody preached on the subject "Looking for Jesus," using Titus 2:13 as his text. Vivian Moore gave a report on the Christian Supply. She and Brother Moore were selling books and supplies as they traveled for the state and were planning to open a walk-in book store in Sherman, which they eventually did. Former executive secretary Jim Williams brought greetings from the work in Mexico.

The body voted to ask Roy Norie to express the state's disappointment to the Board of Trustees of Hillsdale Free Will Baptist College over the release of Reford Wilson as mission's professor. Bill Jones was commended for his eight years of service as president of Hillsdale. The body passed a resolution expressing disapproval of Reader's Digest printing a condensed version of the Bible.

No one should ever question whether Allen and Vivian Moore loved the Free Will Baptist work in Texas and worked very hard for the Free Will Baptist people of Texas. Their love and work are reflected in Brother Moore's 1980 report as executive secretary, which is given here in part. This partial report will lay the groundwork for our understanding some of the things which occurred at the 1983 state meeting in Amarillo.

> I want to thank each Church for their Prayers and for allowing me to be a part of their Work. To the many individuals who open their homes and hearts to the wife and I as we traveled more than Forty Thousand (40,000) miles, spent Two Hundred Forty Nine (249) days out of the Office. Visited Fifty (50) of our Churches this year 1978. Preached Ten (10) Revivals, in Twenty Three Districts, State Meeting and in some of our Churches. Prepared and mailed over Sixteen Thousand (16,000) copies of the Challenge, more than One Hundred Fifty (150) personal letters. Prepared the Digest Report and Programs for the State Meeting. Printed the Minutes 1978. I represented our State in Four (4) Board Meetings in Nashville, Tenn.[126] One (1) State Meeting Oklahoma. One (1) National Meeting in Kansas City, MO. This is only a summary of the work and of the Blessings of God. Now it is time to look forward and to expect Greater Blessings, as we continue to work together in Unity.[127]

The minutes report that the Executive Committee had spent several minutes discussing the laxity of standards and the dress code at Hillsdale Free Will Baptist College during the 1978-79 school year. Roy Norie was asked to express the committee's sentiments to the Hillsdale Board of Trustees which were to meet the following week.

The Inspiration Debate Concludes - Charlotte, North Carolina

---

[126] Brother Moore served one term on the Board of Foreign Missions.
[127] Minutes of the 1979 state meeting, printed as written, page 17.

The inspiration statement, the addition to chapter one in the *Treatise*, along with the footnote, presented by the General Board in Kansas City in 1978, was again presented to the body by the General Board and adopted in 1979 at the National Association, which met in Charlotte, North Carolina. This definition of inspiration and inerrancy was taken from the resolution on inspiration adopted by the 1977 National Association, which in turn had been taken from the position paper adopted by the Texas State Association in 1977, meeting at Corpus Christi.

Also, the proposed appendix to chapter one in the *Treatise* was again presented by the General Board to the national body. It, too, was adopted.

Furthermore, the General Board presented to the body a statement, written by the Executive Committee, clarifying the statement in the *Treatise* on whether the three men preferring charges against an erring minister had to be from the local association in which the accused minister was a member, or if they could be men in good standing from anywhere. This had been an integral part of the whole inspiration debate. The General Board presented the following clarifying statement:

> We recommend the following statement to be entered in the minutes as the inter-pretation of paragraph B, Section II, page 57, of the Treatise, "Discipline of a Minister."
> In most cases accusations against a minister should be brought by the local church to the association.
> Concerning the only exception stated in paragraph B, Section II, the "fellow minister" refers to any minister or ministers at large, and "three ministers jointly," refers to ministers within the association of the minister in question.

This clarification of the statement in the *Treatise* dealing with the discipline of an erring minister was adopted by the national body. It did not become a new rule of practice, it simply clarified the rule which was already in place. The important thing is that the National Association of Free Will Baptists was saying that three ministers, not two, all from the local association, in this case the Midessa Association, were required in order to bring charges against Dusty Cooksey. Thus, the National Association had confirmed that Dennis Haygood and I were correct in that three ministers from the Midessa Association would have been required in order to bring charges against Dusty Cooksey for his errant views.

A Postlude

Dusty left Abilene and moved back to Oklahoma in 1978, joined the First Free Will Baptist Church of Norman, and applied to the First Oklahoma District Association for membership as an ordained minister. The association's Credentials Board examined Dusty and submitted the following report to the association on Saturday, November 18, 1978:

CREDENTIAL BOARD

> 6. The Board examined Dusty Cooksey for acceptance into the Association as an ordained minister. Motion was carried to ask him to write in plain language answers to questions regarding statements made in his letters regarding inspiration, and that he denounce any leaning toward pseudonimity (*sic*). October 21 the Board postponed action on his case until the meeting of November 10. Motion was carried by a majority vote (Rev. Dan Farmer voting No) to recommend that the Association not seat Dusty Cooksey as an

ordained minister due to his failure to comply with the Board's request to answer in writing, questions concerning inspiration.[128]

Item 6 of the board's report was referred back to the Credential Board to bring back a recommendation at the next quarterly meeting. The Credential Board met again on January 10, 1979, and decided to prepare a statement regarding inspiration of the Bible, approve it at the next meeting, and ask Dusty Cooksey to sign it. At a subsequent meeting of the board, February 13, 1979, the board agreed upon the following recommendation: "That the association refuse to seat Dusty Cooksey on the grounds that he did not write a statement nor sign the statements prepared by the Board pertaining to inspiration of the Bible."[129] Another motion concerning Dusty Cookey, which passed, was that the matter be referred back to Dusty's local church to give him the opportunity to surrender his credentials.[130]

On Saturday, May 19 1979, the First Free Will Baptist Church of Norman submitted the following request to the First Oklahoma Association:

> WHEREAS, the First Oklahoma Association of Free Will Baptists at the last Quarterly Meeting, February 14, 1979, voted to refuse to ratify the credentials of REV. DUSTY COOKSEY; and,
> WHEREAS, the same association voted to refer him back to the FIRST FREE WILL BAPTIST CHURCH OF NORMAN to allow him opportunity to voluntarily relinquish his credentials; and,
> WHEREAS, he has not chosen to do so; we, the NORMAN FIRST FREE WILL BAPTIST CHURCH, request the following:
>> That a committee of fifteen (15) persons be selected to examine MR. DUSTY COOKSEY regarding his doctrinal beliefs at a hearing to convene at the FIRST FREE WILL BAPTIST CHURCH in Norman at a time convenient to the parties concerned.
>> That the committee submit a written report to the next quarterly meeting of the FIRST OKLAHOMA ASSOCIATION precisely specifying their findings and their conclusions; that this report is to be examined by the local association and voted upon with the final conclusion being either exoneration or suspension of MR. COOKSEY'S credentials.
>> That the examination by the committee be conducted by the moderator of this local association.[131]

The request from the First Free Will Baptist Church in Norman was discussed at length and a motion was made and passed that charges be presented against Dusty Cooksey and that a trial be conducted with a minimum of fifteen (15) on the jury, conforming to the request of the Norman church. It was stipulated that a simple majority was all that was necessary to convict or exonerate, and that the decision of the jury would be ultimate and final. The men chosen to be the jury were: Joe Blair, moderator, James Puckett, Dan Farmer, Harold Haas, Reford Wilson, Joe Grizzle, James Murray, DeArthur Yandell, Burl True, Edwin Wade, J. R. Hall, Dan Harper, Wyman Straughan, Jerry Dudley, Frank Wiley, Bill Jones, and Frank Giles.

---

[128] Minutes of the First Oklahoma District Association of Free Will Baptists, Proceedings of the Eighty-Second Annual Session, February 17, 1979, page 11.
[129] Minutes of the First Oklahoma District Association, 1978-1979, page 13.
[130] Minutes of the First Oklahoma District Association, page 12.
[131] Minutes of the First Oklahoma District Association, Proceedings of the Eighty-Third Annual Session, February 16, 1980, pages 5-6.

The formal charges brought against Archie Joe "Dusty" Cooksey, and on which he was tried, were as follows:

1. Archie Joe "Dusty" Cooksey has departed from the traditional and contemporary Free Will Baptist position of "verbal and plenary inspiration" in his insisting that scriptural inspiration is to interpret "generically." Generically interpretation is understood to be that the Bible is accepted as a whole and not necessarily in all its parts. We charge Archie Joe "Dusty" Cooksey is in error in his position of verbal and plenary inspiration.

2. In direct examination Archie Joe "Dusty" Cooksey affirms the Bible to be acceptable and authoritative only in matters of faith and cannot be trusted in other matters; i. e., science, history, cosmogony. This is in open conflict with traditional Free Will Baptist position that the Scriptures are "God's revealed word to man," and that inspiration extends even to the choice of words. The "expressed words" (I Timothy 4:1) are of extreme importance and not just a general principle as affirmed by Archie Joe "Dusty" Cooksey. Thus, we charge Archie Joe "Dusty" Cooksey [is] in error in his view of Biblical inerrancy.

3. Our examination of Archie Joe "Dusty" Cooksey has revealed that he sees contradictions in the Word of God. Traditional Free Will Baptist (*sic*) hold the Word of God to be true and correct in all its teachings and is without error or contradiction. We, therefore, charge Archie Joe "Dusty" Cooksey with error in his view of Biblical inerrancy in charging the Bible to hold certain contradictions.

4. Archie Joe "Dusty" Cooksey has affirmed the position that the Bible is not the "Word of God as it lies on a table, it is just another book full of so many words." The traditional view of Free Will Baptist (*sic*) is "All scripture is given by inspiration of God, and is profitable for doctrine, for reproof, for correction, for instruction in righteousness" II Timothy 3:16. It (the Bible) is the revealed Word of God whether there is human interaction or not. Thus, we charge Archie Joe "Dusty" Cooksey to be in error in his statement disputing the reality of the revealed Word of God.

5. Our examination reveals that Archie Joe "Dusty" Cooksey leans toward pseudonymity, declaring that "there is much evidence to merit consideration of this view." This is in open conflict with the Free Will Baptist position that the Bible is correct in all of its statements and all books declaring authorship are accepted as truth and without question. We, therefore, charge Archie Joe "Dusty" Cooksey with being in error in casting doubt upon the authenticity of the declared authorship of certain books of the Bible.

6. Our examination has revealed Archie Joe "Dusty" Cooksey to be in gross error in his interpretation of Christian ethics, particularly as it applies to the absolutes of God. Free Will Baptists hold the Word of God to teach the "devil is the father of all lies," a lie is a sin, "all liars shall have their place in the lake of fire." This is an absolute and never viewed as relative nor subject to situational interpretation. To view the possibility that a "lie" is acceptable to God, is contrary to any positive teaching in the Scriptures. We, therefore, charge Archie Joe "Dusty" Cooksey with error in his position of Christian ethics.

Credential Board:
Dan L. Farmer, Chairman
Jerry Dudley, Secretary
James Puckett, Jim Cearley and Dan Harper, members[132]

---

[132] From the report of the Credential Board of the First Oklahoma District Association.

The formal trial of Dusty Cooksey occurred on June 9, 1979, at the First Free Will Baptist Church of Norman, Oklahoma. A lengthy discussion and full explanation by Dusty Cooksey of his doctrinal and ethical views was conducted in a good Christian manner. The jury, voting by secret ballot, by a vote of ten (10) to six (6), found Archie Joe "Dusty" Cooksey to be in error in his doctrinal and ethical persuasion. The jury recommended that he surrender his ministerial credentials to his church.[133]

Three observations are in order. First, when Dennis Haygood and I, upon hearing Dusty's views on the inspiration and inerrancy of the Bible, informed the Midessa District Association in Texas that Dusty's views were unscriptural and unacceptable to Free Will Baptists, and Dusty was allowed to informally defend his views to the association, the other pastors saw no problem with his views. The reason was that they were men who were either not trained or were insufficiently trained for the ministry. They were oilfield workers or automotive mechanics by vocation who were pastors by avocation. They were, therefore, not able to discern any error in Dusty's theological views. The state moderator and state executive secretary met at length with Dusty in Abilene, but they, too, discerned no error because they, too, were untrained or insufficiently trained. The moderator stated that he was "not well read" on the subject.

Second, when Dusty moved to Oklahoma and applied for admission to the First Oklahoma District Association for membership as an ordained minister, the pastors there, who were well aware of Dusty's views, were for the most part well trained men in Bible and theology and thus capable of discerning the errors of Dusty's theological views.

Third, though Dusty's ministry was ended among Free Will Baptists, thus he paid a high price for his errors, the men who paid the highest price were Dennis Haygood and I. That statement may sound self-serving, yet it is true. It is shocking how many false reports and vicious rumors were spread across the denomination verbally and in writing, especially about what "troublemakers" we were. The effect of all of this negativity toward us for doing what we knew to be right greatly curtained our ministries for the better part of forty years, costing us numerous ministerial opportunities.

Thus came to end the inspiration debate which had started in the Midessa District Association in West Texas in 1976, had moved on to the Texas State Association in 1977, and had finally been settled by the National Association in 1979, and the First Oklahoma District Association. The entire story was an unfortunate part of the history of the Free Will Baptist work in Texas. It is unfortunate that it spilled over into the entire denomination. At least one good thing came out of it, Texas Free Will Baptists influenced the modification and expansion of the simple statement in the *Treatise* on the subject of the inspiration of the Scriptures, clarifying what we had always believed about inspiration and inerrancy.

Sixty-Sixth Annual Session - 1980

The sixty-sixth annual session of the Texas State Association convened with the East Texas District Association, meeting at the Community Center in Henderson, June 4-6, 1980. The theme was "This Is the Victory." The following district associations represented: Northwest Brazos, East Texas, Midessa, Mission, West Fork, and Central Texas. Sixty-four local churches represented by letter and fees, fourteen more than the previous year. One of the reasons for this was perhaps the existence of some new or nearly new churches and missions, such as United in Bryan, Lighthouse in Temple, Cornerstone in College Station, First Church in Grand Prairie, the Garland Church,

---

[133] Minutes of the First Oklahoma District Association, 1979-80, page 8.

Levelland, Forest Park in San Angelo, Seventh Street in Abilene, First Alto, and First Church in McAllen. Raymond Lee was moderator[134] and Billy Walker was the clerk. Don Ellis brought what the clerk called "a tremendous message" on "It Is Finished" on Wednesday evening. Apparently Thursday was spent conducting the CTS competition and possibly a youth service. The clerk did not record these events. Two hundred fourteen people registered for the meeting.

The business part of the state meeting began on Thursday evening, June 5. Mike Wade preached on the subject "It Is Written," using Matthew 4:4 as his text. Brother Wade and Betty Kelly then presented the Church Training Service competitive awards. The body voted to give the following directive to the Mission Church-Extension Board:

> That any property or properties purchased or obtained by or for a joint project of this State and the National Home Mission Board include in its deed or title to said property a stipulation that in the event said church or mission cease to be an active Free Will Baptist church or mission, control of said property reverts to the Texas State Mission and Church Extension Board.

The body voted to delete the Temperance Committee from the constitution. H. Z. Cox preached on the subject "It Is I," using Matthew 14:27 as his text. The clerk noted "A good lunch was enjoyed by all, thanks to the Holiday Inn." The body voted to ask each church in the state to raise one hundred dollars toward the cost of entertaining the National Association in 1982 in Fort Worth. The body voted to purchase the Cornerstone Book Store in Sherman, which would serve as a walk-in book store. Executive secretary Allen Moore reported that the state association had more than met its 1979 budget.

Sixty-Seventh Annual Session - 1981

The sixty-seventh annual session of the Texas State Association convened with the Midessa District Association, meeting at the Westside Free Will Baptist Church in Midland, June

Building the Church of God
Beverly K. Welch
Texas State Association 1981
Matthew 16:18

---

[134] Former moderator Earl Scroggins had moved to Ardmore, Oklahoma.

3-5, 1981. Raymond Lee was the moderator and Billy Walker the clerk. The theme was "Building the Church." Brother Lee's daughter, Beverly Welch, had written a chorus for use at the state meeting, entitled "Building the Church of God." It went:

All six district associations reported (Northwest Brazos, East Texas, Midessa, Mission, West Fork, and Central Texas), along with fifty-four of the state's seventy-two Free Will Baptist churches. The theme chorus "Building the Church," written by Mrs. Beverly (Lee) Welch,[135] was sung throughout the meeting. On Wednesday evening the message was delivered by Dr. Melvin Worthington on the subject "Building the Church," using Matthew 16:13, 20 as his text. Thursday was used for the state CTS competitive activities and youth service, which were not recorded in the minutes.

The session was called to order on Thursday evening by clerk Billy Walker. Awards for the winners of the CTS competition were given in the service. Brother Lee's moderator's message emphasized that Texas Free Will Baptists needed influence, good leaders, more faithful support, members who were not lazy, faithful members, and each other. Dr. Melvin Worthington, executive secretary of the National Association of Free Will Baptists, preached a second sermon, this one entitled "Building the Church Through the Great Commission."

On Friday morning the devotional continued for so long that Moderator Lee literally pulled on the man's coat tails and told him it was time to stop, which he did reluctantly. In the business session the body authorized executive secretary Allen Moore to borrow up to fifteen thousand dollars for stock and working capital for the Cornerstone Book Store, 107 South Travis Street, in Sherman. A related motion passed stating that if Brother Moore was to be relieved of his duties as executive secretary, the Texas State Association would assume all liabilities of the book store, which were in his name, because the liabilities had been authorized by the state association. Allen Moore was elected to the position of executive secretary for an indefinite term. Dr. Melvin Worthington brought a third message, this one entitled "Building the Church of God In Light of the Organization That Has Been Given to Us," using Acts 1:8 as his text.

There was somewhat of a movement, on the quiet, among some of the young pastors to oust Allen Moore from his position as executive secretary. About half a dozen of them met in a hotel room to try to find a way to get him removed from the office.[136] They discussed the possibility of anonymously printing and mailing a parody of *The Texas Challenge* to the churches, emphasizing his shortcomings as an editor. Nothing ever came of this meeting, but it did indicate that there was growing opposition to Brother Moore.

LaVerne Lee, the wife of moderator Raymond Lee, was present in a wheel chair, suffering from Amyotrophic Lateral Sclerosis (Lou Gerhrig's Disease). She went home to be with the Lord on June 19, 1982, just over a year later.

Sixty-Eighth Annual Session - 1982

The sixty-eighth annual session of the state association convened with the newly formed Rio Grande Valley District Association, meeting at the First Free Will Baptist Church of McAllen, June 9-11, 1982. Raymond Lee was the moderator and Billy Walker was the clerk. The theme was "Add to Your Faith." Larry Powell was the host pastor. Six district associations represented. The clerk did not name them, but they would have been East Texas, Central Texas, Midessa,

---

[135] Wife of Lee Roy Welch and daughter of moderator Raymond Lee.
[136] I was invited to the meeting but was present only as an observer, not wishing to be part of any subterfuge.

Mission, Northwest Brazos, and West Fork. The Rio Grande Valley District Association petitioned the association for membership and was admitted. Forty-three churches represented.

Three sermons were preached during the state meeting worship services. They were "Add Distinctives to Your Faith" by Tom Hampton, Wednesday evening; "Add Directions to Your Faith" by George Hyatt, Thursday evening; and "Add Demands to Your Faith" by Dennis Henderson, Friday morning. On Thursday morning, during the youth service, Jim Mullen preached a memorable sermon on the fact that what one is known for is often what one does early in life, therefore all young people should be careful to not make serious mistakes which will brand them for life. This was a rather remarkable sermon.

James Munsey brought a large contingent of the members of the Templo Free Will Baptist Church, which would later be called the Primera Iglesia Bautista Libre, in Weslaco.

Moderator Raymond Lee presented a plaque to Vivian Moore, recognizing and lauding her service through the Cornerstone Christian Book Store in Sherman. A large contingent of young people attended to participate in the CTS competitive activities.

Most of the business was routine, but one resolution concerning Free Will Baptist Bible College was presented due to what was then simply being called "the wine issue." The resolution read:

> Whereas, Free Will Baptist Bible College has recently been the subject of severe criticism by some brethren in our denomination; and Whereas, we believe that such criticism is without validity; therefore, Be it resolved, That the Texas State Association of Free Will Baptists reaffirm its confidence in the administration, faculty, and staff of Free Will Baptist Bible College. Be it further resolved, That a copy of this resolution be sent to *Contact*[137] for publication.

The controversy had begun when a student asked professor Leroy Forlines in class if the wine Jesus turned the water into in John 2 was real wine. Mr. Forlines answered, correctly, honestly, and truthfully, that it was. After class the student called his pastor in Alabama and told him what Mr. Forlines had said. That particular pastor was well known for seizing upon any issues available and making them matters of major controversy in the denomination. He was soon joined by a large number of other influential and vocal pastors in vicious attacks upon Mr. Forlines and Free Will Baptist Bible College. To those pastors the idea that Jesus turned water into real wine was "an intolerable position." This controversy eventually gave birth to Southeastern Free Will Baptist College in Wendell, North Carolina.

A second resolution, which failed, indicates that there was considerable discussion or even debate over whether the position of the state executive secretary should return to a part-time situation. The resolution read:

> Be it resolved, That the Texas State Executive Committee take a written poll of our Texas ministers concerning their feelings about returning to a part time situation for our Executive Secretary, and that the results of this poll be shared with the state by way of the *Challenge*.

A third resolution called upon the Free Will Baptist people of Texas to remember Brother and Sister Raymond Lee in prayer. Brother Lee's wife, LaVerne, had been diagnosed with

---

[137] *Contact* was the name of the denominational magazine before it combined with departmental newsletters and became *One Magazine*.

Amyotrophic Lateral Sclerosis, commonly known as ALS or Lou Gehrig's Disease. She went home to be with the Lord on June 19, 1982.

National Association of Free Will Baptists

The National Association of Free Will Baptists convened July 18-22, 1982, at the Tarrant County Convention Center in Fort Worth, the third time the convention had met in Texas. The theme of the annual convocation was "Fundamentals of the faith." 3,172 registered for the convention, each attendee counted only once. All in all it was a wonderful national convention with good preaching, great music, and wonderful fellowship. However, for some time there had been fomenting an issue which was bringing serious divisiveness to the denomination: the wine issue. The issue had exploded across the denomination like wildfire, revealing the fact that the Free Will Baptist denomination was divided into two camps on the wine issue, and bringing Free Will Baptist Bible College, and specifically Leroy Forlines, under severe and often unchristian attack.

The wine issue became the *de facto* theme of the 1982 national convention. For one thing there was a rather large gathering of hundreds of pastors and interested parties for the purpose of discussing the wine issue and its implications. The attendees were introduced to the idea, born in the minds of the disgruntled pastors, mostly from the Southeast, of starting a new Free Will Baptist college which would teach that the wine Jesus made was not fermented wine, along with some other issues on which these pastors disagreed with the position of Free Will Baptist Bible College, and the denomination at large.

The wine issue dominated much of the discussion in the association's business sessions, as well as smaller discussions in the hallways of the convention center, the exhibit area, and the lobbies of the various convention hotels. Several resolutions were introduced through the Resolutions Committee relative to the wine issue. One resolution called for a seven member study committee, consisting of people who represented all sides of the issue, be appointed by the moderator to deal with the issue and report back at the 1983 session of the National Association. This resolution met such opposition that it was tabled, effectively killing it. Another resolution recognized the deep concern over the wine issue as evidenced by a large number of resolutions passed by various state associations and local groups on the wine issue, and recognizing that all sides of the issue believed in total abstinence from alcoholic beverages, and the complete sinlessness of Christ. The resolution called upon all parties to accept the statements in the Free Will Baptist Covenant as an adequate answer to our concerns on the wine issue. This resolution was adopted.

Another resolution condemning Free Will Baptist Bible College for distributing a printed explanation of their stand on the wine issue, called "The Record Speaks," was introduced. Due to the divisiveness of the resolution and the caustic attitudes of many, a motion was made to object to the consideration of the question. The motion was sustained and the subject was dropped. The issue wasn't over, however. Southeastern Free Will Baptist College was established in 1983 in the Gateway Free Will Baptist Church in Virginia Beach, Virginia. Soon land was purchased and a campus built in Wendell, North Carolina. A further effect of the wine issue was that many churches redirected their financial support, and students, from Free Will Baptist Bible College to Southeastern, along with their support for other denominational ministries, such as Foreign and Home Missions. For all practical purposes the wine issue created a split in the denomination, greatly weakening an already small denomination.

Sixty-Ninth Annual Session - 1983

The sixty-ninth annual session of the state association convened with the Northwest Brazos District Association, meeting at the Ramada Inn in Amarillo, June 8-10, 1983. Raymond Lee was the moderator and Billy Walker was the clerk. A request from a Fellowship Association for membership in the state association was presented to the General Board. The General Board passed a motion that the request for membership be referred to the Executive Board for clarification and recommendation. There is no further mention of this association in the 1983 minutes. In the executive board meeting, January 20-21, 1984, in Garland, the board decided that since they had had no further communication from the Fellowship Association they would have no recommendation to the state association concerning them.

The theme of the 1983 meeting was "Lift Up a Standard - God's Word." The theme chorus "Lift Up God's Standard" was written by Clarence Hearron. The West Fork, Central, Mission, Midessa, East Texas, and Northwest Brazos districts were represented. Ron Ivey, pastor of the Free Will Baptist Church in Lubbock, voiced his opposition to the seating of the Faith Free Will Baptist Church in Lubbock because the pastor had been divorced and remarried. The church was seated.

The sermons delivered were "Jesus Christ Our Standard" by Bill Jones, on Wednesday evening; "Proclaiming the Word of God - Our Standard, Jesus Christ" by Don Ellis, on Thursday evening; and "The Practiced Standard" by Clarence Hearron, on Friday morning. Thursday was occupied with the CTS competitive activities and youth service. On Thursday night Bobby Ferguson introduced a song which had been written by one of the ladies of his church, "I'm Going to Climb Right Up Those Mountains."

The body voted to adopt a recommendation forwarded through the General Board that the state association sponsor a family oriented old fashioned camp meeting in 1984. This idea had originally been to have a two or three days meeting of leaders in the state for the purpose of making both short term and long term plans for a workable program to improve and advance the Free Will Baptist work in Texas. However, it was then suggested that what the state needed most was unity and that the best way to achieve that would be a camp meeting with the leaders of the state and their families present.

One of the most significant things to happen at the state meeting in 1983 was that Ron Ivey voiced his opinion strongly that executive secretary Allen Moore be terminated. Pastor Ivy presented a number of complaints. Several people stood to speak, some for retaining Brother Moore and some for letting him go. The discussion wasn't always sweet and Christlike. In the end Brother Moore was able to retain his job. However, at a called meeting of the Executive Board at the Garland Free Will Baptist Church, on September 17, 1983, Allen Moore submitted his resignation as executive secretary, effective October 15, 1983. The responsibility of overseeing the Cornerstone Book Store was given to Clarence Hearron. The task of handling the state office finances was given to Billy Walker.

There was another called meeting of the executive board, November 18-19, 1983, again at the Garland Free Will Baptist Church. The board spent the day and evening on Friday the 18th discussing the office of executive secretary. They continued their meeting on Saturday, November 19th. They hired Billy Walker as the new executive secretary, subject to the ratification of the state association at the next state meeting in June of 1984.

Another Fellowship Association

A request from a Fellowship Association for membership in the state association was presented to the General Board in 1983. The General Board passed a motion that the request for membership be referred to the Executive Board for clarification and recommendation. There is no further mention of this association in the 1983 minutes. However, in the executive board meeting, January 20-21, 1984, in Garland, the board decided that since they had had no further communication from the Fellowship Association they would have no recommendation to the state association concerning them.[138]

Seventieth Annual Session - 1984

The seventieth annual session of the Texas State Association met at the First Free Will Baptist Church of Duncanville, June 6-8, 1984. Raymond Lee was the moderator and Larry Cox served as the clerk. Billy Walker had been appointed as executive secretary on November 19, 1983. Theme was "Let's Get Together," which was reflected in the sermons preached by Dr. Jack. L. Wlliams, editor of *Contact* magazine: "Learning to Labor Together." "Learning to Live Together," and "Learning to Give Together." The theme chorus was" Learning to Lean." The following district associations represented: Central, Mission, Midessa, and West Fork.

The body voted to close the Cornerstone Christian Bookstore in Sherman and voted to elect Billy Walker as State Executive Secretary, replacing Allen Moore. The body adopted a resolution that the Free Will Baptist churches of Texas endeavor to increase their membership by 15% during the following year and report the results at the next state meeting. No plans as to how they should do this were mentioned.

There was a large number of young people participating in the Church Training Service competitive activities, under the direction of James Munsey. The Thursday morning worship service was a youth service and Thurmon Murphy preached on the subject "Can a Young Person Live a Christian Life Today?"

The Board of Christian Education had surveyed the sixty-six Free Will Baptist churches in Texas in an effort to ascertain attendance figures. They reported that the average Sunday school attendance of the sixty reporting churches during 1983 had been 37. The number would have been smaller if the six non-reporting churches had responded to the survey. Each of those six non-reporting churches were smaller in attendance than 37[139]. Only two churches had an average attendance in Sunday school of over 100. Seventeen churches averaged 50 or better. Forty-three churches averaged lower than 50. Thirty-four churches had 30 or less in Sunday school. One church reported having no Sunday school at all. The Christian Education Board announced that the Minister's and Laymen's Retreat had been changed to the Men and Women's Retreat. The annual retreat had become so popular that the women wanted to be able to attend, too. Speakers for the retreat, to be held at the Lazy Hills Guest Ranch near Ingram, were announced as Mrs. Mabel Willey and Dr. Jack L. Williams.

The association promoted a family oriented, old fashioned camp meeting to be held at the Piney Woods Camp in East Texas in August. The stated purpose of the camp meeting was to foster unity in the state association as a prelude to involving all of the Free Will Baptist churches

---

[138] 1983 state minutes, page 7; 1984 state minutes, page 5.
[139] How did the board know they were small? I was the one who took the survey and I knew about how many these churches were running in Sunday school.

in Texas in the state work.

The camp meeting was held as planned but attendance was small, with many of the pastors not attending at all. One East Texas pastor came for one service because he was scheduled to preach. This small attendance created a financial shortfall to the extent that some of the churches had to raise funds to pay for the meeting.

Seventy-First Annual Session - 1985

The seventy-first annual session of the Texas State Association convened with the Fellowship Free Will Baptist Church, 1406 Ursuline Avenue, Bryan, Texas, on June 5-7, 1985. Raymond Lee was the moderator and Larry Cox was the clerk.

Sermons were preached by Bobby Ferguson, Larry Cox, and James Munsey.

Executive Secretary Billy Walker reported that forty-four of Texas' sixty-four churches had reported to the state association, along with seven districts, which were not named in the minutes. Those district associations would have been the Midessa, East Texas, Central Texas, Mission, Rio Grande, Northwest Brazos, and West Fork. Thirty-one ministers, fifty-five delegates, and one hundred nine registered attendees were counted. The estimated attendance on Wednesday evening was 275, and 215 for Thursday evening. Attendance was very good.

The General Board recommended to the body that the State Home Missions Board take James Munsey under their supervision and advice for home mission operations in Texas and Mexico, and that he be accountable to the mission board for his operations. The body voted that the mission board act in an advisory capacity to Brother Munsey.

James Munsey reported that, compared to recent years, participation in the Church Training Service (CTS) competition was tremendous. He also stated that Texas had been represented in twenty different categories in the national C. T. S. competition, with 17 of the 20 receiving a number one rating.

The association voted to invite the National Association of Free Will Baptists to have their annual convention in Texas in 1996.

Seventy-Second Annual Session - 1986

The seventy-second annual session of the Texas State Association convened June 11-13, 1986, at the First Free Will Baptist Church of Henderson. H. Z. Cox, chosen by the Executive Board and General Board, served as moderator for the session, Raymond Lee having left the state. Larry Cox was the clerk. The honorable Lester Brown, mayor of Henderson, welcomed the association. Dr. Stanley Outlaw, professor of Bible at Free Will Baptist Bible College, preached three sermons during the association.

Executive Secretary Billy Walker reported that giving to outside causes was up $15,000 dollars over the previous year, but that support for the state office was down by $4,000.00, preventing him from serving full-time. Outside giving for the year was $117,813.67, and giving to the state office was $23,694.06.

The Board of Christian Education reported that participation in the C. T. S. competitive activities was excellent, with good results, and reported that the Men's and Women's Retreat at the Twin Elms Guest Ranch in Bandera, with Dr. Ken Riggs, professor at Free Will Baptist Bible College, as speaker, had been exceptionally successful.

Seventy-Third Annual Session - 1987

The seventy-third annual session of the state association convened with the Midessa District Association, meeting at the Odessa Hilton in Odessa, Texas, June 17-19, 1987. The date of the state meeting had been changed in order to get the use of the Hilton for the meeting. Bobby Ferguson served as moderator and Thurmon Murphy as the clerk. Bobby Ferguson was acting executive secretary, Billy Walker having left the state. The theme of the meeting was "Exalting Christ," which was developed in the sermons preached at the meeting: "Christ in You, the Hope of Glory" by Ron Parker, "The Pre-eminence of Christ" by Dwain Crosby, and "The All-Sufficiency of Christ" by Frank Cope. Moderator Bobby Ferguson gave the moderator's message entitled "They Understood the Times and They Knew What to Do" (1 Chronicles 12:32). Charismatic of Brother Ferguson, this message was insightful and powerful.

The following associations represented: East Texas, Central Texas, Midessa, Mission, and West Fork.

A large number of young people were present at the state meeting to participate in the CTS competitive activities and the Music and Arts Festival. These young people, both individuals and groups, ministered to the delegates through music and a puppet show.

The Executive Board had been working since January on a budget and a revised job description for the position of executive secretary. These were presented through the General Board and adopted by the body. They listed the duties of the executive secretary under five headings: Representation, Communication, Counselor, Treasurer, and Accountability.

Seventy-Fourth Annual Session - 1988

The seventy-fourth annual session of the Texas State Association convened with the Mission District Association, meeting at the Ramada Inn-Bayfront in Corpus Christi, June 8-10, 1988. Bobby Ferguson was the moderator and Thurmon Murphy was the clerk. Brother Ferguson was also acting executive secretary. With the state not having an executive secretary, Bill Jones served as acting editor of *The Texas Challenge* and Frank Cope served as acting treasurer. The following district associations represented: Mission, West Fork, East Texas, and Central Texas. Sixty churches were members of the state association.

The theme of the 1988 state meeting was "Holy Living." This theme was extremely well developed in the Wednesday evening message, "The Holiness of God," by F. Leroy Forlines, professor of Bible and Theology at Free Will Baptist Bible College. It was a classic, foundational sermon, and thoroughly practical in its application. Mr. Forlines followed up with two more sermons during the meeting: "Building Convictions" and "Maintaining Sexual Purity."

Attendance for the meeting was good. There were 250 people present for the Wednesday evening worship service, and 150 present on Thursday evening. The state reported 60 churches in Texas, with 29 full-time pastors and 14 part-time pastors. The Woman's Auxiliary presented missionary to Japan Dwain Crosby with a check in the amount of $3,455.85. The state association was riding a several years crest of high attendance, not only in general attendance but also in the young people who attended for the C. T. S. competitive activities.

Once again there was a large contingent of young people present, participating in the C. T. S competition. They body voted for the Board of Christian Education to conduct future C. T. S competition separate and apart from the state meeting. *This was, therefore, the last state meeting at which there was a large number of young people present.* The body also voted for the Executive Committee to begin planning for state meetings two years in advance.

I had been asked to design a full color brochure which would be suitable for each local church to use to advertise its presence and ministry in their communities. It contained blank areas on one side which could be filled in by each local church to make the brochure personal to that church. They were attractive and inexpensive to the local churches.

Planning Session

Later in the year, September 29-30, 1988, the Executive Board, the Missions-Church Extension Board, and the Board of Christian Education met at the West Fork Youth Camp, near Vashti, Texas, to formulate a ten year program of growth for the last decade of the twentieth century, culminating in the year 2000. The theme "TOGETHER WE GROW: A Decade Dedicated to Discipleship and Development" was adopted. Much of the discussion concerned a strong ten year mission's emphasis. The goal of planting three new churches by the year 2000, in San Antonio, Austin, and the Dallas-Fort Worth Metroplex was adopted. The joint group decided to recommend to the state association that the following printed material be written and made available to the churches:

- Visitation brochures (the one mentioned above was already available)
- A brochure and/or booklet on who Free Will Baptists were historically and doctrinally (Never completed)
- New converts' lessons (never completed)
- Discipleship lessons for use in home Bible studies (never completed)
- Elective Sunday school lessons on tithing and stewardship (never completed)
- A self-evaluation brochure for churches wanting to grow (never completed)
- A booklet explaining the ten year program, along with suggestions for individual churches, to be given to each Free Will Baptist church in the state (completed)
The Executive Board adopted themes for the next five state association meetings as follows:
    - 1990 - Missions
    - 1991 - The Church and Its Pastor
    - 1992 - Church Growth and Evangelism
    - 1993 - Leadership
    - 1994 - Stewardship

Executive Board Meeting

The Executive Board met at the All Boards Meeting, January 27-28, 1989, in College Station to plan the 1989 state meeting. Assistant clerk Frank Cope had moved to Arkansas and the board appointed me, as clerk, to serve as acting treasurer. Thus began the expansion of my responsibilities. The boards agreed to finish their business on Friday evening so they could attend the funeral of Brenda Joann (Bankhead) Arnold, eldest daughter of Jack and Wanda Bankhead, the next day.

Seventy-Fifth Annual Session - 1989

The seventy-fifth annual session of the Texas State Association convened with the Rio Grande District Association, meeting June 7-9, 1989, at the First Free Will Baptist Church, 3801 North Second Street, in McAllen, and the Templo Free Will Baptist Church in Weslaco. Bobby Ferguson served as moderator and acting executive secretary. Thurmon Murphy was the clerk. He gave a brief history of the Texas State Association before calling the session to order. He presented commemorative coffee mugs celebrating the 75th session of the association. Colorful bumper stickers were also available which said "I Love My Free Will Baptist Church." Commemorative letter openers were distributed.

Six district associations represented: Central Texas, East Texas, Mission, Northwest Brazos, Rio Grande, and West Fork. Forty-two of Texas' fifty-five churches represented by letter and dues. One hundred fifty-three people registered for the meeting. Moderator Bobby Ferguson, in his moderator's message, stated that to be faithful one had to have the following abilities: compatibility, adaptability, responsibility, dependability, availability, and sociability. Continuing the association's theme of "Faithfulness," three sermons were preached during the meeting. Arnold Shrewsbury, pastor of the First Free Will Baptist Church of Carthage, preached on "God Is Faithful." David Sutton, pastor of the First Free Will Baptist Church of Duncanville, preached "God Requires Faithfulness." Roy Wilson, pastor of the Northcrest Free Will Baptist Church in Victoria, preached "God Rewards Faithfulness."

The music was especially good at the seventy-fifth session of the association, and the body expressed hearty appreciation. Mark and Tracy Jones, Mark Brawley, Everett Hellard, and

Templo Free Will Baptist Church, Weslaco, Texas, founded by James Munsey. The name was later changed to Primera Iglesia Bautista Libre, under Munsey's leadership.

Hilarino Gonzales all sang specials and/or led the congregational singing. Ava Hellard, her daughter Everyl Getz, and Everyl's daughter Tanya Getz, three generations in one family, sang "All Because of God's Amazing Grace."

The Pastor's Conference, part of the ten year program, met for the first time. Joel Kircher, pastor of the Cornerstone Free Will Baptist Church in Denison, formerly the First Free Will Baptist Church, preached the inaugural Pastor's Conference sermon entitled "Knowing God." James Munsey, pastor of the Templo Free Will Baptist Church in Weslaco, preached "Keep the Doors Open."

In the business sessions the body adopted the ten year program, "TOGETHER WE GROW: A Decade Dedicated to Discipleship and Development." Rita McDuffie was elected to serve the association as assistant clerk. Though one state officer said that a woman had no business being on a board with a bunch of men, no one could have served with greater distinction. Bobby Ferguson gave up his position as moderator. The body stood to their feet to show their appreciation for the work of the executive board the last three years under his excellent leadership. In his report of the State Mission Board pastor David Sutton expressed sincere appreciation to Roy Norie for his long and faithful years of service on the board.

Several missionaries were present and participated in the meeting, contributing greatly to the spirit of the services: Ken and Marvis Eagleton, who announced that their next term in Brazil would be their last before retirement, Darryl Nichols (Ivory Coast), and Dwain Crosby (Spain).

It was stated that the 75th session of the state association was the best in recent memory. There was a special spirit of unity and purpose. Delegates were joyful to be meeting in two new Free Will Baptist churches in the Rio Grande Valley, both of which had constructed outstanding facilites. The preaching was excellent and, as noted above, the music was outstanding. A special commemorative coffee mug was sold as a memorial of the 75th annual session of the association.

Seventy-Sixth Annual Session - 1990

The seventy-sixth annual session of the Texas State Association convened with the West

First Free Will Baptist Church, McAllen, Texas, founded by Larry Powell
The name of the church was changed to McAllen Community Church in 1992 under the
leadership of Pastor Raymond Getz, who eventually took the church out of the denomination.
The church last reported to the state association in 2002.

Fork District Association, meeting at the First Free Will Baptist Church of Duncanville, June 6-9, 1990. Bill Jones was the moderator, and acting executive secretary, and Thurmon Murphy was the clerk. The last several state meetings had been unusually good and that would continue through this meeting and for more than ten years to come. In a sense the association was in its heyday, its stage or period of greatest vigor, strength, and success.

Seven district associations represented, which were the West Fork, East Texas, Central Texas, Northwest Brazos, Mission, Rio Grande Valley, and the Midessa. This was the last year the Mission District reported. It would cease to exist because most of its churches died. The Permian Basin District Association was admitted to membership in the state association. It consisted of the First Free Will Baptist Church of Odessa, the First Free Will Baptist Church of Kermit, and the Landmark Free Will Baptist Church of Odessa. Interestingly, a motion was made and passed directing the moderator to contact and attempt to reconcile the churches of the Midessa and Permian Basin associations, both of West Texas. Forty-nine of the fifty-five churches in the state association represented by letter. The theme of the session was "Missions: The Necessity." Expounding on that theme Fred Warner, Director of Missionary/Church Relations of the Free Will Baptist Foreign Missions Department, spoke three times. His messages were "Missions: The Necessity of a Strong Home Base," "Missions: The Necessity of Fulfilling the Great Commission," and "Missions: The Necessity of Sacrificial Support."

The Pastor's Conference featured two sermons. Dr. Charles Thigpen, retiring president of Free Will Baptist Bible College spoke on "The Church: Its Message." Keith Stewart, pastor of the Garland Free Will Baptist Church, spoke on "Presence of Mind." Brother Stewart soon left the denomination and took the Garland church with him.

Business conducted at the meeting consisted of the usual committee and board reports. Some of the highlights were:
- The mission board announced plans to start a new church in Austin (with missionary Keith Woody) and announced plans to purchase property in Plano for the mission church there (with missionary Don Guthrie).
- Plans were announced to have the next state meeting in Austin in order to focus the attention of Texas Free Will Baptists on the city of Austin as the next target city for the State Home Missions Board.
- With Texas not having an executive secretary, Bill Jones was acting executive secretary, Dale Smith was acting editor of *The Texas Challenge,* and Thurmon Murphy was acting treasurer.
- Everyl Getz, president of the Woman's Auxiliary, announced that their state project for the following year would be to raise $6,000.00 for missions and missions students, with the money for missions going to Mike and Deleen Cousineau (Africa) and Darryl and Lila Nichols (Africa).

It must be noted that once again the preaching and devotionals were outstanding, the music was superb, the fellowship was sweet and upbeat, and the business was conducted in unity and harmony, with an atmosphere of confidence and high expectations. Delegates left the meeting with a sense that they had been revived and that good days were ahead for the Free Will Baptist work in Texas. These were good times.

Chapter 6

1991 to 2000

In 1989 the state association had adopted the ten year theme: "TOGETHER WE GROW: A Decade Dedicated to Discipleship and Development." It was in many respects a bold plan for the future growth of the Free Will Baptist work in Texas. Part of the plan was already being implemented early in the decade, with intentions of carrying out all of the plan over the ten year period. Texas at least had a plan and was working to achieve the adopted goals of church growth and church planting. The state association had a plan and knew the direction in which they were supposed to be going. The themes of the various state meetings initially reflected the "TOGETHER WE GROW" program.

Seventy-Seventh Annual Session - 1991

The seventy-seventh annual session of the state association convened with the Central Texas District association, meeting at the Airport Ramada & Conference Center, 5660 N. Interstate 35, Austin, Texas, June 5-7, 1991. This was the first of several state meetings in Austin, all of which were for the purpose of focusing attention on Austin as the location for the planting of the next Free Will Baptist church under the auspices of the State Home Missions Board. Bill Jones served as moderator and Thurmon Murphy as clerk. The following district associations represented: Central Texas, East Texas, Northwest Brazos, Permian Basin, Rio Grande Valley, West Fork, and the Midessa. This was the first year the First Free Will Baptist Church of McAllen reported under the name Valley Community Church.

The theme of the 1991 state meeting was "Church Growth and Evangelism," which had originally been adopted as the 1992 theme. The preaching followed that theme carefully. Bobby Ferguson preached "Ten Reasons Why Evangelism Should Be the Number One Priority of the Church." In actuality he listed seventeen reasons. Doug Little, pastor of the First Free Will Baptist Church in Russellville, Arkansas, preached "Prayer: Unlocking God's Power for Evangelism." Luther Sanders preached on "Discipleship: the Neglected Part of Evangelism." During the Pastor's Conference Doug Little preached "Making Worship More Meaningful in the Local Church." He listed six things which would make our worship more meaningful: prayer, praise, participation, preaching, planning, and patience. Deleen Cousineau and Mabel Willey spoke to the Woman's Auxiliary.

In addition to the usual committee and board reports the association conducted the following business and/or shared the following information:

- The state voted to purchase a Macintosh desktop publishing system, the price not to exceed $7,492.95, for use in the "state office."
- A budget of $16,700.00 was adopted for the state office.

- Outside giving through the state office for 1990 was $99,189.49.
- Missions giving for 1990 totaled $173,323.41.
- Of the 27 churches reporting on Texas'own Roll Call Sunday, two churches had more than 200 in attendance (Houston First - 257; Duncanville First - 219) and three had more than 100 in attendance (United Bryan - 162; Evergreen - 132; and Fellowship Bryan - 109). Nine of the remaining churches had more than 50 in attendance, and the rest had less than 50.
- The Mission Board announced that the monies from the sale of the Faith Free Will Baptist Church in San Antonio, being held for another work in San Antonio, had been released by trustee H. Ray Berry for use in the new church to be planted in Austin.
- The Mission Board announced that they were diligently seeking the best possible location in which to purchase property for the new mission work in Austin.

The job of acting state treasurer was given to me by the Executive Board, further adding to my responsibilities to the state association and to my church.

Seventy-Eighth Annual Session - 1992

A Short Planning Session

The Executive Board of the Texas State Association met on Thursday, March 12, 1992, at the First Free Will Baptist Church of Duncanville. The board had been asked to come prepared to stay for three days primarily to make plans and proposals on how best to provide adequate funding for local church, district, state, and national ministries. It had been announced that the meeting would last from Thursday evening through Saturday morning. Many varied and diverse opinions were given on the subject but no consensus could be reached on what to suggest or present to the state. The board did reach a consensus on two things: (1) to emphasize every church involvement, and (2) that each church had the freedom of several alternatives as mechanisms for giving. Those alternatives were: (a) the Cooperative Program, (b) designated giving, (c) budgeted giving, and (d) special offerings.

The three day meeting lasted only one evening because two of the men on the board wanted to go golfing on Friday and then go home. This was not taken well by the other board members, particularly assistant moderator Raymond Getz who had come all the way from McAllen to attend the meeting and do some serious work. This was a major turning point in his involvement in the state work. This short planning session was perhaps the chief reason the elective Sunday school lessons on tithing and stewardship, which had been adopted as part of the ten year program to undergird and strengthen giving, were never written and made available to the Texas churches.

The State Meeting

The seventy-eighth annual session of the state association convened with the East Texas District Association and met June 10-12, 1992, at the Quality Hotel and Conference Center in Tyler. The theme for the meeting was "The Church and Its Pastor." Bill Jones served as moderator, and was also acting executive secretary. Thurmon Murphy was the clerk, and was also serving as acting treasurer and editor of *The Texas Challenge*. The following seven district associations represented: Central Texas, East Texas, Midessa, Northwest Brazos, Permian Basin, Rio Grande Valley, and West Fork. Forty-four of forty-nine churches represented by letter and fees.

It was noted that this was the first state meeting in fifty years which had been missed by H. Z. Cox, who was suffering from cancer. Special music was provided by numerous people and groups, including the Rejoice Ensemble from Free Will Baptist Bible College. Tom Malone, president of Free Will Baptist Bible College preached three messages: "The Preacher Saving Himself," "The Preacher Saving Those Who Hear Him," and "The Preacher Broken and Blessed." David Sutton preached at the Pastor's Conference on "Encouragement."

Don Guthrie announced that the goal of the Collin Creek Free Will Baptist Church was to be self-supporting by January of 1993. Keith Woody, who had recently been hired as a church planter, reported the good progress of the new mission in Austin and announced there was a good possibility that land for the church would soon be purchased in the northwest Austin area. They were currently meeting at 13812 N. Highway 183, Suites 2 & 3, in Austin.

Delegate fees were raised to $25.00 for each local church and to $50.00 for each district association. A recommendation from the General Board to change the constitution to allow churches in isolated areas, many miles from any other church, to be members of the state association without necessarily being members of a district association, was postponed until 1993. Total outside giving for the year was reported at $125,935.64. The adopted State Office budget for the following year was $20,000.00. It was noted that a desktop publishing system for the state office had been purchased at a cost of $4,960.16.

Among the deceased recognized in the obituary report was Philip Jeff Easley, 105 year old deacon in the Easley's Chapel Church in Comanche and son of the church's founder, R. B. Easley. Also listed was Ruel Conner, former pastor and Texas state missionary.

The Texas State Woman's Auxiliary reported that they had surpassed their $6,000.00 goal by $2,000.00, with a total of $8,351.64. They further announced that their state project for the coming year was $4,000.00 to be given to Ken and Marvis Eagleton for the retirement fund, and that the following year's project would be to raise an additional $6,000.00 for the Eagletons, bringing their total contribution to the Eagleton's retirement fund to $10,000.00.

Seventy-Ninth Annual Session - 1993

Both the Northwest Brazos and the Midessa district associations had declined their turns hosting the annual state convention. As a result the seventy-ninth annual session of the Texas State Association convened with the Rio Grande Valley District Association, meeting in the grand ballroom of the McAllen Airport Hilton Inn, in McAllen.[140] Bill Jones served as the moderator, and was serving as the acting executive secretary. Thurmon Murphy was the clerk, and he was serving as acting treasurer and editor of *The Texas Challenge*. Five district associations, down from seven the previous year, represented: Central Texas, East Texas, Midessa, Northwest Brazos, and the West Fork. Forty-two churches represented. The registration report noted that there was a decline in attendance from previous years.

The theme of the meeting was "Stewardship, You Can Make a Difference." This theme was developed in the sermons and in other presentations. Dale Smith spoke on "Giving, the

---

[140] The fact that the association met at a hotel in McAllen, rather than at the First Free Will Baptist Church, was an indication that the pastor of the church, Raymond Getz, and perhaps the church itself, was beginning the departure from the denomination. Very few members of the church attended the meeting.

Biblical Concept - Is It Right?"[141] David Sutton preached on "The Responsibility of the Steward to the Whole Task." Keith Woody preached on "Principles of Giving," drawing heavily from 2 Corinthians chapters eight and nine. Ken Harris, a deacon in the Collin Creek Free Will Baptist Church in Plano, spoke on "The Joy of Giving." Music for the meeting was again outstanding.

The proposed constitutional change which would have allowed churches in isolated areas, far removed from a district association, to be members of the state association without necessarily being members of a district association, failed in the General Board meeting. The body voted to pay clerk Thurmon Murphy $350.00 per month as a part-time employee of the state association for his work as acting state treasurer and editor of *The Texas Challenge*.

The Mission Board reported that three acres of prime land had been purchased in the Austin suburb of Cedar Park for the new church and that the first phase of the building would be completed, barring any unforeseen problems, by the time of the 1994 state meeting. Keith and Neva Woody were highly commended for their excellent work as church planters. It was noted that $90,000.00 had been transferred to the board for the work in Austin by H. Ray Berry, trustee of the funds from the sale of the Faith Church in San Antonio. An addition $21,000.00 would soon be transferred to the board from the sale of the Lighthouse Free Will Baptist Church in Temple. An additional $1,000.00 had been given by Earl Nettleton who had helped dispose of the First Free Will Baptist Church property in Austin, which had been closed for some time. The deed to the property of the Lifegate Free Will Baptist Church in Tyler was released to the church, since it had reached full-time status.

The association voted to adopt "The Together Way Plan" of the National Association of Free Will Baptists, a plan which accepted all forms of financial support, including cooperative giving and designated giving.

James Munsey provided a bus tour to Reynosa, Tamaulipas, Mexico, for delegates to see several of the Free Will Baptist churches there and to meet many of the members and pastors of those churches.

A few weeks after the association H. Z. Cox passed away on July 28, 1993.

Eightieth Annual Session - 1994

The eightieth annual session of the Texas State Association of Free Will Baptists convened with the West Fork District Association, meeting at the Sheraton Inn in Wichita Falls, June 8-10, 1994. Keith Woody served as moderator due to the fact that Bill Jones had moved to Oklahoma. Thurmon Murphy was the clerk. Five district associations represented: Central Texas, East Texas, Midessa, Northwest Brazos, and the West Fork, along with forty-two churches.

The theme of the meeting, "Leadership," was developed by the guest preacher, Dr. Alton Loveless, Director of the Sunday School and Church Training Department of the National Association of Free Will Baptists. He spoke on "The ABC's of Human Management," "Motivation," and "Communication." The congregation gave him a standing ovation at the conclusion of his final message. Don Guthrie gave a workshop on "The Seven Most Important People in Your Church." The people, in order of their importance, were: 1) the visitor, 2) the greeter, 3) the nursery worker, 4) the person you sit by, 5) the presider/master of ceremonies, 6) the music leader, and 7) the pastor.

---

[141] Pastor Smith had been asked by the Executive Board to speak on whether the concept of stewardship of possessions was taught in the Bible. Perhaps he misunderstood what he was asked to do or simply assumed that by stewardship the Executive Board had meant "giving." It was, however, an excellent sermon on giving.

Music for the meeting was again outstanding and it included a large number of people.

The association voted to move into phase 3 of the four phase plan which had been adopted at the 1987 state meeting in Odessa and to pay Thurmon Murphy $500.00 per month for his work as clerk, treasurer, and editor of *The Texas Challenge*.

A special offering was received for Judy Posner, wife of Robert Posner, whose purse had been stolen by a purse snatcher who had grabbed it and exited the hotel on the run. The clerk noted that 44 people were present for the Thursday morning worship service, 57 for the Thursday evening service, and 30, including 11 pastors, for the Friday morning business session.

Helen Sanders, president of the state Woman's Auxiliary, announced that the name of their organization had been changed to Texas Women Active for Christ (TWAC). She reported that their goal of raising $2,000.00 for Dwain and Debbie Crosby, missionaries to Spain, had almost been doubled and that they had presented to them a check in the amount of $3,500.00.

The association voted to have the next three state meetings in Austin as a convenient location for the delegates from across the big state.

Eighty-First Annual Session - 1995

The eighty-first annual session of the state association convened with the Central Texas District Association, meeting at the Holiday Inn South in Austin, and at the Lakehills Free Will Baptist Church in Cedar Park, June 7-9, 1995. Business sessions and other activities were conducted in the Holiday Inn South and the evening worship services at the Lakehills Free Will Baptist Church. David Sutton was the moderator and Thurmon Murphy was the clerk. Four district association represented: Central Texas, Northwest Brazos, Rio Grande, and West Fork, along with thirty-six churches. The East Texas District Association boycotted the convention because it was being held in a Holiday Inn which made objectionable movies available to those who purchased them on their in-room televisions.

The theme for the meeting was "Free Will Baptists - Who We Are." This theme was developed in a number of ways. Carl Cheshire, pastor of the Cavanaugh Free Will Baptist Church in Fort Smith, Arkansas, and assistant moderator of the National Association of Free Will Baptists, was the featured speaker for the convention. He spoke on "A Call to Commitment," and "Loyalty." Two workshops were conducted. The first was by Thurmon Murphy, who spoke on "Why We Believe in the Possibility of Apostasy." The second was by Luther Sanders, who spoke on "Free Will Baptists and Feet Washing." Mike Cousineau, missionary to Africa, spoke on "Our Mission As Free Will Baptists."

At the recommendation of the Executive Committee and the General Board, the body approved constitutional changes which eliminated the General Board. This action was taken for a number of reasons: 1) the General Board had become unnecessary. Its purpose had been to filter business items which would be the cause of heated and divisive debate on the floor of the association. No such heated and divisive debate had been experienced in many years. 2) the General Board created a redundancy at the state meetings. All of the reports presented to the General Board were also given to the state body in the business sessions, where the reports and business items were adopted or defeated. 3). Other state associations had seen the wisdom of eliminating their general boards.

Outside giving for the year was reported at $162,914.66. The body adopted a budget for the State Office totaling $26,000.00. The Mission Board reported that the new church facility in the Austin suburb had been completed. They reported that Earl Nettleton had given an additional

$6,000.00 for the Austin work. Helen Sanders, president of the Texas Women Active for Christ reported that $8,954.78 had been given toward their state project, exceeding their goal for the year. The monies went to Dwain and Debbie Crosby ($3,661.00), Earnest and Elaine Holland ($2,972.20), and to the Women Nationally Active for Christ toward the hosting of the WNAC at the National Association in Fort Worth in 1996 ($2,321.58).

Eighty-Second Annual Session - 1996

The eighty-second annual session of the state association convened once again with the Central Texas District Association, meeting at the Lakehills Free Will Baptist Church in Cedar Park, June 5-7, 1996. David Sutton served as moderator and Thurmon Murphy was the clerk. The following six district associations reported: Central Texas, East Texas, Midessa, Northwest Brazos, Rio Grande Valley, and West Fork, along with 39 local churches. An unusually large crowd was in attendance. 187 people registered for the convention. As was normal for those years, the music was exceptional.

The theme was "Every Day with Jesus." Robert Posner, pastor of the Lifegate Free Will Baptist Church in Tyler, preached Wednesday evening on that very theme: "Every Day with Jesus." There were three preaching services on Thursday morning. David Ferguson, pastor of the Westfield Free Will Baptist Mission in Katy, preached on "Man on the Move." Dr. Thomas Marberry, professor at Hillsdale Free Will Baptist College, preach on "How to Handle Life's Second Best." The third preaching service was a joint worship time with the Texas Women Active for Christ. Everyl Getz presided. The message was brought by Dr. Ken Eagleton, medical missionary to Côte d'Ivoire, West Africa, and son of Texas' own Kenneth and Marvis Eagleton, missionaries to Brazil. His message was entitled "Hold the Light High." Special music for the service featured Brenda Doffing, Elaine Holland, and Sharie Surface, each singing solos. On Thursday evening James Munsey, coordinator of the Free Will Baptist Work in Mexico and pastor of Primera Eglesia Bautista Libre (First Free Will Baptist Church) in Weslaco, Texas, spoke on "Called from on High."

The Board of Christian Education returned the Church Training Service (CTS) competitive activities to the state meeting after several years of having them meet separately.

Total outside giving through the State Office for the year was $131,960.14. The budget adopted for the State Office was $21,800.00.

Among those listed on the Obituary Committee Report were Helen Sanders, wife of Luther Sanders, and Gaston Clary.

Considerable emphasis was placed on preparation for the Free Will Baptist National Convention which was scheduled to meet in Fort Worth in July. Bobby Ferguson reported that the Mission Board's obligation to the Austin mission project, the Lakehills Free Will Baptist Church, would continue through September. The spirit of the state meeting was very high.

The National Convention

The National Association of Free Will Baptists convened in Texas for the fourth time, meeting once again at the Tarrant County Convention Center in Fort Worth, July 21-25, 1996, for its sixtieth annual session. The theme of the convention was "I Will Build My Church." Total registration for the convention numbered 6,771, each delegate and visitor being counted only once under the new registration system. Numerous Texans were involved in the convention activities.

As a member of the Executive Committee of the General Board I presided over the Monday evening service and welcomed the delegation to Texas. I was elected to serve another two year term on the General Board. David Ferguson led the benediction on Monday evening.

Collin Creek pastor Will Harmon, a member of the Sunday School and Church Training Board, preached at the highlight service of the convention, Wednesday evening, the missionary service. His sermon was "Our Time Is Now." David Sutton, pastor of the First Free Will Baptist Church of Duncanville, was elected to another six year term on the Sunday School and Church Training Board. Nancy Copeland, daughter of Pastor Jack T. Bankhead, sang "He the Pearly Gates Will Open." Lynn Wood, pastor of the Fellowship Free Will Baptist Church in Bryan, served on the National Home Missions Board. Everyl Getz served as president of the Woman's National Auxiliary Convention and JoAnn Wood, wife of Lynn Wood, served as secretary of the WNAC. Everyl Getz also conducted a Minister's Wives Seminar on "Privileges and Responsibilities of Holding the Light in the Parsonage." Bettie Ferguson and Artelle Cox served on the Registration Committee of the WNAC. Pastor Jack T. Bankhead served as Chauffeur for the convention. Raymond Lee, Owen Barger, and Charles Denman were faithful in their annual ministry as ushers and vote counters of the convention. Others served on the Hospitality Committee assisting convention delegates with directions and information as needed.

Eighty-Third Annual Session - 1997

The eighty-third annual session of the state association convened with the Central Texas District Association, meeting at the Fellowship Free Will Baptist Church in Bryan, June 4-6, 1997. Four district associations represented: Central Texas, East Texas, Northwest Brazos, and West Fork, along with 40 local churches. David Sutton was the moderator and Thurmon Murphy was the clerk. One hundred eighty-one people were present as the Wednesday evening service began.

Thurmon Murphy preached on Wednesday evening on the subject "The Power of Unity." The Pastors' Conference was on Thursday morning, and there were three sermons preached. Brad Hanna, pastor of the SouthPointe Church in Arlington, spoke on "The Acts of a Growing Church." Dwain Crosby, former missionary to Spain and pastor of a new mission in The Woodlands, spoke on "Breaking the Barriers." The third sermon was at a joint service with the Texas Women Active for Christ. Leroy Forlines, professor of theology at Free Will Baptist Bible College, spoke on "Six Ways God Has Manifested His Goodness to Us." On Thursday evening Trymon Messer, director of the National Home Missions Department, preached on "God's Concern for the City." Once again music for the association was exceptional.

Everyl Getz reported that the Texas Women Active for Christ (TWAC) had once again exceeded their goal for the state project. $6,254.87 had been divided between Ernest and Elaine Holland (Côte d'Ivoire), Dwain and Debbie Crosby (North Pointe Fellowship, The Woodlands) and the offices of the Women Nationally Active for Christ in Nashville. In addition, $3,254.87 had been channeled to various missionaries. Professor Leroy Forlines spoke to the TWAC, as did Dr. Mary Ruth Wisehart, the WNAC Executive Secretary/Treasurer.

The Texas Mission/Church Extension Board reported on the progress of missionary Dwain Crosby, who had returned from Spain and who had been hired to plant a church in The Woodlands, near Conroe. The mission was making good progress.

A resolution was passed which condemned the New NIV[142] translation of the Bible. The resolution contained nine charges against it. See the 1998 state meeting below.

Eighty-Fourth Annual Session - 1998

The eighty-fourth annual session of the Texas State Association convened with the West Fork District Association, meeting at the First Free Will Baptist Church in Duncanville, June 10-12, 1998. David Sutton was the moderator and Thurmon Murphy the clerk. Four district associations represented: Central Texas, East Texas, Northwest Brazos, and West Fork. Ministers were present from the Rio Grande and the Midessa but the two associations sent no letter or fees and were not seated. Thirty five churches represented by letter. However, attendance for the meeting was excellent. This was the first state association meeting in which the *Texas Free Will Baptist Yearbook* was distributed. The *Yearbook* was a combination of the 1997 State Minutes and the 1998 Digest of Reports, combining the two into one for convenience and lower costs.

Both the Wednesday evening and Thursday evening worship services were preceded with extended special music. On Wednesday evening the youth group from the Primera Iglesia Bautista Libre in Weslaco conducted a pre-service concert from 6:45 to 7:15. On Thursday evening the Levan Hubbard family conducted another thirty minute concert. Both concerts were very well received by the delegation.

The theme was "Little Is Much When God Is in It." During the Wednesday evening service Sandy Anderson sang "Take America Back" and received a standing ovation. Don Bailey, pastor of the Forest Park Free Will Baptist Church in San Angelo, preached "Seeking the Anointing." Dwain Crosby spoke to the Texas Women Active for Christ, a joint service with the state body, on the subject "Dare to Believe." Louis Nettleton, pastor of the Western Hills Free Will Baptist Church in Fort Worth, spoke on "Little Is Much When God Calls."

On Thursday morning Mrs. B. J. Worth, of Worth Tax and Financial Services and author of *Income Tax Guide for Ministers and Religious Workers*, conduced two workshops for the benefit of pastors and churches. These workshops had helped pastors and church worker save hundreds of dollars in taxes in states where they had been conducted. But unexpectedly and unbelievingly, only seven people attended these Texas workshops and there was considerable criticism of the Executive Committee for having tax workshops instead of workshops or seminars on soul winning.

This was the first association meeting after the elimination of the General Board. Business items which had previously been presented through the General Board were presented through the Executive Committee.

Three items of potentially historic significance were voted upon by the body. The first, a resolution presented from the Midessa Association by the Resolutions Committee, concerned Bible translations. In short it called upon the state body to instruct all speakers at the Texas State Association meetings to use only the King James Version of the Bible, and the editor of *The Texas Challenge* to use only the King James Version of the Bible in all scriptural references. This resolution was tabled indefinitely, effectively killing it.

---

[142] The actual name of the translation under question was *The Holy Bible, New International Version, Inclusive Language Edition*, published by Hodder & Stoughton: London, Sydney, and Auckland.

The second, also a resolution which originated with the Midessa Association,[143] called upon the state association to avoid contemporary music, emphasize good Bible preaching, and called upon the state association to conduct only workshops/seminars/conferences which were aimed at soul winning and revival. The last part of that resolution was aimed at preventing the state association from having any more tax seminars to help pastors and churches, or any such thing. This resolution was also tabled indefinitely, effectively killing it.

The third item was a recommendation from the Executive Committee that the Texas State Association adopt the TEAM (Texans Excited About Missions) Plan, a plan formulated by the Executive Committee and the Home Missions/Church Extension Board over a two year period, and that the TEAM Plan be implemented January 1, 1999. The TEAM Plan was adopted by the body but never put into practice. It had the potential to enormously increase funding for missions, as similar plans have done and continue to do. The term "TEAM Plan" is used but not the plan.

Clerk Thurmon Murphy, having been asked the previous year to write a report on the *Holy Bible, New International Version, Inclusive Language Edition*, included a six page written report in the *1998 Yearbook*.[144] The report addressed all nine of the charges which had been brought against it, basically stating that the charges made against it by the Midessa Association were not true, though not stating that the version was a perfect translation.

Eighty-Fifth Annual Session - 1999

The eighty-fifth annual session of the state association convened with the Central Texas District Association, meeting at the Lakehills Free Will Baptist Church in Cedar Park. Keith Woody was the moderator and Thurmon Murphy was the clerk. Brenda Doffing served very capably as the assistant clerk. Six district associations represented: Central Texas, East Texas, Midessa, Northwest Brazos, Rio Grande, and West Fork. Forty-three local churches represented. The registration report stated that 143 people registered, though, as always, not everyone registered. As had been the case for a number of years, the music was exceptional.

The theme of the meeting was "The Power of Teamwork." Dr. David Crowe, Director of Missionary Assistance with the National Home Missions Department, spoke on "Hands Held High, the Power of Teamwork," using Exodus 17:8-13 as his text. The entire altar area was filled with people at the invitation. The Thursday morning Pastors' Conference featured three speakers. Ernest Harrison, Jr., Executive Secretary of the Oklahoma State Association of Free Will Baptists, spoke on "The Outline of the Believer's Prayer Life." Randy Puckett, missionary/church planter to Sugarland, Texas, spoke on "Obedience in God's Eyes Is Success. Using 1 Samuel 15:13-23 as his text. Levan Hubbard, pastor of the Fellowship Free Will Baptist Church in Bryan, spoke on "People," using Luke 19:1-10 as his text.

The Thursday morning worship was a joint service with the Texas Women Active for Christ. Everyl Getz, president of the TWAC, presided. Raymond Getz, pastor of the Valley Community Church[145] in McAllen led the prayer. Justin Banks, missionary appointee to the Kuna Indians of Panama, spoke on "God's Master Plan, Pass It On." On Thursday evening David Crowe spoke on "But What Are We Among So Many," using John 6:1-9 as his text.

Dr. John Chang, missionary to Korea, spoke briefly on his work in Korea and appealed for financial and prayer support.

---

[143] These two resolutions can be found on pages 37-38 of the *1999 Yearbook*.
[144] See pages 41-46 of the *1998 Texas Free Will Baptist Yearbook*.
[145] The Valley Community Church was formerly the First Free Will Baptist Church of McAllen.

At the urging of the East Texas District Association, particularly by Allen Moore and Harold Teague, the state association voted to re-establish the General Board.

I resigned my position as executive secretary, thus ending my years of service to the Texas State Association of Free Will Baptists. I had been serving simultaneously as clerk, treasurer, editor of *The Texas Challenge*, and promotional man, all while serving as pastor of the First Free Will Baptist Church in Wichita Falls. When I failed to include in *The Texas Challenge* an article sent to me by Pastor David Holguin about his church, the United Free Will Baptist Church in Bryan, much to his disappointment, I knew I was trying to do too much. I decided it was time to focus on my ministry as pastor and my writing ministry.

Among those listed on the Obituary Committee report as having passed away during the previous year were Roy Norie, Jr. and Mrs. Mabel Willey, wife of legendary missionary Thomas "Pop" Willey.

The Executive Committee asked Dwain Crosby, church planter in The Woodlands, to serve as editor of *The Texas Challenge*, Sally Wilcox to serve as graphic designer for *The Challenge*, Dava Willis to serve as treasurer, while moderator Keith Woody would do some of the promotional work for the state association. According to the minutes Ken Mayo was elected clerk. Let it be said here that *The Texas Challenge*, which had come to be considered by many as the best state paper in the denomination, became even better, thanks in large part to the excellent work of Sally Wilcox who put her professional touch to it.

Eighty-Sixth Annual Session - 2000

There was a lot of confusion in the country as the calendar rolled around to January 1, 2,000. Some argued that A.D. 2,000 was the end of the Twentieth Century and the beginning of the Twenty-first Century, while others maintained that the Twenty-first would begin on January 1, 2001. Those who argued that the Twenty-first century would begin on January 1, 2001 were correct, of course. Then, there was much angst about Y2K, short for the year 2,000. Many were predicting the second coming of Christ. Others were predicting colossal disasters caused by computer failures. Still others took the position that nothing unusual at all would happen and that all should remain calm. As it turned out, of course, it was just another year.

The minutes of the state meeting were not in the 2001 Yearbook. The meeting was held June 7-9, 2000, at the First Free Will Baptist Church in Henderson. "Building for the New Millennium" was the theme of the meeting. Keith Woody served as moderator. James Forlines, General Director of the Free Will Baptist Foreign Missions Department, spoke Wednesday and Thursday evenings on the subject "Building for the Next Millennium."

The Pastor's Conference featured three speakers. Allen Moore spoke on "Building Through Encouragement," James Puckett spoke on "Building Through Leadership," and Jackie Farmer spoke on "Building Through Prayer."

Judy Posner served as president of the Texas Women Active for Christ. Danita High, pastor's wife at the First Free Will Baptist Church in Henderson, sang a special song at the TWAC convention and another special in the Thursday evening worship service. She would later become the Director of the Women Nationally Active for Christ in Nashville, Tennessee. Dr. Thomas Marberry, President of the Seminary of the Cross in Reynosa, Tamaulipas, Mexico, spoke to the women, who were also joined by the pastors from the Pastor's Conference.

Ken Mayo resigned as clerk and was replaced by Rick Futch.

At the end of the year, December 31, 2000, the momentous and historic Twentieth Century came to an end. The United States had gone through a number of great wars: World War I, World War II, the Korean War, Vietnam, and Desert Storm in Iraq, to name the major ones. These wars changed the United States and the world forever. The Civil Rights Movement also changed America forever, for the good.

Free Will Baptists had been strong and numerous at the beginning of the century in 1901, and were a presence, a denomination of influence, a name well known, at the time. Church rolls had included the names of presidents, congressmen, governors, as well as leaders of commerce and industry. Then came the merger with the Northern Baptists in 1910-11, which largely eradicated the name Free Will Baptist from America's consciousness, leaving only a remnant of churches in the South, Midwest, and Southwest. The numerous colleges and graduate schools which trained our ministers and missionaries were gone, every one of them. An aggressive foreign missions program, including all monies and properties, had been turned over to the Northern Baptists. What was left of the denomination was weak, struggling, scattered, and for the most part, the remaining churches were pastored by untrained men and women.

But they began to pull themselves together as a remnant, a remnant ready to continue the noble work of the Free Will Baptist denomination. Regional and state associations were formed. The Texas State Association of Free Will Baptists was formed in 1915. Slowly and surely they began to rebuild, strengthening existing churches, and planting many new ones. The times were right for such a rebuilding. People were still responsive to the gospel in large numbers. By 1935 the scattered remnants were ready to come together again as a national organization. As a result, and fulfilling the dreams of many men and women in the ministry, as well as a host of laypeople, the National Association of Free Will Baptists was formed in November of 1935. New schools were started to train pastors and other church workers. Free Will Baptist Bible College, owned and operated by the denomination, opened its doors in the fall of 1942. Smaller schools, owned and operated mostly by state associations, also came into existence, most notably Oklahoma Bible College (later called Hillsdale Free Will Baptist College and then Randall University) and California Bible College. Southeastern Free Will Baptist College came into existence as a result of denominational strife, but it is turning out a number of influential pastors.

It has often been said that the growth of the Free Will Baptist denomination since the merger has been remarkable, and in many ways it has. We have churches in most of the fifty states and in more than a dozen foreign countries and an aggressive home missions program. There are some large Free Will Baptist churches, with attendance in the hundreds, though they are few and far between. The number of pastors who are trained for the ministry is increasing, and there is forming a group of ministers who can truly be called scholars. There is definitely a lot of potential for denominational growth in the Twenty-first Century.

Chapter 7

2001 to 2014

Eighty-Seventh Annual Session - 2001

The eighty-seventh session of the Texas State Association met at the First Free Will Baptist Church of Houston, June 6-8, 2001. Keith Woody served as moderator and Rick Futch was the clerk. Three district associations represented by letter and fees; though not listed they would have been East Texas, Central Texas, and West Fork.

The theme of the 2001 state meeting was "Reclaiming the Promised Land (a Texas Revival)." Larry Powell, General Director of the National Home Missions Department, spoke twice on the subject "Building Through Evangelism." The Thursday morning Pastors' Conference featured sermons by Bill Adkisson, pastor of the Evergreen Free Will Baptist Church, Keith; Frank Gregory, First Free Will Baptist Church, Duncanville; and Dale Smith, pastor of the Folsom Free Will Baptist Church, Coleman, Oklahoma. The 11:00 a.m. service consisted of a special report on the TEAM Plan by the Missions/Church Extension Board.

David Ferguson, of Katy, was serving as State Office Coordinator.

The Obituary Committee reported that, among the deceased for the year 2000, were Alvin F. Halbrook, James Munsey, and Juanita Marie Hearron, wife of Clarence Hearron. The State Office report was given by State Office Coordinator Dwain Crosby. He reported that during the year 2000 $220,320.49 had been received by the State Office and spent and/or disbursed to state and national ministries.

Eighty-Eighth Annual Session - 2002

The eighty-eighth annual session of the Texas State Association convened with the West Fork District Association, meeting at the First Free Will Baptist Church of Duncanville, June 5-7, 2002. Keith Woody served as moderator and Rick Futch was the clerk. Minutes of the meeting were extremely brief. The theme was "Past Time or Perfect Time," based on Romans 13:11. On Wednesday evening Dr. Tom Malone, Chancellor of Free Will Baptist Bible College, preached on the subject, as recorded by the clerk "Witness: Testimony God Is Faithful." Dr. Malone spoke again on Thursday evening but his sermon subject was not noted by the clerk.

The Thursday morning Pastors' Conference used the theme "God's Spiritual Habitation." Following that theme Bobby Ferguson, of Houston, spoke on "The Focus of God's Spiritual Habitation," Clarence Hearron, pastor of the Cornerstone Free Will Baptist Church in Denison, spoke on "The Framework of God's Spiritual Habitation," and Mike Hutsell, pastor of the Grace Free Will Baptist Church in Broken Arrow, Oklahoma, spoke on "The Future of God's Spiritual Habitation."

No report is given on which district associations reported to the state association, but the district associations in existence at the time were East Texas (11 churches), Central Texas (18 churches), Northwest Brazos (1 church, Oakdale First in Amarillo), Rio Grande (1 church), and the West Fork (15 churches) and the new West Texas District Association (3 churches). The state minutes do not record when the West Texas District Association joined the state association. However, since the association is listed for the first time in the directory of churches in the 2003 Yearbook, they apparently joined in 2002. The West Texas District Association consisted of the Bible Church in Odessa, the Faith Church of Lubbock, and the First Church of Kermit. They were later joined by the Canyon County Church in Canyon, the First Church in Pampa, and the Heritage Parks Church in Abilene. The First Free Will Baptist Church in McAllen, which had become the McAllen Community Church, had left the denomination, leaving only the Primera Iglesia Bautista Libre in Weslaco as the only church in the Rio Grande Valley District Association.

$227,205.88 was channeled through the State Office, with $134,075.94 going to outside causes. Giving for the year 2002 was a record year. However, the State Office operated $5,000.00 below its budget. The Executive Board reported that they had appointed Marcus Brewer, a layman from the Fellowship Free Will Baptist Church in Bryan, to the position of State Office Coordinator. Sally Wilcox of Conroe took over the full responsibilities of editing *The Texas Challenge,* Dwain Crosby having been dismissed because of moral improprieties. Dava Willis was given the task of doing the bookkeeping.

Eighty-Ninth Annual Session - 2003

The eighty-ninth annual session of the Texas State Association met at the Doubletree Hotel Airport, hosted by the North Oaks Free Will Baptist Church, in San Antonio, June 4-6, 2003. Keith Woody served as moderator and Chuck Vaughan served as assistant clerk. Once again the minutes are brief. The theme for the meeting was "Forever Forward." Darryl Nichols, former missionary to Côte d'Ivoire in West Africa, recently transferred to Panama, was the keynote speaker on Wednesday evening. On Thursday evening he spoke again, this time on "Deciding Our Strategy," using Acts 1:8 as his text.

Two men spoke at the Thursday morning Pastors' Conference: Robert Posner and retired pastor/missionary Luther Sanders.

The body voted to extend an invitation for the Free Will Baptist National Convention to meet in Texas as the earliest date available. That turned out to be 2014, when the National met once again in Fort Worth.

The number of district associations which reported to the state association is once again not given. However, there were still six district associations in existence: Central Texas, East Texas, Northwest Brazos. Rio Grande, West Fork, and West Texas. Fifty-one churches were listed in the directory.

Marcus Brewer, State Office Coordinator, was elected clerk.

The Missions/Church Extension board reported three mission projects, which were all doing well: The Woodlands, under the ministry of Jarvis Reed and wife Kelly, who had taken over following the dismissal of Dwain Crosby; the Sugarland mission in southwest Houston, under the leadership of Randy Puckett and wife Shelly; and the North Oaks Free Will Baptist Mission in San Antonio, under the leadership of Don Bailey and wife Sonja. They announced that funds from the sale of the Zion Free Will Baptist Church in Corpus Christi had been made available.

Ninetieth Annual Session - 2004

The ninetieth annual session of the Texas State Association of Free Will Baptists convened with the East Texas District Association and met at the First Free Will Baptist Church in Henderson, June 9-11, 2004. Keith Woody served as moderator and Marcus Brewer served as clerk. The theme of the meeting was "Practicing His Precepts." Tim York, moderator of the National Association of Free Will Baptists, was the featured speaker. He spoke on "Feeding the Flock" and "Leading the Flock." One hundred ninety-seven people registered for the meeting, including thirty-one pastors.

The Thursday morning Pastors' Conference used the theme "Christian Unity." Jack T. Bankhead presided. Bill Van Winkle spoke on "The Unity of Experience" and Russell Johnson spoke on "The Unity of Expectation." Deleen Cousineau, missionary to Côte d'Ivoire in West Africa, spoke to the Texas Women Active for Christ. The association adopted budgets totaling $83,050.00.

Two constitutional amendments were approved by the voting body: the first clarified the structure and duties of the state's Executive Board; the second changed the amount of state representation fees per church to equal the amount of national representation fees per church.

Ninety-First Annual Session - 2005

The ninety-first annual session of the Texas State Association convention convened with the West Fork District Association, and met June 8-10, 2005, at the First Free Will Baptist Church in Duncanville. Keith Woody was the moderator and Marcus Brewer was the clerk. The opening prayer was by Dr. Larry Cox, pastor of the First Free Will Baptist Church in Bowie. The featured speaker was Dr. Matthew Pinson, president of Free Will Baptist Bible College. He spoke on "Consider Christ's Person," using Philippians 2:5-11 as his text, and "Consider Christ's Passion," using Philippians 2:1-11 as his text.

The Thursday morning Pastors' Conference also used a theme, "Consider Christ." It met at the Mountain Creek Community Church of Dallas.[146] Jeff Cates spoke on "Consider Christ's Drawing Power," using John 12:32-34 as his text. Dr. Eugene Richards spoke on "Consider Christ's Desire," using John 17:24-26 as his text. The joint session with the Texas Women Active for Christ featured the theme "Soul Pursuit - Sole Purpose," and the speaker was Mick Donahue, missionary to the Muslim community in Southern Spain and Northern Africa. He spoke on "The Call of God," using Judges 6:36-40 as his text.

Texas home missionaries Jarvis Reed, North Point, Conroe; Don Bailey, North Oaks, San Antonio; Nick Stewart, Lighthouse, Victoria; and Secundino Urena, Iglesia Bautista Libre, Houston; gave reports on the progress of their works.

The State Office finished the year 2005 $1,600 in the black. It was noted that *The Texas Challenge*, edited by Sally Wilcox, continued to receive accolades for its excellence.

Ninety-Second Annual Session - 2006

The ninety-second annual session of the state association convened with the Rio Grande District Association, meeting at the Primera Iglesia Bautista Libre and the Best Western Palm Aire

---

[146] This was not a Free Will Baptist church. It was a beautiful facility with a beautiful view in a solitary location and was used while the WNAC was using the First Free Will Baptist sanctuary.

Hotel in Weslaco, June 7-9, 2006. Keith Woody served as moderator and Marcus Brewer as the clerk. Five district associations represented: East Texas, Central Texas, Rio Grande Valley, West Fork, and West Texas. One hundred forty people registered for the convention.

The them of the meeting was "The Basics of Christianity." The featured speaker was Larry Powell, founder of the First Free Will Baptist Church in nearby McAllen and director of the National Home Missions Department in Nashville, Tennessee. He spoke on "Conditions of Salvation," and "Conduct of the Saved." During the Thursday morning Pastors' Conference, which met at the Weslaco Church, Luis Felipe Tijerina preached on "Our Holy Endeavor," and Faron Thebeau spoke on "A Heavenly Entrance."

The body adopted a constitutional amendment which stated conditions for employment by the state association and encouraged local churches and district associations to adopt similar statements. That amendment stated:

> We believe that the Bible forbids any intimate sexual activity outside of marriage between a man and a woman and that all forms of homosexuality, lesbianism, bisexuality, bestiality, incest, fornication, adultery, and pornography are sinful perversions of God's gift of sex. Any employee of this association engaging in any of these activities and/or becoming pregnant as a result of consensual intercourse outside of the marriage relationship shall be terminated from employment. No one known to be engaged in such activity shall be considered for employment by this association (Gen. 2:24; Gen. 19:5, 13; Genesis 26:8-9; Lev. 18:1-30; Romans 1:26-29; 1 Cor. 5:1; 1 Cor. 6:9; 1 Thess. 4:1-8; Heb. 13:4).[147]

There was another amendment to the constitution presented as a recommendation to the body by the General Board which would have allowed churches in remote areas of Texas to report directly to the state association without being members of a district association. The proposed amendment failed.[148]

Among the deceased listed by the Obituary Committee was Nell Stell, of the Pleasant Mound Free Will Baptist Church in Buffalo Spring. Jeff Cates, pastor of the Primera Iglesia Bautista Libre in Weslaco, announced that he would be moving to Canyon, Texas, to start a new Free Will Baptist Church.

Ninety-Third Annual Session - 2007

The ninety-third annual session of the state association convened with the Central Texas District Association, meeting at the Fellowship Free Will Baptist Church in Bryan, June 6-8, 2007. Keith Woody was the moderator and Marcus Brewer was the clerk. Five district associations represented: Central Texas (19 churches), East Texas (11 churches), West Fork (12 churches), Rio Grande Valley (1 church), and West Texas (5 churches). The registration total for the meeting was 203.

The theme of the meeting was "Personal Discipleship." Tim Campbell, Executive Director of the Arkansas State Association of Free Will Baptists was the featured speaker. He spoke on "The Foundation of Faith," and "The Focus of Faith." His two sermons were remarkably well prepared and delivered. The Thursday morning Pastors' Conference featured sermons by Richard

---

[147] ARTICLE XII in the constitution of the Texas State Association of Free Will Baptists
[148] Page 11 in the *2007 Yearbook of the Texas State Association.*

Terry, "The Faithfulness of the Church," and by Dr. Kenneth Mayo, "The Fellowship of the Church." The TWAC met at 8:30 a.m. and heard missionary Ruth Bivens.

Good reports were given by the Missions/Church Extension Board, namely, that the attendance in Abilene had doubled since the previous year, the Cates were full-time in Canyon, the plat for the Bailey's work in San Antonio had been approved, the Eagle Heights mission had closed on a piece of property in Sugarland and was fully supporting the Puckett's salary, the NorthPointe Church in Conroe, under Jarvis Reed, was close to being self-supporting, and that the new Cross Life Mission in West San Antonio was just underway, under the leadership of Jeremy Lightsey. The Missions/Church Extension Board was doing an excellent job under the leadership of Pastor Robert Posner of Plano.

The body voted to amend the constitution to reflect that the association had become incorporated, to change the date of the state meeting from starting on the second Wednesday of June to the third Wednesday, and to change the title of the Executive "Committee" to the Executive "Board."

Ninety-Fourth Annual Session - 2008

The ninety-fourth annual session of the Texas State Association of Free Will Baptists convened with the West Fork District Association, meeting at the Collin Creek Free Will Baptist Church in Plano, June 11-13- 2008. Keith Woody served as moderator and Marcus Brewer was the clerk.

The theme of the meeting was "Manifestations of Greatness." The featured speaker for the convention was Keith Burden, Executive Secretary of the National Association of Free Will Baptists, Nashville, Tennessee. He spoke on "A Great God," using Psalm 47:2 as his text, and "A Great Grace," using Ephesians 2:8-9. The Pastors' Conference featured speakers who were new state missionaries. Jeremy Lightsey, of the CrossLife Mission in San Antonio, preached on "A Great Salvation," using Hebrews 2:3-5 as his text, followed by Michael Scott, Crossroads Mission in Lubbock, who preached "A Great Inheritance," from 1 Peter 1:3-5.

The State Office reported that $120,495.67 had been channeled through the office for outside ministries. Total expenditures and disbursements for the year was $236,773.11.

Ninety-Fifth Annual Session - 2009

The ninety-fifth session of the state association convened with the West Fork District Association, meeting at the Hilton Garden Inn in Abilene, June 10-12, 2009. Keith Woody served as moderator and Marcus Brewer continued as clerk. Five district association represented: East Texas (10 churches), Central Texas (19 churches), West Fork (11 churches), West Texas (5 churches), and Rio Grande Valley (1 church). 136 people registered for the convention.

The keynote speaker was William Smith, Executive Secretary of the Georgia State Association of Free Will Baptists. He spoke on "Christ's Preparation of His People," and "Christ's Perfection of His Purpose." The Thursday morning Pastors' Conference featured two Texas pastors. Jimmy Dickinson, Bible Church, Odessa, preached "Exalting Christ Publicly," and Charles Jones, pastor of the First Free Will Baptist Church in Kermit, preached on "Exalting Christ's Personality." Keith Woody spoke to the Texas Women Active for Christ on the subject "Knowing the Time," using Romans 13:11-14 as his text.

The body voted to change the starting time of the state meeting back to the second Wednesday of June. They voted that the Executive Board would consist of the moderator, assistant moderator, clerk, assistant clerk, and one member at large, eliminating the Hillsdale Trustee and Executive Secretary as members of the board. The parliamentarian has been eliminated from the board already.

The list of the deceased given by the Obituary Committee for the year 2008 included the name of Luther Sanders, missionary and pastor.

Perhaps the most significant presentation at the 2009 state meeting was Keith Woody's moderator's message. Learning from the past and looking to the future he listed ten things Texas Free Will Baptist must do to survive. They are listed in this book in the chapter on Evaluation and Outlook for the Future.

Ninety-Sixth Annual Session - 2010

The ninety-sixth session of the Texas State Association convened with the Central Texas District Association, and met at the Eagle Heights Free Will Baptist Church, 16718 West Bellfort, in Richmond, a Houston suburb, June 9-11, 2010. This was the first opportunity many of the delegates had to see the large and beautiful Eagle Heights Church, founded by and pastored by Randy Puckett. The theme for the meeting was "Knowing the Unknown."

The body adopted a 2011 budget for the State Office in the amount of $32,700.00. Total expenditures and disbursements for the state association for the year 2009 were reported at $213,536.80, which included $143,636.54 to outside ministries. The Executive Board had replaced Dava Willis with John Davis as treasurer of the state association.

The report of the Missions/Church Extension Board was particularly encouraging. Reporting on their ministry for 2009, they listed:
- The North Pointe Free Will Baptist Church in Conroe, under the leadership of Jarvis Reed and his wife, Kelly, had become self-supporting in January.
- The Heritage Parks Free Will Baptist Church in Abilene, under the leadership of Freddie Gillentine and his wife, Katherine, had become self-supporting.
- The Crossroads Free Will Baptist Church in Lubbock, under the ministry of Mike Scott had started a Sunday school and was making good progress.
- The Canyon Country Free Will Baptist Church in Canyon, under the leadership of Jeff Cates and his wife, Sondra, had paid for their land and were expecting to construct a building on it in the near future.
- The North Oaks Free Will Baptist Church in San Antonio, under the leadership of Don Bailey and his wife, Sonya, had poured a concrete slab and were planning to erect a building on it soon.
- The Crosslife Free Will Baptist Church in San Antonio, under the direction of Jeremy Lightsey and his wife, Jill, was growing and had gone to two services because the congregation had doubled in size.

Ninety-Seventh Annual Session - 2011

The ninety-seventh annual session of the Texas State Association of Free Will Baptists met at the First Free Will Baptist Church of Duncanville, June 8-10, 2011. Keith Woody served as moderator and Marcus Brewer was the clerk. Five district associations represented: Central Texas (20 churches), East Texas (10 churches), West Fork (11 churches), West Texas (6 churches), and Rio Grande Valley (1 church). Total registration was 133.

Larry Powell, Director of the National Home Missions Department, spoke twice to the meeting. On Wednesday evening he preached on "Longsuffering Love," using Colossians 1:9-11 and Galatians 6:9-10 as his texts. On Thursday evening he spoke on "Living by Faith," using Hebrews 11:1-3. Two Texas pastors spoke at the Thursday morning Pastors' Conference, which used the theme "Reaffirming Our Difference." Doug Dickey, pastor of the Fellowship Free Will Baptist Church in Bryan, spoke on "The Gospel Ordinances," listing three: water baptism, the Lord's Supper, and feet washing. Randall Wright, pastor of the new Clearview Free Will Baptist Church in McKinney, spoke on "Life After Death," using Jude 3-23, and Luke 16:19-31 as his texts. In his moderator's message Keith Woody spoke on "The Pastor," using 1 Timothy 1:3-8 as his text.

Host pastor, Richard Terry, along with Jared Oaks of Duncanville, gave a presentation on the history and 400th anniversary (1611 - 2011) of the King James Version of the Bible.

The 2012 Digest of Report, reporting on 2011, stated that *The Texas Challenge* had published four issues, and that *The Challenge* had been made available online. The State Mission/Church Extension Board reported great progress in the mission works being supported by the board:

- The Crosslife Free Will Baptist Church in San Antonio, under the leadership of Jeremy Lightsey, had outgrown their facilities and were needing to remodel and expand.
- Jeff Cates and the Canyon Country Free Will Baptist Church was averaging over 90, with a high over 100, and were looking to build an educational building.
- Randall and Collette Wright had begun a new work in McKinney and had 67 in their opening service, meeting in a school.
- Michael Scott had added new facilities in Lubbock and they were looking to grow.
- Don Bailey had finished their building at North Oaks in San Antonio.
- Greg Yacobian and his wife, Ana, had started a new English speaking work in McAllen.

The State Office reported that contributions through the office had totaled over $211,000.00 in 2011. However, overall giving had declined in nearly every category. Giving to the State Office had declined to the extent that the office was left with a negative balance at year's end of about $4,000.00. This resulted in salaries going unpaid for the final three months of the year.

Ninety-Eighth Annual Session - 2012

The ninety-eighth annual session of the Texas State Association of Free Will Baptists convened with the East Texas District Association, and met at the First Free Will Baptist Church in Henderson, June 13-15, 2012. Keith Woody served as the moderator and Marcus Brewer was the clerk. The following five district associations represented: Central Texas (18 churches), East Texas (10) churches, West Fork (11 churches), West Texas (6 churches), and the Rio Grande Valley (2 churches). Total registration for the meeting was 148.

The theme of the meeting was "End-Time Absolutes: Agreement Without Controversy." The featured speaker for the association was Dr. Garnett Reid, of Free Will Baptist Bible College. Dr. Reid spoke on "Christ's Return and Our Hearts," and "Christ's Return and His Glory," on Wednesday and Thursday nights, respectively. The Thursday morning Pastors' Conference heard him twice more. The theme of that conference was "Reaffirming Our Difference." Dr. Reid spoke on "Christ's Return and Our Salvation," and "Christ's Return and Our Living."

State treasurer John Davis reported that contributions through the State Office totaled $231,533.680 in 2012, an increase of nearly $20,000.00 over 2012. However, support of the State Office had remained nominal, leading to a negative balance at year's end of $1,302.00. This resulted in salaries going unpaid for several months during the year. Texas churches gave nearly $100,000.00 for the World Missions Offering, a record.

The body stood to express their special thanks to Keith Woody who was retiring as moderator after sixteen years of faithful service. Marcus Brewer was elected moderator and Doug Dickey, pastor of the Fellowship Free Will Baptist Church in Bryan, was elected clerk.

The Collin Creek Free Will Baptist Church of Plano

Ninety-Ninth Annual Session - 2013

The ninety-ninth annual session of the Texas State Association met with the Collin Creek Free Will Baptist Church in Plano. Marcus Brewer was the moderator and Doug Dickey was the clerk. The following district associations represented: Central Texas (16 churches), East Texas (10 churches), West Fork (11 churches), West Texas (6 churches), and Rio Grande Valley (2 churches). Twenty-two churches represented by letter.

The theme of the meeting was "No Apologies." Will Harmon, pastor of the Cavanaugh Free Will Baptist Church in Fort Smith Arkansas, and former pastor of the Collin Creek Church, spoke twice to the meeting. On Wednesday evening he spoke on "No Apologies: The Three I

Am's of Paul." On Thursday evening he spoke on "No Apologies for the Passion We Have in our Christian Work." The Thursday morning Pastors' Conference followed the theme with two sermons. Randall Wright, pastor of the Clearview Free Will Baptist Church in McKinney, spoke on "Why Apologize for Perseverance," and Howard Bass, new pastor of the First Free Will Baptist Church of Tomball, formerly the First Free Will Baptist Church of Houston, spoke on "Why Apologize for Eternity." That sermon was on the subject of eternal punishment in hell.

The Missions/Church Extension Board reported good progress, even outstanding progress, in the various mission projects underway: the Light of Life mission in McAllen with Greg Yacobian, Clearview Free Will Baptist Church in McKinney with Randall Wright, North Oaks Free Will Baptist Mission in San Antonio with Don Bailey, Crosslife Free Will Baptist Mission in San Antonio with Jeremy Lightsey, Lubbock with Michael Scott, and Canyon Country Free Will Baptist Church in Canyon with Jeff Cates. They announced that Heath Ferguson was in Texas and starting a new work, the Woodforest Free Will Baptist Mission in the North Houston area. Heath Ferguson was present and gave the report of the National Home Missions Department. Randy Puckett, pastor of the Eagle Heights Free Will Baptist Church in Richmond, and member of the State Home Missions/Church Extension Board, recognized Jeff and Sondra Cates for their work in Canyon, leading the church to self-supporting status. They were given a plaque and applause from the congregation who deeply appreciated their work.

Host pastor Robert Posner, and chairman of the Home Missions/Church Extension Board, asked a panel of three revered and renowned men, Keith Woody, Bobby Ferguson, and Clarence Hearron, the following questions:
1. What two events in ministry do you look back on with the most joy?
2. What two events in ministry do you look back on with the most regret?
3. What role do you feel your marriage has played in your ministry?
4. What three short words of advice would you give a pastor serving in the current generation?
5. How can we best pray for your ministry at this time?
6. What in the current generation of pastors most excites you and what most concerns you?
7. What theological trends most worry you today? The questions themselves were highly significant and the answers were very instructive. The 2014 budget adopted for the mission board was $72,000.00.

The body adopted a 2014 budget for the State Office in the amount of $28,400.00, which was $1,500.00 less than for 2013. Sally Wilcox, editor of *The Texas Challenge*, reported that both print and online issues had been published, but that in the future it was likely that only online issues would be published due to funding limitations. She stated that online issues could be read at www.texasfwb.org, the state association's website.

One Hundredth Annual Session - 2014

There was a sense of anticipation as delegates gathered from the vast regions of Texas for the one hundredth annual session, the centennial session, of the Texas State Association of Free Will Baptists. From the Chihuahuan Desert of West Texas, the High Plains of the Panhandle, the Rolling Prairies of North Texas, the Piney Woods of East Texas, the balmy Rio Grande Valley and Gulf Coast of South Texas, and the beautiful Hill Country of Central Texas they came to celebrate the occasion, to fellowship joyously, and to do the Lord's work. They convened with the Central Texas District Association, meeting at the Fellowship Free Will Baptist Church, 1228 West Villa Marie, Bryan, Texas, June 11-13, 2014. Layman Marcus Brewer served as moderator and Doug Dickey was the clerk. Texas did not have an executive secretary; Marcus Brewer was serving as state office coordinator. The honorable Ann Horton, mayor *pro tempore*, welcomed the association to Bryan and read a proclamation about the ministry of Free Will Baptists in Texas.

The following district associations represented: Central Texas (16 churches), East Texas (9 churches), West Fork (12 churches), West Texas (6 churches), and Rio Grande Valley (2 churches). 164 people, including out of state guests, registered for the meeting.

Allen King and Marcus Brewer served as the congregational song leaders, accompanied at the piano by Mitzi Burks. Numerous special songs were performed during the course of the meeting. The Rejoice ministry team from Welch College was present and performed several musical numbers.

Befitting the occasion, moderator Marcus Brewer, in his moderator's message, spoke on "It's About Time" dealing with changes in the state, country, and world over the past 100 years and the difficulty of predicting changes which would occur in the future. Nevertheless, he stated that we had to be prepared and ready to take the timeless message of the gospel to an ever-changing world that needed Christ.

The theme of the meeting was "Sendtennial." Also befitting the occasion, Dr. Kevin Hester, of Welch College, spoke twice to the Ministers' Conference, conducted at the historic Bright Light Free Will Baptist Church in the Harvey Community, outside of Bryan. His two part presentation covered the history of the Free Will Baptist denomination and the history of Texas Free Will Baptists. It was a superb presentation of Free Will Baptist history. Dr. Hester also spoke to the Texas Women Active for Christ at the Bright Light church on the subject "Heritage from the Past, Horizons for the Future: Free Will Baptists in America."

Mark Headrick, editor of *The Texas Challenge*, who had been publishing an online edition of the *Challenge* reported that he was trying to get a print edition published again.

Attorney David Gibbs, of the National Center for Life and Liberty, gave a seminar on the legal challenges churches faced in the early Twenty-first Century. The Wednesday and Thursday evening sermons were preached by Dr. David Crowe, Director of the National Home Missions Department. He spoke on "Sending" and "Tending" the People of God.

There was considerable excitement over the fact that the National Association of Free Will Baptists would be meeting in Fort Worth, Texas, in July.

The State Office reported receiving and distributing $289,764.03, which included $65,000.00 received from the sale of the Westside Free Will Baptist Church property in Midland, which was placed into a state office endowment fund at Free Will Baptist Foundation in Nashville, Tennessee. The 2015 budget adopted for the State Office was $29,000.00, up $600.00 over the previous year.

The Missions Board announced the sale of several church properties of closed churches, with considerable sadness. Those included properties in Amarillo, Wichita Falls, Midland, and The Woodlands. They also announced the closing of the Cross Roads mission in Lubbock. The new missions and churches in Magnolia, McKinney, San Antonio (two works), and McAllen were reported as doing very well, some exceptionally well.

Assistant clerk Mark Headrick had ordered and made available several items as souvenirs of the one hundredth session, most notably a coffee mug. Robert Posner and the Home Mission Board provided a travel coffee mug. A photograph of the Thursday evening congregation was taken by Thurmon Murphy, though several of the delegates had gone home prior to the service due to health, pressing obligations, or other factors.

Among the people listed by the Obituary Committee as passing away during the previous year were Mrs. Margaret Richards, wife of Herbert Richards, who was present, and Billy Decker of the Lifegate church in Tyler.

As always there was a large representation from the Free Will Baptist national offices in Nashville, Tennessee, and other ministries outside of Texas. Welch College in Nashville, Tennessee, was represented by Dr. Matthew Pinson and his family, Dr. Kevin Hester, along with Susan Forlines and the Rejoice Ministry Team. The other National departments were represented by Dr. David Crowe, Home Missions; Ken Akers, Master's Men; Clint Morgan, International Missions; Ryan Lewis, Executive Office; Ray Lewis, Board of Retirement; and Brandon Roysdon, Randall House Publications. Dr. Tim Eaton represented Hillsdale Free Will Baptist College in Moore, Oklahoma.

Moderator Marcus Brewer made some excellent observations about the past and future of Free Will Baptists in Texas, most notably observing that things in the future will not be as they were in the past (they never are) and that they had to prepare to make the necessary adjustments without changing the timeless gospel message.

Chapter 8

Character Profiles

This chapter contains short, brief biographies or profiles of the men and women who were the early leaders in the Free Will Baptist work in Texas, along with many of the leaders who followed after the pioneers and continued the work, and many of the present leaders who carry on the work today.

Jack Bankhead

Jack Trent Bankhead was born on August 16, 1935, to Charlie B. and Irma Clara (Weddle) Bankhead in Los Angeles, California. He was the fourth of six children. His father worked in the shipyards in Long Beach. Charlie's health did not permit him to remain in California for long stretches of time and so they moved several times from California to Fort Worth, Texas, finally settling for good in Fort Worth. Charlie worked as a boner for the Armour Packing Company, cutting meat from the bones of slaughtered cattle. Jack attended Diamond Hill High School but did not graduate. He said he got too big for his britches and quit. He needed only a credit and a half when he dropped out of school.

Jack & Wanda Bankhead

On October 31, 1953, Jack met Wanda Janelle Gilly at a Halloween party at the home of his friends Haze and Hazel Winkle. Wanda was very active in the Trinity Free Will Baptist Church, pastored by M. L. Sutton. She had a beautiful singing voice and was the church pianist. Trinity was a large church located at the corner of 28th Street and Azle Avenue. Jack and Wanda were married on Tuesday, July 13, 1954, in the living room of her parents. The ceremony was performed by Jay White, a friend of the family. From this marriage came three girls, Brenda Joann, Betty Darlene, and Nancy.

Jack wouldn't attend Trinity with Wanda because Brother Sutton always preached at him, or so Jack thought. So they began attending Dixie Heights Baptist Church. It was here that Jack was converted to Christ. They soon left Dixie Heights, however, and began attending Love Temple Free Will Baptist Church, which was near their home. Love Temple was pastored by Doc Baber. It was here that Jack surrendered his life to preach the gospel at the age of twenty-six. Pastor Baber took him under his wings and taught him homiletics and other things he knew about preaching and pastoring. On Tuesday nights Jack would preach a prepared sermon, with only the Lord and Brother Baber listening. Brother Baber would critique the sermon and the delivery. This helped Jack tremendously and was the only thing in the way of training for the ministry that he

Jack Bankhead at Mesa Verde, Colorado

ever had. He was licensed to preach by the Fellowship Association of Free Will Baptists and then ordained by the West Fork District Association in 1961. His ordination certificate was signed by A. J. Worley, M. L. Sutton, and Doc Baber. Jack made his living working for Meadow Gold Dairies.

The first church Jack pastored was the Friendship Free Will Baptist Church in Fort Worth, but he didn't remain as pastor very long. He accepted the call to pastor the First Free Will Baptist Church in Denton. The Denton church was struggling and had pretty much already decided to close, which it did in a few months. Jack then accepted the call to pastor the First Free Will Baptist Church in Weatherford and had a very successful ministry there. He, however, learned some hard lessons about pastoring and the behavior of some church people when, at the height of his ministry there, he was suddenly voted out as pastor as a result of some shenanigans on the part of others. He accepted the pastorate of the Philadelphia Free Will Baptist Church, also in Weatherford. Things were going well there until one of the men of the church told Jack that he owned the deed to the church property and that Jack wasn't to change anything. He did change one thing, he changed pastorates.

Jack made his mark in life as pastor of the Friendship Free Will Baptist Church in Fort Worth, which he pastored for forty-two years. His second tenure at the church began in July of 1974. The church grew and became strong. Jack was able to go full-time as pastor in 1979, leaving a good job at Dannon, formerly Meadow Gold. The congregation filled the church building at 3054 Schadt Street. In 1989 Friendship purchased a larger church building at 4200 McKibbon Street in Haltom City.

Jack Bankhead and Thurmon Murphy walking from Wichita Falls to Waco in 1984

Jack did his fair share of work in the district association. He held every job in the West Fork except clerk. His greatest contribution was made while he was a member of the Christian Education Board of the West Fork. As a member of that board he was a trustee of the West Fork Youth Camp in the south end of Clay County. He worked long and hard to improve both the ministry and the facilities of the camp. Improvements were made in about every area. New bathrooms were built in both the boys' and girls' dorms. The chapel was built in 1980. A large new building was constructed in 1985 which contained a large dining room, kitchen, lodge, four bath rooms, two sleeping rooms for staff, and two decks. This building was named Covington Hall in honor of the legendary Tiff Covington. To raise money for this building Jack and I walked from Wichita Falls to Waco, from the north end to the south end of the West Fork. Dr. Jack L.

Williams, editor of *Contact* magazine, and longtime friend of Jack, came and preached at the West Fork Annual Meeting when the building was dedicated. The Ed Thompson gazebo was also constructed. The camp ground was cleaned up and a live-on-campus caretaker, Harry Collins and his wife, Myralyn, moved to the camp and lived in a mobile home. Jack usually served as camp cook during camp, serving large helpings of delicious, nourishing food to the campers and staff. The chapel was filled to capacity for the camp worship services. With his good humor and gregarious personality Jack had a wonderful rapport with the campers.

During the National Association meetings in Fort Worth in 1982 and 1996, Jack worked with hosting the big conventions. Few people know Fort Worth the way Jack did and, because of that, he was especially helpful as the convention driver, shuffling denominational dignitaries wherever they needed to go. No one could have been better.

As the years rolled by Jack, as all pastors must, reached the conclusion that his days as a full-time pastor were over. He retired from Friendship in 2004, at the age of sixty-nine, slowed by the years, miles, and by the replacement of both knees and both hips. But the preaching bug was still in him. He soon accepted the pastorate of the New Salem Free Will Baptist Church in Decatur, driving up from Fort Worth each weekend to preach. The church built an addition, including a prophet's chamber, a room where he and Wanda could spend the night.

On May 7, 2006, Jack was honored at the annual meeting of the West Fork District Association. Speeches were made, flowers were given, and a brief biography of Jack was given to each person present.

On July 5, 2011, Jack's beloved wife, Wanda, passed away from heart disease and related complications. She had been a faithful companion, friend, and pastor's wife for fifty-eight years. Her musical talents had greatly helped his ministry. She is buried in the Family Cemetery in Azle, Texas.

On September 23, 2012, Jack married Billie Crosby, widow of the late M. L. Crosby and mother of former Free Will Baptist missionary to Spain, Dwain Crosby. The ceremony, which took place in Jack's living room, was performed by her pastor in Waco, J. E. Jean, and myself. Jack and Billie lived where Jack had lived for decades, 2812 Roosevelt in Fort Worth. Jack continued to pastor the New Salem church for as long as he was able.

Jack Trent Bankhead was an unusual personality, full of humor, wit, and common sense. He possessed the kind of passion, compassion, dedication, commitment, humility, and integrity that every pastor needs, but not everyone has. He was loyal to his Lord, to his church, and to his friends. He never held high office in the Texas State Association of Free Will Baptists or in the National Association, but Free Will Baptists all over the country knew and admired him.

H. Ray and Asa Berry

Hubert Ray Berry was born May 26, 1912, to Fonza Monroe and Mary Ann (McGeHee) Berry in rural[149] Rusk County, Texas. Brother Berry was a twin to Eudie M. Berry. He attended Kilgore Business College. He served the Free Will Baptist denomination for fifty-four years, all of it as a bi-vocational pastor, working as an accountant. Brother Berry founded the First Free Will Baptist Church of Houston and served many years as a member of the Texas Home Mission

---

[149] His obituary states his birthplace as Laneville, Texas.

H. Ray and Asa Berry

Board. Many of his pastoral years were spent as pastor of the Faith Free Will Baptist Church in San Antonio. When that church closed and was sold, he held the money in trust for the church. He released those funds to the State Mission Board for use in the planting of the new Free Will Baptist Church in Austin, the Lakehills Free Will Baptist Church, planted by Keith Woody.

Asa Cornelia (Hillin) Berry was born February 21, 1910, in Rusk County, Texas. She was a graduate of Compton District School and of the Stephen F. Austin Teachers College. She was an officer in the Woman's Auxiliary and served as its president in Texas. She retired from the Texas Department of Human Resources. She passed away January 5, 2001, in Virginia Beach, Virginia, living there under the care of her daughter Jane Burden.

Brother Berry was named the Outstanding Minister of the Year in 1967. He was a stalwart in the Free Will Baptist work in Texas, ever faithful, persevering, an encourager of others, serving wherever needed, and true to his commitment to Christ until the day of his home going.

H. Ray passed away on July 2, 1999, in Birmingham, Alabama. The Berry's lived the last two years of his life in Birmingham to be close to their son, H. Ray Berry, Jr., and his wife Sharon (Roberts). H. Ray and Asa are buried in Neeley Cemetery, Rusk County Texas.

H. Ray, Jr. Born November 10, 1943; died June 9, 2014, in Hoover, Alabama. Daughter Norma Jane is married to Dale Burden, now retired, one of the denomination's best known pastors, and editor of *The Gist,* a paper which gave his personal views on Free Will Baptist issues. In their earlier years Dale pastored a Free Will Baptist church in Louisiana, often coming to Texas for fellowship. Jane was so well known and recognized in Texas that at first Dale was known as the husband of Jane Berry.[150]

Jane Berry Burden

Allen Bowen

Daniel Allen Bowen was born on August 12, 1972, in Raleigh, North Carolina, to Jimmy Elton and Lois Emmie (Bingham) Bowen. Mr. Bowen works as a technical specialist at AT&T. Allen attended the Wake Christian Academy in Raleigh, graduating in 1990.

Allen was converted to Christ at the age of twelve at a revival meeting held by Evangelist Bobby Jackson at the Haven Free Will Baptist Church in Raleigh. At the age of twenty he sensed God's call to the ministry and preached his first sermon in 1991 at the Garner Free Will Baptist Church, Garner, North Carolina, pastored by Jim Turnbough. Allen was licensed to the gospel ministry by the Palmer Association in North Carolina and the Cave Creek Association in Thayer, Missouri. He graduated from Welch College in Nashville, Tennessee, in 1994. He also attended Campbell University for a year.

---

[150] Dale himself gave me this information in a telephone conversation on March 3, 2015.

While a student at Welch College he attended Cofer's Chapel Free Will Baptist Church, the church at which the National Association of Free Will Baptists was formed in 1935. At Cofer's Chapel in 1992 he met Jennifer Erin Hampton, daughter of Dr. Charles and Peggy Hampton, professor at Welch College. The Hampton's had worked in the Austin Mission which had been started by Harvey Henderson in 1965, while Charles worked on his doctorate at the University of Texas. Two years later, on March 12, 1994, Allen and Jennifer were married at Cofer's by her father, Dr. Charles Hampton. Allen and Jennifer have three children: Emma Katherine, Karah Elizabeth, and Josiah Sullivan Bowen.

Jennifer and Allen Bowen

Allen served in the United States Air Force. He served in the 118th Air Lift Wing of the Tennessee National Guard as a crew chief for a C-130 aircraft. He supported missions to New Orleans for Hurricane Katrina Evacuations, Operation Iraqi Freedom, and Operation Enduring Freedom. During his stint in the Air Force he was temporarily stationed at Sheppard Air Force Base in Wichita Falls, Texas, for intensive, short term technical training, from February to August of 2005. During this time he attended the First Free Will Baptist Church in Wichita Falls. He received a medical discharge from the Air Force in 2008.

Churches he has served include the Trinity Free Will Baptist Church, Greenville, North Carolina, as Youth and Outreach Minister, 1995 to 1998. From 1998 to 1999 he served the Horton Heights Free Will Baptist Church in Nashville, Tennessee, as Youth Minister. Moving west he worked with the Thayer Free Will Baptist Church, Thayer, Missouri, from 2000 to 2002 as Associate and Youth Pastor.

In 2002 Allen took a break from full time ministry due to a difficult ministry position split, although he continued to work as a youth sponsor and Sunday school teacher. He went back to Welch College and received his teacher certification and taught in the Metro Nashville public schools, mainly in inner city schools. He then taught at Christ Presbyterian Academy for a year.

In February of 2014 the Lakehills Free Will Baptist Church in Cedar Park, Texas, called him as pastor. Jennifer's parents had assisted in an Austin mission in the late 1960's. The fact that her parents had worked in an effort to plant a church in Austin years earlier influenced their praying as they prayed about whether to accept the Lakehills Church. Allen and Jennifer began their ministry there on June 1, 2014, succeeding the founding pastor, Keith Woody. Allen had never sought ordination during his earlier years working in associate ministry positions. The natural thing for him to do, then, was to be ordained when he began his ministry as pastor at Lakehills. In June of 2014 he was ordained by the Central Texas District Association at the Lakehills Church. His ordination credentials were signed by Charles Denman, Dr. Kenneth Mayo, and Dr. Eugene Richards.

Brother Bowen resigned as pastor of the Lakehills Church in July of 2016.

John A. Brooks

John Andrew Brooks was born on June 9, 1893, to Fannie (Foster) and Benson Berry Brooks, in Gravette, Arkansas. His father was a farmer. The family migrated to Texas and John attended elementary school in Prospect, Texas, completing the third grade, about 1900. In 1912 he married Lavina Edith Covington, the sister of legendary Free Will Baptist pastor Tiff Covington. John and Edith had a large family: Letha Maggie, Mary Evylan, Gracie Lee, Callie Lorain, Bessie Alma, Willie Jo, John Thomas, Tommie Rae, William Leslie, and John A. Jr.

John and Edith Brooks

John was licensed to the gospel ministry by the West Fork District Association of Free Will Baptists. On August 14, 1912, John was ordained by the West Fork at the Pleasant Valley Free Will Baptist Church. The Pleasant Valley church would later move from the valley to the mound and become the Pleasant Mound Free Will Baptist Church at Buffalo Springs, Texas. The church is known far and wide in Clay County as the Rock Church because the new sanctuary on top of the hill was constructed of field stone. His ordination certificate was signed by W. M. Coggins, J. W. Shultz, founder of the Pleasant Mound Free Will Baptist Church, and M. C. Covington, father of Tiff Covington. At some point in the 1920's he attended one semester at Decatur Baptist College. The school would later move from Decatur to Dallas and become Dallas Baptist University. In 1970 Dallas Baptist College awarded him an honorary doctorate degree.

John A. Brooks had a long and fruitful ministry in Texas. All of the churches he pastored were in the West Fork District Association. The churches he pastored include the Pleasant Valley Free Will Baptist Church, Silver Creek, Prospect, New Salem Free Will Baptist Church at Decatur, First Free Will Baptist Church in Weatherford (twice), Dott, Longbranch, Gartman's View in Comanche (twice), First Free Will Baptist Church in Fort Worth (twice), New Hope Free Will Baptist Church near Weatherford, and the Pleasant Mound Free Will Baptist Church at Buffalo Springs, the one that used to be Pleasant Valley. John A. Brooks preached the very first sermon preached at the Easley's Chapel at Gartman's View Free Will Baptist Church in Comanche. His preaching ministry extended beyond the borders of Texas. He held several revivals in Oklahoma, and at least three in Hobbs, New Mexico.

The minutes of the tenth annual session of the Texas State Association of Free Will Baptists, held at the Easley Chapel Free Will Baptist Church in Comanche, October 28-30, 1924, record that John A. Brooks brought a devotion from 2 Corinthians 1 on Thursday afternoon and that later in the session he gave an address: "The Joys of the Ministry."

Early in his ministry he moved his family to West Texas to work in the cotton fields. There was no Free Will Baptist church in the area and so they joined a Nazarene church. Before long the Brooks family moved back to Clay County and he was reissued Free Will Baptist credentials by the West Fork District Association.

At the Thirty-second annual session of the Texas State Association of Free Will Baptists, which met at the North Zulch Free Will Baptist Church, October 29 through November 1, 1946, John preached the introductory sermon on Tuesday evening.

In 1952 John organized the First Free Will Baptist Church of Wichita Falls. His own family formed much of the nucleus of the church. In addition to John and his wife Edith, there were four of his children, two sons-in-law, and three grandchildren. Free Will Baptists moving to Wichita Falls from the Buffalo Springs and Bowie areas helped the church grow.

During the long years of his ministry he worked to support himself and his family mostly by doing manual labor. All the children worked to help out. They would plant crops, chop the weeds out of the cotton and peanuts in the spring, and then work in the harvest in the fall. John Jr. remembers: "I well remember the fall of 1941. My dad picked 500 pounds of cotton per day and myself, my brother, and sister could pick 500 pounds per day and we received 35¢ per 100 pounds picked, and that made all of $3.50 for the four of us. That was great, wasn't it?" The churches which he pastored sometimes paid him with a little food, but most of the time it was just small donations. A few times he was not paid at all. In 1947 he moved to Fort Worth to pastor the First Free Will Baptist Church, which was the first church to pay him a salary. The church paid him $50.00 per week and provided a parsonage in which the Brooks family could live. They thought that was all the money in the world. At the time gasoline was 20¢ per gallon, and ground beef was 25¢ per pound. The parsonage family at the time consisted of John and Edith, and the two sons, W. L., and John, Jr.

One of the things for which John Brooks is best remembered is his work in the youth camp. Before the West Fork acquired a camp of their own, they held camp at Camp Holland, a rented facility in Weatherford. He taught some there. Then, in the mid 1950's the West Fork District Association bought some land in the south end of Clay County for a youth camp all their own, the Broom farm. John was probably the largest contributor of work at the camp for the first ten years or so. He went to Parker County and tore down the old New Hope Free Will Baptist Church building after the church closed. John and his son-in-law, Slim Jackson, hauled the lumber to the new youth camp and he, Tiff Covington, John Jr., and Tiff's son Shorty Covington, used the old lumber to construct the first new building at the camp, the kitchen and dining hall. The kitchen area was enclosed but the dining area was a screened in section, allowing the wind to blow rain all the way through it during a fierce storm. John's daughter Gracie was the first cook for the camp. He loved the camp so much, and for many years, well into his old age, his white head could be seen bobbing around the camp, helping wherever he could.

Sometime in the late 1930's, John and his brother-in-law, Tiff Covington, held a brush arbor revival at Pleasant Mound Free Will Baptist Church that lasted for six weeks. During this time one of Tiff's sons, either Granvel or Shorty, said after about a month of going to church every night, that he was kind of getting tired of trying to live a Christian life! After the meeting closed John and Tiff baptized about one hundred twenty people in a stock tank.

In 1942, during World War II, there were not enough preachers for all of the small, rural Free Will Baptist churches to have pastors. John pastored four churches at one time, preaching at each church only once a month: Dott, Long Branch, Gartman's View, and Weatherford. During the war tires and gasoline were rationed, so about half the time he would have to ride the bus to Weatherford. When he would come back home to Dott he would have to get off the bus in Eddy, Texas, about ten or twelve miles from home, and walk from Eddy to his house. During the winter of 1942 it was so cold as he walked home one day that his ears froze. He almost lost them, but never missed a Sunday at his churches.

He always believed that God would provide, but sometimes he didn't know how. He would get on his knees and pray and everything would turn out right.

John A. Brooks, Jr. said about his father, "He was the greatest man I ever knew, and that was said by lots of his peers. I never saw my father get mad. He always told us that when we get mad we always do or say something for which we later have to say we're sorry."

The first church he pastored was the Pleasant Valley Free Will Baptist Church, south of Buffalo Springs. The last church he pastored was the Pleasant Mound Free Will Baptist Church, the same church with a new name and a slightly different location. He was seventy-six years old when he retired. He passed away on February 24, 1973, at the age of seventy-nine. His wife Edith passed away on September 22, 1985, at the age of ninety-five. At the time she was living with her daughter Gracie and attending the First Free Will Baptist Church in Wichita Falls, which John had started thirty-three years earlier. They are both buried at the Pleasant Valley Cemetery, near the original site of the Pleasant Valley Free Will Baptist Church.

Carl Cheshier

Carl Cheshire

Carl Everett Cheshier was born in Lindsey, Oklahoma, on July 2, 1938, to Paul and Pauline (Comstock) Cheshier. Carl was converted to Christ at age fourteen. Six months later he answer the call to preach. He was issued a license to preach by the First Oklahoma District Association and the Central Avenue Free Will Baptist Church, now the Southern Oaks Free Will Baptist Church in Oklahoma City. He was then ordained to the gospel ministry on December 2, 1956, when he was eighteen years of age. His ordination credentials were singed by his pastor, Jack Dodson, and the deacon board of the Central Avenue Church.

As any young minister should, Carl saw the need for a good education and so he attended the University of Arkansas, and then graduated from Hillsdale Free Will Baptist College with a Bachelor of Arts degree. Early in his ministry Carl pastored the Prague Free Will Baptist Church in Prague, Oklahoma, and the Pine Hill Free Will Baptist Church in Star City, Arkansas.

At this point in his life he moved to West Texas to pastor the Westside Free Will Baptist Church in Midland, Texas, which he pastored from 1967 to 1968. The high point of his ministry in Midland was having over two hundred people in Sunday school and winning the Free Will Baptist national Sunday school campaign in their division. Carl was a very promising young preacher, only about thirty when he left Midland, but one has to understand the difficulties of pastoring in an isolated place such as West Texas. There is first the isolation from areas where Free Will Baptist churches are plentiful, where fellowship with other Free Will Baptist preachers is very limited, where the name Free Will Baptist is not well known, and where the culture is noticeably different. Many young pastors, therefore, return to greener pastures.

Carl left the Westside Church after one year and took the Cavanaugh Free Will Baptist Church in Fort Smith, Arkansas. This pastorate was, in many ways, his signature ministry. He pastored there for twenty-eight years, from June 15, 1969 to July 31, 1997. During this time the Cavanaugh Church became one of the leading churches in the Free Will Baptist denomination.

The average attendance at the time Carl left the church was 478, and the high attendance during his time there was 762.

As any good pastor should be, Carl was active in the wider ministry of the denomination beyond the limits of his own local pastorate. In addition to his district and state work Carl served for thirteen years as a member of the Sunday School and Church Training Board of the National Association. This meant that he was on the board which supervised Randall House Publications. He also served as assistant moderator of the National Association of Free Will Baptists for nine years. He was chosen to preach at the National Association conventions at Louisville, Kentucky, in 1981 and again when it met in Memphis, Tennessee, in 2002. He served with distinction as moderator of the National Association from 1997 to 2004. Carl served as president of Hillsdale Free Will Baptist College, in Moore, Oklahoma, from 1997 to 2004, while still serving as moderator of the National. During his administration at Hillsdale the school was able to get on its feet financially, the campus was remodeled, the Barber Building, which consists of two auditoriums, a cafeteria, classrooms, a conference room, and an office complex, was constructed. Additionally, the school added new degrees to its program.

In commenting on his involvement in his denominational work Carl says, "I have always attended all the denominational meetings from the district to the state to the National. We are servants and it is a privilege to serve. We have a great heritage that must be passed down and this is a great work that must be done. I love our denomination and am privileged to get to serve." Would that every pastor, young and old, had that same sense of responsibility.

Barbara, Carl's wife of fifty-eight and a half years, passed away of brain cancer on April 24, 2014. He then married Virginia Lee Akin on March 22, 2015.

At this writing Carl is pastoring the Cornerstone Free Will Baptist Church in Muldrow, Oklahoma. One piece of advice Carl would pass along to all young people aspiring to the ministry: get a good education. He says, "It is imperative in this day and time."

Gaston Clary

Willie Gaston Clary[151] was born in Iola, Texas, on July 21, 1916, to Dr. Curtis and Media (Williams) Clary. His father, Dr. Clary, was a medical doctor, a surgeon. Gaston grew up in the community where he was born and graduated from Iola High School. Gaston married Lela Josephine (Richards) on September 4, 1937. The wedding took place in the parsonage of the First Free Will Baptist Church in Bryan, and the ceremony was conducted by J.O. Fort, pastor of the Bryan church. Lela is the sister of Walter Herbert Richards.

Ten years later, in 1947, Gaston sensed that God was calling him into the ministry, and he answered that call. That same year he was licensed to the ministry by the Central Texas District Association of Free Will Baptists. He realized the need for training for the ministry and wanted to go to school for that purpose. He was working at the time for Texas A&M University in College Station, had an eight year old son and a four year old daughter. He and Lela sold their house and went to Nashville, Tennessee, to attend Free Will Baptist Bible College. People thought they were crazy, according to Lela. At the time the college was a two year school and he graduated in 1949, along with his sister Margaret Richards and her husband Herbert. He had returned to Bryan in the summer of 1948 and was ordained to the gospel ministry by the Central Texas District Association. He ordination credentials were signed by Pastor J. O. Fort, Norman Kinne, and a Mr. Holmes. The

---

[151] Much of the information about Gaston Clary was gleaned in an interview conducted with his wife Lela on June 10, 2014, in the home of her niece, Marilu McDonald, in Bryan, Texas.

ordination service took place at the First Free Will Baptist Church in Bryan. During the next several years he pastored the Cross Free Will Baptist Church in Iola, three times, the Good Hope Free Will Baptist Church in Henderson, and the Buncombe Free Will Baptist Church, out of Carthage, Texas. He was chosen to preach on the radio program sponsored by the East Texas District Association for a time, taking turns with some of the other East Texas pastors. He served his churches full time until he retired from the ministry. It must be noted that there were times when his churches could not pay his salary. During these times he sold insurance in order to make ends meet.

Lela was the ever busy pastor's wife. Churches often unfairly consider the role of the pastor's wife to be somewhat of an official position in the church, with numerous responsibilities but no extra pay for her. Lela filled her role admirably, teaching children's classes at times and adult classes at other times. She considers herself a better teacher of adults than children. She was active in the youth work in the local church and in the district, and served as president of the Woman's Auxiliary on both a district and state level.

Gaston was elected as president of the East Texas District Association, back in the days when moderators were called presidents, and also served as district clerk. He served as president of the Master's Men in East Texas. Additionally, he served as moderator and clerk of the Texas State Association of Free Will Baptists.

There are usually some very trying times in the life of a pastor and he must do on occasion what he would rather not do. This was the case with Old Testament prophets and New Testament apostles. A situation arose in East Texas when two of his fellow pastors began to preach doctrines contrary to Free Will Baptist positions. The pastors in question were Noah Tuttle and Huey Gower. There were several areas of concern. One of them was that Pastors Tuttle and Gower began preaching that one couldn't go to heaven if he did not practice feet washing.[152] Whether one washed feet or not wasn't a concern to Gaston because the church he pastored, the Good Hope Free Will Baptist Church, did not practice feet washing. However, saying that washing feet was essential to salvation was a perversion of the gospel. Another area of concern was that Pastor Tuttle began preaching and encouraging the practice of speaking in tongues, as practiced by the various charismatic groups. Gaston filed charges against his two fellow pastors at the 1954 77th annual session of the East Texas District Association.[153] The charges read as follows:

> I, Gaston Clary, a minister in good standing in the Texas District Association of Free Will Baptists and a member and pastor of Good Hope Free Will Baptist Church, make the following charges against Noah Tuttle and Huey Gower and request this association to deprive them of their credentials as Free Will Baptist Ministers if these charges are found to be true.
>
> They are advocates of a second work of Grace to which our church is definitely opposed.
>
> They brought in individuals who are not licensed or ordained to preach and are not

---

[152] While I was pastoring in West Central Alabama, at Northport, in the 1960's and early 1970's, most of the Free Will Baptist churches in the area did not practice feet washing and never had. It was a surprise to me one Friday evening at a quarterly meeting of the Progressive Association that one of our pastors made the same assertion, that one could not go to heaven unless he washed feet.

[153] It was at this session that the name of the association was changed from Texas Association to East Texas District Association.

Free Will Baptists and are advocates of doctrine contrary to Free Will Baptist belief and practice and sponsored their appearance in several of our churches.

They are teaching and preaching that Divine Healing is Co-equal with Salvation and was provided for in the bruised body of Christ to the extent that those who believe can grow limbs that have been severed from the body.

That Infirmity in the Christian is caused by sin and if they would not sin they would not be sick.

Through preaching of doctrine contrary to Free Will Baptist belief they have caused reproach on the Free Will Baptist denomination and have caused irreparable damage to the Texas District Association and to Free Will Baptists of this Area.[154]

The association found Pastors Tuttle and Gower guilty of the charges and revoked their credentials. This was done even though Gower was moderator of the association at the time. The vote was 17 for and 14 against adoption.

After Gaston had retired from active pastoring and moved back to Bryan, the First Free Will Baptist Church asked him if he could serve them in the capacity of deacon. Gaston consented and became one of the few Free Will Baptist preachers who later became a deacon. It usually works the other way: many Free Will Baptist deacons have stepped up to become pastors.

Gaston and Lela donated part of the land for the cemetery in Iola, which is the Clary-Nevill Cemetery. Their land joined the Nevill property and so the two families each gave a portion. Gaston passed away on March 24, 1995, and is buried in the cemetery which bears his name. Lela passed away in September of 2016 and was laid to rest next to Gaston on September 11th.

H. Z. Cox

Harry Zirl Cox was born on November 30, 1919, in Antelope, Texas, to Robert Ebbie and Margaret Sue (Blackmon) Cox. He attended elementary school at Buffalo Springs and attended high school in Bellevue, through the tenth grade. He was licensed to the gospel ministry in 1941. He received a Bachelor's degree in Bible from Dallas Bible College, and in 1953 he earned a Master of Theology from Bible Baptist Seminary. He married Artelle Barnette who would be his faithful companion for fifty-one years. They would have three children: Robert Dewayne, Michael Lee, and Cynthia Ann.

World War II interrupted his ministry as it did many other young Free Will Baptist men. During the war he served in the United States Army from 1943 to 1945 as a medic and chaplain's assistant. During the latter months of the war he served in Germany as the powerful Allied Armies destroyed the Third Reich and brought Hitler's dream of a thousand year

H. Z. Cox

---

[154] Minutes of the East Texas District Association, 1954, Proceedings of the 77th Annual Session, page 6.

empire to an end. Back in the United States, after the war, he returned to his wife Artelle and son Robert.

Brother Cox's first pastorate was the New Salem Free Will Baptist Church, just south of Decatur, which he pastored from 1945 to 1947, preaching every other Sunday. In those days many churches held worship services only twice a month, either the first and third Sundays or the second and fourth Sundays. If a month had a fifth Sunday there were usually no services, though some did have Sunday school.

In September of 1947 he became pastor of the First Free Will Baptist Church in Dallas and embarked on a long and productive ministry which would make him well known, not only in Texas, but in the denomination at large. To support himself and his family Brother Cox worked for the Lone Star Gas Company. In 1954 the church had grown to the extent that they could put Brother Cox on full-time. That pastorate would last until his retirement in November of 1986, a ministry of forty years at the church. He was on an annual call, that is, the church voted each year to call him as pastor. That is the way he wanted it, which was different from what most pastors preferred.

At first the First Free Will Baptist Church of Dallas was located 1803 Browder Street. Then it relocated to the corner of Beaumont and Browder Streets. As the church grew and sought a better location, Brother Cox led them in 1971 to build a second beautiful new church building, at 1711 Reynoldston Lane in Dallas. By 1982 the growing church under Brother Cox's leadership relocated to 1415 W. Wheatland in Duncanville, a suburb on the south side of Dallas, building an even larger and more beautiful church. This move was made, not only to accommodate a growing congregation, but to locate it closer to where a large number of the church members lived. In the 1970's and 80's the church had a very large group of young people, many of whom were involved in the competitive activities of the Church Training Service (CTS). Individuals and teams competed in Sword Drill, Declamation, Bible Tic Tac Toe, and Bible Bowl on a district, state, and national level, winning many trophies over the years. When CTS added the Music and Arts Festival the youth of First Duncanville continued to excel in that area, too.

Brother Cox was active on a wider scale than just as pastor of the church. He was very active in the ministry of the West Fork Youth Camp, even before the association purchased land for a camp in the south end of Clay County. In his earlier years the West Fork rented a youth camp near Weatherford, Texas. He served the West Fork Youth Camp in many capacities over the years, from being a member of the Christian Education Board which operated the camp, to being camp director, teacher, counsellor, and camp evangelist. One of the things he loved to do was take the campers on the morning hike before breakfast and lead the morning devotional. As long as he was physically able he attended the camp, spending the entire week, even though he had no specific duties.

Also in the West Fork District Association he served in many capacities as well, perhaps most notably as moderator. On a state level he served as moderator of the Texas State Association of Free Will Baptists and as a member of the State Mission Board. Whether on the district or state level he promoted and emphasized that each church should support all denominational causes through the district association and the Cooperative Plan of support. In his earlier years as pastor of the Dallas church he led them to give five percent of their general fund income to denominational causes. When he felt the church was more able to do so he led them to give ten percent to those causes. In the 1960's he served as a member of the National Board of Home Missions and Church Extension.

In the late 60's when the matter of the state of the backslider became a hot, controversial issue, threatening to endanger the unity of the Free Will Baptist denomination, each state association was asked to send two representatives to Nashville, Tennessee, to meet with the Executive Committee of the General Board of the National Association, and find a solution, if possible. Brother Cox and Rashie Kennedy, who was Texas' Executive Secretary at the time, were sent by the Texas State Association to represent Texas at the meeting. The meeting was held in the warehouse of Randall House Publications, behind the National Offices building at 1134 Murfreesboro Road in Nashville. The delegates to that meeting agreed to recommend to the National Association a statement written by Dr. Robert E. Picirilli, professor of Greek and New Testament at Free Will Baptist Bible College, now Welch College, for inclusion into the *Free Will Baptist Treatise*, clarifying how Free Will Baptists stood on the issue. The National Association adopted that statement in July of 1969 and placed it in the *Treatise*, thus ending, at least outwardly, the controversy. The statement didn't change anyone's theological position, and didn't intend to, but it did state a common ground on which all Free Will Baptists could work together while still holding their differences on the issue.

H. Z. retired from the pastorate in 1986. Brother Cox passed away on July 28, 1993, and is buried in the Vashti Cemetery at Vashti, Texas. The conference room in the Barber Center at Hillsdale Free Will Baptist College in Moore, Oklahoma, is named the H. Z. Cox Conference Room.

Tiff Covington

Tiff Covington

Anderson Tifton (Tiff) Covington was born near Panola, Kentucky, on August 25, 1895, to Milton Conner and Charlotte Covington.[155] The Covington family moved to Texas, arriving by train in Henrietta on September 3, 1908. Tiff was thirteen. The family settled in the Buffalo Springs community and began working in the fields, mostly picking cotton in season. He attended school in Buffalo Springs and in Deer Grove, getting the equivalent of a seventh grade education.

Word reached Tiff that J. W. Schultz was preaching a revival meeting in the Pleasant Valley School house, south of Buffalo Springs. On Sunday morning he put his pony to the buggy and made his way to church and continued attending the services throughout the week. Finally, on Saturday morning he committed his life to Christ. He was then baptized in Billy Hilburn's stock tank.

Pastor Schultz, who had helped organize the West Fork Association, had a daughter by the name of Carrye Dell. She and Tiff began dating. After a courtship of a year and a half they were married on July 29, 1917, less than a month before his twenty-third birthday, in her home in Post Oak, Texas. Carrye was always called Carrye D. after that to distinguish her from Tiff's sister, Carrye. During the first year of their marriage Tiff and Carrye D. lived in a ten by twelve foot tent. It had a dirt floor and their furnishings consisted of a bed, cookstove, cabinet, and a trunk. Tiff did job work and worked as a farmer growing cotton,

---

[155] Much of the biographical information about Tiff came from interviews I conducted with him in his home on Lake Wichita in 1983.

corn, hay, and raising some livestock. Tiff and Carrye D. had four children: Granvel Wayne, Mauvereen (Mickey), Willburn Conner (Shorty), and Ramona Latrell.

For several years Tiff fought the call to the ministry. He considered himself too illiterate to take on the ministry and, besides, he was timid and downright afraid of the public, as he told me in a personal interview. For a while he served as a deacon, but that did not satisfy his calling. During this time he suffered several setbacks. One year he lost all of his crops, as well as his chickens and turkeys, in a great hailstorm. Another year he lost twenty-seven head of livestock, including his horses, cattle, and hogs. Every day he began to run a low grade fever.[i] His sister Carrye Morgan told me, "Nothing made his faith in the Lord waver, no matter what happened to him."[156] As a result of the constant fever he saw four different doctors and each of them told Tiff that he had tuberculosis in his right lung. One doctor said that he had only six months to live. This news resulted in him going out on the plains of West Texas where he spent seventeen days with his sisters Carrye and Bessie and his brother Jephthah. Soon he received a letter from Carrye D. which said in part, "Tiff, you don't have tuberculosis." He knew Carrye D. was a praying woman and that no one had more faith than she had. Carrye D. had saved her nickels and dimes until she had six dollars, enough to buy Tiff a Bible. She mailed it to him out on the plains. As Tiff related the story to me tears flowed down both cheeks and he spoke very softly, "I opened the Bible, laid it on the bed, and laid my face in it and said, 'Lord, I'll do it. I'll preach your Word. I may not have but six months, but as long as I live I'll preach your Word.' "

Soon he went to the hospital in Lubbock and took a battery of tests. When he met with the doctor to get the text results, the doctor said to him, "Young man, who told you that you have tuberculosis? You don't have a germ in your body, though you do have scars on your right lung."

Tiff returned home from Lubbock and told his pastor, Tom Newsome, that he had surrendered to preach. He was licensed by his home church, Pleasant Valley Free Will Baptist Church, in 1928. Soon the time came for the West Fork quarterly meeting and Tiff went to Weatherford to attend. While there he was asked to speak and so "he made a little talk, just sort of gave my testimony," as he recalled to me. The first sermon he preached was at the next quarterly meeting at the New Salem Free Will Baptist Church, just south of Decatur. He preached at the Saturday morning session and his text was "…What shall I do then with Jesus which is called the Christ?" (Matthew 27:22). As he preached the sermon he was extremely nervous, his body was trembling, he held onto the pulpit with both hands to secure himself, and his knees were shaking something fierce. "It wasn't that I was afraid of the people, I was afraid that I would fail God," he recalled. That afternoon the deacons of the New Salem church called him aside and asked him to pastor the church. He told them that he couldn't do it, that when they had seen him preach that morning they had seen all the experience he had as a minister. However, the deacons prevailed and the church called him as pastor and he accepted.

In 1932 it was time for him to be ordained as a Free Will Baptist minister. His ordination took place at the Silver Creek Free Will Baptist Church near Azle. The ordaining council consisted of J. C. Hodges, T. W. Newsome, and a Brother Haney. They sat Tiff down on the piano stool before the whole congregation and examined him. They passed on him right then and proceeded to ordain him. He continued as pastor of the New Salem church for seventeen and a half years, driving down from Buffalo Springs to preach for them one Sunday each month.

Shortly after beginning his ministry at New Salem, he was also called as pastor of the Pleasant Valley Free Will Baptist Church at Buffalo Springs. J. C. Hodges had been serving the church until one day he resigned "in favor of Brother Covington." Tiff pastored both churches

---

[156] From an interview conducted in Joy, Texas, 1983.

until he was asked to pastor the Buffalo Springs church full time. "Full time" meant every Sunday rather than just one or two Sundays a month. During this time he worked as a carpenter and farmer to supplement his income and provide for his wife and four children, which is what most Texas Free Will Baptist pastors did at the time.

Tiff's ministry at Buffalo Springs during those early years, while he also pastored at New Salem, extended until 1949. In 1936 the Pleasant Valley Free Will Baptist Church constructed a new church building on a hill closer to Buffalo Springs. Built of field stones the church became widely known as The Rock Church. The actual name of the church was changed from Pleasant Valley to Pleasant Mound. That year, 1936, there was an outstanding revival conducted at the church. M. L. Sutton began the meeting and preached for two weeks, morning and night. During the third week of the meeting Tiff and a Methodist minister by the name of Felix Kendall continued the meeting, taking turns morning and night. Tiff finished out the meeting by himself. Altogether the revival lasted a total of thirty-one days. There were eighty-two conversions and rededications. A long line of converts were baptized in a nearby stock tank.

There was another notable revival meeting in Buffalo Springs when Tiff and his brother-in-law, John A. Brooks, preached under a brush arbor which had been built in the pasture of Teague Forman. There were sixty-six conversions during the meeting and Tiff baptized forty-nine of them in a stock tank owned by a Mrs. Flinn.

In September of 1948, Tiff and Ruel Conner established a Free Will Baptist church in Bowie, Texas. Brother Conner served as the first pastor. Then, in May of 1949, the church called Tiff as pastor and he accepted, leaving the church in Buffalo Springs. He moved his family to Bowie on August 15, 1949. Under his leadership the church purchased some property and constructed a church building. Attendance in the church averaged from sixty to eighty during all the time Tiff served as pastor, except at the last when Carrye D., as a result of a series of strokes, became an invalid and required much of his time. During this time he conducted many funerals and performed so many weddings that he became known as "the marrying and burying preacher of Bowie." The funeral home directors said he preached more funerals than all the other pastors in Bowie combined. The funeral home directors would call on Tiff to preach funerals for people he didn't even know. He became well known for his funeral ministry. An article in the Bowie News referred to him as a "real living legend."[157] Often he and his co-workers were called to come down off the house on which they were working as carpenters to conduct a funeral. The men would serve as pall bearers and Tiff would preach the funeral. He pastored in Bowie for eight and a half years.

In 1957 Tiff accepted the pastorate of the First Free Will Baptist Church in Wichita Falls in order to be near the doctors. He served as pastor there until 1960. He lived in Bowie all this time except for one year. Church attendance was down at first but he was able to build the attendance back up to an average of fifty to sixty. In 1960 he returned to Bowie as pastor of the First Free Will Baptist Church there. Then some of the members of the church in Wichita Falls went to Bowie and asked him to return as pastor. He told them that he had to take care of Carrye D. The men promised that they would install a speaker in her bedroom of the parsonage next door to the church so she could hear the services. He consented and returned to Wichita Falls as pastor. He moved into the parsonage in December of 1961. Carrie D. was moved by ambulance. The men of the church kept their promise and she was able to hear the services each Sunday from her bedroom. A little more than a year later, February 12, 1962, Carrye D. passed away of a heart

---

[157] The Bowie News, February 9, 1984, front page.

attack. She had been his faithful companion for more than forty-four years. This was a great personal loss to Tiff. He said she had been the sweetest, holiest wife any preacher could ask for.

Even in a time of deep personal sorrow Tiff continued his ministry. There were many conversions and new members came into the church regularly. Attendance reached into the seventies and then into the eighties. The church became debt free, the parsonage was paid for, facilities were expanded, and the church was in good shape spiritually. Almost a year after losing Carrye D., Tiff married Ethel Inman, January 1, 1963.

Tiff accepted the call from the Pleasant Mound church and he and Ethel moved to Buffalo Springs in 1967 and resumed the pastorate of the church which he had already pastored for over twenty years. Tiff led the church in a remodeling program to improve the facilities and attendance began to pick up. There was renewed interest and cooperation among the congregation. He pastored Pleasant Mound until May 1, 1980, when, at the age of eighty-four, he asked the church not to elect him for another year. He and Ethel moved to Wichita Falls to live next to his son Granvel, on the north shore of Lake Wichita. In retirement Tiff and Ethel attended the First Free Will Baptist Church. Ethel passed away in 1983, followed by Tiff on November 3, 1984. It was my privilege to be standing by his bedside when he passed.

Tiff was active in the work of the West Fork District Association of Free Will Baptists, taking on various leadership roles in the association, such as the West Fork Youth Camp. All of the fifty-two years of his ministry were spent in the West Fork. He was also active in the Texas State Association, preaching as requested, serving on various boards and committees, such as the State Home Missions Board, and working to promote the Free Will Baptist Children's Home in Ringling, Oklahoma.

Perhaps his greatest claim to fame, not that he would claim any, was his funeral ministry. When pressed to give an estimate of how many funerals he conducted he estimated the number at three thousand. He averaged doing two funerals a week. During one February he did fourteen in that one month, and he was seventy-seven years old at the time. He often preached two a day and on multiple occasions he preached double funerals. His brother Cheese once said to me, "The reason he preaches so many funerals is because he knows so many people and they think no one else can preach a funeral like he can."[158] Riding home from a funeral just preached by Tiff, his nephew, John A. Brooks, Jr., said, "Uncle Tiff is the best funeral preacher I ever heard."
After hearing several funeral messages by Tiff, I can say that he had a sweetness about him which endeared him to the people. He always seemed to know exactly what to say to comfort and console the family. There was a certain pathos and empathy in his funeral messages. I can personally verify that right up into his eighties people were asking him to live another twenty-five years so he could preach their funeral.

While visiting with him in his home on Lake Wichita I asked him if he had any advice to pass on to the younger generation of preachers. He thought a minute and then said, "Preach the Word, preach the Bible. Don't preach your opinions, tell them what the Bible says. Get all of the education you can, and then ask God to help you use it. Read lots of books and observe nature, observe all that goes on around you. I still feel that God calls men. If anyone is going to preach, he must have a divine calling. I'm so glad God let me be a part of His ministry."

---

[158] From a personal interview at Cheese's home in Joy, Texas, circa 1983.

M. L. Crosby

Milburn Lee Crosby was born on February 23, 1933, to May Bell (Swanner) and William Floyd Crosby, in Falls County, Texas. He was one of four children. His father worked in a cotton gin. His parents were not members of a Free Will Baptist church, but they did attend one. The Woodlawn Association of Free Will Baptists was located in the area in and south of Waco in the 1930's and 40's. The pastors lived in Killeen, Bruceville, Waco, Dott, and Eddy, along what is now the I-35 corridor from Waco to Killeen. The pastors usually drove in from wherever they lived, often coming by bus, to preach on Sundays that had worship services. Billie Jean Martin was the daughter of Oran McKenzie and Ollie Leola (Calvery) Martin. Her father was one of sixteen children, and her mother was one of thirteen siblings. Mr. Martin was a deacon in the Liberty Free Will Baptist Church at Dott, and later in the First Free Will Baptist Church in Waco. He owned the Martin Grocery Store in Dott, and later owned one by the same name in Waco, on LaSalle Street near the church. Billie and her sister Glendene often worked in the store in Waco. Billie's first year of elementary school was in Dott, but she finished her elementary education in Chilton, where she graduated from Chilton High School in 1950.

Milburn graduated from Chilton High School and then attended Baylor University for one year. In addition he took some correspondence courses. He and Billie Jean Martin were married on August 31, 1951. Elic Marecle performed the ceremony. It was raining at the time, and consequently, Marecle stood on his front porch while Milburn and Billie sat in a wagon, which had a top to shield them from the rain. From this marriage came two children: Edward Lee and Allen Dwain.

Milburn was converted to Christ at the age of eighteen. Ten years later he answered the call to preach the gospel, at the age of twenty-eight. He was licensed to the ministry on September 9, 1961, and ordained on August 31, 1962, by the West Fork District Association of Free Will Baptists. His ordination papers were signed by J. E. Marecle, R. E. Conner, and John A. Brooks.

Brother Crosby pastored a number of churches during the twenty-one years of his ministry. In 1964 he filled in as pastor at the New Hope Free Will Baptist Church in Fort Worth. In 1966-67 he pastored Faith Chapel Free Will Baptist Church in Carlsbad, New Mexico. From October of 1967 to March of 1972 he pastored the First Free Will Baptist Church of Crowell, Texas, in the Northwest Brazos District Association. In October of 1972 he moved to the Gulf Coast and pastored the Zion Free Will Baptist Church until October of 1973. Zion Church was in the Mission District Association. In December of that year he returned for a second tenure at the First Free Will Baptist Church in Crowell, once again serving for five years, until May of 1978. In June of 1978 he became the pastor of the First Free Will Baptist Church of Waco, serving for eight years, until September of 1986.

In March of 1984, when Jack Bankhead and Thurmon Murphy finished their walk from Wichita Falls to Waco, to raise funds for the construction of Covington Hall at the West Fork Youth Camp, Brother Crosby and Billie were waiting for them at the Brazos River Bridge as they completed their walk.

Brother Crosby was always a bi-vocational pastor, consistently having to work for a living at a secular job to support his family. He was a master carpenter. He passed away on July 1, 1990, and is buried in Waco Memorial Park.

Their son Dwain was a missionary to Spain under the auspices of Free Will Baptist International Missions. Billie went to Spain to visit him and his family for two weeks in 1991, and again for two weeks in 1995. Dwain and Debbie were living in the city of Mostales at the time.

Z. B. Dally

One of the couples whose ministries in Texas needs to be preserved in our history is Zell Byron Dally and his wife Annie. They were both born in Ohio. Annie was born on December 22, 1867, and Z. B. was born on March 12, 1870. They were married in 1894. In 1910 they lived in Penfield, Monroe County, New York. They were both involved in the General Conference of Free Will Baptists, the Randall Movement, which was strong in both Ohio and New York. By 1916 Z. B. and Annie were living in Weatherford, Texas, where he published the *Free Will Baptist Sentinel*.

Dally tombstone in Algoma cemetery, Marshall, Texas

Z. B. was an educated man. Annie had not been to school but could read and write. They worked as colporters, that is, people who traveled to sell books, bibles, and tracts. As such they were given the "full privileges of the house" at the January 1917 session of the state association. He reported that they had organized five Sunday schools and furnished literature to numerous others. They were unusually active in that second session of the state association. He gave a presentation on "Our Relations with the American Baptist Publications Society" and later read a paper on "Preparation for Life's Work". The paper was so well received that the association had it printed in book form for distribution to the churches. Mrs. Dally gave a lecture on "World Wide Missions" and showed a number of curios from India and discussed them. During the Women's Missionary Society part of the meeting she gave a reading called "Twins." They were singers, also, singing duets twice during the session. They were elected to serve the association as Sunday School and Young People's Society missionaries, with a view to strengthening and improving both ministries in the state and introducing the most up to date methods for Sunday school work. He was elected state moderator and she was elected to a position on the Woman's Missionary Society leadership team. They continued to serve Texas Free Will Baptists for years. In 1930 they were living in Slayton, Lubbock County, Texas. Annie passed away on July 11, 1938, in Marshall, Texas. Z. B. died on March 24, 1958, also in Marshall.

Bobby Joe Davis

Bobby Joe Davis[159] was born to Sanford Harold and Mary Pauline (Lowery) Davis on October 16, 1934, at Navasota, Texas. Bobby Joe's father worked in the oil field for eleven years and then became a farmer. Bobby Joe accepted Christ as his savior at the age of twelve and devoted his entire life to him. As a young man he answered the call to preach and was licensed to the gospel ministry in November, 1951, by the Central Texas District Association of Free Will Baptists, at the age of seventeen. He received his license at the Blue Lake Free Will Baptist Church in the Piedmont community of Grimes County. He graduated from Navasota High School in 1952

---

[159] The information about Bobby Joe Davis came from an interview in his home on July 19, 2013, from written answers to questions in writing submitted to him, from personal correspondence, and telephone conversations.

and enrolled at Free Will Baptist Bible College that fall. He graduated from the Bible College in 1956, completing the four year program of study. While still a student at the Bible College, Bobby Joe was ordained by the Central Texas District on July 3, 1954, at the age of nineteen. The men who signed his ordination certificate were Alvin F. Halbrook, H. M. McAdams, and J. L. Bounds, a Who's Who among Texas Free Will Baptists.

Bobbie Joe and Barrie Sue Colson were introduced by their pastors at a Central District Association quarterly meeting at the Pine Prairie Free Will Baptist Church. Barrie Sue had grown up in the First Free Will Baptist Church in Bryan, and was very active in the church. She often attended quarterly meetings and, while a teenager, gave a devotion at one of the meetings. She graduated from the Bryan High School in 1954, along with Bill Jones and John Moehlman, both of whom would become Free Will Baptist foreign missionaries. When Bobbie Joe and Barrie Sue were married, on August 18, 1956, the ceremony was performed at the First Free Will Baptist Church in Bryan by John Moehlman. The best man was Bill Jones. From this marriage came John David, Peter Daniel, Susanna (deceased, before she was two full days old), Joel Andrew (deceased, 1971-2009), James Samuel, and Joanna (Schorre).

Bobbie Joe and Barrie Sue Davis

Bobby Joe entered the United States Army and served from 1956 to 1959. He was stationed at Fort Jackson, located in Columbia, South Carolina. All of his time in the service was stateside.

Bobby Joe pastored a number of churches during his long years of ministry in Texas, and all of them in Texas, we might add. The churches he pastored were:

      Pine Prairie Free Will Baptist Church, out of Huntsville
      Huntsville Free Will Baptist Church, Huntsville
      Evergreen Free Will Baptist Church, Keith
      Fellowship Free Will Baptist Church
      Zion Free Will Baptist Church, Corpus Christi
      Northcrest Free Will Baptist Church, Victoria
      Thomaston Free Will Baptist Church, Thomaston

Bobby Joe remembers that when he was pastoring the Huntsville Church Lizzie McAdams was a member of the church in her later years. She used to interrupt the sermons of the young pastor, saying, "Pastor, let me explain a little further so it will be clearer to the members." He was more patient with her than many pastors would have been.

All the years of his ministry were bi-vocational. He worked as a carpenter, school teacher, and counsellor. He worked fourteen years for the Texas Rehabilitation Commission. He was always active in the district and state ministries in Texas. He served on the district ordaining council, as parliamentarian, and served as a member of the State Christian Education Board. He was perhaps especially active with the youth camp ministry, serving on the Central District Camp Board. During the weeks of camp he served as camp director, teacher, dorm parent, and helped in the kitchen. During the year, as well as during camp, he worked at camp maintenance, both at Camp Carlos and Camp Sonshine.

Bobbie Joe and the churches he pastored have always been supporters of Free Will Baptist Bible College and missions. In 1993 he moved the Northcrest Church from Victoria to Thomaston, and it became the Thomaston Free Will Baptist Church. The Thomaston Church helped establish the Lighthouse Free Will Baptist Church in Victoria, paying the salary of the missionary pastor there, Rev. Nick Stewart, providing the Lighthouse Church with rent free facilities for the past thirteen years. In addition, they paid Brother Stewart $3,000.00 per month in salary for the first year and then continued paying him a reduced salary for another eighteen months. They also provided free housing for Nick and Angie for a few years. Before three years had passed the mission church in Victoria had more members than the supporting Thomaston Church. Brother Stewart has recently resigned to accept a pastorate in Mississippi. The church has elected Rev. John Hancock, from the Midland-Odessa area, to be their new pastor, though at the time of this writing he has not moved yet due to his obligations as a building contractor. Under Brother Davis' leadership, the Thomaston church has sent large amounts of funding to other Free Will Baptist mission churches in Texas. Remarkably, with only fourteen members, the Thomaston Church has given $777,839.30 to colleges and missions through the church treasury between its beginning in 1993 and the end of 2013. Personal giving by members of the church, given directly, brings the total to more than $800,000.00.

W. E. Dearmore

The faculty of Tecumseh College, left to right: Mr. and Mrs. S. L. Morris, Mr. and Mrs. G. W. Lawrence, Mr. and Mrs. Samra Smith, W. E. Dearmore, John and Delia Wolfe.

William Edward Dearmore was born at Charleston, Arkansas, on May 25, 1881. He married Ada Ann Baze (born 1885) on December 28, 1900. From this marriage came seven children: William Henry (1902-1909), Ethel Idel (1903-1975), Grace Lilly (1910-1992), James (1914-1914, August 30 to September 26), Floydette E. (1917-2002), Joy Yvonne (1921-1985), and Mildred Marie (1923-1925). It is not known when he came to Texas or when and by whom he was ordained, but we learn that he was active in the Free Will Baptist work in Texas prior to the organization of the state association. His home association was the West Fork. In 1914 he, acting as associational missionary, went to Clay County and gave the new Pleasant Valley Free Will Baptist Church, now the Pleasant Mound Church, a thorough examination before they were organized into a church. He found them to be sound in the faith and the organizational service was conducted.[160]

He was well enough known and respected that he was placed in several important positions in 1915 when the Texas State Convention, now the Texas State Association, was organized. He was one of the most active men in the first session of the Texas State Convention of Free Will Baptists, which met at Bradley, Texas, October 8-9, 1915. We glean from the minutes of that meeting, written in Dearmore's own beautiful handwriting, several pieces of information about him. He was chosen to preach the "introductory sermon" at the meeting. The introductory sermon was the initial sermon preached at meetings in those days. They were what we today might call a keynote sermon or keynote address. This was a very distinct honor and indicates something of the

---

[160] *Buffalo Springs Community History*, edited by Louise Maxwell and Louise Reeder, not dated, page 117.

high esteem in which Dearmore was held by his fellow Texas ministers. He was first appointed temporary clerk until the association could be organized, and then was elected permanent clerk. In addition, he was elected treasurer and was appointed to serve with J. J. Tatum and C. C. Wheeler on a committee to draft a constitution for the fledgling association. With numerous other ministers present, and with him being appointed and/or elected to so many positions of great responsibility at the first session of the association, we learn something of the abilities with which he was gifted. At the time Dearmore lived in Boyd, Texas, located on State Highway 114 seven miles south of Decatur, in southern Wise County.

At the second session of the Texas State Convention, held in January of 1917, Dearmore was not present. He had made, or was preparing to make, a move to Oklahoma to be involved in the first year of operation of Tecumseh College, a Free Will Baptist school owned and operated by the Cooperative General Association of Free Will Baptists. He was a teacher in the preparatory department, specializing in History and Mathematics. It seems that he took on more and larger responsibilities of ministry in Oklahoma. In addition to his years of service to Tecumseh College, where he served on the teaching faculty, he served a number of churches as pastor in Oklahoma, such as the Box Church and the Wolf Church, and he served for many years moderator of the Oklahoma State Association. In 1932 he was present in Vernon, Alabama, at the twelfth annual session of the General Conference. He was given the floor to present the cause of the Western Free Will Baptist Publishing Company, "which he did in an impressive way" noted the clerk.[161] He was a delegate to the Cooperative General Association which met in Denison, Texas, in 1934. In 1935 he served as a delegate to the organizational meeting of the National Association of Free Will Baptists in Nashville, Tennessee. He was active in several sessions of the National Association thereafter.

Dearmore and William Arthur Hearron baptized M. L. Sutton's first converts. Sutton had been working as an associate of Lizzie McAdams but had to leave his association with her because of inadequate finances. He preached a revival meeting in Oklahoma, as a licensed minister, and had several converts. Not yet being ordained he called in Dearmore and Hearron to baptize the converts for him.

Dearmore was also the owner of an insurance agency. His wife Ada was also active in the Free Will Baptist work, especially in Oklahoma. She was a teacher at Tecumseh College and served briefly as president of the school. She was a delegate to the Cooperative General Association of Free Will Baptists in 1934 when it met in Denison, Texas. She died on November 23, 1936, in Wanette. Brother Dearmore passed away on December 12, 1945.

---

[161] Minutes of the Twelfth Annual Session of the General Conference of Original Free Will Baptists of the United States, 1932, Vernon, Alabama, page 7.

Doug Dickey

Doug Dickey is another one of the men who came to Texas after having pastored in another state, and in his case several states, and immediately became involved in the Free Will Baptist work in the state. Douglas Wayne Dickey was born on October 19, 1968, in Florence, Alabama, to James Edward and Gladys Kathleen (Springer) Dickey. Doug became affiliated with Free Will Baptists through the ministry of the First Free Will Baptist Church in Florence. Pastor Tom Malone, who pastored the Florence Church before becoming president of Free Will Baptist Bible College, was instrumental in leading Doug to the Lord when he was seven or eight years old. Doug graduated from Central High School in Florence in 1987.

Doug and Sharon Dickey and children

At first Doug was unsure about his call to the ministry and had a certain lack of confidence that he would be able to serve God in that capacity. However, he enrolled at Hillsdale Free Will Baptist College in the fall of 1988, majoring in Theology, with a minor in Missions. He served as Missions Chaplain and played on the school's baseball team.

Several life changing events happened while a student at Hillsdale. First, he met Sharon Renee Becker in 1991 and they were married on December 19, 1992. Interestingly, they were married at the Fellowship Free Will Baptist Church in Bryan, Texas. The ceremony was performed by friend Wesley Bigalow, pastor of the Cornerstone Free Will Baptist Church in College Station. From this marriage would come three children: Douglas Alexander, Danielle Faith, and Elizabeth Chayllie. Second, Doug gained valuable ministerial experience by serving as youth pastor at two local churches: the Kingsview Free Will Baptist Church, in Moore, 1989-1990, and the Northwest Free Will Baptist Church, 1992 to 1994. Third, Doug was licensed to the ministry by the First Oklahoma Association in 1993. He graduated from Hillsdale in 1994 and became youth pastor at his home church, the First Free Will Baptist of Florence, Alabama, where he served from 1994 to 1999. During these years he was ordained to the gospel ministry at his home church, the First Free Will Baptist Church of Florence, on May 7, 1995. Leaving Alabama Doug returned to Bryan, Texas, where he had been married, and served as youth pastor there from 1999 to 2001.

From Texas Doug moved his family to Tennessee where he became pastor of the Flatwoods Free Will Baptist Church of Lawrenceburg, where he pastored for nine years, from June of 2001 to October of 2010. Having gained considerable experience, Doug then became pastor of the Fellowship Free Will Baptist Church in Bryan in December of 2010, and moved his family back to Texas.

Doug is one of those young pastors who correctly understands that his ministry extends beyond his local congregation, though it remain his primary focus. Knowing that he is a part of something larger than himself, and larger than his local church, he serves his denomination and the kingdom of God in several capacities. He has served as moderator of the Central District Association of Free Will Baptists, and currently serves as clerk of the Texas State Association of Free Will Baptists, one of the more important positions in the state work. He also serves as a trustee of Randall University, formerly Hillsdale Free Will Baptist College, a position he has held since 2011.

Doug and his wife Sharon share an interest in working with young people. He has been involved with coaching them through public recreational leagues for about fifteen years. At church he teaches the Junior High and High School Sunday school class and teaches the church's junior age and up Wednesday night youth class. He loves working with youth and trying to have a positive influence and giving guidance in their lives. Sharon is very involved in the ministry of the church, as well. She serves as Vacation Bible School director, teaches a Sunday school class, teaches a primary age group on Wednesday nights, leads a ladies' Bible class, is Women Active for Christ (WAC) Central Texas president, and serves as vice president of the Texas Women Active for Christ (TWAC).

Doug says he dislikes the Texas heat and how far most of our churches are from each other. But he loves his church, stating, "I like how responsive the people of our church are, how generous they are to missions, and the sweet fellowship we enjoy. Our church is pretty diverse and a pleasure most times to pastor."

R. B. Easley

Robert Burnett Easley was born on September 1, 1850, in War Eagle, Arkansas. He married Mary Ann McGuire in 1869 and moved to Texas in October of 1871. Robert and Mary had eleven children: Zorah E., Orpha, Dicie, Deffie, John Martin, Tommy, Simon Peter, Robert Burnett, Jr., Philip Jeff, William Paul, and Luke Ellery. Philip Jeff, ninth of the eleven children, lived to celebrate his one hundredth birthday on March 25, 1986. Brother Easley is best known for founding the Easley's Chapel Free Will Baptist Church, just north of Comanche, Texas, in September of 1886. Lumber for the first church building was hauled by team

R. B. and Mary Ann Easley. This picture presented and unveiled to the church September 17, 1967

and wagon from Dublin, Texas, and Brother Easley helped construct the building. This is one of the older Free Will Baptist churches in Texas and it continues today. At the second session of the Texas State Association brother Easley gave a presentation on "Why a State Association." He passed away on December 26, 1940, at the age of ninety.

J. L. Edge

James Lee Edge was born in Americus, Georgia, April 5, 1868.[162] From about the age of ten he lived in Brazos County, Texas, for the last sixty-two years of his life. For fifty of those years he was a very successful merchant in the city of Bryan, where he was considered to be one of Bryan's leading citizens. He was a lifelong member of the Free Will Baptist Church, which later became the First Free Will Baptist Church, and served for years as senior deacon. He was married to Lillie F. Edge. Both were charter members of the church. J. L. Edge, as he was known, being a successful merchant, owning the Edge Dry Goods Company, was able to give a great deal of his time to the Free Will Baptist work in Texas beyond his local church. He was moderator of

---

[162] *The Bryan Daily Eagle*, Bryan, Texas, July 22, 1941, page 1.

the Texas State Association in 1928.[163] The Executive Committee, of which Edge was chairman, met in Clayton, Texas, on September 1, 1927, to begin making plans for their work for the year. They met again in a called meeting on March 17, 1928, in Edge's office in Bryan. The clerk noted "we discussed the work of the Free Baptist[164] in the State from every angle."[165]

At the tenth annual session of the General Conference of Free Will Baptists, which convened June 11-12, 1930, in Vernon, Alabama, J. L. and Lillie Edge served as corresponding delegates representing the Texas State Convention. They were received into the conference and elected to sit as members of the body.[166] The Texas State Convention was not yet a member of the conference. The conference's Field Secretary, J. L. Welch, noted the presence of Mr. and Mrs. Edge in his report and expressed hopes that Texas would soon be a member. Brother Edge, President of the Texas State Convention, requested that an elected delegate from the conference be sent to the Texas State Convention in November of that year. A motion passed to that effect and J. L. Welch of Tennessee and M. L. Hollis of Alabama were elected as delegates. As a result of Brother Edge's efforts, the General Conference held its twelfth annual session at the Free Will Baptist Church in Bryan, June 15, 1932.

Edge was president of the state convention of Free Will Baptists for several years, including 1929. That year the convention presented him with a nice fountain pen in appreciation for his service as president.[167]

His love for his church, and his generosity, was shown in 1939 when he and his wife Lillie announced that they would donate the money for the construction of the new brick sanctuary needed for the growing congregation.[168] The new sanctuary was completed and dedicated in 1940. As a footnote to history it should be noted here that another prominent citizen of Bryan, Mr. Walter J. Coulter, donated the land on which the sanctuary was built, at West 30th Street and Parker. Brother Edge passed away in July of 1941 of a heart attack suffered in his home. His wife Lillie, who had been born in Brazos County December 12, 1873, passed away December 1, 1976, at the age of 103. Both are buried in the Bryan City Cemetery.

Jackie Farmer

Jackie Wayne Farmer was born on October 4, 1945, in Odessa, Texas. His father Paschal was a house painter. Jackie had three brothers and four sisters. Growing up in Odessa he graduated from Odessa High School in 1973. He was converted to Christ in 1965, at the age of 20, under the ministry of Gene Zoellers.

---

[163] State Convention Minutes, 1928, page 1.
[164] It is interesting that the clerk still used the name Free Baptist as late as 1928.
[165] Texas State Convention Minutes, 1928, page 4.
[166] Minutes of the tenth annual session of the General Conference of the Original Free Will Baptists of the United States, 1930, when convened at Vernon, Alabama, page 4.
[167] 1929 state minutes, page 4.
[168] *Bryan Daily Eagle*, Bryan, Texas, December 1, 1939.

In 1970 Jackie sensed that God was dealing with him about the ministry. The call kept tugging at his heart and would not go away. It was at the Westside Free Will Baptist Church in Midland, Texas, while Glen Hood was pastor that he surrendered his heart to God to preach and to begin to make preparation for the ministry.

Another monumental event took place in Jackie's life, this time on July 1, 1972. This is when he married Patsy Havner, who was raised in Midland, and a good Free Will Baptist, at the Westside Church, by Pastor Glen Hood. From their marriage came three children: Jackie Wayne, Jr., Kimberly Sharon (Herring), and Christopher David.

Jackie Wayne and Patsy Sharon Farmer

To Jackie preaching and preparation went together, like a hand in a glove. In 1973 he enrolled at Free Will Baptist Bible College in Nashville, Tennessee. While attending the Bible College Jackie worked at night for the Nashville Tennessean newspaper as a pressman to support his family and pay for his tuition. He attended the full four year program of study and graduated in 1977. All of his tuition was paid by the time he finished college. Jackie was licensed to the gospel ministry in 1982 by the Northwest Brazos District Association. A year later he was ordained by the Northwest Brazos. His ordination credentials were signed by Junior Blackwood, Bob Gill, and Troy Harp.

It would be common for a young preacher to begin his ministry by accepting a small church where he could preach and gain pastoral experience. Jackie did it differently. The same year he was licensed to the ministry, 1982, he started the Faith Free Will Baptist Church in Shallowater, Texas, a suburb of Lubbock. He was not supported by a mission board, he did it on his own, with God's help. He continues as pastor of that same church.

Faith Free Will Baptist Church, Lubbock, Texas

Faith Church is not a full-time church, so he had to work as a bi-vocational minister to support his family. He worked as a pressroom supervisor for the Lubbock Avalanche Journal, from which he is now retired. He does some part time work as a meter technician.

In addition to pastoring the Faith Church, Jackie has served as moderator of the Northwest Brazos District Association. He and James Qualls, of Odessa, founded the West Texas District Association when the Northwest Brazos folded.

Bobby Ferguson

Bobby Gene Ferguson was born on April 18, 1936, to Charlie Floyd and Emma Mae (Duggins) Ferguson at Flippin, Marion County, Arkansas. Flippin is a small town in north central Arkansas, just south of Bull Shoals Lake. Bobby attended the elementary school in Flippin, but did not attend high school at all. His family attended a General Baptist church. Bobby's father led him to the Lord.

The Ferguson family moved to Houston, Texas, where Bobby went to work in the meat department of a grocery store. As a meat cutter he made fairly good money for the time and for a teenager. In the spring of 1953 his family became involved in the First Free Will Baptist Church, which he joined in August of 1953. Within two years he announced that God had called him to the ministry, which seems to have come as a surprise to no one. His pastor, Everett Hellard, recommended that he go to Free Will Baptist Bible College for training for the ministry. He packed his bags and went to Nashville, Tennessee, starting his freshman year in 1955.

Bobby and Bettie Ferguson

During his years at the Bible College Bobby sang in the Bible College Quartet, singing bass. Other members of the quartet were Jimmy Hughes, Dean Dobbs, and Ronnie Peele. The quartet traveled to seven states representing the college. He served on the Student Council, was president of the John Bunyan Literary Society, and was president of the junior class. He also earned his GD at Vanderbilt University. He graduated from the Bible College in 1959.

His first pastorate after graduation was the Mount Olive Free Will Baptist Church near Henderson, Texas, which he pastored in 1959-60, a full-time church. He was licensed to preach by the East Texas District Association of Free Will Baptists and then ordained by the East Texas District Association. It was during this time that he met and married Bettie Gene Hunt. The wedding ceremony was conducted at the Mount Olive church by H. Ray Berry. From this marriage came two sons: David Wendell and John Randall.

Several short term ministries followed in quick succession. From Mount Olive he went to Dallas and became associate pastor under H. Z. Cox. This ministry lasted only one year. He says that he did not know how to be an associate pastor and that Brother Cox did not know how to use an associate, not at all an unusual situation. From Dallas he went to Tyler, Texas, in an attempt to establish a church there in 1962-63. In 1963-64 he pastored the Good Hope Free Will Baptist Church in Henderson, Texas.

In 1965, at the age of twenty-nine, he was called as pastor of the First Free Will Baptist Church in Houston, Texas, a ministry that would last until his retirement. He started on the first Sunday of May, 1965. He suddenly found himself to be the pastor of one of the denomination's best known men, C. B. Thompson. At the time Brother Thompson was already showing signs of dementia and was living with his daughter. Before the end of the decade it was Pastor Ferguson's responsibility to preach the funeral of Brother Thompson. The church grew under Pastor Ferguson's leadership and became the flagship church of Texas Free Will Baptists for a number of years. In 1973, due to the increased growth, the church relocated and built a very nice facility at 10331 Stuebner-Airline Road. More growth required the construction of a yet larger sanctuary and additional classroom space connected to the same facility. It was the premier Free Will Baptist Church in Texas.

The methods used by Pastor Ferguson to build the congregation included a home Bible study ministry, conducted in the homes of prospects for about six weeks at a time. At the conclusion of the study Bobby would give the family a family Bible. He eventually realized that giving the families a Bible was not necessary to get them to have the study. Visitation was also one of the methods he used, and, of course, there was his preaching, which was exceptional. The church also provided a full, well-rounded ministry to the entire family. For many years there was a very active youth group which participated in the Church Training Service competitive activities: declamations, sword drill, Bible Tic Tac Toe, and Bible Bowl. Eventually music and arts were added. Teams and individuals often went to the state and national competitions and were often winners. All of this made the church attractive to people. Then, there was one more important ingredient of church growth: Brother Ferguson's personal charisma and good humor.

Pastor Ferguson always found time to do his fair share of work outside the church, a responsibility every pastor has. That was part of his ministry, too, the work of Christ on a broader scale within the denomination. He served in many capacities in the Central Texas District Association of Free Will Baptists, such as a member of the credentials committee/ordaining council and a dozen terms as district moderator. On the state level he served four terms as state moderator, was the state clerk, a member of the State Home Missions Board, the state's executive secretary, and was editor of *The Texas Challenge* in 1970-71. As moderator of Texas State Association of Free Will Baptists he was more than just an objective moderator, conducting business impartially, he brought leadership and ideas to the position. Because of the excellence and effectiveness of his preaching he preached numerous revival meetings in the state. In 1993 he preached at the National Association of Free Will Baptists when it met in Louisville, Kentucky. His text was Matthew 16:13-19 and his subject was "Storming the Gates of Hell."

Bobby had a real passion for missions, which was evident whether he was on the mission board or not. He was very instrumental in the establishing of the Lakehills Free Will Baptist Church in Cedar Park, a suburb of Austin. One of his biggest contributions to the Free Will Baptist work in the state of Texas was the fact that while he was pastor of the First Free Will Baptist Church in Houston he, on several occasions, sent out a number of the families in his own church to other parts of the greater Houston metropolitan area to start new churches, reducing the size of his own church and losing valuable, talented, and dedicated members. However, this resulted in the establishment of several new Free Will Baptist churches, such as Westfield, Magnolia, Eagle Heights, and Wildwood. He would help the new group secure a pastor, purchase land, erect a building, and help them become self-supporting, autonomous churches. This may not have been duplicated any place in the Free Will Baptist denomination. He was not just building churches to establish his own little kingdom over which he ruled as bishop, he was reaching the city of Houston for Christ, building the Free Will Baptist work in Texas, and building the kingdom of God in fulfillment of the Great Commission. However, it must be observed in good humor that some of his best friends jokingly refer to him as Bishop.

Due to a changing community and changing demographics, in 2006 he led the First Free Will Baptist Church in Houston to move to the suburb of Tomball. The church built a beautiful church facility on an ideal piece of property at 12251 Northpointe Boulevard. The larger sanctuary back in Houston became the Iglesia Bautista Libre de Houston (First Free Will Baptist Church of Houston), a Hispanic church pastored by Bobby's friend Secundino (Dino) Urena. The older and smaller sanctuary at that site became the Liberation Free Will Baptist Church, pastored by Dino's son Jezer Urena.

Brother Bobby continued pastoring the First Free Will Baptist Church of Tomball until he retired from the pastorate at the end of 2012 at the age of seventy-six, after pastoring for fifty-three years.

When asked who were the people who influenced his life the most, especially his Christian life, he named H. Ray Berry, Everett Hellard, and his father, Floyd Ferguson. It must also be observed that during all the years of his ministry his wife Bettie was very much a part of his work, being encouraging, supportive, and involved in the work of the Free Will Baptist women of Texas, particularly the Woman's Auxiliary.

It would be hard to name anyone who has done more for the Free Will Baptist work in Texas than Bobby Ferguson.

Allie Ferguson

Allie Fennel Record Ferguson was born in Memphis, Tennessee, November 8, 1909. His father was a carpenter and tenant farmer. His mother became involved in the Christian Science cult and became very neglectful of Allie and his sister Irene. His parents divorced when Allie was about six years old. During Allie's growing up years the family moved almost every year. From Tennessee they moved to Arkansas, to Texas, to Oklahoma, back to Arkansas, and then back to Texas. While working as a carpenter between Alvarado and Cleburne, Texas, Allie's father met and soon married Miss Willie Bell Head. Allie said, "This was my real mother as she turned out to be." His stepmother was the godly influence in his life. He accepted Christ as his savor when he was sixteen years old and he committed his life to Christ. Those are more than just nice sounding words as Allie showed for the duration of his long life that he really was fully committed to his Lord. They were a poor family and often lived with relatives.

Allie and Jesse Ferguson

The Fergusons moved to a small community called Cedar Mills, in Grayson County, five miles from Gordonville and northeast of Gainesville. They rented the Potts farm which was about two and a half miles south of the Red River. Word spread through the community that young Allie was going to be a preacher. In those days that made him much more attractive to the young single ladies, even though he was already a handsome young man. At church one Sunday Allie noted the eyes and smile of a young lady by the name of Jessie Zeona Van. They couldn't seem to keep their eyes off each other. Within a couple of weeks Allie asked if he could walk her home from church and she said yes. About eighteen months later, November 29, 1931, Allie and Jessie were married at the courthouse in Durant, Oklahoma. Allie's father had died just a month before the wedding.

They soon moved, with the family possessions loaded into the family wagon, pulled by a team of horses, to Fort Worth. The family consisted of Allie's stepmother, whom he always referred to as mother, one brother and two sisters. Jessie assumed the responsibilities for caring for Allie's three younger siblings because Allie's mother had become too ill to take care of them.

Allie worked for the Justin Boot and Shoe Manufacturing Company, working fifty-four hours a week for the sum of nine dollars. That wasn't bad pay for 1932. The Great Depression had hit full force, but at least they had a job, an apartment in which to live, and were able to eat regularly.

Allie and Jessie affiliated themselves with the First Free Will Baptist Church of Fort Worth, pastored by M. L. Sutton. It was a good, growing, active church where the Word of God was taught and preached. Allie and Jessie grew up spiritually in the West Fork District Association. Allie's mentor was his pastor, Brother Sutton, one of the best men at the time from whom he could learn about preaching and pastoring. His peers were men such as Tiff Covington, Ruel E. Conner, and Bill McPhail. H. Z. Cox and Clarence Hearron were two of the upcoming younger ministers who would go on to have long and distinguished ministries in Texas and beyond.

Allie and Bill McPhail began going over to Parker County to preach for the New Hope Free Will Baptist Church, out of Weatherford. Here the two young men were able to do a lot of "practice preaching" as they called it. Allie and Bill were ordained to the gospel ministry at the same time, in the same service. They became fast friends for life. Jessie was licensed to the ministry herself by the First Free Will Baptist Church in Fort Worth, her home church, on September 1, 1934. Soon an opportunity came for Allie to pastor at a mission church in Dallas, which met in a store front. He continued living in Fort Worth, working at the Justin Boot Company, and driving to Dallas each Sunday to preach. The mission disbanded in 1938.

When they left the Dallas mission Allie accepted three rural churches to pastor at the same time, preaching for each of them one Sunday a month. He continued working for Justin during the week and then on Sundays he and Jessie would drive to one of the three churches: Gartman's View Free Will Baptist Church in Comanche, the Liberty Free Will Baptist Church at Dott, or the Woodlawn Free Will Baptist Church in McLennan County. Each of these churches were a hundred miles or more from their home in Fort Worth. They spent three years pastoring those three rural churches, 1938 to 1940.

In 1940 they took a mission church on Commerce Street in Dallas and pastored it until 1942. During the War many things were rationed, such as tires, gasoline, sugar, and butter. The mission called H. Z. Cox as pastor in 1942 and the church became the First Free Will Baptist Church of Dallas, now the First Free Will Baptist Church of Duncanville. By this time Allie and Jessie had two children, Norman and Glenna.

The First Free Will Baptist Church of Weatherford, Texas, called Allie as pastor in 1945 and Jessie and Allie moved here. The church offered to pay twenty dollars a week for three weeks of each month. Allie said he would preach the other Sundays for free. He quit his job at the Justin Book Company and moved to Weatherford, living on a salary of sixty dollars a month. They perhaps had their greatest ministry in Weatherford. They had an unusually successful ministry with the young people of the town due, in part, to Jessie's hard work in building a large class for them in the church. Another factor was their involvement with the Youth for Christ organization in town. It was in Weatherford that Allie and Jessie began to be called Ma and Pa Ferguson. The church grew to the extent that a new sanctuary became necessary and the new sanctuary was constructed under their leadership. The Ferguson's left Weatherford after ten good years of ministry there, 1945 to 1955. At the end of the ten years the church was paying them forty dollars per week — for all the weeks of the month.

Allie and H. Z. Cox were two of the main men who helped organize and have the first summer youth camp for the West Fork District Association, first at Camp Holland at Weatherford and then the newly purchased camp near Vashti in southern Clay County.

After Weatherford Jessie continued her enthusiastic and able ministry with her husband. They spent two years at the First Free Will Baptist Church in Denison, two years at the Pleasant Mound Free Will Baptist Church at Buffalo Springs, and then moved to Odessa, in West Texas, to start a Free Will Baptist Church there. Going on their own, without being under a mission board, they were able to establish the Faith Free Will Baptist Church and pastored it for nine years, 1957 to 1965.

Over the next several years they pastored the Liberty Free Will Baptist Church in Comanche, and then the Good Hope Free Will Baptist Church in Henderson. Two interesting things happened at the Good Hope Church. One concerned the practice of feet washing. The church, one of the oldest Free Will Baptist churches in Texas, had never practiced feet washing, which was true of most or all of the earliest Free Will Baptist churches in Texas. However, through Allie's encouragement they agreed to start observing the ritual, which Allie considered to be an ordinance of the gospel. The other thing occurred as a result of Allie asking the church for a two weeks vacation after he had been been pastoring the church for sixteen months. The church said they could not afford to give him a paid vacation. He told them that he would go on vacation without pay. The church voted that he could not go, even without pay. To all appearances Allie and Jessie seemed to take the vote in stride, no problem. Then, a few weeks later, they had the car packed when they came to church on Sunday night. Allie preached that evening, read his resignation as pastor, and announced that they would be leaving the next morning for a two weeks vacation in California.

Allie and Jessie Ferguson
50th Wedding Anniversary

While visiting their old friend Bill McPhail, who had by now been pastoring in California for some time, Allie was asked to preach at the Free Will Baptist Church in Shafter. After hearing him preach the church asked if he would consider moving to California to pastor their church. He said he would and in less than a month Allie and Jessie were living in Shafter, pastoring the church.

Allie and Jessie pretty much finished out their pastoral ministry by pastoring the Mt. Olive Free Will Baptist Church, near Henderson, Texas; the Murry Spur Free Will Baptist Church in Spiro, Oklahoma; and the Fellowship Free Will Baptist Church in Richton, Mississippi.

They moved back to Texas, living near Tyler for the remainder of their lives. Jessie's health was bad in her later years and she passed on before Allie did. They are buried in the Tyler Memorial Park Cemetery in Tyler, Smith County, Texas.

During more than sixty years of active ministry, Allie pastored sixteen churches, in four states. He was officially full-time much of his ministry, even though his salary did not always reflect that he was full-time. He was active in every phase of the ministry as a Free Will Baptist preacher. He served in about every office or position available on both the district and state levels. He always served with enthusiasm, recognizing that this was a part of his ministry too. Several things motivated him to work as long and as hard as he did: 1) he had a strong sense of having been called to the ministry, 2) he loved his Lord, 3) he loved the Free Will Baptist denomination, and 4) he always knew he would face an accounting for his ministry.

Karen Ferguson

Karen Ann Ferguson was born to Bonnie (Keeney) and Paul Thomas Carson in Watertown, New York. She was raised an army brat, as she says, and travelled extensively and lived in about seven states and Germany as a result. Karen graduated from Copperas Cove High School in Copperas Cove, Texas, in 1972. She was captain of the Copperettes Drill Team and marched with the marching band. She married her high school sweetheart of four years, Franklin Alexander Ferguson, on December 28, 1972. He was in the Air Force and this contributed to her world travels. Karen became a Christian on September 5, 1976, at the First Free Will Baptist Church in Flint, Michigan, under the ministry of Rudy Shankle. She and Frank have two children: Cory Alexander Ferguson and Heath Franklin Ferguson. At present there are two granddaughters: Katelyn Nicole Ferguson and Ashlyn Nicole Ferguson.[169]

Karen Ferguson

Karen has worked at a number of jobs over the years. She was an escrow agent in Alaska, an insurance secretary in Wyoming, a teller in Copperas Cove, Texas, a sales agent and receiving clerk for Lifeway Christian Book Stores in Houston, as well as a dental assistant, also in Houston. She quit her job so she could teach ladies Bible studies, and to devote more of her time to being a housewife and grandmother. As a teen she worked in a theatre. Her husband Frank works for EMC, a data storage company, as a field engineer.

Karen is qualified to teach Precept by Precept Bible courses, and has taken classes at the College of Biblical Studies in Houston. She also took some Child Evangelism courses.

Karen and Frank came to the First Free Will Baptist Church in Houston, Texas, on July 4, 1982, from the Community Free Will Baptist Church in Westland, Michigan. This move was Michigan's loss and Texas' gain. She almost immediately became a leader in the Free Will Baptist work in Texas, at all levels. She became a children's teacher, children's choir director, CTS sponsor/teacher, puppetry director, sang alto in the adult choir, and played the piano in Dino Urena's Spanish church, which also met at the First Free Will Baptist Church of Houston. When her boys were teens she worked with the church's youth group. She is most noted, however, for her work with the Woman's Auxiliary, which later became the Women Nationally Active for Christ. In January of 1983, only six months after coming to the First Free Will Baptist Church in Houston, they made her the president of the church's Woman's Auxiliary. The Woman's National Auxiliary Convention (WNAC) was soon changed to the Women Nationally Active for Christ (still WNAC). She subsequently also served as Missions Action Chairman, Missions Study Chairman, Missions Prayer Chairman and Social Committee Chairman. That same year, 1983, she became active in the women's work of the Central Texas District Association of Free Will Baptists. She served as Prayer Chairman and Study Chairman, and became president. She eventually became president of the state organization, the Texas Women Active for Christ. As president of the broader group she leads the Texas women

---

[169] Note that both granddaughters have the middle name Nicole. So does Karen's daughter-in-law, Heath's wife Jamie, and Jamie's sister and her daughter.

in various missions' projects, women's retreats, state convention meetings, and budget development.

Most of the women's retreats focus on spiritual growth and fellowship. One of the retreats was a First Lady's Retreat which honored the wives of the state's pastors. There was an Appreciation Tea where they were given gifts, entertained, and made to feel special. Karen said, "I felt it was very important to let our pastors' spouses know they were appreciated, loved, and supported." She adds that one of the most meaningful retreats they ever sponsored was the joint retreat with the TWAC and our Hispanic ladies in Mexico. The women in Texas paid for the ladies in Mexico to attend the retreat while the women in Texas served at the retreat. Karen had the privilege of going with the WNAC to the first ever Women's Prayer Conference in Almaty, Kazakhstan.[170] The women of the Texas Women active for Christ gave financially so the women of Kazakhstan, Tajikistan, Turkmenistan, Uzbekistan, and Kyrgyzstan could attend. Karen has been active in the WNAC on a national level, as well. She attends the national convention and taught a class at a national women's retreat in Glorietta, New Mexico, and spoke at a WNAC meeting on prayer.

When asked about her motivation in being so active in the Women Nationally Active for Christ, she said:

> I believe the WNAC is the voice for our missionaries, keeping them and their needs before the churches while they serve on the field. My goal is to help raise funds for missionaries, as well as help women to grow spiritually and fulfill the purpose to which God has called us. I desire to teach the Word and help women fall in love with God and his Word. As a new Christian I was introduced to Woman's Auxiliary and it was during this time I learned about missions, missionaries, and serving. It also was a means to help me learn how a Christian is to live. I think WNAC is important to our home and foreign missionaries, as well as our local churches, to equip us to better fulfill the Great Commission in Acts 1:8. Our missionaries need our women's help to keep their ministries before the people for financial and prayer support. I think WNAC is a great way to mentor women on how God says a woman ought to live.

One of the notable things done by the First Free Will Baptist Church in Houston, under the leadership of Pastor Bobby Ferguson, was to send a portion of the congregation out into another area of Houston to be the nucleus of new churches. In 1994 Karen and her family left the First Free Will Baptist Church to go to Katy, Texas, and be part of a new church pastored by David Ferguson (no relation) and his wife Rhonda. The new church became the Westfield Free Will Baptist Church. Karen served not only as part of the nucleus of the church, but also ministered as the women's Bible study teacher, president of the Women active for Christ, VBS teacher, Sunday school teacher, sang in the ladies ensemble, directed the children's choir, was First Place 4 Health co-director/teacher, and various other jobs.

After fifteen years at the Westfield Free Will Baptist Church, Karen and Frank moved their family to the Eagle Heights Free Will Baptist Church in Sugarland, Texas, to help with the planting of yet another church. This one was pastored by Randy Puckett and his wife Shelly. At Eagle Heights Karen served as ladies Bible study teacher.

---

[170] The Republic of Kazakhstan is a contiguous transcontinental country in Central Asia, extending into Eastern Europe, and bordering on Russia and China. It is the world's largest landlocked country by land area and is the ninth largest country in the world. The religious majority is Islamic.

Then, Karen and Frank became a part of the Woodforest Free Will Baptist Mission in Woodforest, Texas, which is a joint project of the Texas State Home Mission Board and the Free Will Baptist National Home Missions Board. This new mission effort is under the leadership of Karen's and Frank's son Heath Ferguson and his wife Jamie. That is where Karen and Frank are serving now and, undoubtedly, Karen is making her normal ministry contributions.

Perhaps the best way to end this brief biography of Karen is to once again use her own words. She says it best.

> I was raised in a "religious" home and learned reverence for God and that He sent His Son to die on the cross for the sins of the world; but not about a personal relationship with Him or what the Christian life is to be. I was saved in 1976 at the age of 22 and knew nothing about the Christian life or the Word of God. From the moment I was saved God changed me and gave me a hunger to study His Word. I have never doubted my salvation because of the inward change God has done and continues to do in me. I had no abilities or talents to offer Him but He choose to give me the gift of teaching and allowed me to study under great pastors and women who mentored me and who would be willing to allow me to share what I was learning with the ladies of our churches. I'm forever grateful for the relationship I have with the Lord and all that He has done for me.
>
> Life has been very rewarding as a Christian and though I have failed God at times, He has never failed me. I'm very grateful for Free Will Baptists because it was through Free Will Baptists that my sisters became Christians and led me to Christ. It is through Free Will Baptists that I have learned how to live for the Lord and how to develop an intimate relationship with Him. It has been through Free Will Baptists that I have been able to serve, teach, and speak at various retreats, meetings, conventions, etc. I'm grateful for Dr. Robert "Bob" Porter, my very first pastor at the Community Free Will Baptist Church in Westland, Michigan, and Brother Bobby Ferguson at the First Free Will Baptist Church in Houston, Brother David Ferguson, my pastor at Westfield Free Will Baptist Church in Katy, Texas, and Brother Randy Puckett at Eagle Heights Church in Sugarland, Texas. At the foot of each of these pastors I learned a great deal about the love of God and His Word and will forever be grateful for their testimonies and their pastoring me.
>
> I can never get over the privilege that I am being given the opportunity of serving the Lord with my son, Heath, and daughter-in-law, Jamie, in the mission work recently started in Woodforest, Texas. God heard the desires of my heart and I am enjoying watching the Lord use my son to minister to me as He has faithfully done through the rest of these godly men that God has given me as pastors. The Lord has given me the privilege of serving Him in ways I never dreamed and with people I will deeply love forever. Teaching women is my passion. There is nothing better to me than enjoying the study of the Word of God with women who love Him and His Word, and then going out to lunch together (unless, of course, it is time with my family doing the same).

All of us, both men and women, know how vital the presence and ministry of women are in our churches. Where would we be without them? Where would we be without their prayers? It is a privilege to recognize their contributions to the Free Will Baptist work in Texas. Karen Ferguson is one of the special women of Texas, though she would probably be the first to deny it.

T. C. Ferguson

T. C. Ferguson

Thomas Campbell Ferguson (January 10, 1870—March 28, 1957) was born in Ratna, Ontario, Canada. He attended Moody Bible Institute in Chicago for a year and part of a second year, from October 1896 to December 1897. He became affiliated with the Free Will Baptist denomination and was licensed to preach at the New Salem Church in southern Kansas, then ordained to the gospel ministry at the Free Will Baptist Church in Lincoln, Nebraska, sometime around 1900. He married Myrtle Henderson of Augusta, Kansas, on February 26, 1902. To this marriage were born three children: Jesse, who died as an infant, Jewel Elizabeth, who sang in their campaigns, and John William. For several months in 1907 Brother Ferguson pastored the Free Will Baptist Church in Bryan, Texas. He once noted that, though the church paid six hundred dollars per year, they had been unable to find a pastor for the better part of a year. He preached often at the First Free Will Baptist Church of Fort Worth. Starting in 1909 he and Myrtle served for at least three years as evangelists for the Southwestern Convention, with both of them sharing the preaching responsibilities. They conducted numerous evangelistic campaigns in Texas. Altogether they served for eighteen years as traveling evangelists. He was described as a ready, off-hand speaker, a fire and brimstone preacher who spoke with eloquence and persuasive power. He averaged about a thousand converts a year and was able to steer the majority of them into existing Free Will Baptist churches or organize new ones.[171] Thus he helped strengthen the Free Will Baptist work. He helped organize at least one church in Texas. He preached the gospel in a dozen states, as well as in Canada and Mexico. He became a United States citizen in December of 1924.[172]

Myrtle Ferguson, fifteen years younger than her husband, was an accomplished musician and ministered in the campaigns with her playing, singing, and hymn compositions, as well as with her preaching. Ferguson was one of several men, among whom was John H. Wolfe, who spoke out strongly in opposition to the merger with the Northern Baptists and voted against the merger at the 1910 General Conference. The minutes of the 1917 General Conference noted that Ferguson "bitterly opposed the union in the General Conference in 1910."[173]

Brother Ferguson and his wife Myrtle were divorced in 1919, with the divorce becoming final on July 6, 1920. They both, however, continued their preaching ministries, though separately and she left the Free Will Baptist denomination. He married Odessa Reed, called Dee, in 1933, when he was sixty-three. He also pastored churches in Kansas, Nebraska, Iowa, and Missouri.

J. A. Ford

J. A. Ford, the brother of the founder of the New Salem Free Will Baptist Church near Decatur, J. W. Ford, played a part in the Free Will Baptist work in the Decatur area. He, too, had

---

[171] *The Morning Star*, January 26, 1911, page 18.
[172] I owe a debt of gratitude to Gail (Ferguson) Mitchell of Missouri, a granddaughter of Brother Ferguson for much of the information about him.
[173] *Minutes of the Thirty-sixth General Conference of Free Baptists*, held at Ocean Park, Maine, August 22-23, 1917, (Merrill and Webber Company, Auburn, Maine, 1917) page 51. Even after the merger of 1910-11 the General Conference continued to meet as sort of a paper organization because of legal and financial issues which had to be resolved.

come from Missouri. A letter he wrote to the *Morning Star* in 1901 sheds a great deal of light on him and the work in general. Because of that it is included here:

> DECATUR.-- As I have never written a line to any paper in my life I thought I would make the effort, as I have never seen any paper that comes so close or rather gets so hold of my heart as the MORNING STAR. God bless it and all its efforts for good, and may God send it where it is not, and may it grow and spread like the palm tree of until it will fill the universe with its glad tidings of free salvation, as it teaches. Dear brothers in Christ, I am a member of the Free Baptist denomination and one of its so called back woods preachers. I am sixty years old, and in 1900 I traveled 1300 miles, sometimes in wagon, sometimes on horseback, other times on foot, to fill my appointments. Many times I felt that it was more than I was able to bear, yet I was like Paul, I felt woe is me if I preach not the gospel. We organized the West Fork Association in 1890. We have had a long, hard struggle, though God has blessed every effort until our denomination is coming to the front. Though we have not the advantages of church houses as you have, we hold our protracted meetings under bush arbors or in some shady grove. But the people are becoming awakened to duty and we are making hard struggles for church houses. While other denominations have tried to keep us under in this part of the world yet Truth crushed to earth will rise again, the eternal years of God are hers, and now that the Free Baptist people are preaching and practising (*sic*) just what Christ and the apostles taught, then if God is for us who can be against us? Christ said, "Lo I am with you alway, even unto the end of the world." Then let us earnestly contend for the faith once delivered to the saints. I want to tell you that our people in this part of the world are poor people as a general thing. Though they are rich in faith they are not able to help their ministers. I am a poor man, work five days out of the week, then in my weakness try to preach Saturdays and Sundays. And I have a very weakly wife and a blind son to support. I oftentimes when I have to start to my appointments turn my back on them with tears streaming from my eyes and with an aching heart. But Christ said, "Go, fail not to declare the whole counsel of God." I am praying that all our sorrows will wind up in death. Brothers, pray for us that when Christ shall come again without sin unto salvation, he may gather many precious jewels from the Free Baptist denomination, and that we may be as numberless as the sands on the seashore. Now in conclusion I want to say, please excuse bad writing and misspelled words, as I was like our blessed Saviour, born of poor parents, raised on the frontier, had not the chance of schooling; all I know I learned at home as my sainted mother had time to teach me. God bless a mother's influence. It will live parallel with God. Brothers, pray for me that I may blow the gospel trumpet what few more days I may live.
>
> Yours in Christ, J. A. Ford

J. W. Ford

Josephus Wesley Ford was born on January 31, 1848, in Washington County, Arkansas, to Martha (Patsy) Barham (Middleton) and Richard E. Ford. Richard was a farmer, wagon maker, and a Free Will Baptist minister. Richard travelled from Tennessee to Arkansas and Missouri in a cart pulled by oxen. Josephus married Elizabeth (Eliza) Ann Young (1854-1929), daughter of Lurana A. (Davis) and Uriah S. Young, on March 20, 1870. They were married by Thomas Skaggs, Justice of the Peace. From this marriage came thirteen children.[174] That year, 1870, Josephus W. Ford was listed as the head of a family in the 1870 census of McDonald County, Missouri. He is also listed in the census of 1880, which lists him as a farmer, thirty-eight years of age, born in Arkansas, and his religious preference was "Freewill Baptist." Three of Josephus' brothers were also Free Will Baptist preachers: James Alexander Ford, William Henry Ford, and Markley Stanford "Sandy" Ford.[175]

J. W. and Eliza Ford

His ordination to the gospel ministry is recorded on page 633 of the McDonald County Records. It says:

> This certifies that the bearer, J. W. Ford, of the County of McDonald and State of Missouri, a regular member of the Free Will Baptist Church in said county has this day been publicly set apart to the work of gospel ministry by prayer and laying on of hands according to the usage of the Freewill Baptist Denomination and is hereby authorized to preach the Gospel and administer its ordinances wherever God in his providence may call him.

His credentials were signed by L. H. Roberson and William H. Ford, Ordaining Council. It is dated August 15, 1880, but it was filed and recorded on May 4, 1887, by John Black, Clerk. Goodspeed's 1888 *History of McDonald and Newton Counties* shows the Free Will Baptist church of Gooden Hollow as organized in September of 1886, with J. W. Ford as moderator. The membership of the church was nineteen at the time it was organized. The Western Mount Zion quarterly meeting convened on July 8, 1887, with the Pleasant Hill Free Will Baptist Church, on White Rock Prairie, with a delegation from eight churches and seven ministers. J. W. Ford served as moderator.

At some point between 1888 and 1893, Josephus Wesley Ford brought his family from Jane, McDonald County, Missouri, to Wise County, Texas.

According to the Ford family history he passed away at the church when they were having dinner on the grounds. He had run a foot race, after which he took a spoon of honey, and then passed away, according to his son "Pate" Ford. He was not yet fifty years old. *The Wise County Messenger,* July 22, 1898, mentioned his death on page one, but did not state that it happened at

---

[174] The findagrave.com memorial lists twelve children, five girls and seven boys.
[175] This information was supplied to me by Rev. Alton Loveless.

the church. His tombstone gives the date of his death as July 19, 1898, but the *Wise County Messenger* lists it as occurring on July 17, 1898. The *Messenger* also states that he left a wife and eleven children. His body is interred in Pleasant Grove #1 Cemetery, Decatur, Wise County, Texas.

From Josephus' son Roy's daughter, Goldie Mae Wood, of Dodge City, Kansas, comes a partial copy of the obituary of J. W. Ford. Though the first part of it is missing, it is worthwhile to include it here because it is so touching. The part we have says:

> ...in the beautiful home of the soul. To the bereaved family and church the beautiful sentiments of the poem come as a welcome greeting in this hour, and we, too, will
> Judge not the
> Lord by feeble sense,
> But trust him for his grace,
> Behind a frowning providence
> He shows a shining face.
>
> A Free Will Baptist himself, Brother Ford came from a race of Freewills and Methodists, and his warm friendship came from the fact that he recognized God's children of all churches. He was born in Washington County, Arkansas, in 1848. He has been in the ministry 18 years; was married in 1871 to Miss Eliza Ann Young, and to them were born 13 children 12 of whom are now living and 5 of whom are now trying to meet their father in that happy land. It is hard to realize that our [as this place the newspaper clipping had deteriorated] _ _ _ _ _ _r (father?), our friend, and our pastor beyond is a_ unknown land. To all our inquires the still small voice replies, do your duty to God, to yourself, and to your fellowman, and leave the rest to him who doeth all things well. He is gone from among us and a grateful church mourns his loss and honors his memory. The church tenders its heartfelt sympathy to her whose sorrow is the deepest, and to the bereaved family. We gently fold the drapery of his couch about him and lay him down to sleep where immortals and forget-me-nots will bloom over his grave. We try to bow with resignation to the summons that calls him away. And we leave him with the angels who will stand by his tomb and keep watch over his slumbers; and we invoke Him who is above all angels, principalities, and powers, to care for her whom his dispensation has left widowed and alone in the world. The life boat is coming by the eye of faith I see. As she sweeps through the waters to rescue you and me, she will land us safely in the port with the friends we love so dear. Get ready cries the Captain. Oh look! She is almost here.
> John T. Sanford

Rosalie Gregg reported as a result of an interview with Mr. Will Phillips, one of the deacons of the New Salem Church, on October 12, 1964, that James A Ford made the coffin for Josephus Wesley Ford as he had once requested.

Clyde Goen

Clyde F. Goen

Clyde Goen was a rancher, a genuine cattle working, horse riding, lasso throwing, branding iron using, Texas cowboy. He was in no way the silver screen variety, though he had the looks to equal those of Roy Rogers, Gene Autry, or Tim Holt. He was born Clyde Forrest Goen on May 21, 1893, in Brazos County, Texas. His parents were Will and Nancy Goen who were founding members of the Bright Light Free Will Baptist Church, which was organized in 1886. Will was one of the church's first deacons. Clyde accepted Christ as his savior at an early age and had a lifelong commitment to Christ and to the Free Will Baptist denomination.

Clyde was the first of his family to graduate from college, graduating from the Agriculture and Mechanical College of Texas in 1912. The school would be renamed Texas A&M in 1963. His field of study was agriculture. While in college Clyde worked for E. J. Kyle, dean of agriculture and the man for whom Kyle Field, the football field, is named.

Clyde married Grace Erin McSwain and they had one child, Oliver, born September 26, 1921.

As a young college graduate Clyde had no money to speak of. He worked breaking horses and mules to help him earn enough money to purchase one hundred fifty acres of ranch land, the beginning of the Goen Ranch. Over the years he expanded the size of his ranch as money and nearby ranch land became available, eventually building his spread to approximately seventeen hundred acres. He was a cattle raiser and it was his ambition to raise the best cattle which could be raised.

Being a cowboy can be tough work. Sometimes it requires seeing the herd though an especially rough winter, though a drought, helping the cows drop calves occasionally, and doctoring them as needed. In the spring of 1955 Clyde had a steer which was bloated as a result of eating clover. The normal course of action in such a case was to pour kerosene down the animal to break down the gas bubbles so the steer could belch the gas out. In the process of doing this the steer knocked Clyde down, puncturing both of Clyde's lungs, and breaking ribs in both of his rib cages.

Above everything else, though, Clyde was a Christian. His commitment to Christ and his beloved denomination were reflected in many ways. His name is spread all over the minutes of the Central Texas District Association of Free Will Baptists, the Texas State Association of Free Will Baptists, and the National Association of Free Will Baptists. He served on a number of committees at all levels and was moderator of the Texas State Association of Free Will Baptists. He was present in Bryan, Texas, during early efforts to bring Free Will Baptists from the East and the West Together. He was present at the Cofer's Chapel Free Will Baptist Church in Nashville, Tennessee, in November of 1935, when the two groups came together and formed the National Association of Free Will Baptists. He was elected to the Executive Board of the newly formed National Association, which indicates the high stature in which he was regarded. He was a member of the National Board of Foreign Missions when the National met in Bryan in 1939.[176] He attended

---

[176] Damon C. Dodd, *The Free Will Baptist Story*, page 127.

the Free Will Baptist national conventions faithfully until he was no longer physically able to do so.

He was always generous to the Lord's work. He was known for coming home from various meetings with empty pockets, having given all the money he had with him in the offering or to one project or another. One of the burdens of his heart was the need for a Free Will Baptist school to train young ministers. Not many Free Will Baptists went off to receive training for the ministry in those days, one reason being that the denomination had no school for them to attend. Those young men who did seek training had to attend the Bible colleges and seminaries of other denominations. This resulted in many of them leaving the denomination and ministering in the denomination whose school had trained them. Clyde recognized that this drain on the Free Will Baptist denomination needed to be stopped, and he also recognized that young Free Will Baptist preachers needed training for the ministry, as most Texas Free Will Baptist ministers were uneducated. He was fervently devoted to the founding of Free Will Baptist Bible College, which opened its doors in 1942 in Nashville, Tennessee.

During the late 1940's Clyde, as he always did, attended the National Association of Free Will Baptists. He was moved by the report of a distressing situation at Free Will Baptist Bible College. The small but growing school had purchased some property in order to expand their facilities. The college had started out in a three story old mansion on Richland Avenue, which they named Davidson Hall after J. R. Davidson, who pastored the First Free Will Baptist Church in Bryan, Texas, from 1937 to 1942. As the student body grew, and the need for more dormitory space and class room space increased, the school would simply buy another of the big houses on Richland Avenue and convert it into a college facility. The note came due on one of these buildings and the school could not pay it. This precipitated a crisis and the Bible College was in danger of closing. Clyde took this distressing situation to heart. He promised to help the school even though he didn't have the money to do so. This was heavy on his mind and heart as he made his way back to Texas from the National Convention. Arriving back home he went into Bryan and talked to his banker, telling the banker that he wanted to borrow ten thousand dollars to give to the Bible College. The banker strongly advised Clyde not to do it, pointing out that the money might not be able to save the college and could be a large lost investment. However, Clyde had faith in God, faith in the Bible College, and faith in the Free Will Baptist denomination. He was persistent and the banker granted him the loan of ten thousand dollars, which Clyde quickly sent to the Bible College, saving it from closing. He continued to faithfully support the college.

Years later, in the 1960's, when the college was building a new three story men's dormitory, the college was appealing far and wide across the denomination for contributions for the much needed new dorm. One day a check from Clyde Goen arrived in the mail, addressed to the school president, Dr. L. C. Johnson. The check was for thirty-five thousand dollars. Dr. Johnston took the check into the office of academic dean Charles Thigpen and just laid it on his desk. Dr. Thigpen looked at the check, saw the amount, saw who it was from, and exclaimed, "I think we ought to name the new dormitory Goen Hall." Dr. Johnson said, "I agree with you and I will propose that to the board of trustees when we meet." The rest is history. Clyde and Grace were present for the dedication of Goen Hall, along with many denominational dignitaries. The dormitory is still the main residence of the young men who attend Free Will Baptist Bible College, now named Welch College. The college has purchased a little more than one hundred twenty-five acres in nearby Gallatin, Tennessee, and is building an entirely new campus. Clyde Goen would be in full agreement with this move to establish Welch College on a regular, spacious campus, rather than it continuing to be a series of old mansions converted into a college.

Clyde's wife, Grace, was committed to and active in the denominational work, right along with her husband. She gave a report on women's work, which she had written, at the Fourteenth Annual Session of the Texas Free Will Baptist Convention, held at the Woodlawn Free Will Baptist Church in McClellan County in 1928, which drew a special vote of thanks from the body for such a splendid report. The report is so noteworthy that it is included in the chapter on Texas Women Active for Christ in this book as an example of her work.

J. M. Goode

Another of those names which are written all over the minutes of the East Texas District Association and the Texas State Association is J. M. Goode. Joseph Murray Goode was born on December 5, 1908, to Robert Ross and Mae Behringer Goode, in Lexington, Lee County, Texas. His father was a farmer. J. M.'s maternal grandfather was from Baden Baden, Germany, and had homesteaded land between Lexington and Giddings, Texas. J. M. grew up in that area and was the oldest of seven children. His father became ill and J. M. had to step up to be the man of the house and do the farming. As a result he was able to finish only the eighth grade in school at the Lexington Elementary School. He was converted to Christ at the age of twenty-three at a revival meeting. He had gone to the meeting because he wanted to date a girl by the name of Viola Pearl Johnson, but she wouldn't date him because he didn't go to

Pearl and J. M Goode

church and wasn't a Christian. This was no "conversion" just so he could date the girl of his dreams; he gave his whole life to Christ and served him faithfully the rest of his life.

Pearl agreed to date him and they were married in Lexington, on July 19, 1933. From this marriage came a slew of beautiful girls: Volree June Goode Wilkinson Hersey, Shirley Joan Goode Sharpston, Barbara Sue Goode Dunning Bodnar, Mary Katherine Goode Yance, and Paula Rae Goode. Every one of them attended Free Will Baptist Bible College and Brother Goode was justifiably proud of this. June and Shirley married preachers. June married Sam Wilkinson and, after his death, Fred Hersey. She spent most of her life as a missionary in Brazil, and served for a short time in Japan. Shirley married Billy Sharpston who pastored in Texas, Mississippi, Alabama, and Ohio. Brother Goode would have been glad if all of his daughters had married preachers.

Brother Goode sensed the call of God to preach shortly after he became a Christian. For several years he was a lay preacher, but eventually devoted himself fully to the ministry. In 1945 he was licensed to the ministry by the Fellowship Free Will Baptist Church in Henderson, and then ordained by the Texas Association later that same year. One of the men who signed his ordination papers was C. B. Thompson. Over the ensuing years he had a large impact on the Free Will Baptist work in Texas, especially in East Texas.

He set out immediately to pastor churches in East Texas. In 1945-46 he pastored several churches, all at the same time, which wasn't at all unusual in those days. He preached at the Mt. Olive Free Will Baptist Church (Compton) in Laneville, on the first and third Sundays. On the second Sunday mornings he preached at the Dirgin Free Will Baptist Church near Tatum. On the second Sunday afternoons and evenings he preached at the Stewart Free Will Baptist Church near Tatum. He preached at the Centerpoint Free Will Baptist Church near Tatum on the fourth

Sundays. During this time he also preached at the Good Hope Free Will Baptist Church in Henderson on Sunday afternoons.

The Mt. Olive Free Will Baptist Church in the Compton Community went full time in 1948, meaning that they had services each Sunday. The Goode family moved from Overton to the Compton Community to pastor that church. During this time he preached at the Stewart Free Will Baptist Church, conducting services there in the afternoons. Then, in the summer of 1950, they moved again, this time to Kilgore, with the intention of starting a church there. This mission effort did not materialize so Brother Goode became pastor of the Buncombe Free Will Baptist Church, near Clayton, Texas. For a while the Goodes continued to live in Kilgore, driving to Buncombe on Sundays and Wednesday nights. They moved to Clayton in 1953.

Brother Goode started the First Free Will Baptist Church in Carthage in November of 1956, meeting first at the Community Center and then at the H & H Lumber Yard. Charter mem- bers of the church were: Elbert and Pauline Nations, Mrs. Verna Marshall, Mrs. Delmer Dukes, Melton and Ruth Boggs, Mrs. Donnie Clark, Mrs. Jetti Wainwright, Mrs. Gladys Kelly, Mrs. Ethel Carmichael, Mr. V. J. Johnson, Jr., Mr. and Mrs. Gravis, Mrs. Levi Heath, and the Goode Family - J. M. and Pearl Goode, and daughters Shirley, Barbara, and Mary. In December of 1956 they purchased the old Missionary Baptist Church on the Henderson Highway and moved the building to Beverly Drive in Carthage. This church planting effort was not supported by any mission board. The church grew and prospered and Brother Goode pastored it for a number of years.

The Goode family left Texas in 1972 because he felt that the Carthage Church needed someone younger and he needed something different. He moved to Montgomery, Alabama, where he pastored the First Free Will Baptist Church from 1972 to 1975. Several pastorates followed: Okefenokee Free Will Baptist Church, Waycross, Georgia, 1975-76; New Salem Free Will Baptist Church, Colquitt, Georgia, 1976-78; Union Free Will Baptist Church, Abbeville, Alabama, 1978 until he had a stroke.

During the years of his pastoral ministry Brother Goode was bi-vocational, except in Montgomery, Waycross, Colquitt, and Abbeville. He worked mostly as a butcher to support his family during his years as a part time pastor, though he did work for a while as a barber.

Brother Goode was a simple person, and one of those people who never met a stranger. It was his practice, when he met someone for the first time, to ask them if they were a Christian. Folks who knew him best say he was pleasant, cordial, warm, and polite. He was a good family man and was very supportive of the girls and their decisions. His wife Pearl was very involved in the various phases of his ministry.

Brother Goode passed away on Thanksgiving Day, November 28, 1985. Pearl died on November 8, 1996. They are buried in the Haleburg Community Cemetery, Columbia, Alabama.

Cindy Grimes

Cynthia Ann Cox was born to H. Z. and Artelle (Barnett) Cox on July 16, 1956, in Dallas,

Left to right: Thurmon Murphy, KFDX news anchor Rachel Wheat, Cindy Grimes

Texas. Her father was her pastor from the time of her birth until his retirement from the pastorate in November of 1986. Cindy attended youth camp from the days of her earliest childhood. An old photograph shows her as a babe in arms at Camp Holland, the rented camp the West Fork District Association used for several years in Weatherford, Texas. In 1962 she was converted to Christ at the West Fork Youth Camp under the ministry of her father and E. E. (Gene) Zeollers.

She graduated from Carter High School in 1974, and attended Texas Tech University during her freshman year in college, 1974-75. She then attended the University of North Texas in Denton, earning her Bachelor of Science degree in 1977. She went on to earn a Master of Education degree in education, with a minor in reading, in 1987.

Cindy and Douglas Keith Grimes were married on December 27, 1975. The ceremony was performed by her father, H. Z. Cox. From this marriage came two children: Roby Douglas, 1979, and Britney Ann, 1984.

Cindy has always been very active in the First Free Will Baptist Church of Duncanville. She has served the church as pianist, choir director, Sunday school teacher, church clerk, Church Training Service (CTS) coach and sponsor, coaching Bible Tic Tac Toe and drama teams. The work with the CTS groups took her to state meetings in McAllen, Bryan, and Dallas, and the National Association meetings in Arkansas, Tennessee, and Texas. Her church, she feels, is her heritage from her father who pastored the church for so many years. She wants to hear, "Well done," from her heavenly Father and from her earthly father.

For a number of years Cindy served as a member of the Christian Education Board of the West Fork District Association. As a member of that board she was a trustee of the West Fork Youth Camp, near Vashti, Texas, in the south end of Clay County. This was a position of responsibility and opportunity for ministry with the youth camp, which was run and operated by the Christian Education Board. The years on the camp board were years of numerical growth of the camp as well as a time of development and expansion of the camp facilities. She was converted to Christ at the youth camp in June of 1962. It was at camp that she first realized that she was a sinner and needed to be saved. Part of that realization was that she was not going to heaven just because of who she was or who her father was, and that there were no free passes through the pearly gates. She says it was a devastating realization for her. Though she is no longer a member of the camp board, she continues to attend camp and work hard in it every year, fulfilling responsibilities as needed. It is the normal thing for her to be at camp working just as hard as anyone, and harder than many, on camp work days cleaning and preparing the camp for use in the spring and summer. With her positive attitude and consummate energy Cindy can be seen from early morning until late at night participating in every aspect of youth camp: planning, praying, hiking, singing, teaching, counseling, laughing, learning, interacting with the campers, pitching in a softball game (as a musician playing softball she has perfect pitch), swimming, shooting BB's, archery, and just helping the campers have a rich, enjoyable, spiritual, life-changing experience at camp. At other times of the year she works hard at promoting the camp. She was interviewed about her work with the camp on the noon news program on NBC affiliate television station KFDX in Wichita Falls, by news anchor Rachel Wheat. Just as Cindy grew up attending the West Fork Youth Camp, so did her two children, Roby and Britney.

In 1985, at the young age of twenty-nine, Cindy was diagnosed with Multiple Sclerosis, a chronic degenerative, often episodic disease of the central nervous system. Through her strong faith and the wonders of modern medicine she was pretty much recovered from it two years later, in 1987. She still shows some symptoms as a result of it, however. She has a limp when she is tired, or has been inactive for a long period of time, and has a slight hearing loss.

After graduation from college she became a school teacher in 1977 at the Neal Ray McLaughlin Elementary School in the Carrollton/Farmer's Branch Independent School District. Over the next thirty-one years she also taught in both Cedar Hill, where she lives, and in Irving. She retired from teaching in June, 2011. After a couple of years off she has resumed teaching as a substitute teacher when needed. Her husband Doug retired from Vought Aircraft in 2006, and now works for Keefe Group Commissary.

Alvin Halbrook

Alvin Floyd Halbrook[177] was born to Mary Malissia (Daniel) and George Anderson Halbrook, in Womack, Missouri, on May 27, 1914. Alvin had a twin brother, Albert. Their father, George, was a truck farmer. Alvin graduated from Esther High School in Esther, Missouri, in 1932, during the Great Depression. As a youth he attended the Leadington Free Will Baptist Church in Leadington, Missouri, Missouri's Lead Belt area.

Ida and Alvin Halbrook

Alvin began pastoring even before he was licensed to preach. He pastored the Richwoods Free Will Baptist Church and others from 1933 to 1939. During this time he attended a Junior College in Flat River and taught school. He was licensed to preach the gospel on July 31, 1936, by the St. Francois County Quarterly Conference of Free Will Baptists. He was twenty-two years old. They were meeting at his home church, the Leadington Free Will Baptist Church. He was ordained to the gospel ministry by that district association in 1938, when it met at the Parkview Free Will Baptist Church in Desloge, Missouri. One of the names on his ordination certificate is illegible, but the names of the other people who signed it are Elder James F. Miller, of Flat River, Missouri, and Elder Tommie Franklin of Desloge, Missouri. This is Texas' own Miss Tommie Franklin who pastored the Parkview Free Will Baptist Church at the time.

As some young ministers did, Alvin realized the need for specific training for the ministry. As a result he enrolled at Free Will Baptist Bible College, Nashville, Tennessee, and began classes in 1944 during World War II. Already a student there was Miss Ida Frances Tinnin of North Carolina. She had enrolled a year earlier, in 1943, the second year of operation of the college. While in Nashville Alvin served as interim pastor of the East Nashville Free Will Baptist Church, one of the denomination's foremost churches in the 1930's and 40's.

Alvin finished his schooling at the Bible College and graduated, in 1945, as did his future wife, the aforementioned Miss Ida Frances Tinnin. Alvin and Ida were married on July 7, 1945, in Durham, North Carolina. The ceremony was performed by Rev. R. H. Wooly. From this marriage came four children: a stillborn son, and then Alvin Earnest, Timothy Morris, and Melanie Lynn.

In August of 1945, the same month World War II ended with the surrender of Japan, Alvin and his new wife moved to Texas. For the next several years Alvin pastored several churches on a rotating basis. These included the North Zulch Free Will Baptist Church, the Evergreen Free

---

[177] Most of the information about Alvin Halbrook was supplied by his daughter-in-law, Kathy Halbrook of Bryan, Texas.

Will Baptist Church, in Keith, Texas, the Blue Lake Free Will Baptist Church in Piedmont, Texas, and the Bright Light Free Will Baptist Church in the Harvey Community out of Bryan-College Station. In 1947 Bright Light built a parsonage so the Halbrooks could live and serve near the church, and they moved there. He continued to preach on Saturdays and Sunday afternoons at churches which did not have a pastor for almost all of his time at Bright Light.

During the early years of his ministry Alvin preached some revival meetings. He mostly thought of himself as a teaching pastor and did not do revivals in his later years. Mrs. Halbrook often said that in their early years in Texas people were on fire for the Lord. The altars were often full and sometimes people would come to the altar during the services because they couldn't wait for the invitation.

Alvin never pastored a church full-time, always having to work at a secular job to support his family. During his tenure at Bright Light he worked full-time in the library at Texas A&M. He graduated from A&M in 1955. He wrote his thesis on rural churches. Because of having to work at a secular job while pastoring, Alvin rarely was able to work in the youth camp. He couldn't get off work to do so.

In the meanwhile, his twin brother Albert was pastoring in Missouri and Tennessee. Albert's last pastorate was in Jackson, Tennessee.

Alvin was a studious sort of person, and that's what enabled him to be a teaching pastor. Biblically, every pastor should be a teacher of the Word, but some are just not good at it, partly because some ministers are not inclined to do the required studying. Alvin was. He loved to study God's Word and memorize Scripture. Even in his older years he studied and read continually. The Lord was both his passion and his hobby. He loved people, too. It was his practice to carry a little notepad in his pocket and whenever he met people, he would write their names in it so he could remember them and pray for them.

Alvin held a number of positions in the Central District Association: Assistant Clerk, Ordaining Council, Credentials Committee, Foreign Missions Board, and Moderator. He served for several years as Clerk of the Texas State Association of Free Will Baptists, beginning in 1950, served on the Superannuation Board (retirement board), and served on the Foreign Missions Board. His wife Ida worked right alongside of him. She was elected Treasurer of the Texas State Association in 1946, when the meeting was held at the North Zulch Church.

He retired from Bright Light in 1968. He then worked at the Bryan Municipal Golf Course. During his retirement years he pastored the North Zulch Free Will Baptist Church, though he continued working at a secular job.

Alvin passed away on July 23, 2000. Ida then passed away on April 5, 2006. They are buried beside each other in the Bryan City Cemetery. Their daughter Melanie passed away in 2004, son Alvin E. died of a heart attack in 2007, and Tim passed away in 2013.

D. C. Hargrove

Dolphus Crawford Hargrove[178] was born on November 5, 1868, in Hopkins County, Texas, to James William (1823-1877) and Dorinda E. (Couch) Hargrove (born 1827). He married Anna Ophelia Gressett in Grimes County, Texas, on November 27, 1889, and they had four children. Anna passed away on December 16, 1899. He subsequently married Anna Artelia Young in Grimes County on January 11, 1905.

---

[178] Find-a-grave.com

D. C. Hargrove was very active in the Free Will Baptist work in Texas, mostly in the Central District Association and in the Texas State Association. The Central District sent him, along with Rev. John Swanwick, as a delegate to the Southwestern Free Will Baptist Convention in 1908.

He passed away on September 8, 1946, at the Brazos Valley Hospital in Navasota, Grimes County, and is buried in Zion Methodist Cemetery, Iola, Texas.

W. D. Haston

W. D. Haston[179] was born on May 10, 1860. At about thirty years of age he entered the gospel ministry and affiliated with the Free Will Baptists. He married Sallie McLemore on September 16, 1880, in Yell County, Arkansas. He and Sallie later moved to Texas where they raised a large family, six boys and two girls. He passed away on June 4, 1929. The July 1929 issue of the Missouri *Gem* contained a brief obituary of Elder Haston, written by Elder J. A. Edmondson. Edmondson wrote that he was called to conduct the funeral of his fellow minister in Paducah, Texas. He stated that Elder Haston "had preached and organized churches for over forty years." He is buried in the Buck Creek Cemetery, Cottle County, Texas. The cemetery, beautifully kept, is on a dirt road several miles south of Paducah, overlooking miles and miles of empty prairie off to the west.

W. D. Haston Tombstone, Buck Creek Cemetery, Cottle County, Texas

Mark Headrick

Mark Anthony Headrick was born to Samma Dwight and Irma L. (Derr) Headrick in St. Louis, Missouri, on December 4, 1972. Mark's father worked as a mechanic for McDonnell Douglas, manufacturer of famous commercial and military aircraft. Mark's mother worked as an accountant for several corporations, but spent the last twelve years of her working career as a daycare teacher. Mark grew up in the St. Louis suburbs of Overland and Edmundson. During the first years of Mark's life the family attended the West Side General Baptist Church in St. Ann, Missouri, and then the Edmundson Road Baptist Church in Edmundson. He accepted Christ as his savior when he was five years old at the West Side church under the ministry of the Children's Pastor, Bud Parrent. The pastor of the church, Lloyd A. Stone, was like a grandfather to him due to the fact the two families spent a lot of time together outside of church. When Mark was in the tenth or eleventh grade the family began attending the Overland Free Will Baptist Church, Overland, Missouri, where Bill Coffman was the pastor.

As a teenager Mark led the children's ministry, preached in the monthly youth led services at the church, and felt the nudging of his pastor to go into full-time ministry, but was not yet sure God was calling him to preach. Technically he preached his first sermon about 1990 at the

---

[179] Information about W. D. Haston came from the *Missouri Gem*, Vol. 1, No. 7, July, 1929, and from the *Handbook of Historical Free Will Baptist Burial Places*, by Dr, Alton Loveless, FWB Publications, Columbus, Ohio, 2013, page 402. The photograph of his grave was taken on March 1, 2014.

Overland Free Will Baptist Church. It was on the topic of "Satan and His Methods of Deception." He graduated from the Ritenour High School in St. Louis in 1991.

Mark met Miss Vickie Lynn Maple at the Trinity Free Will Baptist Church in Bridgeton, Missouri, in 1991. They were married on May 11, 1996, the ceremony being performed at Trinity Church by Pastor Lynn Davenport. Mark and Vickie have two children: Anthony Joseph and Allison Nicole Headrick.

It wasn't until Mark was thirty years old that he firmly knew that God was calling him to preach. The first sermon he preached after announcing his call was at the First Free Will Baptist Church in O'Fallon, Missouri. His text was Romans 10:14. Finally knowing for sure that God had called him to preach, he attended the Missouri State Association meeting shortly thereafter. He knew that he had a lot to learn and short time to do it, and knew that if he did go to school it would be at Welch College, the denomination's college. He was somewhat hesitant to quit his career and move his family to Nashville, but he received much encouragement from missionaries and pastors at the state meeting. With much prayer, and the enthusiasm of his wife Vickie, he made the decision to move to Tennessee to attend Welch. Son Joseph was nine years of age at the time, and daughter Allison was five. He began classes in the fall of 2003. During his years as a student he was licensed to preach by the Mid-Rivers District Association of Free Will Baptists of Missouri, on October 29, 2006. Mark excelled as a student and received several scholarships. He was elected Senior Class Chaplain by the student body, and was awarded the Picirilli-Outlaw Excellence in Greek Award in 2006. In 2008 he graduated *magna cum laude*, with a Bachelor of Arts in Pastoral Ministry. While in Tennessee he served as Minister of Education at the Hendersonville Free Will Baptist Church, Hendersonville, Tennessee, in the Cumberland Association.

Shortly after his graduation from Welch College Mark moved his family to Henderson, Texas, where he became the pastor of the First Free Will Baptist Church, beginning June 21, 2008. It was after he came to Henderson that Mark was ordained. This occurred on November 8, 2008, when he was ordained by the East Texas District Association of Free Will Baptists. His ordination credentials were signed by Harold Teague and David Rudd. In addition to serving as pastor of the Henderson church he is moderator of the East Texas District Association and assistant moderator of the Texas State Association of Free Will Baptists. He is also the editor and designer of *The Texas Challenge*. Mark's hobbies include acting, collecting coffee mugs, and dabbling in art. His style is more "cartoony," he says, and most of what he does is computer graphics and layout.

Clarence Hearron

Clarence John Hearron[180] was born on January 17, 1923, in Tecumseh, Oklahoma, to William Arthur and Celestia Jane (Collops) Hearron, commonly known as Essie. Clarence didn't come alone as his twin sister Clara Mary arrived seven minutes ahead of him. Clarence and Clara were the last of eleven children born to his parents, though two of them had died before Clarence and Clara got to know them. The Hearron's Scotch-Irish ancestry traces back to Robert the Bruce, the first king of Scotland. Older brothers Arthur and Luther took the new twins across the street to Tecumseh College to show them off. Clarence says that he attended college before he could walk.

---

[180] The information in this profile came from a small booklet I wrote about Brother Hearron when he was honored by the West Fork District Association in May of 2005, and from additional information he supplied to me in personal interviews.

Three of Clarence's siblings attended the college: Arthur, Luther, and Sybil. William Arthur Hearron had a big impact on the Free Will Baptist denomination. Though he only had a third grade education he was able to teach himself Greek, which says a lot about his intelligence. During the long years of his ministry William pastored a number of churches in Arkansas, including Pleasant Grove, New Hope, Mt. Joy, and Glenwood. In Oklahoma he pastored at Tecumseh, Francis, Box, Spring Hill, Bryant, Dibble, Hawkins, Sulphur, and others. Sometimes he pastored more than one at a time since many of the churches did not have preaching services every Sunday. He served as moderator of the Cooperative General Association, when it convened in Glenwood, Arkansas, the Arkansas State Association, the Dibble Association in Oklahoma, and assistant moderator of the Oklahoma State Association, in 1926. His name appears frequently in the old minutes. It should be mentioned, too, that Clarence's brother Arthur pastored for many years in Texas, including at Gartman's View in Comanche, and Oklahoma.

Clarence Hearron

Clarence's formal schooling began when he was seven years old, when his father pastored at Box, Oklahoma, in Cleveland County. He and Clara, along with other sisters who were already enrolled, attended a one-room school house, starting with the Primary class, similar to kindergarten. Soon Clarence and Clara were promoted to the first grade. Then, in the middle of that school year, they were promoted again, to the second grade. During that same school year they moved to Payne, Oklahoma, and were promoted again, this time to the third grade. In 1931 the Hearron family moved to a small community two miles north of New Hope, Arkansas, about thirty-two miles from DeQueen. They arrived at their new home late at night due to car trouble. They discovered that the house into which they were to move was still occupied, causing them to have to move into a smaller house until the occupants moved out. While others unloaded the furniture, Clarence's mom prepared a meal. The house had a fireplace with a large flat rock serving as the hearth. Older sister Grace stepped on the hearth and fell into the cellar beneath the floor. One moment she was there, and the next moment she was gone. Consternation reigned until Grace found her way up the outside steps back into the living room. Before long they were able to move into the other house. Clarence's dad said he thought the family could weather the Great Depression better in Arkansas than in Oklahoma. He helped a farmer gather his crop in return for being moved to Arkansas.

That area of Arkansas was a land of forests. Clarence's mother thought the woods were full of wild animals and, since they had to walk to school a mile though the woods to catch the school bus, she arranged with the school officials to have Grace, Clara, and Clarence taught at home. Clarence found that his older sisters, who did the teaching, were hard and demanding teachers and he was glad to eventually get back into public school. Grace was valedictorian of her graduating class and, since he couldn't let her beat him, Clarence accomplished the same feat, graduating from high school in 1941.

After graduation Clarence joined the Civilian Conservation Corps, the CCC, for a six month term. In July of 1942, at the age of nineteen, he went with his mom and dad to Mount

Pleasant Free Will Baptist Church, near Hamburg, Arkansas, where the elder Hearron was conducting a revival meeting. It was during this meeting that Clarence accepted Christ as his savior and was baptized. The creek in which he was immersed was very cold due to the fact that it had its origin in a spring. He joined the church and kept his membership there until he became pastor of the First Free Will Baptist Church in Waco, Texas, regularly sending his tithes to his home church.

Clarence joined the United States Army in March of 1943 while World War II was raging in Europe, Africa, and in the Pacific. He was assigned to the Signal Corps in 1944 and received his training at Camp Crowder near Joplin, Missouri. His older sister lived in Joplin and he visited her on weekends and attended the Webb City Free Will Baptist Church. During that time he enrolled in the Army Specialized Training Program. While much of the world was at war, there was a war raging inside of Clarence; he was battling the call to the ministry. It was a battle, in part, because he had seen his preacher father treated in such a manner that he didn't want to be treated that way. He saw things the ordinary child could not see, and many of those things were unpleasant. He saw that some church people could be cruel, unChristian, and hypocritical. He told the Lord he would teach Sunday school, be a deacon, lead singing, or do anything except be a preacher. However, in May of 1944, he surrendered to the call to the gospel ministry and decided to tell his parents. He notified them by letter but, to his surprise he received a letter in return from them informing him that they had been praying for the Lord to call one of their boys into the ministry. Later that year, 1944, his older brother Arthur surrender to preach, giving his parents twice what they had asked for. Clarence was licensed to the gospel ministry in 1944 by Mount Pleasant Church, which was a member of the Saline Association in Arkansas. They renewed the license in 1945. After considerable training the Army sent him to the Territory of Hawaii, where he was assigned to Schofield Barracks on the island of Oahu serving as a telephone installer and repairman. He preached his first sermon to a small group of wartime soldiers in Hawaii. While there he met Howard Gage who later became a Free Will Baptist missionary builder in Ivory Coast, Africa. With the war going on, and thousands of military people moving through Hawai'i in those days, Clarence and Howard both saw foreign missions in action. As a result Clarence has believed in world evangelism ever since. He says that he and Howard were the first Free Will Baptists to preach the gospel in Hawai'i. He often practiced his sermons in the chapel on the base when it was empty.

In June of 1944 Clarence was seriously injured when the driver of the telephone truck in which they were riding lost control of the vehicle. The truck rolled and Clarence was ejected, and the truck landed on top of him, fracturing his pelvis in four places. In July he was sent to the Veteran's Hospital in Temple, Texas. After several months of rehabilitation he was able to walk. He soon discovered that there was a Free Will Baptist church in Bryan, Texas. Contacting the pastor, J. O. Fort, he was given directions to the church and began attending services there. Pastor Fort told him about the First Free Will Baptist Church in Waco, Texas, that had split and needed a pastor. Clarence visited the church and they asked him to preach that afternoon, and then asked him to preach several more times after that. A few months later the church called him as pastor. That call came on the Sunday before he was discharged from the Army on Wednesday.
Thus began a long ministry of preaching the gospel and giving much needed leadership to the Free Will Baptist denomination.

His home church, Mount Pleasant, authorized any ordaining council to ordain him. So he went to Oklahoma and was ordained on January 26, 1946, at the Capitol Hill Free Will Baptist Church in Oklahoma City. His ordination credentials were signed by his brother, James Arthur

Hearron, and by E. A. O'Donnell and Harry Stairs. He assumed the pastorate of the First Free Will Baptist Church in Waco the following Sunday. The church paid him $10.00 a week but, since he was receiving one hundred percent disability compensation as a result of his injury while in the Army, he was able to pastor the church full-time. Later his compensation was reduced to twenty percent and he became a bi-vocational pastor.

Wesley Calvery, who would later serve as a Free Will Baptist missionary in Japan, suggested to Clarence that he date a beautiful young lady by the name of Juanita Marie Jackson. Clarence took the advice and began dating Juanita. They were married on March 17, 1947. The ceremony was performed by M. L. Sutton in Arlington, Texas. From that union came two beautiful daughters, Judy Wynell (Smith) and Martha Lucille (Wells).

Clarence went on to pursue a formal education, believing strongly that he needed it since he was now a minister of the gospel. His dad said of him, "Clarence will be a better preacher because he is going to college." He earned a Bachelor of Arts Degree in Religion at Baylor University in 1950, and also completed ten hours toward a Master's Degree from Baylor. He earned a Master of Education Degree, with a permanent secondary teacher's certificate, from Texas Wesleyan University in Fort Worth, Texas, in 1964. He was able to do post graduate work at the University of Florida in 1966.

The churches Clarence J. Hearron pastored include the following:
First Free Will Baptist Church, Waco, Texas   1946-1948, 1949-1950
Easley's Chapel Free Will Baptist Church of Gartman's View, Comanche, Texas 1950-1952
United Free Will Baptist Church, Bryan, Texas 1953-1955
First Free Will Baptist Church, Weatherford, Texas   1955-1957
First Free Will Baptist Church, Fort Worth, Texas,   1957-1960
Liberty Free Will Baptist Church, Comanche, Texas   1960 - 1962, 1965-1966
First Free Will Baptist Church, Bowie, Texas   1963-1965
Blanchard Free Will Baptist Church, Blanchard, Oklahoma   1966-1972
First Free Will Baptist Church, Denison, Texas   1979 - 1985
University Free Will Baptist Church, Durant, Oklahoma   1985 - 1995
Cornerstone Free Will Baptist Church, Denison, Texas   1995 - 2000
(Formerly First Free Will Baptist Church)

The First Free Will Baptist Church of Fort Worth, Texas, called him as pastor in October of 1957. The church had just experienced another big split. On his first Sunday as pastor there were only nineteen people in attendance, but by Easter Sunday of 1958 they had one hundred and four in attendance. Sure it was Easter, but over a hundred people after a big split is a good showing.

Clarence always had an affinity for smaller churches which could not afford a full-time pastor. Since he had a teacher's certificate he was able to teach school to support himself and his family while pastoring. He taught for years in junior high and high school. While pastoring in Bowie, for instance, he taught for four years at nearby Goldburg.

In 1966 Clarence became a teacher and Academic Dean at Oklahoma Bible College in Moore, Oklahoma, where he served for nine years. The position is now called Vice-President of Academic Affairs, a title which he had suggested but was adopted later. He taught from twelve to fifteen class hours a week, teaching such subjects as Bible, English, History, Social Sciences, Greek, and Literature. He is perhaps best known for having taught Parliamentary Law to a lot of young ministerial students who are now, or have been, in positions of leadership throughout the denomination. Part of his job was arranging the academic requirements and the subjects the instructors were to teach, and to help the half failing students meet their requirements. One of the great contributions he made during his years at the college was his work securing accreditation for the school. He knew that the college, which became Hillsdale Free Will Baptist College, was not accredited but needed to be so their work would be accepted by other colleges. This would, among other things, allow Hillsdale's students to continue their education. Hillsdale was a junior college at the time. Clarence was able to obtain recognition from Oklahoma University, which opened the door for Hillsdale's students to most of the colleges in Oklahoma, as well as in other states.

The time came when accreditation was required by the North Central Accrediting Association. Clarence obtained a copy of a self-study and assigned portions of the study to the Hillsdale faculty. During some of that time he served as acting president when Dr. J. D. O'Donnell was injured in a plane crash, and again between Dr. O'Donnell's departure and the hiring of Bill Jones as president. He worked diligently to see that Hillsdale offered the correct subjects which would be accepted by other colleges, and still keep the Bible and Christianity central in the school's academic and spiritual life. By his persistence and hard work Hillsdale received accreditation from the Oklahoma Board of Regents. When Hillsdale became a four year institution they were accredited as such without any problem.

His peers have shown their respect for him by electing him to about every office available over the years. He served as moderator of every district association in which he pastored, except one, and clerk of some. He served as assistant moderator and moderator of the Texas State Association of Free Will Baptists, moderator of the West Fork District Association in Texas, moderator of the Dibble Association and the Hopewell Number One Association in Oklahoma. He ably served as parliamentarian of both the Texas and Oklahoma state associations, as well as the West Fork District Association. He has served as a member of the West Fork Home Missions Board and the Home Missions Board of the Texas State Association. He was a very active member of the Board of Christian Education of the West Fork District Association, which owns and operates the West Fork Youth Camp, and served as a member of the Education Commission of the National Association of Free Will Baptists. Beginning in 1946, when he was mentioned in the minutes of the Texas State Association for the first time, his name is spread all over the minutes of both the State Association and the West Fork District Association. He has been one of the most active leaders in the state of Texas and has left an indelible mark upon the work.

Clarence grew up in a musically gifted family and it is not surprising that he took a great interest in music himself. At the age of fourteen he began to teach himself to play the guitar, which he does very well, never having had a formal lesson. He learned how to read music by attending a three week singing school in New Hope, Arkansas. The Hartford Music Normal taught these three week schools, traveling from place to place. He learned sight reading, harmony, and versification. Though he had written poetry from childhood, it was the Hartford Company which taught him to write songs. In 1940 he wrote his first one. The first song he had published was "The Lord Is with Me," published by the Hartford Music Company, now owned by the family of the late Albert E. Brumley, author of "I'll Fly Away" and dozens of more songs popular from the early 1930's until the present. Other songs written by Clarence have been published by the National Music Company. Altogether Clarence has written nearly fifty songs and choruses, with five of them being published. Of the songs which he has written his favorites are: "Forgiven, Forgotten, Forever," "Jesus Walks with Me," "Hidden Beauty," and "I Want to Stand Before My Father." Two of his songs have been recorded. They are "A Touch of Heaven," and "I'm Back with My Father." He finds inspiration for his songs in the incidents of his life and things he heard. He says he has tried to learn to play the piano but has not mastered that yet.

His beloved wife Juanita, after fifty-three years and almost eight months of marriage, passed away of a pulmonary illness on November 8, 2000. At the time he was pastor of the Cornerstone Free Will Baptist Church in Denison, Texas. He was very grateful for the many expressions of sympathy he received from Cornerstone, friends from the national offices of his beloved denomination, from Oklahoma and, of course, from Texas, and for the large attendance at her funeral. Three years later, in February of 2003, he began dating Artelle Cox, widow of the late H. Z. Cox, whom he had known since 1948. Both were convinced that the Lord had brought them together. They were married on October 25, 2003, at the First Free Will Baptist Church of Duncanville.

Since retiring from the pastorate he has had the opportunity to supply pulpits when and where needed. He remembers with great fondness the Sundays he has spent with the Pleasant Mound Free Will Baptist Church at Buffalo Springs. He continues serving the Lord through the First Free Will Baptist Church in Duncanville, Texas, where he serves as Sunday school superintendent. Though born in Oklahoma he considers himself a citizen of Arkansas as is reflected in this sentiment: "God has been might good to a country boy from Arkansas and I am grateful for His calling me into the ministry. Whatever the future holds will be fine because I know who holds the future and me." Now in his nineties, he and Artelle live in an assisted living facility in Cedar Hill.

James Arthur Hearron

James Arthur Hearron was the oldest son of William Arthur Hearron and the older brother of Clarence J. Hearron. James was born on September 10, 1905, in Porum, Indian Territory/Oklahoma. He married Opal Dunn in 1928. His connection to Texas is that he pastored the Easley's Chapel Free Will Baptist Church in Comanche, which over the years was also pastored by his father and his little brother. All three of the Hearron preachers mentioned here pastored in the West Fork District Association and were active in its ministry. As was the case with his father and younger brother, James pastored for many years in the State of Oklahoma in the Nineteenth Century.

James passed away on March 27, 1968, at a hospital in Brownwood, Texas, at the age of 62, after a long illness. The memorial service was conducted at Easley's Chapel by John A. Brooks, but he was buried in Chickasha, Oklahoma, where he had pastored for ten years prior to his pastorate at Easley's Chapel. He was survived by his wife, three daughters, one son, and 12 grandchildren.

James Arthur Hearron

William Arthur Hearron

William Arthur Hearron was born on August 28, 1882, in Paintsville, Kentucky. Those being the days of the great western expansion the family moved to Indian Territory, where William grew up in Briartown, very near Porum. He married Essie Colleps on October 10, 1901, and from this union came eleven children, nine of whom were reared to adulthood. James Arthur, the oldest, and Clarence John, the youngest, became Free Will Baptist ministers. William himself was ordained to the gospel ministry on April 27, 1903. The ordination took place at Peggs, Indian Territory.

William was a self-taught student of the Bible, and he also taught himself New Testament Greek. He became a leader in the Free Will Baptist work in Indian Territory/Oklahoma, Arkansas, and Texas. In Oklahoma he pastored churches in the South Grand River Association, Dibble Association, and First Oklahoma. In Arkansas he pastored in the Little Missouri River Association. His Texas pastorate was at the Easley's Chapel Church in the West Fork District Association, a church pastored over the year by himself and both of his preacher sons.

William Arthur Hearron

William conducted many revival meetings and baptized over one thousand converts during his ministry. Due to a shortage of teachers during World War II, he and Mrs. Hearron taught in a small elementary school at Daisy, Arkansas.

William moved to Tecumseh, Oklahoma, to become editor of *The New Morning Star*, a denominational magazine named after *The Morning Star*, one of the magazines of Free Will Baptists prior to the merger with the Northern Baptists in 1910-11. *The New Morning Star* had originally been started in Weatherford, Texas, where it was published for one year. It was moved to Tecumseh, Oklahoma, when Tecumseh College, owned and operated by the Cooperative General Association of Free Will Baptists, opened. An article in the *New Morning Star* has an enlightening paragraph on Brother Hearron. It reads:

> Bro. Hearron couldn't half live on what he got out of the Star office, so had to resign. Yes, Bro. Hearron has a large family, but whoever edits our paper is entitled to a living from it. If we starve another editor out, it will be hard indeed for us to have a paper.

An article in *The Ada Weekly*, December 3, 1925, gives us a short glimpse of some of the work of Brother Hearron: "Rev. W. A. Hearron and John Baker went to Red Oak last Thursday, attending a meeting of a committee of which Bro. Hearron was chairman to revise a church treaty."

After a long and fruitful ministry as a pastor, evangelist, editor, and denominational leader, William Arthur Hearron passed away on September 1, 1957.

Everett Hellard

Everett and Ava Hellard

Everett D Hellard was a different sort of man, a Free Will Baptist preacher who was cut from a different cloth, so to speak. Perhaps that was reflected in the fact that the D in his name did not have a period after it and it was not the initial for Donald, Dale, or Dwight. Everett D Hellard was one of six children born to Delbert and Martha Hellard. He was born on September 9, 1923, in Tulsa, Oklahoma. Everett's father was a Free Will Baptist preacher who pastored the Bluebell Free Will Baptist Church out of Sapulpa, Oklahoma, and was also a dairy farmer. This provided Everett with the opportunity to learn good work ethics during his growing up years, and to some degree learning about the ins and outs of pastoring a church. He was converted to Christ at the age of fifteen while attending youth camp near Drumright, Oklahoma. He graduated from Kellyville High School in Kellyville, Oklahoma, in 1942.

Ava Irene Matlock was born on October 2, 1926, in Bristow, Oklahoma, to Riley and Rebecca Matlock. She was one of seven children. Ava and Everett were married on June 17, 1943, in Tulsa, Oklahoma, by Rev. Melvin Bingham, pastor of the First Free Will Baptist Church. Ava was sixteen years old and Everett was nineteen at the time. Ava dropped out of school to become a homemaker. By that time World War II was raging in full force and so Everett became a member of the United States Navy. He served for two years on the island of Okinawa as a Pharmacist Mate. Their first child, Everyl Irene (Hellard) Getz was born while he was in the service. She was nine months old before he got to see her. He was discharged from the Navy in 1946.

After his discharge from the Navy at the end of the war he attended Free Will Baptist Bible College in Nashville, Tennessee, which was a two year college at the time, and from there he graduated. The Hellards, Everett, Ava, and young Everyl, moved to Breckenridge, Michigan, where he pastored his first church from 1948 to 1950. Their son, David Gentry, was born while they lived in Michigan. During this time Everett attended college while pastoring, majoring in music.

In 1950 the Hellards left Michigan and moved back to Oklahoma where Everett pastored the First Free Will Baptist Church in Cushing, from 1950 to 1952. Then, for three or four months the Hellards lived on a small farm near Sapulpa, Oklahoma. Everett sold Singer sewing machines during that time. This brief time away from pastoring provided Everett and Ava with a much need refreshing break before they took on their next ministry. From the farm Everett moved his family to Houston, Texas, where he assumed the pastorate of a small mission church. The mission was meeting in a temporary building which had a dirt floor and screens for windows. It looked more like a hen house than a house of worship. The Hellards were always a cultured, well-dressed, refined, distinguished looking couple and yet in true humility they worked together, and worked very hard, to establish a Free Will Baptist church from that lowly beginning. Eleven years later, when he resigned as pastor, there was a nice church building, with an educational wing, and a growing congregation known as the First Free Will Baptist Church of Houston. It was located on Schneider Road on the north side of Houston. Bobby Ferguson was one of the preacher boys, who later pastored the church and relocated it to Steubner-Airline Road, where an even larger church building was constructed as the church continued to grow.

Raymond and Everyl Getz

In 1962 Brother Hellard moved his family to West Texas, to Midland, where he became pastor of a small, struggling church, probably the First Free Will Baptist Church of Midland. After eight months he discovered that the man to whom they had been making payments for the property did not have the deed to the property. This resulted in the small church merging with the Westside Free Will Baptist Church of Midland, pastored by E. E. (Gene) Zoellers. Brother Hellard then moved his family to Farmington, Missouri, where he had accepted a call to pastor the Farmington Free Will Baptist Church. In the fall of 1963 daughter Everyl enrolled as a freshman at Free Will Baptist Bible College. This Missouri pastorate was for two years, from 1963 to 1965. Brother Hellard soon moved back to Oklahoma, accepting the call to pastor a church in Turley, Oklahoma, which he pastored from 1965 to 1967.

This brings us to his second and final move to Texas. Brother Hellard, his wife Ava, and son David, moved to Conroe, Texas. In Conroe he started the Conroe Free Will Baptist Church in 1968, which initially met in the Hellard's home and in the home of Steve and Jewel Gregory. He pastored the church until 1973, but the Hellards lived in Conroe for the rest of their lives. To supplement their income while the church was still part-time, the Hellards owned and operated the Christian Book Shoppe and Piano Service. Ava ran the store while Everett tuned, serviced, and rebuilt pianos as his services were needed. This was not only a means of supplementing their income, it was a ministry to help others spiritually. They built a house outside of Conroe where Brother Hellard ran the Pine Log Christian Day Camp for several summers. In 1973 Raymond and Everyl Getz moved to Conroe from Fort Worth to help with the Free Will Baptist work there. About a month later Brother Hellard resigned as pastor and his son-in-law, Raymond Getz, became the pastor. The church was still a part-time church.

The Hellards, however, continued an active ministry. He pastored the North Zulch Free Will Baptist Church, a part-time church, on two separate occasions. He pastored the Bright Light Free Will Baptist Church, out of Bryan-College Station, part-time, traveling on weekends to fill the pulpit of one of the oldest Free Will Baptist churches in Texas. Afterwards, Everett and Ava pastored the senior citizens, known as the Victors, at the First Free Will Baptist Church in Houston for several years. Everett and Ava led this special group on numerous outings and kept up with the members and their needs.

When the First Free Will Baptist Church in Houston began sending groups of their members to various areas of Houston to establish new Free Will Baptist churches, the Hellards became members of the Tomball Free Will Baptist Mission. When the Northpointe Free Will

Baptist Mission was formed in The Woodlands, they moved their membership there, encouraging, helping, and assisting with the new mission effort. Another ministry initiated by Brother Hellard was the organizing of the Golden Nuggets of Encouragement, a ministry which sought to encourage others. He published a paper in Spanish and English, soliciting others to be encouragers, and sharing articles designed to encourage the readers to grow spiritually.

Brother Hellard may have been known in the denomination more for his singing than his pastoring. This was true even though his signature ministry may have been growing a small, lowly mission into the First Free Will Baptist Church of Houston. He had a beautiful tenor voice and he used his musical gift for the Lord throughout his life. Clarence Hearron said that perhaps his most requested song was *Ship Ahoy*. His daughter Everyl said, "Music was a big part of his life and our family's." As a Free Will Baptist minister Everett, as well as Ava, was active in the denominational work. He participated in the district and state work and faithfully attended the National Association meetings. He was always missions minded and often had missionaries into his home and churches. One of the other things for which he was known is that he did not believe in or practice feet washing. He was a Christian gentleman in the best sense of the term and a southern gentleman. Ava was active all of her adult life in the ministry of the Woman's Auxiliary, as it was known then. She was always a sweet, thoughtful, gracious and beautiful Christian lady. We quote Everyl again: "She might not have had a formal education, but she was self-educated far above many who have a formal education. She was an excellent cook, hostess, seamstress, florist, pianist, teacher, homemaker, wife, and mother. She loved the position the Lord had placed her in as a pastor's wife and fulfilled her job with joy. She loved her Lord dearly and his people."

Ava went to be with her Lord on August 1, 2004, and was joined by Everett on February 11, 2007. They are both buried in Garden Park Cemetery in Conroe, Texas.

Ed Hobbs

Ed Hobbs founded the First Free Will Baptist Church in Odessa and pastored it from February 3, 1952, until June 2, 1954. While preaching a revival meeting in Midland he had seen the need for a Free Will Baptist Church in Odessa, twenty miles to the west. The church was started at 1600 South Grant Street in a truck barn were E. M. "Red" Montgomery and Jess Hobbs worked on their oil field trucks during the week. The church grew, relocated to 2203 West 7th Street, and became a leading Free Will Baptist church in the state of Texas.

Ed was born in a tent under a grove of old pecan trees to David A. and JoAnna (Parker) Hobbs in Bixby, Oklahoma. He served in the Seventh Armored Division of the United States Army during World War II. His division fought from the invasion of Normandy in 1944 until V-E Day in 1945. Ed came ashore at Normandy in the second wave. The Seventh Division, also known as the Lucky Seventh, participated in most major battles of the European theater, including Northern France, Rhineland, Ardennes, Central Europe, and the Battle of the Bulge. The men crossed 2,260 miles during combat, traveling from the Normandy beaches all the way to the Baltic Sea. They destroyed 2,653 enemy vehicles, captured 3,517 enemy vehicles, and captured 9,054 prisoners. In addition to being called the Lucky Seventh, they earned the names "Ghost Division," because they haunted the Germans all the way across Europe, "Stonewall Seventh," because of their defensive ability, and the "Rattlesnake Division," because the enemy never knew where they would strike next. Ed was awarded the Bronze Marker and the Battle Over, Victory At Last medals. He served under General George Patton and General Bernard Montgomery, and others. He was honorably discharged in 1945 at the rank of sergeant. He retired from Western Hughes in Tulsa, Oklahoma, and is buried in Woodland Memorial Park Cemetery in Tulsa.

Barry Kelly

Barry Lane Kelly pastors the First Free Will Baptist Church of Bowie in the West Fork District Association. Barry was born on October 16, 1982, in Florence, Alabama. He was converted to Christ at the age of 13 in a Baptist church and graduated from Wilson High School, in Florence, in 2001.

He married Kelli Savannah Jones on August 6, 2005. She graduated from Bradshaw High School, also in Florence, in 2004. Barry and Savannah have three children: son Taylor, born in 2006, and twin girls Paislee and Preslee, born in 2009. Savannah came from a long line of Free Will Baptist preachers, including her grandfather who had started and constructed the Jones Chapel Free Will Baptist Church with which she is closely connected. She was converted to Christ in 1994, at the age of eight, in the Jones Chapel Church.

Barry & Savannah Kelly & children

For a number of years Barry resisted the call to preach the gospel. He preached his first sermon on June 3, 2012, at the Jones Chapel Church, before he had actually surrendered to preach. He eventually accepted the call to preach two months later, in August of 2012, at the age of twenty-nine. He was licensed to preach that same month by the Progressive District Association of Alabama. He was called as pastor of Jones Chapel, preaching his first sermon as pastor on April 10, 2013. He was ordained by the Progressive Association, the ceremony being conducted on September 8, 2013, at Jones Chapel. His credentials were signed by Jack and Allen Jones, both of Jones Chapel. As stated above, Savannah is closely connected with Jones Chapel.

Barry pastored Jones Chapel until April of 2015. Some of the people of the church observed to him that he needed to pastor somewhere else, away from the Jones family, in order to allow his ministry to develop and flourish. This led to him trying out at the First Free Will Baptist Church of Bowie, Texas. On April 29th the Bowie Church called him as pastor. He commuted back and forth for a month, moving his family to Bowie on April 15, 2015. The reason for the delay in moving was so their children could complete the required state testing before they left Alabama.

First Free Will Baptist Church, Bowie

The Bowie Church, which had been the largest Free Will Baptist Church in Texas in attendance, running about three hundred people, had had some serious trouble and had lost a large number of people, including their pastor, Dr. Larry Cox. The attendance the week before Barry tried out was only forty. Barry has been able to stabilize things at the church and, after a little more than one year, the church is growing again.

Barry was active in the Progressive Association while he was still in Alabama, serving as the district clerk. In Texas he continues his involvement in his church's ministry outside the immediate community. He has already served as director of the West Fork Youth Camp and serves on the district's Executive Committee. He plans to be involved in the state work as opportunities arise. Savannah serves as assistant clerk of the West Fork Association.

J. W. Loftis

J. W. Loftis was born on November 8, 1869. He was one of the early pastors in the Brazos Quarterly Meeting, which was started in 1887. He passed away on January 8, 1906, and is buried in the Jacksonville City Cemetery, Jacksonville, Cherokee County, Texas.[181]

James Pierce Lunsford

James (Jim) Pierce Lunsford was born in Tennessee in 1834. According to the 1850 census he was living in Wayne County, Tennessee, at the age of sixteen. His parents were Aris and Mary Lunsford, who were from South Carolina. James married Sarah Ann Walters of Georgia, in Chattahoochee County, Georgia, on June 27, 1855. James and Sarah Ann moved to Covington County, Alabama, about 1862. They raised eleven children, two of them being born in Texas.

James was a Confederate soldier in the American Civil War, serving between 1862 and 1865. He served in the First Alabama Heavy Artillery Battalion, Company D, and fought in the Battle of Mobile Bay (August 6, 1864) and the Battle of Spanish Fort. The Battle of Spanish Fort took place from March 27 to April 8, 1865 in Baldwin County, Alabama, as part of the Mobile Campaign of the Western Theater of the war. He was wounded, captured, and then released at the end of the war.

James Pierce Lunsford

His family came to Texas in a wagon train after the Civil War, about 1876, and settled in Cherokee County. Later they lived in Rusk County and the Sand Flats of East Texas, where he started the Old Prospect and Mount Union Free Will Baptist Churches.

James Lunsford had two brothers who migrated to Texas with him in 1876. One of them, Isacc Hillard Lunsford, was also a minister, and was possibly the I. Lunsford mentioned as one of the early ministers of the Mt. Union Free Will Baptist Church in the program of the centennial celebration of the Mt. Union Church in 1987. Isacc's granddaughter, Mary A. Wharton, told me that she had been told that James had attended a Methodist Episcopal Seminary in Greenville, Mississippi (or Alabama), in 1875. She says that a relative had his ordination papers but that she does not have access to them. She also says that her grandfather, Isacc, was ordained in 1877 at the First Free Will Baptist Church in Cherokee County, Texas.

In addition to the Old Prospect Church and the Mt. Union Church, James reportedly started the Lone Star Freewill Baptist Church in the Lone Star community of Cherokee County (but Mary isn't sure). When James founded the Old Prospect Church in Rusk County 1887, it was started in

---

[181] *Handbook of Historical Free Will Baptist Burial Places*, page 403.

a building shared with the Methodists. The original building still stands beside the newer Baptist church next to it. There is a petrified wood marker beside it.

James' wife, Sarah Ann, died in 1908 and James himself passed away on November 27, 1918. Both are buried in the Old Prospect Cemetery. His grave spot in the cemetery is unknown, but many other relatives are buried there, presumably beside him.[182]

According to Dr. Eugene Richards in *History of Free Will Baptist State Associations*, the first Free Will Baptist Church organized in Texas was in the community of Clayton[183] in Panola County, deep in the piney woods of East Texas, in 1876. Dr. Richards does not give the name of that first church. It was organized by A. M. Stewart, the name which first appears in the records of Texas Free Will Baptists. Stewart also organized the Union Chapel and Beckville churches in Panola County. Also in East Texas, Stewart organized the Good Hope Free Will Baptist Church and the Union Springs Free Will Baptist Church in Rusk County. James (Jim) Pierce Lunsford organized the New Prospect Free Will Baptist Church in Rusk County in 1887. Later, when they met in the Mount Union school house, the name was changed to Mount Union Free Will Baptist Church. Rev. Lunsford also organized a church at Mount Pleasant, Texas. Again, for those not familiar with East Texas, Henderson is the county seat of Rusk County. Then, in Cherokee County, Stewart organized the Lone Star Free Will Baptist Church and the Rape's Chapel Free Will Baptist Church. Rusk, the county seat of Cherokee County, is 130 miles southeast of Dallas.

Stewart's influence extended far beyond East Texas. He and his wife were charter members of the Free Will Baptist Church in Bryan,[184] Texas, which was organized in 1894. The book on the history of the church, which the church published in 1957, does not specify whether he was the founder or just a charter member, but it does list him as the first pastor. The Free Will Baptist Church of Bryan would go on to become one of the leading churches, not only in Texas, but in the entire Free Will Baptist denomination. Another church in central Texas which was organized by Brother Stewart is the Evergreen Free Will Baptist Church, which was organized in 1895. He was assisted in organizing the church by J. J. Tatum, another preacher of note in the early Free Will Baptist work in Texas. The Bright Light Free Will Baptist Church and the Christian Home Free Will Baptist Church were both organized in 1886 by T. H. Adams, with the assistance of Brother Stewart. Both of these churches were in Brazos County. The Bright Light and Evergreen Churches continue to this day.

The first association of Free Will Baptist churches in Texas was organized in 1878. It was called The Texas Association.[185] The *Free Baptist Cyclopedia* lists seven member churches in 1887: Good Hope, Union Springs, and Old Prospect in Rusk County; Union Chapel in Panola County; Lone Star in Cherokee County; and Bright Light and Christian Home in Brazos County; the Beckville and Rape's Chapel churches already having closed.[186]

---

[182] Much of the information about James Pierce Lunsford was supplied by Mary A. Wharton of Nacogdoches, Texas, via telephone conversation and personal letter received on January 17, 2014. She also supplied the photograph of James P. Lunsford. The copy of the photograph had to be made through the glass cover of the frame because the photo itself was too brittle to remove from its frame.

[183] Clayton, Texas, located at the junction of State Highway 315 and Farm Road 1970, sixteen miles southwest of Carthage in southwestern Panola County, was first settled around 1845 by Jacob Cariker, a native of Georgia.

[184] Originally called Bryan Free Baptist Church, it was later named the First Free Will Baptist Church of Bryan.

[185] This association would later become the East Texas District Association of Free Will Baptist Churches.

[186] *The Free Baptist Cyclopaedia*, by G. A. Burgess and J. T. Ward (Free Baptist Cyclopaedia Company, printed by the Woman's Temperance Publication Society, Chicago, Illinois, 1889) page 642.

Dr. Thomas Marberry

Dr. Thomas Marberry

Thomas Luther Marberry was born to Luther Fagan and Ruby Estelle (Sheffield) Marberry in Houston, Texas, on May 3, 1949. His father was a professional golfer and the family did not attend church during Thomas' childhood years. The family moved to Bryan and Thomas began attending the Fellowship Free Will Baptist Church as a teenager. He accepted Christ as his savior at the age of seventeen, having been led to Christ by his pastor, Don Ellis. Thomas had meant business when he gave his life to Christ, something which has been evident throughout the remainder of his life.

Thomas was the academic sort growing up and he loved learning. He graduated from Stephen F. Austin High School in Bryan in 1967. He answered the call to the ministry in 1968 and was licensed to preach by the Central Texas District Association. To Thomas a call to the ministry was a call to prepare. Consequently, he attended Oklahoma Bible College in 1968-69, taking courses which could be transferred to Baylor University. His grades and test scores became legendary. He did not graduate from Oklahoma Bible College, choosing rather to enroll at Baylor, which he attended as an undergraduate student in 1969-71, and as a graduate student from 1974 to 1982. He earned a Bachelor of Arts in Religion in 1971. With years of hard work and dedication he earned a Ph.D. in Religion with a New Testament concentration in December of 1982. He wrote his dissertation on "The Place of the Natural World in the Theology of the Apostle Paul." He was now officially Dr. Thomas Marberry.

With his B.A. in hand, but still working on his Ph.D., Thomas returned to Oklahoma in 1975 to teach at Hillsdale Free Will Baptist College, the former Oklahoma Bible College. Out of necessity he also worked as a dormitory supervisor. The courses he taught in those early years were Greek, Church History, Theology, and Bible. Thomas was a rare mind and it soon became evident that he was in a position to make a special contribution to the cause of Christ through Free Will Baptists.

Thomas met Wilma Lee Ussery and they began dating and soon they were in love. They were married on July 22, 1983, at the Central Free Will Baptist Church in Grandview, Missouri. The ceremony was performed by their friend Howard Gwartney.

Thomas and Wilma had been making trips to Mexico for about ten years when a crisis developed at El Seminario Biblico La Cruz, the Seminary of the Cross, in Reynosa in the state of Tamaulipas. God moved on the hearts of Thomas and Wilma to go and serve at the seminary. Thomas went to Mexico as president of the school. The position required a great deal of travel, both in the United States and Mexico, to promote the work of the seminary. In the classroom Thomas taught English, Greek, Theology, Hermeneutics, and Bible. His ministry also involved working with groups from various churches in the United States who travelled to Mexico on mission trips. In time Thomas came to believe that it was time to put the seminary entirely in the hands of the Mexican Free Will Baptists. He and Wilma returned to Hillsdale on August 1, 2008.

At Hillsdale Thomas served as Vice President for Academic Affairs from 2008 until 2013. Beginning in 2013 he has been serving as Professor of New Testament, teaching Greek, Theology, Church History, and Bible.

Over the years Thomas has pastored three churches. From 1973 to 1975 he pastored the United Free Will Baptist Church in Bryan, Texas; from 1976 to 1992 he pastored the Prairie Bell Free Will Baptist Church in Putnam, Oklahoma; and from 2014 to the present he has been pastoring the First Free Will Baptist Church in Oklahoma City, Oklahoma.

Thomas continued to further his education over the years. He completed a Master of Divinity degree at Southwestern Baptist Theological Seminary in December of 1973. He has taken courses at Sam Houston State University, Texas A&M University, Rose State College, Oklahoma City Community College, and Oklahoma University.

As a legitimate scholar Thomas has had an extensive writing ministry. For twenty years he wrote Top Shelf, a book review column, for *Contact* magazine. His book reviews were excellent and helpful, especially to Free Will Baptist pastors who were inclined to read books. He wrote the commentary on Galatians in the Randall House Bible Commentary, and co-wrote the volume on the Johannine Epistles with Dr. Craig Shaw.[187] He is currently writing the volume on the Book of Luke.

In addition to his ministry in Oklahoma and Mexico, Thomas has been active in the work of the National Association of Free Will Baptists. He served on the Historical Commission for several years, and taught the Sunday morning Sunday school class at the National Association on two different occasions. He has been a frequent speaker at district and state meetings in Texas and Oklahoma and preached several times at the Mexican Association. Several years ago he taught training conferences for pastors in the Ukraine.

Every young person considering the ministry, and every person who is already in the ministry, should pay careful attention to the following words by Dr. Marberry:

> In my mind there is no doubt that a young man who plans to enter the ministry should go to college and seminary. The ministry is different today from what it was years ago. College and seminary training will help a minister face the challenges of the modern world.

Isaac Martin

As in the case of many of our Texas Free Will Baptists, Isaac Martin was born in some other state and migrated here. He was born on December 31, 1812, to James (1788-1869) and Hester Bogan Martin (1789-1867). James and Hester were the parents of four preachers, one of whom started the Martin Association in Georgia. They are both buried in Georgia. Isaac was one of the early ministers in the Chattahoochee Association of Free Will Baptists in Georgia. He is listed in the 1842 minutes of that association. He married Mary Polly Truitt on June 6, 1834, in Jasper County, Georgia. Isaac and Mary had eleven children. After migrating to Texas Isaac was one of the early pastors in the Texas Association, which in 1954 became the East Texas District Association of Free Will Baptists. Mary passed away in 1890 in Cherokee County, Texas. Isaac passed away on November 2, 1888, and is buried in the Alto City Cemetery, Alto, Cherokee County, Texas.

---

[187] We could write a profile on Craig Shaw because he pastored the Western Hills Free Will Baptist Church in Fort Worth while attending Southwestern Baptist Theological Seminary. Dr. Shaw later taught at Hillsdale.

Samuel Crawford Martin

Samuel Crawford Martin was born on January 20, 1825 in the state of Alabama, in "the heart of Dixie." He was one of the four preacher brothers born to James and Hester Martin, mentioned above. He also migrated to Texas, first to Tyler County and then to Brazos County. The *Bryan Eagle* carried the following obituary on Thursday, December 24, 1903:

> REV. S. C. MARTIN DEAD. Venerable Pioneer Baptist Preacher Gone to his Reward. Brazos County mourns the loss of one of her oldest, noblest and best citizens, and the holidays have been darkened in the homes throughout the length and breadth of the county, where his name was a household word, by the death of Rev. S. C. Martin at his home in the Steep Hollow community on Wednesday morning, December 23, 1903, at 8:30 o'clock. Rev. Martin, infirm with the weight and labors of 79 years, has been in failing health for some time and ill for several weeks, so that his death was not unexpected. Nevertheless, it was a sad blow to the family and a host of friends when the news came from the darkened chamber that his noble spirit had taken its flight.
>
> Rev. Martin was a native of Alabama and came to Texas before the Civil War, locating in Tyler County. He moved to Brazos County more than thirty years ago and has since resided in the Steep Hollow community. For more than half a century he preached the gospel and his labors were graciously blessed in the salvation of souls. Not only did he serve as pastor of nearly every Baptist church in Brazos County, but throughout his life he did much successful revival work. He was sincere, honest, uncompromising, unselfish, and consecrated. He labored as faithfully without reward as when his labors were abundantly rewarded. In deed his best service was given to the Master with numerically weak and struggling churches, and it may be truly said that he gave his life to the gospel, the church, and humanity. His brother was the founder of the Martin Association in the state of Georgia and he had at least two other brothers who were Free Will Baptist preachers as well. His ancestry has roots in South Carolina, with one of them buried in the Horse Branch Free Will Baptist Cemetery.

It is nice to read such high praise for one of our older Free Will Baptist preachers. Incidentally, the Horse Branch Free Will Baptist Church, Turbeville, South Carolina, mentioned at the end of the obituary above, is to this day one of the leading Free Will Baptist churches not only in the state of South Carolina, but in the entire denomination as well.

Jerry McArthur

Jerry Allen McArthur is one of those multitalented men who have ministered in Texas, as well as in a number of other states, and has made some valuable contributions to the work. He was born on September 2, 1944, to J. A. and Ada Allene (Neal) McArthur in Fort Worth, Texas. Jerry's father was a furniture builder. Jerry graduated from Polytechnic High School in 1963.

During his high school years he played on the baseball team and was a two year letterman.

Jerry married Barbara Louise Durham on December 30, 1966. They had gone to high school together and she had joined the United States Air Force. She took her basic training at Lackland Air Force Base in San Antonio and was assigned to the 3700 Personnel Processing Squadron. She served her entire time in the Air Force at Lackland, from July 1963 to June of 1965. Reconnecting with Jerry after her discharge from the service, they were married in the home of her parents, with Baptist pastor J. D. Fenn officiating.

Barbara and Jerry McArthur, Ruidoso, NM

Jerry was eighteen years of age when he sensed that God was calling him into the ministry. Accepting the call he was licensed to preach on June 7, 1967, by the West Fork District Association. He accepted the call of the Good Hope Free Will Baptist Church in Henderson, Texas, in 1970. He was then ordained to the gospel ministry on January 16, 1971, at the Friendship Free Will Baptist Church in Fort Worth. During the summer of 1971 he took summer classes at Free Will Baptist Bible College in Nashville, Tennessee. He continued as pastor at Good Hope until 1972.

He then pastored the Trinity Free Will Baptist Church in Fort Worth from 1974 to 1975. He left Trinity to attend Hillsdale Free Will Baptist College in Moore, Oklahoma, graduating in 1982 with a B. A. degree. After graduating from Hillsdale Jerry had a long succession of pastorates, always willing to go wherever the Lord in his providence called him. He pastored the First Free Will Baptist Church in Wichita Kansas, from 1982 to 1984; The Ambassador Free Will Baptist Church in Cincinnati, Ohio, 1987-1992; the Cornerstone Free Will Baptist Church in Denison, Texas, 1993-1998; the New Salem Free Will Baptist Church in Colquitt, Georgia, 2001-2003; and the Northgate Free Will Baptist Church in Hobbs, New Mexico, 2003-2015, his longest pastorate. While in Hobbs Jerry led in the relocation of the church to a newly constructed building on the north side of town, in 2008, and changed the name of the church from First United Free Will Baptist Church to Northgate Free Will Baptist Church. He retired from the pastorate in 2015.

During the years of his ministry Jerry was always active in the denominational work in and beyond his local community. He served as chairman of the Board of Trustees of the West Fork Board of Christian Education, which operated the West Fork Youth Camp. He was responsible for the construction of the concrete slab for the basketball court. He also served on the Credentials Committee of the West Fork. He served as secretary-treasurer of the State Mission Board in Kansas. In Ohio he was instrumental in establishing the Tri-State Conference, and served as it's moderator, and served on the state's General Board and Executive Committee. Back in Texas he served as clerk of the West Fork and as assistant clerk for the state association, as well as assistant moderator. In New Mexico he served as clerk of the New Mexico District Association and as assistant moderator.[188] For ten years in Hobbs he served as chaplain for the Police and Fire Departments and the hospital.

Jerry and Barbara both are talented musicians, not so much at playing music but at writing and singing. Jerry has written ten songs and co-written six more. Barbara co-wrote one of the

---

[188] In New Mexico the only organization broader than the local church is the one district association.

songs with him. They have recorded three CDs and one Christmas song, which was released nationally. They have been regular singers at churches, quarterly meetings, and state association meetings.

Although Jerry is retired from the pastoral ministry, he currently works as a field representative for Free Will Baptist Family Ministries and lives in Bowie, Texas. He passes along the following advice for younger ministers: Get all the education you can and don't let anyone change your mind as to what God has called you to do in his service. "Go forward with a purpose, always looking to Jesus as your guide." Because of his gregarious personality he never met a stranger, and he loved and enjoyed people.

S. L. Morris

Schooley Lemmon (or Lemon) Morris was born April 5, 1856, in Zanesville, Morgan County, Ohio, to David and Rachel Ann (James) Morris. He was converted at thirteen years of age and entered the ministry at age twenty-eight. In the 1880 census he was listed as a photographer. Later references in the censuses list him as a Free Will Baptist minister. Morris was widowed twice in his lifetime. In the 1880 census his wife was listed as Josephine Morris, and they had a three month old son, Corral W. Morris. On March 4, 1891 he married Belle Adams. In the 1900 census he is listed as having three children: Corral W., Hallie, and Nellie. He joined the Free Baptist Church at Ava, Illinois, in 1896. He was ordained in 1897, at Tamaroa, Illinois. He organized the Lone Oak Church and then pastored the Tamaroa Church where he had a very successful ministry. After the death of his second wife he married Grace Irene Topping on March 24, 1901, in Ashley, Illinois.

Morris began to make his mark on Texas Free Will Baptists when he moved to Bryan, Texas, where he became only the second pastor of the Free Baptist Church, later to be named the First Free Will Baptist Church. He followed the founding pastor, A. M. Stewart, whom, you will remember, started the first white Free Will Baptist Church in Texas at Clayton in 1876. Morris left Bryan to take the pastorate of the Free Baptist Church in Alvord, Texas, in 1906.[189] It was in connection with his work that he established that same year the monthly denomination paper, the *Free Baptist News*, later called the *Free Will Baptist News*, which he eventually published in Weatherford, Texas. Morris had contemplated plans for the *News* for some time He had moved north from Bryan in order to cover a larger field, which included Texas and the Indian Territory north of the Red River. He also pastored the First Free Will Baptist Church in Weatherford. He was a friend and mentor to the younger Lizzie McAdams, who often referred to him as "father Morris." In 1912 he was an agent for the Southwestern Freewill Baptist General Convention. At the 1912 convention he gave a talk on *The Free Will Baptist News*.

He continued publishing the *News* for several years. In 1916 Free Will Baptists in Texas, Oklahoma, and Missouri organized the Cooperative General Association of Free Will Baptists at a meeting at the Philadelphia Church, near Pattonsburg, Missouri. Morris was present and was chosen to preach during one of the evening services. The moderator appointed him to be on a committee to devise reporting forms for the association. Morris also preached at a called session of the association on December 26, 1917, at the Northview Church near Tecumseh, Oklahoma.

The Cooperative General Association at its organizational session voted to purchase the *Free Will Baptist News* from Morris and to name him the editor and publisher. They paid him $350.00 for the *News* and $913.00 for the printing equipment and other assets, and voted to change the

---

[189] *The Morning Star*, March 8, 1906, page 13.

name of the *News* to the *New Morning Star*. It was printed in Weatherford, Texas, for about a year before it was moved to Tecumseh, Oklahoma.

In 1919 Samra Smith, a native of North Carolina, merged his publication, the *Biblical Beacon*, with the *New Morning Star* and became co-editor with Morris. At about the same time W. C. Austin merged his paper, the *Gospel Pruning Hook*, with the *Star*, thus three papers became one, with a much larger circulation. At first the *Star* was published twice a month, then weekly for a time, and then back to twice a month.

The Cooperative General Association opened Tecumseh College on September 2, 1917. The *New Morning Star* was moved from Weatherford, Texas, to Tecumseh, Oklahoma. The latest printing equipment was purchased for the *Star*, such as Linotype, a larger cylinder press, a large job press, a motorized paper cutter, and a mailer. Morris made the move with the *Star*, and became the first pastor of the Tecumseh College Church, which had been organized earlier in the year. Morris and his wife Grace were also on the faculty of Tecumseh College. He served as a lecturer in the Department of History and Apologetics. She was the head of the Department of Mathematics and Physics. Their salaries were $70.00 per year for each of them.

S. L. Morris passed away May 19, 1922, in Ashley, Washington County, Illinois, at the age of 66. In November of 1924 his widow, Grace I. Morris, became the president of Tecumseh College.

Thurmon Murphy

Thurmon Murphy

I was born in a log cabin in Overton County, Tennessee, to Charlie and Rachel Murphy on August 6, 1941. I usually say I am from Hanging Limb, Tennessee, which was the nearest village. My father was a coal miner and tenant farmer. Most of my youth in Tennessee was spent in Sunk Cane, also in Overton County, in a mountain valley below Hanging Limb. We never had electricity, gas, or inside plumbing. We drew our water from a well, cooked on a wood burning stove, and heated the house with a potbellied coal burning stove. My siblings and I attended the one room Sunk Cane School, which had one teacher, all eight grades, and twenty-something students. My father was a deacon in the Columbia Hill Free Will Baptist Church, which belonged to the old Stone Association of Tennessee. There was no church in Sunk Cane.

On January 9, 1953, we moved to Dayton, Ohio, where dad found work with General Motors. At first we lived in an upstairs three-room apartment in a ghetto, or slum, though we did have electricity, running water, and a bathroom, albeit with no bathtub. I started school at Emerson Elementary in the fourth grade, a school which had over thirteen hundred students. I was one lost country boy. I discovered the public library and devoured three books every two weeks.

My family and I attended the First Dayton Free Will Baptist Church. I graduated from Stivers High School in 1960 and enrolled at Free Will Baptist Bible College in Nashville, Tennessee, in the fall. I sat under some of the greatest teachers in the Free Will Baptist denomination: Laura Belle Barnard, Leroy Forlines, Dr. Robert Picirilli, Ralph Hampton, Dr. Charles Thigpen, and Dr. J. D. O'Donnell, graduating in 1964.

My early pastorates were in Midland City and Northport, Alabama. I married Karen Tylene Terry on August 14, 1964. I started the First Free Will Baptist Church in Austintown, Ohio, a suburb of Youngstown. After attending the National Association of Free Will Baptists in Fort Worth, Texas, in July of 1972, I decided to move my ministry to Texas. I located my family to White Settlement, a suburb of Fort Worth, in October of 1972, and pastored the Grace Free Will Baptist Church, a mission church, a split off of the Rock of Ages Free Will Baptist Church. I soon realized the mission should never have been started. I also worked as a bookkeeper for the Town and Country Village Shopping Center, part time. Grace was the only church I ever pastored which wasn't full time. I planned to attend Southwestern Baptist Theological Seminary to earn a doctorate. My ambition was to teach Bible and theology.

Finances were tight and Karen became ill. As a result I accepted the call to pastor the First Free Will Baptist Church in Odessa, in West Texas, which I pastored from 1973 to 1978. Leaving there was the worst mistake of my entire ministry. I left to become the Minister of Christian Education at my home church in Dayton, Ohio, pastored by Dr. Hobert Ashby. That brief ministry lasted only one year and I moved my family back to Odessa. I worked about six months as a personnel consultant with Bennett Personnel Services.

Keith Woody told me that the First Free Will Baptist Church in Wichita Falls was in need of a pastor and so I had my name passed along to the church by Roy Norie. The church called me as pastor and I started in March of 1980 and pastored until my retirement from the pastorate in 2006, twenty-seven years. Altogether I had pastored for forty-five years.

During the years of my pastoring I was active in the district, state, and national work, feeling that every pastor should do his fair share of denominational work. In Alabama I had served as chairman of the Progressive Association's Board of Christian Education as well as chairman of the state Board of Christian Education. I was moderator of the Progressive Association for a time. I was active in the Progressive Association's youth camp, Camp Proyuca, as well.

In Texas I served as moderator of both the Midessa Association and the West Fork. I served for years as chairman of the Board of Christian Education which operates the West Fork Youth Camp. On the state level I served as chairman of the State Home Missions Board, chairman of the Board of Christian Education, clerk, treasurer, and editor of the *Texas Challenge*. These last three were finally combined for me under the title State Executive Secretary. Four things during that time I am particularly proud of: 1) the state meetings were exceptionally well organized and operated efficiently and harmoniously, 2) plans were made for the state work for both the short term and long range, which provided direction and goals for the state association, 3) the quality of printed matter, such as the *Digest of Reports*, was raised to where it was first class, and 4) *The Texas Challenge* was improved to where it was said to be the best state paper in the denomination. I must hasten to say that the *Challenge* became even better after Sally Wilcox became the editor.

On the national level I served for six years on the General Board of the National Association of Free Will Baptists, four of those years as a member of the Executive Committee, often wrongly called the Executive Board, of the General Board. It was my privilege to serve as presider during several of the evening worship services. I preached at the Pastor's Conference of the National Association in 1998, when the convention met in Tulsa, Oklahoma. I wrote *The Bible Teacher* for Randall House Publications for one quarter and then turned down a request that I do more.

I retired from pastoring and from my district and state work in 2006, at the age of sixty-five, because I was physically, mentally, emotionally and spiritually spent, having given everything I had to give. I needed time for healing. Since 2006 I have been involved in a writing, Bible teaching, and occasional preaching ministry.

I have a number of hobbies. One of them, which I have been involved with since I was about twelve years old, is studying the history of Native Americans. In the process I have acquired a rather large collection of Native American artifacts.

At the request of Dr. Teressa Voltz, the final proofreader of the manuscript of this book, the following has been added by her:

> Thurmon Murphy has played a vital role in the history of Texas Free Will Baptists. He has been faithful and has served where called and needed. As the author of this book he has spent hundreds of hours, months, years, researching and interviewing to make sure he captured the history of the Texas Free Will Baptists to the best of his ability and as accurately as possible. I would like to extend the deepest gratitude to Thurmon for taking on this project in response to many inquiries and requests for him to do so. He has diligently and prayerfully completed a written history of the Texas Free Will Baptists, serving God as He calls.

Judson B. Palmer

Judson Palmer was born on April 25, 1851, in Orangeville, Ohio. He attended Hillsdale College in Hillsdale, Michigan, the premier college of the northern movement of Free Will Baptists, the school after which Hillsdale Free Will Baptist College in Moore, Oklahoma, was named. He graduated from the theological department at Hillsdale and was ordained to the gospel ministry in May, 1873. A. A. Smith and A. H. Chase, along with others, served on the ordaining council. He served as a teacher at the mission in Cairo, Illinois, for two years and as a state missionary. He pastored in the states of Michigan, Wisconsin, and Iowa before coming to Texas. He conducted many revival meetings and baptized over one hundred fifty converts. He became the general secretary of the YMCA at Galveston, Texas, where he died in 1937. He is buried in the Galveston Memorial Park, Hitchcock, Galveston County, Texas.[190]

Robert Posner

Robert Julius Posner, Jr. was born in Cherry Point, North Carolina, on May 1, 1964, to Robert Julius Posner, Sr. and Julie Jane (Henderson) Posner Pernell. His father served in the United States Marine Corp for twenty years and then as an insurance agent until his retirement. His mother was a homemaker for eight years, then salesperson and manager of Belks department store for over twenty-five years. Robert grew up in several places, namely, Cherry Point, North Carolina; Yuma, Arizona; Raleigh, North Carolina, and Virginia Beach, Virginia.

In March of 1979 Robert met Judy Mary Accongio at a skating rink in Raleigh. On April 15th they began dating exclusively. They have continued to date ever since. They were married on April 14, 1984, at Robert's home church, the First Free Will Baptist Church of Raleigh, North Carolina, with Pastor Randy Cox performing the ceremony. Robert and Judy have three children: Bethany Gayle Posner Lopez, Anna Jane Posner Keller, and Nathan Robert Posner. As of this writing they have three grandchildren.

---

[190] *Handbook of Historical Free Will Baptist Burial Places*, page 405.

Robert graduated from W. G. Enloe High School in Raleigh in 1982. He was named to Who's Who Among American High School Students, was president of DECA (Distributive Education Clubs of America) and won a local speech contest. He was converted to Christ in October of 1979 under the ministries of his pastor, Randy Cox, and youth pastor, Doug Henderson[191] at the First Free Will Baptist Church of Raleigh, North Carolina.[192]

Robert and Judy Posner

Shortly after surrendering his life to Christ, he sensed a calling to be a preacher of the gospel, but was very nervous and unsure about it. Youth pastor Doug Henderson encouraged him by giving him opportunities to teach the teens in Sunday school and other ministry opportunities, but after a rather embarrassing failure in the DECA state speech contest he turned away from that calling. Later, after marrying Judy in 1984, his faith grew substantially and he sensed the calling again. The final obstacle to surrendering to the call was attending college. After a short and distasteful experience at the Wake County Community College he rejected the whole idea of higher education. This rejection was never encouraged or condoned by his pastor or parents. One Sunday in September of 1985, during the worship service, he sensed a strong urging to surrender his stubbornness in this area and prayerfully told the Lord he would go to college if he wanted him to go. A great burden was lifted and his faith grew even more in the days ahead. He shared his thoughts about the Lord's calling with then youth pastor, Doug Rabon. They committed together to pray daily for ten minutes, solely about the Lord's calling and career direction for his life. While driving home after a Sunday morning worship service in October of 1985, he was overwhelmed with the need to answer the Lord's call to pastoral ministry. By the time he arrived home he was fully surrendered.

He preached his first sermon in late 1985 in the children's worship service at the First Free Will Baptist Church of Raleigh. He was subsequently licensed to preach by his home church in 1986, and ordained by the same church in May of 1992. His credentials were accepted by the Randall Association, but he never went before them or attended an associational meeting. His credentials were signed by Dr. Randy Cox, Tim Rabon, Danny Dwyer, and various deacons of the church.

As one can see above, the call to the ministry to Robert meant that he would have to get a college education at a good Christian school. To get his preparation for the ministry he enrolled at Southeastern Free Will Baptist College in Wendell, North Carolina. The reason he went to that particular school was because his pastor told him to. He started classes in the fall of 1985 and graduated in May, 1992. During those several years of college he was named to Who's Who Among American College Students, and was recognized for three years of service to Southeastern Free Will Baptist College as Dean of Men and Men's Dorm Supervisor.

After earning his bachelor's degree in Pastoral Administration in May of 1992. Robert and Judy moved their family, consisting of Beth and Anna at the time, to Texas. Robert and Judy believed that it was the Lord's leading and calling for them to minister in the state of Texas, though they don't know why specifically. Robert began his first pastorate at the Lifegate Free Will Baptist Church in Tyler on June 7, 1992, and continued as pastor there until January 25, 1998. As with most incoming pastors, the Free Will Baptists in the state of Texas received the Posners well and

---

[191] Doug is the son of Harvey Henderson who worked in Austin in the 1960's as a Project 30 missionary.
[192] This church is now the Beacon Baptist Church.

made them feel right at home. When he first came to Texas Robert had never attended a national, state, or district association meeting. His sole denominational experience had been his home church in Raleigh and his time as a student at Southeastern Free Will Baptist College. Again, as most incoming pastors do, he experienced numerous cultural differences in Texas. For instance, they found Texas pastors to be more relaxed and inviting. Friendships were encouraging and supportive. Texas became home very quickly. The King James Version of the Bible, in Proverbs 18:24, says "A man that hath friends must shew himself friendly." Robert's relaxed manner, warm smile, humility, acceptance of others, and friendly demeanor made it easy for him to gain acceptance and establish friendships.

Robert became pastor of the Collin Creek Free Will Baptist Church on February 1, 1998, and continues what appears to be a very successful ministry there at this writing. He has some unique philosophies about preaching, music, and youth work. When asked to share those he said:

> With regard to preaching: it must be biblically based, in general expository, and have a clear bridge of application to the present day. Our points must have a biblical text to back it up, otherwise it is opinions. I believe the preacher must have lived in the text for some time, meaning he has studied it fully, made practical application to his own life, sees the relevance to those of his congregation and community, and is able to clearly and passionately express the principle(s). With regard to church music: it must be biblical above everything else. The style must connect with the listeners and clearly communicate the message. I agree with Rob Morgan who said, "Every generation must create their own music. If they don't, then the gospel has stopped touching lives." With regard to youth ministry: it should be about building disciples, helping parents love, lead, and spiritually disciple their own children. The church should complement what the parents are doing at home (Deuteronomy 6).

As many pastors' wives do, Judy is very involved in the work of the local church. Her primary role is to be a follower of Jesus, above everything else. Her primary ministry at Lifegate and Collin Creek has been in children's ministry, which includes teaching a children's program on Wednesday evenings. All other ministries are temporary until someone else can take on the responsibility. She serves the church mostly by loving Jesus, supporting Robert, and being a godly example for all to follow. She serves in the Texas Women Active for Christ, TWAC, largely as an encourager to others, encouraging other ladies to lead the women of Texas for the glory of God.

The Posner children are all involved in the Lord's work in various ways, of their own free will. Beth and her husband, Chris, serve on the praise team ministry at Collin Creek. Beth helps as a leader of the Vacation Bible School each summer and helps Judy consistently on Wednesday evenings with the children's program. Anna is a mother, serves in short-term leadership roles in different ministries, such as outreach, congregational care, and children's ministry. Anna's husband, Mason, is the lead voice for Collin Creek's praise team and serves to disciple others for Jesus. Nathan, or Nate as he likes to be called, serves on the praise team as the lead guitar player and serves on various other ministry opportunities as they become available, such as outreach, teens, and assistant teaching the 5th and 6th graders. All three of the Posner children have served in mission efforts in Mexico and Cuba. Robert has made numerous mission trips, himself.

Because Robert focuses his ministry efforts on three areas, the church he pastors in Plano, the work of the State Home Mission Board, and the Board of International Missions, he has sometimes been criticized for not holding an office in the West Fork District Association. When asked about this he indicated that he had to establish priorities and make choices. Other than God, his first priority and obligation is to his family. The church is his next priority and after that comes his responsibility to his mission's ministry. Robert serves as chairman of the State Mission Board. He was elected to the Board of Free Will Baptist International Missions at the 78th session of the National Association, which met in Fort Worth, Texas, July 27-30, 2014. He serves as state liaison for International Missions' annual World Missions Offering (WMO). He is pursuing a Master's Degree from Randall University in Moore, Oklahoma. This gives him a full load. He further stated, "Words cannot express how much I love and respect the pastors of the West Fork District Association. Many of them are wiser, more skilled and, quite honestly, more competent at leading our district. I enjoy sitting under the leadership of those involved. Hopefully, I can encourage them to serve on."

For a fuller account of his work with the Texas Home Missions Board see the chapter on Home Missions.

Tom Quinones

Tomas Quinones III is a two hat man, a term understood by Texans, meaning that he has two professions or careers. He pastors the Friendship Free Will Baptist Church in Fort Worth at this writing and is a practicing attorney, with law offices in Hurst, Texas, part of the Dallas-Fort Worth Metroplex.

Tom was born on August 10, 1958, in Fort Worth to Tomas Bermudez and Lucille (Zaskoda) Quinones. Tom's father was born in Ponce, Puerto Rico, and his mother was born in El Campo, Texas, of Czech descent. For the first eight years of his life Tom lived in New York, New York. His family moved back to Texas in 1966. Tom was raised a Roman Catholic. He attended local Catholic churches in New York and Fort Worth, and attended Nolan Catholic High School in Fort Worth, graduating in 1976.

Pastor Tom Quinones gives an assignment to an Impact Fort Worth

Tom worked at the Sears at Seminary South in Fort Worth from 1977 to 1983, while attending college. During those years he was around numerous seminary students, both men and women, including his wife to be, Michele Ann Pedigo, who worked part time at Sears. He recounts here how he came to faith in Christ:

> I was not aware of what Free Will Baptists were until I met Michele and her parents, Ed and Charlene. I came to faith in Christ not in the traditional southern gospel church setting or background. I was raised a Catholic, was an altar boy, and tried very hard to be moral and ethical. That is how we were taught. I loved to read history, politics, and theology. I had many Christian friends while working at Sears that directly influenced me to seek the truth and Christ. The evangelical church community was foreign to me so I was very skeptical. I had to research on my own and was very fortunate to have the witness of about twenty seminary students and other strong believers at Sears. In short, I had read and heard enough that it became

very clear that I must step out in faith and personally believe and act upon the truths I had come to accept. I read C. S. Lewis and Francis Schaeffer, among others. I knew there would be no turning back; though there have been times of great weakness and coldness. I cannot emphasize enough the importance of a biblical worldview that is consciously developed by the Word of God.[193]

Tom accepted Christ as his savior in the fall of 1981 and committed his life to Christ. He began attending Friendship Free Will Baptist Church with Michele occasionally in 1982 and became a regular attender in 1983. His growth in his new faith in Christ was evident to all who knew him. Michele and her family were active in the Friendship Church, pastored at the time by Jack Bankhead. In addition to her active participation in Friendship, Michele went to France in the summer of 1983 and was active in the West Fork Youth Camp. She attended Hillsdale Free Will Baptist College from 1980 to 1984, graduating in May of '84 with a Bachelor's Degree in Theology.

Tom and Michele was married on August 16, 1986, at the Friendship Church, still located at the time on Schadt Street in Fort Worth. Pastor Bankhead performed the ceremony. They have two children: Caleb and Jessica, who are both active in the Lord's work.

In 1987 Tom sensed that God was calling him into the ministry. He was licensed to preach in the late 1980's or 1990. He was then ordained to the gospel ministry by the New Salem Free Will Baptist Church, near Decatur. His ministerial credentials were signed by Jack T. Bankhead, Thurmon Murphy, and Deacon Ronald Womack. Tom pastored the New Salem Church from 1998, just after former pastor Roy Norie died, until 2004. He was called as pastor of the Friendship Church in Fort Worth in August of 2006, after having filled in for them as needed, and continues as pastor at this writing.

Tom is also active in politics as a Republican. He has been a precinct chairman since 1996. He has held the small precinct conventions and has participated in and/or chaired several senatorial district conventions since 1996. He has regularly attended state conventions since 1994 and was elected to be a delegate to the Republican National Convention in 2004. Michele is active with him and served as a delegate to the 2000 Republican National Convention. He says, "I have read all my life and believe it is important that Christians take their citizenship in God's kingdom and in this world seriously. The wealth and knowledge and good Bible teaching renders us without excuse."

In addition to her degree from Hillsdale, Michele earned a Master's Degree in Math at Texas Women's University in Denton. She is a teacher in the Fort Worth Independent School District.

---

[193] From written answers to questions posed to him in writing.

Walter Herbert Richards

Herbert & Margaret Richards

Some leaders are recognized as being great because of two or three outstanding things they do or have done. Some leaders are recognized as being great because they do or did their jobs faithfully over a long period of time, without fanfare, and sometimes without much notice. This, to some degree, describes Herbert Richards.

Herbert was born to W. A. and Mary Jane (Keefer) Richards on January 14, 1920, at Edge, Brazos County, Texas, about twenty miles from Bryan. His father worked as a farmer.

When Herbert was four years old the family moved in two covered wagons from Edge to Bronte, in Coke County, on the edge of West Texas, where his father had rented some farm land. At the time the family consisted of Herbert, his father and mother, four brothers, Claude, Otho, Luel, and Wesley, and two sisters, Lela and Beulah. Lela would later marry Gaston Clary, a well-known Free Will Baptist minister in Texas in his own right. On the trip west the family camped out at night, just as had earlier pioneers. The Richards family lived in Bronte for two years and then moved back to Edge. Mr. Richards traded the mules and wagons and bought a Model T Ford.

Herbert attended elementary school at Edge, Steep Hollow, and A&M Consolidated. He attended A&M Consolidated High School in College Station, though he did not graduate.

Herbert and Margaret Denton were married on January 20, 1940. Herbert was twenty years of age and Margaret was nineteen at the time. From this union were born two children: Eugene and Marilu.

During World War II he served in the United States Navy from 1943 to 1945 in the Pacific. During this time he served for twenty-two months and fifteen days in the Philippines. He was a Radarman Second Class, serving on the *USS Alshan*, known as an AKA, an amphibious cargo attack vessel. He was involved in six invasions: Guam, three in the Philippines, Leyte, and Okinawa. The first invasion of the Philippines was at Luzon, to seal off Bataan. The *Alshan* came under kamikaze attack by the Japanese four times, each time escaping sinking. However, the ship next to the Alshan was sunk by one of the diving kamikaze planes. During an attack it was Herbert's job to load 20 mm anti-aircraft guns. He was in New Guinea when the Japanese surrendered in 1945. All of the medals he received during the war were stolen about fifteen years ago when he lived at Keith, Texas. Now in his 90's he cannot remember which medals he had earned.

Herbert was licensed to the gospel ministry in 1947 by the Central Texas District Association at the Bright Light Free Will Baptist Church, one of the oldest Free Will Baptist churches in Texas. Then, in 1948, at the age of twenty-eight, he was ordained at the North Zulch Free Will Baptist Church. His ordination certificate was signed by Hiram M. McAdams, Joe Fort, and Clyde Goen.

Herbert and Margaret moved to Nashville, Tennessee, in August of 1947 and enrolled as students at Free Will Baptist Bible College, now Welch College. Eugene was four or five years old when they moved to Nashville. They were able to go to college because of monies received through the GI Bill. Herbert and Margaret both graduated in 1949. They were members of the school's fourth graduating class. This class was distinguished, not only because Herbert and

Margaret were members of it, but because of such people as Billy Melvin, Joe Haas, Gaston Clary, their brother-in-law, and Wesley and Aileen (Mullen) Calvery who were also members of it. Herbert served as vice president of the class. During this time he received his GED from Vanderbilt University.

In years to come both of their children, Eugene and Marilu, would attend Free Will Baptist Bible College, as did Marilu's oldest daughter Megan. Eugene's son, Colby, attended Hillsdale Free Will Baptist College in Moore Oklahoma.

Upon graduation from the Bible College Herbert and Margaret, along with Eugene, moved back to Texas. Then began his long career of ministry, all of them in the state of Texas.

His first church was the Southside Free Will Baptist Church in Comanche, Texas, one of many Free Will Baptist churches no longer in existence. While there he took the opportunity of attending Howard Payne University in Brownwood. Then followed a term as pastor of the First Free Will Baptist Church of Denton, Texas. The church was in a storefront but soon bought land with a house on it, which was converted into a church building. The church was in the West Fork District Association. It was at Denton that Eugene was saved and Marilu was born. After Brother Richards left, the church built a nice, big, new church in the early 1960's.

He next pastored two churches at the same time: Evergreen and Blue Lake, out of Bryan. He resigned the Blue Lake church so he could pastor the Evergreen church alone, feeling that he could serve one church better than two.

Over the next several years he pastored the Cross Free Will Baptist Church in Iola, where he supported his family by teaching school, the First Free Will Baptist Church in Huntsville, the North Zulch Free Will Baptist Church, and Christ's Free Will Baptist Church in Corpus Christi, where he remained for fourteen years. During the time in Corpus Christi he taught the fifth and sixth grades at the elementary school in Rockport. Next, he pastored the Zion Free Will Baptist Church in Flour Bluff, and then returned as pastor of the Evergreen Free Will Baptist Church, where he remained for eight years. Then he pastored the Bright Light Free Will Baptist Church for fourteen years. He preached his last sermon at Bright Light in August of 2012. Altogether, Brother Richards pastored in Texas for sixty-five years, which is a rare accomplishment for a minister anywhere.

In addition to teaching school as a means of supporting his family, as he had at Iola and Rockport, he worked at a furniture factory in Bryan and for the Lone Star Gas Company in Dallas.

Brother Richards held many offices during his long years of ministry in Texas, on both the district and state levels. He served as moderator of the state association for two years and was the moderator of the Central Texas District Association. He served on the State Mission Board and on the Credentials Committee of the Central District.

He says that the highlight of his ministry was preaching the moderator's message at the National Association of Free Will Baptists when it met in Atlanta, Georgia, in 1999. It was the responsibility of moderator Carl Cheshire to preach the message but, as a means of recognizing and honoring Brother Richards, moderator Cheshire graciously extended the opportunity to him, which was an unselfish and Christlike gesture.

His beloved companion of seventy-three years, Margaret, passed away on January 28, 2013. She is buried in the Evergreen church cemetery. At this writing Brother Richards lives with his daughter, Marilu, in Bryan. He has four grandchildren and seven great grandchildren. He recently said, at the age of ninety-three, "If I've accomplished anything good in my ministry its been because of Jesus. I want him to get all the praise."

David Rudd

David Connally Rudd was born on November 28, 1962, in Tyler, Texas, to Gerry Connally and Loretta Lynn (Dozier) Rudd. David's father was an architect. David grew up in the Bascom community, east of Tyler, though he lived for a time in Tyler, Mesquite, and Pine Tree (now a part of Longview). He attended twelve years of school at Chapel Hill, east of Tyler, graduating in May of 1981, in the top ten of his class. He was a member of the National Honor Society and was voted Most Likely to Succeed in the Field of Drafting.

David and Adethia Rudd

David's maternal grandfather, Elwood Dozier, was a Southern Baptist pastor in Smith County for over fifty years. He was converted to Christ at the County Line Baptist Church, pastored by his grandfather, on October 31, 1971, at the age of nine.

Adethia Lynne Watson, who would become David's wife, also attended all twelve years of school at Chapel Hill. Graduating one year after David, in May of 1982, she, too, was a member of the National Honor Society, graduating third in her class. She was chosen as the English Department Student of the Year and was elected Band Sweetheart. David and Adethia met in high school when he was sixteen and she was fifteen. They were married at her home church, the Bascom United Methodist Church, on May 12, 1994. The ceremony was performed by Rev. Elwood L. Dozier, his grandfather, and Richard Luna, Adethia's pastor. From this marriage came three children: Regina Gaille, Bethany Anne, and David Westley.

David and Adethia were first introduced to Free Will Baptists shortly after they were married. They were invited to the Russell Road Free Will Baptist Church, a small upstart church north of Whitehouse, Texas, attending but never joining. They moved to Hackett, Arkansas, in 1986 so David could take a job in Fort Smith. David was twenty-four years old at the time and Adethia was expecting their first child. They joined the Pleasant Hill Free Will Baptist Church, pastored by Danny Owenby. David had been sensing God's call to the ministry for some time, but he wanted to be sure. He did not mention this to Adethia, which he says is not recommended. Finally, in May of 1987 he surrendered to preach one Sunday evening. Adethia was not present, having stayed home because she was not feeling well because of her pregnancy. When he arrived home after the service he dropped the bombshell on Adethia. He relates that it was not a pleasant experience at first. However, she got over the shock and became his most ardent supporter.

In 1988 or 1989 he was licensed to the ministry by the Arkansas District Association in western Arkansas, and then ordained on May 19, 1990. By then he had accepted the pastorate of the Brooklyn Free Will Baptist Church in Ratcliff, Arkansas. The ordaining council consisted of Danny Owenby, and Deacons James Earl Hawkins, Dale Green, Boyd W. Cox, and John Paul "Sparky" Musa, of the Brooklyn church.

David preached his first sermon at Pleasant Hill Free Will Baptist Church in Hackett, Arkansas, on Sunday evening, June 21, 1987. Other than high school David says he attended Hard Knocks University. He is currently working on completing a Bachelor's degree on-line through Hillsdale Free Will Baptist College.

His pastorates include the Brooklyn Free Will Baptist Church, mentioned above, Faith Free Will Baptist Church, Fort Smith, Arkansas (August 1991 to December 1991); First Free Will Baptist Church, Barling, Arkansas (October 1992 to August 1995); Good Hope Free Will Baptist

Church, Henderson, Texas (beginning April 1997). In the East Texas District Association he has served on the camp board, as moderator, and assistant moderator. Currently he is a member of the Texas Home Missions/Church Extension Board, serving as secretary/treasurer.

David has always been a bi-vocational pastor, working at a secular job to support his family while also pastoring. His secular career is in the fire sprinkler trade. He is a fire sprinkler designer and holds a Level VI certification as a senior engineering technician. He is currently general manager of his family owned business, Rudd Contracting Company, Inc. The company specializes in plumbing, fire sprinklers, and electronic alarms.

Richard Rust

Richard Wayne Rust is a prime example of a bi-vocational pastor. From his youth he dreamed of being a pastor but for all of his ministry he has made his living primarily as a carpenter. Richard was born at home on August 26, 1947, at Shady Point, Oklahoma. His mother was a devout Christian but his father did not attend church until, when Richard was eight years old, he was converted to Christ. Richard himself was saved at the age of ten at the Panama Free Will Baptist Church. Panama is part of the Fort Smith, Arkansas-Oklahoma Metropolitan Statistical Area.

Richard and Kareen Rust

While attending the Eureka Association Youth Camp, at the age of twelve, Richard answered the call to preach the gospel. He preached his first sermon the very next night at the youth camp. He says he didn't have a whole lot to say. He was licensed to preach at the age of eighteen, in 1965, by the Panama Free Will Baptist Church. The Poker Bend Free Will Baptist Church was about five miles west of Panama and Richard would go over early Sunday mornings and preach and teach Sunday school for them before going to his home church at Panama. The Panama Church ordained him to the ministry in 1966.

Richard graduated from Panama High School in 1966 and then attended Oklahoma Bible College, now Randall University, from 1966 to 1968. Afterwards he attended Northeastern State University at Tahlequah, Oklahoma, for one and a half years. He majored in business with two minors: history and music. During the next few years he took classes at four additional colleges.

Richard's pastoral ministry was from short term to long term. He pastored the Barnsdall Free Will Baptist Church for three years, the Red Oak Free Will Baptist Church for seven years, and the Alleck Free Will Baptist Church for three years. He came to the Faith Free Will Baptist Church in Wichita Falls, Texas, in 1987, and has pastored there for the past thirty years, where he continues his ministry at this writing.

While pastoring his first church, the church in Barnsdall, Oklahoma, he married Faye Reed. They were married for ten years and then she divorced him. There were a number of reasons for the divorce, but a familiar one to several pastors was as she stated to him, "I can't stand being a pastor's wife." As a result of the divorce Richard quit pastoring for about a year. Then the Alleck Free Will Baptist Church called him and he pastored there for three years as a single pastor.

Richard eventually moved to Texas and became the music director at the Garland Free Will Baptist Church. He has a star quality singing voice, if it may be stated that way. He was working in construction as a carpenter. During this time he met Kareen Ann Middlekauff of Austin and they were married on June 29, 1985.

He soon became the pastor of the Faith Free Will Baptist Church in Wichita Falls, where he continues to pastor. During those years he worked as a superintendent for Bratcher Construction Company as a builder. Richard has served in several capacities with the West Fork District Association: Credentials Committee; Chairman of the Board of Christian Education, which owns and operates the West Fork Youth Camp; Clerk; and as Moderator.

Luther Sanders

Robert Luther Sanders was born on May 18, 1922, in Emma, Kentucky, to Matthew and Anna Belle (Woods) Sanders. His father was a circuit riding Methodist minister and barber, who passed away with typhoid fever when Luther was six years old. After the death of his father, Luther and his brother started attending a Free Will Baptist church at Cow Creek, Kentucky, where they lived with their grandparents. His affiliation with Free Will Baptists would last a lifetime. He was converted to Christ in his early teens and was preaching by the time he was fourteen. Isaac "Ike" Stratton was his mentor who exerted a strong influence on his early Christian life.

Luther and Helen Sanders

Luther's life, as were the lives of many other young men, was interrupted by World War II. He served proudly in the United States Navy, fighting in the Pacific Theatre against the evil empire of Japan.[194] This, of course, acquainted him with the Hawaiian Islands, where he would later return to plant a church.

He met Helen Elizabeth Brown when they were both students at the school in Cow Creek, Kentucky. She walked up to him on the school playground and said she was going to marry him. He took a lot of ribbing from that over the years. She was five years younger than he was, having been born on December 25, 1927. They were married on April 8, 1945, in Helen's home in Cow Creek.

After World War II he was able to pursue an education in preparation for the ministry. He received a general education diploma (GED), not having completed high school, and enrolled at Free Will Baptist Bible College in the fall of 1946. He completed the two year program, graduating in 1948, and then enrolled at Bob Jones University in Greenville, South Carolina, where he graduated in 1951. He pastored the Haven Free Will Baptist Church[195] in Florence, South Carolina, from 1951 to 1954. From South Carolina he moved to Cordova, Alabama, to pastor the Cordova Free Will Baptist Church, from 1954 to 1956. He pastored in Monet, Missouri, from 1956 to 1959. It was in 1959 that he went as a home missionary to Hawai'i. While raising financial and prayer support for his missionary work he came to Dayton, Ohio, and spoke in my home church. He was the very first missionary I ever saw. The Sanders family arrived in Honolulu,

---

[194] That description could accurately be used during the war but would now be inappropriate since Japan is a friendly ally.
[195] Now the First Free Will Baptist Church

Hawai'i, in August of 1959, the month and year Hawai'i became the fiftieth state. He founded the Waipahu Free Will Baptist Church on the island of Oahu, near Pearl Harbor. When he left the church in 1977 it was averaging one hundred fifty people in attendance and was a very successful home mission project. From Hawai'i he went to Garner, North Carolina, where he pastored from 1977 to 1982. He returned to Hawai'i and pastored the Waipahu church once more, this time from 1982 to 1986.

When their daughter Brenda was sixteen years old Helen and Luther adopted a son, Robert Luther Sanders, Jr. He lives in College Station, Texas.

One of the men in the church in Hawai'i, Colonel Fred Dollar, retired from the Marines and moved to College Station, Texas. Knowing that Brother Sanders was leaving Hawai'i Colonel Dollar was instrumental in securing his services as pastor of the relatively new Cornerstone Free Will Baptist Church in College Station. After his term at Cornerstone Brother Sanders accepted the position of interim pastor of the North Zulch Free Will Baptist Church in 1998. The historic old church had been closed for about five years. Some of the members of the church decided to reopen it and they turned to Brother Sanders to lead them. He led them in an extensive remodeling program, and pastored it until his retirement from active ministry in 2002.[196]

Helen was active in Luther's ministry during the fifty years of their life together. The usual duties and responsibilities of a pastor's wife were faithfully fulfilled by her at each pastorate. In addition to those responsibilities Helen was active in the work of the Woman's National Auxiliary Convention, now Women Nationally Active for Christ. For instance, in 1956 the WNAC executive committee asked her and Helen Ketteman to write a manuscript for a new GTA[197] manual. The manuscript was actually written by Helen and Luther and in January of 1957 it was accepted for publication. The women of the WNAC executive committee were so pleased with the work that they asked Helen to write a new YPA[198] manual, which she did, again with the help of her husband.[199] In 1959 she served as the Youth Chairman of the WNAC and had several articles and reports in the *1959 Woman's Auxiliary Yearbook*.[200] She was active in the Texas Women Active for Christ. She passed away on April 18, 1995.

In March of 2003 Brother Sanders married Virginia Vaughn, a Texas resident for most of her adult life.

Brother Sanders exhibited a number of talents. One of them was writing poetry, what daughter Brenda calls "his silly rhyming." He used these poems or rhymes for birthdays, anniversaries, special events at church, or just to tease Brenda, and often worked them into his sermons. His friends talked him into self-publishing his poetry in a printed booklet. Brenda's favorite is "Living with Me."

---

[196] The July-August 1994 issue of the *Texas Challenge* had a one page article about this remodeling effort.
[197] Go-Tell Auxiliary, with the stated purpose of bringing all girls aged 9-14 into service in God's kingdom by bringing them to Christ, building them up in Him, and sending them forth to do His work.
[198] Young People's Auxiliary, for single young ladies aged 14-18.
[199] *Sparks Into Flames, a History of the W.N.A.C.*, by Dr. Mary Ruth Wisehart, (published by the Woman's National Auxiliary Convention, Nashville, Tennessee 1985) pages 90-94. Thanks to Brenda Spruill for putting me onto this information.
[200] *YEAR BOOK 1959*, Compiled by Mrs. Eunice Edwards, Pages 13-14, 30-32, 98-99, 118, 123 .

It goes:

> My daily task is not trivial to see
> For I am responsible to God and me;
> So today if I do what I should
> And honestly feel that I've done all I could
>
> If I can enjoy both work and play
> And collect my pay at the end of the day;
> With heart and mind both light and free
> Then I truly enjoy living with me
>
> If my course in life is rough indeed
> And I wait for others to take the lead
> If my task at dusk remains undone
> And my day was spend in leisure or fun
>
> I may shrug my shoulders in jest and say,
> "O, well, there will be another day."
> But inside I feel like a churching sea
> And I find it hard to live with me.

Luther Sanders was a man fully committed to the gospel ministry. That's what he did. That's why he was trained. It's how he made his living. He didn't sell insurance, work in construction, or operate a business. The gospel ministry was his business.

As noted above son Bobby lives in College Station. He works as an excellent mechanic. Brenda and her husband, Wayne Spruill, moved to Hawaii as tentmakers to help with the mission church there in 1985 and remained there until 1999. Presently they live and work at Welch College in Nashville, Tennessee. Brenda is Business Administrative Assistant and Wayne is Director of Institutional Research.

Brother Sanders passed away on September 9, 2008. He and Helen are buried side by side in the Veteran's Cemetery in Bryan, Texas.

T. A. Searcy

Tom Asa Searcy was born November 15, 1866, in Madison County, Texas. He graduated from Madisonville High School and then from Baylor University, which at the time was located at Washington on the Brazos. His primary occupation for a time was as a teacher, though he also owned and managed a farm. In 1885, he married Martha Amanda Zulch. To this union were born nine children. He was converted to Christ at the age of 27 and immediately became an active Christian, serving in whatever capacity he could.

He moved to Bryan in 1894 to become co-owner of a grocery business. He continued in that business only for a short time because at heart he was an educator, not a business man. In 1894 he helped A. M. Stewart organize the Free Baptist Church of Bryan, the church known to us as the First Free Will Baptist Church of Bryan. Initially he served as Sunday school superintendent but soon entered the ministry and followed that calling for the rest of his life. He pastored the

Bryan Church from 1907 to 1909. When he left the Bryan Church he moved to Iowa and preached there for the rest of his life, expect for the last five years which he spent in Kansas. He passed away in August, 1933, at the age of 67. [201]

Earl Scroggins

Earl Dean Scroggins served as state moderator during a particularly difficult time for the Texas State Association. It was during the inspiration debate involving Dusty Cooksey. Earl was born on December 30, 1947, in Ada, Oklahoma. As a teenager Earl sensed that God was calling him into the ministry, and he answered that call in 1964 at Oklahoma's August Center Youth Camp.

In preparation for the ministry he attended Oklahoma Bible College in 1967-1968 and graduated. At OBC he met Sandra Kay Davenport and they were married on September 6, 1968. Early and Sandy have three children: Paul, Michele, and Michael.

Earl Scroggins

Earl was licensed by the Center District Association of Oklahoma and then, on July 20, 1969, was ordained to the gospel ministry, also by the Center Association. He first served as Youth Pastor at the First Free Will Baptist Church of Ada. His early pastorates in Oklahoma were the First Free Will Baptist Church of Weatherford and the Eastside Free Will Baptist Church in Duncan.

He received a call to the First Free Will Baptist Church in Wichita Falls, Texas, and moved his family there in June of 1970. He devoted nine years of his life to the pastorate in Wichita Falls, leaving in April of 1979. During his years in Texas Earl was very active in both the West Fork District Association and the Texas State Association of Free Will Baptists. He was particularly active in the West Fork Youth Camp. In the church he established regular missionary conferences, bringing in numerous missionaries to speak at the church, and developed a much needed youth ministry. In the district association he served as clerk, as a member of the Credentials Committee, and as a member of the West Fork Mission Board.

Earl was elected to the Board of Christian Education of the Texas State Association during a time when that board was unusually active with the Church Training Service competitive activities, minister's retreats, and training institutes designed to train Sunday school teachers and other church workers. He then was elected as assistant state moderator and then moderator, a position he held for several years. He says his most difficult task during his ministry in Texas was moderating conflicts between various pastors during the inspiration debate. He considers the highlight of his ministry in Texas to have been hosting the National Association of Free Will Baptists in Fort Worth in 1972. Another highlight occurred at the 1978 National Association of Free Will Baptists, meeting in Kansas City, Missouri, when he presided over the Monday evening worship service.

Earl left Texas to pastor the First Free Will Baptist Church of Ardmore, Oklahoma, which he pastored from 1979 to 1988. He then pastored the Bethel Free Will Baptist Church of Allen,

---

[201] The information about T. A. Searcy was taken from *A 63 Year History of First Free Will Baptist Church*, by Charles L. Sapp, 1957, pages 20-21.

Oklahoma, from 1989 to 2013. He currently pastors the Faith Free Will Baptist Church of Holdenville, Oklahoma, beginning in 2013. Not yet seventy, he says he will continue to pastor until he is too old to do so anymore.

J. W. Shults

Joseph Wilburn Shults was born in Missouri on March 11, 1853, to W. C. and Melinda Shults, who had migrated west from Kentucky. In the 1860 census, when J. W. was 7, the family was living in Spring Creek Township, Dent County, in South Central Missouri. J. W. married Comilla Frances Bowles (1859-1935), but little else is known about her except that she was born in Texas in June of 1859. In 1900 J. W. and his family were living in Denton County, Texas, on a rented farm with seven children. Their daughter Carrye Dell had been born in Indian Territory in 1894.

In late December of 1913 Shults moved his family to Post Oak, Texas. Less than five months later, on May 1, 1914, he organized the Pleasant Valley Free Will Baptist Church, three miles north of Post Oak and three miles south of Buffalo Springs in Clay County, Texas. The church services were held in the Pleasant Valley School, which was a one room schoolhouse. He pastored the church from 1914 to 1919, and again from 1921 to 1924. The church would go on to become one of the better known Free Will Baptist churches in Texas.

Joseph and "Fannie" had seven children: George L., Maggie B., Effie B., John P., Carrye Dell, Clyde A, and William P. Carrye Dell married Tiff Covington who twice pastored the church Brother Shults had started (1928-1949; 1967-1980). Tiff had been converted at the Pleasant Valley Church when Brother Shults was preaching a revival in August of 1916. Tiff would go on to become a legend in North Central Texas. In 1936 the Pleasant Valley Church built a new sanctuary one mile north of Pleasant Valley. The new church was on higher ground than at its previous location in the valley and its name was changed to the Pleasant Mound Free Will Baptist Church, affectionately known in the community as the Rock Church, because it was constructed of local field stones.

Shults died on April 2, 1926. He and Fannie are buried in the Buffalo Springs Cemetery in Buffalo Springs, Clay County, Texas.

A. M. Stewart

Angus McAllister Stewart was born on August 25, 1853, and passed away on September 17, 1913. He was one of the very earliest, if not the earliest, white Free Will Baptist ministers in the state of Texas. He was a missionary sent to Texas by the General Conference of Free Will Baptists, that is, the Randall Movement of Free Will Baptists. An account of his work and the churches he started are found in chapter one of this book. Brother Stewart was present at the 1912 Southwestern Freewill Baptist General Convention, which met at Earlsboro, Oklahoma, a few months before his death. He must have been held in high esteem as seen in the fact that he opened or closed the services in prayer three times and preached in the Sunday morning service.[202] Mrs. Clara Cole described him as "a brilliant and godly Christian gentleman of great and winning personality. It seems to those who remember the zeal and fervor of his utterances that truly God had given him of his wisdom and words of eloquence to bring many into his kingdom."[203]

Stewart founded the Liberty Church, Clayton, the Union Chapel and Beckville Churches in Panola County, and Good Hope and Union Springs in Rusk County, all in East Texas. The Lone Star Church in Cherokee County, and the Rape's Chapel Church were also founded by Brother Stewart. In Central Texas he assisted T. H. Adams in the founding of the Bright Light and Christian Home churches in Brazos County. **See Heritage from the Past, Horizons for the Future in Additional Research notebook.** He passed away on September 17, 1913, and is buried in the Odd Fellows Cemetery in Carthage, Panola County, Texas.

A. M. Stewart marker, Odd Fellows Cemetery, Carthage

David Sutton

David Myron Sutton was born on March 6, 1940, in Ada, Oklahoma, to Alfred Herman and Edith Carmen (Farr) Sutton. David's father was a carpenter/builder. David grew up in the Pickett Community, five miles west of Ada. This young man who would years later be one of the leaders in the Free Will Baptist denomination was raised as a Methodist. David was converted to Christ at the age of fifteen under the ministry of Ernest Grose, a Methodist minister. David graduated from Vanoss High School, located thirteen miles west of Ada.

It was at the age of twenty-five that David sensed that God was calling him into the ministry. He was licensed to preach as a Free Will Baptist minister in May of 1965, by the Center Association of Oklahoma. Less than two years later, on February 19, 1967, David was ordained to the gospel ministry by that same Center Association. The ordination service took place at the First Free Will Baptist Church, Ada, Oklahoma. His ordination credentials were signed by Ministers F. M. Wood, Lynn Wood, J. R. Hall, and Deacons Earl Collins, James L. Barnes, and John Wood.

David Sutton

David married Kathleen Sue Reeves on August 27, 1965, at the First Free Will Baptist Church in Ada. The ceremony was performed by E. M. Pannell. From this marriage came two children: Faron Kyle and Cheré Daleen. David knew that he needed preparation for the ministry and so he attended Oklahoma Bible College, starting classes in 1966 and graduating in 1969. During the next several years he pastored the following churches in Oklahoma: the Northeast Free Will Baptist Church, Shawnee; the Jenks Free Will Baptist Church, Jenks, which he founded as a

---

[202] Minutes of the Southwestern Freewill Baptist Convention, 1912, pages 8-10.
[203] Mrs. Clara Cole, "History of Bright Light Free Will Baptist Church," 1954, from notes made by Mrs. Alice Cole.

home missionary working as a joint project worker under the Oklahoma State Association and the National Association; and the First Free Will Baptist Church, Ada. He further developed and honed his leadership skills while also serving on the Oklahoma Church Training Service (CTS) Board, State Executive Board, the Board of Trustees of Hillsdale Free Will Baptist College, and as Moderator of the Oklahoma State Association of Free Will Baptists.

In February of 1987, when he was almost forty years of age, David and Kathleen moved to Duncanville, Texas, to pastor the First Free Will Baptist Church, following the long ministry there of H. Z. Cox. He served the church capably for eleven years. Pastoring was always his first love in the Lord's work. However, during those years in Texas, he, as he had in Oklahoma, did his fair share of ministry in the district and state associations. He served as Moderator of the West Fork District Association and was active in the West Fork Youth Camp. He served as Moderator of the Texas State Association of Free Will Baptists for a number of years, which placed him in the important position of being chairman of the state's Executive Board. David took his position as Moderator seriously, conducting the meetings of the state association and executive board fairly, honestly, and according to good parliamentary procedure. He was more, however, than just an impartial moderator, he was a true leader. He had ideas. He wasn't satisfied just to operate the status quo efficiently. He could say, "Let's go in this direction," pointing the way to progress, and rally people to follow. He made those around him better. One example is that he realized there was no need for the state's General Board, the board that met prior to the state meetings to smooth out possible problems that might arise over various issues. He knew that the state meetings were running smoothly and that the various reports of boards and committees were unnecessarily duplicated by being given in the General Board and then repeated on the floor of the state association itself. He successfully led the effort to eliminate the General Board, something which was also done by a number of other state associations. The Texas State Association of Free Will Baptists was running perhaps at a peak performance under his leadership. He and Kathleen helped select the site for the construction of the Lakehills Free Will Baptist Church in the Austin suburb of Cedar Park. David served for fifteen years on the board of Randall House Publications, the publishing arm of the National Association of Free Will Baptists. He served as chairman of that board for eight years.

After over a decade as pastor of the First Free Will Baptist Church in Duncanville, Texas, David resigned to accept the pastorate of the Southern Oaks Free Will Baptist Church in Oklahoma City, Oklahoma. He and Kathleen left Duncanville on July 4, 1998. David pastored the Southern Oaks Church until his retirement from the pastorate in September of 2008. Soon thereafter he published *The Tender Touch*, a book designed to give assistance to other pastors during times of special ministry, such as funerals. David and Kathleen moved back to Texas, buying a home in McKinney, Texas, because they loved Texas, and to be near their grandson at nearby Princeton, Texas. Though retired, David and Kathleen continue an active ministry. They attend the Clearview Free Will Baptist Church, a new mission church in McKinney. David serves as treasurer of the church. He conducts funerals for a couple of funeral homes in the North Texas area when they need someone, and he supply preaches at various Free Will Baptist churches in the area when they need someone to stand in for the pastor.

Two interesting anecdotes illustrate some of the unusual things which happened during his ministry. While he was pastoring the First Free Will Baptist Church in Ada, Oklahoma, he conducted the funeral of a man whose name was Dwight L. Moody. While pastoring the Southern Oaks Church he baptized a man whose name was Billy Sunday, and later conducted his funeral. He first met Billy in the hospital and led him to the Lord. When Mr. Sunday got out of the hospital he was not expected to live more than a month or so. David baptized him at the South Oaks Church.

M. L. Sutton

M. L., Clara, and Willis Sutton

Milton Laneheart Sutton was born on January 25, 1899, Natchitoches Parish, Louisiana, to Thomas H. and Malinda Sutton. He served in the United States Army from 1917 to 1918 during World War I. The 1920 census lists his residence as Fort Worth, Texas. It was there that he made his mark in the world. He married Clara Willette McFeely, who was about sixteen years old, in Fort Worth in 1919. Clara was born on April 28, 1903, in Alvarado, Texas. They had one son, Willis Layne Sutton, born May 14, 1920.

We find no record of his ordination to the ministry. We first see him working as an assistant to Lizzie McAdams in her evangelistic campaigns, serving mostly as her song leader and as a counselor. In the 1920's he left her ministry and returned to Fort Worth to begin a ministry of his own. We don't know if he started the First Free Will Baptist Church of Fort Worth, which was founded in 1927, but he served as pastor of the church until about 1934. The church grew and prospered under his able ministry. Brother Sutton always gave great emphasis to the Sunday school as an evangelistic arm of the church. Additionally, he emphasized teacher training for those involved in that ministry, holding teacher/officer training institutes on a local, district, and state level, calling upon other qualified people to assist him with the training. Fortunately we have located a couple of pictures of these institutes. He demonstrated in his own churches the possibilities for evangelism and church growth through the ministry of the Sunday school.

He knew the importance of good gospel music in his services and utilized that facet of worship to great advantage. He himself was a good singer and he was a member of a very good quartet in his church. He often sang in pick up quartets, if we can call them that, at quarterly and state meetings. He was a multi-talented man. He also knew the importance of advertising. He printed a number of booklets for distribution, not only about his church but about Free Will Baptists in general.

In the spring of 1934 a child was acting out in the Sunday morning worship service and Brother Sutton called the child down, upsetting the child's mother. That afternoon the deacons met with Brother Sutton and asked him to apologize to the mother and child. He refused to do so and told the deacons that he was leaving the church as their pastor. That evening he met with a

Adult Sunday School Class taught by Pastor M. L. Sutton April 3, 1932

number of the church members who wished to go with him. On the evening of May 6, 1934, the Trinity Free Will Baptist Church of Fort Worth was born. With a good nucleus to start with, and under the capable leadership of Brother Sutton, Trinity became a large and influential church in the West Fork District Association. A beautiful church building was constructed on Azle Avenue on the northwest side of Fort Worth.

A sizeable number of ministers, Christian workers, and missionaries came out of the Trinity Church, including Ken Eagleton, missionary to Brazil, Lonnie Palmer, missionary to Ivory Coast, Africa, and Lila Nichols, missionary to Ivory Coast, African, and Panama.

Brother and Sister Sutton suffered a great loss on May 5, 1959, when their son, Captain Willis Sutton, who was a test pilot in the United States Air Force, died when the plane he was testing disintegrated in the skies over Florida.

During Brother Sutton's long years in Fort Worth he was active in the West Fork Association and in the Fellowship Association during its brief existence. He was a leader in

M. L. Sutton, (left, in the water) baptizing converts in the Trinity River

the Texas State Association, serving in many capacities. He was a valuable member over the years on several boards and committees, and as moderator. It was said that when people thought of Free Will Baptists in Texas they thought of M. L. Sutton. He published a paper for the Trinity Church called the *Free Will Baptist Trumpet*, which went not only to his church members but to the other churches, as well. He was active in the work outside of Texas, too. He was active in the Cooperative General Association of Freewill Baptists in the late 1920's and early 1930's. He preached at the twelfth annual session of the General Conference of Original Free Will Baptists, which met at Bryan, Texas, in 1932.[204]

---

[204] Minutes of the Twelfth Annual Session of the General Conference of Original Free Will Baptists, Bryan, Texas, June 15, 1932, page 7.

Records have not yet been located which would tell us when Brother Sutton's pastorate ended at Trinity. We do know that Brother Sutton pastored the Faith Free Will Baptist Church of Wichita Falls from July 19, 1964, to March 30, 1966.

J. J. Tatum

J. J. Tatum

John Julian Tatum was born May 22, 1863, in Steeleville, Illinois. He was the son of William B. and Emily Tatum. Growing to young manhood in that community and attending school there, he served his apprenticeship as a blacksmith and practiced this trade. He entered the confectionary business and also the grocery business until he returned to school to receive his theological education at Hillsdale College in Michigan. This fulfilled his life-long ambition to enter the ministry, and he was ordained in 1889 in his home church in Steeleville.

On June 22, 1886, he married Hettie K. Mason (1862-1934) in Pinkneyville, Illinois. They had five children. Together the Tatums served churches in Illinois, Indiana, and Iowa. In 1905 Tatum preached a ten days revival in the Free Baptist Church of Bryan, Texas, and was called as pastor of the church. He left the Free Baptist Church of East St. Louis, Illinois,[205] to move his family to Bryan. The Tatums came to Texas with their children: Morris, Georgia, Emily, Bernelle, and Earl, in 1905 and remained until 1907. Pastor Tatum's influence was felt, not only in the church, but in the entire community of Bryan. His ministry thus extended into every part of the city life.

In 1907, the Tatum family returned to Oelwein, Iowa. In 1910, they came back to Bryan and served this church until 1913. At that time they answered a call to the church in Perry, Iowa.

The minutes of the 1914 session of the Southwestern Convention of Freewill Baptists contains a report of Brother Tatum. It indicates that at the time he was serving as agent for both the Southwestern Convention and the General Conference of Free Baptists and that his salary was paid exclusively by the General Conference.[206] In 1916 Tatum and Z. B. Dally were still involved with the General Conference and were publishing a paper called the *Free Will Baptist Sentinel.* In 1918, he came back to Bryan and lived there until his death.

According to the minutes of the first annual session of the Texas State Association of Free Will Baptists, J. J. Tatum was appointed by moderator E. L. Hill to serve on a committee to draft the first by-laws and constitution for the state association. He served on the committee with W. E. Dearmore and Charles C. Wheeler. That meeting was held October 8-9, 1915, at Bradley, Texas. The minutes of the first several sessions of the Texas State Association reveal that Tatum served on numerous committees and that he displayed considerable literary skills in his written reports to the association.

Tatum was serving as State Secretary,[207] which was a promotional ministry, much like our later Executive Secretary. He served as an agent of the General Conference of Free Baptists, as

---

[205] *The Morning Star,* March 8, 1906, page 13.
[206] Minutes of the 1914 session of the Southwestern Convention of Freewill Baptists, page 24.
[207] Minutes of the 1929 state convention, page 3.

well. In 1917 the Home Mission Society requested a salary increase for him in the amount of two hundred dollars.[208]

During these years Tatum was pastor of the Bryan church from 1918-19. He also served many rural churches in the area, and he was Field Secretary of the Southwest for the Free Will Baptist denomination, serving Texas, Oklahoma, Arkansas, Missouri, Kansas, and Nebraska. He passed away on March 10, 1931, at the age of sixty-seven and is buried in the Bryan City Cemetery.

Richard Terry

Richard Calvin Terry is somewhat of a new breed of Free Will Baptist preachers. That's not to say that he is the only one or even the first one, for there have been others before him. It's just that he is one of a growing number of men in the denomination who are scholars. Free Will Baptists have not exactly been overrun with them, especially since we lost all of our schools in the merger of 1910-11. The fact that Richard has seven thousand books in his personal library is an indication of his uniqueness.

Richard C. Terry

Richard was born in Joplin, Missouri, on August 7, 1946. He grew up in Kansas City, Missouri, graduating from Grandview High School. His father was attached to the American Embassy in Rio de Janeiro, Brazil, and Richard was able to spend three years there, along with his mother.

Richard was converted to Christ on Easter Sunday in 1967 at the Central Free Will Baptist Church in Kansas City, Missouri. Shortly thereafter, in June of 1967, he sensed God's call into the ministry. He was licensed to preach while a member of the Central Church. Recognizing the adage that a call to preach is a call to prepare, he enrolled at Oklahoma Bible College in late August of 1967 and earned his Associate of Arts Degree in 1969.

In 1969 he married Thelma Haws in Sapulpa, Oklahoma. Thelma was born in Hominy, Oklahoma, in 1948 and graduated from the Sand Springs High School.

In 1970 he was pastoring the Faith Free Will Baptist Church in Kansas City, Kansas. During that pastorate he was ordained by the East Kansas Quarterly Conference. He was able to earn his Bachelor's Degree from Hillsdale Free Will Baptist College, formerly Oklahoma Bible College, in 2002. Over a period of several years he accumulated hours at a number of schools: Mid-American Nazarene University, Olathe, Kansas; Washburn University, Topeka, Kansas; and Southern Nazarene University, Bethany, Oklahoma. He earned a Master of Divinity in Biblical Languages, MDiv.BL, at Southwestern Baptist Theological Seminary in Fort Worth, Texas, and has worked several hours on a Masters of Theology, also at Southwestern.

His pastorates include the Faith Free Will Baptist Church in Kansas City, and First Free Will Baptist Church in Topeka, Kansas. In Oklahoma he pastored the Lake Area Free Will Baptist Church, Cleveland; First Free Will Baptist Church, Pryor; First Free Will Baptist Church, Wewoka; the Southwest Free Will Baptist Church, Oklahoma City; and served as interim pastor of the First Free Will Baptist Church, Ada. He moved to Texas in 2006 when he became pastor of the First Free Will Baptist Church in Duncanville.

---

[208] Though the General Conference of Free Will Baptists had merged with the Northern Baptists in 1910-11, for a number of reasons they continued to exist more or less as a paper organization until a number of legal and financial issues were resolved. See the Minutes of the Thirty-sixth General Conference of Free Baptists, August 22-23, 1917.

Starting 1986 Richard served as Director of Development at Hillsdale Free Will Baptist College, now Randall University, in Moore, Oklahoma. He served as an adjunct professor at Hillsdale, teaching Personal Evangelism, Hermeneutics, Pastoral Internship, and Systematic Theology.

As with many busy pastors he has served beyond his local community in denominational work. While in Kansas he served as State Treasurer, State Home Mission Board member, and as Kansas' representative on the Hillsdale Board of Trustees. In Oklahoma he served as a member of the State Board of Christian Education and was elected to the Hillsdale Board of Trustees, though he never served this term because he moved to Texas. He has been active in Texas by serving on the State Executive Board, and the Credentials Committee of the West Fork District Association. He has worked with a number of Free Will Baptist youth camps in Oklahoma, New Mexico, and Texas, serving either as camp director or camp evangelist.

Back in the days when churches had revival meetings, Richard preached lots of them in Kansas, Oklahoma, and Texas.

Richard and Thelma have three sons: Richard, Michael, and Stephen. Richard (Dick) pastors the First Free Will Baptist Church in Sulphur, Oklahoma.

C. B. Thompson

C. B. Thompson

Charlie Bev Thompson was born March 17, 1890, in Carrollton, Texas, and went on to become one of the most popular and influential preachers in the state. He received his theological training at Lon Morris College, Jacksonville, Texas, and at Duke University, Durham, North Carolina. He was ordained by the West Fork District Association at the New Salem Free Will Baptist Church near Decatur on February 16, 1913. In East Texas he pastored Good Hope, Union Arbor, Harper, Mount Olive, and the Liberty Church in Clayton. In the Central District he pastored at North Zulch, Kurtin, Cross, Keith, Evergreen, Edge, Plainview, and the (First) Free Will Baptist Church in Bryan. He pastored the Bryan church from 1920 to 1926. It was while pastoring at Bryan that he met and married Annie Lawless[209] (1897-1988). In 1928, while simultaneously pastoring four of these churches he reported preaching 243 sermons. Four years later he was pastoring six of the Central Texas District churches and received a total salary of $900.25.

The Bryan Church, out of appreciation of and love for their pastor, presented him with a car, a Ford roadster. He used this vehicle for the promotion of the Lord's work in the community. He once said that he was the first pastor in the city of Bryan to own an automobile. When he received the gift he didn't yet know how to drive.

In the West Fork he pastored the First Free Will Baptist Church in Fort Worth. Later in life he served the West Fork as associational evangelist.

Outside of Texas he pastored at Bennington, Oklahoma. Following this pastorate he served in the United States Army, 39th Infantry, during World War I. He also pastored churches in Goldsboro and Ayden, North Carolina, and the Trinity Free Will Baptist Church in Nashville, Tennessee.

---

[209] Presumably the sister of Lizzie (Lawless) McAdams.

He served in many capacities other than pastoring. He was always active in the district, state, and national work, ever trying to enlarge, improve, and expand the Free Will Baptist work in Texas, as well as the United States. He served on the Texas State Home Missions Board, in the capacity of President and Treasurer. He served as moderator of the General Conference of Free Will Baptists, the eastern body of Free Will Baptists, when it joined with the Cooperative General Association of the West to form the National Association of Free Will Baptists in 1935. He served as a member of the all-important Treatise Revision Committee which presented the *Treatise* to the assembled body for adoption. He had been one of the driving forces which brought about the formation of the National Association. Perhaps it was this effort which resulted in him being chosen to preach at the organizational meeting of the National Association at the Cofer's Chapel Free Will Baptist Church in Nashville, Tennessee. On the other hand he could have been chosen because of his eloquence in the pulpit, being one of the ablest pulpiteers in the denomination. He preached during the concluding service of that first Free Will Baptist National Convention. The minutes of the meeting state that "Rev. C. B. Thompson of Bryan, Tex., brought a splendid message in sermon." That C. B. Thompson was chosen to preach this sermon is an indication of the high esteem in which he was held as a preacher of the gospel. The minutes further state that after the sermon a season of praise and testimony was enjoyed, and the congregation was dismissed. He served on the Foreign Missions Board of the National Association for ten years and also served on its General Board.

Charlie Bev Thompson's name has almost been forgotten in Texas. But his name should not slip into oblivion. As a matter of fact, we should build a monument to him. C. B. Thompson is truly one of Texas' leaders of special note. To introduce us to the stature the man held in the Free Will Baptist denomination we will start with his work at the organizational meeting of the National Association of Free Will Baptists. Therefore, we will digress for a moment, but what follows is extremely important to all Free Will Baptists and especially to Texas Free Will Baptists.

For three days, November 5-7, 1935, thirty-three delegates, representing twelve states and fifteen district associations, sixty Free Will Baptist ministers, and many laypersons, came together from far and wide for the purpose of uniting the General Conference of Free Will Baptists, in the East, and the Cooperative General Association of Free Will Baptists, of the West. The meeting took place at the Cofer's Chapel Free Will Baptist Church in Nashville, Tennessee. The Free Will Baptist movement had been badly shaken and greatly reduced in numbers by the merger of the majority of Free Will Baptists with the Northern Baptist Convention in 1910-11. The Free Will Baptists who refused to participate in the merger, and remain true to Free Will Baptist principles and convictions, worked for almost twenty-five years to bring about an organization of the remnant groups into one body. On Tuesday evening, November 5th, after a lively devotional service of songs and prayer, Winford Davis, of Monette, Missouri, brought a splendid gospel message to the large congregation of anxious delegates and visitors. The organization of the National Association was postponed so that all of the expected delegates might have part in the organization.

At 10:30 A.M. on Wednesday morning, November 6th, after a "spiritual devotional service," by which is meant the singing and prayers, the assembly enjoyed a very inspiring sermon by S. H. Styron of Pine Level, North Carolina. The National Association had not yet come into being. In the business session during the afternoon the delegates were recognized and seated. The Texas State Convention was represented by Texas rancher C. F. Goen and E. Sterl Phinney, who was pastor of the First Free Will Baptist Church in Bryan, Texas, from 1935 to 1937. The Central Texas District Association was represented by J. L. Bounds and C. B. Thompson. Other existing Texas district associations did not send delegates. Four committees were appointed and approved.

The Committee on Constitution and By-Laws included E. Sterl Phinney of Texas. The Program Committee and the Publicity Committee did not include any Texans. However, the Treatise Revision Committee, perhaps the most important of the four committees, included C. B. Thompson.[210] Various and sundry other reports and business items were taken care of as the afternoon business session continued.

On Wednesday evening a large delegation assembled to hear the Thomas Willey, of Durham, North Carolina, preach. The man who would later be a missionary to Cuba and become affectionately known as "Pop" Willey, preached on "Foreign Mission Work in South America." Then, on Thursday morning, November 7, 1935, business was resumed. There was a report from a joint education committee which recommended that Nashville, Tennessee, be accepted as the location for a Bible School to be opened soon.[211] A board of trustees for the school was elected. Next, a report on foreign missions was given and I. J. Blackwelder, who pastored the First Free Will Baptist Church in Bryan, Texas, from 1932 to 1935, was elected as National Secretary Treasurer of Foreign Missions. Then, something historic happened. Mrs. Lizzie McAdams, one of Texas' own, who had worked for years for this moment, stood and made a motion that the report of the Treatise Revision Committee be adopted.[212] Her motion passed and this action brought the Free Will Baptists of the East and West together and formed the National Association of Free Will Baptists.

C. B. and Annie (Lawless) Thompson

The business of the Association was discontinued at 11:00 o'clock for worship, and Millard F. Vanhoose of Paintsville, Kentucky, stirred the large congregation with an old-time gospel sermon. After lunch the business session continued throughout the afternoon. One of the items of business was the adoption of the proposed constitution and by-laws. Since the new constitution required the election of an executive board, the association proceeded to elect: Elder J. W. Alford of Kenly, North Carolina; Elder E. B. Joyner of Lake Butler, Florida; Brother C. F. Goen of Bryan, Texas; Elder D. F. Pelt of Abbeville, Alabama; and Elder B. F. Brown of Purdy, Missouri, as members of the very first Executive Board of the National Association of Free Will Baptists.[213]

Another noteworthy item was that the association, having heard of the death of Evangelist Billy Sunday, stood in a moment of silent prayer in recognition of the passing of the great gospel evangelist. The association asked John L. Welch,[214] pastor of the host church, to send a telegram of condolences to Mrs. Sunday. Mrs. Sunday responded with the following note addressed to J.

---

[210] Other members of the Treatise Revision Committee were: J. C. Griffin (North Carolina), M. L. Morse (Nebraska), W. B. Davenport (Tennessee), H. E. Post, E. E. Morris (Oklahoma), Ralph Staten (advisory, Arkansas), E. B. Joyner (Florida), Millard F. Van Hoose (Kentucky), Winford Davis (Missouri), and J. S. Fredrick.
[211] Free Will Baptist Bible College began classes in 1942.
[212] Lizzie's motion was that the report of the Treatise Revision Committee be adopted without the reading of the proposed *Treatise*. However, it was read later.
[213] In later years Keith Woody and I both served on what came to be called the Executive Committee of the General Board of the National Association of Free Will Baptists.
[214] This is the John L. Welch for whom Welch College in Nashville, Tennessee, is named. In July of 2012 the name of the school was changed from Free Will Baptist Bible College to Welch College.

L. Welch, dated November 16, 1935, 11:00 P.M. : "The family of William A. Sunday acknowledge with grateful appreciation the kind expression of your sympathy."[215]

After a break for the evening meal the association reassembled for the last service of the session. The devotional service was conducted by. S. T. Shutes of Blakely, Georgia. Now we return to the story of C. B. Thompson. The minutes of the meeting state that "Rev. C. B. Thompson of Bryan, Tex., brought a splendid message in sermon." That C. B. Thompson was chosen to preach this sermon is an indication of the high esteem in which he was held as a preacher of the gospel. The minutes further state that after the sermon a season of praise and testimony was enjoyed, and the congregation was dismissed. It should be noted that Thompson preached the very first sermon to the National Association of Free Will Baptists after it was formed.

Brother Thompson passed away September 2, 1977, at the age of 87, at the Vista Nursing home in Pasadena, Texas. He is buried in the Bryan City Cemetery.

Dr. Teressa Voltz

Dr. Teressa Voltz

Teressa Joan Voltz was born to Dorothy Faye (Nickerson) and James Harles Smith in Houston, Texas. Her father was Postmaster General for the United States Postal Service, now retired. She graduated from Nimitz High School in the Aldine ISD in 1982. During high school she was Colorguard Captain of the Marching Band. She married Morris Shafer Voltz, Jr. on January 4, 1986, at the First Baptist Church in Aldine, Texas. They have three children: Jessica Michelle, Chelsea Danielle, and Jacob Daniel.

Teressa attended Sam Houston State University in Huntsville, Texas, earning a Bachelor of Arts Degree in 1986. In 1995 she earned a Master's Degree in Reading, also from Sam Houston State. In 2012 she earned an Ed.D. an Educational Doctorate, in Executive Leadership from the University of Houston. She has certification in: Teaching K-6, Principal K-12, Reading Specialist K-12, and Superintendent. She recently retired from Bryan ISD in Bryan, Texas, as the Assistant Superintendent of Curriculum and Instruction. She completed a 30-year career in public education. She is now employed as an education therapist as The Woodlands Christian Academy, The Woodlands, Texas, where she works with students who have Dyslexia. Her husband also recently retired as band director in the Bryan ISD, completing a 29-year career in public education.

She accepted Christ as her savior when she was in the fifth grade at age ten, while attending the Parkwood Baptist Church. She was baptized by Raymond Getz in the former First Free Will Baptist Church in McAllen. She and Morris were living in the Rio Grande Valley the year after they were married and she had not been baptized previously. Back in the Houston area they attended the First Free Will Baptist Church, pastored by Bobby Ferguson. Teressa served as youth leader, Sunday school teacher, Church Training Service (CTS) leader, and sang in the choir. She and her family moved to help begin the Magnolia Free Will Baptist Church. They felt that God was leading them to reach more people for Christ and establish more Free Will Baptist churches in the Houston and suburban areas. They are now helping to establish the new Woodforest Free

---

[215] The original note is in the Free Will Baptist Historical Collection at Welch College in Nashville, Tennessee.

Will Baptist Church in the Woodlands/Magnolia area, pastored by Heath Ferguson. In Woodforest she serves as youth leader and CTS leader.

Teressa serves on the Christian Education Board of the Texas State Association. She has been enthusiastically involved with the ministry of that board since being elected to it in 1999, and continues to make her mark there. The board serves to further Christian education in many areas for Texas Free Will Baptists. They provide a men's retreat, a youth retreat, the CTS competition, children's and youth activities and service projects at the annual state meeting, and they provide leadership training. The board also assisted with several youth and children's related activities and projects in conjunction with the National Youth Conference of the National Association of Free Will Baptists' annual convention in Fort Worth, July 27-30, 2014. Teressa is a vital part of and a valuable contributor to all of these ministries. She and her family attend the National Association of Free Will Baptists just about every year, missing very few.

This lady who is so valuable to the work of Texas Free Will Baptists is involved with the youth because she feels she is following God's calling. She was not part of a youth group that could have given her support growing up and that fact has given her a burden to work with youth and teach them how important they are to Christ and how they can work through their youth years having Christ as their guide. She loves the Lord and feels that all people should serve Him in some capacity.

She says that the people who have influenced her Christian life the most are her grandmother, who raised her and her siblings to know the Bible and who Jesus is; her mother, who sent them to church on Sundays on a bus ministry, and later became very faithful herself; and her husband Morris who has been a faithful spiritual leader to her and to the children.

Teressa is one of four girls raised by their mother. All of them love and serve the Lord.

Her oldest daughter, Jessica, was on the Truth and Peace staff in the summer of 2014. She was on Truth and Peace for four years as a student, and served on E-Team for two years. Chelsea served on E-Team for three years. Jacob served on E-Team for three years, and on the College Missions Program (CMP). He is attending Welch College in Nashville, Tennessee, majoring in international business and missions.

When asked what advice she would give to young people, she responded with the following, with some added emphasis for young women. It is best quoted as she stated it:

> The advice I would give any young person, male or female, about their discipleship and involvement in the church is TO SERVE. Do not stand back and think others will do it. Pray about what God would have YOU do. Every person is important to God and He wants to use all to serve Him in specific ways. Once you feel God calling you to a certain area of service in the church, step forward and don't let anything stand in your way. Never run from Christ - run towards Him! It is also very important to be a part of the church's youth group so you can learn how to handle the pressures of being a young person in a godly way. It is also important for others your age who are also Christians.
>
> I would give young women the advice to follow God's lead for your future careers. Make sure you pray about what God wants you to do and follow that calling. It may be a full-time ministry position, a doctor, lawyer, school teacher or a stay-at-home mom. I think that everyone should go to college or to a trade school to get some kind of training and education. Even if it is not used, it is good to have the experience.

To find your place as a young woman in the church, you must first pray. Seek what God would have you to do. Even if it is beyond the ordinary, if God wants you to do it, He will provide the way. Women are an important part of the ministry of God and in the local church. Don't let anything hold you back.

Teressa Voltz represents an all too rare form of Christian leadership in Free Will Baptists; she is deeply qualified spiritually and highly qualified intellectually and academically.

John Voss

John Dewayne Voss was born on July 6, 1970, in Jacksonville, Texas. He grew up in Henderson and graduated from Henderson High School in 1988. He was a member of the National Honor Society. He was converted to Christ at the age of nine under the ministry of James Dawson. He felt the call of God on his life at the age of fourteen. He was licensed to the gospel ministry in 1994 by the East Texas District Association of Free Will Baptists. Subsequently, he was ordained at the Youngblood Free Will Baptist Church, under the direction of Leroy Anderson, Jr., Forrest Welch, Ken Austin, Gordon Thompkins, and Carl Anderson.

John and Helen Voss

In 1994 he became the assistant pastor of the Youngblood Free Will Baptist Church out of Beckville, Texas. In 1995 John became the pastor of Youngblood, where he served until 2001. The Friendship Free Will Baptist Church in Fort Worth called him to serve as assistant pastor, a position he held from 2001 until 2002. He left Fort Worth to become the pastor of the Union Arbor Free Will Baptist Church, where he served until 2004. From there he went to Mount Union Free Will Baptist Church, where he continues to serve as pastor.

John has always been a bi-vocational pastor. While working at Kroger Food Store he met, and won to the Lord, a young lady by the name of Helen Ann Welch in 1988. The following year, June 9, 1989, they were married at the West Main Street Baptist Church in Henderson. John and Helen have three children: Dustin, Lydia, and Joshua. Helen's father, F. B. (Buddy) Welch, was also a pastor in East Texas. John and Helen consider it a privilege to have pastored several of the churches her father pastored.

Billy Walker

Billy Brown Walker was born in a two room log house on May 6, 1932, in Thomasville, now Pleasant View, Tennessee. He was premature and when he was seen by a doctor, the doctor did not expect him to live. A black mid-wife came to stay with his mother and take care of him. He lived and after thirty days the doctor filled out a birth certificate for him. His father, Cecil Jerome Walker, was a farmer until he was disabled in 1950 at the age of thirty-nine by an accidental gunshot to the leg. This resulted in the leg being amputated four inches above the knee. However, in the fall of 1951 Billy's father got a job at the Tennessee State Highway Maintenance Shop in Nashville and was able to work for twenty-five years before his retirement.

Billy fought the call to the ministry for two years, but he finally surrendered to preach in August of 1951, at the age of nineteen. He preached his first sermon at his home church, the Oaklawn Free Will Baptist Church, Chapmansboro, Tennessee, August 19, 1951. In the spring of 1952, Billy, in consultation with his father and grandfather, realized that he could not operate the farm by himself and so they agreed to lease the farm to someone else at the end of the crop year. Billy then enrolled at Free Will Baptist Bible College in September of 1952. One June 28, 1953, Billy married Miss Geneva Winstead of Rocky Mount, North Carolina. Billy became the pastor of his first church, the Oakwood Free Will Baptist Church, Stroudsville, Tennessee, in July of 1953. Three months later, on October 15, 1953, he was ordained to the gospel ministry by the Cumberland Association of Free Will Baptists. With Billy being a student at the Bible College, married, ordained, and pastoring his first church, things seemed to be moving right along for Billy and Geneva and the future was looking bright.

Billy and Geneva Walker

Then, on November 25, 1953, the day before Thanksgiving, Billy and Geneva were involved in an automobile accident in Cheatham County on Old Clarksville Pike. Geneva was seriously injured with two fractured vertebrae and one disc. To keep her from being paralyzed she was placed in a body cast from the top of her head to her hips. Her arms, legs, ears, and the front part of her face, from her eye brows to the lower lip, were the only parts not covered. Geneva's health and immobile condition required Billy to resign from his church so he could care for her and continue his studies at the Bible College. In April of 1954 Geneva's body cast was removed and a neck brace was placed on her shoulders to allow the vertebrae and disc to fit together again. This gave her the ability to travel once more. The next month, May 1954, Billy and Geneva both began to help the Oaklawn Church with music and teaching.

In June of 1956 Billy was able to finish his college courses at the Bible College. Then, in August of 1956, he began pastoring the First Free Will Baptist Church of Rocky Mount, North Carolina. He graduated from the Bible College on May 30, 1957, with a Bachelor of Arts, with a major in Bible and a minor in Christian Education.

Over the next several years Billy pastored churches in Virginia, North Carolina, Missouri, and Tennessee. Then, in August of 1976 Billy and Geneva were called to pastor the Eastside Free Will Baptist Church in Houston, Texas. Thus began their involvement in the Free Will Baptist work in Texas. They came as seasoned veterans to the work. After about seven years as pastor of the Eastside Church in Houston Billy accepted the pastorate of the Grand Prairie Free Will Baptist Church in Grand Prairie, Texas, in May of 1983. In 1984, while serving on the Executive Board of the Texas State Association, Billy was chosen to be the Executive Secretary of the Texas State Association of Free Will Baptists, following the resignation of Allen Moore. For the next one and a half years Billy travelled the state of Texas promoting the Free Will Baptist work. He attended quarterly meetings faithfully, preached in a great many of the churches, often preached revival meetings, and endeavored to give leadership to the State Association. During his time in Texas Billy served in many capacities: clerk, youth camp board member, mission boards, State Executive Board, Hillsdale Trustee, and as Texas' representative on the General Board of the National

Association. For two years he served on the Executive Committee of the General Board, the most powerful board in the National Association.

Billy is noted for his work as an usher at the National Association conventions, serving for ten years as Usher Coordinator. This gave him the responsibility for counting the votes at the National. Today he and Geneva work in the convention registration.

Billy and Geneva have three children: Kevin, born March 5, 1957; Michael, born October 4, 1960; and Shannon, born April 27, 1965.

Billy continued to pastor churches in Texas, Oklahoma, and Tennessee until his retirement from the pastorate in February of 2002. As of August of 2016 Billy has spent sixty-five years in the ministry. Geneva has been right alongside him as a faithful companion in his ministry. One more thing should be said of Billy Walker, he was always willing to go wherever the Lord in his providence called him to go. At this writing Billy and Geneva reside in Smyrna, Tennessee.

C. C. Wheeler

Charles Cody Wheeler was born on January 28, 1886, in Weatherford, Parker County, Texas, the son of George Washington and Amy Elizabeth (Moody) Wheeler. He received his theological training at Westminster College[216] in Tehuacana, Texas. He pastored the Bryan Free Will Baptist Church from 1913-1915, and again from 1917 to 1918. He pastored several of the Free Will Baptist churches in the Bryan area, including North Zulch, Kurten, Wellborn, Cross, Bright Light, and Keith.[217] He pastored several of these churches simultaneously. He was a beloved and well known man in Bryan. In addition to his Texas pastorates he also pastored in Geneva and Sutton, Nebraska.

Being an educated man, Wheeler was appointed to a committee to draft the first constitution of the Texas State Association at its initial session in 1915 at Bradley, Texas. He served along with J. J. Tatum and W. E. Dearmore, two other well educated men of unusual abilities.

Brother Wheeler married Maude Ellie Gant (1887-1963) and they had six children: Ruby Lee, George Ewell, Charles Teresa, Imaree Egbert, Mohnike, and Florence Edge. Brother Wheeler was described as a man with a sunny smile.

Wheeler's ministry was brought to an early end when he died in a train wreck at Hammond, Robertson County, Texas, on January 14, 1918, at the age of 31 years. Hammond was a small station ten miles north of Calvert. The North Bound Owl passenger train, train number 17 of the Houston and Texas Central Railroad, crashed into the steam engine of a south bound freight train parked on a side rail so the passenger train could pass. The engine and baggage car passed safely but the coach and chair car left the track and plunged into the boiler and caused an outpouring of steam and boiling water that immediately covered the unfortunate passengers. The cause of the

---

[216] Westminster College was originally located in rural Collin County, seventeen miles southeast of McKinney. In 1902 the college moved to Tehuacana in northeastern Limestone County. The school was a preparatory school for Methodist Protestant ministers. It closed in 1950. Tehuacana is located at the intersection of State Highway 171 and Farm Road 638, six miles northwest of Mexia, Texas. Tehuacana was named for the Tawakoni Native American tribe, who lived in the area until the 1840's.

[217] *A 63 Year History of First Free Will Baptist Church, Bryan, Texas*, by Charles Sapp, 1957, page 23.

wreck was a split switch. Seventeen people were killed, many of them badly mutilated.[218] J. J. Tatum signed Wheeler's death certificate.

Wheeler was living in Tehuacana while he was attending Westminster College. At the time he was pastoring the Free Baptist Church in Bryan as well as the churches in Kurten, Wellborn, and Bright Light. He took the train down to Bryan each weekend to fulfill his pastoral duties. Wheeler is buried in the Bryan City Cemetery and has a large monument.

Keith Woody

Wendell Keith Woody was born in Norfork, in rural Baxter County, Arkansas, on August 26, 1940, to Author M. and Lidia (Kirley) Woody. His father was a farmer. The family moved to Littlefield, Texas, when Keith was in the fifth grade. He says that his mother and father had the greatest influence on his life by far because they kept him in church and lived a life of example before him all of his life. He graduated from Whitharral High School in 1958. Whitharral is a small community in north central Hockley County, in the Llano Estacado region of West Texas. It is located on U. S. Highway 385 ten miles north of Levelland. Whitharral is pronounced "WHIT-hair-ul."

Keith Woody

Keith married Neva Jo Mowery in 1960. Keith was in the United States Army at the time and was home on leave. They were married by the Justice of the Peace in Levelland, Texas, since they were not Christians and did not know a preacher. They have two children: Danny Eugene and Kimberly D. Woody. Both Keith and Neva accepted Christ as their savior under the ministry of Lionel Cooksey at the First Free Will Baptist Church in Lubbock, Texas, in 1964.

Keith was working at the Post Office in Midland, Texas, and he and Neva were attending the Westside Free Will Baptist Church. In 1968 they attended a revival meeting one night at the First Free Will Baptist Church in Odessa, Texas, when Rev. Lionel Cooksey was pastor and Rev. Tom Malone was the evangelist. God had been dealing with Keith for some time, calling him into the gospel ministry. He went forward in that service and answered God's call to preach. In 1970 he was licensed to the ministry by the Midessa District Association of Free Will Baptists.

Shortly thereafter Keith and Neva moved to Oklahoma City, Oklahoma, to attend Oklahoma Bible College, now Hillsdale Free Will Baptist College, located in Moore, Oklahoma. They initially attended the Sunnylane Free Will Baptist Church in Del City, Oklahoma, where he was ordained by the First Oklahoma District Association of Free Will Baptists. His ordination certificate was signed by E. E. Morris,[219] Jim Cearley, and Charles Flynn. He attended Hillsdale for two years. Keith pastored the Bible Free Will Baptist Church in Odessa, Texas, for one year in 1971.

The First Free Will Baptist Church in Lubbock had been closed for some time. It was where Keith and Neva had accepted the Lord, and they both were from the Lubbock area. They both had a burden to start a church there. They left Odessa and moved to Lubbock, Texas, in 1971, and started the Lubbock Free Will Baptist Church. The Midessa District Association Mission

---

[218] *Bryan Daily Eagle*, January 14, 1918, front page
[219] This is the same E. E. Morris who served on the Treatise Revision Committee at the organizational meeting of the National Association of Free Will Baptists in 1935.

Board backed them financially. At first they met in a park, with twelve people present. They were able to rent the Carpenters' Union Hall and started having services there. Then, for a year, they had services in the Alcoholics Recovery Building. By this time they were able to purchase a church property from the Evangelical Methodists. The Lubbock Free Will Baptist Church became a self-supporting church in four years. During this time he graduated from Texas Tech University, having earned a Bachelor's Degree.

He then moved to Searcy, Arkansas, and pastored the First Free Will Baptist Church for one year. During this time he took classes at Harding University. In 1975 he moved to Norman, Oklahoma, and pastored the Straight Street Free Will Baptist Church until 1977. During this tenure he also attended the University of Arts and Science. Then he moved back to Lubbock to pastor the Lubbock Free Will Baptist Church because it was about to close. He pastored there until 1981. Then, Keith and Neva returned to Oklahoma City where Keith pastored the Capital Hill Free Will Baptist Church for ten years.

Keith and Neva took a few days leave from their work in Oklahoma City and were going to San Antonio, Texas, for a few days of rest and relaxation. People come there from all over the world for just the same reason. On the trip down they got as far as Austin where they got a room in a hotel on Lady Bird Lake, at the south side of downtown Austin. They were standing on the balcony of the hotel and Neva asked if there was a Free Will Baptist church in Austin. Keith said, "No, I think there used to be one here but it has long been closed."

Neva said, "Someone should come here and start a church in this beautiful city." Not long after that Bill Jones, moderator of the Texas State Association of Free Will Baptists, approached them to see if they would be interested in starting a church in San Antonio. Faith Free Will Baptist Church in San Antonio, which had been started by H. Ray Berry, has closed. Faith Church had sold its property and wanted the money to be used to start another Free Will Baptist church in San Antonio at some point in the future. Brother Berry was made the trustee of the money. Keith told Brother Jones that he and Neva had no burden to start a church in San Antonio, but that if they ever decided to plant one in Austin they might want to go. Within a week Brother Jones called and said that Brother Berry had released the money from the sale of the Faith Church in San Antonio so it could be used to start a Free Will Baptist church in the Austin area. The Texas State Mission Board hired Keith and he and Neva were commissioned at the Texas State Association meeting at the Ramada Inn in Austin in June of 1991.

By this time Keith was a well-known and widely respected pastor, excellent preacher, proven church planter, and denominational leader. In July of 1991 he preached at the National Association of Free Will Baptists, which met that year in Charleston, West Virginia. *The Texas Challenge* gave Keith and Neva front page coverage in its September-October issue, and continued to promote the cause through the whole church planting effort. Pretty much the entire contingent of Free Will Baptists in Texas got behind the project and it became one of the best mission success stories in the history of the Free Will Baptists in Texas.

It should be observed that a young couple, Wes and Marsha Hood, moved from Oklahoma City to Austin to help form the nucleus of the new church. Wes had been Youth Pastor at the Capitol Hill Free Will Baptist Church in Oklahoma City, where Brother Woody had just served as pastor. Marsha was the daughter of Phil and Fannie Ellis of Grand Prairie and members of the First Free Will Baptist Church of Duncanville, Texas. Wes was the son of Glen and Nadine Hood, who had formerly pastored the Westside Free Will Baptist Church in Midland, Texas. Wes and Marsha both had deep Texas roots. They both continue as active workers in the new church in Cedar Park to this day.

The mission met in a rented facility for the first three years and had about forty people coming when they found suitable property and in Cedar Park. It was an ideal piece of property across the street from Austin Community College. *The Austin American Statesman* referred to Cedar Park as "Boom Town" because of the enormous growth the area was experiencing. Construction of a beautiful church building was begun, with the exterior of the building made of white Austin stone, perfect for the area. The Master's Men Helping Hands building team, working under the direction of missionary builder Howard Gwartney, gathered from several states and spent several weeks constructing the building. The completed building was dedicated on February 4, 1994. The Central Texas District quarterly meeting met at the church the day of the dedication, the choir from the First Free Will Baptist Church in Duncanville came to sing, and the *Austin American Statesman* did another article about the church. The original building was 8,600 square feet and a new 4,000 square feet addition was added in 2009.

Over the forty-five years of his ministry Keith served in many positions of leadership in the denomination, having an impact that few men do. On a district level he served as moderator of the Midessa District Association in Texas, member of the Mission Board and as moderator of the First Oklahoma District Association, and assistant moderator and moderator of the Central Texas District Association. On the state level he served as a member of the state Mission Board, a member of the State Executive Committee, and was moderator of the Texas State Association of Free Will Baptists from 1997 to 2012. He did not allow himself to be reelected as state moderator because he simply had too many irons in the fire, and had for too long. He came to the point in life at the age of 73 that he needed to wind down - and Neva needed it, too. On the national level he served as a member of the General Board from 1996 to 2012. He was a member of the Executive Committee of the General Board of the National Association from 2003 to 2012. He resigned from the Executive Committee of the General Board in 2012 because he was missing meetings because of the sickness of his father-in-law and because of the increased demand of the Lakehills Free Will Baptist Church. At the time he was moderator of the State Association, assistant moderator of the Central District Association, and pastor of a growing, active church. The demands on his time and energy became too much. He resigned as pastor of the Lakehills Free Will Baptist Church in Cedar Park in November of 2013, at the age of seventy-three.

Pastor Woody was widely known as a good pulpit preacher. His sermons were always carefully prepared, well outlined, and practical. He was noted for beginning each sermon with a very funny joke. He used these to break the ice and make people feel comfortable in the service. He believed that it was healthy for God's people to laugh and that people tend to take themselves too seriously. How many men ever get to preach at the National Association of Free Will Baptists twice? At stated above he preached at the National Association in 1991 when it met in Charleston, West Virginia. He preached again in 2014 when the convention met in Fort Worth, Texas. That was an honor very few men ever receive, and think of all the preachers who are never invited to preach at the National.

He and Neva moved back to Lubbock, where Neva was from and where they had family and friends. They had remodeled the house which Neva's mother had owned. Their daughter Kim teaches at South Plains College in nearby Levelland. They planned to devote their remaining years to helping a local Free Will Baptist church, gardening, golf, and traveling. Keith said he hadn't seen nearly all of the Big Bend he would like to see. However, Neva had a heart attack in November of 2013. She subsequently had by-pass surgery from which she did not recover. She died on Sunday morning, March 23, 2014. Their pastor, Jackie Farmer, and Steve Loveless, of

Tulsa, Oklahoma, conducted the funeral. Neva was buried in Peaceful Gardens Memorial Park in Lubbock.

The First Free Will Baptist Church of Pampa, in the Texas Panhandle, needed a pastor and so Keith started going up on weekends to preach for them. The church prepared a room for him in the basement of the church so he could spend Saturday nights there.

We quote Keith once again: "I am not worthy of the high calling God has given me. I am not worthy of the confidence that my brothers and sisters in Christ have placed in me. It has been a joy to work in Texas and if I had it to do over I would spend all of my years in Texas and I would try to build more churches in our state. Texas has been good to me and given me a place to work for God among Free Will Baptists."[220]

Brother Woody passed away quietly in his sleep on July 20, 2016.

~~~~~~~~~~

I'm reminded of what the author of the Book of Hebrews said as he drew near the close of his great chapter of faith. He said, "And what more shall I say? I do not have time to tell about Gideon, Barak, Samson, Jephthah, David, Samuel and the prophets…" (Hebrews 11:32). That he could leave out such giants of the faith as David, Samuel, Isaiah, Jeremiah, and Daniel is incredible, from a human standpoint. But there just wasn't time, he said. That is the primary reason some have been left out of these profiles, but there are other reasons. One is that some chose, through neglect or procrastination, to not respond to the requests for information sent to them, sometimes repeatedly. Another reason is that information on those who have passed on to their reward simply hasn't been available, though we know the names of many of them. So we echo the words of the writer of Hebrews: we cannot tell about W. T. Wood, R. A. Roberts, E. L. Hill, E. J. Vaughn, J. E. Raney, E. S. Jameson, Miss Minnie Jimmerson, Roy Norie, J. L. Payne, John Swanwick, R. E. Conner, Tommie Newsom, Jack Turrentine, Bob Gill, and a host of others.

---

[220] Almost all of the information about Keith Woody came from answers to questions submitted to him in writing. Other information came from *The Texas Challenge*, starting with the September-October, 1991, issue.

Chapter 9

Notable Churches

Blue Lake Free Will Baptist Church

The Blue Lake Free Will Baptist Church was organized in the Piedmont Community of Grimes County in 1899, by Hall Miller. Charter members of the church were W. H. Miller, W. A. Bounds, S. A. Miller, E. R. Bounds, and W. J. Bounds. Many different preachers pastored Blue Lake over the years, many of them men who pastored other churches at the same time. Several of the men who pastored the First Free Will Baptist Church in Bryan also preached at Blue Lake. The church closed in 1979. John Ray Maxwell wrote the following obituary for the church, still standing at the time, which could serve as a eulogy for a hundred Texas churches:

> About four miles down a winding road in rural Grimes County, Texas, there stands a small church. It stands alone amid overgrown lawns. The paint that was once so fresh and white has begun to chip. The front door has no lock to deny entry, and man and beast can come and go at will. The floor which once was clean is now filthy. Leaves, paper, and a variety of other refuse litters the floor. A rear window is missing which accounts for part of the clutter. But once it was not so. Once these walls resounded to the voices of men and women, boys and girls all raising their voices in praise to God.
>
> She did not die all at once. Perhaps that would have been more merciful. But instead it was a slow, lingering death. The young were the first to go. The city beckoned, the city called and they obeyed. The older members, one by one, passed on to their eternal reward. Families who could have stayed left for larger churches. The membership continued to drop. Finally a few old ladies, together with a man or two, constituted the congregation. She no longer had her own minister. She had to share one. The worship hour was changed to mid-afternoon. But it was a losing battle. Finally the last message was delivered. The preacher stepped from behind the pulpit for the last time. The two or three members that remained shook his hand. Perhaps a few tears were shed. They walked down the aisle, the same aisle which many people, saints and sinners, had walked before them. Tears of joy and tears for sorrow of sins were the tears of the day, but those tears of sorrow were not for tears for sins but instead were tears for what had been lost. The doors were closed, forever.[221]

Bright Light Free Will Baptist Church

The Bright Light Free Will Baptist Church is the oldest Free Will Baptist Church in Central Texas, having been started in the summer of 1886 by P. H. Adams. The church is located in the Harvey Community, Brazos Country, Texas, a few miles out of Bryan. The church began when a

---

[221] The information about Blue Lake was supplied by John Maxwell.

Bright Light Free Will Baptist Church

small group of people met under a large oak tree under the leadership of P. H, Adams, who would be their first pastor. The group felt that the Free Will Baptist doctrine was in accord with their belief and they pledged themselves to work for the cause of Christ under the banner of the Free Will Baptist denomination.

Soon after the group was organized into a church a revival was held in a brush arbor with A. M. Stewart serving as the evangelist. Brother Stewart was a missionary from the Randall movement of Free Will Baptists who had already started churches in East Texas before moving to the Bryan area. Brother Stewart was gifted with a winning personality, a good education, and fervent eloquence. It was Brother Stewart who gave the church its name, Bright Light, that it would always be a bright and shining light for Christ in the community. Material for the first church building was hauled by wagons from the sawmills of East Texas by A. B. McSwain, Green Buchanan, and Will Goen. This building was razed around 1900 and a second building erected on the same site.

The second pastor of the church was W. T. Wood, whose remains lie peacefully in the cemetery next to the church. It is sad that we cannot do a profile on him because he seems to have had a wonderful ministry in Texas. Then came the notable A. M. Stewart, James Tipton, S. L. Morris, T. H. Newsom, T. C. Ferguson, and J. J. Tatum. C. C. Wheeler, with his sunny smile, had his ministry come to an early end in 1918 when he died in a train wreck. All of these men were of outstanding ability and highly gifted for the ministry. Each of them left huge footprints on the Free Will Baptist work in Texas. Then came Ollie Smith and J. P. Brown, who labored with his own hands to restore the church building after a tornado blew it off its foundation. Other notable pastors were Sam Thomas, J. L. Bounds, J. W. Handy, Robert Wiggs, R. E. Conner, and J. B. Lovering. Up to this point the normal thing was for the pastors to live somewhere else, such as in Bryan-College Station, and make mostly weekend trips to the Harvey Community to preach at Bright Light. Most, if not all of them pastored other churches while also serving Bright Light. Many churches shared their pastor with other churches.

As was often the case in those days' services were held one Sunday a month and was called a quarter-time church. In 1942 the church became a half-time church, meaning that worship services were conducted two Sundays each month, in this case the first and third Sundays. Beginning at this point in 1942 the church shared its pastor with only one other church.

Then Alvin F. Halbrook, of Leadington, Missouri, and a graduate of Free Will Baptist Bible College, came to Texas to pastor Bright Light, beginning in August of 1945. In 1946 he began to promote the idea of a parsonage so that the pastor could live in the community and better serve the church. That year General Howard Davidson donated five acres of land next to the church cemetery for that purpose. A three bedroom house was constructed by remodeling a former Woodmen Lodge building which had been donated to the church and moved to the property near the church. Brother Halbrook and his wife moved into the new parsonage in April of 1947. Living

An old picture of a Bright Light congregation

in the community made it possible for the pastor to do more than just make weekend visits to the church. He not only could preach there, he could now pastor there as well. He became the church's first full-time pastor. Brother Halbrook served the church longer than any other pastor to date; from 1945 to 1968, twenty-three years. J. L. Bounds had the second longest tenure as pastor, fifteen years, although he simultaneously pastored other churches.

In 1953 the church unanimously voted to construct its third church building, on the same site as the first two. A building fund goal of $4,000.00 was set and a building committee elected, which consisted of N. C. Cole, Clyde F. Goen, J. J. Foster, Bud Graham, and Arnold Schultz. The new sanctuary was dedicated on Sunday, April 28, 1957. A fellowship hall and baptistry were dedicated in 1974.

After Alvin Halbrook, the church was served by Don Lombard, Albert "Bud" Keech, William Don Ellis, Everett Hellard, Gary "Buzz" Bird, Mike Mize, Paul Dean, Mike Fields, Herbert Richards, Danny Davis, and Matt. G. Calhoun.

Bright Light was the earliest Free Will Baptist light to shine in Central Texas and it continues to shine well into the Twenty-first century. The church continues to be an integral part of the Central Texas District Association, the Texas State Association, and the National Association of Free Will Baptists. The church has always been a faithful and generous supporter of missions and Free Will Baptist Bible College, now Welch College.

Evergreen Free Will Baptist Church

Evergreen Free Will Baptist Church, Keith

The Evergreen Free Will Baptist Church,[222] at Keith, Grimes County, Texas, is one of the oldest Free Will Baptist churches in Texas. It was organized in 1895 by A. M. Stewart, with seven members. They were W. Hall and Sallie Miller, Mr. and Mrs. Huff Oldgrand, Pa Hunter (William?), Mrs. Ed Hunter, and one other member whose name has been forgotten. William Thomas (Tom) Wood was the first pastor. It is believed that he served from 1895 until 1909. According to Mrs. Lizzie (Flynt) Trant, who died in 1950, J. J. Tatum also participated in organizing the church, as did W. T. Wood.

---

[222] Much of the information about Evergreen is taken from *Evergreen Free Will Baptist Church History Digest*, Vol. 1, Issue 2, June 4, 1995.

The earliest minutes available at this time are dated April 7, 1906. The pastor was W. T. Wood. The major item of business conducted at this meeting was to appoint a committee to raise funds "for the purpose of building a church at this place." Those appointed to the committee were J. S. Harrison, Ben Smith, Alice Conlee, and Kate Flynt. The sum of $54.00 was subscribed for building purposes. This sum, plus $9.00 collected by July 7, 1906, brought the total to $63.00. On July 11, 1908, a committee consisting of Brothers Harrison, Cook, and Pyle were appointed to confer with the school trustees about purchasing the Trant School house to be used for church purposes. A month later the church voted to purchase the school house. By December of 1908, the sum of $52.80 was collected and paid to the school board for the Trant school house. Land was purchased from Preston C. and Susan A. (Vaughn) Conlee. This parcel of land was part of Susan's inheritance from her grandfather, Samuel Andrew Jackson Pyle, who died in 1873. On March 6, 1909, the church purchased one acre for $1.00. The deed states in the description of the land "on which sits the Trant School House and the cistern thereto." On August 25, 1909, the church purchased land for the cemetery for $5.00. The deed states about the cemetery, "and for that purpose only."

The pastor from 1909 until 1910 was A. W. Mayes. J. J. Tatum served as pastor from 1910 until 1911. To put this in historical perspective, the merger of Free Will Baptists with the Northern Baptists occurred in 1910-11. In January of 1910 a collection was made to raise money to pay interest on a note owed by the church to Sister N. A. Thomas. The necessary amount was raised and the note was carried for another year. The sum of $22.51 was paid, April 30, 1910, to reduce the amount owed. Evidently, up to this time they had repaired the old Trant School House and were meeting therein.

The pastor from 1911 until 1914 was J. H. Dowell. At a meeting, December 2, 1911, the subject of a new church building was discussed. On March 2, 1912, the church agreed to hold its Sunday school and prayer meeting at Double Branch School during construction of the new church building. The first lumber for the church was hauled by Charles W. Cook and Homer E. Vaughn. The carpenter was a Mr. Brown. A collection of $6.40, along with pledges of $12.00, was received and presented to Sister Rose Craft for expenses incurred in the burial of her husband, Henry Lee Craft. He was the first person buried in the church cemetery. In March of 1913 the total amount owed on the church was $229.00, which was due on November 1, 1913. John Swanwick served as pastor in 1914. He was followed by D. C. Hargrove, who served from 1914 until November, 1916. On April 11, 1915, Josh Mitchell Flynt made a motion that the lots in the cemetery be given to all free of cost, except in cases where parties desired to pay. In such cases the church retained the right to receive a sum of 50¢ up to $3.00 per lot, which was to be used in the interest of the cemetery. The motion carried.

At the close of 1915 the sum of $80.60 had been paid to the pastor, D. C. Hargrove, leaving a balance due of $44.40. The only pastor to die during his pastorate at Evergreen was Charles C. Wheeler. He was elected November 1, 1916, and died in a train accident at Hammond, Texas, January 14, 1918. Hammond is on State Highway 6 between Calvert and Bremond in northwestern Robertson County. Wheeler was buried in the Bryan City Cemetery.

For the next several years the Evergreen Free Will Baptist Church was served by the following pastors:

J. J. Tatum, January to August, 1918, supply pastor

D. C. Hargrove, November, 1918, to October, 1920

T. T. Payne, November, 1921 until ?

J. W. Cook, March, 1922 - October, 1922

J. L. Bounds, December, 1922 - October 1924

J. P. Brown, October, 1924 - May, 1926

E. J. Vaughn, September, 1926 - October, 1929

C. B. Thompson, October 1929 - October 1937

> The church agreed in 1930 to remain with the Northern Baptist Convention. In 1935 the church joined the newly formed National Association of Free Will Baptists. The pastor, Rev. C. B. Thompson, served at that meeting as a member of the Treatise Revision Committee and then preached the first sermon to the newly organized National Association. The church paid Pastor Thompson the sum of $5.00 for expenses to attend a Free Will Baptist convention in 1936, which met in Georgia.[223]

Two legendary Free Will Baptist missionaries spoke at Evergreen in the early 1940's. Thomas H. "Pop" Wiley spoke at the church on March 17, 1940. Brother Wiley was at the time missionary to South America. He would later do his signature work in Cuba. In March of 1941, Free Will Baptist missionary to India, Miss Laura Belle Barnard,[224] spoke on her work in India.

In September of 1940 a collection was taken to obtain funds for a deposit enabling the church to obtain electric lighting. In August, 1941, another collection, in the amount of $7.40 paid for the electric wiring for the church building. The wiring was done in December, 1941, by Kennard Trant, Joe Brotherton, and Stewart Rice. Clyde and Ruby Maxwell made a special contribution toward the project. The first month's payment for electricity was $1.95.

Ruel E. Conner served as pastor from October, 1941, until October, 1942, roughly the first year of America's involvement in World War II. The pastor's salary was raised to $225.00 per year in November. T. W. Smith served as pastor from October, 1942, until 1944. In 1945 Alvin F. Halbrook came on board as pastor and remained in that position until 1953, roughly from the end of World War II through the Korean War. The last funeral to be held in the old church building was Hazel Trant. In the fall of 1949 the old church building was torn down and the new one was begun early in 1950. During construction of this building, church services were held in the Keith School house. The funeral of Lizzie Flynt Trant, who died February 25, 1950, was the first one held in the new building even though it was not completed at the time. Among those who assisted in the construction of the building were Charlie Wesley Cook, who was the head carpenter, Ray Tatum Trant, Harold B. Trant, Joe Brotherton, Calvin Stewart, Clyde Ray Maxwell, Kennard E. Trant, Alton M. Flynt, and Russell Finley. Charlie Cook was offered payment but refused.

Walter Herbert Richards served as pastor from 1954 until July, 1962. In 1957 two Sunday school rooms, along with a storage closet and bathrooms, were added to the rear of the building. Volunteer labor, supervised by Charlie Cook, was used to build this addition. He again refused payment for his services. Talmage Blount drilled a water well to supply water for the restrooms. A. J. Keech served as pastor for a while. Bobby Joe Davis pastored Evergreen from 1962 to 1968. Eugene Richards served as interim pastor in 1969. Then, from 1969 to 1981 Keith L. Phipps pastored the church. A fellowship hall was added to the building in 1981, which was as large as

---

[223] The First session of the National Association met at the Cofer's Chapel Free Will Baptist Church in Nashville, Tennessee, in 1935, but did not meet again until 1938, when the second session convened at the East Nashville Free Will Baptist Church in Nashville, November 15-18.

[224] After retiring from her missionary work in India, Miss Barnard taught Bible and Missions courses at Free Will Baptist Bible College. She was my Bible Survey professor. It was my privilege to visit with Miss Barnard in her campus apartment, have tea with her, listen to her counsel, and then hear her say one of her wonderfully inspiring prayers before returning to my dorm. She graciously made time for all of the students who wanted to visit with her and seek her counsel.

the sanctuary. Those assisting in this construction were A. J. Shaw, Russell Finley, Doyle Finley, James Ray Trant, Mike Trant, Tim Burns, and John Ray Maxwell.

Herbert Richards returned as pastor in 1981. Eugene Richards served as associate pastor from 1987 to 1989. On February 7, 1988, the church began to consider long range plans for the church's growth. The deacons recommended that an architect be hired to plan the proposed expansion. The planning continued until August 14, 1988, when the church voted to go forward with the following: construction of a new sanctuary, building a wing on the fellowship hall, remodeling the exterior of the existing building, and adding a shell for an additional bathroom. This new construction was completed at a cost of $167,721.00, and the first service was held in it on the first Sunday of March, 1989. There were 145 people in attendance.

Now in 2017 the church is almost 120 years old and continues its ministry in the Keith community and beyond. At present the church is not in fellowship with the Central Texas District Association of Free Will Baptists. Hopefully the difficulties will be worked out so it can return to active participation in the district, state, and national associations. Evergreen Free Will Baptist Church is too valuable, and too much a part of Free Will Baptist history to lose.

The Easley's Chapel Church

The Easley's Chapel Free Will Baptist Church, also known as Gartman's View Free Will Baptist Church, Comanche

The Easley's Chapel Free Will Baptist Church, located on Highway 16 just north of Comanche, is one of the oldest Free Will Baptist churches in Texas still in operation. The church was organized on September 18, 1886, by thirty-six year old R. B. Easley.[225] He founded the church in his pasture across the creek on a hill south of his home under an old fashioned brush arbor. The church held meetings in the Duncan School House, Arbor Springs, and at Old Salem for a time. In 1889, they built a church building as a meeting place of their own. Lumber for the building was hauled from Dublin, Texas, by team and wagon. The church was constructed by Pastor Easley, the deacons, and other members of the church. Pastor Easley asked the ladies of the church to write down suggested names for the church. Aunt Dorothy Hasley suggested the name "Easley's Chapel," and the church has carried that name ever since.

---

[225] Much of the information about Easley's Chapel comes from the paper "The First One Hundred Years of Easley's Chapel, by James and Sue Rainey, written for the one hundredth anniversary of the church.

R. B. and Mary Ann Easley. This picture presented and unveiled to the church September 17, 1967

Initially, Easley's Chapel was a member of the original West Texas Association and is listed as a member in the 1910 minutes of that association. When the West Texas Association ceased to exist Easley's Chapel joined the West Fork District Association.

Pastor Easley was a lover of gospel music and he and a Brother Emert ordered an old fashioned pump type organ from Sears and Roebuck to be used in the song service. Sister Lona McGuire played the organ during the revival meeting that summer. People came from miles around to attend the revival.

A fire broke out in the woods and burned up to the fence line near the church. Soon afterwards the church building was moved to Vandyke, just north of the church's present location. Mr. J. C. Fritts donated the land for the church.

During this time it was normal for people of every denomination to worship together. The church organized a union Sunday school. As mentioned elsewhere a union Sunday school was a Sunday school for members of several churches or denominations. A union Sunday school fit the needs of the day and such schools were very common. This Sunday school proved to be very successful.

In 1902, revival services were held under a brush arbor until a tabernacle could be built. Tabernacles were usually roofed structures, with a pulpit and benches, but with no walls. These open-air tabernacles provided suitable meeting places for summer revivals. The tabernacle proved to be good for the church as people traveled great distances to attend services, as was common in those days. The church grew and prospered.

The church minutes record that one of the men of the church was disciplined by being voted out of the church. His infraction? He was accused of riding his horse too fast on church property. After being voted out of the church he repented of his misconduct and was admitted back into full fellowship.[226]

An annual all day singing on the third Sunday in May was organized and continued until the 1990's. People from music companies were invited to come and representatives came with song books and helped make this a success. In the early 1900's Pastor Easley, W. A. Irby, and Jimmie Brinson hired a music teacher from Tennessee to teach a singing school. The teacher cost $140.00, but everyone was invited to attend free of charge. These singing schools, popular until the 1950's, taught people how to read music and sometimes introduced new songs. At the end of this particular singing school, the annual revival was held, and forty people were baptized as a result of the meeting.

Easley's Chapel continued to grow and prosper, and a new addition was built onto the church to meet the needs of a growing congregation. In 1934, the church building burned. No one knew the cause of the fire. Pastor Easley expressed his concern for this tragedy by saying, "I only wish it had been my house, instead of the house of God." The congregation met for worship under the tabernacle for some time.

---

[226] Told to me by James Rainey on September 19, 2014, in his furniture store in Comanche, Texas; Jim is a deacon in the church and sometimes fill-in when the church has no pastor.

In April, 1935, the congregation bought three acres of land from Mrs. J. E. Gartman, where the church is presently located, and the tabernacle was moved from Vandyke. Pastor Easley said, "We will call this place Gartman's View." Hence, the reason some call the church Easley's Chapel and others, Gartman's View. The tabernacle was boxed in on the sides, and the services of the church were carried on. When Pastor Easley passed away on December 26, 1940, his funeral was held under the tabernacle. Before his death he expressed his desire for the people to build a church building. This was done in 1942. John A. Brooks preached the first sermon in the new church. In 1950, four new classrooms were added, and since then there have been numerous other improvements. The interior of the sanctuary was paneled with knotty pine, and new floors, pews, pulpit, communion table, and altar were installed.

In 1964, a parsonage was moved to the church property, and a full-time pastor was called to live in the community and be close when needed. This proved to be a good thing for the church. In 1967, a complete remodeling of the church sanctuary was done, along with a new baptistry and 1230 square feet of new Sunday school classrooms, a kitchen, and modern restrooms were installed as well.

Now, well into the Twenty-first Century, the church has been in decline for some years as the demographics of the community have changed. The town of Comanche has grown some and new, larger churches offering more ministries to families, have been established. Easley's Chapel remains a country church, but continues carrying on faithfully.

The following pastors have served the church:

R. B. Easley, founder	Ted Patton (supply pastor)	Paul Morris
Henry Jones	A. F. Ferguson	Elvis Fielding
A. J. Cox	C. J. Hearron	Homer Tumbleson
A. J. Barnette	W. A. Hearron	Roy Norie
R. B. Easley	Alvie Hudson	David Medley
J. E. Raney	Roy Norie	D. H. Rudd
J. C. Hodges	Huey Gower	J. L. (Pat) Burttram
E. J. Vaughn	Homer Tumbleson	D. H. Rudd
A. J. Ferguson	Arthur Hearron	Eugene Richards
Lizzie (Lawless) McAdams	Homer Tumbleson	Elvis Fielding
John A. Brooks	J. E. Jean	Marcus Nettleton
J. L. Brandon, interim	Larry Cox	James Rainey,

Faith Free Will Baptist Church, Wichita Falls

The Faith Free Will Baptist Church in Wichita Falls was organized on September 8, 1956, by Ruel E. Conner. The church was a split off the First Free Will Baptist Church. The present pastor is Richard Rust, who has been pastor of the church since April 26, 1987, which is by far the longest tenure of any previous pastor of the church. Pastor Rust was a carpenter by trade. He attended Hillsdale Free Will Baptist College in Moore, Oklahoma, from 1966 to 1968 and received an Associate's Degree. His area of study was church music. He also attended Northeast State University for one and a half years. He has what many would call a "star quality" singing voice.

The men who have pastored the Faith Free Will Baptist Church are:

R. E. Conner	September 8, 1956 to March 29, 1964
M. L. Sutton	July 19, 1964 to March 30, 1966
Roy Norie, Jr.	May 8, 1966 to October 22, 1969
Randall Johnson	December 31, 1969 to April 7, 1971
Roy Norie, Jr.	May 19, 1971 to June 5, 1974
Lester Davis	August 25, 1974 to June 1, 1975
Lewis Nettleton	July 30, 1975 to October 6, 1976
M. L. Sutton	December 5, 1976 to May 13, 1979
Larry Cox	August 12, 1979 to October 15, 1979
Don Davis	April 6, 1980 to October 15, 1980
Vince Williams	March 1, 1981 to November 23, 1984
Richard Bowden	May 19, 1985 to November 16, 1986
Richard Rust	April 16, 1987 to the present

First Free Will Baptist Church, Henderson

First Free Will Baptist Church, Henderson, photo courtesy of Kelly Johnson

The First Free Will Baptist Church[227] in Henderson is one of the youngest Free Will Baptist churches in East Texas. The church was organized on May 26, 1952, under the direction of Noah Tuttle. The organizational meeting was held at the Calvary Baptist Church in Henderson, Texas. Two members of the State Home Mission Board were present: Mr. Noah Cole and Mr. Clyde F. Goen, deacons of the Bright Light Free Will Baptist Church in Brazos County, and one visiting minister, Robert B. Crawford, pastor of the First Free Will Baptist Church of Bryan, Texas. The newly organized church was named the Jameson Memorial Free Will Baptist Church in honor of E. S. Jameson.

The charter members of the church were: Mamie Flanagan, Tennie King, Homer Flanagan, William L. King, Lucille Green, Emma Gibson, Homer Green, Val B. Stone, Leeman King, Estelle Stone, Mollie Watson, and Lennie Watson.

During the first few months of its beginning the church experienced rapid growth. However, difficulties soon developed over the pastor becoming involved in the charismatic movement that was spreading from California across the United States and touching most every denomination. These teachings and practices were contrary to the Bible and to the *Treatise of the Faith and Practices of the Original Free Will Baptists*. As a result of the ensuing difficulties that developed among the membership of the church and with the East Texas District Association, the church considered withdrawing from the denomination. In conference on April 15, 1955, the decision was made to remain affiliated with Free Will Baptists. Since that date the church has remained loyal to the Free Will Baptist *Treatise* and in support of the denomination.

In August of 1957 the name of the church was changed from Jameson Memorial to the First Free Will Baptist Church of Henderson, Texas. Before they moved into permanent facilities at their present location in April, 1953, the church met in the American Legion Hut from July to November, 1952. In November the church moved its meeting place from the American Legion Hut to the District Court Room, and then to 305 Truman Drive, where they met until a church building was built. On November 5, 1952, the church voted to purchase property on Richardson Drive as a building site for a church building. On November 12, 1952, the trustees presented an estimate to the church for the building. On November 25, 1952, the church approved the building plans and construction was begun. The building at 913 Richardson Drive was completed in 1953. Although the church was not fully completed inside, the first service was held in the new building on Easter Sunday, April 5, 1953. The finishing of the interior of the sanctuary and Sunday school classrooms was completed later. Because of the church's concern for the comfort of its members, especially the elderly and those in poor health, the decision was made on July 22, 1959, to air-condition the sanctuary. The classrooms were air-conditioned later after the parsonage had been constructed. This building served the church well for several years and holds many memories for many of the present members.

On August 31, 1960, the decision was made to construct a parsonage as a residence for the pastors. Leeman King, Tennie King, Charlie Dunn, Velma Strong, Bill Thrasher, Ronny King, and Lewis Jordan were elected as the building committee. Charlie Dunn was employed as the carpenter to build the building. Leeman King was designated to work with Brother Dunn in helping supervise the work. Many members of the church volunteered their time to do part of the construction, such as installing the roof, nailing up the paneling, etc. Jordan Plumbing did the

---

[227] Most of the information about the First Free Will Baptist Church in Henderson came from a special paper published by the church on May 27, 2007, in celebration of the church's 55th homecoming celebration. Additional information came from the minutes of the East Texas District and the Texas State Association.

plumbing and Ned Youngblood did the electrical wiring. Central heat was installed during construction. Central air-conditioning was added in September, 1972.

An opportunity was offered to the church to purchase approximately 2.4 acres of land east of the church property, along Carter Creek, by Russell Jones, owner of the property, for the sum of $10,000.00. After negotiations, the price of $7,500.00 was agreed upon. In April, 1980, the church agreed to purchase the property. Russell Jones then donated $500.00, making the final cost to the church of $7,000.00. This property was to prove invaluable to the later growth and expansion of the church facilities. By 1980 the church was outgrowing its facilities. On September 3, 1980, in regular church conference, the deacons recommended that the church expand its facilities. After much discussion and planning Chris King was elected by the church on March 3, 1982, to draw up plans for a new sanctuary and classroom building. After considering several architectural designs, the plans for the present building were approved on October 6, 1982. The pastor, deacons, and trustees were elected as the building committee. In October, 1982, a resolution was passed to the effect that they were to construct the new building as soon as possible. The sanctuary was completed and dedicated on Easter Sunday, April 7, 1985. The old sanctuary was converted into a fellowship hall, with a new kitchen built and furnished in 1986.

The First Free Will Baptist Church in Henderson has always been involved in supporting the work of the Free Will Baptist denomination. Support of missions began with the church's first budget when the church designated $5.00 per month for missions. Regular monthly offerings were set aside to help support the Ken Eagleton's and Judy Smith, both families' members of the church. The church continues to support missions. The church supports other state and national work such as Women Active for Christ, state and national home missions, and Whispering Pines Youth Camp, the youth camp owned and operated by the East Texas District Association. Some of the members of the church are actively involved in the work and ministry of the Texas State Association, namely Mitzi Burks, president of the Texas Women Active for Christ; Allen King, previous member of the Christian Education Board, and Pastor Mark Headrick.

The First Free Will Baptist Church has been served by the following pastors:

Pastor	Dates
Noah G. Tuttle	May 1952 to July 1955
J. M. Herald	October 1955 to February 1956 (interim)
William Don Ellis	June 1956 to February 1962
Clyde Cain	March 1962 to September 1962
Dan Parker	October 1962 to July 1964
Roy Norie, Jr.	November 1964 to February 1965 (interim)
Rashie J. Kennedy, Jr.	February 1965 to August 1967
Harold Teague	October 1967 to February 1969
William Don Ellis	May 1969 to February 1992
Leroy Blankenship	August 1992 to April 1998
John High	September 1998 to March 2001
Harold Teague	March 2001 to August 2001 (interim)
Harold Teague	September 2001 to- July 2007
Clyde Tucker	July 2007 to May 2008
Mark Headrick	June 2008 to the present

Other historical nuggets include the following:
- The first revival service was held June 16, 1952, in the Calvary Baptist Church building.
- The first offering was taken on May 26, 1952, in the amount of $11.61 and was for the purpose of meeting the immediate needs of the church.
- The first monthly budget was presented and adopted on August 27, 1952, as follows: Pastor's salary, $150.00; Janitor, $12.00; Rent, $40.00; Foreign Missions $5.00; Miscellaneous, $13.00, for a total of $220.00.
- The first communion service was held on November 1, 1952.
- The first baptismal service held in the sanctuary on Richardson Drive was November 8, 1953.
- The church voted to print its first bulletin September, 1953.
- The first state association meeting was hosted by the church October 3-5, 1954. Homer Green and Darnell Stone were delegates to the meeting.
- The church's first radio program began on January 4, 1953, at 1:15 p.m. It was a fifteen minute program to continue for a period of three months.
- In August, 1963, the recommendation was made by Brother Parker that the church tithe the Sunday school offerings to fund the youth to camp each summer. This funding method continues to this day.
- On January 4, 1954, the church budget was set at $6,000.00.

First Free Will Baptist Church, Bryan

A. M. Stewart, the missionary from the Randall Movement of Free Will Baptists, who had founded the Liberty Free Will Baptist Church in Clayton, Panola County, Texas, in 1876, along with a number of other Free Will Baptist churches in East Texas, moved his center of operations to Central Texas by the early 1890's.[228] He owned and operated the Bryan Academic and Collegiate Institute, a grade school in Bryan. He was both an educator and a church planter. A small group of people interested in forming a Free Will Baptist church began to meet in the First Christian Church in 1893. The group consisted of Mr. and Mrs. A. M. Stewart, Mr. and Mrs. J. L. Edge, a prominent businessman in Bryan, Mrs. Roe Edge, Mr. and Mrs. T. A. Searcy, who would later be one of the pastors, and Mr. and Mrs. Jim Mike. When the group was ready to organize into a church, the organizational service was conducted in the Bryan Academic and Collegiate Institute in 1894. Services continued to be conducted in the school building until a church building could be erected. A. M. Stewart was named the first pastor.

Simply called the Bryan Free Baptist Church at first, the church grew and became one of the most prominent churches in town. The church was able to attract some of the most capable Free Will Baptist pastors in the denomination. The list reads like a Who's Who among Free Will Baptists: S. L. Morris, editor of the *Free Will Baptist News*; J. J. Tatum, a prominent promotional man for Texas Free Will Baptists and the Southwestern Conference of Freewill Baptists; T. C. Ferguson, prominent opponent of the merger with the Northern Baptists, and evangelist for the Southwestern Conference, and whose wife, Myrtle, was also a preacher; W. T. Woods, about whom we wish we knew more; R. E. Lawless, single at the time but later became famous as Lizzie McAdams; C. C. Wheeler, an outstanding young minister who died tragically in a train wreck in

---

[228] Most of the information about the Bryan church was taken from the book *A 63 Year History of First Free Will Baptist Church, Bryan, Texas*, by Charles L. Sapp, printed by The Scribe Shop, Bryan, Texas 1957.

1918; C. B. Thompson, one of the most outstanding preachers of his time; M. L. Hollis, who was well known for having started twenty-four Free Will Baptist churches in Mississippi and Alabama, many of them still going strong well into the Twenty-first Century; I. J. Blackwelder, songwriter and denominational leader for decades; E. Sterl Phinney, who became a foreign missionary; L. C. Johnston, founder and longtime president of Free Will Baptist Bible College; J. R. Davidson, denominational leader for whom Davidson Hall, the first building at Free Will Baptist Bible College, was named; J. O. Fort, mostly known for his work in North Carolina, served as editor of the *Free Will Baptist*; N. Bruce Barrow, graduate of Moody Bible Institute and Northern Baptist Seminary in Chicago, moderator of the National Association of Free Will Baptists; R. B. Crawford, who served as Executive Secretary of the denomination, and a host of others.

An interesting note in one of the issues of *The Morning Star* in 1909 mentioned that the church, although it paid six hundred dollars a year in salary, had failed for several months to obtain a suitable pastor.[229]

One of those notable pastors mentioned above was M. L. Hollis of Mississippi. He did not know how the church got his name out in Texas, but they wrote him several letters urging him to come. Finally they telegraphed him asking how much it would take to get him to come for a trial sermon. Brother Hollis had never heard of a "trial" sermon, and he really didn't intend to come, but he wired back that it would take one hundred dollars. To his surprise they insisted, and he came. Later he was equally surprised that they agreed to pay one hundred fifty dollars per month and to build a parsonage, so he became their pastor. It was about 1929. When he came to Bryan, the church was affiliated with the Northern Baptists (as a result of the 1910 merger, of course), and he told them plainly he wasn't a "Northern Baptist," but a "Free Will Baptist"; and they said that's exactly what they wanted. Soon the Texas churches asked Brother Hollis to be a delegate to the Northern Baptist Convention. He asked that, instead, they send delegates to the Eastern General Conference of Free Will Baptists that would be meeting soon. They agreed. It is surprising to learn that some Texas Free Will Baptists had stayed with the merger as late as 1927. Here, too, is apparently the explanation how Texas came to be in fellowship with the Eastern General Conference rather than the Western Cooperative General Association.[230]

During the ministry of the notable J. R. Davidson the church grew spiritually, new members were added, and the church prospered financially. Due to crowded conditions in the sanctuary and in the classrooms the church decided to erect two new buildings. One was to be a new brick sanctuary and the other was to be a frame educational building. Walter J. Coulter donated the downtown property at the corner of West 30th Street and Parker. Mr. and Mrs. J. L. Edge donated the money for the construction of the new sanctuary. The new facilities were completed and dedicated in 1940. At the dedication service Walter J. Coulter spoke of the high regard with which the church was held in Bryan.

The Bryan Free Will Baptist Church served as host for a number of various denominational gatherings including local, district, state, regional, and national meetings. The National Association of Free Will Baptists met at the church July 11-14, 1939, for its third session. In 1950 the church hosted the National Sunday School Association.

From the church a whole host of young people went out to serve the Lord in many capacities. Herbert Richards was ordained from the church in 1948; Jesse Hensarling grew up in the church, went into the ministry, but left the denomination; Bill Jones was ordained at the church,

---

[229] *The Morning Star*, January 28, 1909, page 13.
[230] Information in this paragraph came from "The History Corner" by Mary Wisehart and Robert Picirilli in *Contact Magazine*. The photocopy page I have is not dated.

served for many years as a missionary in Ivory Coast, Africa, served as president of Hillsdale Free Will Baptist College, and numerous other ministries; John E. Moehlman was ordained at the church, married Barbara Willey, daughter of "Mom" and "Pop" Willey, served as a foreign missionary, and now lives in Bryan; Gaston Clary was ordained at the church and pastored for many years in Texas; and Bobby Joe Davis, who has pastored for most of his life in Texas. Jim Jones, brother of Bill Jones, also grew up in the church and for several years edited *Contact,* the official magazine of the denomination. Jane Jones, sister to Bill and Jim, graduated from Free Will Baptist Bible College, as did her two brothers, married a young man from North Carolina and moved there. There were numerous others. Wesley Calvery served as assistant pastor and educational director for the church while awaiting his visa from Japan.

Two other Free Will Baptist churches came out of the Bryan church. The Fellowship Free Will Baptist Church was organized on March 24, 1955, by a group of twenty-four members from the First Free Will Baptist Church, who went out with the blessings of the First Church to expand the cause of Christ in the city of Bryan, particularly in the eastern part of the city. The Fellowship Church has also done well and has an excellent facility at 1228 West Villa Marie Road. The United Free Will Baptist Church, with a nice property at 2177 N. Earl Rudder Freeway, also has its roots in the First Free Will Baptist Church. The church is now called the New Beginnings Free Will Baptist Church. (This property has been sold and the church is currently meeting in a new location.)

The First Free Will Baptist Church of Bryan had a long and fruitful ministry which extended to the entire denomination and the world, through the young men and women who went out from the church, and were supported by the church.

While Dennis Henderson was pastoring the church, the church, in its endeavor to purchase new property and relocate, was seeking to raise the necessary funds for the project. Members of the congregation contributed large sums of money to an investment firm which turned out to be a bogus firm, operating a scam. The invested money was lost. Consequently, the First Free Will Baptist Church of Bryan, Texas, one of the most prominent Free Will Baptist churches in the country, closed. Many of the members moved their membership to the Fellowship Free Will Baptist Church. The old church site on the corner of W. 30th Street and Parker is now the location of a large Roman Catholic Church.

First Free Will Baptist Church, Duncanville

The following comes from a hand written account of the First Free Will Baptist Church of Dallas, written by H. Z. Cox on October 10, 1967.[231]

> First Free Will Baptist Church of Dallas, Texas, was organized the first Sunday in December, 1940 by Rev. M. L. Sutton, Rev. A. F. Ferguson, and Rev. W. B. Riley, with 9 charter members. Mrs. F. E. Walling, Sr., being the only one of these members remaining on the day of organization. Rev. W. B. Riley was called as pastor. The church was organized at 400 W. Commerce, Dallas, in a small

---

[231] I have purposely left the wording and punctuation as in the original.

20 X 30 building, which was rented for $10.00 per month. The first Sunday meeting had 9 present and $3.14 offering. The pastor was paid $1.35 per week which took care of his travel by bus from Fort Worth each Sunday.

Brother Riley served as pastor until Nov. of 1941, at which time Rev. A. F. Ferguson, of Fort Worth, was called as pastor, at a salary of $3.00 per week, which was to care for his expense to come from Ft. Worth each Sunday.

First Free Will Baptist Church, Duncanville

Brother Ferguson served as pastor of the church until Nov. of 1942, at which time R. E. Connor was called as pastor, at a salary of $30.00 per month. In Feb. 1943 a special drive was put on to raise money to make a down payment on some church property which was available at 1803 Browder, Dallas, Tx. On March 1, 1944 a down payment of $1200 had been raised and the church bought property at 1803 Browder and moved to it. The pastor's salary was raised to $50.00 per mo. and April 1, 1944 found a balance of $701.15 in the church treasure. Attendance was 25 per Sunday and the offering was about $55.00 per Sunday. In October 1945 the pastor's salary was raised to $75.00 per month. There was a balance in the treasure of 799.00 at that time.

In November 1946 the pastor's salary was raised to $90 per month. The average attendance was 45 and the offering $58.00 per week. April 2, 1947 Bro. R. E. Connor resigned as pastor of the church.

July 2, 1947 Rev. Tiff Covington was called as pastor of the church. He did not accept.

October 14, 1947 Bro. H. Z. Cox was invited to preach at the church in view of a call as pastor. September 10, 1947 the church voted to call Rev. H. Z. Cox as pastor at a salary of $100 per month. At this time the attendance was about 45 per Sunday and the offering about $50 per Sunday.

April 7, 1948 the new pastor, Rev. H. Z. Cox in regular business meeting requested the church to be much in prayer about re-locating the church.

February 1952 some church property had been located at 3419 Michigan Ave. The church voted to buy the property and a $2,000.00 down payment was made on it. In July 1953 the land had been paid for and the church set about trying to get a loan to put up a new building finding money hard to come by. The pastor, Rev H. Z. Cox, made a personal note and borrowed $6,500 for the new building. Dallas Federal Loan loaned $6,500.00 and the church raised $3,500 through the sale of bricks at $1.00 each. Feb. 14, 1954 the church moved to its new location at 3419 Michigan.

In October 1956, the church seeing a need for larger quarters voted to take steps toward erecting a new auditorium. The congregation voted on and sold a $40,000.00 issue of building bonds and the new auditorium was started. By October of 1957 the new auditorium was finished and on October 6, 1957 the auditorium was occupied.

In January 1966 the church voted to build a fellowship hall on the back of the old building. This hall was completed and ready for use in late 1966 at a cost of $4,500.00.

At present the church indebtedness is $12,000.00, and finding our neighborhood taken over by the colored, we are seeking a new location for the church. We covet your prayers and financial help in this endeavor. We are sure the Lord will see us through -- after all He always has.

Rev. H. Z. Cox
10-10-1967

The pastors who have served the First Free Will Baptist Church of Duncanville to date:

W. B. Rylie, 1938 to 39	David Sutton, 1987 to 98
Allie Ferguson, 1939 to 42	Frank Gregory, 1998 to 2006
Ruel Conner, 1942 to 1947	Richard Terry, 2006 to the present
H. Z. Cox, 1947 to 1987	

From its inception in 1938 until the present the First Free Will Baptist Church of Dallas, now the First Free Will Baptist Church of Duncanville, has met in a number of locations, moving now and then to meet the demands of a growing congregation.

1. 715 Commerce, Dallas
2. 1803 Browder, Dallas
3. 3415 Michigan, Dallas
4. 1711 Reynoldston, Dallas
5. Temporary Facility, S. I-35
6. 1415 W. Wheatland, Duncanville

For many years the First Free Will Baptist Church of Duncanville has served as the flagship church of the West Fork District Association. It has been the leading church in giving to outside causes and has supplied many volunteers for the various ministries of the West Fork, especially the West Fork Youth Camp.

First Free Will Baptist Church, Carthage

The First Free Will Baptist Church of Carthage, Texas, was organized on November 11, 1956. J. M. Goode was the founding pastor. Charter members of the church were J. M. Goode, Ethel Carmichael Goode, Barbara Goode, Shirley Goode, Mrs. Marshall, Marvin Wright and his mother Mrs. Wright, Myrtle Evans, and Elbert and Pauline Nations. Mother Mrs. Wright, Myrtle Evans, and Elbert and Pauline Nations.

*First
Free Will Baptist Church
Carthage*

First Free Will Baptist Church, Kermit

The First Free Will Baptist Church of Kermit,[232] Texas, had its beginning in 1954 when Nolan Roberts came to Kermit and looked up Ernie and Virginia Fielding whom he knew to be Free Will Baptists. Ernie Fielding was the brother of Elvis Fielding. The small group initially met for worship at the old Texan Theater for about a year. A congregation was gathered and they soon purchased a property from the Kermit Chamber of Commerce, The Hut, which was a small fast food place, located at 1019 West Campbell. The church group paid $350.00 for

First Free Will Baptist Church, Kermit

it. In 1957 the church building was built around The Hut. When the church's outside structure was nearing completion, The Hut was torn down, and the inner part of the church completed. The charter members of the church were Ernie and Virginia Fielding, Mr. and Mrs. David Allen, Mr. and Mrs. Elmer Westfall, Talmadge S. Minton, and Mr. and Mrs. W. M. Kiser. The first pastor was Nolan Roberts. Other men who have pastored the church are: Lonnie Hall, Homer Tumbleson (1964 & 1978), Dean Thompson (1966), James Reddick, George Hyatt, John Kruger (1980), Max Morris (15 years), and Charles Jones (10 years).

The Kermit Church was for many years a member of the Midessa District Association of Free Will Baptists. When all of the other churches in the Midessa Association died, the Kermit Church, being isolated as it was, did not belong to any association, simply because it was not close enough to any association, even by West Texas standards. People have sometimes remarked that Kermit lies just before the edge of the world. Currently the church is a member of the West Texas District Association of Free Will Baptists, associated with the Faith Free Will Baptist Church in

---

[232] Information on the Kermit Church was supplied by Betty Edwards, a longtime member of the church.

Lubbock and the Canyon Country Free Will Baptist Church in Canyon, Texas. Mainstays of the church include Ken and Betty Edwards. Ken is a deacon and sometimes has to fill the pulpit. Currently the church has no pastor.

Kermit is a quiet old field town, surrounded by pump jacks and oil tank batteries. Just to the east of town are thousands of acres of sand dunes. East of the dunes is the Caprock, then what used to be the town of No Trees. About forty-five miles east of Kermit lies the city of Odessa. If you drive west from Kermit, and drive long enough, you will come to Wink and Mentone. Mentone is in Loving County, with a population of 19 according to the 2010 census. Loving County is known for having no water system (water is hauled in). Nor does it have a bank, doctor, hospital, newspaper, lawyer, civic club, or cemetery. Loving County is the most sparsely populated county in the United States, with a population in 2012 of 71.

First Free Will Baptist Church, Midland

There is little information about the First Free Will Baptist Church in Midland. At first it was simply called Free Will Baptist Church, and it was located on Mineola Street in Midland. Burton Hughes was the pastor in 1952. After Brother Hughes left the church was pastored by Jake Armstrong. Everett Hellard was pastor when the church closed.

First Free Will Baptist Church, Nacogdoches

First Free Will Baptist Church, Nacogdoches

The First Free Will Baptist Church of Nacogdoches, Texas, had its beginning on the third Sunday of June, 1980, when a group of about thirty people decided to start a Free Will Baptist church in the area of Nacogdoches. The group started meeting at the home of Larry Nations and continued meeting there for four Sundays. Then about the fourth Sunday of July they moved to a rent house belonging to Junior Lunsford. The congregation met in the rent house until it became too small to accommodate the people. The group then rented a large church on Highway 21 at a cost of $180.00 per month. Services continued there for about three months, until they decided the rent money would be better spent on the construction of their own church building. The Hollis Springs Community Church invited the group to conduct their services in their church facility until the new church building could be finished. The congregation moved into the new church home on May 17, 1981. The church was formally organized in 1980 with the following charter members:

Lillie Key	James Kee	Betty Lunsford
Winnie Lunsford	Virgie Margon	Tammy Lunsford
Keith Hutto	Kevin Hutto	Kim Hutto
Taylor Lunsford	Gladys Lunsford	Brandi Butler

Sharon Housley	Tammie Housley	Jeannie Pinson
J. M. Bales	Elmer Boatman	Mary Lou Boatman
Rhonda Chatman	Danyell Lunsford	Charles Lunsford
Bill Housley		

James Kee was ordained to the gospel ministry on August 23, 1987. His ordination certificate was signed by H. Ray Berry, Deacon Elmer Boatman, and church clerk, Gladys Lunsford.

H. Ray Berry served the church several years as pastor. On October 18, 1986, he submitted his resignation, which included his wife Asa, in writing as follows:

Dear Brethren:

The first Sunday in November will mark the 5th anniversary of our coming to the church as pastor. During this time we have been blessed with your fellowship and love. There have been times of joy and times of heavy-heartedness, but our Lord has been most gracious. However, we have not seen the church grow as we had hoped, but God is still on the throne. There is hope yet.

October 31st will mark the completion of 54 years in the service of our Lord as an ordained minister. He has blessed beyond words for us to express as we have served wherever He has called. Souls have been saved along the way, not as many as we would have liked to have seen, but His name be praised for those who were saved and are serving Him in daily living.

Now we see the day drawing to a close for us in the pastorate and time to make way for fresh leadership in the field that is white unto harvest. Therefore, we are retiring from the pastorate of the church as of the beginning of the year 1987. If however, you can obtain the services of a pastor before that time it will be satisfactory with us.

May the lovely Lord continue to bless in the life of the church, bringing many into the fold of God before it is too late.

Thank each one of you for the love and support you have given to us. May God bless you bountifully.

Yours for Christ,

H. Ray and Asa H. Berry

The First Free Will Baptist Church of Nacogdoches, Texas, closed in the spring of 2014. The church property was donated to the Texas State Home Missions Board by Lillie Key, who at the last attended the otherwise empty church alone.[233]

---

[233] Information about the First Free Will Baptist Church in Nacogdoches was supplied by Lillie Key.

First Free Will Baptist Church, Odessa

The First Free Will Baptist Church of Odessa,[234] Texas, had its beginning with the ministry of Eldon "Ed" A. Hobbs (1918-2010), who had been ordained at Mounds, Oklahoma. After holding a revival meeting in the Midland church he saw the need for a Free Will Baptist Church in Odessa. The church was started at 1600 South Grant Street, in the garage of the Red Montgomery Trucking Company, owned by Ed's brother-in-law, Red Montgomery. Both Ed and his brother, Jess Hobbs, worked there, too. Trucking took place six days a week.

First Free Will Baptist Church, Odessa

On Saturday evenings the trucks were removed from the garage, except for the ones broken down and couldn't be moved. The ladies would sweep the place out, mop the floor, hose it down, and set the benches, piano, and pulpit in place. During services the mechanical tools were in place and perhaps a broken down truck or two were on one side of the garage. At times Red and his wife Dolly could not make the payroll to pay their help. They prayed about it and promised the Lord that if He would help them make the payroll they would provide a curtain to separate the trucks and parts from the church. They made the payroll and purchased a black curtain with huge red roses on it, the only thing they could afford. No one seemed to notice that it was a garage converted into a church on weekends. The building was heated by a homemade stove made out of stove pipes which kept it warm enough.

The church was organized on February 3, 1952. J. A. C. Hughes was elected chairman of the organizing council. Other members were: Brother Rogers, Brother Savage, Brother McDaniel, and Brother Burton Hughes. An invitation was given for those wishing a home in the church. Fourteen people came forward. The organizational rules were read by Brother Rogers and the Church Covenant was read by Brother Medart. Brother Ed Hobbs led the prayer of consecration. The hand of fellowship was given the members of the new church. Bernice Huckeba was elected as church clerk, Dorothy Hobbs as treasurer, and Ed Hobbs as pastor. Four men, Vester Burton, Ray Wood, son of Vard Wood of Oklahoma, W. A. Lansford, and James Qualls, were appointed to serve as deacons. The charter members of the church were: E. M. Montgomery, Dolly Montgomery, Vera Mae Montgomery, Vester Burton, Sarah Burton, W. A. Lunsford, Lottie Lunsford, Joan Lunsford, Ray Wood, Beverly Wood, Ed Hobbs, Dorothy Hobbs, Bernice Huckeba, James Qualls, W. G. Smart, and Marie Smart. Brother and Sister Smart joined one week later but were counted as charter members because the charter membership was left open for thirty days. Pastor Hobbs was paid a salary of $25.00 per month. Once a child locked himself in the restroom. Some of the men took the hinges off of the restroom door while Brother Hobbs kept on

---

[234] Most of the information about the First Free Will Baptist Church of Odessa came from the obituary of the first pastor, Ed Hobbs, and from a booklet written by me in 1980 for the 28th anniversary of the church.

preaching. Many, if not most, of the early families in the church had roots in Oklahoma and had come to West Texas to work in the oil industry.

By June, 1952, the church was well on its way and on June 15, 1952, it joined the Northwest Brazos District Association, the Midessa District Association not yet having been organized. That year land was purchased at 7th and Vine, 2203 W. Seventh Street. Building materials were hauled out of New Mexico on a truck furnished with drivers paid for by Jess Hobbs and Red Montgomery. Friends and members of the church helped build the church building, working in the evenings. The church building was finished in 1954 and the church bought a parsonage. Brother Hobbs resigned as pastor in April 1954, but agreed to stay on until a suitable pastor could be found.

On June 2, 1954, James Minor was elected as the new pastor. During his ministry the old parsonage was sold and a new one obtained and moved to the lot next to the church. A baptistry was purchased and installed in the church.

The next pastor was Ed Wilson, who served from August 1, 1955, to 1956. Bailey Thompson served the church as pastor from May 2, 1956, until 1959. Roy Hearron served as pastor from 1959 to July 14, 1963. During his tenure additions were added to the church building and parsonage, and pews were installed in the church. Gene Jackson served the church as pastor from December 1963, to 1964. During this time the educational rooms and kitchen were built.

Kenneth Brandon came to serve the church as pastor on June 21, 1964. He remained until September 3, 1967. During this time the steeple, which was a memorial to Scott Ogle, was installed on the church. Earl Judd served as pastor from October 11, 1967, to November 15, 1970. Brother Judd and Loyd Stout put paneling in the church sanctuary. Boyd Phillips was ordained a deacon and Jerry and Barbara Hamman began attending during this time.

Lionel Cooksey served as pastor from January 3, 1971 until November, 1973. Brother Cooksey established a short lived Sunday school mission on East 13th Street and was instrumental in getting the Lubbock Church started. Brother Cooksey resigned and moved to Abilene to help start a mission church there.

Thurmon Murphy arrived and began as pastor on November 17, 1973. A nice new parsonage at 2513 Cambridge had been purchased and was ready for the Murphys when they arrived from White Settlement, Texas. Soon the indebtedness on the church and old parsonage was paid off. The church had four very good deacons at the time: Weldon Houston, father of missionary Deleen Cousineau; Ray Wood, son of the late Oklahoma pastor, Vard Wood; Glen Wood, brother of Lynn Wood of Oklahoma, and Boyd Phillips. A Hammond organ was purchased, which proved to be a wonderful addition to the worship services. During his tenure annual youth retreats became a regular part of the ministry for the young people. Youth groups were taken to Fort Davis, Big Bend National Park, and the Lazy Hills Guest Ranch in Ingram for fun, recreation, and spiritual training. Billy Brown, a student at Free Will Baptist Bible College served as a summer intern in 1976. The church had a number of television programs broadcast all over the Permian Basin on Sunday mornings, courtesy of the CBS affiliate station in Odessa. Bob Shockey, Roy Thomas, Joseph Ange, Dr. Stanley Outlaw, and Tom Malone preached revival meetings during these years. Murphy served the church as pastor longer than any of the Odessa pastors. He left on September 24, 1978, to become Minister of Education at his home church in Dayton, Ohio. He says that leaving the church in Odessa was the single greatest mistake of his ministry.

The church had money with which to pay a pastor a good salary. They announced far and wide that they were looking for a good pastor. Many telephone calls were made inviting preachers to come try out for the church, or simply asking denominational leaders to recommend someone.

No one responded. It was difficult to get preachers to consider moving to isolated West Texas. After three months of searching for a pastor, the church called Rev. Dennis Haygood, former pastor of the Westside Free Will Baptist Church in Midland, who had joined the church some months earlier. Dennis became pastor on December 10, 1978. Mark Riggs, a student at Free Will Baptist Bible College, came and served as a summer intern in 1979. During 1979 the church had twenty-nine conversions and received twenty-six new members. The high attendance for the year was 97 in April and 95 in October. The highlight of 1980 was the church's 28th anniversary service, which was held March 9th. Former pastors Earl Judd and Lionel Cooksey returned to take part in the service. There were 133 people in attendance. Rev. Keith Woody preached in the morning service and there were seven decisions made. In June, 1981, Mervin and Daphne Pugh, along with their daughter Hilary, came to help the church in the education and youth departments. On November 7, 1981, the old parsonage, next to the church, being used as the children's Sunday school department, was destroyed by fire, leaving the church severely cramped for Sunday school space. During pastor Haygood's ministry several men came and preached revival meetings: James Pauley, E. A. Riggs, Keith Woody, Paul Ketteman, and Ron Ivey.

After Dennis Haygood resigned as pastor and returned to his home state of Alabama, the church called Lynn Beck as pastor. By the time pastor Beck left in 1987 the church attendance was very low. The church called Troy Burney from Missouri and he served the church from 1988 to 1989. After Brother Burney left the church was not able to find a pastor and the three remaining families voted to close the church. The Hammond organ was given to the First Free Will Baptist Church in Pampa, Texas, along with a considerable amount of funds. The pews were donated to the First Free Will Baptist Church of Kermit, and the remaining funds were given to the missionary account of Mike and Deleen Cousineau. Deleen had grown up in the church, the daughter of Weldon and Sissie Huston. Weldon was a deacon and the church's song leader.

First Free Will Baptist Church, Pampa

The First Free Will Baptist Church of Pampa, Texas, began when L. C. (Lester) Lynch and his family were transferred from Taft, California, where Lester and his wife Letty had been active in organizing and pastoring churches. The Lynch family arrived in the Texas Panhandle town, fifty-five miles northeast of Amarillo, on September 4, 1959. There was no Free Will Baptist church in the area and they began praying that God would lead them to people who were interested in getting one started. They ran some ads in the *Pampa Daily News* advertising their intentions and asking if there were any Free Will Baptists in town and if there were any people interested in starting a church. The J. E. Forbes family called, stating that they were Free Will Baptists from Oklahoma and that they were interested in starting a church. They began visiting and working and found that there were others, acquaintances of the Forbes, that would help.

First Free Will Baptist Church, Pampa, Texas

They were able to identify Brother and Sister Harless, Louie and Imogene Parham, Sister Chaudion and her mother, and the Haskel Medley family as potential church members.

Lester and Letty Lynch

On September 16, 1959, the third Wednesday night, a prayer meeting was held in the Lynch home, with twelve people present. There was an inspiring testimony service, after which Brother Lynch preached. The group prayed about the beginning of a new church and it became evident to them that their prayers were being answered. On the following Sunday, September 20, 1959, services were held in the Harless home, on U. S. Highway 60 seven miles southwest of Pampa. Prayer meetings continued on Wednesday nights. Soon a building was rented on South Barnes, very small but suitable for the time being. The group located four lots of land on North Rider Street and donations began to come in toward the purchase of the property. When enough money was raised the four lots were purchased. Next, they had to tackle the issue of a building. They discovered that the Humble Oil Company had a recreation building for sale, by bid, to be moved to another location. The church people met and agreed on the amount of a bid, which was submitted to Humble Oil. It was some time before the bids were opened.

In the meanwhile, the church people continued progress toward organizing as a church. On November 8, 1959, the people assembled under the leadership of Lynch and proceeded to organize a Sunday school and elect teachers and officers. Sunday school and church services continued for three months and the body voted to call the Texas State Home Missions Board to organize them into a Free Will Baptist church. In answer to this call Tiff Covington, chairman of the Home Missions Board, and Bud Parr, came and met with the body on February 10, 1960 to formally organize the group into a church. The service was opened by Brother Lynch, "Amazing Grace" was sung, prayer was offered by Brother Forbes, and a sermon delivered by Parr. He preached a timely message on "Church Duties and Growth," using Ephesians 6:11-17 as his text. After the sermon Brother Lynch called Tiff Covington to organize the church. Brother Tiff gave a brief talk on Free Will Baptist doctrine and gave instructions to the body. Twenty-four people, nine men, eleven women, and four young people under nineteen years of age, presented themselves for membership. A call was given for ordained ministers and deacons to come forward and three people came to the front: L. C. Lynch, H. M. Medley, and H. E. Forbes. The Bible was presented as the only rule of faith and practice, and the church covenant was read and adopted. A prayer of consecration was offered, and all applicants for membership were called to the altar for this prayer. Brother Tiff then offered the hand of fellowship. Then he announced that nominations for church officers were in order. L. C. Lynch was elected as pastor. Covington then turned the service over to Brother Lynch for the election of other officers. Rachel Forbes was elected church clerk, Imogene Parham as treasurer, and H. M. Medley and H. E. Forbes as deacons. A call for a song and handshake was given and brother Lynch later reported that "a wonderful time was enjoyed by all." The organizational service was dismissed by Ted Skaggs. The charter members of the church were:

L. C. Lynch	Letty Lynch	Lester Lynch
Ronald Lynch	Peggy Lynch	Betty Carter
J. E. Forbes	Rachel Forbes	Dorothy Forbes

Willie Harless	Alma Harless	Louie Parham
Imogene Parham	Haskel Medley	Essie May Medley
Edd Leon Neely	Regina Neely	Ted Skaggs
Delphia Skaggs	Sister L. E. Pool	Amy Chaudion
Ocie Smith	Jessie Smith	Thomas Green

Finally, the church people were notified that they had won the bid on the building, as it was a cash bid. Pastor Lynch and his two deacons had made previous arrangements with the Citizens Bank for a loan to cover the bid and to move the building to the recently purchased lots. The foundation was run and the building was moved to the church property in February of 1961. The group began to modify the former recreation building into a church building. All work on the church was donated and soon it was evident that a Free Will Baptist church had come to Pampa.

L. C. Lynch continued to pastor the church through 1992, thirty-three years. Willard Kiper pastored for a few months, June of 1993 through May of 1994. Thomas Smith pastored from April, 1999 through May of 2002. Missionary Ernie Deeds came and preached during this time. The church was pastored by Raymond Stowers from August 2004 through March of 2005. The church has often gone without a pastor, as it is currently. The church never had a full-time pastor except for Willard Kiper who was full-time for only six months.

Initially the church joined the Northwest Brazos District Association, in which they were members from November of 1961 through February of 1971. In 1972 they formed the Texas High Plains Association, which dissolved in February of 1973. Then they joined the Union Association of Oklahoma because it was closer to travel to the quarterly meetings. They continued their membership in the Union Association for many years. When the Union Association changed their meetings to Sunday the Pampa church could no longer attend because of elderly people in the church. When the West Texas District Association was formed the Pampa church joined. The church did not have a pastor and the new association wanted to take it under its wings. Pastor Jeff Cates, from Canyon, Texas, south of Amarillo, went up to Pampa to preach for them several times. Newly licensed John Crabtree, also from Canyon, preached for them some.

The church is now located at 731 Sloan Street, which was formerly a Mormon church. At one time the church had an attendance of from sixty-five to seventy. At the present they have five faithful people. Mrs. Melba Lynch says, "We are going to continue as long as we can hold on."[235]

---

[235] Information about the Pampa Church came from a brief history of the church written in 1990 by Pastor Lynch for the church's 30th anniversary celebration, and from a letter from and personal conversation with Mrs. Melba Lynch, daughter-in-law of Pastor L. C. Lynch.

First Free Will Baptist Church, Weatherford

First Free Will Baptist Church, Weatherford

The First Free Will Baptist Church of Weatherford is one of the most historic Free Will Baptist churches in the state of Texas. Founded sometime around 1900 the first pastor was Tommie Newsom.[236] Both the town and the church were important to Free Will Baptists in the early 1900's. The Southwestern Convention met in Weatherford in 1910, although they met in the Free Will Baptist "tabernacle," a large tent which seated about three hundred people. The *New Morning Star* was published there edited by S. L. Morris, before it was moved to Tecumseh, Oklahoma in 1917. Regional Sunday School training institutes were held at the church occasionally for the purpose of training Sunday school leaders and teachers, as well as Free Will Baptist League workers.

A list of pastors supplied by deacon Morris Brandon, grandson of two of the pastors of the church, James and Verda Walker, is as follows: Tommie Newsom, James M. Walker, John A. Brooks, Verda Walker, E. J. Vaughn, J. Henry Measures, Allie Ferguson, James M. Walker, John A. Brooks, Verda Walker, E. J. Vaughn, J. Henry Measures, Allie Ferguson, Clarence Hearron, Jake Estes, Jack Corrinder, Sonny O'dell, Alvy Hudson, Alton (Blackie) Kirkland, J. C. Alexander, Jack Bankhead, Owen L. Barger, Billy J. Aulds, Bob Brown, Bill Bacon, Jarvis Reed, Dennis Kiser, Cory Thompson, Jay Andrews, Mark Stanzyk (interim), Josh Provow, and Eric Halleran. Attendance at the church seems to have been at its greatest under the ministries of Allie Ferguson and Jack Bankhead.

In about 2015, under the leadership of Eric Halleran, the church changed its name to Victorious Messiah Fellowship and left the Free Will Baptist denomination.

First Free Will Baptist Church, Wichita Falls

The First Free Will Baptist Church of Wichita Falls was organized on November 15, 1951.[237] John A. Brooks was the founding pastor and he had the families of several of his daughters and one son, John Jr., in the church to help form the nucleus of the new congregation. The initial location of the church was near downtown but they eventually moved to the corner of Arthur and Arizona Streets, two streets which ended where they intersected. Even though the church was located only two blocks off busy Kemp Boulevard, it was a difficult location to reach, one having to go around his elbow to get to his thumb, so to speak.

---

[236] The spelling of the first name as Tommie may lead you to incorrectly assume he was a woman. The last name is often spelled Newsome, but Newsom seems to be correct.
[237] 1952 West Fork Minutes, page 16

Most of the history of the church during its early years was lost when the clerk threw away the first book of minutes when the book of minutes was full. There were several pastors over the years, including founder John Brooks, Tiff Covington, Tom Sunday, Dean Burpo, Earl Scroggins, and Thurmon Murphy. In 1972 the church was running around one hundred twenty-five while Earl

First Free Will Baptist Church, Wichita Falls

Scroggins was the pastor. On April 10, 1979, eleven families in the church lost all they had to a category five tornado that swept across town. Later that year, or in early 1980, the church had a bitter split from which it never recovered. When Thurmon Murphy began pastoring there in March of 1980 there were nineteen people present for the first service, though they soon reached a high attendance of 98. The oil field practically died in 1984 taking a heavy toll on the church as nine members lost their jobs. Momentum was pretty much lost as a result of all that. Members moved away or died off and they were not able to replace them, though many different things were tried. As a result the church eventually closed. The property was sold and the proceeds given to the Texas State Mission Board. There were a number of things in the church which marked them as an unusual church. One of them was that they had two women deacons: Pamela Thompson and Marilyn Morgan.

Good Hope Free Will Baptist Church

The Good Hope Free Will Baptist Church was organized in 1875 and was located on the Laneville Highway out of Henderson. In 1916 land was donated to the church on FM 840 and the church was moved to its present location. The church records were kept in the home of the church clerk and her home burned in the early 1950's, resulting in the loss of all of the church's early records. Being one of the very earliest Free Will Baptist churches established in Texas, the Good Hope Church did not practice feet washing until well into the Twentieth Century. Pastor Allie Ferguson introduced them to it and was the first pastor to get them to begin practicing it.[238]

Good Hope Free Will Baptist Church, Henderson

---

[238] This information comes from the unpublished autobiography of Allie Ferguson.

Mount Union Free Will Baptist Church

The Mount Union Free Will Baptist Church is one of the oldest Free Will Baptist churches in Texas. It was founded by James Pierce Lunsford in 1887 under the name Old Prospect. The church was located in Rusk County, about seven miles west of Garrison, just a few miles off FM 1087 (Camp Tonkawa Road). The name was later changed to Mount Union when it began meeting in the Mount Union school house. Mount Union moved to a larger building in the 1930's. One of the members of the church purchased the land and building for Mt. Union.

*Mount Union Free Will Baptist Church
Garrison*

In 1954 the church building was moved a few miles away to its present location at 7509 Camp Tonkawa Road (FM 1087). The building was enlarged and remodeled. Later another remodeling program resulted in the addition of new Sunday school rooms, a fellowship hall, and a new, larger sanctuary. The church was a member of the Texas Association of Free Will Baptists, which later became the East Texas District Association of Free Will Baptists.

The attendance of the church ranged from twenty-five to fifty-three in the early years. However, in the 1990's, attendance was around one hundred thirty. In the early days church was held monthly, which was quite normal for the time. The church met on Saturday night and Sunday morning, before the first Sunday of the month. In 1951 services were held twice a month, on the first and third weekends. In 1952 the church began having services each Sunday. Pastors were bi-vocational; the church has never had a full-time pastor. Other pastors who have served the church include:

T. L. Porter	Ira Harper	B. A. Grant
U. J. Vaughn	L. K. Brashier	Chester Sachtleben
Leroy Anderson, Sr.	Leroy Anderson, Jr.	Larry Monday
John Voss	F. B. "Buddy" Welch	L. M. Parton
Gaston Clary	Burl Ferguson	Larry Dunning
Donald Jackson	Paul Jett	Loyce Plunkett
Bro. Williams		

New Salem Free Will Baptist Church, Decatur

The New Salem Free Will Baptist Church, just south of Decatur, in Wise County, Texas, is one of the oldest Free Will Baptist churches in the state of Texas.[239] It was organized on April 22, 1893. The founding pastor was Josephus Wesley Ford. At some point between 1888 and 1893, Josephus Wesley Ford had brought his family from Jane, McDonald County, Missouri, to Wise County, Texas. It was in the old Perrin school house, located about 1.1 miles north of the present location, that Brother Ford organized the New Salem Free Will Baptist Church.

New Salem Free Will Baptist Church, Decatur

Brother Ford was forty-five years old at the time. There were a number of relatives and others who came from Free Will Baptist churches in Missouri and became part of New Salem. The nine founding members were: Josephus Wesley Ford and wife, James Alexander Ford and wife, Richard S. Ford and wife, Jessie Garrison and wife, and Sister Jessie L. Phillips. Three individuals, members of the Arnett Family, who previously lived in Jane, would become members by letter from the Sulphur Springs Free Will Baptist Church of McDonald County. Other families from McDonald County who had one or more family members to become members of the church included: Cleveland, Davenport, Goff, Horner, Walker, and Young. James Alexander Ford and Jessie Garrison served as the first deacons. Richard S. Ford was the first clerk. A church roll dated September 1, 1906, listed thirty-eight male members and forty-three female members. Twenty-five of those members were related to the founding minister, Josephus Wesley Ford. Records indicate that members of the Ford family have held membership in the church since its organization.

In the early years the church met only once per month, beginning with a business session at 2:00 p.m. on Saturday before the second Sunday of each month and concluding on Sunday. This was fairly common practice for the day. Finances must have been a major problem in those early years of the church. Minutes of a business meeting held in 1899 record a resolution passed by the church which required each male member to pay 15¢ into the treasury during the quarter.

The government of the church was very strict at the time. An undated hand written document, titled "Local Government of New Salem Church of Freewill Baptist," lists the following eleven resolutions, written here with original spelling and grammatical errors:

> Resolved 1st, that we will watch our oneself both in word and in action so that the cause of Christ be not Reproached on our account
> Resolved 2nd that we will watch over each other in the Spirit of true charity always being careful of each other's moral and Christian character and usefulness
> Resolved 3rd, That we will report ourselves in person at each covenant meeting on Saturday unless we can render a providential excuse for our absence.

---

[239] Most of the information about New Salem was furnished by Ronald Womack, a deacon in the church for many years.

Resolved 4th, That we will strive to maintain true Pity in our own hearts and recommend the religion of our lord and Savior Jesus Christ to others not only by word, But by an exemplary life and corresponding practice

Resolved 5th, That we will hold up the Doctrine of Church before world as the true Doctrine of the Bible as taught and Practiced by Jesus Christ and the apostles

Resolved 6th, That we will look after the wants and necessities of the poor and needy widows and orphans and especially those of our own church

Resolved 7th, That we will patronize our own publishing houses and Support our own denominational papers and literature in preference to all others

Resolved 8th, That we will contribute to the Support of the gospel ministry to the best of our ability according as God may prosper us

Resolved 9th, That we will give heed to any respectable rumor regarding any member walking disorderly and will accept the evidence even of an outside person who has always been accounted good for true and veracity

Resolved 10, That any male member, absenting himself for 3 consecutive covenant meetings shall be waited upon by a committee and the cause reported at the next regular meeting

Resolved 11, That it is the sense of this church, not holding pastor to Serve more than 2 years in Succession

One young minister preached his first sermon at New Salem during a quarterly meeting in 1928 and was hired by the deacons as the pastor that afternoon. He served until 1946. Obviously the two year limitation on pastors was not in effect or the church did not adhere to it. The name of that young preacher was Tiff Covington.

The church joined the West Fork District Association, which had been formed in 1891, and hosted the eighth annual session of the association in 1898.

One of the former deacons, George Burns, was a member of the "Lost Batallion" during World War II. During his captivity in Burma, he helped build the railroad that led to the bridge over the river Kwai, made famous partially by the movie "Bridge Over the River Kwai," starring William Holden.

Services were held at the place of organization until about 1907. At that time a new church was built, almost directly across the road from the present location. However, that new structure was used for only a few years before it was condemned as being unsafe by the Wise County Commissioners Court. The problem was that the roof was too heavy, resulting in the walls bulging out, according to W. D. Phillips, who was a member of the church for about seventy-five years, and who served the church as a deacon for many years. The Perrin school had moved to the present location of the church, built the building, and conducted classes there for a short time. Perrin school was soon consolidated with the Decatur Independent School District, making the school building available. New Salem purchased the property and moved in. Modifications have been made over the years, but the building is still the former Perrin school house. A state historical marker was erected in front of New Salem on April 27, 2013.

Church records indicate that ten or twelve Free Will Baptist churches existed in Wise and surrounding counties during the latter part of the Nineteenth Century and early part of the Twentieth Century. All of those other Free Will Baptist churches have closed, though some new ones have been started.

Josephus W. Ford worked closely with his brother, James A. Ford, and James' son, R. S. Ford, who married Josephus' daughter Menecy. They would have been first cousins. In family papers given to Bob Ford of Montgomery, Alabama, by his grandmother, Menecy, there were church records and a journal which are now in the Wise County Museum in Decatur, Texas.

North Zulch Free Will Baptist Church

The North Zulch Free Will Baptist Church[240] was organized in August, 1907, on the front porch of the George W. McGill home. There were seven people present: George and Emma Lou McGill, Tom and Sarah Keefer, Plummer and Lizzie Taylor, and Tom Searcy. The November 21, 1907 Morning Star indicates that J. J. Tatum also assisted with the organization of the church.[241] After the organization of the church, worship services were first held at the Houston and Texas Central Railway Depot in North Zulch, where many others united with them. They were the first followers to erect a church building in North Zulch, and the first school in North Zulch was held in that church building. On August 28, 1907, Mr. T. J. Keefer, Mr. G. W. McGill, and Mr. W. P. Taylor signed a promissory note in the amount of $925.00 from Mr. S. H. Dunlap in Bryan, Texas, to erect the first church building. The North Zulch School was held in that building beginning in 1908. In 1937, the first church building was torn down and the second building was constructed.

North Zulch Free Will Baptist Church and mobile home

In 1923 and 1924, there was a very active Christian Endeavor Group made up of young people of the church and an adult leader. The thirty-second annual session of the Texas State Association of Free Will Baptists met at the church, October 29-November 1, 1946. M. L. Sutton was the moderator, Alvin F. Halbrook was the clerk, and the introductory sermon was preached by John A. Brooks. Attendance for the meeting was very good. Some of the early church records were burned in a home fire in 1950, but one class record book later found from 1952 recorded twenty-three pupils in one of the adult classes.

Some of the ministers who served North Zulch are Tom Searcy, John Swanwick, J. L. Bounds (three times), H. Ray Berry, W. F. McDuffie, Luther Payne, E. S. Jameson, C. B. Thompson, J. B. Lovering, C. C. Wheeler, R. C. Wiggs, L. J. Foreman, Troy McDonald, E. E. Zoellers, Bert Rogers, Clyde Burney, R. N. Frye, John H. Moehlman, Riley Morrisett, Herbert Richards, J. W. Arnold, Everett Hellard, A. F. Halbrook, Phil Snell, W. E. Richards, and Kurt Hoch. Others supplying the pulpit at different times were Jimmy Jones, Ed Morris, Jessie Ellis, Fred Dollar, David Holguin, Keith Phipps, William Don Ellis, and Billy Walker. Kurt Hoch served from 1982 through 1984. After Brother Hoch left, Roger Yates, from Conroe, supplied until December, 1985. At that time the church was unable to obtain a pastor, so only Sunday school services were held until February of 1987. There were very few members attending, and

---

[240] Almost all of the information about the North Zulch Free Will Baptist Church was supplied to me by Doris McGill, church clerk.
[241] *The Morning Star*, November 21, 1907, page 12.

no pastor to preach. Therefore, members began attending other churches throughout the district. Although services were no longer held at the church, district, state, and national dues were always paid.

Several meetings were held in homes of North Zulch church members trying to find a way to get the church started again. Then, Luther Sanders agreed to serve as interim pastor for the church. On August 6, 1989, Billy Walker preached the reopening services for the church. His text was Matthew 16:18. Luther Sanders served as interim pastor until February of 1993, when he agreed to serve as full-time pastor.

Upon the reopening of the church, after no services had been held there for almost two and a half years, there was much, much work to be done. The inside of the church was cleaned and readied to use, but many renovations needed to be made. A new roof was put on the church in October of 1989. Then, in November, the building was completely scraped and repainted. In April of 1990, ceiling fans were added. During the next two and a half years renovations were put on hold, but in June of 1993 work really began! The old windows were removed and new, slimmer windows were installed, along with aluminum siding. In July, new front doors were added and workers began installing paneling. In August, air conditioning and heating units were installed. In September, the inside of the building was completely repainted, and in October new carpeting and vinyl floors were installed. The cloth banner Scripture verse that had always hung over the baptistry was reprinted on vinyl and put back in place. New hymnals were purchased. The old pictures were re-matted and framed and hung in the vestibule. The antique furniture was cleaned, restained, and varnished. The pulpit chairs were recovered, and the altars and communion table updated. A new piano was purchased from the United Free Will Baptist Church in Bryan, and was tuned and leveled. A new public address system was installed, along with American and Christian flags. Indoor/outdoor carpet was installed on the front porch and steps. Cushions were also installed on the pews, making them a lot more comfortable.

A portable building was purchased and installed to serve as a nursery. A member donated an organ to the church, and a lighted steeple was installed on the roof. Sidewalks were poured around the church, and shrubs were planted. The outdoor lighted sign was completed in April of 1993 and a flower bed was arranged around the sign. A new concrete handicapped ramp and railing were completed in 2004. There were days that were very, very tiring, but they were uplifting. All of this work brought the North Zulch church closer together and made them stronger Christians. Sometimes it seemed as if no funds were available, but the church was reminded that if they were faithful, kept working and praying, God would supply. He did just that, not just a little, but abundantly, time after time.

During the time Brother Luther Sanders was pastoring the church, he would realize the church needed additional items. He would check with the church treasurer about the finances, and if funds were not available in the treasury, he would contact his dear friends in Raleigh, North Carolina, Rufus and Joan Moore. In a week or two there would come a check for the amount of the needed item, or most of the time, more. From 1993 through 2006, Mr. and Mrs. Moore donated more than $45,860.00 to the church.

Brother Sanders retired in June of 1997 and the church called Danny Davis as the pastor. He served from July, 1997, through December, 2000. Brother Sanders continued attending the church. In July, 2001, Heath Norris was called as pastor and served in that capacity until January 31, 2004. Warner Collier is the current pastor.

Church clerk Doris McGill says, "Through these one hundred years of our church's history, there have been good times and sometimes a feeling of bad times. On the mountain top and down in the low valley, God has always helped us through these times and, with His help, we will continue to serve Him in this place for many years to come." Doris' husband, James L, McGill, was the son of one of the church's founding families, George W. and Emma Lou (Baines) McGill. Some of George's and Emma Lou's descendants, including their great great grandchild, still attend the church.

Pleasant Mound Free Will Baptist Church

*Pleasant Mound Free Will Baptist Church, Buffalo Springs
"The Rock Church"*

In the year 1911, Elder W. E. Dearmore of Bowie preached a series of messages near the Pleasant Valley School House, south of Buffalo Springs, in the south end of Clay County.[242] The meeting was conducted under a brush arbor, as many such meetings were in those days. Dearmore set forth the Bible doctrines held by Free Will Baptists. Though feet washing wasn't practiced by many Free Will Baptist churches in Texas at the time, Brother Dearmore espoused it, along with the possibility of falling from grace. There were several conversions during the course of the meeting. On May 1, 1914, the small congregation, meeting in the Pleasant Valley school house, was organized into a church with eight charter members. They were: Mr. and Mrs. J. C. McGowen, Mr. and Mrs. J. H. Bevers, Mr. and Mrs. C. B. Johnson, and Mr. and Mrs. J. J. Johnson. The little group struggled along, meeting when they could. Though not having anyone to preach for them for a long time, they gained a few members, among them Mrs. M. D. Sparks and Mrs. Etta Lawler. The church was called the Pleasant Valley Free Will Baptist Church. The little valley was dotted with small farms and ranches.

In 1914, J. W. Shults moved into the community. W. E. Dearmore returned and helped him conduct a revival meeting, which proved to be a revival indeed. Though there have been some low times, the fire that was kindled in the hearts of these early members has never gone completely out. During this revival which began on May 1, 1914, the Shults family united with the church. Carrye D. Shults united with the church by letter on September 6, 1914. Mr. and Mrs. M. C. Covington united with the church by statement from Buffalo Springs Baptist Church.
He was a deacon in the Baptist church and was accepted as one when he joined the Free Will Baptist church. M. C. Covington was the father of Tiff and Edith Covington.

As the new church grew, B. B. Brooks and family were added to the list of members. Brother Brooks' name remained on the church roll until his passing in 1946. The church got a much needed boost when John A. Brooks, Sr., and C. A. Shults announced their call to the ministry. J. W. Shults wrote to a minister in Oklahoma, W. M. Coggins, to help with the ordination service. He and Deacon M. C. Covington laid hands on the two young men.

In 1919, John A. Brooks was called as pastor of the church, which was worshipping in the Pleasant Valley school house. The following year, 1920, J. W. Shults was called once again to be the pastor. The pastors for the first fourteen years of the church were: J. W. Shults, 1914-19; John A. Brooks, 1919-21; J. W. Shults, 1921-24; T. H. Newsome, 1924-26; and J. C. Hodges, 1926-28. T. H. Newsome, whose name is usually spelled as Newsom, was a school teacher and

---

[242] Most of the information about the Pleasant Mound Church comes from

he never let his people forget it. J. C. Hodges served until 1928 when he resigned in favor of a young preacher by the name of Tiff Covington.

Tiff Covington served as pastor longer than any other preacher, from 1928 to 1949, and from 1967 to 1980, about thirty-four years. In 1934, in the heart of the Great Depression, under the leadership of Pastor Covington, the church decided to build a church building. In January of 1935, an offering was received and a building fund was started. The congregation decided to move the church from Pleasant Valley where it was located to a more suitable location up on a hill two miles south of Buffalo Spring. The property was donated by the Campbell family.[243] Prior to the starting of the building a revival meeting was conducted on the property under a brush arbor by Pastor Covington and his brother-in-law, John A. Brooks. There were a large number of converts and they were baptized in a nearby stock tank. An offering was taken and the construction of the building began. It was 1936. The largest contribution given was ten dollars. Because it was such a large gift, Pastor Covington acknowledged it in the services. Both men and women from the community came to help work on the building, whether they were members of the church or not. The exterior of the building was composed of field stones gathered from nearby fields and pastures. Ninety year old Lillie Belle White once put her hands on the side of the building and said to me with fond memories and deep emotion, "I helped put these stones into place." She had been the wife of Deacon Ben White.

In July the cornerstone was laid and the building was completed in September of 1936. There were no Sunday school rooms and no bell tower yet. The name of the church while it was located in Pleasant Valley was the Pleasant Valley Free Will Baptist Church. Now that it had moved upon the hill, or mount, the name became the Pleasant Mound Free Will Baptist Church. It has been fondly known throughout the area ever since simply as The Rock Church. That fall the Texas State Association of Free Will Baptists met at the church, with several denominational dignitaries from Nashville, Tennessee, in attendance.

At this time Pleasant Mound also had a branch of the church, called Liberty, which met on the Perkins property between Buffalo Springs and Vashti.

In 1939 twenty-one year old Cleo Dalton from Denison was ordained to the gospel ministry at the Pleasant Mound Free Will Baptist Church by the West Fork District Association. She made her mark in the denomination as Cleo Purcell and served from 1963 to 1985 as Executive Secretary-Treasurer of the Woman's National Auxiliary Convention. See her profile in the chapter on women preachers from Texas.

In 1946, four Sunday school rooms, a room which is now the kitchen, and a bell tower were added. The bell had previously served as the school bell at the Buffalo Springs School.

On April 23, 1949, Pastor Tiff Covington presented his letter of resignation to the congregation. On May 21, 1949, R. E. Conner was called to serve as pastor and he served until July of 1955. Many improvements were made under the leadership of Brother Conner. In 1952, the church voted to drill a water well and a pump. There was no air conditioning in the church building and revival meetings were usually held outdoors under a brush arbor. Revival meetings were annually conducted under an open tabernacle that was constructed in 1953. Church members sat in straight-backed chairs, cooled themselves with funeral parlor fans, and listened to "a lot of good preaching."

In 1949, the church began to feel a responsibility to pay their pastor a salary. When the church was first organized no salary was paid the pastors, just a freewill offering, or perhaps a

---

[243] Apparently M. G. Campbell

piece of meat, a sack of dry beans or peas, or perhaps a few days' work on a farm. The first salary was one hundred dollars per month.

On September 18, 1955, Allie Ferguson was called as the new pastor and he served until August 14, 1957. Two more Sunday school rooms were added during Brother Ferguson's pastorate. From August to October the church was without a pastor. On October 23, 1957, the church called Paul Argo as pastor. He served until September 1, 1959.

T. J. "Bud" Parr served as pastor from October of 1959 until January 25, 1964. Several more improvements to the building were made during Brother Parr's pastorate. Most notably perhaps were indoor restrooms which served far better than the outhouses.

John A. Brooks was called as pastor in March of 1964. In May of 1965 Bud Parr was again called as pastor and he served until May 24, 1967. That year Tiff Covington left the First Free Will Baptist Church of Wichita Falls and returned as pastor of Pleasant Mound, this time for a thirteen year stint. Brother Tiff had been the pastor when the church building was constructed and, now that he was pastor again, many improvements were made to the building. In November of 1967 the church voted to make some major improvements to the church facilities. These included carpeting, central heating and air conditioning, new pews, a new bannister, and new outside doors.

Brother Tiff could see the future well enough to know that his time for active service was soon drawing to a close. He wanted to bring in a younger man and slowly work him in as pastor. In December of 1979 the church called Larry Cox as associate pastor. Larry served in this capacity until April 23, 1980, when Tiff resigned as pastor due to health reasons. Larry then stepped up as the new pastor. That fall the church voted to remodel the sanctuary and make many necessary repairs to the building. The walls were insulated and paneled, and new metal outside doors were installed. The congregation grew quickly under the ministry of the charismatic Brother Cox. For several months people sat in folding chairs in the aisles and every other available space. On at least two occasions the doors were opened and people were seated outside during the worship services. On one occasion fifteen people were counted sitting just outside the front door. All this growth produced a need for a larger sanctuary. So, in April of 1982 the church voted to construct a new sanctuary joined to the old one. Land was donated by Billy Don Campbell, grandson of M. G. Campbell. In December, a groundbreaking ceremony was held and construction on the new sanctuary began. Even though the work was hired out to carpenters outside the church, the able members of the congregation pitched in to do what they could to help. The first service in the beautiful, spacious new sanctuary was held on April 3, 1983.

Progress continued as the church voted in July, 1984, to build a parsonage. Land for it was donated once again by the Campbell family. The new residence for the pastor was completed in March, 1985, immediately north of the sanctuary.

Darryn McGee became the assistant pastor in June of 1985 and served in that capacity until April of 1986, when he became pastor of the church, with Larry Cox serving as associate pastor. This relationship continued until October of 1986, when they switched positions again. Both of them resigned in 1987. Billy Brown, of Northport, Alabama, and graduate of Free Will Baptist Bible College, became the pastor in 1987. There were a number of short term pastors after Billy: James Taylor, Steve Harris, John Hays, Russel Johnson, and Lynn Beck. As of January, 2017, Billy Waller, an Independent Baptist bi-vocational pastor, continues as leader of The Rock Church, after having been there several years.

The community in which Pleasant Mound is located has changed a great deal since the inception of the church. During the first part of the Twentieth Century the area was dotted with small farms and ranches and the population was fairly dense for a rural area. Now the small farms are mostly gone, with much of the land being used to graze cattle. The population has thinned out considerably. Several families of the church moved to town, many of them joining the three new Free Will Baptist churches in Bowie and Wichita Falls. Since then, members have simply joined other churches or died off, leaving the church to struggle for survival, as is the case with many Texas Free Will Baptist churches.

Trinity Free Will Baptist Church, Fort Worth

The Trinity Free Will Baptist Church in Fort Worth is now only a ghost, gathered with a hundred other Free Will Baptist churches which have gone to join together with other ghost riders of the sky. But in its day it was one of the most remarkable Free Will Baptist Churches in Texas. M. L. Sutton walked out of the First Free Will Baptist Church, following a dispute with the church, and a large number of people left with him. From this ready-made congregation the Trinity Church was formed. During it's about thirty year history it had a ministry which eventually reached to three continents through the missionaries who went out from the church, and the pastors and members who went out to serve in the kingdom of God.

In 1971 someone in the church wrote a brief history of the Trinity Church. Jack. T. Bankhead supplied me with a copy of that history, which is included here in its entirety.

CHURCH HISTORY OF
TRINITY FREE WILL BAPTIST CHURCH
1934-1971

Thirty-seven years ago on May 6, 1934, a group of Christians met on the north side of Fort Worth in the home of Mrs. Anna Bell Arnold in the 2000 block of Prairie Avenue. Under the direction of Rev. M. L. Sutton, the Trinity Free Will Baptist Church was organized. The 33 charter members were:

M. L. Sutton	Mr. Jack Lucas
Clara Sutton	Mrs. Verna Lucas
Willis Sutton	Mrs. Lillie McFeely
Mrs. Anna Bell Arnold	W. V. McPhail
Mrs. Edna Howard	Mrs. Opal McPhail
Mr. W. H. Howard	Mr. Bill Taylor
Mr. H. H. Howard	Mrs. Worthea Taylor
Mrs. Sarelda Ausgsburger	Mrs. Chester Pannell
Mrs. Lena Dilleshaw	Mrs. Louise Sheppard
Mr. George Bassham	Mr. Claude Sheppard
Mrs. Marie Bassham	Mrs. Vera Sheppard
Mr. C. B. Weir, Sr.	Mrs. Flossie Sheppard
Mrs. Maudie Weir	Mr. Frank Sheppard
Mrs. Merle Waldrop	Mrs. Oma Burton
Mr. A. G. Gardner	Mrs. Jesse Ferguson
Mrs. Johnnie Herron	Mrs. Fay Young
Mrs. Mary Lucas	

The group first met in the home of Mrs. Arnold and then rented a building where Hills Grocery is located now. At this time under the leadership of the pastor, ground was purchased at 2320 Azle Avenue, and construction was begun on a frame church building. These charter members had a spiritual vision of the future of Trinity Church, and now May 2, 1971, Trinity Church still holds that vision. Bro. Sutton, being the main carpenter, spent endless hours working and planning and all the members helped when they could. In the beginning, the church has a dirt floor and was heated by a potbellied stove which the members sat around.

These were busy but happy times because God was leading and blessing. Weekly prayer meetings were held in the members' homes and baptismal services were held at the Trinity River.

Bro. Bill Kirk was the first deacon. Other deacons were Martin Howard, Earl Eagleton, Sr., Bill Taylor, George Bassham, Jack Lucas, J. P. Lowery, George Wetzel, Frank Smith, George Rice, Rill Reeder, Dave Wilkes and Ray Sheppard.

Bro. Charlie Wier was the first treasurer of Trinity Church. He served well in this capacity. He also helped out in the music for the church. His wife, Sis. Maudie Wier, was very faithful in teaching a large Sunday School class.

Sis. Verna Lucas started a class of young people with one member and it later grew to a membership of 60.

Trinity was blessed with two large families: the Eagleton family of nine and the Gardner family of ten. As these children grew up and married and began their families, the church increased in number and spirit. From these two families came wonderful singers, teachers, a pianist and a foreign missionary. This missionary is Bro. Kenneth Eagleton who is now serving our denomination in Brazil.

Another missionary also came from Trinity Church, Bro. Lonnie Palmer, son of Mrs. Minnie Palmer. Bro. Lonnie and his family are now serving in Ivory Coast, Africa.

In 1947, Sis Clara Sutton helped organize the Women's Auxiliary with approximately 15 members. Monthly lunch meetings were held where the ladies brought their lunches and ate and fellowshipped together.

During World War II, Trinity Church had an honor board which hung in the vestibule. Names of servicemen from the congregation were placed on this board. As Trinity prayed for these men in each and every service, God heard their prayers and brought them all home safely.

In 1959, Trinity Church - 2320 Azle Avenue - underwent a major re-modeling. The auditorium was extended and refurbished with new pews, altar, pulpit stand, and various other improvements were made. Dedication for the new construction was held on Oct. 4, 1959.

In 1959 grief came to Bro. and Sis. Sutton and to our church. The Sutton's only son, Capt. Willis Sutton, was killed in a plane crash.[244] Together we wept and looked to God for comfort. During Bro. Sutton's pastorate, several ministers were ordained in Trinity Church. Among these were A. F. Ferguson, John Lucas, Ray Stanford, Jack Turrentine, Bill McPhail; Braxton Chaffin, Owen Barger and James Bandy.

When Bro. Sutton left the church in 1964, he had served Trinity for thirty years. Shortly after that, he accepted to pastor the Faith Church in Wichita Falls.
Bro. Braxton Chaffin served as interim pastor until such time as the church called Bro. Odus Eubanks.

While Bro. Eubanks was pastor, Trinity moved to its present location, 3715 Flory in North Richland Hills. He served as pastor for two years and left the church to go to Fresno, California to serve as Dean of Men in the California Bible Institute.

From 1967 to 1970 our pastors were Clayton Moore, Owen Barger and Burton Hughes.

---

[244] Brother Sutton told me in 1980 that his son Willis was a test pilot and that an airplane he was test flying disintegrated in the skies during a test flight.

In March 1970, the church was again without a pastor. The congregation had dwindled. As - in the beginning of Trinity Church - we met in our homes to pray that God would lead us and send us a pastor. God answered and Bro. Bob DuVall was called as pastor the last part of April. By June, Bro. DuVall had his family moved from Arkansas and was able to assume full time pastoral duties. Under his leadership, the church has grown spiritually and numerically. We have witnessed many new conversions and re-dedications. 25 new members have been placed on the roll which now totals 63. A good working spirit is now among us. Prayer meetings are being held each Friday night in members' homes. The Ladies Auxiliary is progressing steadily. A CTS has recently been organized and many young people are participating.

Like all churches, Trinity has had its share of problems, but God has always made a way for us. The testing's have made us depend more on God.

Today we are very grateful for George and Marie Bassham who have been in the church since its organization in 1934. Their faithfulness and testimonies have been a source of strength to us all. The Dave Wilkes family - members for 25 years - have also served the church in many areas. Bro. and Sis. J. T. Reeder has been a member for 22 years.

God has been so good to Trinity Church. We now have a spirit of unity and love among us. We should always exalt, teach and preach Jesus Christ and Him crucified.

I'd like to conclude with the first verse of the hymn, The Church's One Foundation.

> The Church's one foundation is Jesus Christ her Lord;
> She is His new creation by spirit and the Word;
> From heaven He came and sought her to be His holy bride;
> With His own blood He bought her, and for her life He died.

The Trinity Free Will Baptist Church closed in the late 1970's. The property was sold and the proceeds given to the West Fork Youth Camp. The money was used to build Trinity Chapel, the building in which chapel and evening services are held during camp, and Bible classes. It is also used as the meeting place for the annual meeting of the West Fork District Association of Free Will Baptists each May. The cornerstone on the building says: "TRINITY CHAPEL, JUNE 1980, IN MEMORY OF TRINITY F. W. B. CHURCH." See the photograph on the next page.

*Trinity Chapel, West Fork Youth Camp
Built in 1980*

Union Arbor Free Will Baptist Church

The Union Arbor Free Will Baptist Church[245] was organized "sometime between 1876 and 1878." Don Austin, one of the members of the church, dates the organization circa 1877. This makes Union Arbor one of the oldest Free Will Baptist churches in Texas. The church was organized by Angus M. Stewart, but the first pastor was J. J. Tipton. At first the church was called Union Chapel, but the name was later changed to Union Arbor because the church was initially a brush arbor. This church still serves faithfully.

Union Arbor Free Will Baptist Church, Beckville

Other pastors who shepherded the church were:

E. S. Jameson	Robert Kimball	Harold Teague
A. R. Harper	Floyd Ferguson	Donald Scott
H. T. Sizemore	Ivan Godwin	John Voss
J. H. Gholston	LeeRoy Anderson	James Edwards
W. R. Clark	Lee Fears	
Barney Grant	L. K. Brashier	
E. J. Vaughn	Mace Perry	
A. A. Young	Ernest Holland	
Huey Gower	Edwin Miles	

Westside Free Will Baptist Church, Midland

---

[245] Much of the information about the Union Arbor Free Will Baptist Church came from Don Austin, who did research, conducted personal interviews, and went over old church records.

Jake Armstrong left the First Free Will Baptist Church in Midland and started the Westside Free Will Baptist Church. Everett Eugene "Gene" Zoellers[246] was the second pastor of the church and the pastor under which the church experienced the most growth. Brother Zoellers' wife, Barbara, though she was blind, was very active in the church, serving as pianist, working with the Woman's Auxiliary, and in the Sunday school. The church built an exceptionally nice and spacious sanctuary, with an attached two story educational building, in a prime location in the city of Midland, 4031 W. Illinois. The church was for many years a member of the West Fork District Association of Free Will Baptists, but joined the Midessa District Association after it was formed. After Brother Zoellers resigned and moved to California, the church was pastored by Leslie Rowe, Carl Cheshier, George Stitt, Glen Hood, Dennis Haygood, Danny Potter, Patrick Dickens, and a few others. During the pastorate of Patrick Dickens the church name was changed to the Puritan Covenant Free Will Baptist Church, at least temporarily. The church began a slow but steady decline and finally closed, leaving the Odessa-Midland area without a Free Will Baptist church.

Westside Free Will Baptist Church, Midland

---

[246] Gene Zoellers and his wife Barbara both died in a house fire on Saturday, January 2, 2010, in Dallas, Texas. They were buried at Hillcrest Memorial Park Cemetery, Ardmore, Oklahoma.

Chapter 10

Texas Home Missions

Despite some setbacks resulting from the merger with the Northern Baptists in 1910-11, the Free Will Baptist work in Texas made some rapid progress in planting new churches during the next several years. The Southwestern Freewill Baptist Convention, meeting at the North Zulch Church in 1914, the year before the organization of the Texas State Association of Free Will Baptists, reported such growth. The Church Extension Report stated:

> We, your committee on Church Extension, after investigation find that our church extension in the past year has been very great, for which we wish to thank the Lord. The great extension of our church [denomination] in the past year gives us the assurance that the Lord has been in the great Freewill Baptist move. We commend our brethren and sisters for their great efforts and faithfulness in extending our church work. But when we look out and see the great opportunities for Freewill Baptist churches to be organized, we urge our people to put forth a great effort during the next year to promote our church extension, and also to secure church houses for the places where we are using school houses as places of worship. We wish also to urge the laity of our churches to stand by our ministers in this great work.
>
> J. W. Diserens
H. M. McAdams
W. P. Taylor[247]

The Report on the State of the Denomination gave a similar report: "We find that more new churches have been organized than any year possibly. Most of our churches own their own houses of worship, and we are advancing faster than ever before in number, having more increase, or as much as any year in our history."[248]

As we noted earlier in this book the General Conference of Free Will Baptists continued as a paper organization for a few years following the merger of 1910-11. In 1919, J. J. Tatum was employed as a "missionary" by the General Conference. However, he was not a church planter as such, but more of what we would call a promotional man serving the churches of Texas. In a letter dated November 1, 1919, to Alfred Williams Anthony in New York, administrator of the paper organization, Tatum reported that "our churches show some progress for the past year. Most of them have had an increase in membership. The most encouraging feature to me is they are calling for a more efficient ministry and better church buildings. They seem willing to pay better salaries also."[249] Tatum's statistical report for the month of October, 1919, reveals something of the nature of his work:

Bryan, Texas, Oct. 31, 1919

---

[247] Minutes of the Southwestern Freewill Baptist Convention, 1914, page 10.
[248] Minutes of the Southwestern Freewill Baptist Convention, 1914, page 11.
[249] A copy of this letter was supplied to me by David Crowe of National Home Missions.

Missionary report for the month of Oct, 1919.

Churches visited		6
Associations visited		3
Homes visited		26
Sermons and addresses delivered		12
Institutes conducted		2
Collected on missions (Holder)	Foreign	$32.00
Collected on missions	Home	8.00
Collected on	education	4.00
Collected on	state work	15.00
Collected on	Charity	25.00
Miles traveled	1,200	
Expense	$15.00	
Collected on Salary	$12.00	

There is now due me from Gen. Con. of Free Baptist $98.00

Receipt in full here in acknowledged,

J. J. Tatum (Missionary)

We have copies of additional reports from Tatum which were mailed to Dr. Anthony dated July 20, 1917; April 2, 1920; June 1, 1927; December 31, 1929; and April, 30, 1930. The statistical reports are all pretty much the same. The letters which accompanied his reports reveal that some of the associations in Texas, though not all, were still affiliated with the General Conference of Free Will Baptists, which was only a paper organization at the time, and through it to the Northern Baptist Convention as late as 1927. However, a vote seemed to be looming which would sever that relationship.

In 1929, the Texas State Association gave the Executive Board the responsibilities of being a Home Missions Board during its annual meeting.[250] The report of Home Missions at that meeting is so informative that we include it here. It states:

> While there are some who are really interested, in general there is not the interest in Home Missions that should be. In fact, we feel that the condition at present is rather deplorable. The attitude of many of our people toward the Home Mission program is such that it is impossible for it to go forward as we feel that God wants us to. As we see it, there are different causes for this condition; one cause is that old enemy which we all know--too self-centered--another is ignorance concerning the program. But the main trouble is selfishness on the part of the individual; not everyone of course, but such expressions as, "What do we get out of it," "It won't help us any," and other expressions meaning the same thing justify the statement. We would call attention to the fact that such selfishness is unchristian, and should be discouraged by this body.
>
> We further recommend that a Home Mission Board consisting of three members be elected by the body, that they may formulate plans for our Home Mission work. An amendment to this report was adopted making the Executive Board the Home Mission Board..   -C. B. Thompson, James Lang, A. L. Roberts

---

[250] 1929 state minutes, page 3.

Donald Bailey

Don Bailey is a Texas pastor and home missionary. He and his wife Sonya, along with their children, are currently in the process of planting a Free Will Baptist Church in San Antonio, the North Oaks Free Will Baptist Mission. Don is a second generation preacher of the gospel, following in the footsteps of his father, Fred Bailey. He was converted to Christ in January of 1983, in Odessa, Texas, where his father pastored the Bible Free Will Baptist Church. He has been preaching the gospel for over a quarter of a century. Don and his wife, Sonya, who is from Odessa, have five children who are all active in the work of the Lord. Don received his Bachelor of Biblical Studies from Southeastern Free Will Baptist College in Wendell, North Carolina. He pastored the Bible Free Will Baptist Church in Odessa, which had also been pastored by his father. Don also made yet another attempt to plant a Free Will Baptist Church in San Angelo, Texas, which has proven to be a difficult place for Free Will Baptists to get a foothold.

Don and Sonya Bailey and their five children

Don is an energetic preacher of the gospel, preaching with a great deal of evangelistic fervor.

The church is currently located at 13703 Bulverde Road in San Antonio.[251]

Bud and Ruth Bivens

North Oaks Free Will Baptist Mission, San Antonio

Bud and Ruth Bivens are included in this history of the Free Will Baptist work in Texas because they are well known to Texas Free Will Baptists, one or both of them annually attending the Texas State Association, they maintain a residence in Pharr, Texas, in the Rio Grande Valley, and because they are home missionaries to Mexico. Their story is rather remarkable.

Martin Leon "Bud" Bivens was born in Wirt, Oklahoma, in the southern oil fields, on November 30, 1940. Ina Ruth was born on November 19, 1942, in the first permanent white

---

[251] Information on Don Bailey came mostly from the North Oaks website: www.northoaksfwb.org.

settlement in Oklahoma, Salina. Bud's father, Marlin Monte Bivens, was a deacon in the First Free Will Baptist Church in Healdton, Oklahoma. He worked as a superintendent for an oil company and oversaw the maintenance of the pipelines throughout the area.

Ruth's father, Howard Gage, was a pastor. He founded the Greenbrier Free Will Baptist Church a few miles from Adair, Oklahoma. Brother Howard was also a dairy farmer for many years, then when he pastored in the Checotah Free Will Baptist Church he built houses to supplement his salary. In 1967 he and his wife Willie went to Africa where he built a hospital for Dr. Lavern Miley in the Ivory Coast. They made three two year trips to the Ivory Coast where, in addition to the hospital, Brother Howard built homes for missionaries, churches, and a dorm at the boarding school where the missionaries' children went to school.

Bud and Ruth Bivens

Bud and Ruth met at the Central Avenue Free Will Baptist Church in Oklahoma City. She was studying nursing at the St. Anthony School of Nursing and he was studying for a teaching degree at Central State College in Edmond, Oklahoma. They were married in Checotah on August 18, 1963. After working for a year, they went into the Peace Corps in 1964 and were sent to Bolivia, South America. They worked there for two years, making many precious friends and nailing down their skills at speaking Spanish. That has impacted their lives ever since.

After a few years, Bud left his teaching career and went to work as a State Farm agent in Tulsa, Oklahoma. He had a great business, one reason being that he was the only insurance agent in the area who spoke Spanish. After twenty-three years in a prosperous business, one of his clients asked him to please pray for his family in Mexico. He wanted Bud to pray that the Lord would send someone to tell them about Jesus. They prayed together and before the man left his office Bud promised that he would continue to pray for the Lord to send someone to his people.

At that time the Bivens were making frequent trips to the City of Reynosa, just across the border from McAllen, Texas. They would leave his office at five o'clock Friday, drive all night and get to Reynosa at 10:00 a.m. Saturday. They would visit with the pastor and his family, deliver the goods they had brought to them, then attend church with them on Sunday morning. Then they had to leave by 3:00 p.m. That would take them to the front door of his office at 8:00 Monday morning, where he would go in, change his shirt, and open for business. They made thirty-four weekend trips in 1994.

Bud never mentioned the conversation he had with his client to Ruth. But, one Wednesday, when he came home, he said, "We've got to go to Mexico."

"We just got back Monday," Ruth answered. "When do you want to go?" It was then that he told her about his conversation with his Mexican client. He said that every time he prayed for the Lord to send someone to the man's family in Mexico the Holy Spirit whispered in his ear, "You can go, you speak Spanish." Ruth told him that she was ready to go when he was. They had worked for seventeen years, heading up the children's church at the East Tulsa Free Will Baptist Church. Then, when Bud bought Ruth her dream home they began to attend the West Side Free Will Baptist Church in Pryor.

That year State Farm had offered early retirement to agents who turned fifty-five. Bud was fifty-five on November 30th, so he qualified. He was one of only a handful of agents across the country who accepted the offer.

They put their dream home, a huge two-story house on ten acres west of Pryor, on the market. They had a two day auction, which was even advertised in the *Antique Trader*. They had collected antiques all of their married life. When their pastor knew of their plans he put them in touch with Free Will Baptist Home Missions, and they headed for the border as Free Will Baptist home missionaries.

Bud had bought a little house in Pharr, Texas, with a credit card, so you can guess what condition it was in. It had belonged to a drug dealer. He had pulled everything loose that he could sell: light fixtures, switch plates, even the electric cook top. He had tried to get the oven pulled out, but could only get it pulled out far enough to disconnect the light. It took them a while to get the little house livable, but it provides a home base for them today.

Bud and Ruth helped with the construction of the Seminary of the Cross in Reynosa, then they both served as teachers there. The local missionary in charge of the Mexican work had moved it from Altamira. Fred and Barbara Jones had served there for many years at the Free Will Baptist Bible Institute of the Cross, "IBLAC." It had been established in 1984.

In 1998 Trymon Messer asked the Bivens to go to Puerto Rico to try to rescue a work there. The local pastor had run off with his song director and the thirty year old work was down to six people. He suggested that they would only be there six months until he could find a pastor for the work. Then, when he thought it over, he said, "Maybe a year." The Bivens served in Puerto Rico for five years. During the time the Bivens were serving in Puerto Rico there was a split in the Mexican National Association of Free Will Baptists, and National Home Missions pulled out of Mexico.

National Home Missions had paid for a lot for the construction of a church in Carolina, a city near San Juan, Puerto Rico. But the previous pastor had not even finished the paperwork for the purchase. Bud went to work getting that taken care of, then encouraged groups to come and help build a church, while "pastoring" the little congregation that met under a metal roof. The little shelter was right in front of the house where the previous pastor had lived, and his abandoned wife still lived there with their grown sons.

One of the men who came down to help put down the tile floor in the new building was a young minister who had grown up in the Bivens' children's church in Tulsa. He suggested that when Bud and Ruth were finally able to move on they should consider moving to Missouri. The district where he worked had bought an abandoned Methodist church out in an open field. They wanted someone to come and start a work with the Hispanic people in the area. There were large chicken processing plants there and most of the employees were Hispanic. Bud and Ruth moved to Missouri and got the work going.

When a young minister and his family came to work at the church Bud and Ruth moved to Monet, Missouri, and quickly established a Hispanic work there. When they had a congregation of about fifty, they called Fermin Sanchez, one of their former students, who was pastoring a work Bud and Ruth had started in Reynosa. They asked him to come and take over the work. They went right to work on the paperwork they needed to do. As soon as possible, Fermin brought his family and they are still laboring in that church in Monet.

With that work in good hands, Bud and Ruth moved back to Pharr, and quickly on down to Altamira, Tamaulipas. The director of Home Missions warned them that if they returned to Mexico they would have to go on their own. So, they did. The churches in that area had not approved of moving the Bible Institute to Reynosa so they asked the Bivens to come back and reopen the work there.

They continued in that area from 2006 to 2015. With the beautiful facility there, even housing for married students, for the past six semesters there have not been full time students enrolled. They currently only have classes Tuesday and Thursday nights. So, the Bivens went from there to the state of Coahuila where their son John and his Mexican wife, Paulina, founded the Getsemani Children's Home.

The Bivens currently spend most of their time there. Bud fixes supper every evening for the whole tribe, and Ruth's main job is hugging the kiddos. The children are placed by the Department of Family, and they come from situations of terrible abuse, or often, being abandoned on the street. They need to be taught that they are valuable and most of all, that the Lord loves them.

The danger of the drug cartel in the area is great. At times Bud and Ruth hear shootouts at night in the nearby town of Morelos. The local cartel completely occupied a small town that is five miles west of the children's home. However, they seem to respect the home. One year they even brought Christmas gifts to the children and told Paulina who they were. When a strange car pulls through the gate she goes out to see who it is before she permits John to step outside. His blond hair and blue eyes are a giveaway that he is a Gringo, and that sometimes puts him, and also Bud and Ruth, at risk.

The Bivens covet the prayers of their fellow Christians for their safety and the safety of the staff at the children's home. Ruth often tells folks, "When you eat Mexican food you are required to pray for Mexico and the Bivens."[252]

Bobby Beavers - Grand Prairie

In January, 1975, Bobby Beavers and his wife were hired as joint project workers with the West Fork District Association and the National Home Missions Board to start a new church in Grand Prairie. A convenience store was converted into a suitable meeting place for the startup mission. The mission grew into the First Free Will Baptist Church of Grand Prairie and did well for a time, showing great promise. It is a sad part of Texas history, however, that this church died as a result of the first two pastors, Bobby Beavers and Tom Hampton, both running off with other women.

Jeff Cates

Jeff Cates is currently planting a new Free Will Baptist church in Canyon, Texas. Canyon is a city in, and the county seat of, Randall County. The population was 13,303 at the 2010 census. It is part of the Amarillo, Texas, Metropolitan Statistical Area. Just to the east is Palo Duro Canyon, Texas' version of the Grand Canyon. Canyon is a college town, home of West Texas A&M University. And it is cowboy country.

Jeff and his wife Sondra, and their two daughters, came to Canyon from the Templo Free Will Baptist Church in Weslaco, Texas, down on the border in far South Texas. He had followed

---

[252] I owe a debt of gratitude to Ruth for writing their story for me, from which I borrowed heavily, verbatim in places.

the late James Munsey as pastor there. Canyon, just south of the Texas Panhandle, offered Jeff the opportunity to do something he really wanted to do, establish a Free Will Baptist church which would be patterned after the cowboy churches, churches in the Western Heritage movement of churches. These churches are springing up all over the West, and usually with great success.

Jeff is working under the National Home Missions Department and the Texas State Home Missions Board. The name of the church is Canyon Country Free Will Baptist Church and it is located at 3400 FM 3331. The new congregation has purchased land and constructed a church facility on the property.

Jeff and Sondra Cates and their two daughters

And sure enough, it is patterned after the cowboy churches. It is, however, a Free Will Baptist church. The congregation has showed good growth under Jeff's leadership.

Sanford Davis - Temple

Sanford Davis graduated from Free Will Baptist Bible College in the spring of 1977. Almost immediately he was hired by the National Home Missions Board, in cooperation with the Texas State Home Missions Board, to plant a church in Temple, one of the nation's fastest growing areas at the time. Sanford was a more mature student, with a family, when he was hired and should not necessarily be considered a novice. However, for a number of reasons the mission did not succeed and become a strong church. The church was named the Lighthouse Free Will Baptist Church, located at 1614 W. Avenue L in the Central Texas town of Temple.

Heath Ferguson - Montgomery

Heath Ferguson currently serves as a home missionary, commissioned with the task of planting a church in the city of Montgomery, Texas, about thirty miles west of Conroe. Employed as a joint project worker with the Texas Home Missions Board and the National Home Missions Board, Heath began his missions work in February of 2013. Three and a half acres of land have been purchased as the future location of the Woodforest Free Will Baptist Church, but at present they are meeting in a store front facility. A congregation is being established and prospects for a thriving church are looking good.

Heath Franklin Ferguson was born to Karen Ann (Carson) and Franklin Alexander Ferguson on July 31, 1978, in Farmington Hills, Michigan. His father Franklin is an engineer with EMC2 Corporation, and his mother Karen is a homemaker. From age three Heath grew up in Houston and graduated from Cypress Falls High School in 1996. He was listed in Who's Who Among America's High School Students. When he was five years old he gave his life to Christ under the ministry of Bobby Ferguson (no relation) at the First Free Will Baptist Church in Houston. Heath grew up being involved in the Church Training Service (CTS) competition, competing in Bible Memorization, Puppetry, Sword Drill, Bible Tic-Tac-Toe, Vocal Music, and

Charcoal Drawing. At the age of eighteen he sensed that God was calling him into the gospel ministry. To prepare for the ministry Heath attended Southeastern Free Will Baptist College in Wendell, North Carolina, from 1996 to 2000. During his college years he served as a Prayer Captain and as vice-president of the Sigma Chi Society. He preached his first sermon at the Charity Free Will Baptist Church, Wendell, North Carolina, in October of 1998.

Heath met his future wife, Jamie Nicole Smith, while he was in college, in 1996. Jamie attended the Raleigh Christian Academy, graduating in 2000. She was salutatorian of her graduating class, received an honors diploma, and was homecoming queen. Heath and Jamie were married on September 22, 2001, at the First Free Will Baptist Church in Raleigh, North Carolina. The wedding ceremony was performed by Pastor Tim Rabon. Heath and Jamie have two children: Katelyn Nicole Ferguson (2006) and Ashlyn Nicole Ferguson (2011). Jamie's father retired as assistant director of the North Carolina State Bureau of Investigation and currently serves as police chief in Fuquay-Varina, North Carolina.

Heath and Jamie Ferguson and girls Katelyn and Ashlyn

After graduating from college Heath served as youth pastor of the First Free Will Baptist Church in Amory, Mississippi, from August of 2002 until November of 2004. He became pastor of the church in 2004 and served until July of 2008. He was licensed to the gospel ministry on November 18, 2002, by the Northeast Mississippi Association of Free Will Baptists, and then ordained on December 26, 2003, at the Westfield Free Will Baptist Church in Katy, Texas. His ordination credentials were signed by David Ferguson, Bobby Ferguson, David Holguin, Frank Ferguson, and Chuck Vaughn.

Clyde Gillentine - Mesquite

Clyde Gillentine was hired as a joint project worker by the National Home Missions-Church Extention Board and the West Fork District Association in 1971 to plant a church in the fast growing Dallas suburb of Mesquite. A location was selected and a new, small, brick church building was constructed. However, after a short time the mission church closed and the property was sold.

Harvey Henderson - Austin

Harvey Lee Henderson, Sr., was born on December 9, 1924, in Houston County, Alabama. His father, William Dolphus Henderson was a tenant farmer. Harvey married Edna Mae Cloud on November 29, 1942. From this marriage came seven children: Harvey Lee Henderson, Jr., Myra Sue Etterling, Charles Douglas Henderson, twin to James Donald Henderson, Carol Jean Caine, Edna Merle Williams Jordan, and Paula Lanette Gilbert. Harvey didn't finish high school, but he did receive his GED diploma, and he attended summer school at Free Will Baptist Bible College a few summers.

Harvey was ordained to the gospel ministry in October of 1953 by the Salem Association of Florida. Starting in 1954 and for the next dozen years he pastored three churches in Florida: the Damascus Free Will Baptist Church in Marianna; Grace Church, Pensacola; Shiloh Church, Bratt, just south of Atmore, Alabama. It was while Harvey was pastoring the Shiloh Church that I first met him and we became friends.

The Home Missions-Church Extension Department of the National Association of Free Will Baptists came up with what appeared on paper to be a good plan for starting new churches. The plan was called "Project 30" and it involved working jointly with state mission boards. Project 30 was a plan to put a missionary on the field and pay him for thirty months, with the goal of having a full-time, self-supporting church at the end of the thirty months. The plan called for the church planter to be paid a full-time salary by the mission board for twelve months. Then, after the first year his salary would be cut incrementally after six months, eighteen months, twenty-four months, and finally terminated at the end of the thirty months. The plan was for the mission church as it grew to pick up the difference in salary each time the mission board cut it. The goal was to have the new mission church paying him a full-time salary by the end of thirty months. As stated above the plan appeared on paper to be a good plan. Several states adopted the plan and endeavored to make it work. It was as a Project 30 home missionary that I went to Youngstown, Ohio, in the fall of 1965 to plant a church there.

Harvey and Edna Henderson

There may have been some differences in the salary package I had in Ohio and the plan Harvey had in Texas. Perhaps my situation in Youngstown can throw some light on Harvey's situation in Austin. My monthly starting salary for the first twelve months was $520.00, total. Out of this monthly salary of $520.00 I paid the rent and utilities on the church facility we rented, paid for all of the advertising and promotion of the mission, and then paid for our own housing and utilities, food, and all other living costs. At the end of the thirty months I was suffering from malnutrition and exhaustion.[253]

Texas was looking to start a new church in the capital city of Austin, where there were no Free Will Baptist churches. The Texas Home Missions-Church Extension Board met on July 9, 1965, and with the recommendation of the National Home Missions Board, and other men who were contacted for further recommendations, they hired Harvey Henderson, of Atmore, Alabama, to be their church planter in Austin under the Project 30 plan. "Operation Capital" was launched, which was a plan to have every Free Will Baptist in the state contribute one dollar per year to the project. The Mission Board announced that the work would begin by September 1, 1965.[254]

Harvey resigned as pastor of the Shiloh Church and moved his family to Austin, Texas, in August of 1965. He sold a forty acre tract of land he owned in Marianna, Florida, and used part of the money to move his family to the Lone Star State. Part of the money went for securing a house in which to live and for living expenses early on. His three youngest children, Carol,

---

[253] It must be noted that there is a strong Free Will Baptist church in Youngstown today as a result of that beginning. The credit, however, for the success of the work must be given to such men as Clarence Newman, Billy McCarty, and Tom Dooley, who followed me.

[254] 1965 state minutes, page 14.

Merle,[255] and Paula, made the move with him and his wife Edna. Myra was married to Blaine Etterling who, along with her brother Doug, were students at Free Will Baptist Bible College. Doug's twin, Don, had his own family and did not make the move right away, but he did join them for a while before also going on to Free Will Baptist Bible College.

The first services in Austin were conducted in the Henderson's living room. Harvey would play the guitar and lead the singing. Carol and Merle played a "chord" organ. Several families from the neighborhood began to attend the mission and form the nucleus of a church. A new meeting place was secured in 1966 at 507 Radam Lane, at the corner of South First Street.[256] Charles and Peggy Hampton, of Oklahoma, along with their two children started attending and lending their help. Charles was the son of a Free Will Baptist pastor and brother of Professor Ralph Hampton of Free Will Baptist Bible College. Charles became the song leader and Peggy played the piano. Charles was doing post graduate work at the University of Texas and would later become a professor himself at the Bible College. As a footnote to history it should be noted that Jennifer Hampton, daughter of Charles and Peggy, born after they left Austin, was the wife of Allen Bowen who briefly pastored the Lakehills Free Will Baptist Church in Cedar Park following the retirement of Keith Woody.

Starting a new church in a large city where there were few or no Free Will Baptists to gather as the nucleus of a church, is a difficult proposition and the going can be slow at first, and discouraging. Harvey and his family held steady in their efforts at planting a church. However, the church did not grow and pick up his salary as the Project 30 Plan called for. With his salary decreasing at regular intervals, Harvey had to rely on the rest of the funds from the sale of that forty acres in Florida He also went to work at Browning Airfield, repairing and doing decorative painting on airplanes. He also worked part-time painting houses. This, of course, took time and energy away from his church planting efforts.

The 1966 report of the Texas Home Missions-Church Extension Board indicated that they would continue supporting Brother Henderson under the "Operation 30" project at $75.00 per week for the following six months, and then $50.00 per week for the following six months. The board planned to review their plan at the end of six months to see if the church could pick up the difference in salary of $50.00 per week at that time.[257]

The Austin mission was organized into a church and the Texas Mission-Church Extension Board was present for the organizational service. Actively involved in this effort were Bobby Ferguson, Allie Ferguson, H. Ray Berry, and Allen Moore. *Mission Grams* reported in 1968, "The First Free Will Baptist Church of Austin is now self-supporting and meets in beautiful facilities."[258] That statement was questionable at best.

The Report of the Texas Missions Church-Extension Board in 1968 reported that Harvey Henderson had resigned and that Charles Hampton had been leading in the mission effort in Austin.[259] Charles Reeves pastored the church for a while, as did Louis Nettleton. The church was located on Eberhart Lane when it closed.

---

[255] Merle (Henderson) Jordan helped me with much of the biographical information on her father.
[256] 1966 State Minutes, page 8.
[257] 1966 State Minutes, page 8.
[258] *Mission Grams*, published by the National Home Missions Department, Nashville, Tennessee, Volume 18, Number 3, May-June 1978, page 2.
[259] 1968 State Minutes, page 17.

For the next forty years after leaving Texas in 1968, Brother Henderson pastored nine churches in Florida, Alabama, Tennessee, and Georgia. Altogether he served as a pastor for a total of fifty-five years. He passed away on November 5, 2008, at his home in Donaldsonville, Georgia, at the age of 83. The cause of death was severe bone cancer which had metastasized from prostate cancer. His wife Edna passed away on March 19, 2006, at the age of 81, also of cancer. They are both buried in the Damascus Free Will Baptist cemetery, Marianna, Florida.

Merle (Henderson) Jordan, Fort Worth, 2014

All seven of the Henderson children are active in church and involved in some form of ministry to this day. They serve as ministers of music, associate pastors, pastor's wives, Bible teachers, youth workers, counselors, etc. All of them are musically inclined. That they are all active in ministry is a tribute to their parents. At the 2014 national convention of the National Association of Free Will Baptists, which met in Fort Worth, Harvey's old 1951 Chevrolet pickup, beautifully and fully restored, was displayed at the "Reach That Guy" National Youth Convention outreach and at the Master's Men booth in the Fort Worth Convention Center. The truck is used as a promotional tool to encourage the starting of new Master's Men chapters and in their Disaster Relief efforts. Harvey's daughter Merle, shown at the right, is active in the First Free Will Baptist Church of Dothan, Alabama.

Hispanic Churches

During the 1966 state meeting the body adopted a resolution which purposed to encourage each district association in the state to seek ways and means of sponsoring a "Latin American work," i.e., Hispanic churches, in their districts.[260] However, not much has been done in establishing Hispanic churches in Texas to minister to the vast numbers of hispanics in the state. The most notable work would be the Iglesia Bautista Libre de Houston, pastored by Secundino Urena, and the Liberation Free Will Baptist Church, pastored by Jezer Urena. Both of these churches are part of the complex of what used to be the First Free Will Baptist Church, 10331 Veteran's Memorial Drive, Houston.

Tom Hunt - Houston

Tom Hunt was employed in March of 1974 as a joint project worker with the National Home Missions Board and the Central Texas District Association to begin a new work in Houston. The church became self-supporting in eighteen months, which seems remarkable. It must be remembered, however, that many families who helped form the church came out of the First Free Will Baptist Church in Houston. The church is the Eastside Free Will Baptist Church.

---

[260] 1966 State Minutes, page 9.

Jeremy Lightsey - San Antonio

Jeremy Lightsey grew up in the Fellowship Free Will Baptist Church in Bryan. His father Michael was music director and a deacon there. His mother Marcia was a children's director, teacher, and a clown. Jeremy was born on March 26, 1978 in Bryan. He was led to the Lord at the age of five by his parents, under the ministry of Pastor Bill Jones. He married Jill Nix on September 3, 1994. He and Jill have three children: Adria, Hope, and Josiah. At the age of eighteen he sensed that God was calling him into the ministry, and he preached his first sermon at Fellowship in the summer of 1996, the same year he graduated from Bryan High School.

Jeremy and Jill Lightsey with their children

In 1996 Jeremy entered Hillsdale Free Will Baptist College in Moore, Oklahoma, to begin his preparation for the ministry. It was during his college years that he was licensed and ordained, 1999 and 2001, respectively. This was done by the Union District Association. He graduated from Hillsdale with a major in Theology and a minor in Pastoral Studies.

He gained important ministry experience while serving as Youth Pastor at Fellowship during the summer of 1996; Youth Pastor at the First Free Will Baptist Church in Carthage, Texas, from August of 1997 to October of that year; and as Youth Pastor of the Woodward Free Will Baptist Church in Woodward, Oklahoma, from June of 1998 to December of 2006.

Jeremy and Jill saw the need for a Free Will Baptist church in San Antonio, Texas, a city of over a million people, with no Free Will Baptist church there at the time. After receiving confirmation that this was God's will for them they contacted Home Missions in January of 2007 and soon were on their way to San Antonio, moving there in May. They are employed jointly by the National Home Missions Board and the Texas State Home Missions Board. They are entirely supported financially by the Total Support Program of Oklahoma.

Lots of ground work was done toward planting a new church in San Antonio and their first preview service was held in October of 2007, with their actual launch service being March 23, 2008. Their preview services were conducted in two elementary schools and their launch service was in a movie theater. Advertising and promotion was done by mailing postcards, ads shown in the theater before the movies, servant evangelism, by conducting festivals, putting out door hangers, and by being listed on Craigslist. There were forty-one people in their first service.

The church has been able to pick up most of their salary and cover all other expenses. They are meeting in a leased facility and as of this writing have not purchased land for their permanent location. They are averaging about sixty people in attendance.

Jeremy describes CrossLife Church as a more modern style of church, not traditional at all. He says they tried to come to the project with a clean slate with plans to create a church which matches the culture of the people to whom they are ministering. He further says, "We want to be a church that holds a high view of Scripture, emphasizes prayer, loves each other, and is passionate for those outside the church."

Longview

Numerous attempts at starting a Free Will Baptist church in Longview had failed. In 1986 a mission effort in Longview, under the direction of missionary Harold Teague, had become one of them. At the January 16, 1987 meeting of the State Executive Board, the outstanding balance on the property which had been purchased for the mission was a primary concern. The balance on the property was $50,442.07. The loan for the purchase had been secured from the Board of Retirement and Insurance of the National Association of Free Will Baptists. Herman Hersey, director of the department, was present to meet with the Executive Board. Although the Texas State Association had not authorized the purchase of the Longview property, moderator Bobby Ferguson assured Mr. Hersey that the association would do whatever was right and proper. In the end the Executive Board voted to offer the deed on the property to the Board of Retirement in lieu of the outstanding balance, thus disposing of the property.[261]

Larry Powell - McAllen

Larry Powell

The Mission District Association pushed for a church to be planted in the Rio Grande Valley of Texas and their efforts paid off, starting in 1976. Larry and Wanda Powell, who had successfully started churches in both Puerto Rico and the Virgin Islands, were employed in August, 1976, as joint project workers with the Texas State Mission Board and the National Home Missions Board to plant a church in McAllen. With Larry's training, success as both a pastor and church planter, charismatic personality, incredible work ethic, and superb preaching, a congregation was quickly gathered, even while meeting initially in an elementary school. Dr. Wilford Lee, who was a professor at nearby Pan American University, and his family were very helpful in the work. Felix and Lucy Lima, of Cuba, and their daughters were also helpful in the work. The First Free Will Baptist Church of McAllen, located at 3301 N. Second Street, was at first a member of the Mission District Association, but when James and Mitzi Munsey established the Primera Iglesia Bautista Libre, an hispanic church, in nearby Weslaco, the two churches formed the Rio Grande Valley District Association.

Larry Powell was one of the most successful church planters in the denomination, not necessarily in the number of churches he established, but in the quality of the churches he planted. He later served successfully as pastor of the Cofer's Chapel Free Will Baptist Church in Nashville, the church at which the National Association was formed in 1935. After Cofer's Chapel he served as General Director of the National Home Missions Department in Nashville, Tennessee, until his retirement.

Here is another sad note to Texas Free Will Baptist history. Raymond Getz, who followed Larry Powell as pastor, eventually took the church out of the denomination. It seems there were two contributing factors. One was that Raymond began to change some of his doctrinal beliefs. Another was that he came to feel that he could have a better ministry if he was out of the Free Will

---

[261] Minutes of the Executive Board meeting contained in the minutes of the 1987 state minutes, page 8.

Baptist denomination. The church is currently the McAllen Community Church. Raymond passed away in 2016.

A Planning Session

For most of the early years the attempts to start new Free Will Baptist churches were underfunded, understaffed, and underplanned. One method was for an evangelist or a very evangelistic preacher to go to an area and hold a protracted revival meeting, perhaps lasting for several weeks. From the converts in these meetings a local Free Will Baptist church was organized. Lizzie McAdams used this method in several states. M. L. Hollis used it very successfully in Alabama and Mississippi, at least in the number of churches established, twenty-four in all. A few churches in Texas had their beginnings with this method.

Another method was simply for a preacher, on his own, to move to an area in which he wanted to start a church, get a job, find a place to meet, and begin inviting people to the new "church." There was usually no funding for these projects by any mission board. A few churches were established by this method, the success of the effort being determined by the abilities of the preacher, the size of his family, the number of reachable people in the area, etc. There were more failures than successes.

A third method was for a district association, or even the state association, to send a preacher to a target area, and pay him almost enough money to live on while he did the ground work of getting a congregation together and organized into a church. This resulted in a few churches being started but, again, there were more failures than successes. East Texas would send out a missionary to start a new church, yet provide him with very limited funding, and virtually no other assistance. The West Fork would do the same. The Central district did it, and so did other associations in Texas. Over the years this method resulted in failure after failure. It was a discouragement to all.

Several district and state leaders began to seek a better way. Executive Secretary Jim Williams and state moderator Allen Moore arranged for a planning session to meet at the Fellowship Free Will Baptist Church in Bryan in the spring of 1975. This was to be a "think tank" gathering at which the State Mission Board, the State Executive Board, and various representatives from each district association could mull over the problem and come up with a proposed solution. Each district association was asked to send a delegate. After an open and honest review of the multiple problems Texas faced in starting new churches, the gathering hit upon an idea: instead of having several underfunded projects going on at the same time, as district association projects, why not pool our resources and efforts and put one qualified church planter in a target area, give him the assistance he needs, and build new churches one at a time. Eugene Richards expressed it this way, "It is time for us to put all our eggs in the same basket." One new church planted over a five year period would be better than five or six failures. In hindsight, better planning could have gone into the subsequent missions projects, there could have been a lot more assistance given to the church planters, and more funding could have been provided to cover not only the church planter's salary, but the necessary expenses of advertising, providing a meeting place, and other miscellaneous expenses incurred by the projects. But it was a good start, a step in the right direction, a new kind of thinking. It was after that meeting in 1975, and after another failure or two that Free Will Baptists in Texas began to get the hang of starting new churches.

District associations slowly began to cease their efforts at starting new churches, some associations even eliminating their mission boards. More and more the effort to plant new churches in Texas became the responsibility of the Texas State Home Missions Board. By making the church planting efforts a joint project between the State Mission Board and the National Board of Home Missions, a number of benefits were realized. For instance, if the state board didn't have the money to pay the missionary's salary, the salary was paid on time by the National Home Missions Department. As successes mounted, and enthusiasm for home missions in Texas grew, the state reached the ability to have several church planting projects going at the same time. There continued to be, however, some local, underfunded projects.

In 1980 Keith Woody, who was chairman of the Texas Missions Church-Extension Board reported to the state meeting in Bryan that there were a number of mission churches in the works. The First Free Will Baptist Church in McAllen, one of the all-time great successes in Texas, had become self-supporting under the leadership of Larry Powell. A new work had been started in Longview. The Forest Park Free Will Baptist Church in San Angelo had completed their building. Sanford Davis was working hard to establish a church in Temple, and Wesley Bigelow had moved to College Station to start Cornerstone Free Will Baptist Church. George Hyatt had moved to Levelland in yet another attempt to start a church there. There was a good deal of excitement about these works and also a good deal of optimism about the future of the Free Will Baptist work in Texas.[262]

Another Planning Session

The State Executive Board met at the Aggieland Inn in Bryan on January 22, 1988. During the meeting the board had a lengthy discussion of possible future mission sites in Texas. With moderator Bobby Ferguson leading, the board listed the following cities as possible places to plant new churches: Texarkana, Austin, San Antonio, and the Dallas-Fort Worth Metroplex. The Missions-Church Extension Board came and joined the discussion, stating that they were considering Bandera, as well as Austin and San Antonio.[263] This meeting laid the groundwork for several church planting projects for the next two decades.

Robert Posner and the Texas Home Mission Board

In 1995 Robert Posner was elected to the Texas Home Missions Board and soon became chairman of the board. The Texas State Mission Board was already involved in an aggressive project in Austin, which resulted in the planting of the Lakehills Free Will Baptist Church in the Austin suburb of Cedar Park, under church planter Keith Woody, when Robert was elected to the board. Robert rolled up his sleeves, so to speak, and went right to work with the mission board, continuing the aggressive effort of church planting in Texas.

During his tenure on the board, up to this point, the following churches have been planted, or are being planted, in Texas:

- Eagle Heights Free Will Baptist Church in Richmond/Sugarland, Texas
    Randy and Shelly Puckett
- Heritage Park Free Will Baptist Church in Abilene, Texas
    Freddie and Katherine Gillentine

---

[262] 1980 state minutes, page 29.
[263] Minutes of the 1988 state meeting, pages 10-11.

- Canyon Country Free Will Baptist Church in Canyon, Texas
    Jeff and Sondra Cates
- Northpointe Free Will Baptist Fellowship in The Woodlands, Texas
    Dwain and Debbie Crosby
- CrossLife Free Will Baptist Mission in San Antonio, Texas
    Jeremy and Jill Lightsey
- North Oaks Free Will Baptist Mission in San Antonio, Texas
    Don and Sonya Bailey
- Light of Life Free Will Baptist Mission in McAllen, Texas
    Greg and Ana Yacobian
- Clearview Free Will Baptist Mission in McKinney, Texas
    Randall and Collette Wright
- Woodforest Free Will Baptist Mission in Woodforest, Texas
    Heath and Jamie Ferguson

I put the following question to Robert: "Please give us a little insight into your philosophy of missions in Texas. It seems that you are (properly) concentrating the missions' efforts in population centers, as did the Apostle Paul. A hundred years ago most of our churches were being planted in rural communities, which is one of the reasons so many of those churches are no longer in existence." He replied:

> First, I want to make it clear, from my perspective, we as Texas Free Will Baptists would be in far worse shape had those early pioneers not blazed a trail for us all to follow. Yes, in hindsight, some things could have been done better, but as a whole they demonstrated a powerful Christ honoring faith, sacrificial spirit, and a passion for the lost. Now with regard to a philosophy of missions: share the gospel, demonstrate a Christ-like life, and pray for laborers. As a board we seek to do this personally, in our leadership with our local congregations, and throughout our state, nation, and world. Primarily, I and the board pray often for laborers to come to Texas or be raised up in Texas. That way they would have an honest calling from the Lord and a specific call to the city in which they will serve. I believe this simple approach allows the Lord to work freely, instills confidence through hard times for the missionary and his family, and, in the end, gives the credit to Whom it is deserved.

In 2014, at the National Association of Free Will Baptists meeting in Fort Worth, Robert was elected to the Free Will Baptist International Missions Board. Robert was elected to this important position because of his reputation as a promoter of home missions in Texas and because of his commitment to world-wide missions. When asked to tell us about his efforts to promote and support foreign missions he said:

> I must confess my passion for foreign missions has not always been as it is today. The promotion and support of foreign missions in Texas has, for the most part, been strong. My prayer is that we can strengthen it financially and prayerfully throughout the coming years. Much of this will take a hands on approach to lovingly guiding fellow pastors to seeing their part in supporting foreign missions. This will largely happen through the

efforts of not one person but a team/group of people who will proclaim the Macedonian Call to all Texas pastors.

Because of his involvement and leadership in Texas Home Missions, Robert was invited back to speak to the missions and pastoral students at Southeastern Free Will Baptist College in Wendell, North Carolina. He spoke to them for an hour about the needs in Texas.

Randy and Shelly Puckett

Randy and Shelly Puckett seem to be one of the real success stories in Texas home missions, having planted the Eagle Heights Free Will Baptist Church in the Houston suburb of Richmond. Randy and Shelly both come to Texas with good bloodlines and good experience. Randy's father, Jim Puckett, a 1963 graduate of Free Will Baptist Bible College, is a well-known Oklahoma pastor. Jim was a mission pastor in his first pastorate in a suburb of Miami, Florida. In addition, Jim served for seven years as the Director of Oklahoma Missions, after having served on the Oklahoma State Mission Board before taking that position. Jim also served for eighteen years on the National Home Mission Board, including seven years as chairman. His mother, Judith, is the sister of Jim Combs who served as a Free Will Baptist missionary in Brazil for well over thirty years. Randy's maternal grandfather, W. C. Combs, was a Free Will Baptist pastor of renown in West Virginia for decades. Shelly's father was a U. S. Army veteran of the Vietnam War, decorated with a Purple Heart and a Bronze Star with Valor. Later he was an administrator at Tinker Air Force Base in Midwest City, Oklahoma.

Randy and Shelly Puckett

James Randall Puckett was born in Deerfield Beach, Florida, on February 8, 1971. His growing up years took him from Florida to Georgia, and then to Oklahoma. He graduated from Moore Christian Academy, Moore, Oklahoma, in 1989. He was a captain of his high school football team. He accepted Christ as his savior at the age of eight under the revival meeting preaching of Elro Driggers, in his father's church and ministry at the Southern Oaks Free Will Baptist Church in Oklahoma City. At the age of nineteen he sensed that God was calling him into the ministry. He preached his first sermon at the Harrah Free Will Baptist Church, Harrah, Oklahoma, during a Sunday night youth service in 1991. He was licensed to preach in 1992 and then ordained in 1993 by the First Oklahoma District Association.

The other half of this team is Shelly Nicole (Arther). She and Randy first met while they were both students in middle school in Moore, Oklahoma. She graduated from Moore High School in 1989. She was a member of the National Honor Society and a homecoming attendant. She received her degree in Elementary Education from the University of Central Oklahoma in Edmond, Oklahoma in 1995 and a Master's Degree in Library and Information Science from the University of North Texas.

Shelly and Randy were married in December of 1990 and they have three children: Torre Nicole, Taryn Mikelle, and Tatum Elyssa.

Randy's training for the ministry formally began by interning under his father as a youth pastor at the Harrah Church from 1991 to 1996. During these years he attended Hillsdale Free Will Baptist College in Moore, Oklahoma, graduating with a Bachelor's Degree in Biblical Studies in May of 1993. He then served as an associate pastor under David Archer in Glenpool, Oklahoma, interning under his leadership. He served as Director of Student Recruitment at Hillsdale Free Will Baptist College in 1996 and 1997. Then, he served as Associate Pastor of Faith Free Will Baptist Church in Glenpool, Oklahoma, from 1997 to 1999. Though he had never pastored a church he came to Texas with a lot of training under his belt. It was in 1998, while serving the Faith Church in Glenpool, that Trymon Messer, Director of the National Home Missions Department, approached him about planting a church in the Houston area. In February of 1999, he and Shelly moved to Sugarland and began the process of founding the Eagle Heights Church.

Financing for this church planting venture wasn't much of a problem for Texas. This was a joint project of the National Home Missions Department and the Texas State Home Mission Board. However, they were funded by the Oklahoma Total Support Program until the church went self-supporting on January 1, 2008.

Eagle Heights Free Will Baptist Church is a large, beautiful church in an excellent location. The Puckett's are proud of the fact that the church is a multi-racial church. Eagle Heights has twelve to fourteen different nations represented as first or second generation citizens in the United States who are regularly a part of the congregation. A quick list of nations currently involved in the church include: the United States, Venezuela, Nigeria, Korea, India, El Salvador, Canada, Mexico, the Philippines, South Vietnam, Haiti, Thailand, and Syria. The incredibly diverse congregation is a reflection of the church's mission to fulfill the Great Commission.

Randy and the church minister outside the walls and beyond the community. For several years Randy has served as chaplain in the local hospice. He has served several terms on the State Mission Board. Eagle Heights has been involved in Free Will Baptist churches and ministries in Mexico for approximately twelve years. Each year they have made at least one trip south of the border to deliver toys, clothing, and monetary donations. They partner with other Texas Free Will Baptist churches to deliver their donations to the ministries in Mexico.

The TEAM Plan

In 1996 members of the Executive Committee and the Home Missions/Church Extension Board began working together to find a solution to the growing need of providing adequate funding for Texas missionaries, both home and foreign, a daunting task. On September 8, 1997, the state's Executive Committee met in Duncanville with the Texas Home Missions/Church Extension Board to continue formulating a comprehensive plan designed to accomplish that objective. After three and a half hours of discussion, the group asked me to go home and write out a plan utilizing the ideas discussed by the two boards. The written plan was to be presented to the two boards at the All Boards Meeting at the Stagecoach Inn in Salado in January of 1998. The All Boards Meeting, however, was cancelled due to the lack of a quorum.

In October of 1997, Jerry McArthur (assistant clerk) and I (clerk and executive secretary) attended a mission's support forum in Antioch, Tennessee, at the new national offices building. The forum involved a number of denominational leaders, particularly the promotional men/executive secretaries of over a dozen states who explained plans which their states had successfully adopted or were in the process of formulating. This meeting was extremely informative and challenging.

After consulting with numerous Texas pastors, members of the Texas Home Missions/Church Extension Board, and leaders from other states, a comprehensive plan was written and presented to the body for adoption at the 1998 Texas State Association. The plan called for as many families in Texas as could be recruited to voluntarily commit a set amount each month to give to The TEAM Plan, above and beyond their tithes to their local churches.[264] The amount suggested as a monthly contribution would be set each year by the Executive Committee and the Texas Home Missions/Church Extension Board, based on budgetary needs. The plan included support for Texas Home Missions, National Home Missions, and Free Will Baptist International Missions, with a focus on foreign missionaries with strong Texas ties. The State Association adopted The TEAM Plan, though not without a dissident voice here and there. A large number of copies of a booklet explaining The TEAM Plan was printed for distribution to the Texas churches.

For all of the time, effort, and money which went into formulating The TEAM Plan, it was never promoted among the churches, though the name is still used in reference to monies given to the Texas Home Missions/Church Extension Board. As a result the Texas State Association has never realized the potential for increased giving in support of Texas Home Missions, National Home Missions, and Free Will Baptist International Missions. In truth, the major blame for the lack of success of The TEAM Plan lies with me. Due to factors I will not mention here, I resigned as clerk/executive secretary shortly after the plan was adopted. It would have been largely my responsibility to promote it. States, such as Arkansas and Missouri, which have similar plans continue to raise large amounts of money for missions.

Tyler

Several attempts to start Free Will Baptist churches in the city of Tyler were attempted over the years. All of the early attempts, even one pastored by Bobby Ferguson, eventually closed. A primary reason these early attempts did not take hold and survive was lack of financial support, including inadequate salaries for the pastors. In 1984 Ron Parker and his wife Elaine were hired as joint project workers by the Texas Home Mission Board and the National Home Missions Board to make yet another attempt at planting a church in the East Texas city. The Parkers converted their two-car garage into a small meeting facility and gathered a group together to form the nucleus of a church. When they outgrew that space they started meeting at the Tyler Activities Center for a while. Soon Ron located a vacant church at 12532 Greenland Boulevard for sale and the mission purchased it and moved in. The mission became the Lifegate Free Will Baptist Church. At the 1988 state meeting, David Sutton, chairman of the Missions-Church Extension Board announced that a target date for the Tyler Mission to go self-supporting: January 1990. Following the resignation of Pastor Parker the church hired Robert Posner as their pastor and Posner began his ministry there on June 7, 1992 and continued to serve until January of 1998, at which time he became the pastor of the Collin Creek Free Will Baptist Church in Plano. The Lifegate Church continues its ministry at this writing.

Randall Wright

In 2010 Randall and Collette Wright moved from Kinston, North Carolina, to plant a Free Will Baptist church in McKinney, Texas, a joint project between the Texas State Home Missions Board and the National Home Missions Board. Curtis Randall Wright was born on November 19, 1971, in Tuscaloosa, Alabama. He grew up in the First Free Will Baptist Church of Fayette, Alabama, as did Collette.

---

[264] The TEAM Plan is explained in detail on pages 27-40 of the *1998 Texas Free Will Baptist Yearbook*.

Randall received Christ as his savior while attending the Trinity Free Will Baptist Youth Camp near Guin, Alabama, on August 3, 1983. He subsequently answered the call to the ministry at the same camp when he was fifteen years old. He preached his first sermon at his home church in Fayette in 1985. After moving to Virginia Randall graduated from high school at the Gateway Christian School in Virginia Beach, Virginia. Preparation for the ministry then took him to Southeastern Free Will Baptist College in Wendell, North Carolina, where he graduated in 1995. It was during his junior year at Southeastern that he was licensed to the ministry in 1994 by the First Free Will Baptist Church of Raleigh, North Carolina. He went on to earn a Master's Degree from Liberty University in Lynchburg, Virginia.

Randall and Collette Wright and children

After graduating from Southeastern Randall married Collette Lenore Cheney on June 26, 1995, at the First Free Will Baptist Church in Fayette, Alabama. Randall and Collette have three children: Joshua, Rebekah, and Leah.

Prior to coming to Texas Randall gained considerable pastoral experience for fifteen years. He started in 1995 by serving three years as assistant pastor at the First Free Will Baptist Church of Amory, Mississippi. It was during this ministry that he was ordained by the Northeast Mississippi District Association in 1996. Following in rapid succession were pastorates at the First Free Will Baptist Church of Columbus, Mississippi; the Oaklawn Free Will Baptist Church, Pleasant View, Tennessee, near Nashville; and the Bethel Free Will Baptist Church of Kinston, North Carolina, as associate pastor. He left the Bethel Church to come to Texas.

Hired by the Texas State Home Missions Board in 2010, Randall and his family moved to McKinney, Texas, and began the work of planting the Clearview Free Will Baptist Mission. These days church planters wisely do months of preliminary work before actually holding their first worship services. This usually involves tons of advertising, forming relationships with as many families as possible, finding a suitable meeting place, etc. In the fall of 2011 Clearview began having regular Sunday morning worship services. The number of services they could have was limited by the fact they were using rented facilities. The mission is doing very well and at this writing they are averaging forty-five to fifty people in attendance. They now have their own meeting place.

In August of 2016 Chris and Beth Willhite, of Pleasant View, Tennessee, came to the Clearview Mission to assist with the ministry. Chris serves in a dual role as associate pastor and as student pastor. As student pastor he leads the ministry to the youth of the church. Chris is employed by the Home Missions Board, just as is Randall.

Greg Yacobian

Gregory Giragos Yacobian is an unusual Free Will Baptist home missionary in a number of ways. He was born on January 11, 1946, in Quincy, Massachusetts, with no acquaintance with Free Will Baptists until well into his adulthood. He graduated from Thayer Academy, a private high school in Braintree, Massachusetts, and subsequently graduated from St. Lawrence University in upstate New York.

Greg eventually ended up in Mexico where he lived for several years. During this time he met Ana Elvira Carranza Sanchez, who had been born in Acapulco. They were

Ana and Greg Yacobian

married on June 28, 1992, and they eventually had two children: Gregory Blake and Joshua Josiah. Both sons are active Christians who have been deeply involved in the Free Will Baptist youth work. Gregory is a student at Randall University.

Greg had been a member of a Baptist church but eventually became Arminian in his theology, though he had never heard of Free Will Baptists. While still living in Mexico he and his family made a trip into the United States, driving up the coast of California. During their travels through the Golden State they ran across the Salinas Free Will Baptist Church and attended a service. When they returned home to Mexico Greg looked up Free Will Baptists on the internet to learn more about them. This led to him entering into communications with Larry Powell, Director of the National Home Missions Department. Powell put him in contact with the Seminary of the Cross in Reynosa, Tamaulipas, just across the Rio Grande from McAllen, Texas. This led to Greg being ordained as a Free Will Baptist minister on January 11, 2008.

Greg and his family moved from Mexico to McAllen to start a Free Will Baptist church in the city where Free Will Baptists had recently lost the First Free Will Baptist Church. Greg did not go as a missionary hired and supported by the National Home Missions Department or the Home Missions Board of the Texas State Association. He was in an unusual situation. He had the funds to be self-supporting and he has used his own money to plant a Free Will Baptist church in McAllen. The church is called the Light of Life Free Will Baptist Church. At present they are sharing a church building with another congregation, renting part of the facilities, and using the sanctuary and gym for Saturday evening and Wednesday evening services.

Their ministry has been especially fruitful with young people. The church needed a bus with which they could provide transportation to the services for a lot of the young people. Greg heard of a bus in Florida which was available. The man who owned the bus donated it to Greg and Ana for use by the church. The bus was in good running condition. Greg and Ana went to Florida and drove the precious gift all the way back to McAllen, Texas, where it is being used to help bring numerous young people to Christ.

Miss Bessie Yeley

Miss Bessie Yeley worked among the Native Americans and Mexicans on the Texas-Mexico border in Laredo in 1955.[265] Miss Yeley, who was from Ohio, had previously served as a missionary in Venezuela and Cuba. She would later serve for many years in India and is usually associated with that country.

Miss Bessie Yeley

---

[265] *Mission-Grams*, published by the Department of Home Missions and Church Extension, National Association of Free Will Baptists, Nashville, Tennessee, Volume 18, Number 3, May-June 1978, page 2.

Chapter 11

Missionaries from Texas

The Free Will Baptist work in Texas began as a result of missionaries coming from the Randall Movement to start Free Will Baptist churches here. The Randall Movement, centered in New England and in the northern tier of states, was strong on missions, what we tend to call both home and foreign. Perhaps that is the reason Texas Free Will Baptists have similarly been strong on missions from our beginning. Even though the state is huge, the denomination is small here compared to many other states. However, the emphasis on missions takes a back seat to no one. You may be surprised at how many missionaries have gone from Texas to the far flung mission fields of the world. Here is a brief account of those who have been on the front lines, fulfilling the Great Commission.

Justin and Leslie Banks

Leslie Morene Brown was a girl who pretty much grew up attending the West Fork Youth Camp and participating in Church Training Service (CTS) competitive activities. Sword Drill, Bible Tic Tac Toe, Bible Bowl, you name it and she was involved in it. Leslie was born March 3, 1975, to Sylvia (Fulce) and Charles (Charlie) Brown in Denison, Texas, and grew up in the First Free Will Baptist Church of Denison. It was her mother, Sylvia, who led her to Christ at church when she was five years old. Her entire life has been committed to Christ ever since. The Denison Church often brought in missionaries to speak and to appeal for prayer and financial support. Leslie attended the West Fork Youth Camp every summer from the time she was in the first grade until she graduated from high school.

She graduated from Denison High School in 1993, the top girl in her class. That fall she started attending Oklahoma University on a full ride scholarship, with a math major. She was simultaneously attending Hillsdale Free Will Baptist College. It was at Hillsdale that God turned her heart toward a vision

Leslie and Justin Banks

of ministry. She dropped her classes at OU and started attending Hillsdale full-time. She would later graduate from Southern Nazarene University with a Bachelor of Science in Elementary Education, *magna cum laude*.

While at Hillsdale she met Justin Banks, son of missionaries Jerry and Janice Banks, who had served as missionaries from 1974 to 1991. The Banks had planted a church in Kita Hiroshima, Hokkaido, Japan. Though born in Norfolk, Virginia, Justin lived in Japan from the age of six months until he went to college at the age of seventeen. He served as youth pastor at the First Free Will Baptist Church in Cushing, Oklahoma, from 1994 to 1997. He graduated from Hillsdale in 1995 with a Bachelor of Arts in Missions. The friendship between Leslie and Justin turned to love and they were married at the Cornerstone Free Will Baptist Church, in Denison, Texas, formerly the First Free Will Baptist Church, May 20, 1995.

Leslie and Justin were commissioned to missionary service at the First Free Will Baptist Church, Cushing, Oklahoma, January 29, 2000. Bound for missionary service in Panama they had to tackle the language issue first. They attended the New Tribes Language School in Camdenton, Missouri, to learn the basic of linguistics. This was to prepare them to learn a tribal language and potentially reduce that language to a written language in order to one day translate the Bible into that language. They made two trips to Panama for exploration of the targeted areas in 1997 and 1998. They moved to Panama on February 2, 2000. They attended the University of Panama in Panama City in order to learn Spanish.

Specifically, their targeted area was a tribe of indigenous Native Americans called Kuna, sometimes spelled Cuna, on the Bayano Lake in the reservation area called Madungandi. Working with Free Will Baptist teammates Ed and LaRhonda Bowman, they began by making efforts to gain trust and build relationships with the tribe, especially the chiefs of three villages in order to be granted permission to live in a village.[266] They were required to live outside the reservation and make trips, only for a few nights at a time, into the villages.

The Kuna villages surrounded a huge lake and were accessible only by boat, dugout canoes in this instance. Some of the villages had once had a running water system of PVC pipes on top of the ground, but most never did or no longer worked. Most villages had one outhouse. There was no electricity and the Kuna lived in thatch roofed huts.

Leslie and Justin got e-coli on their first trip into the villages. As it turned out, Justin had a genetic condition that was dormant until the severe bacteria turned on his immune system, and it will never turn off. It attacks his body (an autoimmune issue). His symptoms continue today and are like arthritis, fibromyalgia, chronic fatigue, and GI issues all rolled into one. After six months Justin's health was broken down and the missionary council recommended that they return to the states, which they did in July of 2000.

Upon returning to the states, Justin went through intense physical therapy in order to regain some of his strength and health. He was at best walking with a cane, but often using a walker and barely able to perform daily routines. After about six months of rehab, and being under great medical care, he started working on his Master's Degree from the University of North Texas, in Denton. He received his Masters of Information and Library Science and has been working as the Archivist at Austin College in Sherman. Leslie teaches Kindergarten with the Denison ISD.

Leslie and Justin were involved in the Home Missions plant of the Clearview Free Will Baptist Church in McKinney, planted by Randall and Collette Wright. Mission trips have taken one or both of them to Japan and Mexico. They served as camp evangelists for the West Fork

---

[266] Even years after Leslie and Justin left the field, the Bowermans were never granted that permission.

Youth Camp one summer. Leslie and Justin have adopted four children: Simeon Cole, Sadie Morene, Seth Robert, and Susannah Joy.

Disappointed that she could not serve indefinitely as a foreign missionary, Leslie says, "Our experience in Panama made me realize what we often say: some plant, some reap. But it is very humbling when you are not the one to reap or even to get to witness others reaping. Just trusting that I have done what God has asked…and that doesn't have to be defeating. Our experience in living in the states since, has taught us that God has a purpose for us. We have a mission field in our own home. We have adopted four children out of foster care. Four children who would not have grown up in a Christian home, but now are."

Ronald and Linda Callaway

Ron Callaway wasn't born in Texas but he came here as soon as he could, as the saying goes. Ronald Joseph Callaway was born July 27, 1944, in Hannibal, Missouri, to Beulah May Grishow Callaway and Sidney B. Callaway, his adopted father. Ron was three years old when his mother married Mr. Callaway, a Texan, and they moved to Lometa, Texas. Lometa is located in Lampasas County and is part of the Killeen-Temple-Fort Hood Metropolitan Statistical Area. Ron's adopted father was a rancher and then owner of an irrigation-water well business in North Texas.

Ron and Linda Callaway

Ronny, as he was called in his high school yearbook, graduated from Dumas High School in 1962. He played football there and during his senior year his team won the 3-A state championship. He also attended Amarillo College when it was a junior college, and then joined the United States Navy during the Vietnam War. It was during his stint in the Navy that he accepted Christ as his savior at the Fairmount Park Free Will Baptist Church, now the Gateway Free Will Baptist Church in Norfolk, Virginia, under the ministry of Pastor Dale Burden. He and his future wife, Linda Carol Williams, were active in the church's bus ministry, choir, visitation, and teaching Sunday school. They were married in June of 1972 at Fairmount Park. Ron soon sensed God's call to the ministry and the call to be a missionary, and he and Linda were off to Free Will Baptist Bible College in Nashville, Tennessee. While a student at the Bible College Ron was licensed to the gospel ministry by the Woodbine Free Will Baptist Church in Nashville and preached his first sermon at the Poplar Grove Free Will Baptist Church in Iuka, Mississippi.

He graduated from Free Will Baptist Bible College, now Welch College, in 1975. He was ordained to the ministry that same year by the Randall Association of North Carolina when he was thirty-one years old. Ron and Linda were commissioned for missionary service at the First Free Will Baptist Church of Raleigh, North Carolina, in 1976. Missionary to Brazil, John Stewart Craft, preached the sermon and Eugene Waddell, Director of the Free Will Baptist Foreign Missions Department, did the commissioning. The Callaway's did itinerate work in Texas prior to departing for their ministry in Spain. Their daughter, Rachel Leigh Callaway, was nine months old when they departed for Spain. They spent 1976-79 at a language school in Madrid, Spain, then Linda studied Spanish with a private teacher and Ron attended the University of Madrid for one year of cultural studies and additional language study.

Upon the completion of their language studies Ron and Linda went to work in church planting, evangelism, and leadership training. Linda was also involved in youth and children's ministry. Linda, being a licensed teacher, taught Rachel in grades 1-3. Ron pastored the Alcalá de Henares Church for one and a half years while Lonnie and Anita Sparks were on furlough. In 1989 the mission board asked Ron to travel to Cuba to assist two North American Free Will Baptist pastors who were going to attend the Cuban Free Will Baptist National Association meeting. Then, in 1991, the mission board asked him to return to Cuba to teach a class at the newly reopened Cuba Bible Institute, *Los Cedros del Libaño*,[267] Cedars of Lebanon. These visits and the friendships made placed a burden on Ron's heart to try and enter Cuba on a full-time basis. This was (and still is) not possible at this writing. In hope of entering Cuba, Ron and Linda requested a transfer from Spain to Panama to work with Steve and Judy Lytle in the Bible Institute in Panama and, at the same time, be more and more involved in the Cuban work. Their request for transfer was granted and they left Spain in 1995 and entered Panama in 1997.

Ron's ministry in Panama was multifaceted, as it had been in Spain. As he had requested to do, Ron served as the director of the Bible Institute and pastored the First Free Will Baptist Church in Panama City, Panama. He was also involved in evangelism and leadership training. In addition, he was the last Protestant chaplain on the last U. S. Army base in the Panama Canal Zone, as the United States closed the bases there. Linda co-founded the ladies Tuesday Morning Prayer ministry at the church. Somehow Ron managed to earn a Master of Divinity Degree from Southeastern Baptist Theological Seminary in 1997. From 1998 to 2002 Ron and Linda worked and lived in Cuba during the months of January and February, partially fulfilling their desire to work in Cuba. When home on furlough they continued to do itinerate work in Texas. By the time they left Free Will Baptist International Missions, somewhere between 16% and 18% of their financial support was coming from the Lone Star State.

In 2003, Dr. Matthew Pinson, president of Free Will Baptist Bible College[268] requested that Ron come to Nashville, Tennessee, to become the Missions Program Coordinator for the college. Thus there was another shift in the ministry of the Callaway's, though the focus was still on missions. Ron continues to be an adjunct professor at *Los Cedros del Libaño*, serving as assistant professor of missions and coordinator of their master's degree program. He still travels to Panama to teach in the institute there. He invests himself in the promising mission's students at Welch College and the results of that may reach many countries and countless souls in the future. He has translated several Free Will Baptist theological books into Spanish and continues that ministry. Ron and Linda both teach Sunday school classes at Cofer's Chapel Free Will Baptist Church in Nashville. Ron earned a Doctor of Ministry Degree from Mid-American Baptist Theological Seminary in 2014. He has gone to Russia (twice) and India to teach in addition to his continuing trips to Panama and Cuba.

Their daughter, Rachel, and her husband, Aaron DeMerchant, and three children, live in Canada. Aaron pastors the Grace Free Will Baptist Church in Plaster Rock, New Brunswick, which is in the Atlantic Canada Association.

---

[267] This school was founded by legendary missionary Thomas "Pop" Willey, another missionary with a Texas connection.
[268] Free Will Baptist Bible College became Welch College in 2012.

Wesley Calvery

Marvin Wesley Calvery was born in Eddy, Texas, on May 27, 1929, the youngest son of Ellis and Lela Calvery. He grew up in Waco where his family attended the First Free Will Baptist Church. His father owned a grocery store one street over from the church. Wesley attended Free Will Baptist Bible College, in Nashville, Tennessee, graduating in 1947, from their two year program of study, along with fellow Texans Herbert and Margaret Richards, and Gaston Clary. Also in that graduating class was a young lady by the name of Aileen Mullen, from Arkansas, whom he would later marry. Wesley went on to earn a Bachelor's Degree in biology from Vanderbilt University, in Nashville, in 1954.

Aileen and Wesley Calvery

Wesley was ordained to the gospel ministry in 1948 and commissioned as a foreign missionary. He served as assistant pastor and educational director at the First Free Will Baptist Church in Bryan, Texas, while he and Aileen were awaiting visas from Japan. In 1954 he and Aileen arrived in Japan as the first Free Will Baptist missionaries to that nation. He and Aileen both attended language school in Yokohama, after their arrival in Japan. He planted several churches on the island of Hokkaido from1956 to 1987, when his service with the Free Will Baptist Mission Board was terminated due to moral issues, which resulted in he and Aileen getting a divorce. From 1987 to 1990, he continued missionary work, this time in Hawai'i. From 1991 to 2002, he was with the Christian Bridal Mission and pastor of Sharon Gospel Church in Maebashi, Japan. He passed away on Monday, January 14, 2002. He is buried in Japan. In 2002 his son Michael Calvery lived in Round Rock, Texas, and his son Jonathan Calvery lived in Cameron, Texas. A daughter, Rebecca Arthur lived in Snow Hill, North Carolina.

Dwain Crosby

Allen Dwain Crosby was born to Milburn Lee and Billie Jean (Martin) Crosby in Waco, Texas, on November 30, 1956. His father was a Free Will Baptist pastor and a master carpenter. Dwain graduated from Crowell High School, Crowell, Texas, in 1975. During high school Dwain excelled and received awards in Band and Drama. While attending the West Fork Youth Camp, while still in high school, Dwain sensed that God was calling him into the ministry. He was licensed to the gospel ministry by the Northwest Brazos District Association of Free Will Baptists in 1973. He was then ordained by the Northwest Brazos in 1974. Having a desire to prepare for the ministry, Dwain enrolled at Hillsdale Free Will Baptist College,

Dwain and Debbie Crosby

Moore, Oklahoma, in 1975, and graduated in 1980. While in college Dwain met and married Debbie Ann Carol, of Mustang, Oklahoma, on June 10, 1977. From this marriage came two children: Michelle Elizabeth and Matthew Allen Crosby.

While still a student at Hillsdale, Dwain became the pastor of the Stroud Free Will Baptist Church, Stroud, Oklahoma, and pastored it until 1981. He then pastored Christ's Free Will Baptist Church, Corpus Christi, Texas, from 1983 to 1985. His next pastorate was the Chapel Hill Free Will Baptist Church in Brownwood, Texas, which he pastored from 1985 to 1987.

Dwain first sensed God's call to be a missionary while a student at Hillsdale, and this call was renewed during his pastorate in Corpus Christi. He and Debbie were commissioned for missionary service at the First Free Will Baptist Church in Waco, in 1989. They arrived in Spain in December of that year and began language school in Madrid. During their ministry in Spain they lived in Galapagar, Mosteles, and Majadahonda, in the Madrid Province. They ministered alongside Ron and Linda Callaway, Steve and Linda Reeves, Jeff and Susan Turnbough, Lonnie Sparks, and Lynn Midgett. Their primary missionary work was church planting and training national workers. Dwain also taught in a seminary. The Crosby's resigned from Free Will Baptist International Missions in June of 1996 and left Spain to return to the United States.

They were hired by the State Missions Board of the Texas State Association of Free Will Baptists and began a church planting project in The Woodlands, Texas, north of Houston. This work, which began in August of 1996, was a joint project between the Texas Mission Board and the Mission Board of the National Association of Free Will Baptists. The church they started was the North Pointe Fellowship Free Will Baptist Church and it did well under Dwain's leadership. During this time he also edited *The Texas Challenge*, the state paper of the Texas State Association of Free Will Baptists, from June 1999 to 2001. Dwain then left the ministry, and surrendered his credentials, to deal with family issues privately, with a desire to not hinder the work in any way. He lives in Nassau Bay, Texas, and operates his own business.

Deleen (Huston) Cousineau

Deleen Huston was born on August 1, 1954, to Weldon and Sissie Huston in Odessa, Texas, two of the finest people who ever lived on the face of this earth. Her father was at first a mechanic. Later he worked for France Products in Odessa, working his way up to Regional Manager. Then he founded and was president and owner of Compressor Components, an oilfield supply company in Odessa. Weldon was also the song leader and a deacon in the First Free Will Baptist Church of Odessa. The Texas State Association of Free Will Baptists named Weldon the "Layman of the Year" in 1971. While Kenneth Brandon was preaching a revival meeting at the Bible Free Will Baptist Church in Odessa, Deleen went forward and gave her heart to Jesus when she was eight years old.

Mike and Deleen (Huston) Cousineau

After graduating from Permian High School in 1972, Deleen went to Hillsdale Free Will Baptist College in Moore, Oklahoma, for her freshman year. She transferred to Howard Payne University in Brownwood, Texas, for the fall semester in 1973. While a student at Howard Payne she drove from Brownwood to Abilene on Sundays and played the piano in the Free Will Baptist mission pastored by Robert Scroggins. After the one semester she returned to Hillsdale. Deleen attended Hillsdale because she wanted to find God's will for her life. At the time she was not thinking about becoming a missionary. She graduated in May of 1976 with a Bachelor's Degree in Theology.

In June of 1974 she served as a camp counselor at the West Fork Youth Camp near Vashti, Texas, making a huge impression on, not only the campers, but the adult workers, as well.

It was during her Junior year at Hillsdale in 1974 that Deleen met Mike Cousineau. Mike was the son of Maurice and Marie LaBelle Cousineau, both French Canadians by birth, who served for a time as Free Will Baptist missionaries in Ivory Coast, Africa. Maurice also served for a time as a home missionary pastor in Billings, Montana. Deleen's interest in being a missionary started with her relationship with Mike. She knew he was planning on returning to Ivory Coast where he had spent his teen years. Deleen and Mike were married on December 22, 1975, at the First Free Will Baptist Church in Odessa, her home church.

After being commissioned as missionaries by the Free Will Baptist Foreign Missions Board in June of 1979, Deleen and Mike went to Albertville, France, for language study, where they studied French, the national language of Ivory Coast. They sailed on a freighter from Marseille, France, to Abidjan, Ivory Coast, West Africa, arriving in Abidjan on October 31, 1980. The country is now called Côte d'Ivoire. Brooke Michelle was born in 1980, thirteen days after they arrived in Côte d'Ivoire. Kristina Renee was born in 1985, also in Côte d'Ivoire.

Mike and Deleen served in the city of Bouna from 1980 to 1998. They started out working with the youth ministry with Eddie and Sandra Payne, and then worked in village evangelism. In 1987, Mike and Clint Morgan created a Bible institute in leadership training for Ivorian Christians. At one time in the Bouna church there were eleven tribes represented. Mike taught in French since the national language was French. In 1995, Deleen graduated from Southern Nazarene University with a Master of Science in Counseling Psychology. Later they served at the International Christian Academy in Bouake, a school for missionary children, from 1998 to 1999, and from 2000 to 2002. Mike worked at the school as the business manager and Deleen as a counselor. Daughters Brooke and Kristina were students at the school. Mike was involved in the planting of a church in Bouake, the second largest city in the country.

On July 17, 2002, two months before the civil war in Ivory Coast, seven armed men attacked the campus at International Christian Academy.[269] Mike suffered several blows to the head, one of them inflicted by a blow with a 9mm pistol. He was then kidnapped at gunpoint and taken off campus in his own car by seven men. The seven kidnappers stopped the car and ordered Mike to get out so they could kill him. In the split second that it took the driver to reload his gun, Mike took off running behind the car in a zigzag fashion. More than a dozen bullets were fired at him, whizzing by as he ran, but Mike escaped into the bush unharmed, except for the several blows he had received at the school. On September 23, Free Will Baptist missionaries met at Bouna to discuss evacuation plans. On October 1 all Free Will Baptist missionaries, except the Cousineaus, left Côte d'Ivoire for the United States. On Thursday, October 3, 2002, Mike and Deleen left Côte d'Ivoire for the States, too. Seventeen year old Kristina left for Dakar, Senegal, where other missionary children from International Christian Academy went to complete the school year. Twenty-two year old Brooke was in nursing school in Athens, Georgia, at the time. After a short trip to the United States the Cousineaus returned to Dakar to finish the school year. Deleen spent the school year doing member care and Mike would return to the International Christian Academy,

---

[269] Some of this story was taken from the November/December 2002 issue of *Heartbeat*, the bimonthly magazine of Free Will Baptist Foreign Missions.

in rebel controlled territory, working to keep the campus intact under the control of the French military.

Deleen was herself a missionary, not just a missionary wife and mother. She and Mike lived their lives with the national people and grew to love them dearly. They served together as missionaries from 1980 to 2005. They were evacuated out of Africa a second time in 2004 due to the continuing civil war. In 2005 Mike took leadership of the Hanna Project, the humanitarian branch of International Missions, the new name for the Free Will Baptist Foreign Missions Department. They established residence in Moore, Oklahoma, and Mike traveled back and forth between the United States and Côte d'Ivoire.

In May, 2010, Mike founded 1040 Initiative, a non-government organization that ministers to people in Morocco and Côte d'Ivoire in the areas of water, health, and education. He leads several teams each year to both African countries. Deleen worked on the senior unit as a mental health therapist at a local hospital, an acute care facility for diagnosing and evaluating geriatrics. She took an early retirement in October, 2015, due to the progression of Parkinson's disease. Mike and Deleen are grandparents, with a growing number of grandchildren. She lost her father, Weldon Huston, on December 23, 2015.

Paul and Tanya Dean

Included among the missionaries with strong Texas connections are Paul and Tanya Dean, who pastored the Bright Light Free Will Baptist Church in Brazos County, out of Bryan-College Station from 1984 to 1994 and served in the position of assistant pastor from 1997 to 1998. While pastoring at Bright Light Paul Aubrey Dean also served on the Christian Education Board of the Central Texas District Association. Paul received his education at Old Dominion University, Norfolk, Virginia, receiving a Bachelor of Arts in History in 1979. He was engaged in non-degree studies at Free Will Baptist Bible College (1980-1982), focusing on Bible and International Missions, and at Tennessee State University (1982-1983). From 1991 to 1994 he earned a Master of Science in Adult Education from Texas A&M University, College Station, Texas.

Paul and Tanya Dean

Wanting to reach across cultures and countries to share the gospel with others Paul and Tanya accepted a position with the English Language Institute in China, teaching English. Missionaries as such were barred from China, so the Deans used a different strategy to take God's word to a country considered closed to the gospel. China did not want missionaries but they did want their citizens to learn English. Through the means of an independent sending agency, ELIC, Paul and Tanya went to China in the summer of 1998. They had the status of associate missionaries with Free Will Baptist International Missions. Sometimes Paul taught at the Qingdao Agricultural University, Qingdao, China, and sometimes as an independent teacher. In 2013 Paul and Tanya returned to the States. At this writing Paul pastors in Tennessee.

Ken and Marvis Eagleton

Kenneth Paul Eagleton was born to Earl Edwin and Bertha (Perkins) Eagleton in Fort Worth, Texas, on July 1, 1928. His father was a carpenter. Ken graduated from Northside High School and then joined the United States Air Force for four years. He served in Korea during the Korean War, although he was not involved in combat. He was discharged as a Staff Sergeant. It was after his service in the military that Ken became a Christian, attending the Rock of Ages Free Will Baptist Church in Fort Worth. The church later changed its name to the Western Hills Free Will Baptist Church. He sensed that God was calling him to preach the gospel and he answered the call. He was licensed and ordained by the West Fork District Association. His ordination certificate was signed by Clarence Hearron, C. B. Thompson, and one other person whose name is not recalled. He went to Nashville, Tennessee, to attend Free Will Baptist Bible College, starting in 1953.

Ken and Marvis Eagleton

Marvis Nell Anderson was born to James Lauderdale (Lod) and Ella Frances (Beard) Anderson, in Henderson, Texas, on April 27, 1926. Her father was also a carpenter. Marvis grew up in the Good Hope Free Will Baptist Church near Henderson in East Texas. Marvis attended Free Will Baptist Bible College, starting in the fall of 1952 and finishing the school's two year program in 1954. It was at the Bible College that the two Texans, Marvis and Ken, met and fell in love. She worked in the school's administration office until Ken graduated in 1957.

Ken and Marvis were married on August 28, 1954, in Marvis' home church, Good Hope. From their marriage came four sons: Kenneth Paul Eagleton is a Free Will Baptist missionary, living in Campinas, Sao Paulo, Brazil; Terry Wayne Eagleton, program director at Tennessee Primary Care Association, living in Nashville, Tennessee; Andrew James Eagleton, Inspector for the Federal Aviation Agency (FAA), living in Colorado; and Stephen Philip Eagleton, engineer with Honeywell International, living in Chandler, Arizona.

Ken went on a mission's trip to Cuba in the summer of 1956 with Tom Willey, Jr. and five college students, including Dave Franks from Alabama. All of the students, except for Ken and Dave, were intending to be missionaries. Ken and Dave went with a new convert to the state of Minas Gerais, where the man has family. They made the trip in a Volkswagen van. In one of the towns they held open-air meetings in the town square. The local Catholic priest did everything he could to stop them. He threatened the population, telling them not to sell food or give lodging to the Protestants. One night after the service some boys came up to them and asked to take their shoes off -- they wanted to see their pig's feet. The priest had told them that Protestants had pig's feet. Ken and Dave, who were not intending to be missionaries, ended up in Brazil as Free Will Baptist missionaries, while the three young men who were intending to be missionaries never made it. Ken had a growing conviction, wrought by Scripture, the summer spent in Cuba, and the encouragement of Tom Willey, Jr., that he should be a missionary. He once said, "As I studied the Bible and read that all men are lost and doomed to an eternal hell without Christ as their savior, that they cannot have faith in Christ unless they hear the gospel, and they cannot hear without a preacher, I then knew God would have me personally go tell them that Christ saves." Ken sought further training for the mission field by attending Winona Lake School of Theology at Winona Lake, Indiana, and Bob Jones University in Greenville, South Carolina.

Ken's friend Dave Franks arrived in Brazil on January 1, 1958, while still single. Thomas "Pop" Willey had made a survey trip about a year earlier, and had come in contact with a Brazilian Baptist pastor who had started an independent (unaffiliated) work in his home. Dave followed up on that contact and the pastor became a Free Will Baptist and organized his work as a Free Will Baptist church in April of 1958. This was the first Free Will Baptist church in Brazil. Ken and Marvis arrived on July 3, 1958, as Free Will Baptists' second missionaries in Brazil, with one son in tow and Marvis seven months pregnant with Terry. They quickly found a need to fill in the Campinas church and Bible institute. Over time Ken took over responsibilities in the Campinas church. He soon led in a construction program to build a new sanctuary for the congregation.

Following their first furlough, Ken and Marvis settled in Jaboticabal, Brazil, where they purchased land for youth camps and a new Brazilian Bible Institute. Through the next many years Ken taught full-time at the institute, teaching Bible classes and training national workers. Marvis assisted at the library when she was not busy with their four boys. She was also bookkeeper for the Mission in Brazil, and worked with various auxiliary ministries such as the women, Sunday school, etc. Ken was also a church planter, though he usually followed another missionary in these efforts. He pastored three churches altogether: Campinas, Jaboticabal, and Araras.

Ken's greatest gift was teaching. He had good insight into the Scriptures and ably communicated his knowledge to his students. His greatest legacy is the denominational leadership he disciplined and taught. Many of the first Brazilian pastors sat under his teaching. Almost all of the leaders in the First Free Will Baptist Church of Araras, where he pastored the longest, were trained by him.

Over the years several more missionary families joined the work in Brazil. At present Free Will Baptists have churches in two states: São Paulo and Minas Gerais. There are eighteen organized Free Will Baptist churches in Brazil, eight mission churches, with an attendance of twenty-one hundred people, and one regional association. There are thirty-three ordained Bazilian pastors and three Bible institutes, with approximately seventy enrolled. Brazil has sent out six cross-cultural missionaries: one in Turkey, three in Uruguay, and two in India, plus one couple that teaches at a New Tribes school for missions.

Ken and Marvis moved from Brazil to the United States in 1990, where he worked in the home office of International Missions. Ken developed an idea which has proven effective. He was certain that if Free Will Baptist students were exposed face-to-face with the mission field they would respond in service and support. He proposed TEAM, Teens Equipped and Active in Missions. With the approval of the board of Free Will Baptist International Missions, a new era of student missions blossomed. Bringing together teens and cross-cultural ministry, TEAM proved an immediate success. Dozens of students continue to train and travel each year as a living legacy of Ken's vision. Each year TEAM sends groups of dedicated youth to places such as Cuba, Mexico, France, Brazil, Panama, as well as countries in Eastern Europe and Asia. TEAM eventually became E-TEAM in honor of Ken Eagleton.

In the early 90's they returned to Brazil about three times to teach each year for about three months. In 1994 Ken and Marvis accepted a short term assignment of six months to help out in Côte d'Ivoire (Ivory Coast, Africa) due to personnel shortages there. They spent a trimester at International Academy, a school for missionary children, as dorm parents for twenty teenage boys. Then they spent another three months in Doropo doing maintenance on the Mission property, which included the hospital. They were in their late 60's by then.

They were still employed by International Missions when Ken passed away on August 26, 1999, at the age of seventy-one. Marvis retired after Ken's death and lived in Kingston Springs, Tennessee, with their son Terry. She was an invalid during that time. Her last months were spent in a retirement home under special medical care. She passed away on February 21, 2003, at the age of seventy-six. They are buried together in the Middle Tennessee State Veterans Cemetery in Nashville.

Anthony Edgmon

Anthony Stephen Edgmon was born to Cletis C. Jr. and Claret Sue (Jones) Edgmon on June 15, 1971, in Pensacola, Florida.

Anthony and Lea Edgmon

The Edgmon family was attending the Oak Park Free Will Baptist Church in Pine Bluff, Arkansas, when Anthony was saved at the age of five and baptized. Through the influence of his mother, who is very mission-minded, Anthony developed a burden for missions at an early age. The Edgmon family moved to Denison, Texas, in 1984 and became active in the First Free Will Baptist Church. Anthony and his siblings were active in the Church Training Service (CTS) competitive activities in the Denison church, the West Fork District Association, the Texas State Association, and the National Association of Free Will Baptists. They were always active as campers in the West Fork Youth Camp. It was when Joel Kircher pastored the church in Denison, and under whose leadership the church changed its name to the Cornerstone Free Will Baptist Church, that Anthony answered the call to preach.

Needing to prepare for the ministry, Anthony enrolled at Free Will Baptist Bible College in Nashville, Tennessee, and began classes in the fall of 1989. Anthony answered the call to missions while a student there. After his graduation in 1994, he served as a student missionary to Panama during the summer. In the fall he began serving as associate to Pastor Larry Montgomery at Calvary Chapel Free Will Baptist Church in Hollywood, Florida. He was both youth minister and music minister. It was during this time that Anthony was licensed to the gospel ministry by the South Florida District Association of Free Will Baptists. He was ordained by the South Florida District Association on November 25, 1995. His ordination certificate was signed by Lonnie Buser, Bill Wilson, Jose L. Rodriguez, and his pastor Larry Montgomery.

Lea Cheryl Southwell was born in Arlington, Virginia. Her father, Rev. Murray L. Southwell, was the pastor of the Bloss Memorial Free Will Baptist Church there for seventeen years. Lea was led to the Lord by her children's church teacher. She answered the call to missionary service during her sophomore year at the Bible College. She was part of the Go and Be Team that traveled to Côte d'Ivoire in 1993. She graduated from the Bible College in 1996 with a degree in Elementary Education and Missions.

Lea and Anthony met while in college and were married at the Cross Timbers Free Will Baptist Church in Nashville. They have two children: Emily Hope and Marc Andrew.

The Edgmons were appointed as career missionaries to Spain by the Free Will Baptist Board of Foreign Missions in April, 1997. They arrived on the field in October, 1998. Following language study they worked in the areas of teaching and preaching in Villalba.

Anthony and Lea are currently working in the town of Alpedrete, which has more than doubled in population in the last decade. When the Edgmons arrived in Alpedrete there was no evangelical church there of any kind. The Alpedrete team, consisting of the Edgmons and Tim and Kristi Johnson, opened an Outreach Center in December 2005, beginning with activities for children, women, and families. The first regular worship service was held on Sunday, February 5, 2006. Since then, a vibrant congregation with a desire to reach others with the gospel has grown in Alpedrete. The church seeks to reach out to friends and neighbors in the community, but also has been very involved in giving to send the gospel around the world. The Edgmons are currently working to train leaders in the church and prepare them for their role as a church-planting movement in the country of Spain.

June Goode Wilkinson Hersey

Volree June Goode was born to Viola Pearl (Johnson) and Joseph Murray Goode on June 29, 1934, in Lexington, Lee County, Texas. She was of German descent. Her paternal great grandfather, whose last name was Behringer, came from Baden Baden, Germany and homesteaded some land in Giddings, Texas, where he and his wife are buried. June's father, J. M. Goode, was a Free Will Baptist pastor in East Texas. She was converted to Christ at home when she was somewhere between the ages of ten and twelve. The Goode family lived in Overton, Texas, at the time. June was baptized and joined the Mt. Olive Free Will Baptist Church when she was thirteen. She is the oldest of five girls: June, Shirley Sharpston, Barbara Bodnar, Mary Katherine Yance, and Paula Goode.

June Goode

June's parents always entertained visiting missionaries when possible. A book, *Terry's Call*, which she received from the Bible Memory Association for doing their memory program, made a life changing impression on her. She made a public commitment to be a missionary at Piney Woods Camp when Wesley Calvery was the speaker. In the summer of 1949, when June was fifteen, Henry "Pop" Melvin brought a quartet from Free Will Baptist Bible College to East Texas. The quartet consisted of Wesley Calvery, Myrtis Carnes, Darrel West, and Billy Melvin. That was her introduction to Free Will Baptist Bible College. They had a service at Mt. Olive and had an evening meal at June's house.

June's father also held Sunday afternoon services and Sunday school at Good Hope Free Will Baptist Church, near Henderson. Marvis Eagleton's father gave her five dollars for playing the piano there for a revival meeting once. She says it was the only time she ever got paid for playing the piano except when their present piano player in Georgia is absent, and she gets paid for playing.

June graduated from Kilgore High School, Kilgore, Texas, in May, 1951. In her graduating class was the pianist Van Cliburn. They sat at the same table in the chemistry lab for homeroom. After graduation from high school she attended Kilgore Junior College during the 1951-52 school year. She then worked for Cahahan-Gage Insurance and Accounting Firm from 1952 to 1953. In September of 1953 she entered Free Will Baptist Bible College in Nashville, Tennessee. She had met Stan Mooneyham when she was president of the East Texas League Rally and he was their speaker on a couple of occasions. Now in Bible College, she went to work as secretary to W. S.

Sam and June Wilkinson

Mooneyham, Executive Secretary of the National Association of Free Will Baptists, whose offices were about three blocks down Richland Avenue from the college. She worked there from 1953 to 1957. June did not graduate from the Bible College but went there from September, 1953, to May, 1955.

It was while she was a student at the Bible College that she met Sam Wilkinson who had been born and reared in Glennville, Georgia. Sam was a senior and graduated in May, 1954. He and Evelyn, Fred Hersey's first wife, were in the same graduating class. June and Sam were married July 22, 1955, at the Buncombe Free Will Baptist Church where her father, Rev. J. M. Goode, was the pastor. Eugene Waddell was holding a two week revival at Buncombe but cancelled the Friday night service for the wedding. Leah Waddell sang, though she was seven months pregnant with Rhonda. Ken Eagleton, Bill Jones, and Elro Driggers were in the wedding. The next night June and Sam attended the wedding of Dale Burden and Jane Berry at the church near Huntsville where Jane's father, Rev. H. Ray Berry, was pastor. June sat next to Rev. Mrs. Lizzie McAdams. June and Sam had to give up the bridal suite after they registered at the motel because it had been reserved for guess who? Dale and Jane! June and Sam, and Dale and Jane, all went to breakfast together the next morning.

After graduating from Free Will Baptist Bible College in 1954 Sam attended Columbia Bible College, now Columbia International University, in Columbia, South Carolina. He was the first pastor of Horton Heights Free Will Baptist Church, first known as Palmer Memorial, in Nashville, Tennessee. Sam's and June's original plans were to go to India as missionaries, where one of his distant relatives, Miss Laura Bell Barnard, had spent most of her life as a missionary. In 1957, after their visas to India were denied twice, Sam and June moved to Jesup, Georgia, where he pastored the Spring Grove Free Will Baptist Church.

Their plans to become missionaries came to fruition when they went to Brazil December 16, 1959. Their ministry in South America's largest country involved some church planting, but some of the time they were gypsy missionaries, filling in for those on stateside assignment, that is, for missionaries who had gone home on furlough. During their latter years in Brazil they lived on the missionary property and were responsible for conferences, retreats, youth camps, and mission meetings. June home schooled the children part of the time and part of the time they attended public schools. In addition, she was mission bookkeeper several times, played the pump organ for worship, taught Sunday school, planned menus, and bought food for the meetings, sometimes for as many as over a hundred people. Sam and June ministered mostly in the State of Sao Paulo, but lived down south in Tubarao, Santa Catarina, for a year. June's and Sam's children consider Jaboticabal, where the mission property is located, as home. During furlough time, Sam received a Masters of Education Degree in Guidance and Counseling from Middle Tennessee State University, Murfreesboro, Tennessee, in 1971. June graduated from São Luis Faculdade de Educacao (St. Louis College of Education) in Jaboticabal, with a degree in Letters (language related subjects).

In August, 1964, while June and Sam were flying home from Campinas, Brazil, to the states for furlough, four young men who had boarded when June and Sam did, came and stood around them. One of them asked, "What is that religious song we know?" They then sang "Swing Low Sweet Chariot." It was the Beatles on their first trip to the States. The four got off in Lima,

Peru, and June and Sam found out later who they were. June didn't even get an autograph on a napkin or ticket.

June and Sam had three children: Kevin, Kimberly, and Kenan, all born in Brazil.

After serving almost twenty years as missionaries to Brazil, Sam and June resigned from the Free Will Baptist Foreign Missions Department, now International Missions, in March, 1979. Sam became pastor of the Surrency Free Will Baptist Church in Surrency, Georgia, where he and June served until 1985. Sam was then offered a teaching position at Hillsdale Free Will Baptist College in Moore, Oklahoma. They moved to Oklahoma in July, 1985. Sam died from a massive heart attack on April 11, 1988, while mowing the lawn. He had not been sick but knew he had some heart vessel problems. It was a genetic problem since his mother's youngest brother died at fifty-five, and Sam's sister just older than he, died a similar death. Sam and June had been snow skiing with a church group from the First Free Will Baptist Church in Norman, Oklahoma. June believes that the extreme exertion made one of the vessels weak. Sam would have been fifty-five years old on May 13, 1988. He is buried in the Ebenezer Free Will Baptist Church cemetery in Glennville, Georgia, near Miss Laura Bell Barnard.

Fred and June Hersey

Following Sam's death, June remained at Hillsdale until July, 1991. She was cashier in the business office, taught some, and finished her Bachelor of Arts Degree. In July, 1991, June moved to Nashville, Tennessee, to work for International Missions in the business office. At this point June's life took another turn. Fred Hersey's wife, Evelyn, died of cancer in October, 1993, while they were living in Nashville. June and Fred had known each other at Free Will Baptist Bible College in 1954 when he came there for one semester. Fred had graduated from Bob Jones University and wanted to know more about Free Will Baptist missions. He had joined the Free Will Baptist denomination in Gastonia, North Carolina, while he was a student at Bob Jones. He and Evelyn had gone to Japan as missionaries in April, 1956, and Sam and June had gone to Brazil in December, 1959. Consequently, their stateside assignments very rarely coincided. June and Fred, now both widowed, began dating in the spring of 1994, but he went back to Japan for six months. For those six months they had a phone-letter courtship. They were married January 21, 1995, at the Rudy's Restaurant at Opryland (Mrs. Rudy was a personal friend) with immediate family and few friends in attendance. Eugene Waddell, who had cancelled the Friday night revival service back at Bumcombe in 1955 for June's first wedding, and former director of Free Will Baptist Foreign Missions, performed the ceremony. June and Fred had a reception at Donelson Free Will Baptist Church for extended family and other friends. On the following Monday, June and Fred left for Japan, with a one week stopover in Hawaii. June was once again a missionary.

After having been a missionary to Japan for nearly thirty-nine years, Fred was now joined by June. Their work involved ministering in four different churches in Japan. He preached in three of them and they held English classes in three of them. Two of the churches were in the Sapporo area, on the west coast of the island of Hokkaido, and the other two were all the way across the island, about a five hour drive east, on the Pacific Ocean. She was in Japan two and a half years, until 1998, just long enough to begin to feel at home. It was difficult for them to get up and down on the floor to sleep and eat in some cases. In Fred's earlier years in Japan he had been involved in church planting. June never expected to like the Orient, but she loved Japan. Fred says she misses it more than he does.

June and Fred went back for the fifty year celebration of the Free Will Baptist work in Japan, and for the forty year celebration of the church he started in the Tokyo area. June and Fred currently live in Dothan, Alabama. Fred pastors the Blakely Free Will Baptist Church in Blakely, Georgia, about a forty minute drive from Dothan.

June says she is the only person alive who has worked at all three of the Free Will Baptist National Offices. In 1953-1957 she was secretary to Stan Mooneyham at 3801 Richland Avenue, down the street from the Bible College; 1970-1971 she was secretary to Henry VanKluyve and receptionist for International Missions at the Murfreesboro Road location; 1991-1994 she worked in the business office of International Missions at the present location on Mt. View Road in Antioch, Tennessee.

Back in the 1940's a beautiful young teenage girl in East Texas made a commitment to be a missionary. Lots of young people do that in the spirit of the moment at youth camp or at a youth rally, but June Goode did it. She actually did it. As a matter of fact, she served as a missionary twice, for many years in Brazil, and then for a time in Japan. June, Texas is really proud of you.

Mrs. Ida B. Holder

Several minutes mention a missionary to India by the name of Mrs. Ida B. Holder who was supported by the Southwestern Freewill Baptist Convention, which included most of the churches in Texas. The 1914 minutes of the convention refer to her as the "Lone Star Messenger." What that meant is not certain, but in all probability it meant that she was from Texas. We do know that the Southwestern Convention and the Free Will Baptists of Texas continued supporting the Free Will Baptist work in India even after the merger of 1910-1911.

Ernest Holland

Ernest Ray Holland was born on May 21, 1961, in Comanche, Texas, to James and Barbara (Kirkland) Holland. Ernest's father, James, worked for the United States Postal Service. The Hollands were members of the Liberty Free Will Baptist Church in Comanche and were there every time the doors were open. Ernest was nine days old the first time he attended church there. Ernest's mother, Barbara, taught Sunday school. Ernest became a Christian in 1968 at the age of seven, under the ministry of Pastor Cotton. Ernest remembers that when he was young missionary Bill Jones came to speak at the church. While the missionary to Africa was speaking, Ernest felt that God was calling him to be a missionary.

Ernest attended Comanche High School, graduating in 1979. He played football in high school and was valedictorian of his graduating class. While still in high school he began working in the hospital and that is what led him to go to Cotê d'Ivoire as a summer missionary. He had planned on being a doctor and the medical mission work was interesting to him. It was during his high school years that he answered

Ernest and Elaine Holland

the call to preach the gospel. His uncle, Blackie Kirkland, who pastored the First Free Will Baptist Church in Weatherford, Texas, and his cousin by marriage, Larry Cox,[270] was also a Free Will Baptist pastor, and they both had an influence on his call. Ernest was licensed to the gospel ministry by the West Fork District Association of Free Will Baptists in 1979. After high school, he attended Tarleton State University in nearby Stephenville, Texas, for one year. During that year at Tarleton State Ernest felt that God was calling him to attend Hillsdale Free Will Baptist College, at Moore, Oklahoma, to prepare for the ministry. He enrolled at Hillsdale in the fall of 1980. He was ordained to the gospel ministry that same year, 1980, by the West Fork District Association. One of the men who signed his ordination certificate was Burton Hughes, pastor of the Liberty Church at the time. Three years later, 1983, Ernest graduated from Hillsdale.

During the summer after his graduation he went to Côté d'Ivoire, the new name for Ivory Coast, as a summer missionary. Two important things happened that eventful summer that changed Ernest's life forever. First, he felt God's call to be a missionary. Second, he met Miss Elaine Allen of Tulsa, Oklahoma, who was working at the Free Will Baptist hospital in Côté d'Ivoire, where he himself was working that summer. Elaine had become a nurse in order to go to Doropo to work in the Free Will Baptist hospital. Her parents had helped start the Bethany Free Will Baptist Church in Broken Arrow, Oklahoma, in 1962. Elaine was baptized at the time and became one of the charter members. Bethany supported her throughout her mission work and continued to support her and her husband after they were married. Elaine returned to the states for furlough at the end of the summer and Ernest returned to the states and started working at Hillsdale. Elaine came to Hillsdale, from which she had graduated in 1975, for a mission's conference in November of that year, 1983. Ernest and Elaine started dating. They were married on May 19, 1984 at Bethany Free Will Baptist Church in Broken Arrow, Oklahoma. The ceremony was performed by Elaine's uncle, J. C. Morgan. From their marriage came three children: Joshua James Holland, born August 18, 1985, in Longview, Texas; Leah Joy, Holland born April 30, 1987, in Albertville, France; and Elissa Morgan Holland, born November 19, 1991, in Tulsa, Oklahoma.

Ernest became pastor of the Union Arbor Free Will Baptist Church in Beckville, Texas, in May of 1984, and served in that position until October of 1985. Ernest and Elaine loved serving at this church. The members of Union Arbor helped them in many ways. They were employed by Free Will Baptist International Missions in October of 1985 and began deputational work to raise financial support to go to Côté d'Ivoire, Africa.

Ernest's and Elaine's missionary commissioning service was conducted at the Pleasant Mound Free Will Baptist Church, at Buffalo Springs, Texas. It was conducted by Rev. Larry Cox. Ernest did his language study[271] in Albertville and Nantes, France, from July 1986 to June 1987. Ernest and Elaine returned to the states briefly to raise more financial support before leaving for Africa. They arrived in Côté d'Ivoire in July of 1987.

They were first assigned to work in the area of Doropo, Côté d'Ivoire, and served there from July 1987 to May 1992. Ernest worked with church planting and village ministry. Elaine worked as a nurse at the clinic/hospital. They were transferred to Bondoukou, in May of 1992 and served there until 2000. There they worked with church planting and also worked to develop the Free Will Baptist National Youth Ministry in Côté d'Ivoire. Elaine also worked with the music and children's ministry at the church and taught health clinics in various villages and at Bondoukou. She also home schooled the children. Additionally, Ernest helped start the Free Will

---

[270] Larry Cox married Jacque Kirkland, daughter of Rev. Blackie Kirkland.
[271] French is the national language of Côte d'Ivoire.

Baptist church in the capital city of Abidjan, Cotê d'Ivoire. Ernest would travel six hours from Bondoukou to Abidjan once a month to begin meetings with university students in Abidjan. With this group they started the first Free Will Baptist church in the capital city.

The Holland's work in Africa brought them alongside other missionaries, some of whom are now legendary. Separately or together they worked with Dr. Lavern Miley, Sherwood and Vada Lee, Jerry and Carol Pinkerton, Kenneth and Rejane Eagleton, and several others. Kenneth is the son of Fort Worth's own Kenneth Eagleton, who was for so many years a Free Will Baptist missionary to Brazil.

Ernest and Elaine resigned from missionary service in May of 2001. Why did they resign and return to the states? There were several reasons. The Free Will Baptist work had developed a strong national youth ministry. The church at Bondoukou had a national pastor. Other Ivorian graduates from the Bible Institute were beginning to take leadership of the ministry. They felt that God was leading them into another ministry, but didn't know what at the time. He says that leaving the mission field was very difficult, even harder than the decision to go to the field. But God gave them a peace about the decision and they continue to be involved in mission work today. Almost as soon as Ernest and Elaine returned to the states Ivory Coast began to go through a civil war. This civil war resulted in the recalling of virtually all of the Free Will Baptists from Cotê d'Ivoire for their own safety.

While Ernest and Elaine were attending the Bethany Free Will Baptist Church in Broken Arrow, Oklahoma, a position as mission's pastor opened up at the church and they felt that God was leading them to take on that ministry. At present Ernest continues as Missions and Outreach Pastor of the church. Ernest leads the church in outreach ministries locally, nationally, and internationally. The church's goal is to have every member involved in outreach. He teaches missions on a regular basis through conferences and mission trips. Elaine is an elementary school nurse and works at one of the local hospitals. She is very involved in the ministry at Bethany. She also sings on the praise team. They feel that their mission's ministry is a joint ministry.

Ernest says, "We are so thankful for Free Will Baptists in Texas. They supported us faithfully while we were on the mission field. Even though we are now living in Oklahoma, we still feel that the churches in Texas are a major part of who we are today."

Heath Hubbard

Heath Levan Hubbard was born in Fort Smith, Arkansas, to Dewey Levan and Vicki Elaine (Self) Hubbard on August 8, 1984. Heath's stay in Texas was for about five years while his father, Levan, pastored the Fellowship Free Will Baptist Church in Bryan, 1998 to 2002 or 2003. He gave his life to Christ at the age of four during a revival meeting conducted by Roy Thomas and Trymon Messer. After graduating from high school in Bryan, Heath enrolled at Free Will Baptist Bible College, now Welch College, and then graduated in 2006 with a double major: Theology and International Business, combining missions and business. This was, of course, to prepare him for missionary service.

Heath married Joni Lynn Thomas and they have three children: Eli McKendry, Micah Heath, and Emma Kathleen. Heath was licensed and ordained by the Cumberland Association of

Tennessee, the services being conducted at the Donelson Fellowship Free Will Baptist Church and his credentials signed by Pastor Rob Morgan. His ordination occurred in 2011. Heath and Joni were commissioned to missionary service, also by the Cumberland Association, at the Donelson Fellowship Church.

Heath and his family arrived at their field of service on January 17, 2013. Specifically, they serve at the Kaimfukuoka Christ Church in Saitama-ken, Kawagoeshi, Japan. Heath serves as leader of the church, which is a relatively new church plant. Still in the early stages of planting a church in Japan, Heath and Joni teach English classes to both children and adults as a means of building relationships with Japanese people. Using this method they get to a point of influence where they can share the gospel with those around them.

Heath and Joni Hubbard

Having been active in the Fellowship Church in Bryan during his growing up, teen years, a good percentage of their missionary support comes from the church.

Bill and Joy Jones

Billy Marion "Bill" Jones was born February 3, 1937, in Houston, Harris County, Texas to Marion E. and Ruth (Spencer) Jones. His father worked as a line foreman for Rural Electric Association (REA). Bill had four siblings: Dale Jones Sawyer, sister (deceased); Cindy Jones Vance, sister (deceased); Jane Jones Duke, sister; and Jim O. Jones, brother.[272] Bill and his family attended the First Free Will Baptist Church in Bryan, Texas, where he was converted to Christ at about the age of twelve. He graduated from Stephen F. Austin High School in May of 1954, and then attended Free Will Baptist Bible College, Nashville, Tennessee, from 1954 to 1957. Bill completed the four year program of study in three years and graduated *cum laude*.

Bill and Joy Jones

It was near the end of his high school career, in 1954 that Bill sensed that God was calling him to the ministry. He was licensed to preach by the Central Texas District Association. Later that year, in the fall of 1954, while attending a Billy Graham Crusade in Nashville, that he was called to be a missionary. During his first semester at the Bible College, in 1954, he met Miss Joy Wilenne Arnold. Joy was the daughter of John William (Jack) and Ora (Barnhill) Arnold. Jack worked for Mobile Oil Company as a roustabout in his early years and then as a pumper. He was also a bi-vocational preacher. Joy was born in Holdenville, Oklahoma. Joy has three siblings: Jack W. Arnold, Dr. Connie Ray Arnold, and Dan C. Arnold. Jack and his family were transferred to Gainesville, Texas, when Joy was nine years old. She graduated from Gainesville High School in 1954, and entered Free Will Baptist Bible College that fall. She attended the Bible College for three years, until 1957, but did not graduate. She, however, promised her mother that she would graduate but just didn't know when since she and Bill were getting married soon and looking

---

[272] Jim Jones, a 1965 graduate of Free Will Baptist Bible College, served as editor of *Contact*, the monthly magazine of the National Association of Free Will Baptists. Jane also graduated from the Bible College, in 1963.

forward to the mission field. Joy had not thought about the mission field until she started dating Bill. She really did not want to go to the mission field at the time, but Bill told her that he was going with or without her, though he really would like for her to go with him. After about a week of soul-searching, she decided that God had put them together, and that she would go wherever Bill went. She loved God and loved Bill, so if that was God's will for them, she was ready to go wherever God directed. Bill and Joy were married on June 10, 1957, in Whitesboro, Texas. Her father, Rev. Jack Arnold, performed the ceremony.

Bill was ordained to the gospel ministry in 1955 by the Central Texas District Association of Free Will Baptists. He pastored the First Free Will Baptist Church in Denison, Texas, from June 1957 to the summer of 1958. Bill and Joy were commissioned as missionaries at the First Free Will Baptist Church in Bowie, Texas, because they were pastoring there at the time. It was early spring of 1959. They attended the Alliance Francaise language school in Paris, France. It was set up as a year's course but, as usual, Bill was in a hurry, so he got his diploma in nine months. As soon as Bill had received his diploma from the language school, they were off to Africa. They sailed on a French liner from Marseille, France, to Abidjan, Cotê d'Ivoire. They arrived in January, 1960.

The only other Free Will Baptist missionaries in Cotê d'Ivoire at the time were Lonnie and Anita Sparks and their son, Paul, as permanent missionaries. Dan Merkh, along with wife Margaret and their children, was there in the capacity of missionary builder. When Bill and Joy arrived, Dan had completed Lonnie and Anita's house and had just moved to Koun Abronso. They found a dried-mud-brick house at the edge of the village and had moved in with a few changes. A block bathhouse was built beside the main house, with a porta-potty, shower from a bucket, and a partition moved so the kitchen would be a part of the main house. Dan had found a 6' X 12' homemade house trailer for the Jones' "place." Bill and Joy ate with the Merkhs; they hardly had elbow room to do otherwise. Dan began building a rather small house for his family so they could live up on the property while he built the Jones' house. Bill and Joy then graduated from the small trailer to the dried-mud-brick home, but they were glad to get out of that hot trailer.

They lived in Koun Abronso among the Agni tribe, about a thirty minute drive to the nearest market village. There was a small church in this village with a group of Christians. A man from their village had gone to Ghana about twenty years previously and had been converted. He learned a few songs and a few Scripture verses. He came home and shared the gospel and several people were saved. However, though they stayed together and built a church building, they really knew very little about Christianity. There had been a Methodist missionary who came about once a year and preached for them. The Christian and Missionary Alliance missionaries came from time to time. So they had some Christian beliefs mixed in with some pagan beliefs and Catholicism. One of Bill's and Joy's first jobs was to teach and train them in the truth. Bill and Joy also began study of the Agni language, which had first to be reduced to writing as it had never been in written form, only spoken. Fortunately, Bill and Joy had studied at the Wycliffe Linguistic School right after they were married. They studied the Agni language and Bill began to reduce it to writing. After they had learned the language fairly well, Bill began translating the Book of Mark, as well as some other useful things, into Agni. Bill used an interpreter who knew his own language, Agni, as well as enough French, so he and Joy could get a better understanding by being able to use a third language when it was needed. They began making contact with some surrounding villages that had no gospel witness. To some villages they went for a service once a week; to others not so often. They would go and spend two or three nights with the villagers and do concentrated teaching and preaching.

Joy began with classes with the children, teaching them, beginning with Genesis to give them some understanding of who the true God was; why there was "bad" in the world, and what God had done for their salvation. She did what she could to get to know the women, as well as all the people of the village. She visited their homes, met the children, including all the members of their household. This was done in the women's compound as the women and men had different households. She also started a medical clinic, ministering as much as she could with what she knew. Household tasks and language study were put in as time permitted.

Bill and Joy came home on furlough in 1964. They rented a small house in Whitesboro, Texas, where her parents were living. They spent most of their time doing itinerary work among the churches. They returned to Africa by a freighter ship and remained until 1969. They returned to the States because of Joy's health. Dr. Laverne Miley, who was by then a medical missionary in Coté d'Ivoire, never made a definite diagnosis. She says that she was having some kind of panic attacks. She had never had anything like this before, and never had anything like it afterwards. She says:

> I was definitely not for returning home. It seems to me God used this to make me come back to the States. It would have been very hard to convince me to come home otherwise. But I can see that even the timing was right. It gave Bill the six months to travel for the Mission Department and then time for God to lead us to Oklahoma Bible College for a year.

Bill became Dean of Men and taught missions at Oklahoma Bible College in Oklahoma City, Oklahoma, while he was working on his Master's Degree in teaching at Oklahoma City University. They adopted their son, Steven, in August of 1969. Bill received his Master's degree in 1970. Joy worked in the library at Oklahoma Bible College. Bill was then called to go to Nashville, Tennessee, to be editor of *Heartbeat* magazine, a job he did for a year.

After almost a year in Nashville as editor of *Heartbeat*, the board members of Oklahoma Bible College began calling Bill asking him to consider returning as president of OBC. At first, he turned them down. But after persistent calls, he finally consented to go to Oklahoma to talk with the board members. The outcome was that Bill and Joy sold the house they had just purchased, but not yet moved into, and went to Moore, Oklahoma, as president of Oklahoma Bible College. One of the first things they did was to change the name to Hillsdale Free Will Baptist College. Free Will Baptists had lost the original Hillsdale College in Hillsdale, Michigan, when the denomination merged with the Northern Baptists in 1910-1911. Bill and Joy arrived back in Oklahoma in the summer of 1971. They remained until 1979. Joy kept the promise she had made to her mother way back in 1957 that she would graduate from college. In 1979 it was her husband, Bill, who, as president of the college, gave her the diploma - and a kiss.

At Hillsdale Bill wore many hats. He was professor of various Bible courses, Greek professor, homiletics professor, systematic theology professor, promotional man on weekends, and whatever happened to be needed at the time. The college was very short on money, staff, and facilities. As the college grew, and the funds grew, Bill was able to give more of his time to other duties. During the eight years of his tenure as president of Hillsdale, a gym was built, which also housed the library, dining hall, and kitchen. Additional new construction included a four-plex for a boys' dormitory, on campus apartments for married students, a president's home, and a duplex for staff housing. The two-year college became a four-year liberal arts college as well as a Bible college. They began working for accreditation. Joy taught French for one year and worked in the library until a certified librarian could be hired. It was a wonderful and busy eight years for Bill and Joy. Bill resigned from the school to go back into the pastorate. He became pastor of the then small Calvary Free Will Baptist Church in Norman, Oklahoma, and served it from 1979 until 1982.

In 1982 they moved to Bryan, Texas, where Bill became pastor of the Fellowship Free Will Baptist Church. In Bryan, Joy trained to become a Fellow in the Academy of Life Insurance Underwriting. She worked in the General Security Life Insurance Company as Chief Underwriter. They remained in Bryan until 1994, a ministry of twelve years.

Bill and Joy returned to Oklahoma in 1994, this time as pastor of the First Free Will Baptist Church of Poteau, Oklahoma, where they remained until 1997. Bill became Director of Oklahoma State Missions in 1997 and served in that capacity until 1999. Then, they returned to Texas, pastoring the Eastside Free Will Baptist Church in Houston from 1999 until 2002. Once again returning to Poteau, Oklahoma, Bill became Senior Adult Pastor of the First Free Will Baptist Church, now semi-retired, where he had previously pastored. Bill continued in that position, working with senior adults, from 2002 until December 19, 2011, when he passed away in a hospital in Fort Smith, Arkansas. Due to his illness the last two or three years, Joy did most of the work, a ministry which she continues until the present.

During his long years of ministry Bill was active in other ways than just being a missionary, pastor, and college president. He served on the National Foreign Missions Board from 1980-1993, and from 1993-2005, many of those years as Chairman of the Board. It has already been mentioned that he was editor of *Heartbeat* magazine, and that he translated the Book of Mark into Agni. He wrote a theology book, *Systematic Theology*, which was never printed except for home printing. This came out of his teaching Systematic Theology at Hillsdale Free Will Baptist College. He wrote *Free Will Baptist Missions, Missionaries, and Their Message*, published by the Free Will Baptist Sunday School Department in 1972. He also helped publish *Women's Footprints on the Pages of History*, published by Hillsdale Publications. He was editor of *The Texas Challenge* briefly, while pastoring in Texas. He served as state moderator for a number of years in the Lone Star State, as well. By virtue of that office, he was chairman of the state's Executive Committee, a position of leadership and considerable influence.

When asked what she would consider to be Bill's most important contribution to the Free Will Baptist denomination, Joy said:

> Bill's most important contributions to the denomination, I believe were: (1) Missions: his many years serving on the Foreign Missions Board. I believe he was the first, or one of the first, returned missionaries to serve on this board. His first-hand insight and wisdom were a great help over the many years he served on this board. (2) His years as president of Hillsdale. His time there was at a most critical stage, a time when many private colleges were closing their doors. He changed the name and expanded the direction of the college, established a support base, built much needed buildings, expanded it to a four-year college, expanded staff, number of professors, and built a strong influence in the area of young preachers and missionary emphasis.

Joy has, herself, made a great contribution to the Free Will Baptist denomination. Perhaps it could be said that she made her greatest contribution by standing with and by her husband during all those years of ministry, being actively involved in his work. However, she had a ministry of her own. For one thing, she accomplished a great deal as a woman, as an active missionary, and as a servant of Jesus Christ. She set an example for other women to follow, for all Christians to follow. Her pleasant demeanor, her full and total commitment to Christ, her support role to an active and influential denominational leader, her encouragement during tough times and hard decisions put her in a position to do what few others could do. She did it well and continues her ministry to others.

Bill's funeral was conducted by Rev. Keith Burden, Executive Secretary of the National Association of Free Will Baptists; Clint Morgan, Director of International Missions; Jim Cook, associate pastor of the First Poteau Free Will Baptist Church, Poteau, Oklahoma; and Barry Reel, pastor of the First Poteau Free Will Baptist Church. He is buried in Steep Hollow Cemetery, in Bryan, Texas.

John Moehlman

John E. Moehlman was born in Bryan, Texas, February, 1936. He graduated from Stephen F. Austin High School in Bryan in 1954. He was converted to Christ at a rural Baptist church during his junior high years. He attended Free Will Baptist Bible College for two years, 1954-1956. In 1956 he married Barbara J. Willey, daughter of the late legendary Free Will Baptist missionaries Thomas and Mabel Willey, well known as "Mom" and "Pop" Willey. He attended and graduated from Columbia Bible College, now known as Columbia International University, in Columbia, South Carolina, in 1957. He earned a Master of Education Degree from Texas A & M in 1960.

John and Barbara Moehlman and children

John attended Spanish Language School in Costa Rica in 1961. He spent 1962 and 1963 doing exploratory development of Free Will Baptist missions in the Republic of Panama. He separated from the Free Will Baptist Foreign Mission Board in 1965. He served as a public school educator, both as a teacher and principal, in Florida and Texas, from 1965 to 2004. He is an elder in the Presbyterian Church in America, and has been active in the Gideons International from 1977 to the present. He and Barbara continue to be active in their local Presbyterian Church in America (PCA) in Bryan-College Station, Texas.

James and Mitzi Munsey

James Alan Munsey was born to Howard Thurman and Mildred (Collins) Munsey, August 10, 1950, in Greenville, Tennessee. James' father Howard worked at Magnavox after serving in the United States military. He rose to the position of plant supervisor. He resigned from Magnavox to become a Free Will Baptist pastor and church planter. He was also a building contractor, constructing both homes and churches.

While James was just a child, the Munsey family traveled in Mexico to visit Free Will Baptist churches. Then, he spent the summer of his fifteenth year living in Mexico with a Free Will Baptist missionary. His heart was touched by the spiritual needs of the Hispanic people.

James' primary and secondary education was anything but normal. He attended ten different schools during his elementary and high school years because of his parents moving so often. He ended up graduating with a General Education Diploma (GED) in 1968. That summer, when James was seventeen years old, his father helped him qualify for an FHA loan and he built his first home for resale. The profits from that sale paid for his first year at Free Will Baptist Bible College.

James attended Free Will Baptist Bible College for two years, 1968-1970, then took a year off to work and save money for further schooling. At the time the "Return to Nature" culture was permeating the country, and James understood the trend. He loved and appreciated antique furniture and log buildings. Most of that year was spent buying and reselling antiques and tearing down and rebuilding old log homes. He studied the craft and taught himself how to do a dovetail notch with a chain saw so he could repair or replicate any log that was not in good shape. He developed a growing business, seeking out old log buildings for renovation. Since these old log buildings were becoming rare, he later would use his knowledge to begin Hearthstone Log Homes, which was new log building construction, using the old techniques. Hearthstone would go on to become one of the largest companies in the hewn log industry.

*James and Mitzi Munsey
Laura, Rachel, and Matthew*

At the age of eighteen James sensed that God was calling him to preach. He was licensed to preach by the Central Quarterly Meeting of the Union Association of Tennessee, in 1969. The Union Association ordained him to the gospel ministry in 1974. His credentials were signed by Marcus Neas, Bobby Otterman, Howard Munsey, and Thurman Pate.

Mitzi Delaine Moore was born to Tunney and Alyce (Stykes) Moore in Newport, Tennessee. Her father was a plant employee at American Enka, a farmer, and served as the Cocke County sheriff for twelve years. Mitzi graduated from the Cocke County High School in 1974, after just three years of high school. She was ninth in her class of over two hundred graduating seniors.

James and Mitzi knew each other from childhood because James' father, Rev. Howard Munsey, had been her pastor when she was a child. They met again at the youth camp of the Union Association in the summer of 1971. She was fourteen years old and James was twenty. He went to her home to visit her and her parents. After a year her parents agreed to allow them to begin dating. James and Mitzi were married on August 4, 1973. Mitzi was only sixteen years old. Her parents had to go to a judge to have her legal age raised to permit the marriage. They were married at the Lowe's Chapel Free Will Baptist Church in Newport, Tennessee. The ceremony was performed by James' father. From this marriage came three children: Laura Ruth, born August 11, 1982; Matthew James, born September 11, 1984; and Rachel Ann, born October 28, 1990.

James returned to Free Will Baptist Bible College for the 1971-72 school year, and then again for the 1979-80 school year. He completed a couple of needed classes at Pan-American University in South Texas and returned for his graduation at Free Will Baptist Bible College in May, 1984. Mitzi attended the Bible College during the 1979-80 school year. She later attended Walter's State Community College, Pan American University, and completed her studies at Carson Newman, a four year, liberal arts Southern Baptist college located in Jefferson City, Tennessee.

After finishing his studies at the Bible College, James and Mitzi moved to South Texas in January of 1980 and began language school at the Rio Grande Bible Institute in Edinburg, Texas.

Their plan was to go to Guatemala to begin missionary service. However, God changed those plans. In addition to being a gifted preacher, James was gifted linguistically and was so fluent in Spanish by the summer that one of the professors recommended him to help out a small Southern Baptist congregation of about twelve people in Weslaco, Texas. James began preaching there every Sunday. After a few months, the Southern Baptists decided to consolidate their small community churches and build one large church. They planned to sell the property and disband the little church where James was preaching. James would not be unethical and so he went before the Southern Baptist mission board and explained that the people of his congregation wanted to stay together. He proposed to vacate the building and purchase property to build a church in Weslaco, but explained that it would be a Free Will Baptist church. The mission board was very agreeable with the plan and even gave them the furniture in the church to use in their building. A couple of those board members became some of James' and Mitzi's best friends throughout their years in South Texas. Representatives of the mission board attended every special function they held at the Weslaco church for years. The group found property in a prime location on Expressway 82. The land was purchased and a new sanctuary was completed in 1981. It was a beautiful log sanctuary, named the Primera Iglesia Bautista Libre (First Free Will Baptist Church). A log church might have seemed out of place in the culture of South Texas, but James still owned Hearthstone Log Homes and they provided the labor for the construction. Most of the actual labor was volunteer labor.

    James and Mitzi were serving under Cross Beams Missions, which would later become Berea Ministries, Inc., with James' father, Howard Munsey, serving as president. Support for James' building projects was raised through Berea Ministries. James and Mitzi also received a small salary from Hearthstone Log Homes until the sale of the company in the 1980's. Later in the 1980's James and Mitzi served under the Free Will Baptist National Home Missions Board. They knew every missionary needed to be accountable to a board.

    The Weslaco church began to blossom. The worship services were conducted in Spanish while the Sunday school was bilingual, Spanish and English. Eventually they began a ministry with the winter Texans[273] and added an early English worship service. The attendance reached a high of four hundred. Mitzi home schooled the children.

    Living in such near proximity to the border with Mexico, it was a natural thing to develop an outreach ministry across the border in Reynosa. The spiritual needs of the Hispanic people created a fertile soil for the gospel. James and Mitzi were able to build the first Free Will Baptist church in the Reynosa area. There are currently about ten Free Will Baptist churches in the area and the work continues to grow. From there they branched out to different areas of Mexico. Eventually the National Home Missions Board named James the Free Will Baptist Coordinator for all of Mexico, making him the liaison between the field and the National Home Missions Board.

    James, Mitzi, and all the children, were unusually talented. James played the guitar and Mitzi was good at the piano. James taught Laura and Matt to play the guitar when they were both very young. Part of the church culture in South Texas and Mexico was the *estudiantina*, a musical group formed to evangelize and enhance the services. The Munseys loved the string instruments and the Mexican music. They also loved bluegrass and their beloved Tennessee. They decided to add that to their homeschool repertoire. Matt was already amazing on the guitar so they bought him a mandolin and a bunch of Bill Monroe tapes. He spent hours copying the Bill Monroe style. James began to learn the banjo. It became a natural progression to add different string instruments to their list. They spend hours working and perfecting their sound together. James played rhythm

---

[273] Winter Texans are northerners who spend the winters in balmy South Texas.

guitar and banjo, Mitzi played the keyboard instruments and upright bass, Matt flat-picked guitar and played mandolin, Laura played rhythm guitar, while Rachel played some piano, some mandolin, and some fiddle. They had an amazing sound and played and sang in the Weslaco church, in the churches in Mexico, and in churches in the States when they were traveling promoting the work in Mexico.

When they initially began the work in Mexico, James would travel into the country for a week at a time to help a national pastor or to work on a church building. He still pastored the Weslaco church, so he tried to be wise in how much time he spent away from his church. Their traveling changed over the years. Since they were home schooling the children, Mitzi and the children were able to accompany James on a lot of the trips into Mexico. However, it became more difficult for Mitzi to go when Rachel was born because of her illness. In later years, as the leadership in Mexico developed, James traveled more in the states to promote the work.

James often travelled with a quartet, which was simply called The Mexican Quartet. It consisted of Felix Zuniga, Lalo Gonzalez, Chuy de la Rosa, and James. They had beautiful four part harmony. The churches which supported the work in Mexico loved seeing tangible results of their generosity. The quartet sang at various state associations and at the Free Will Baptist national convention and were always well received.

James was involved in some part of the actual building of around twenty-five churches in Mexico. He helped in evangelistic work in others. There were a number of different things James did to promote the Free Will Baptist work in Mexico. He enlisted various church groups to go to Mexico from the States to help with church construction and evangelism. These groups became an important part of the ministry in Mexico. In some years there were as many as ten groups per year that would travel below the border to assist in various ways. This required a lot of coordination, but it was well worth the effort. James realized that people are better equipped to pray for a mission field when they have visited it, and they support it better when they have invested their own sweat in it. Some of the young people who visited Mexico are now serving on mission fields all over the world.

The development of national leadership was James' burden. He saw it as essential to the long term success of the work. He always chose to work through the national pastor. He saw the need for training of national workers. He realized the need for a seminary and it was his design and vision that built the Seminary of the Cross. He found the property and oversaw the purchasing of the land. The sanctuary at the seminary has been named the James Munsey Memorial Auditorium.

When daughter Rachel was born in 1990, she was born with autosomal regressive polycystic kidney disease. They knew from her birth that the day would arrive when she would need a kidney transplant. It happened when she was seven years old. Her kidneys were removed in the spring of 1998. James and Mitzi were both good matches to donate a kidney, but James wanted to do it so Mitzi could continue as caregiver. The transplant took place on August 4, 1998, James' and Mitzi's twenty-fifth wedding anniversary. Years later, Rachel would get married on August 4, 2013. It was a beautiful day.

James and Mitzi were both compassionate and dedicated servants of the Lord. They both contributed enormously to the salvation of numerous people, on both sides of the border. Under James' tutelage more than twenty-five churches and institutions were founded and built in Mexico, and dozens of others benefited from his counsel. The Hispanic people considered him to be the best Spanish linguist of his era. He worked tirelessly and ceaselessly to promote evangelism and church growth among the Mexican nationals, whom he loved dearly. He was unselfish in his work.

Though he was highly successful, and a very charismatic personality, he always had a humbleness about him that characterized him as a man of Christ. His only desire was to glorify God. The same things can be said of Mitzi.

At the age of fifty, and in the prime of his life, James was diagnosed with a glioblastoma brain tumor. He had surgery in early January, 2001, and then endured radiation treatment. He passed away on February 3, 2001. He was buried in Union Cemetery, Cocke County, Newport, Tennessee.

Mitzi felt that she needed to move the children back to Tennessee to be closer to their grandparents. So she moved back in August, 2001, and built a house on her father's farm in Newport. Her parents live nearby and her mother-in-law, Mildred Munsey, lives in Morristown, Tennessee.

The children are all doing well. Laura Ruth Munsey Bosworth graduated from Free Will Baptist Bible College. Matthew James Munsey graduated from Tusculum College in Greenville, Tennessee. He later attended Free Will Baptist Bible College while his wife, Juliana, completed her degree. Rachel Ann Munsey Jackson, the youngest, graduated from Welch College in 2013 and is a first grade teacher in an inner-city school in the Davidson County School District in Nashville. She is vibrant, happy, and truly has a heart for service to the Lord. One day she will need another kidney transplant, but hopefully it will be several years in the future.

Mitzi remarried, to Gary Satterfield, on December 26, 2003. Gary and Mitzi are members of Peace Free Will Baptist Church in Morristown, Tennessee, where he serves as adult Sunday school teacher and Mitzi is the church organist and leads a monthly Bible class for the women. Gary is an outside salesman for Dealers Warehouse in Knoxville. Mitzi works as a prenatal coordinator at Rural Medical Services Inc., which has five clinics in Cocke and Jefferson counties. She continues to work with Berea Ministries as financial secretary and serves as liaison between Berea's current president, Chris Dotson, and the Free Will Baptist pastors in Mexico and Costa Rica.

Darrel and Lila Nichols

Lila Denise Everitt was born on October 23, 1956, in Dallas, Texas, to Joyce (Hughes) Everitt and Robert Lidge Everitt. Her father was a barber. The family seldom attended church but Lila became a Christian while attending Vacation Bible School at Oakwood Terrace Southern Baptist Church. She attended Trinity High School in Euless, Texas, graduating in 1975. She then attended Executive Secretarial School in Dallas. In 1977 she joined the Trinity Free Will Baptist Church in Fort Worth, where her sister was a member. While on a trip to Hillsdale Free Will Baptist College in Moore, Oklahoma, to visit her sister who was a student there, she met Darrel Nichols but no courtship started until later.

Darrel Eudean Nichols was born on August 6, 1955, in Pryor, Oklahoma, to third generation Free Will Baptists Marie (Stephens) and Virgil Nichols. Darrel's father was a World War II veteran and an electrician. Darrel was converted to Christ during a testimony meeting at Osage Free Will Baptist Church of rural Pryor, Oklahoma, at age ten. He answered the

Darryl and Lila Nichols

call to preach at age fifteen and the call to missions at the age of seventeen. He graduated from Pryor High School in May of 1973. That same month he was ordained to the gospel ministry at the West Side Free Will Baptist Church of Pryor in the South Grand River Association. The presbytery consisted of Ministers Richard Collison, Jake Gage, Henry Withers and deacons Bill Terns and Bernard Wright. That fall, 1973, he entered Hillsdale Free Will Baptist College to prepare for a career in missions, graduating in May of 1977.

In the fall of 1977, Darrel entered Southwestern Baptist Theological Seminary in Fort Worth, Texas. This is when Lila and Darrel first began dating. Lila had long felt a call to service and she recognized this as a call to missionary activity while she and Darrel were courting. They were married on March 18, 1978, at the Trinity Free Will Baptist Church, during the seminary's spring break. The ceremony was performed by Pastor Jim Shepherd, who was also a student at Southwestern. They resided in seminary housing until Darrel received his MDiv. in May of 1980. During his seminary days, Darrel pastored the New Salem Free Will Baptist Church at Decatur, Texas, about thirty miles northwest of Fort Worth.

In the summer of 1980, Darrel and Lila served as summer missionaries in Cotê d'Ivoire, Africa. In the fall of 1980, they took up residence at Hillsdale, where Lila received her Association of Arts degree, with extra studies in Bible and Missions to fulfill the requirements of the Free Will Baptist Board of Foreign Missions. While Lila attended Hillsdale as a student, Darrel served as adjunct professor of Bible and Christian Education.

Darrel and Lila were appointed to serve as missionaries in Cotê d'Ivoire, Africa, in May of 1982, where they served until 2003 when civil war closed the school for missionary children in the city of Bouake. Virtually all of the Free Will Baptist missionaries were recalled or transferred out of Africa for their own safety during this time of civil war. Darrel and Lila were transferred to the field of Panama, in Central America, where they continued to serve Free Will Baptist International Missions until December 31, 2008.

At this writing Darrel serves as bi-vocational pastor of the Hoyt Free Will Baptist Church in Hoyt, Oklahoma, while also teaching school. Lila is a housewife and pastor's wife.

Lonnie Palmer

Lonnie Palmer was born March 9, 1932, in Pheiffer, Arkansas, to Lonnie and Minnie Esther Lee (Williams) Palmer. Pheiffer is an unincorporated community in Independence County, northeast of Batesville. He began his schooling in a one room school house near Pheiffer. It was when he was just a boy that he knew God had called him to be a missionary to Africa. He graduated from the Cave City High School, in Cave City, Arkansas. It was in high school that he met and fell in love with Lillian Bernice Crow. After graduating from high school, Lonnie went to Akron, Ohio, where he went to work. While in Akron he attended the University of Akron for two years. He sent for his sweetheart Bernice, and they were married in Barberton, Ohio, September 12, 1951. From this marriage came four children: Kathleen, Marion Elaine, Lonnie Stephen, and Martin Stanley. The two boys were born in Africa.

Lonnie's parents had moved to Fort Worth, Texas, so he and Bernice moved there to be with them and some of his other relatives who had also moved there. They attended the Trinity Free Will Baptist Church, which was pastored by M. L. Sutton. Lonnie told Brother Sutton about his call to the mission field and Brother Sutton advised him to get in touch with the Free Will Baptist Foreign Mission Board. Lonnie didn't know there was such a thing as a mission board, but he made the necessary effort to get in contact with them. They told him that if he wanted to be a missionary he would need to attend Free Will Baptist Bible College in Nashville, Tennessee, to prepare for the mission field. It wasn't long after he spoke with Pastor Sutton about his missionary call that Raymond Riggs came to Fort Worth and preached a revival meeting at the Trinity Church. During one of the services Lonnie went forward, rededicated his life to the Lord, announced his call to preach, and announced his call to be a missionary. He talked to Brother Riggs about going to the Bible College and whether it would be a waste of his time if he didn't end up on the mission field. Brother Riggs told him that going to Bible College would not be a waste of time even if he did not end up on the mission field.

Lonnie was ordained to the gospel ministry on December 22, 1952, by the Fellowship Association of Free Will Baptists. The men who signed his ordination certificate were: Clarence J. Hearron, deacon Owen Barger, and deacon J. T. Reeder. Lonnie and Bernice sold their home and moved to Nashville to attend Free Will Baptist Bible College, now Welch College. He graduated in 1960. From the Bible College he and Bernice moved to Norman, Oklahoma, where he attended the Wycliffe Bible Translation School, which was conducted at Oklahoma University. They then went to Lausanne, Switzerland, to language school, where he studied French, the national language of Ivory Coast, Africa.

Lonnie and Bernice Palmer and daughters

After years of preparation Lonnie and Bernice arrived in Ivory Coast, now Côte d'Ivoire, West Africa, on January 12, 1962. Lonnie immediately began learning Koulongo, the native language of the Koulongo tribe with whom he would be working. They lived in the Bondoukou Circle, which is like a county or state, situated in the savannah region just north of the coastal forest. At the time the Koulongou people, which numbered about 200,000, were very primitive, but that was changing quickly due to the fact that the trappings of civilization were penetrating deepest, darkest Africa. Just two years earlier the tribe had gained their independence and this new freedom was enabling them to make rapid advances to a more modern civilization.

Lonnie's work was primarily evangelism, winning the Koulongo people to the Lord, and that remained his primary ministry. However, he realized the need for having the Old Testament in the Koulongo language. Fellow Free Will Baptist missionary Lonnie Sparks had already translated the New Testament into Koulongo, and so Lonnie Palmer set about the task of translating the entire Old Testament, an enormous undertaking. When he completed that project he went over the Koulongo New Testament and made suggestions about spelling so the two testaments would be consistent, plus he made some suggestions about the wording of one verse in the Book of Romans. Eventually both testaments were combined under one cover, giving the Koulongo the entire Bible in their own language. This was a major piece of missionary work in and of itself.

In his evangelism work, Lonnie realized another need, the need for a Bible college where the new Christians could be taught and trained to reach their own people with the gospel. As a result, Lonnie started a Bible college and taught there for nine years. The school is still in existence and as of this writing Lonnie's son Stephen is teaching there. Lonnie and Bernice remained in Africa, even when the other Free Will Baptist missionaries were called back to the States as a result of the violence and danger to them brought about by the country's revolution in 2010-2011.

Lonnie and Bernice spent a total of forty-three years in Africa. Lonnie had a heart attack and subsequent by-pass surgery, which required him to come back to the States for a while. After recovering, he and Bernice returned to Africa to continue their missionary work. However, Lonnie realized that the heart attack and surgery had taken a greater toll on him than he thought. He soon knew that he could no longer do the work required of a missionary. They returned to the United States.

At this writing Lonnie is pastoring the Bethel Free Will Baptist Church in Allen, Oklahoma. His wife Bernice passed away on January 19, 2012, after more than sixty-one years of marriage. Lonnie still has family in Texas. His brother, Joshua Marion Palmer, lives in Fort Worth. His second daughter, Marion Elaine Patterson, named after her uncle, lives in Levelland, and is married to Steve Patterson.

At the 1967 state meeting. the state executive secretary reported that Texas had given more than $3,500.00 toward the purchase of a new Dodge pickup for the Palmer's, which they had taken with them to the field.[274]

Dr. E. Sterl Phinney

E. Sterl Phinney's connection with Texas is that he pastored the First Free Will Baptist Church of Bryan for two years, from 1935 to 1937. He was born in Columbus, Ohio, and married Miss Marie Wilson of Bladenboro, North Carolina. After two fruitful years as pastor of the Bryan church, he resigned to become a missionary to Japan, and then to Columbia. Apparently he did not go out under the auspices of the Free Will Baptist Foreign Missions Board. He served a total of nine years as a missionary, including two years of deputational work here in the states. He went on to become a college and seminary professor.[275] In 1935 he was a delegate from Texas to the organizational meeting of the National Association of Free Will Baptists, which met in Nashville, Tennessee.

Judy Smith

Judy is an East Texas girl who ended up being a missionary to the Far East. Judy Lorell Smith was born to Haskel Hoke, Sr., and Juanita Irene (Miles) Smith in Henderson, Texas, on August 18, 1950. Her father was a carpenter, cabinet maker, and maker of grandfather clocks. Judy gave her life to Christ at the age of fourteen in the church in which she grew up, the Good Hope Free Will Baptist Church, Henderson, Texas, under the ministry of Rev. Bobby Ferguson. She graduated from Henderson High School in 1968.

Miss Judy Smith

A week after she was converted, she knew that it was God's will for her to be a missionary. She was in the back seat of her Sunday school teacher's car on her way to church, and she told her teacher that God wanted her to be a missionary. At youth camp that summer, her first year at camp, she went to the altar and made a commitment to God to be a missionary. Harold Teague was the camp evangelist. Camp

---

[274] 1967 state minutes, page 10.
[275] The information comes mostly from the book *A 63 Year History of First Free Will Baptist Church, Bryan, Texas*, by Walter J. Coulter, published in 1957, page 27.

that year was held at Mt. Olive Free Will Baptist Church in the Compton Community out of Henderson. Knowing that she needed preparation for being a missionary, she enrolled at Free Will Baptist Bible College in the fall of 1968, graduating in the spring of 1972. During the last part of her senior year in college, she went to Japan as part of the Good News Team, working under the direction of Wesley and Aileen Calvery and Jim and Olena McClain.

Before she went to Japan as a full-time missionary, Judy and Arilla Wode, a girl from Oklahoma, went to Ivory Coast, Africa, as the first two summer missionaries there for Free Will Baptists. They spent ten weeks helping the missionaries. They were involved in a number of different ministries. They helped type the Koulongo New Testament, which Lonnie Sparks was translating, and they worked at the Free Will Baptist hospital in Doropo, working with Eddie and Sandra Payne, and Sherwood and Vada Lee. They also spent time working with Lonnie and Anita Palmer, Maurice (Frank) and Marie Cousineau, and Norman and Bessie Richards. They went with Eddie Payne to one village and were the first white women some of the villagers had ever seen.

Judy was commissioned in 1970 as a foreign missionary at the First Free Will Baptist Church in Henderson, Texas, by Foreign Missions Director Rolla Smith. Becoming a missionary involved years of academic preparation and then months of travel raising financial support. This took her to a number of states in addition to Texas: Oklahoma, Arkansas, Mississippi, Louisiana, Ohio, West Virginia, Kentucky, California, Georgia, Virginia, and Illinois.

In 1972, Judy arrived in Japan and began her language study to learn the Japanese language. She attended the Overseas Missionary Fellowship Language School, which was located in the city of Sapporo. She was scheduled to study for two years, but because the missionary staff was shorthanded, she left language school after about a year and a half. She joined the missionary team of Jerry and Janice Banks in a new work that was just starting in the town of Kitahiroshima, outside of Sapporo. She spent the rest of her entire time in Japan in Kitahiroshima, ministering in the church established there, Kitahiroshima Chapel. When the Banks were on furlough stateside, she worked with missionaries Jim and Olena McClain and Dale and Sandra Bishop, who would come on weekends to help in the services. During her time in Japan there were two single ladies who spent several years there, Mirial Gainer and Vivian Waller (Reasoner). Both of them taught in either the international school or university and worked alongside Judy and the other missionaries. Mirial was later commissioned as a full-time missionary and continues her ministry in Japan as of this writing.

As a single female missionary working in the Far East, Judy's ministry was varied. Much of it was simply a matter of building relationships so the gospel could be conveyed to the Japanese people whom the missionaries befriended. She often spoke to the congregation, especially when other missionaries were on furlough. She taught English classes to all age groups and for three years taught at Hokusei Daigaku University, teaching spoken English and composition. She taught guitar for ten years, cooking classes, craft classes, Bible studies, child evangelism, puppet ministry outreaches, and even played on a Japanese city volleyball team.

It was while she was in Japan that Judy learned ventriloquism. She learned this art and skill under Mr. Ichiiroo Harukaze, founder of the Japanese Ventriloquist Association, which is a Christian organization in Japan. Mr. Harukaze was a friend of Edgar Bergen, an American actor and radio performer, best known as a ventriloquist, and also the father of actress Candice Bergen. Judy bought her ventriloquist doll, Ken-Chan, K.C. for short, in Japan for about $500.00.

While on furlough from Japan, doing itinerate work stateside raising funds, she was speaking at several churches in West Virginia and Kentucky. She was to speak at one particular church in Kentucky, but was informed by the pastor that they did not allow women in the pulpit.

They made arrangements for her to speak in the basement at a spaghetti supper. Before the service began the pastor asked Judy if she would like to see the sanctuary. She wanted to. As they walked through the sanctuary she reached out and touched the pulpit...and nothing happened. The following Saturday she was scheduled to speak at a youth rally, with over a hundred youth and pastors present. They actually allowed her to stand up behind the podium to speak with Ken-Chan, her ventriloquist doll. Judy began to notice that any time she spoke and made a statement, there was a complete silence in the room, but when she had Ken-Chan say the same thing, she could hear, "Amen! Preach it, brother!" from all over the room. She played off of that and had Ken-Chan getting amens all evening. The Lord spoke to hearts that night and there were teens saved and decisions made for the Lord.

After seventeen years in Japan, Judy left Japan in 1991 and returned to the States to begin a full-time children's ministry called Korner Kids 'n Company. She received a Master's Degree in 1991 in Social Sciences with an emphasis on Human Resource Development, from Azusa Pacific University, Azusa, California. She had several job offers to support herself while she was trying to build her children's ministry. She lived in southeastern Missouri for three years, subbed in the schools there, and worked part-time for St. Francis Social Services, working with troubled teens. While there she began working as a consultant for Moore Educational Services in Nashville, Tennessee, and traveled extensively throughout the United States, helping people in the medical field get study materials for Associate and Bachelor degrees in nursing. She traveled on weekends to churches in several states and ministered as a Christian ventriloquist. In 1997 she moved to eastern North Carolina, got her real estate license, and worked as a broker for over ten years with United Country/Southland Properties Real Estate. She continued to travel and work with churches all over East Tennessee, North Carolina, and South Carolina with Korner Kids 'n Company. As part of her children's work after returning to the States, she has gone on mission trips to Brazil, to minister to MK's during field council; to India, where she spent time with Carlisle and Marie Hanna; to South Korea, part of a ventriloquist tour; back to Japan twice; and to Israel.

Judy made another move in 1910, returning to East Texas to her sister's farm, and substitute teaching for one year in public schools. She then began working full-time as a field supervisor for Jordan Health Services, which she is currently still doing. Judy offers the following advice to young women:

> Don't let anyone hold you back or tell you that because you are a woman you can't do something. I was told in my lifetime many times to get a "real" job. I know that serving God in any capacity that He calls you, is THE real job He has for you. My life has truly been a God-venture. I challenge young women to wake up each morning and ask God, "Where are You going today? I'm going with You!" And hold on for the ride!!!

Judy further says that the greatest influences on her life were two of her pastors, Rev. Bobby Ferguson and Rev. Harold Teague. She also credits the influence of missionaries Miss Laura Belle Barnard, Mrs. Mabel Willey, and Ken and Marvis Eagleton. She also lists her mother, Juanita, whom she considers to have been her greatest cheerleader and the most sacrificial person she ever knew. Judy is exceptionally talented in many ways. In addition to her skills as a ventriloquist, she is an accomplished guitarist, having learned to play at the age of eleven. She writes children's stories and songs, and released an LP album in 1970 called *OUTLINED*, featuring her original songs. She loves to fish and is a birder.

Judy's current ministry consists of a number of endeavors. She is an active member of International Sports Chaplains, which goes to the Olympics every two years, the Summer Olympics and the Winter Olympics. She has so far been to five Olympics where the team ministers on the streets and in the various Olympic venues. She has been to the Olympics in Sapporo, Japan; Nagano, Japan; Beijing, China; Vancouver, British Columbia, Canada; and London, England. Stateside, she is in the process of building a home/ministry center in Minden, Texas, which will be a place of ministry for women's groups, youth groups, and a place for weary travelers to come, rest, and enjoy.

Jim and Vicki Sturgill

Jim and Vicki Sturgill are not normally thought of as being from Texas, and they weren't. Jim is from Sophia, West Virginia. However, they do have a connection to Texas in that Jim pastored the First Free Will Baptist Church of Seminole, which is about twenty-five miles from the eastern border of New Mexico. Jim had graduated from Free Will Baptist Bible College in 1965 and he and Vicki were preparing to go as missionaries to Brazil. Someone from Seminole, while ordering Sunday school literature from Randall House Publications, asked about someone who might be willing to move to West Texas and open a Free Will Baptist church. Jim was put in contact with Eugene McCown.

Jim and Vicki Sturgill

Jim and Vicki moved to Seminole in the summer of 1967, knowing that this ministry opportunity would help prepare them for missions overseas. They knew their time in West Texas would be relatively short. Not being under any mission board, Jim got a job in the parts department of the local GM dealership. Later he worked as a mail carrier in Seminole to support himself as he did the ground work for opening the church. This ministry gave them a great taste of life in West Texas. Seminole was a small town surrounded by miles and miles of dry land cotton fields, often buffeted by sand storms. Jim was able to open the church, the First Free Will Baptist Church of Seminole. During their brief stay the church building was pretty much filled to capacity. His successful work was recognized by the Texas State Association in 1970 when they named Jim Texas Minister of the Year. That same year Jim and Vicki moved back East because they knew it was time for them to proceed with their calling to the foreign mission field of Brazil. Their three years in Seminole gave Jim and Vicki some good pastoral experience prior to their service as missionaries in Brazil.

They served 40 years total with the missions department. They did mostly church planting in large urban areas, first in Campinas, SP, that had a population of about 750,000, and lastly in Belo Horizonte, MG, a metropolitan region with a population of around 5.5 million total. This actually included several cities that had grown overlapping to form one large metropolis. Between these two major projects, they worked in two smaller locations with a little less than 100,000. The first of these was Barbacena, MG, substituting for the Aycock's during their furlough of 1975-1976, and the second was in Jaboticabal, SP, where they filled in for two years administering a youth camp property and teaching in a Bible Institute. While in Campinas, SP, they also opened preaching points in suburban areas of the city. They also translated and published (using xerox copies) a significant part of the Randall House Sunday school curriculum that wound up being used by several of our churches, as well as by a few other churches of other denominations in different regions of Brazil. During most of the 40 years, Vicki taught young people piano lessons that left musicians adequately trained to help in several congregations. At this writing Jim and Vicki are retired and living in Crab Orchard, West Virginia.

William and Anna Travis

The July 13, 1957, minutes of the East Texas District Association mention that William and Anna Travis, members of a church in the association, had recently been appointed as missionaries to Cuba by the Free Will Baptist Foreign Missions Board. The minutes of the Foreign Missions Board show that on April 30, 1957, a recommendation was made that "Mr. Travis be sent to substitute for Mr. Phenicie" and "that those six months be a test of their ability to fit into the program."[276] William and Anna were to substitute for Herbert and Edith Phenicie, who served in Cuba from 1952 to 1958 and who were on leave for health reasons. William was to meet various needs on the field, even helping the native farmers. Anna substituted for Edith Phenicie as she could where needed. Evidently they were appointed as "fill-in" workers for six months. On October 8, 1957, board minutes state: "letter read from Mr. Travis re his work in Cuba. Motion sustained that the Travises be sent the regular missionary allowance for them and their children for their remaining time on the field."

Thomas and Mabel Willey

Mabel and Thomas Willey

We may not normally think of legendary missionaries Thomas "Pop" and Mabel "Mom" Willey as having any connection with Texas, but they did and do. Neither of them were born in Texas but they both had a close relationship to the state. Prior to leaving for their first missionary assignment in Panama in 1937, they lived in Bryan and had many friends and supporters there. Mom and Pop Willey spent many years in Cuba and did a remarkable work there which is still strong to this day. There is a strong association of Cuban Free Will Baptist churches, and *Los Cedros del Libaño,* the Cedars of Lebanon Free Will Baptist Seminary, still continues to train Cuban Free Will Baptist pastors. "Mom" Willey died in Bryan in 1998 and is buried there

Thomas Jr., who lived in Bryan as a youth, also served for twenty-one years as a Free Will Baptist missionary in Panama and Cuba. Tom Jr. attended Free Will Baptist Bible College and Columbia International University. He has spent the greater part of his life in the cause of world missions, much of it working with World Relief out of Miami, Florida. At this writing he lives in Bronson, Florida.

The Willey's daughter, Barbara, married John Moehlman from Bryan and became Free Will Baptist missionaries for a while. See their profile above. John and Barbara live in Bryan, Texas, at this writing.

---

[276] This additional information about William and Anna Travis was supplied to me via e-mail, dated April 7, 2014, by Deborah St. Lawrence, Communications Manager at Free Will Baptist International Missions, Nashville, Tennessee.

The story of Thomas Willey is told in the book *Never Say Can't,* by Jerry Ballard (1984). The book is advertised as "the inspiring saga of a man's gigantic vision, who used every obstacle to prove the power of God."

Tom Willey, Jr.

The iconic photo of "Pop" Willey

Chapter 12

Texas Women Active for Christ

The women of Texas were always very involved in the Free Will Baptist work of Texas. They were not mentioned in the minutes of the first state meeting in 1915, when the task at hand was simply to organize a state association. However, at the second meeting of the state association in 1917 the women were organized and active at the meeting, under the name "Woman's Missionary Work." Miss Minnie Jimmerson was the leader of the group. From the very first their work was focused on missions, which has continued to be their purpose for all of the years of their existence.

What was often simply called "Woman's Work" the women of the state of Texas kept the churches informed about missionaries and progress on the fields, they promoted missions, raised large amounts of money for missions, and undergirded the work with prayer support. The strong missionary emphasis of Free Will Baptists would likely have waned without the persevering work of the women.

Mrs. Clyde F. Goen, Grace Goen, was very active in the Woman's Work in the earlier days of the State Association. At the Fourteenth Annual Session of the Texas State Association of Free Will Baptists, 1928, she gave a report, which she had written, that made a great impression on the body and elicited from them a special vote of thanks for such an outstanding paper. It was such a noteworthy paper that it is included here in its entirety.

The Importance of Women's Work in the State

The importance of women's work in the State is very apparent. We will first think of her work in the home. The greatest gift that woman can make to her church, her community, and her God is the gift of a Christian home. The home is woman's golden opportunity, her rich privilege, her solemn responsibility, her peculiar stewardship. If the light of the gospel is to shine through the Church to the uttermost parts, then it must shine bright at home and in the home. Luther said, "The hearth is the center of religion and it is more often the mothers than the fathers that keep the fires burning there." No money value can be placed on the woman in the home as she teaches there the character building virtues. Out from the homes of Christian mothers have come a steady stream of ministers, missionaries, business men, teachers, and leaders whose lives and works eternally pay tribute to the greatest gift that woman can make to the world -- the Christian home.

We find woman's work in the Bible times and the early Christian era very important in spreading the gospel. Paul's greeting to women showed how they were essential to the work of the Church. In the time of Christ they did what they could to follow His example and teachings. At the present time He uses a goodly number who are giving of their time, strength, money, and intellect to prosper the great work carried on throughout the ages.

Women, enlisted to put over the program of the church, have wrought wonders. Their work has made marvelous progress and has achieved results that can never be estimated in this world, for we realize that a growing church must be filled with missionary zeal and must be earnestly engaged in these activities that carry out the true spirit of missions. To their credit it must be said that women of the church take loyally and seriously whatever task is assigned to them and devote their whole strength to its accomplishment.

One denomination has said that the two finest assets of the church are women and church papers. They are the great missionary agencies of promotion.

I know that comparisons are dangerous and easily misunderstood, but the best results may be had through them. When we compare the Woman's Auxiliary and the work being done by the women of other states, and even denominations, with our own, we find that we are woefully deficient. They are accomplishing great results for the Master. Why can't we?

When we go to the bottom of it all, we find that we are lacking in education, co-operation, organization, and working for definite set aims.

Other denominations have their woman's work in the states well organized, and the women are realizing more and more the value of parliamentary laws and are seeking opportunities to inform themselves. They may have their summer school of missions, local Bible study, training their youth for leadership, and their state paper in all homes which gives information as to what is being done.

There has never been a time when the gospel of Christ is more needed than in these days of political disorder, international disturbance, and social distress.

So let us as a denomination awaken to our duty, be up and doing. We will either go forward or backward.

We have women of talent, if it is only developed, also women of vision and ability.

So looking unto Jesus for strength, let us give of our time, talent, means, and prayers that we may be a great power in His service for advancing the cause of His kingdom.

Mrs. C. F. Goen [277]

1935

At the Eastern General Conference meeting, June 13, 1935, women from Florida, Georgia, Missouri, North Carolina, Tennessee, and Texas formed a national organization: The Woman's National Auxiliary Convention of Free Will Baptists.[278] In time, these state organizations were joined by auxiliaries from numerous other states, creating a truly national organization of women involved in the Free Will Baptist work.

---

[277] Minutes of the 1928 State Convention of Free Will Baptists, pages 2-4.
[278] http://fwbhistory.com

The following is a history of their work over many years. It was written by Mrs. Elizabeth Brandon, circa 1966, and supplied to us by Mitzi Burks of Henderson, Texas.

History of the Organization of the Texas State Woman's Auxiliary Convention

1950

The Texas State Auxiliary Convention was organized at the Free Will Baptist Encampment at beautiful Pineywoods, Woodlake, Texas, August 15, 1950. A study course on the *Auxiliary Manual of Methods* was conducted by Mrs. Damon C. Dodd, third Vice-President of the Woman's National Auxiliary Convention (W.N.A.C.). After lunching with the campers in the dining hall, the ladies met in the chapel to proceed with their organization.

A nominating committee, composed of Mrs. Dodd, Mesdames[279] A. F. Halbrook, Ruby Gary, V. B. Stone, and H. Ray Berry had earlier been appointed to meet, and upon their recommendation, the following officers were elected to serve for one year:

President	Mrs. A. F. Halbrook
Vice-President	Mrs. Ruby Gary
2nd Vice-President	Mrs. Bill Berry
3rd Vice-President	Mrs. Noah Tuttle
4th Vice-President	Mrs. Ruby Withers
5th Vice-President	Mrs. V. B. Stone
Secretary-Treasurer	Mrs. Asa Berry
Field Worker	Mrs. Lizzie McAdams

There were some thirty-nine delegates from the Central Texas and East Texas District Conventions present, who voted that the Convention set aside Tuesday of each Camp week as the State Woman's Auxiliary Convention Day.

Report of Woman's Auxiliary Board[280]

The watchword of the Woman's Auxiliary for 1950 has been *"Advancing with Christ."* Theme for the year -- *"Speak Unto the Children of Israel, that they go forward."* Ex. 14:15. I believe we can truthfully say that we have gone forward and made greater progress in our Woman's Auxiliary work in the State of Texas this year than has ever been made before. Much is yet to be accomplished. We must remember that God's way is always forward. Christ has commanded us to advance and has never sounded a retreat. There is yet much land to be possessed. May we like Caleb say we are well able to possess the land and go forward in faith to conquer for Christ.

As chairman of the Woman's Auxiliary board I have tried to do my best to promote the work throughout the State. Of course much of this had to be

---

[279] Mesdames is a plural of madam.
[280] This report is taken verbatim from page 17 of the minutes of the 1950 session of the Texas State Association of Free Will Baptists.

correspondence. I have written numerous letters and cards answering questions and encouraging those just beginning in the work. Working with the Camp Committee and after corresponding with the other members of the Auxiliary Board, we planned a day of Manual Study and Fellowship to be held for our women at the State Encampment in August. Fifty form letters were distributed notifying our women of these plans. Following the Manual Study taught on Tuesday of the week by Mrs. Damon C. Dodd of Nashville, Tenn., she helped us organize a Texas State Auxiliary Convention. Two District Conventions were represented in this organization. There were about thirty-five ladies present from these two Districts. We regretted very much, that the other ladies of the State did not participate with us. We hope soon they will join forces with in in this great forward march in Woman's Auxiliary work. The next meeting of the Texas State Auxiliary Convention will be held on Tuesday of the week of the State Encampment. This meeting will be at the Camp. Officers of the State Auxiliary Convention are as follows:

President -- Mrs. Alvin F. Halbrook, Bryan, Rt. 3.
First Vice-President -- Mrs. John Gary, Laneville, Rt. 1.
Second Vice-President -- Mrs. Bill Berry, Laneville, Rt. 1.
Third Vice-President -- Mrs. Noah Tuttle, Henderson, Rt. 2.
Fourth Vice-President -- Mrs. Ruby Withers, Bryan.
Fifth Vice President -- Mrs. V. B. Stone, Henderson.
Secretary and Treasurer -- Mrs. H. Ray Berry, Houston.
Field Worker -- Rev. Mrs. H. M. McAdams, Huntsville.

1951

September 12, 1951, the Texas State Woman's Auxiliary met at the Bryan Free Will Baptist Church, with Mrs. Ruby Withers, Program Chairman, presiding. In this session it was voted that we pattern our state officer's election after that of our National Convention, using two year terms of office, replacing present officers wherever needed and retaining the rest.

An interesting playlet, "Mrs. Prospect Receives Visitors," was given by Mrs. Gaston Clary and various silent helpers. There were two changes in the slate of officers for 1951. Mrs. Gaston Clary of Bryan became 3rd Vice-President, and Mrs. Ray Trant of Iola became 5th Vice-President.

It was voted to adopt the State Constitution and By-Laws from the *Manual of Methods*, with specified changes as follows:

In Article 6, the word "Treasurer" was changed to "Secretary-Treasurer.
In Article 8, the tenure of office was changed from one to two years.
In Article 9, the word National was changed to "State."

1952

The Texas State Woman's Auxiliary Convention met at the Mt. Olive Free Will Baptist Church, near Henderson, Texas, June 10, 1952. An officer's clinic was held at this Convention for the benefit of the new officers. The State Officers for 1952-1954 were:

President	Mrs. Huey Gower, Henderson
Vice-President	Mrs. Alvin Halbrook, Bryan
2ne Vice-President	Mrs. Ruby Withers, Bryan
3rd Vice-President	Mrs. Will Hayes, Henderson
4th Vice-President	Mrs. H. Ray Berry, Houston
5th Vice-President	Mrs. David Reed, North Zulch
Secretary-Treasurer	Mrs. Gaston Clary, Bryan
Field Worker	Rev. Mrs. Lizzie McAdams

During these early years the Convention has steadily made progress and its many achievements are noteworthy. Reports from Central Texas, East Texas, and West Fork districts are recorded which show that enlistments, promotional work, youth work, study courses, support of Bible College, tithing, publicity, support of children's home, evangelism, benevolence, foreign missions, *Co-Laborer* fund, and superannuation are not only being stressed but carried out.

1953

June 9, 1953, the Texas State Woman's Auxiliary Convention met at Bright Light Church near Bryan. Two officers resigned this year and were replaced: Mrs. Joe Ferguson, Youth Chairman, was replaced by Mrs. Ruby Withers; Sister Lizzie McAdams, Field Worker, was replaced by Mrs. Crawford. One of the highlights of the Convention was the declamation contest, which was won by Barbara Williams.

At the executive committee meeting in 1953, Mrs. Gaston Clary was elected to serve on the National nominating committee.

1954

On June 8, 1954, the Texas State Woman's Auxiliary Convention met at the Jamerson Memorial Church, Henderson, Texas. State Officers for 1954-1956:

President	Mrs. Hugh Gower, Henderson
Enlistment Chairman	Mrs. Alvin Halbrook, Bryan
Youth Auxiliary Chairman	Mrs. Bill Berry, Henderson
Study Course Chairman	Mrs. Gaston Clary, Henderson
Program Chairman	Mrs. H. Ray Berry, Huntsville
Personal Service Chairman	Mrs. Everett Hellard, Houston
Secretary-Treasurer	Mrs. Jim Vance, Bryan
Field Worker	Rev. Mrs. Lizzie McAdams

The Convention held a special meeting (workshop), August 19, 1954, at Piney Woods Encampment. There were representatives from the following churches: Bryan, Fort Worth, Good Hope, Keith, Mt. Olive, Houston, Huntsville, Pine Prairie, and Stewart. The duties of the various officers were discussed at this meeting.

1955

The 1955 meeting of the State Convention was held at the First Free Will Baptist Church in Bryan, June 14. This year the Northwest Brazos Association requested membership in the Convention and it was granted. Mrs. C. B. Thompson also requested that the First Free Will Baptist Church of Fort Worth be admitted to the Convention. Her request was granted.

Two students from our Bible College, Miss Barrie Sue Colson[281] and Miss Jane Berry,[282] brought interesting messages at this session.

1956

The State Convention met at the Good Hope Free Will Baptist Church, Henderson, Texas, June 12, 1956, with two districts represented, and with 11 auxiliaries reporting. It is interesting to note the progress of the State Convention, which is indicated by its reaching out in foreign missions, home missions, children's home, contributions to the Calvery fund, the youth encampment, visual aid for the Cronks, Bible College, and *Co-Laborer* fund. State officers for 1957-1958:

President	Mrs. C. B. Thompson
Enlistment Chairman	O. E. Fulton
Youth Auxiliary Chairman	Mrs. Gaston Clary
Personal Service Chairman	Mrs. T. V. Kanky
Study Course Chairman	Mrs. Bob Trant
Program Chairman	Mrs. A. F. Halbrook
Secretary-Treasurer	Mrs. H. Ray Berry
Field Worker	Mrs. Huey Gower

1957

The 8th annual Texas State Woman's Auxiliary Convention met with the Pine Prairie Church, June 11, 1957. In addition to the annual projects which the Convention supports, a canner for the Calvery's and a Tent Fund were added this year. Evidence of the growth of the Convention are the many achievements and spirituality which is manifested.

1958

In 1958, at Bryan, Texas, two district associations represented and also the local auxiliary of the First Free Will Baptist Church of Lake Charles, Louisiana. The Fellowship District Association from Fort Worth was admitted to the Convention.

Officers for 1958-1959:

President	Mrs. Gaston Clary, Henderson
Enlistment Chairman	Mrs. Martha Rice, Fort Worth

---

[281] She became Mrs. Bobby Joe Davis
[282] She became Mrs. Dale Burden

Youth Chairman	Mrs. E. M. Lewis, Bryan
Personal Service Chairman	Mrs. E. D. Hellard
Study Course Chairman	Mrs. Jean Stein
Stewardship Chairman	Mrs. Jane Burden
Secretary-Treasurer	Mrs. Asa Berry

Another step forward was taken in 1958 as the Convention assumed the support of the Wesley Calvery children in the sum of $30 per month, and continued to give for houses for our three missionary families in Japan.

1959

In 1959, the West Fork and Midessa Districts came into the Convention. Mrs. Eunice Edwards, Executive Secretary of the W. N. A .C. Nashville, Tennessee, brought the Convention message and conducted a workshop.

1960

In 1960, three districts represented: Midessa, East Texas, and Central Texas. West Fork sent reports. Twenty-two local auxiliaries were reported to the State. The Calvery's were home on Furlough and Mrs. Calvery brought the message of the hour, expounding on the last words of Jesus, "Go ye." Officers for 1960 - 1962:

President	Mrs. Gaston Clary
Enlistment Chairman	Mrs. S. R. North
Youth Chairman	Mrs. Virgin Holcomb
Study Course Chairman	Mrs. H. Z. Cox
Program Prayer Chairman	Mrs. Dovie Fears
Personal Service Chairman	Mrs. Everett Hellard
Secretary-Treasurer	Mrs. W. O. Withers

An outstanding financial report: Paid Out 1960 to May 31, 1961:

National Dues	34.00
Calvery	100.00
Co-Laborer	222.10
Calvery Children	180.00
Mexico Missions	198.62
Medical Project, Africa	675.80
Medical Project Y. P. A. & G. T. A.	50.00
National Home Missions	76.59
Moehlmans	10.00
Walkers	4.50
Spain	36.50
Japan	10.50
State Home Missions	59.13

Cuba Press	5.00
Student Loan	5.50
Foreign Missions	23.05
Eagletons	6.00
Merkhs	5.00
Pearl Harbor Fund	9.00
Jones	62.95
Shepherd Station, Africa	25.00
Superannuation	2.70
Calvery Fund	54.65
Total	2,145.11

1961

In 1961, four districts and one church answered roll call at the Fellowship Free Will Baptist Church in Bryan. The state project was "Medical Equipment for Station in Africa."

1962

In 1962, the Convention voted to take a special offering to help purchase a Jeep for the Sammy Wilkersons, give $70.00 toward the purchase of a treadle sewing machine for Lonnie Sparks to be used by all the African missionaries, and have each local auxiliary give $30,00 toward the purchase of land for the Boy's Ranch in the India Project. Officers for 1961 - 1964:

President	Mrs. Everett Hellard
Vice-President	Mrs. H. Z. Cox
Secretary-Treasurer	Mrs. Ruby Withers
Youth Chairman	Mrs. E. E. Zoellers
Program Prayer Chairman	Mrs. S. R. North
Study Course Chairman	Mrs. G. M. Goode
Personal Service Chairman	Mrs. Gaston Clary
Field Worker	Mrs. H. Ray Berry

1963

In 1963, the convention voted on the recommendation of the Executive Committee to raise funds by December, 1963, by each auxiliary, to purchase land in Hawaii. The Youth Rally was made a standard part of our Auxiliary Convention, meeting Monday night before the Auxiliary Convention.

1964

In 1964, these state projects were accepted: "Generator for Africa," and "Library for Brazil." A $75.00 love offering was given to the Jones. Officers for 1964 - 1966:

President	Mrs. E. E. Zoellers[283]
Vice-President	Mrs. A. F. Ferguson
Secretary-Treasurer	Mrs. Ruby Withers
Field Worker	Mrs. Gaston Clary
Youth Chairman	Mrs. John Warren
Study Course Chairman	Mrs. Don Ellis
Stewardship Program	Mrs. H. Ray Berry
Personal Service Chairman	Mrs. H. Z. Cox

In 1964, four districts answered roll call with fourteen churches and thirty-seven delegates. Mrs. Joy Jones, Missionary to Africa, was the guest speaker. The Westside Free Will Baptist Church in Midland was the site of the Convention.

1965

In 1965, Caprock, Midessa, East Texas, West Fork, and Central Texas answered the roll call. Caprock District came into the Convention at this session. Officers for 1965 - 1967:

President	Mrs. Asa Berry
Vice-President	Mrs. Oneta Brandon
Secretary-Treasurer	Mrs. Ruby Withers
Study Course Chairman	Morelle Breedlove
Stewardship Prayer	Mrs. John Warren
Personal Service Chairman	Mrs. E. E. Zoellers
Field Worker	Mrs. Gaston Clary
Mission Chairman	Mrs. A. F. Ferguson
Recording Secretary	Mrs. Doyle Baker
Editor-Reporter	Mrs. K. B. Pinson

1966

In 1966, the Convention met in Odessa at the First Free Will Baptist Church. A beautiful Travelers Tea was served by the Caprock District auxiliaries. The project of the year was the Palmer's fares back to Africa.

1967

In 1967, the Convention voted to divide their annual project equally between the Free Will Baptist Bible College Expansion Program and schooling for the Palmer's children. State Officers for 1966 to 1968:

---

[283] Barbara Zoellers was blind, yet she was very active in the Free Will Baptist work in Texas, along with her husband, Gene Zoellers.

President	Mrs. Asa Berry, San Antonio
Vice-President	Mrs. Oneta Brandon, Odessa
Secretary-Treasurer	Mrs. Jean Pennington, Odessa
Assistant Secretary-Treasurer	Mrs. Charlene Denman, Houston
Study Course Chairman	Mrs. Jesse Ferguson, Henderson
Stewardship Prayer Chairman	Mrs. Alton Halbrook, Bryan
Personal Service Chairman	Mrs. Barbara Zoellers
Corresponding Secretary	Mrs. Eloyce Aulds, Weatherford
Field Worker	Mrs. Ila North, Midland
Missions Chairman	Mrs. Lela Clary, Henderson
Historian	Mrs. Elizabeth Brandon, San Antonio

At the end of the above history of the Texas Woman's Auxiliary Convention is the following:

Resolution: That local, district, and state auxiliaries elect a historian whose responsibility is to record the history of the auxiliary of her church.

DUTIES

Prepares history of the women of the auxiliary. Assembles the facts and writes the history of the auxiliary in the local church from the beginning, if this has not already been done. Include sketches of Honorary and Memorial Members.

Writes the supplementary history of the auxiliary.

Submits a history for calendar year, January 1 - December 31. Sends a copy (preferably typewritten) with pictures, to the district historian who compiles a history of the district convention and sends a copy to the state historian. The state historian compiles a history of the state auxiliary convention and sends (with pictures) to the National office where a permanent record will be kept.

If there is a general historian appointed by the church, the historian of the auxiliary will submit a copy of the auxiliary history to that person.

Included with the above history is the following article by Mrs. Asa Berry, in the *Co-Laborer* magazine. It is subtitled "WNAC's First Field Worker.

Portrait of a Great Woman

by Asa Berry

It is very fitting that in this issue of Co-Laborer in which we solicit prayers and gifts for National Home Missions during the Pre-Thanksgiving Season of Prayer that we pay special homage to our *first national home missionary and WNAC's Field Worker*, our beloved Mrs. Lizzie McAdams, who went to be with the Lord, September 1, 1964.

Elizabeth Lawliss was born in Pike County, Alabama, October 1, 1884, one of ten children. She was converted in a revival at the age of seven, and at thirteen she "wanted to be a missionary." Thirteen years later she was called to preach. In her book, *My Experience, and Six Gospel Sermons*, she says, "No woman in our family or near us had ever preached, and people thought I was losing my mind." The Lord gave her courage however and she went about holding revivals. While in a revival at Bryan, Texas, the pastor Rev. Wood died and she remained there several months as interim pastor. Two years later she married Rev. Hiram McAdams and they became an evangelistic team. They had one child, Naomi Rebecca, and when she was six years old they went to the *island of Barbados, British West Indies, as missionaries*. After some disappointments they returned holding revivals and establishing new churches. They were very active in recruiting students and raising funds for the *Free Will Baptist College in Tecumseh, Oklahoma. The Free Will Baptist Church in Desloge, Missouri, was established under their ministry and she served as pastor for a number of years.*

Mrs. McAdams was an active participant in the *organization of the National Association of Free Will Baptists and in the Woman's Auxiliary Convention*. She became a national figure in the convention as she travelled tirelessly from state to state for several years as *Field Secretary*, organizing local, district, and state groups. She instituted the use of the *Jehoiada Chest* (2 Kings 12:9) as a means of raising funds for the work before the *Co-Laborer Plan* came into being.

"Sister Lizzie" was avidly interested in all phases of the Lord's work in the denomination. She worked for support of the *Bible College in Nashville, Tennessee, and was present for the opening*. She loved the cause of missions and never ceased praying and soliciting support for our missionaries.

She had been in the ministry 54 years of her 80 years when she died. Some of our present day pastors were converted under her ministry.

She wrote several books, among which was *My Experience* and *Go Tell That Fox*.

She spent much of her later life in Texas where she pastored the *Huntsville Free Will Baptist Church* until a few weeks before her death.

1989

Everyl Getz served as president of the State Woman's Auxiliary Convention. She reported that the auxiliary had surpassed their goal of $4,000.00 by approximately $2,000.00 in a six month period. The $4,000.00 project for the previous year had been to give $1,000.00 to the Bible Institute in Brazil, where Ken and Marvis Eagleton served, and $3,000.00 to Miss Judy Smith in Japan.

1990

President Everyl Getz reported that during 1990 the State Woman's Auxiliary had channeled $14,753 through their office. Their state project of raising $4,000.00 for the Nichols and Cousineaus in Africa was surpassed with a total $6,292.74. She also announced that they were raising $10,000.00 to be given to Ken and Marvis Eagleton upon their retirement from their mission work in Brazil, the money to be given as a token of love and appreciation for them for their 35 years of missionary ministry.[284]

Unfortunately, time and other demands prevent us from doing a more thorough account of the history of the work of the Free Will Baptist women of Texas. The work has continued, however, under some very capable leadership. Judy Posner contributed her energetic enthusiasm in leading the work for years. Karen Ferguson provided some able and enthusiastic leadership as well. Currently Mitzi Burks gives of her time, energy, and expertise in leading the women as they continue to keep our churches informed of the far flung ministries of Free Will Baptist missionaries around the world. International missions, as well as Home Missions, continues to be one of the strengths of the Free Will Baptist work.

---

[284] Minutes of the 1991 Texas State Association meeting, page 46.

Chapter 13

Free Will Baptist Women Preachers of Texas

The subject of women preachers is a touchy issue with some people and there are those who would prefer that this topic not be addressed in this book. However, this is a book about Texas Free Will Baptist history and women preachers are very much a part of that history. Free Will Baptist history on women preachers was influenced early on. Benjamin Randall and his wife were married by a woman preacher, Sally Parsons. The first Free Will Baptist woman preacher was Mary Savage, who was ordained in 1790, followed by such notables as Clarissa Danforth, and Dolly Quinby, mother of the more famous Hosea Quinby.[285] Texas, of course, is not the only state to have had women preachers. Illinois, Nebraska, North Carolina, Kansas, Oklahoma, Missouri, and Texas are just some of the states in which Free Will Baptist women preachers proclaimed the gospel and pastored churches. Free Will Baptists women preachers are part of our heritage. Attitudes about women preaching the gospel had changed by the early 1960's and the practice pretty much ceased to exist in our denomination after that. This chapter does not advocate for or against women preaching the gospel, it is simply an historical account of their work in Texas and beyond. Women preachers were part of the history of the Free Will Baptist work in Texas and we simply report that history.

Mrs. E. E. Bell

The minutes of the fourteenth annual session of the Southwestern Convention of Freewill Baptists, 1914, list Mrs. E. E Bell of Zulch, Texas, on the roll of ministers in the convention. Her maiden name was Marvelia Ann Nix (1875-1951). She was born in Christian County, Missouri. She married William Bray circa 1895, and had at least two children by him. She later married Ernest E. Bell and they are mentioned in the 1930 census. She passed away in McAllen, Texas, and is buried in the Valley Memorial Gardens there.[286]

---

[285] Hosea Quinby, D.D. (1804-1878) was the first college graduate with the ministry in view who belonged to the Free Will Baptist denomination. He was ordained in 1833. In addition to pastoring several churches successfully, he was principle of several schools, Parsonfield Seminary, Smithville Seminary, and Lebanon Academy. Dr. Quinby was a delegate to the first General Conference in 1827 and was chosen its first clerk. He served as standing clerk for seven years. In 1853 he was assistant moderator. The *Treatise of Faith* adopted in 1834 is understood to have been mainly his work. David Marks refers to him in his journal and seems to have been preaching in a series of meetings when Hosea was converted to Christ. This information is taken from the *Free Baptist Cyclopedia*, pages 550-553.

[286] Minutes of the fourteenth annual session of the Southwestern Free Will Baptist Convention, 1914, page 35.

Mrs. Gladys Beam

Gladys E. (Conner) Beam (1904-1996) was married to Grady W. Beam. They had twin sons and possibly a daughter. There isn't much about Mrs. Beam in the state minutes, but she is listed in the directory of ministers in the 1947 state minutes, though her last name is given as Beane, as being from Huntsville, Texas. Clerks often misspell names. According to the 1943 Central Texas minutes she assisted H. M and Lizzie McAdams in revival meetings. She is buried in the Edom Cemetery, Van Zandt County, Texas.

Mrs. Laura E. Breckenridge

An article in the December 21, 1893, *Morning Star* states that Sister L. E. Breckenridge preached one of the sermons at the eighth annual session of the Denton Creek Association. : Laura E. was born September 10, 1845, place unknown, and passed away on June 27, 1900. She is buried in the Shiloh Cemetery, Corinth, Denton County, Texas.

Mrs. Martha Jane Creamer

Martha Jane Steele was born July 24, 1852 in Georgia. She married J. C. Creamer (1843-1923) and they had at least three children. The Creamers lived in Alabama until October, 1869, when they moved to Texas. After living one year on the Brazos River, they moved to Comanche County, where they farmed and were proprietors of a store in the Creamer Community. They traveled extensively to preach at many churches. The December 7, 1923, Comanche Chief Newspaper carried a front page announcement of Jasper's death, in which it stated: "A minister of the gospel of the Freewill Baptist persuasion, for more than fifty years he had carried the story of Jesus through the pioneer country. Traveling horseback, in a buggy, and often on foot, he was faithful in the discharge of his duty....Earth has one pure spirit less, heaven one pure soul more."

The Creamers are buried in the Indian Creek Cemetery, Comanche, Comanche County, Texas.

The 1910 minutes of the West Texas Free Will Baptist Association contain the following report under Ministers' Reports:

> Sister M. J. Creamer -- To the brothers and sisters of the West Texas Free Will Baptist Association to be held in Vandyke, Texas, greetings, I submit the following report of my work for the year: Preached 35 sermons; received $6.20. May the Lord grant that peace, harmony and fellowship prevail during the association. May the Lord bless you all and pray for me.

At the time she was a licensed minister, not yet ordained and she preached at the Friday evening service of the association, September 2, 1910. The report of her husband, J. C. Creamer, is the first of the ministerial reports in those minutes. His report contained this information: "Have preached 96 sermons and held one funeral service; organized one Sunday school; married five couples; have received $49.25 in money." It seems likely that she primarily assisted him in his work. Mrs. Creamer is listed in the 1909 and 1911 *Free Will Baptist Register* as being a member of the Salt Springs Free Will Baptist Church in Comanche, member of the West Texas Association and member of the Southwestern Free Will Baptist General Convention. She is listed as a licensed minister in the minutes of the 1912 Southwestern Convention.

Mrs. Lelia Estes

M. Leila Cross was born in 1889, location unknown. The 1930 Hall County, Texas, census indicates that she and her husband, James B. Estes, had five children. She passed away in 1971 and is buried in the Clarendon Cemetery, Donley County, Texas. The earliest mention of Mrs. Lelia Estes I have found is in the minutes of the fourteenth annual session of the Southwestern Freewill Baptist Convention, which met in 1914. She is listed there as residing in Burneyville, Oklahoma.[287]

The Ministers' Directory in the 1947 minutes of the Texas State Association of Free Will Baptists lists Rev. Mrs. J. B. Estes, of Memphis, Texas, as one of the ministers in the Northwest Brazos District Association. The devotion at the Wednesday morning worship hour at the 1947 Texas State Association meeting, at the Pleasant Mound Free Will Baptist Church, Buffalo Springs, Texas, was given by Mrs. J. B. Estes, reading Psalm 23, and the clerk noted "with inspiring comments." She is again listed as a minister in the 1950 state minutes. She was a member of the Tex-Homa Ministers' Conference in 1950-1951.

Mrs. Jessie Ferguson

Jessie Ferguson

Jessie Zeona Van was born on September 17, 1912, near Gainsville, Texas, and continued to live there during her growing up years. At about the age of thirteen, in 1925, she accepted Christ as her savior and committed her life to him. Her main ambition for adulthood was to marry a preacher and be a pastor's wife. That ambition began to come to fulfillment when a new family moved into the neighborhood, a family which had a very handsome son. Word spread through the young ladies of the community that the young man was going to be a preacher. That young man was Allie Ferguson, but it was a while before they met. It was at church that the two finally became acquainted. They showed an instant liking for each other. Eighteen months later they were married, which occurred on November 29, 1931, at the courthouse in Durant, Oklahoma. In time, two children were born to this marriage, Norman and Glenna. The Great Depression was in full force during the 1930's and living was hard, harder than most of us could imagine.

Allie took Jessie to live in Fort Worth, along with his family, where he worked for the Justin Boot Company, at a salary of nine dollars a week. With Allie's mother being ill, Jessie became a mother to Allie's younger siblings, a boy and two girls. They affiliated themselves with the First Free Will Baptist Church in Fort Worth, pastored by M. L. Sutton. In some ways Brother

---

[287] Minutes of the fourteenth annual session of the Southwestern Freewill Baptist General Convention, 1914, page 35.

Sutton was one of the best pastors in Texas and a good man from whom to learn, not only about the ministry and pastoring, but about the Bible.

Jessie was ordained to the gospel ministry on January 27, 1946. This was the perfect place for her to be ordained since Lizzie McAdams and Verda Walker had both pastored there. Her certificate of ordination was signed by Elder Allie Ferguson, Elder J. H. Measures, and deacon Jewell Brandon. Jessie seems to have been the perfect complement to Allie's ministry. She assisted him every way possible and she worked extremely hard at all of the responsibilities which she took on. Allie once told me that she "never usurped authority over a man." She never pastored and it is a little difficult to know just how much preaching she did. For one thing, she never mentioned her own preaching in her autobiography, except the one time she filled in for her husband on their radio program in Weatherford, while he was away preaching a revival meeting. But a preacher she was, both licensed and ordained.

Mrs. Myrtle Ferguson

Myrtle (Henderson) Ferguson (1884-1967) was best known as the wife of the renowned evangelist and pastor, T. C. Ferguson. They were usually associated with Missouri but they both had strong ties with Texas Free Will Baptists, serving as pastor of the Bryan Free Will Baptist Church and as evangelists for the Southwestern Convention. The minutes of the third annual session of the Central Texas Association of Free Will Baptists, which met at the Bright Light Free Will Baptist Church, October 1-4, 1908, in the section on Ministers' Reports for 1908, has this report by Mrs. T. C. Ferguson:

> Mrs. T. C. Ferguson - From May 1st, 1908 to Oct. 1st, 1908. I have pastored no churches, but have assisted my husband and others in revival work. I have preached about 75 times. As others have reported the additions to the churches where I have labored, I will not report them. I have travelled over one thousand miles in the work, and have received over $50.00 for my work.

An article by Henry M. Ford in the *Morning Star* informs us that Mrs. Ferguson was examined and ordained at the 1909 meeting of the Southwestern Free Will Baptist General Convention in Weatherford, Texas. At the time, they were serving as evangelists for the convention. Using the convention's large tent, with a capacity of about four hundred, they conducted revival meetings in various areas, organizing the converts and others into Free Will Baptist churches. Ford describes Mrs. Ferguson as "a woman gifted with a sweet spirit, womanly ways, an earnest message and a rare way of telling it."[288] Mrs. Ferguson traveled with her husband and took her turn at preaching in the large "tabernacle," as they called the big tent.[289] She was a gifted musician, singer, and songwriter, often singing songs of her own composition during their evangelistic campaigns. The same issue of *The Morning Star* also reports that "several young men and women have been helped into the ministry."

Following several years as the wife and co-evangelist of T. C. Ferguson, Myrtle divorced him and as a result was dismissed from the Free Will Baptist denomination. She later married J. McAlvane, a preacher, but they were divorced after three or four years. She remarried again and became Mrs. Myrtle Johnson, the name she had at her death. She continued her ministry for many

---

[288] The *Morning Star*, December 16, 1909, Volume 84, Number 50.
[289] *The Morning Star*, January 26, 1911, page 18.

years following her divorce from T. C. Ferguson. She passed away in San Diego, California, and is buried in El Camino Memorial Park there.

Miss Tommie Franklin

Perhaps the best known woman preacher, other than Lizzie McAdams, during the first half of the twentieth century, was Miss Tommie Franklin, who was one of Lizzie's best friends and closest associates. Of all the women preachers in Texas, she was the one with the most tenure as a pastor. Tommie was born in 1897 to Eula Lee (March 31, 1872 to October 2, 1957) and Thomas H. Franklin (December 26, 1868 to September 17, 1937).

Miss Tommie Franklin

On one rainy Sunday morning when Lizzie McAdams was a guest preacher at the First Free Will Baptist Church in Bryan, Tommie met her for the first time. The young Miss Franklin confided in Lizzie that she had been called to preach, but felt that ministry was closed to her. Over lunch the two women had a heart to heart talk about the possibility of Miss Franklin entering the ministry. The next day Tommie joined Lizzie in Mexia, Texas, and went with her to Tecumseh, Oklahoma. There Lizzie dropped her off to attend Tecumseh College, a Free Will Baptist school, for Bible training. When the summer break came, Tommie went to North Carolina and became a member of Lizzie's evangelistic team (R. S. page 50). She would be a member of that team, on and off, for several years. She often preached in the extended evangelistic campaigns.[290]

Tommie pastored several churches during her ministry. She was pastor of a Free Will Baptist church in Washington, North Carolina, for a time. She pastored the First Free Will Baptist Church of Denison, Texas. She pastored the First Free Will Baptist Church in Bryan, Texas, for nine years. From Bryan she went to Henderson, Texas, to become pastor of a Free Will Baptist church there. She also pastored the Parkview Free Will Baptist Church in Desloge, Missouri, the church from which Mrs. Eunice Edwards came. Mrs. Edwards eventually became the Executive Secretary of the Woman's National Auxiliary Convention (WNAC), preceding Cleo Pursell in that position. It was my privilege to hear Mrs. Edwards preach once.

Tommie is buried in the Bryan City Cemetery in Bryan, Texas. Her simple, flat, marble headstone reads only "Tommie Franklin 1897 1977." Resting beside her are Eula and Thomas Franklin. Tommie's funeral was conducted by Dr. Eugene Richards.

It was my privilege to meet Tommie briefly. In the spring of 1974, I was preaching a revival meeting at the First Free Will Baptist Church in Bryan. As people greeted me after one of the services, Tommie came by and introduced herself to me. I had only been in Texas for less than two years and had never heard of her, but it was a pleasure to meet her. She was a sweet and gracious lady, with a kindness in her eyes, as I recall.

Lucy Gressett

Lucy Gressett is listed in the 1909 and 1911 *Free Will Baptist Registers* as being a member of the Spring Hill Free Will Baptist Church, the Plainview Quarterly Meeting, and the Southwestern Free Will Baptist General Convention. She was residing in Iola at the time.

---

[290] *Free Will Baptist Gem*, March, 1936.

Miss Ada Grover

Miss Ada Grover

Ada Grover is pictured with H. M. and Lizzie McAdams, and Miss Tommie Franklin in a photograph elsewhere in this book. On page 27 of *Rolling Stones,* Lizzie mentions several young people in Nebraska who answered the call to preach during her evangelistic meetings there. One of them is "Sister Ada Groves," by which is probably meant Ada Grover, given the number of typographical errors in the book. Ada seems to have been one of the personal workers who worked in Lizzie's evangelistic campaigns. She is briefly mentioned on page 44 of *Rolling Stones* once again.

In the May 1, 1918, issue of the *New Morning Star,* Ada Grover is mentioned as having a church and it is stated that "her church is much in the lead of any in regard to the McAdams' foreign mission fund.[291] Being associated with Lizzie McAdams over a number of years took Miss Grover to a number of states, including Texas, in her ministry.

Mrs. A. R. Harper

This woman preacher is mentioned in the minutes of the 1917 state meeting, the wife of A. R. Harper. We know little else of her.

Mrs. Julia Harper

Julia Keener was born July 7, 1873, to Nancy Matilda Brown and Jesse A. Keener of North Carolina. She married William M. Harper (1871-1956) and they had seven children, including Ira Harper, who was also a Free Will Baptist minister in East Texas. The minutes of the fourteenth annual session of the Texas Free Will Baptist Convention, which met at the Woodlawn Church in McClelland, County, August 28-31, 1928, has a partial list of the ministers in the association. It was a partial list because "It is hard to get a complete list," say the minutes. Listed as one of the ministers of the association is Mrs. Julia Harper, Route 2, Marshall, Texas. She is also listed in the 1929 minutes as living at Route 2, Marshall. Julia passed away January 6, 1944, and is buried in Grace Hill Cemetery, Longview, Gregg County, Texas.

Mrs. Lillie Kelley

The ministers' directory in the 1947 minutes of the Texas State Association lists the name of Mrs. Lilly Kelly but the directory in the 1950 minutes of the Texas State Association of Free Will Baptists spell her name as Lilley Kelley. In both she is listed as being from Huntsville, Texas, as one of the ministers in the Central Texas District Association. The program for the October 15-16, 1948, meeting of the Central Texas District Association lists her as giving the report of the Foreign Missions Director. The 1950 directory of Texas churches lists seven ordained women Free Will Baptist preachers: Lizzie McAdams, Lillie Kelley, Tommie Franklin, Amanda Kester, Jessie Ferguson, Verda Walker, and Mrs. J. B. Estes. All of them are covered in this chapter.

---

[291] *The New Morning Star*, Volume 13, Number 5, Tecumseh, Oklahoma, May 1, 1918, page 3.

Mrs. Amanda Kester

Amanda Jane Crouse was born January 20, 1891, in Miami, Ottawa County, Oklahoma. She married Charles Joseph Kester (1880-1946) and they had four children, one of whom died at birth. She passed away April 5, 1957, and is buried in Lakewood Memorial Park, Henderson, Rusk County, Texas. Mrs. Amanda J. Kester figures prominently in the minutes of the Texas Association of Free Will Baptists in the 1940's and into the 50's. She was the only minister who submitted a report of his/her work and so it is assumed that she was employed by the association in some capacity. Her several reports include the number of sick calls, prayers, and readings in different places, mission work, number of church services conducted, along with the number of funerals conducted and cottage prayer meetings held. The Ministers' Directory in the 1947 minutes of the Texas State Association lists her as being from Wright City, Texas, but the 1950 minutes of the state association lists her as being from Arp, Texas. In both she is one of the ministers in the Texas Free Will Baptist Association, which became the East Texas District Association in1954. She was present for many of the district meetings and very active in them. She is mentioned in the April 9, 1955, minutes of the East Texas District Association as having sent a letter to the association requesting that her name be dropped from the roll. The letter was placed in the hands of the Credentials Committee. In their report they made a motion, which carried, that the moderator appoint a committee of three ladies to talk to Mrs. Kester. The committee members are not named and there is no mention as to why Mrs. Kester wanted her name dropped from the roll of ministers. It seems likely that she was sympathetic to the issue in the Jamerson Memorial Church in Henderson which temporarily caused the church to be out of fellowship with the district. The issue was the charismatic movement which had affected the church.

Mrs. Cora Mann

Mrs. Cora Mann, of Henderson, Texas, is listed as a licensed minister in the minutes of the 1912 session of the Southwestern Convention.[292]

Mrs. Lizzie McAdams

Elizabeth (Lizzie) Rachel Lawless was born on October 1, 1884, near Troy in Pike County, Alabama. She was converted to Christ at the age of six in an old Methodist church at Luverne. Her family migrated to Texas and settled in the area east of Bryan. In August of 1909, at the age of twenty-five, she felt a strong call to preach the gospel. In her memoirs she said:

> It seemed almost impossible for me to believe that He was calling me to
> go out to preach His Word, for I had been taught from childhood that a
> woman had no right to preach the Gospel of our Lord Jesus Christ.[293]

She learned that the Free Will Baptist church in Kurtin, Texas, had recently licensed two young women to preach, so she attended the yearly association meeting at Cross, Texas, in October of 1909. She was invited to preach and was there licensed to the gospel ministry. She would go on to become the most influential and famous of all of the Free Will Baptist women preachers in Texas.

Lizzie McAdams

---

[292] Minutes of the twelfth annual session of the Southwestern Freewill Baptist General Convention, 1912, page 5.
[293] *Rolling Stones*, self-published, not dated, page 5

In the earliest months of her ministry, while she was still only licensed to preach, she served as interim pastor of the First Free Will Baptist Church in Bryan. The pastor, Rev. W. T. Woods, passed away and the church asked Lizzie to serve until they could secure a pastor. The church obtained the services of J. J. Tatum, who served as pastor from 1910 to 1913, the first of three terms as pastor of the church. This would mean that Lizzie's pastoral service of seven months was in the general time frame of 1909-1910. The 1957 book on the history of the First Free Will Baptist Church of Bryan does not give the dates for the pastorates of either Brother Wood or Sister Lawless.

Hiram M, Naomi Rebekah, Lizzie McAdams

Brother R. B. Easley met Lizzie at a convention in Tecumseh, Oklahoma, and asked her to come pastor the Easley's Chapel Free Will Baptist Church near Comanche, Texas, which she did until the following spring, 1911. The Easley's Chapel Church asked for her ordination and she returned to Zulch, Texas, where she was ordained on April 17, 1911. The year 1911 is significant because that was the year the merger of many of our northern Free Will Baptist churches with the Northern Baptists was finalized. Lizzie would, in future years, pastor a church in Kenesaw, Nebraska, and two in North Carolina, at Washington and Belhaven. Those were both short term pastorates because her real work was that of an evangelist. Over the years she pastored a number of churches in Nebraska, North Carolina, and Oklahoma during the winter months.

As noted above her primary ministry was that of an evangelist. Though she preached some revival meetings in churches, she mostly used a large tent for her evangelistic campaigns. Crowds of up to five thousand people came to hear her and sometimes her meetings lasted for weeks. She once pitched her tent on the courthouse lawn in Huntsville, Texas, and preached all winter. Scores of converts normally resulted from the meetings and often churches were formed following the campaigns. She held meetings wherever Free Will Baptists existed but mostly in Texas, Oklahoma, Kansas, Nebraska, Missouri, Illinois, Alabama, North Carolina, and South Carolina. During a three year period in which she held evangelistic campaigns in the lead belt area of Missouri, she had fourteen hundred professions of faith. As a result, she built a church at Flat River and organized the Parkview Free Will Baptist Church in Desloge, which she pastored for a while. Over the years she worked with many Free Will Baptist denominational leaders, men whose names are well known even today: John Wolfe, Winford Davis, James Miller, J. R. Davidson, K. V. Shutes, M. L. Hollis, S. L. Morris, who published a paper called *The Free Will Baptist News*, Melvin Bingham, W. E. Dearmore, L. R. Ennis, Robert Crawford, J. C. Griffin and others. These men were all denominational leaders who accepted her ministry and worked with her or cooperated with her in her evangelistic campaigns.

Some young men, who would later become well known ministers in their own right, worked with Lizzie on her evangelistic team as personal workers or in music. M. L. Sutton, who would later make his mark in Fort Worth, along with his wife, were on her team. Damon Dodd was converted under her ministry in one of her campaigns in Flat River, Missouri, and later joined her team as the campaign song leader and personal worker, as did his wife, Sylvia. Dodd would later ably serve the denomination in many important capacities and wrote the book *The Free Will*

Baptist Story, a history of the Free Will Baptist denomination. Several women also served on her team, including Tommie Franklin who is mentioned above.

Seated: H. M. and Lizzie McAdams
Standing, left to right: Miss Tommie Franklin, Miss Ada Grover

She married Hiram Mullens McAdams on April 19, 1911, at Weatherford, Texas. The service was performed by Miss Verda Smith, who would later become Mrs. Verda Walker. They had one child, Naomi Rebekah, born in 1913 in Texas. Lizzie and H. M. as he was generally known, worked together for the rest of their married lives. So Lizzie Lawless became known as Lizzie McAdams. H. M was ordained at the First Free Will Baptist Church of Weatherford, Texas, though I'm not sure of the year. Lizzie doesn't supply us with many dates in her writings.

She worked at a number of denominational ministries as time permitted during her busy evangelistic campaigns. She was for a time the field worker for Tecumseh College in Tecumseh, Oklahoma, a Free Will Baptist school which she and John Wolfe were instrumental in founding. Tecumseh College opened its doors on September 12, 1917. When the college burned to the ground a few years later it was never reopened. She worked tirelessly for the establishment of Free Will Baptist Bible College and was there for its opening. Lizzie and H. M. were state evangelists for the state of Nebraska and they worked for several months for the Missouri State Association of Free Will Baptists as state missionaries. She is very well known for her work at the Woman's Auxiliary for organizing many chapters all over the denomination and for raising large sums of money for missions through the auxiliary efforts. She designed, had built, and distributed small wooden chests, called Jehoiada chests, for use in churches as a means of raising large sums of funds for missions. The chests were named after the chest made by Jehoiada in 2 Kings 12:9. The National Association of Free Will Baptists appointed Lizzie to serve as field worker for the Home Mission Board, a position she held for one year. She also served a term as a member of the Home Mission Board. Beginning in 1953 the annual missions offering of the Woman's National Auxiliary Convention, WNAC, was named "The Lizzie McAdams Offering." The name of the offering was later changed to "The Benjamin Randall Offering," and 2008 to "The Mission North America Offering" with this parenthesis added (formerly Benjamin Randall and Lizzie McAdams offerings). The purpose of the offering remains to support the general work of the Home Missions Department of the National Association of Free Will Baptists.

She and her husband, along with daughter Naomi, went to Barbados as missionaries, departing by ship on Christmas Eve, 1918, but did not remain there long. She gave only a brief explanation in her memoirs: "We found that our trip to the West Indies was to investigate the Mission Field, instead of remaining as workers. Circumstances existed there that would not permit us to stay" (*Rolling Stones*, page 39). She elsewhere commented, "We went to Barbados, B.W. I, as missionaries, and went with the intention of staying, but the work was not what it was represented to be and we came back" (*My Experience and Six Gospel Sermons*, page 7).

One of the things for which Lizzie is most famous occurred at the organizational meeting of the National Association of Free Will Baptists, which met at Cofer's Chapel Free Will Baptist Church in Nashville, Tennessee, November 5-7, 1935. She stood and made the motion that Free

Will Baptists in the East and Free Will Baptists in the West come together to form the National Association of Free Will Baptists. The motion passed and the National Association became a reality.

At the end of her book *Rolling Stones,* she gave a brief summary of her work: she preached in seventeen states, held about three hundred revivals, had ten thousand confessions of faith, organized eleven churches, numerous Woman's Auxiliaries, and Free Will Baptist Leagues.

Her writings include the following, which are accounts of her experiences or gospel sermons:

- *My Experience and Six Gospel Sermons*
- *Rolling Stones*
- *Go Tell That Fox*
- *Getting a Shave in the Devil's Barbershop*
- *My Trip to the West India Islands*
- *Woman's Bible Rights to Preach the Gospel*

An article about her ministry appeared in the Free Will Baptist Gem. A paragraph which gave the general range of her team's ministry stated:

> Their personal ministry has an unusually wide range. Beginning in southern Texas, they go on preaching tours across the southern states to Florida and Georgia, hence north through the Carolinas, then west to all the states between North Carolina and Southern Illinois, from Illinois to Missouri, Kansas, Oklahoma and back to Texas. Their most extensive ministry is in the Western section of that circuit or in Texas, Oklahoma, Missouri, Illinois, and Tennessee.[294]

Lizzie lived until the age of eighty. She pastored the Huntsville, Texas, Free Will Baptist Church until shortly before her death on September 1, 1964. She outlived her husband by only three months and eight days. She is buried in the Falba Cemetery, Huntsville, Walker County, Texas.

Mrs. B. M. Moody

The minutes of the fourteenth annual session of the Southwestern Convention of Freewill Baptists lists Mrs. Moody of Piedmont, Texas, on the roll of ministers in the convention.[295]

---

[294] *Free Will Baptist Gem*, May 1940, page six.
[295] Minutes of the fourteenth annual session of the Southwestern Freewill Baptist Convention, 1914, page 35.

Mrs. Cleo Pursell

Cleo Wilburn Dalton[296] was born in Fort Worth, Texas, on February 16, 1918, to Charles P. and Eltrie Tice Dalton. She grew up in Denison, Texas, attending the Central Ward Elementary School, and graduating from Denison High School in 1935, the year the National Association of Free Will Baptists was formed in Nashville, Tennessee. Two years earlier, in 1933, when she was fifteen years old, she was converted to Christ at a revival meeting being held at the Denison Free Will Baptist Church. The evangelist was E. C. Morris of Georgia. E. A. O'Connell was the pastor at the time. She dedicated her life to special service the following year and preached her first sermon, at the age of sixteen, at the Denison City Mission. Cleo was licensed to preach the gospel on August 14, 1935, at the age of seventeen, the year she graduated from high school. Four years later, in 1939, she was ordained by the West Fork District Association of Free Will Baptists when she was twenty-one years of age. The

Cleo Purcell, 1939

ordination ceremony was conducted at the Pleasant Mound Free Will Baptist Church at Buffalo Springs, Texas. The ordaining council consisted of W. V. McPhail, pastor of the Denison church; M. L. Sutton, pastor of the Trinity church in Fort Worth; Allie Ferguson, pastor of the Pleasant Mound church; J. C. Hodges, school teacher; and Paul Edgar Pursell.

Cleo and Paul E. Pursell, of Wewoka, Oklahoma, were married February 16, 1939, on her twenty-first birthday, at the Denison church, by W. V. McPhail. Thus she became Mrs. Cleo Pursell and began a lifelong ministry in the Free Will Baptist denomination. She is included in this chapter on women preachers from Texas because she was born here, saved here, licensed to preach, and ordained here. Cleo did not pastor but she assisted her husband in pastoral work in Tecumseh, Burris City, Wirt, Bristow, and Shawnee in Oklahoma, and in Lawndale, California. Cleo became prominent in district, state, and national youth work. She sometimes preached, filling in for her husband but, though she was an ordained Free Will Baptist preacher, she did not make her mark in the world as a preacher. That's not to say that she wasn't a good preacher, it only means that she is most noted for her work with the Woman's Auxiliary.

Cleo was instrumental in organizing the Oklahoma Woman's Auxiliary State Convention in 1941. She served as president of that organization for five or six years. In 1945, she became second vice president of the Woman's National Auxiliary Convention, commonly known as the WNAC. She continued serving with the WNAC in several capacities until 1957. In 1963 Cleo was elected the first full-time Executive Secretary-Treasurer of the WNAC, which required her and her husband to move to Nashville, Tennessee. She arrived in Nashville just in time for the move of the Free Will Baptist national offices from 3801 Richland Avenue, about three blocks down the street from Free Will Baptist Bible College, to the new offices at 1134 Murfreesboro Road. Just as a footnote, she succeeded Mrs. Eunice Edwards, who was also a Free Will Baptist

---

[296] Much of the information about Cleo Pursell was supplied to me by Mrs. Pursell herself before she passed away.

Cleo Purcell as Executive Secretary of the WNAC

preacher. Mrs. Edwards had pastored the Leadington Free Will Baptist Church for a number of years. Another footnote to history is that Eunice Edwards was led to the Lord by her pastor, Tommie Franklin, mentioned above. A major turnaround occurred during Cleo's years of her capable leadership with the WNAC, with many improvements and a huge expansion in the scope of that organization's work and influence in the denomination. The membership reached an all-time high during her tenure. Cleo served as Executive Secretary-Treasurer of the Woman's National Auxiliary Convention from September, 1963, until August 1, 1985, twenty-two years.

Cleo was a gifted and prolific writer. She produced many leaflets, wrote for and edited the Co-Laborer magazine. She wrote a monthly column called "Words for Women" for Contact from 1966-1970. She authored four books:

- Missionary Education of Our Youth, 1955

- Woman's Auxiliary Manual, 1965

- Death and Dying, 1982

- Triumph Over Suffering, 1982

Cleo Wilburn (Dalton) Pursell passed away on December 17, 2009, in Nashville, Tennessee, at the age of ninety-one. She is buried in Nashville. Her husband Paul passed away several years earlier and is buried in Oklahoma.

Ollie Smith

Ollie Smith is listed as a member of the Social Service Committee at the 1928 Texas Free Will Baptist Convention, along with Mrs. John Moody and W. K. O'Brien. The minutes don't specify that she was a woman, but Ollie is generally a woman's name, such as the name of my paternal grandmother, Ollie Murphy. Nothing else is said about her and, so far, this is the only place she is mentioned in the available minutes.

Tommie Smith

Little is known of Tommie Smith. She preached the introductory sermon at the thirty-third annual session of the Texas State Association of Free Will Baptists, which met at the Trinity Free Will Baptist Church in Fort Worth, November 2-4, 1937.

Emma Thomas

The 1909 minutes of the Central Texas District Association list three women who received license to the gospel ministry. Two of them are familiar, Elizabeth Lawless (Lizzie McAdams) and Verda Smith (Walker) but the third is less so. Her name was Emma Thomas and at this point we know little about her. In the 1911 *Free Will Baptist Register,* she is listed as being a member of the Spring Hill Free Will Baptist Church, the Plainview Quarterly Meeting, and the Southwestern Free Will Baptist General Convention. She was living in Cross at the time.

Verda Walker

Verda (Smith) Walker

Verda E. Smith was born on August 19, 1893. She married James Milton Walker. From this marriage came three children: son Fritz Morris Walker, daughter Mattie Elizabeth (Walker) Brandon, and daughter Jimmie Sue (Walker) Yeary. Verda was ordained to the gospel ministry on March 31, 1912, by the West Fork District Association of Free Will Baptists when it met at the New Hope Free Will Baptist Church in Parker County. Her ordination certificate reads:

A MINISTERIAL CERTIFICATE OF ORDINATION

As granted by the usages of the Freewill Baptist Church

This is to certify that the Bearer Verda E. Smith of Singleton, Texas, is an ordained Minister of the Gospel in good standing in the FREEWILL BAPTIST CHURCH and as such we recommend her to God's people everywhere, giving her the authority to preach the Gospel and administer the ordinances of the House of the Lord, and solemnize marriages according to the Bible and the usages of the FREEWILL BAPTIST CHURCH. She was set apart to the Gospel Ministry by laying on of hands by an Ordaining Council appointed by the West Fork Association of the FREEWILL BAPTIST CHURCH at their Parker County Quarterly Meeting at New Hope Church, Parker County, State of Texas, March 31, 1912.

Names of the Ordaining Council	Address
Rev. E. L. Hill	Garner, Texas
Rev. R. V. Whitaker	Weatherford, Texas
Rev. J. M. Walker	Weatherford, Texas
Rev. S. L. Morris	Weatherford, Texas

Preach The Word
This Certificate is for Life Unless Annulled by a Council of *her* Peers.

Many people would object to the wording of the certificate, even if they accepted women as preachers of the gospel. For one thing, the words "Freewill Baptist Church" should be "Free Will Baptist denomination." More importantly, it isn't a local church or an association of churches which gives the authority to preach the gospel, administer the ordinances, or solemnize marriages. The authority to preach and administer the ordinances comes only from God. States can give legal authorization to solemnize marriages. Ordination is simply the church's (or its representatives through the association) official *recognition* that a person does indeed possess the gift and calling of God to the ministry and is therefore entitled to be heard as such.[297] However, our task here is not to discuss theology but to report the history of Free Will Baptists in Texas. So, let's continue with that.

Verda is listed in the 1911 *Free Will Baptist Register* as living in Singleton, Texas, with membership in the Evergreen Free Will Baptist Church, the Plainview Quarterly Meeting, and the Southwestern Freewill Baptist Convention.

Verda Walker was very good friends with Lizzie McAdams. It was Verda Walker who performed the wedding ceremony for Lizzie and H. M. McAdams, who were married at the First Free Will Baptist Church in Weatherford, Texas.

J. M. Walker and his wife, Verda Walker, were elected as evangelists of the Southwestern Convention in 1912. They had the use of a tent which belonged to the convention for use as a meeting place during revival meetings, these meetings generally being for the purpose of establishing churches in new communities.[298]

Verda pastored the First Free Will Baptist Church in Weatherford from August 1940 to September 1942. She and her husband conducted revival meetings at the Weatherford church and the New Hope Free Will Baptist Church near Weatherford. Both she and her husband worked on the *New Morning Star,* the Free Will Baptist paper which replaced *The Morning Star* which was lost to us in the merger with the Northern Baptists in 1910-1911, while it (*The New Morning Star*) was being published in Weatherford and edited by S. L. Morris. She may have assisted her husband when he pastored the New Hope Church in Parker County, Texas, and probably assisted him when he pastored a church in Adams, Nebraska, near Lincoln, according to her grandson Morris Brandon. She is listed in the directory of Free Will Baptist ministers in Texas in the minutes of the 1947 state meeting.

Evangelists James and Verda Walker

She passed away on April 8, 1968, and is buried in the East Greenwood Cemetery in Weatherford, Texas. It is interesting that in the obituary report in the 1968 minutes of the Texas State Association of Free Will Baptists she is simply listed as Mrs. Verda Walker. It was in the 1960's that the Free Will Baptist attitude change toward women preachers had reached its completion. At the time of this writing there are sixteen living descendants of Verda and J. M. Walker. She is the maternal grandmother of Morris Brandon, deacon in the First Free Will Baptist Church of Weatherford, Texas. Morris remembers hearing his grandmother preach but does not remember much about her preaching.

Mrs. H. A. Wheeler

This first woman preacher of Texas did most of her work before she and her husband came to Texas. In the April 1, 1942 issue of *The Free Will Baptist,* she had an article on the early history

---

[297] This definition of ordination was taken from "Ordination To The Ministry In The Free Will Baptist Denomination," page 4, published by the Executive Office/National Association of Free Will Baptists, Nashville, Tennessee.
[298] Minutes of the twelfth annual session of the Southwestern Freewill Baptist General Convention, 1912, page 8.

of Free Will Baptists. The editor, R. B. Spencer, introduced her as a new writer for the paper with the following biographical sketch:

> Rev. Mrs. H. A. Wheeler was formerly Rev. Miss Wilmetta M. Marks of Reynolds, Nebraska. She is a great niece of David Marks of early Free Will Baptist history. Mrs. Wheeler is the only daughter of Rev. William Marks of the Reynolds Nebraska Free Will Baptist church. She is the granddaughter of Rev. Ives Marks who was the founder of Rose Creek City near Reynolds, Nebraska, and who was a pioneer minister as well, and brother of the sainted David Marks of Free Will Baptist history.
>
> Rev. Mrs. Wheeler was called "The Girl Preacher" in 1900 as she pastored churches and did evangelistic work. For the last twenty years she travelled from shore to shore in this country doing evangelistic work together with her husband, Dr. H. A. Wheeler. The work was done under the name "The Wheeler Evangelistic Party." Thousands of souls were saved during these evangelistic campaigns. Dr. Wheeler is now a practicing physician at Port Neches, Texas, where their home is located, and Mrs. Wheeler still goes wherever called to hold revivals.[299]

Mrs. Ola Mae Winters

Ola Mae (Coker) Winters (1913-1992) married preacher W. W. Winters (1910-1971) November 19, 1932, in Tillman County, Oklahoma. We know very little about her. She was chosen by the Divine Service Committee to bring the devotion at the Wednesday evening service of the 1952 Texas State Association meeting[300]. That alone does not mean that she was a preacher, because women were often chosen to bring devotions at district and state meetings. I will admit that I may be wrong about her being a preacher. She is buried in Sunset Memorial Park, Albuquerque, New Mexico..

Members of the Tex-Homa Ministers' Conference

For a short time the ministers of Texas and Oklahoma joined together and formed the Tex-Homa Ministers' Conference for "Inspiration • Information • Fellowship." The minutes of the 1950 session, which met at the Free Will Baptist Children's Home in Ringling, Oklahoma, contain the following list of women preachers who were members of the conference.

From Oklahoma
        Mrs. Faye Bookout, Drumright
        Mrs. Elda Crain, Miami
        Mrs. Ida Dressler, Bristow
        Mrs. Sadie Fincher, Drumright
        Mrs. Leona Mayfield, Tulsa
        Mrs. Hattie Newman, Jennings

---

[299] *The Free Will Baptist*, Volume 57, Number 13, April 1, 1942, edited by R. B. Spencer, published by Free Will Baptist Press, Ayden, North Carolina, page 4. Note: The Wheeler's address was given as 502 S. Commerce Street, Lockhart, Texas.
[300] Minutes of the Texas State Association, 1952, pages 7-8.

Mrs. Cleo Purcell, Bristow
From Texas
Mrs. J. B. Estes, Memphis
Mrs. Jessie Ferguson, Weatherford

Of the forty-seven men preachers who were active members of the conference at the time were such notables as Oklahomans W. S. Mooneyham, J. Reford Wilson, Harry Stairs, Wade Jernigan, Willard Day, Howard Gage, E. E. Morris, E. A. O'Donnell, and Vard Wood. Notable Texans included John A. Brooks, Tiff Covington, H. Z. Cox, Allie Ferguson, W. T. McDuffie, and M. L. Sutton. The fact that they were all members of the Ministers' Conference indicates that they at least had a working relationship.

A further indication that women were accepted as preachers in Texas is the Certificate of Ordination used by the Free Will Baptist denomination back in the 1950's. When this form originated, when its use ended, and how widespread it was hasn't been researched by this author. This particular certificate is slightly different than the one issued by Free Will Baptists in Missouri at the time. Where the one below has a blank space in which was written either the word "*him*" or "*her*," the one in Missouri has written in "*him/her*." Here is a reproduction of the Certificate of Ordination of Bobby Joe Davis, issued to him in 1954.

MINISTER'S
Certificate of Ordination
AS GRANTED BY THE USAGES OF THE FREE WILL BAPTIST CHURCH

This certifies that the Bearer, Elder *Bobbie Joe Davis*[301] of the town of *Piedmont*, County of *Grimes*, State of *Texas*, a regular member of *Blue Lake*

FREE WILL BAPTIST CHURCH
in said County, has this day been publicly set apart to the work of the Gospel Ministry, by prayer and the laying on of hands, according to the usages of the Free Will Baptist denomination, and is hereby authorized to preach the Gospel and administer its ordinances, organize churches, and solemnize marriages according to the usages of the FREE WILL BAPTIST CHURCH, wherever God in His providence may call *him*.

This Certificate of Ordination shall be in full force and effect for life, or during the maintenance of sound doctrine and good moral character. It shall be subject to recall or annullment *(sic)* by a council of at least three ordained ministers appointed by the Church or Association to which *he* belongs, and upon official demand by said Church or Association, *he* is hereby placed under solemn promise to deliver this Certificate.

---

[301] "Bobbie" is incorrect on this certificate. It should be Bobby.

The purpose of inserting this ordination certificate is to show that ordination forms used by the Central Texas District Association, as in many other associations, left blank the spaces where the pronouns "him," "her," "he," and "she" were to be written in, because these associations ordained both men and women to the gospel ministry.

Names of Ordaining Council   **Address**

Rev. Alvin F. Halbrook   Route 3, Bryan, Texas
Rev. H. M. McAdams   Huntsville, Texas
Rev. J. L. Lamb   Houston, Texas

At *Blue Lake* Church, *Grimes* County
State of *Texas*, *July 3*, 19*54*

This Certificate is good for life unless annulled by a Council of Peers
Read 1st Timothy 3:1-13 and 2nd Timothy 4:1-5

Again, this chapter is not to promote or oppose the idea of women preachers, but to report the history of Free Will Baptists in Texas, a history which includes women evangelists and pastors.

For Extra Reading

For anyone interested in reading about other Free Will Baptist women preachers there is an old book recently made available by Alton Loveless, president of Free Will Baptist Publications in Columbus, Ohio. The book, *The Female Preacher*, by Almond H. Davis, is about Salome Lincoln. The back of the book says this about her: "Salome Lincoln died in 1841 at age 34. She married Junis Mowy in 1834 bearing two daughters but losing the first child. He moved to Iowa some years later and had a fruitful ministry. Salome was a very popular preacher, well-educated for her time, and other notable ministers, such as John Colby, traveled together preaching the good news of Christ. She was known as a gracious lady, always modestly dressed. Her voice was inviting to listen to with content and a spirit that penetrated into the hearts of her listeners. Large crowds were always present whenever she preached." Martin Cheney, pastor of the Free Will Baptist Church at Providence, Rhode Island, preached her funeral. The book is available from Amazon.com.

Allie Ferguson and his wife, Jessie Ferguson, both wrote autobiographies of their lives and ministries. Brother Ferguson gave me copies of each of the hand written biographies, which are as yet unpublished. Hopefully these autobiographies of two of the preachers who ministered in Texas will be available in print someday.

Chapter 14

An Evaluation and Outlook for the Future

Free Will Baptists have been present in Texas since 1870 when missionaries from the Randall Movement began planting black Free Will Baptist churches, starting in Lancaster. A. M. Stewart organized the first white Free Will Baptist church in Texas in the community of Clayton in 1876. That is not necessarily to say that Free Will Baptists have been a huge presence in Texas. Free Will Baptists have, for the most part, especially in the early years, been a rural denomination in the Lone Star State, with some churches established in small towns, and fewer still in the large metropolitan areas. We have had few churches in the big cities: Dallas, Houston, San Antonio, El Paso and Austin. Fort Worth has been an exception, even though there is now only one very small church inside the city limits, and it may be closed by the time you read this. Currently, there is an effort to plant churches in the major Metropolitan Statistical Areas of Texas. Getting in the game late, these new churches are normally being established in the suburbs, rather than in the inner cities, and it is these newer churches which seem to be flourishing. There are several reasons they are doing well: most of them have full time pastors, they are experienced men, they are trained for the ministry, and they have adequate or nearly adequate financial support. In addition, they don't have to battle with long established tradition and are, therefore, able to build churches which are prepared to minister in the Twenty-first Century. They do not have to compromise the gospel to do so. And very importantly, the newer churches tend to have excellent locations.

The Free Will Baptist denomination in Texas overall is in decline. This is said despite the fact that some district associations continues to build new churches. The list of closed churches statewide continues to grow, with the prospect that many more will close in the next few years. Several entire associations of churches have vanished. The state association no longer publishes its state paper, *The Texas Challenge*, in printed form, though some hope to revive it soon. The state no longer has an executive secretary to coordinate and promote the work. The state association does have a "State Office Coordinator," Marcus Brewer, who is employed part-time. It was mentioned above that Free Will Baptists have been present in Texas for a long time, but that they do not have much of a presence in Texas. By that I mean that the state of Texas hardly knows that Free Will Baptists exist, except for the immediate communities of some of the local churches. This is not meant to minimize the ministry of Free Will Baptists in Texas. Every soul won to the Lord, and every soul to whom we have ministered, is precious in the eyes of the Lord. It goes without saying that it would have been much better if we had been far more successful in winning converts to Christ and planting more and stronger churches.

Free Will Baptists in some of the neighboring states have done well, very well. The very large state of Texas now has roughly fifty churches. By contrast the much smaller state of Oklahoma lists twenty-five district associations, composed of 216 churches.[302] Though some of

---

[302] These figures are taken from the *2015 Free Will Baptist Yearbook*.

those churches are rural and/or are in small towns, many of them are fairly large churches, by Free Will Baptist standards, and are located in the major metropolitan areas, such as Oklahoma City and Tulsa. As a further indication of the strength of the Oklahoma State Association of Free Will Baptists, they have their own state office building, a full-time executive secretary, a full-time mission's director, a bookstore/supply center, and their own college, recently renamed Randall University. The reason for Oklahoma's strength isn't that the Free Will Baptist work there is much older. The first Free Will Baptist church organized in Indian Territory, now Oklahoma, was the Concord Church, organized in the Buckhorn schoolhouse, in 1892,[303] with the state association being organized in 1908. By comparison the first white Free Will Baptist church in Texas was organized in 1876, and the state association was organized in 1915. The two state associations are not much different in age, the Oklahoma State Association being only seven years older.

The state of Arkansas is another example of a neighboring state doing well. The Free Will Baptist work in Arkansas is about forty years older than the work in Texas. The first Free Will Baptist church established in Arkansas was organized around 1840, and the state association was organized in 1898.[304] Arkansas lists fifteen district associations and 200 local churches.[305] They have a full-time executive secretary, a full-time state mission's director, own their own state office building, and own a sixty-one acre youth camp, Camp Beaverfork, which has a full-time camp director. They do not have a bookstore, but they do sell Randall House Sunday school literature out of the state office, selling around $300,000.00 worth per year. The budget for the Arkansas State Association, excluding designated outside giving to national agencies and outside sources, is about $1,500.000.00. The 2012 *Free Will Baptist Yearbook* indicates that Arkansas gave to national ministries $1,003,613.01 for the year 2011. That same year Texas gave $249,179.54. The churches in Arkansas are located in rural areas, small towns, and big cities.

While the works in Oklahoma and Arkansas are doing well, it must also be noted that the Free Will Baptist work in other neighboring states, Louisiana, New Mexico, and Colorado, are not doing well at all. Louisiana has maybe four churches. New Mexico has two, in Hobbs and Albuquerque. Colorado has about four.

Lack of Leadership

Over the years many people outside of Texas have asked why the Free Will Baptist work in Texas has not flourished as it has in the neighboring states of Oklahoma and Arkansas.[306] Free Will Baptists in Texas have asked the same question. The Executive Board of the Texas State Association has discussed it on several occasions. Let me say here that "God has chosen to bless Oklahoma and Arkansas," and that "God just hasn't blessed Texas," isn't the answer. There are and have been good people in Texas. People have worked hard. People have prayed faithfully for the work in Texas. Several years ago the State Executive Board was discussing this very subject,

---

[303] *Oklahoma State Association of Free Will Baptists, the First 100 Years 1908-2008*, published by the Oklahoma State Association of Free Will Baptists, compiled by Delbert Akin, Nancy Draper, and Edwin Wade, 2009, page 4.
[304] *History of Arkansas Free Will Baptists*, David A. Joslin, editor, Randall House Publications, Nashville, Tennessee, 1998, page 6.
[305] These figures are also taken from the *2013 Free Will Baptist Yearbook*.
[306] I don't want to seem to be obsessed with Oklahoma and Arkansas, but they are neighboring states where Free Will Baptists have done well, much better than in Texas. This is a valid comparison, since Oklahoma is just across the Red River and Arkansas borders the northeastern section of our state. Texas is a great state, a wonderful place to live and work. Texas is the second most populous state in the Union and there are numerous denominations which have done well here.

asking why and what we could do about it, if anything. Several things were listed as contributing factors. I spoke up and said that I thought the primary reason the Free Will Baptist work had not grown in Texas, a very large, populated state, as it had in Oklahoma and Arkansas, was a lack of leadership. The moderator spoke up immediately and said, "That's true, but you can't say that." I didn't know why I couldn't say it. I still don't. So I'm going to say it again. The main reason the work in Texas has not flourished as it has in some states is this: a general lack of leadership.

J. J. Tatum, in his agent's report to the Southwestern Convention in 1914, meeting at the North Zulch Church, stated: "Can we lead our people to higher grounds? Water seeks the level of the fountainhead. So with a denomination. It will be just as strong as its leaders."[307]

Don't be mistaken, Texas has had some good leaders. There were some good leaders when the state association was organized in 1915. There were some good leaders in the 1930's and 40's. There were some good leaders throughout the decades later. There are some good leaders now, a hundred years after we were organized. The problem is that there never have been *enough* good leaders to bring the work along to where it could be and should be. Texas needs good leaders, men and women, who have ideas, who can say, "Let's go in this direction, let's go to this destination, and here's how we're going to get there." We need good leaders who can get people to follow them and rally to the cause. One doesn't necessarily have to hold some high elected office to be a leader. Anyone with good ideas and the ability to lead can have a strong influence in the local church, district, or state association. He or she can make a difference. However, we should expect those in certain positions to be leaders, such as district and state moderators, members of the district and state executive committees, members of various boards, such as the Mission Board and the Christian Education Board, and certainly the Executive Secretary, when and if the state has one.

Ideally, district and state moderators should exert leadership by suggesting various ideas and programs which can improve the work of the associations. However, moderators are often looked upon as having only one job, to moderate the business sessions impartially and see to it that the business sessions are conducted fairly according to a previously adopted standard of parliamentary procedure. You certainly want that, but our districts and state association need more. We need people who not only moderate capably, fairly, and impartially, we need people who can, from their wisdom, experience, training, and creativity, suggest improvements: new and better ways of doing things, and can suggest and promote new programs which will work for the good of all. Some men have served as moderator of district associations or the state association for years yet were not able to propose new ideas. They have seen their job as simply seeing to it that the status quo operates efficiently. It takes more than one or two good leaders to provide proper leadership for an entire association, especially a state association. One or two good leaders can make a difference, of course, but a state association needs good leadership across the board, in the moderator's position, in the Executive Committee, in the General Board, in the Mission Board, in the Christian Education Board, and on any other boards or committees the association may have. Texas has had some good leaders, but they have been too few and far between to bring the Free Will Baptist work along to where it needs to be and should be after a hundred years of existence.

---

[307] Minutes of the Southwestern Freewill Baptist Convention, 1914, page 26.

The Big Country

One of my favorite old western movies is *The Big Country*, starring Gregory Peck. In one scene an old rancher asks Gregory Peck's character, who is an Eastern sailor come west, "Have you ever seen anything so big?" Peck's character startles the old rancher by saying, "Yes, a couple of oceans." The point is that Texas is a big state.[308] That's one thing for which it is famous. How big is Texas? It is by far the largest state in the lower forty-eight, with a land area of 268,580 square miles. Of Texas' 254 counties, forty-two of them are larger than the state of Rhode Island. Brewster County, in the Big Bend country, is larger than the states of Delaware and Rhode Island combined. But those are just numbers. Maybe these numbers will be more understandable: the distance from Dalhart, at the north of the Texas Panhandle, to Brownsville, at the southern tip of Texas, is 763 miles as the crow flies. But if the crow has to drive, it is 864 miles, with a driving time of thirteen hours. Going east to west, from Texarkana to El Paso, it is 815 miles in driving distance, and it takes roughly twelve hours to make the trip. At the National Convention in Fort Worth in 1982, Roy Thomas drew a huge laugh when he commented to the delegation about the size of Texas, "The sun has riz and the sun has set, and here I is in Texas yet."

What does all this have to do with Free Will Baptists? Pastors normally list the size of the state as one of the reasons that the work in Texas hasn't done as well as in some other states. Churches are spread out, there isn't as much fellowship among the pastors, and the churches have less of a sense of belonging together. When I was a pastor in Wichita Falls I sometimes had to drive over two hundred miles to a quarterly meeting in my own district association. Isolation becomes a problem, a problem you may not understand unless you have pastored in San Angelo, Odessa, Amarillo, El Paso, or down in the Rio Grande Valley. If one pastors a church in South Texas, West Texas, or East Texas, it isn't easy to run off to Central Texas for a state men's retreat.

Being so far apart leads to losing the sense of belonging together with other churches. Churches develop a sense of being alone, independent. This is especially natural in Texas because that sense of independence already exists in the culture. That's because Texas was once a Republic, an independent, sovereign nation,[309] before it became one of the United States. Churches can feel they don't need other churches, or even the district and state associations. One of the things that more than fifty years of preaching taught me is that churches need each other, whether they realize it or not. Churches can more easily die without the love, support, help, and encouragement of other Free Will Baptist churches. In Texas, we have seen more than our share of churches die and their voices becoming silent.

Jealousy

This may sounds petty, but it is a fact that in some areas pastors were so jealous of each other that they refused to work together for the common good. This seems to especially have been a problem in Fort Worth. Over the years, beginning with the now extinct Central Brazos Association, and continuing with the West Fork District Association, and even the short-lived Fellowship Association, there have been a dozen or so churches and missions in Fort Worth and Tarrant County. Jack T. Bankhead, who grew up in Fort Worth and pastored there for decades,

---

[308] We Texans don't like to talk much about Alaska, though I spent the summer of 1963 there as a summer missionary, and loved it.
[309] Texas was a sovereign nation from March 2, 1836 to February 19, 1846. The men who served as President of the Republic of Texas were David Burnet, Sam Houston (twice), Mirabeau Lamar, and Anson Jones.

often spoke of the jealousies between the pastors in his younger years. There are various and sundry other reasons so many of the churches in Fort Worth died out, but jealousies between the pastors was one of them.

Differences

What I'm going to say now doesn't fit so much under the category of jealousies as much as it does *petty differences* and *petty behavior*. The Free Will Baptist denomination is a very diverse denomination, and that diversity certainly exists in Texas, as well. That is not a problem in most cases. One of the good things about Texas Free Will Baptists is that they allow you to be yourself, within certain boundaries. Everyone doesn't have to be the same, as if they were all cut out by the same cookie cutter. There isn't as much peer pressure, as there is in some states, to conform to the standards and preferences of certain, outspoken, sometimes self-appointed leaders. Everyone is, however, expected to be evangelical, Bible-believing, and generally hold to the doctrinal positions[310] stated in the *Free Will Baptist Treatise*. Theological liberalism just isn't accepted, nor should it be. There are, however, many differences among us. Worship styles differ. Music styles differ, some clinging to the Stamps-Baxter type music, some prefer the style of hymns in the Free Will Baptist hymnbook *Rejoice*, while others prefer a more contemporary music, and still others try to blend two or more types of music. That's not bad and it is left up to the individual churches. Pastors even dress differently. Some pastors preach with their shirttails untucked, and no tie, or even in a T-shirt, while others insist strongly that a pastor "should dress like a preacher," i.e., with suit and tie. All of this is a matter of taste and preference since the Bible does not specify what it means to "dress like a preacher." Dress doesn't seem to have been a big issue in Texas. But some personal differences have been. Whether we like to admit it or not there have been some pastors in Texas who were extremists, in my lowly opinion. Let me illustrate. Back in the early 1980's the Christian Education Board of the Texas State Association of Free Will Baptists sponsored a Men's and Women's Retreat at the Lazy Hills Guest Ranch near Ingram, Texas, a retreat which turned out to be outstanding and memorable. Prior to the retreat one pastor called me and asked if we had a dress code for those attending. Specifically, he wanted to know if the women were required to wear dresses instead of slacks, and if mixed bathing (he meant mixed swimming) was forbidden in the ranch's Olympic sized swimming pool. He was told that there was no dress code, and that there was no rule about mixed swimming, and that the reason was that those attending the retreat, for the most part, were pastors and their wives, deacons and their wives, along with other active participants in the work in the state. Those attending were the spiritual leaders in our state and we weren't going to impose a dress code upon them. As a result, the pastor who called, and all those he could influence, did not attend the retreat. This story is just to illustrate that there has, at times, been an element of people who refused to work with the Free Will Baptist group as a whole over issues not covered in the Bible. Most of the associations have been affected by this attitude of "unless you do it my way I'm not going to have anything to do with you" at one time or another. This has contributed to the overall weakening of the work in Texas.

---

[310] Some Free Will Baptists believe that humility is the only thing taught by feet washing, while others believe it teaches two things: humble service and the need for regular cleansing from sin's defilements. Free Will Baptists differ openly on the meaning of the atonement; some believe the penal satisfaction view, some hold to the ransom view, i.e., that the ransom price for our salvation was paid to the devil, while others hold to the governmental view.

Part-Time Ministry

The Report on the State of the Ministry adopted by the 1837 General Conference of Free Will Baptists contains the following position and encouragement toward a full-time ministry:

> (9.) That we recommend that our ministers decline political offices, and that so far as their circumstances will permit, they be encouraged to abandon worldly callings that they may give themselves more fully to their work, remembering the words of the apostle, "no man that warreth entangleth himself with the affairs of this life."[311]

By "worldly callings" they, of course, meant secular jobs and secular careers. The denomination continued over the years to adopt a similar position, namely that Free Will Baptist ministers should be full-time, not having to support themselves by secular jobs. This is seen in the 1865 General Conference:

> 5. That it diminishes the influence of pastors, to engage in secular pursuits; and that, to save them from the necessity of so doing, the churches should give them a sufficient support, paying the same fully, punctually, and cheerfully.[312]

The subject of part-time ministry is vitally connected to the subject of ministerial salaries. Each one causes or contributes to the other, but we will discuss them separately. The point addressed here could possibly hurt some people's feelings, but that is certainly not intended. The intent is simply to get at the reasons why the Free Will Baptist work in Texas has not lived up to its potential, why is has not flourished, and why it is in decline overall. Simply stated, Free Will Baptists nationally, including Free Will Baptists in Texas, have been way too accepting of the part-time minister, the part-time pastor, what we tend to call "tent-maker pastors." Of the ten churches currently in the West Fork District Association, the association in which I pastored for twenty-eight years, seven of them have bi-vocational pastors. Three of them have full-time pastors. Except for the pastors who are retired, the pastors of the part-time churches have to work at a secular job to support themselves and their families. It is true that some of them, maybe all of them, would have full-time pastors if they could afford to pay them a full-time salary. I acknowledge that. I appreciate that. However, many of these churches operated as part-time churches when they could have been full-time, have always been part-time, and they expect to continue to be part-time. They have, for the most part, always accepted the idea that a part-time pastor was fully acceptable, that a part-time pastor was fully scriptural. It isn't.

There isn't time and space here, and it is not the purpose of this book, to give a theology of pastoral ministry. However, it might be helpful to give a very brief overview of what the Bible teaches about supporting the ministry. I plan to go into this in great detail in a future book, much of which is already written. Briefly stated, here is what the Bible teaches about those who are involved in the ministry:

---

[311] *Minutes of the General Conference of the Freewill Baptist Connection* (Freewill Baptist Printing Establishment, Dover, New Hampshire, 1859, reprinted by Holleman and Yandell, 1966) pages 142-143.
[312] *Minutes of General Conference of the Freewill Baptist Connection, Volume 2*, Compiled by Rev. I. D. Stewart, D. D., F. B. Printing Establishment, Boston, Massachusetts, 1887) page 143.

- The mysterious priest Melchizedek was given a tenth of the spoils by Abraham, as if giving priest's tithes was the normal thing, Genesis 14:18-20. This was hundreds of years before the Mosaic Law was given.
- God specifically set aside the tribe of Levi to serve at the tabernacle/temple. They were to be supported by the tithes of the other tribes (Numbers 18:21-24; 1 Corinthians 9:13). The priests, later divided into divisions by King David, were supported full-time so they could give themselves fully to their priestly ministry. There were no part-time priests except during times of spiritual declension when the Israelites did not support them. This lack of financial support was, in God's sight, unacceptable. King Hezekiah took action during just such a time: *"He ordered the people living in Jerusalem to give the portion due the priests and Levites so they could devote themselves to the Law of the LORD"* (2 Chronicles 31:4).
- The Old Testament prophets, some of whom were also priests, were full-time for the most part. Daniel held high office in the government of Babylonia. Samuel and Ezekiel were priests, supported full-time. Isaiah, Jeremiah, Elijah, Elisha, and others were full-time prophets. Amos was a shepherd and gatherer of sycamore figs in Judah, but God called him to leave Judah and go to Israel to prophesy. His ministry there was probably short term.
- Jesus and the Twelve Apostles, who were the foundation of the Church, were full-time during the days of Jesus' ministry on earth. Jesus had been a carpenter growing up, and probably into his young adult years, but He did not work as a carpenter during the years of his earthly ministry. The Twelve, who had been fishermen, tax collectors, *etcetera*, left their jobs to follow Jesus and preach the gospel. They were supported by their followers, Luke 8:1-3.
- Jesus taught that those who preach the gospel should make their living from the gospel, Luke 10:7; 1 Corinthians 9:14.
- After the Church was formed, the apostles worked at their ministry of preaching the gospel full-time. They did not support themselves by being carpenters, fishermen, insurance salesmen, by working in the oilfield, or by farming and ranching. They were preachers; that's how they made their living, 1 Corinthians 9:3-6.
- The Apostle Paul taught that those who preached the gospel should be supported by those to whom they preached, 1 Corinthians 9:11-12; Galatians 6:6; 1 Timothy 5:17-18.
- Though Paul, out of temporary necessity, worked as a tent-maker to support himself and his team as the occasion demanded, he devoted himself full-time to the ministry when funds became available (Acts 18:5; Philippians 4:15-16). Accepting the lot of a part-time ministry as a permanent arrangement was not acceptable to the Apostle Paul. The "tent-maker" ministry was always viewed as temporary, less than ideal, not something to be continued indefinitely.
- Paul warned ministers against becoming entangled with the affairs of this life, 2 Timothy 2:4.
- The churches of the New Testament had full-time pastors, either from the very start, or as soon as they were strong enough to support a full-time ministry. Continuing indefinitely as a part-time church, with a part-time pastor, was not acceptable to them, and was not the biblical model.

- This biblical model was continued as the apostles and first century pastors died off. Those who succeeded them continued to be full-time. There were, of course, here and there, men who, as Paul had at times, ministered part-time on a temporary basis. This biblical model of a full-time ministry continues to be the norm in Christendom. To check out this point you will simply need to consult church history.

I have always loved Free Will Baptists. I still do. Long years of experience in the gospel ministry, and sixty years a careful student of the Bible, have made me see some things differently than I did as a youth and as a young adult. In my youth all of my pastors made their living by being farmers, coal miners, carpenters, or factory workers, *etcetera*. None of the ones I knew made their living by preaching the gospel. The very idea of paying the preacher more than a token offering was abhorrent. I attended a Free Will Baptist church from the time I was two or three weeks old. My father was a deacon in the Columbia Hill Free Will Baptist Church in Overton County, Tennessee. Yet I never heard the word tithe until I was about sixteen years old, and then I only heard it because my cousin, Betty Bilbrey, visited a church of a different denomination and happened to hear it there. She came to me the next day and said "Thurmon, do you believe in tying?" I didn't know what she was talking about, partly because she had heard the word incorrectly. She had never heard it either. No pastor of mine had ever mentioned it. All of my pastors up to the time Dr. Hobart Ashby became my pastor, were uneducated, untrained men who made their living by working at secular jobs and preaching on the side, even though they were good, devoted, godly men (and one woman). Sadly, they didn't know enough about the Bible to know what the biblical pattern was. I do not mean to speak ill of them. I loved them all. But that is the way Free Will Baptists were in my part of the country during the days of my youth. Many of them still are.

The fact that from the beginning most of our pastors in Texas were farmers, shop keepers, ranchers, carpenters, school teachers, salesmen, or oil field workers, is one of the main reasons the work did not flourish in the early years. The fact that more than half of the Free Will Baptist pastors in Texas currently make their living from secular jobs, leaving little time and energy for their ministry, is one of the major factors in the current state of affairs in Texas. To put it another way, when the majority of the Free Will Baptist pastors in Texas cannot devote themselves full-time to the ministry, the outcome is predictable, there isn't going to be much growth and there isn't going to be much of an impact on the state of Texas. The work will linger and flicker for a while, but the light will eventually go out, unless some things are changed. We have to get over the "tent-maker" mentality as being an acceptable standard.

Perhaps we need to be reminded of our history, how the denomination stood many years ago. No, I mean well before grandpa's time. It was the practice of the General Conference of Freewill Baptists in the early years to ask questions on denominational polity at the General Conference. At the 1844 General Conference the following question was asked: "Is it thought expedient by this Conference for ministers to indulge the penuriousness of their hearers, by attempting to support themselves by manual labor?" The official answer given and recorded in the minutes was: "We think it is the duty of churches, so far as they have the means, to give a competent support to their ministers who faithfully labor in the gospel among them."[313]

There were too many men who carried the label of minister, preacher, or Reverend who did little in the ministry. The following is a quarterly report of one of the ministers in the West

---

[313] *Minutes of the General Conference of the Freewill Baptist Connection* (Published by order of the General Conference, Dover, New Hampshire, 1859) page 237.

Fork District Association in 1899: "Brethren, I have just preached one sermon to my home church; otherwise have done nothing."[314]

Insufficient Ministerial Salaries

The Report on the Condition of the Ministry which was adopted at the 1837 General Conference of Free Will Baptists contained sixteen position statements and resolutions relating to the ministry. The report was the work of Martin Cheney, one of the pillars of the early Free Will Baptist movement. Three of the position statements are reproduced here, the ones which relate to the compensation of preachers. They are:

> (6.) That it is the duty of every church that engages the services of a preacher, to give him a reasonable and suitable compensation for his labors.
>
> (7.) That we highly approve and earnestly recommend the principle of *Bible equality*; that is, for every member to pay his proportional part, according to his property and circumstances, in supporting the minister, and in all the necessary expenses of the church.
>
> (8.) That it is the duty of every minister of the gospel to faithfully declare, on all suitable occasions, public and private, that part of God's counsel which plainly teaches that it is the duty of churches to support their ministers on the principle of Bible equality -- not as objects of charity, but as laborers who are worthy of "their hire."[315]

It isn't the purpose of this book to give a theology of ministerial salaries. Briefly stated, however, the Bible teaches that those in the ministry should be full-time in the ministry and should be paid a salary which enables them to maintain a normal life for themselves and their families. During the brief years of Jesus' ministry, he and the Twelve Apostles were, of course, full-time and were supported by those who were his followers. One indication of this is Luke 8:3, where some women of means are mentioned. Luke tells us, "These women were helping to support them out of their own means." When Jesus sent out the seventy-two on a preaching mission he told them, "the worker deserves his wages" (Luke 10:7). That the worker deserves his wages would be true of anyone working at a secular job, but the focus of the statement in Luke is on those who go out on a spiritual mission preaching the gospel. The Apostle Paul later quoted Jesus as saying, "In the same way, the Lord has commanded that those who preach the gospel should receive their living from the gospel" (1 Corinthians 9:14). A man who makes his living by being a carpenter (or plumber, or vacuum cleaner salesman, or insurance salesman), and preaches and pastors as time and energy permit, isn't making his living from the gospel, he is making his living from carpentry (or plumbing, selling vacuum cleaners, or selling insurance). This is in violation of what Jesus modeled and taught. A temporary departure from this model is necessary sometimes, as in the occasional case of Paul, but the norm, the standard, the biblical model is that the minister should be paid a full-time salary.

What Jesus modeled and taught is the same as what Paul modeled and taught, except that Paul, being a foreign missionary not being supported by a monthly check from a mission board, had to work as a tent-maker now and then to support himself and his missionary team. In 1

---

[314] Minutes of the Eighth Annual Session of the West Fork Association, 1899, page 6.
[315] *Minutes of the General Conference of the Freewill Baptist Connection,* Volume I, page 142.

Corinthians 9:4-14 Paul argued that he had a right to be fully supported, just as did the other apostles. He used logic and Scripture to state his case. He referred specifically to what Jesus had taught, namely that those who preach the gospel should make their living from the gospel. It should be noted that when funding was provided Paul devoted himself full-time to the ministry. This we see in Acts 18:5: "When Silas and Timothy came from Macedonia,[316] *Paul devoted himself exclusively to preaching*, testifying to the Jews that Jesus was the Christ." An entire chapter, or book, could be devoted to a further explanation of this subject, but we'll have to do that at another place and time.

In writing an evaluation of the Free Will Baptist work in Texas, it is painfully obvious that one of the reasons Free Will Baptists in Texas haven't prospered is that they have not, as a whole, supported their ministers according to the biblical model. A few churches have done well with this, but they are the exception rather than the rule. Even many full-time pastors are insufficiently paid. This is not just a Texas problem, it is a denominational problem. And even more, it is largely an American problem. This mindset of a part-time, low pay ministry developed in this country in colonial days and spread west into the frontier areas as pioneer preachers pushed into new areas to preach the gospel and establish churches. They were largely on their own, depending on God to supply their needs, doing anything they were capable of doing to make a living. This developed a culture, a tradition, which took root and laid the foundation for what we have now, many denominations which accept a part-time ministry where the pastors have to support themselves. Many of these pastors are paid only a token salary by the churches they pastor.

In the minutes of the 1899 annual session of the West Fork District Association, a resolution was passed which made the observation that the Free Will Baptist movement was "retrograding in this country." The suggested answer to the problem: "Deep earnestness and better support of the ministry."[317]

We can easily look back and see how preachers were paid in Texas in earlier days. For example, the 1910 minutes of the West Texas Association report the following amounts paid to the pastors for their years work in the ministry: Salt Springs, $111.16; Liberty Hill, $5.50, and Easley's Chapel, $28.45. We might laugh and chuckle at those figures, but that wouldn't be fair. That was well over a hundred years ago and the economy was completely different then. But, still, those preachers were making their living by doing something other than the ministry and the pattern was being set for the future of Texas Free Will Baptists. A mindset was being developed, not only in the pastors, but in the churches as well.

Is there a solution? Is it too late to change that? It is too late for some churches and they are going to die off, just as hundreds of other churches have died off. One of the things that should be done is that a qualified person author a comprehensive theology of ministerial support specifically for Free Will Baptists, perhaps just for Texas Free Will Baptists. If other states could learn from it that would be well and good, but here we are concerned with Texas. What the Bible teaches about paying the preacher should be taught in every church in the state. This could be done by making the book available for reading and study to all of the adult members of the churches. Additionally, the subject could be written into a thirteen week curriculum which could be taught in Sunday school to young adults on up for one quarter. Using a competent teacher the material could be professionally filmed and made available to each church in a DVD format, or it could be developed into sermon outlines the pastor could use as an entire sermon series on the

---

[316] When Silas and Timothy arrived from Macedonia they brought with them financial support from the church in Philippi, and did so again when Paul was in his first imprisonment in Rome (Philippians 4:10-19).

[317] *Minutes of the Eighth Annual Session of the West Fork Association of Freewill Baptists*, page 2.

subject. The material would need to be promoted by both the district and state associations. This is not impossible and could be done by Texas Free Will Baptists, as weak as we are.

One solution, which would be virtually impossible to pull off, would be for two, three, or more small churches located in geographical proximity to merge together into one church which would then be able to hire a well-qualified pastor, and pay him a sufficient salary. This would provide many benefits to the one congregation, both financially and spiritually. One of the things that make this almost impossible, though, is the fact that two or three Free Will Baptist churches, even though they are located near each other, are likely to be like two or three different denominations. They might not only be different in their worship styles, but in their doctrines and practices. I once mentioned this possibility to one of the pastors of the Faith Free Will Baptist Church in Wichita Falls when I was pastoring the First Free Will Baptist Church, only two miles apart. I soon learned that the two churches were, indeed, like two separate denominations.

Another partial solution would be that when we plant new churches, we should do so with the fully stated intent that they become self-supporting, full-time churches, and that they will pay their pastors a livable salary. Thankfully, this is being done in most of the new churches being established in Texas, if not all of them.

Unqualified Pastors

Let me say again that it is not my intention to hurt anyone's feelings. My intention is to tell the truth, as I see it. The problem of unqualified pastors is, in my opinion, the heart of the problem. It is the major cause of our lack of leadership. It is the main reason the work in Texas has not flourished and lived up to its potential. It is the chief reason so many churches have closed. It is the primary reason the work statewide is in decline, even though a few churches continue to be planted here and there.

What do I mean by unqualified pastors? I'm not talking about those who are not morally qualified, or those who have been thus disqualified. Though that has occasionally been a problem, it certainly isn't unique to Texas, and it is not the main problem. The main problem, as I see it, is this: too many Texas pastors, and this is true nationally, are not intellectually and academically qualified to stand in the pulpit and preach the Bible. I'm not questioning their devotion and commitment to Christ, whether they spend much time in prayer, or if they are good, godly men. I'm simply questioning what they say in the pulpit and in the classroom. In church after church people sit and listen to men preach, men who don't know what they are talking about. The church members themselves, being unfamiliar with the Bible, don't realize they are listening to inept, incompetent preachers proclaiming inaccuracy after inaccuracy. Let me hasten to say that there are some really good preachers in Texas, men who have devoted their lives to a study of the Word and who stand and preach it faithfully and accurately in the power of the Holy Spirit. But they seem to be the exception, not the rule. It is painfully obvious that there are far too many pastors who have little or no training for the ministry, who do not have a working knowledge of the Bible, are basically unfamiliar with theology, and cannot give a clear statement about what the gospel is. In listening to sermons here and there one has to deflect statement after statement in sermons, saying to oneself: "That isn't true," "The Bible doesn't teach that," or "That statement is wrong." These deflections aren't being done by people who are by disposition critical of others. This poor preaching is true of some preachers more than others, of course. However, if one of these pastors exists in our ranks, that is one too many. The fact is, though, there are quite a few of them, there have always been too many of them, and that's a major reason the denomination hasn't grown any more than it has in Texas.

The use of the word "incompetent" in describing some preachers may seem excessive, an overstatement of the case, even arrogant, and egotistical. Maybe. Maybe not. As far back as the 1837 General Conference of Free Will Baptists, this incompetency was admittedly in the ranks of the denomination. The long and excellent Report on the State of the Ministry includes the following recognition and resolution:

> (3.) Whereas, individuals who have gone out into the gospel field with commendations from churches to improve their gifts, have been unqualified and incompetent for this work, and thereby have brought a reproach upon the ministerial office and the cause of God -- therefore,
> *Resolved*, That no brother having a license from a church only, be recognized as a minister in good standing out of the limits of said church, and that to be recognized as such, he must be licensed by a Q. M. Conference.[318]

What is the reason for this inept, inaccurate, incompetent, shallow, superficial preaching? There are a number of reasons. One of them is that, even with our colleges and the presence of a rising number of young Bible scholars and godly, Bible believing intellectuals, there exists an anti-intellectual mindset in our denomination, including in Texas. Some, many in fact, are opposed to education for the ministry. They see no need for it. They see it as the source of problems, particularly in that it tends to lead young ministers away from beliefs and practices long held dear by these uneducated, anti-education preachers. Some even say that education is of the devil, including education received at a Bible college, Christian liberal arts college, or seminary. I was raised in this environment in Overton County, Tennessee, where I was born, and in Dayton, Ohio, where I lived as a teenager. This didn't change for me until Dr. Hobart Ashby became my pastor. It seems to me that the anti-education, anti-intellectual mind set is still very prevalent in those areas. It exists too strongly here in Texas. This anti-education, anti-intellectual mindset is unscriptural and impractical.

A second reason for the incompetent preaching that we often hear is that many preachers mistakenly think that there is no real need to study and be scholarly, believing that God directly gives them the sermons they preach. Does this sound familiar? Of course it does. You've possibly heard it all your life if you were raised in a Free Will Baptist church. I heard it as a boy. I heard it during my teenage years. I've heard it all around the country and I've heard it in Texas. I heard it repeatedly in the last church I attended after I retired from the pastorate. Why is this such a common belief among us? It is based on three things at least. *One* is that the Old Testament prophets received their prophetic messages directly from the Lord. The idea is that, since God doesn't change, he still gives his messengers their messages the same way. There is a certain logic to this kind of thinking, but it ignores the fact that, though God himself does not change, the way he relates to us, and what he requires of us, do change.[319] You can usually tell by listening to the

---

[318] *Minutes of the General Conference of the Freewill Baptist Connection,* page 142.
[319] For instance, (a) at first there was no Mosaic Law, then God established the Mosaic Law at Mt. Sinai, and then he ended the law when Jesus died on the cross (Colossians 2:14; Hebrews 7:18). (b) Before Sinai the heads of families served in a priestly role, then God established the Aaronic Priesthood, but now we no longer approach God through priests because all believers are priests (1 Peter 2:5, 9; Revelation 5:10). (c) In the Old Testament animal sacrifices were required of those who believed in and worshiped God, but now we no longer offer such sacrifices. (d) Changes in the requirement of circumcision illustrate this point. (e) God established what we now call the Old Covenant with

sermons of these men that their messages did not come from God. Two revealing clues that a preacher's message did not come directly from God are: (1) the sermon contains obvious factual errors and (2) the sermon contains doctrinal errors. The *second* reason many believe God gives them their sermons directly, without them having to study hard to prepare a sermon, is a complete misunderstanding of Matthew 10:19-20: *"...do not worry about what to say or how to say it. At that time you will be given what to say, for it will not be you speaking, but the Spirit of your Father speaking through you."* Though these words were said to the Twelve Apostles as Jesus sent them out on a training mission, he was not talking about preaching. He was talking about when they were arrested and taken to local courts conducted by the synagogues. This is indicated by the context: *"But when they arrest you..."* (v. 19). You do not find Paul or any of the other apostles teaching, or practicing, that preachers did not need to study, that God gave them their sermons directly. A *third* reason many believe they do not need to study and prepare sermons, that God gives them their sermons directly, is a misunderstanding of John 14:25-26: *"All this I have spoken while still with you. But the Counselor, the Holy Spirit, whom the Father will send in my name, will teach you all things and will remind you of everything I have said to you."* These words were spoken to the apostles and do not apply directly to you and me.[320] Jesus had taught the apostles many things. They, along with him, would be the foundation of the Church.[321] It was highly likely that in years to come, unaided, they would not remember everything he had taught them. In addition, Jesus had not taught them everything they needed to know because they just weren't up to it yet.[322] The apostles were a unique set of men, in a position no one else would ever hold, and with the responsibility of going out into the world to proclaim the gospel of the kingdom accurately, completely, and authoratatively. Some of them had the additional responsibility of writing books of the Bible and Jesus promised them special help in remembering, understanding, and further learning about what they had been taught by him.

---

his people at Mt. Sinai, but through Christ he established the New Covenant under which we currently live (Jeremiah 31:31-32; Hebrews 8:6-13). This is why there is an Old Testament and a New Testament. (f) In the early chapters of Genesis, God's focus and relationship was with all who believed in him regardless of race or nationality. Beginning with chapter twelve and continuing through the rest of the Old Testament God's focus was almost exclusively on the Jews. Then, beginning in the Early Church his focus was primarily on the Gentiles, where it continues to be today. (g) God used to give new revelations to his people, but when the Bible became complete, he ceased giving them. The written revelation of the Bible is the revelation by which we are to live. (h) During the Old Testament period God did not live in the flesh among his people, though he did occasionally make an appearance, which we call a theophany. Then, Jesus became God in the flesh and lived for a time on earth, after which he returned to heaven and no longer lives among us in the flesh (Philippians 2:6-11).

[320] It is important to discover that not every promise made in the Bible is a promise to you, though you may have been told that they are. Those promises are a benefit to you, though, because by knowing that God made promises to individuals and groups of people, and kept those promises, encourages and strengthens your faith. A couple of promises which God made and kept should suffice to illustrate what I mean. God promised Abraham that He, God, would return in a year and by then Sarah, Abraham's wife, would have given birth to a son (Genesis 18:10). That promise does not apply to me and my wife, though it encourages and strengthens our faith. If you are a middle aged married man you are probably hoping that that particular promise does not apply to you, either, and your wife may certainly be hoping that it doesn't apply to her. Another promise which does not apply to you or me is the promise God made to David that a future son of his, i.e. a descendant, would sit on the throne of Israel and rule over an eternal kingdom (2 Samuel 7:2-13). God has not promised me that one of my future descendants will do anything of the sort. The promise does relate to me in that the descendant of David, future to him, Jesus, is my Savior and Lord.

[321] *"Consequently, you are no longer foreigners and aliens, but fellow citizens with God's people and members of God's household, built on the foundation of the apostles and prophets, with Christ Jesus himself as the chief cornerstone"* (Ephesians 2:19-20).

[322] *"I have much more to say to you, more than you can now bear"* (John 16:12).

We have above referred to the Report on the State of the Ministry adopted at the 1837 General Conference of Free Will Baptists. The report also contained the following two items on an intelligent and studious ministry, which we would do well to note:

> (12.) That the present state of our denomination loudly calls for the labors of an *intelligent, holy, humble, and devoted ministry.*
> (13.) That to *instruct*, or *teach*, as the Bible expresses it, is an essential part of the Christian ministry; and that to do this effectively, it is important that our ministry be *studious*.[323]

After over fifty years of preaching the gospel as a Free Will Baptist preacher, I would give aspiring young preachers the following advice. Don't even think about entering the ministry unless you are also planning on getting a college degree from a good, reliable Bible college or Christian liberal arts college. I would further add, and this comes from experience, or perhaps a lack of it, you should get at least a Master's Degree from a good graduate school or seminary. If I had to do it over again, I would shoot for a doctor's degree. I am not advocating that the denomination set a requirement that young men get a certain level of degree before they can be ordained. However, I do recommend that every young person considering the ministry should voluntarily make definite plans to attain as much education as possible. They're going to need it.

This would be a good time to again remind us of our heritage, our history. From early days Free Will Baptists established colleges and seminaries for the purpose of educating and training those entering the ministry, or those already in it, as well as the lay people. The names of the schools were many and well known by all Free Will Baptist history buffs. The Twenty-first General Conference of Free Will Baptists, 1871, lists the following Free Will Baptist schools:[324] Bates College, Maine Central Institute, Parsonsfield Seminary, New Hampton Institution, Austin Academy, Lyndon Institute, Green Mountain Seminary, Lapham Institute, Whitestown Seminary, Pike College, Hillsdale College, Ridgeville College, West Virginia College, Storer Normal School, Atwood Institute, Randall Academy, Rochester Institute, Evansville Seminary, Wilton Institute, and Prairie City Academy.[325] Rio Grande College, was established later. Early Free Will Baptists believed in an educated ministry. I'm going to reproduce here a resolution on the ministry adopted by the 1850 General Conference of Free Will Baptists. It states:

> 1. *Resolved*, That the Christian ministry was instituted and ordained by God, as a powerful instrumentality in spreading the gospel throughout the world, and that no man should take upon himself the solemn responsibilities of that holy office, unless he is especially called of God.
> 2. *Resolved*, **That it is the duty of every man who is thus called of God, to seek the best education in his power to enable him to preach Christ successfully, and to meet the various and just demands of the age in which he lives.**
> 3. *Resolved*, That every Christian minister, by a holy life and godly conversation [conduct, manner of life], should be an example to the church and the world; and that he should devote himself to the appropriate work of a minister so long as he

---

[323] *Minutes of the General Conference of Free Will Baptists,* page 143, emphasis theirs.
[324] It should be noted that the word seminary was used differently back in the day and was not necessarily a graduate school of theology for the training of ministers.
[325] *Minutes of the General Conference of Free Will Baptists,* Pages 264, 265.

holds his credentials as such.[326]

Three years later, at the next General Conference, 1853, the report from the Maine Western Yearly Meeting, contained these two lines: "Our condition, in many respects, has improved in the last triad of years. The prejudice which has existed against ministerial education is rapidly disappearing."[327]

In 1874, just two years before the first white Free Will Baptist church was established in Texas, the Twenty-second General Conference, after noting that Hillsdale College in Michigan had suffered the loss of three-fourths of its buildings due to a fire, included this item in their Report on Education:

> 10. This Conference, while having no sympathy with the idea that a regular and full course of study in college and theological seminary is the essential or the chief thing as a qualification for the ministry, yet it earnestly desires to impress young men looking forward to that sphere of work with the great importance of using the time and effort requisite to obtain the broadest and most thorough mental culture, before entering formally upon their great and responsible life-work.[328]

The 1928 Texas State Association received the following Report of the Committee on Education:

> We, your Committee on Education beg leave to submit the following report: Realizing the importance of an educated ministry, we recommend and insist that our young people preparing for the great calling of preaching the gospel shall earnestly and persistently endeavor to secure a liberal education whereby their efficiency and usefulness may be greatly increased. We further recommend that we as a denomination render assistance to worthy young people in their efforts to secure an adequate preparation for the work of the ministry.
>
> T. H. Newsom
> John Swanwick[329]

Since I am editorializing rather than just recording history at the moment, let me say this to those aspiring to the gospel ministry. What you will be doing as a preacher of the gospel is more important than what a doctor, lawyer, or president of the bank does. People expect their doctor to be fully competent, to be fully trained for his medical practice. They expect him to be an expert, to know exactly how to diagnose their case and prescribe the proper medication, treatment, and/or surgery. They expect him to be fully qualified when he sees his first patient rather than learning on the job as he goes. They know that if he makes a mistake in prescribing a common pill, or lets the scalpel slip, it could be fatal. Patients could die as a result. What the preacher does is more important than what a lawyer does. If a lawyer makes a mistake his clients could lose their case and all of their money, end up in prison, or even in the death chamber. If the

---

[326] *Minutes of the General Conference of Free Will Baptists*, page 331, emphasis added.
[327] *Minutes of the General Conference of the Freewill Baptist Connection*, page 356.
[328] *Minutes of General Conference of the Freewill Baptist Connection, Volume 2*, page 300.
[329] *Minutes of the Fourteenth Annual Session of the Texas Free Will Baptist State Convention*, 1928, page 8.

preacher makes a mistake, though, people could end up losing their soul, ending up in a fiery hell. It is imperative that the preacher knows his stuff that he be an expert at what he does.

Unsuitable Locations

No one could have reasonably expected Keith Woody to do as well as he did in planting the Lakehills Free Will Baptist Church in Cedar Park, an Austin suburb. It appears that he did an outstanding job in getting a congregation together, building a large, beautiful worship facility, and pastoring the church until his retirement. He wrote an article for *The Texas Challenge* in which the first three words were "Location, Location, Location." Writing on the fact that poor locations have doomed many of our churches, he said, "The location of our churches has contributed greatly to many of our failures."[330] The Cedar Park congregation, Pastor Keith and Neva Woody, State Moderator David and Kathleen Sutton, and the State Mission Board, chaired by Robert Posner, chose a highly visible location across the street from the Austin Community College, in a neighborhood surrounded by hundreds of acres of new homes in a city that was booming. Brother Woody rightfully attributed much of the success of the project to its superb location. Other churches in Texas have had good locations, such as the First Free Will Baptist Church in Duncanville, the First Free Will Baptist Church in Houston, and a few others. These churches are the exception to the rule, however. I have been to every part of the state where Free Will Baptist churches are or were located: from Pampa, high in the Texas Panhandle, to McAllen and Weslaco, near the south end of Texas; from Carthage in East Texas all the way to El Paso in far West Texas; and to just about every place in between. Characteristically Texas Free Will Baptist churches are in very poor locations, some of them in extremely poor locations. They are often found in run down neighborhoods, with low visibility. I recently drove by the former First Free Will Baptist Church of Vernon, Texas, to photograph it. It was located at the conjunction of two dirts streets, across the road from a pasture, at the very edge of town. Even with the use of a GPS the church was hard to find. This isn't meant as a criticism, just a statement of how things are, and one of the reasons Texas Free Will Baptists are the way they are. Good locations alone won't guarantee success, as I once discussed with the last pastor of the Westside Free Will Baptist Church in Midland. There are always other situations and conditions which cause a church to stagnate or die. Location, however, remains a key to church growth.

If one traces the missionary journeys of the Apostle Paul he will discover that it was Paul's *modus operandi* to establish churches in key metropolitan centers. From those strategic locations the gospel would spread to neighboring towns and communities, where churches would also be established. When Free Will Baptists first came to Texas they established churches in rural communities, small towns, and occasionally in mid-sized cities. We were late getting into the large metropolitan cities such as Fort Worth, Dallas, Houston, Austin, and San Antonio. Most of our churches were located in such places as Arp, Alto, Bonami, Bradley, Cego, Chalk Hill, Cedar Grove, Clayton, Darco, Dirgin, Dott, Edge, Elijah, Falba, Keith, Kurtin, Lone Star, Long Branch, Long Prairie, Memphis, Tatum, Pleasant Valley, Vandyke, Wellborn, and the list goes on. Many of those communities no longer exist, and the churches are gone with them.

The Report of the Committee on Church Location at the 1928 state convention contained the following recommendation:

---

[330] *The Texas Challenge*, October-December 1997 issue, page 2.

We further call attention to three points in the west where in our judgment, churches could and should be established, which we believe would soon be of great worth to our denomination and accomplish much for the glory of God. At Lubbock, Texas, Vernon, Texas, and Rotan, Texas, and also in Killeen, Texas. Should these points be developed it would develop many rural churches about each, giving a line of our work through this section adding much strength and rendering great service establishing our work in a most remarkable way in this rapidly developing country.

J. J. Tatum, Chairman

It can now honestly be said that the State Missions Board is making a concerted effort to plant new churches in larger towns and big cities, and in good locations within those cities. If this effort continues, and is successful, it bodes well for the future of Free Will Baptists in Texas.

A Low Self-Image

Back in the mid 1970's I was pastor of the First Free Will Baptist Church in Odessa. The local CBS affiliate television station there offered our church, along with other Odessa churches, the opportunity to participate on a rotating basis in having a free television program to be broadcast all over the Permian Basin. There was a potential viewing audience of many hundreds of thousands. We were told we could do whatever we wished during our half-hour program. I talked to one of our church musicians and a member of the church's quartet, about whether or not we should accept the offer. She was an outstanding Christian lady, and very talented. I was thinking of having the quartet sing and then me preach for our initial program. She said, "No, I don't think we should do a television program, Free Will Baptists don't do those kind of things."[331] It struck me then that her statement reflected a very typical Free Will Baptist self-image, an image which was a low opinion of our denomination. It was reminiscent of when Pastor Owen Barger, founder of the Rock of Ages Free Will Baptist Church in Fort Worth, told his congregation that they were going to build a brick church building. One of his members said to him, "Free Will Baptists don't build brick churches." He said, "They do now." Thankfully, Free Will Baptists have shed much of that poor self-image and have constructed large, beautiful church buildings in some very nice places. There is, however, a hangover of that image, an image that Free Will Baptists don't do and can't do certain things that Free Will Baptists don't and can't do certain things well. That is one of the reasons for the poor quality of workmanship displayed in the printed matter of many of our churches, districts and, formerly, in our state association.

An Outlook for the Future

Predicting the future is a very risky business, unless one has a direct revelation from God as the prophets did. Today none of us have that and about the best we can do is make educated guesses, based on the past and what we currently see trending. Even then our predictions for the

---

[331] We did have several television programs and indeed the quartet sang on it. On one of the programs I chose to have a talk show format and invited Pastor Dennis Haygood, from Midland, Pastor George Hyatt from Kermit, and Allen Moore, our State Executive Secretary, who was also at the time a member of the Free Will Baptist Foreign Missions Board, to appear on the program. I interviewed them and we talked about our churches, the Free Will Baptist denomination, and our world-wide missions program. This provided exposure for our area churches and for our denomination. I still have a recording of the program because it was historically significant for reasons not stated here.

future can be affected by our attitudes and dispositions, which will determine whether our outlooks will be positive or negative. At this point things could go one of several different ways for Free Will Baptists in Texas. It could easily be said that the Free Will Baptist denomination will not exist in Texas a hundred years from now, or that, if it does exist, it will only be a handful of scattered churches. It is entirely possible that the work a hundred years from now will be pretty much as it is today, with many of the churches being closed and about an equal number of new ones having been planted. Some see the future for Free Will Baptists in Texas as being bright and full of promise. That could very well be how things turn out over the next seventy-five to a hundred years. The reasons for this optimism are numerous. One is that there has been an influx of young, bright, very dedicated, godly, young men who are fairly well trained in the ministry. If they will stay with us, assume the roles of leadership available to them on district and state levels, and build strong local churches equipped to minister to people in the twenty-first century, they could be a good, positive influence on the outcome of the work overall. Every pastor should be continually improving himself both intellectually and spiritually. How these young men affect the overall work in Texas cannot be evaluated, though, for about seventy-five to a hundred more years.

Another positive factor could be that the part-time pastor mindset and philosophy will die out as the part-time churches and part-time pastors die off. If this results in the remaining pastors in Texas being fully committed to the ministry, then this could be a very positive factor in the growth and the renewed growth of the work in the state. The great Episcopalian bishop Phillips Brooks once said, "If God has called you to preach, don't stoop to being a king." If our pastors, who feel that God has called them to preach, will devote themselves exclusively to preaching the gospel, rather than, say, selling insurance and padding their own retirement nest egg,[332] this will have a very positive impact on the future of the Free Will Baptist work in Texas. In 1856, at the sixteenth General Conference of Free Will Baptists, held in Mainesville, Ohio, the following resolution was passed: *Resolved*, That this conference recommend that our feeble churches unite, as far as practicable, by organization or otherwise, in securing pastors who shall devote their entire time to the ministry."[333] Perhaps it is time to make that recommendation again.

A third factor that would change the future outlook for Texas Free Will Baptists is that if they, the churches and pastors, would realize that they need each other and begin to make a concerted effort to meet together quarterly for fellowship, to pool their resources, and work together for the common good of all. One of the reasons we have quarterly meetings and state meetings is so that we can do together what we cannot do alone. It is this working together and pooling our resources which enables us to have youth camps, colleges, state offices, an aggressive state missions program, and a world-wide foreign missions ministry. None of us can do any of these alone. We need each other to strengthen and encourage each other and to participate effectively in the great commission.

A fourth factor is to do all we can to improve our self-image, that is, how we view ourselves as Free Will Baptists. There are a number of ways to do this. One is to build more beautiful churches and/or make the churches we have more aesthetically attractive. Thankfully, we have some very beautiful churches now, at least a half dozen of them in Texas. If you need a biblical theology on the beauty of God's house you need to look no further than the tabernacle and temple in the Old Testament. They were aesthetically stunning. When an unknown Levite said, "How

---

[332] Lest you misunderstand, every pastor, no matter how young, needs to be planning for his retirement by investing financially in a definite plan on a monthly basis. If he doesn't, there'll be the devil to pay.
[333] *Minutes of the General Conference of the Freewill Baptist Connection* (Published by order of the General Conference, Dover, New Hampshire, 1859), page 419.

lovely is your dwelling place, O LORD Almighty" (Psalm 84:1) he was talking about the temple in Jerusalem. Our church buildings make a statement, not only about our God, but about ourselves. As suggested earlier, we can improve our self-image by making it a point to produce high quality paperwork, in content, in design, and in printing.

A fifth factor that could be important for the future of Texas Free Will Baptists is this, and it may sound radical to some: allow women to have the same roles of leadership and prominence in our work they used to have, to resume the heritage of Free Will Baptists from generations ago. We recognize the importance of women now to an extent. We see how well the women work in Texas Women Active For Christ (TWAC) and on the Christian Education Board. We can easily see where our churches would be in trouble without the involvement of our women. But we only give lip service to acknowledging the importance of their work. A quick reading of the older minutes of our district associations and our state association reveals that women formerly had much larger roles in the work than presently. They served on more boards and committees. It was perfectly normal for them to bring devotions at district and state meetings. For instance, at the 1940 state meeting, held at Clayton, Texas, the following women brought devotions in the general sessions: Mrs. Leroy Conaway, Mrs. Jessie Ferguson (a preacher), Mrs. Charles H. Moehlman, Miss Tommie Smith (a preacher), Mrs. Clara Sutton, and Miss Eula Mae Martin. Miss Lucille Gardner was clerk and she also addressed the session conducted by the young people on the subject: "The Family Altar a Help to Sunday Schools and Leagues." A number of women served on committees[334]: Mrs. C. H. Moehlman and Mrs. Jessie Ferguson served on the Committee on Committees, along with E. S. Jameson. Mrs. Maude Wheeler was a member of the Credentials Committee, Bernice Jones and Lucille Gardner served on the Committee on Young People's Work, and Mrs. C. H. Moehlman was a member of the Foreign Missions Committee. They weren't relegated just to the Young People's Society and the Woman's Missionary Society. They sometimes preached at district and state meetings, pastored some of our churches, and served as evangelists, and sometimes as field workers, what we might now call promotional men. As stated elsewhere, it is not my purpose here to debate or promote the idea of women preachers; I'm just reporting our history. All Free Will Baptists need to be aware of the heritage Free Will Baptists have in allowing women to participate in the work, whether we agree with it or not. It is part of our history. Aside from preaching, however, women have a lot to offer in terms of leadership and participation in our work. They are highly intelligent, usually well educated, on the average are more skilled than men in some aspects of the work, are good speakers when given the chance to develop that skill, have passion for the work, have leadership abilities, and bring a much needed perspective or point of view to the work that men simply don't have. With a growing vacuum of leadership, we may be forced to turn to women to step up and take more leadership roles in the district and state associations.

Perhaps the most significant presentation at the 2009 state meeting was Keith Woody's moderator's message. Learning from the past and looking to the future he listed ten things Texas Free Will Baptist must do to survive:

1. We must build new churches.
2. We cannot live in the past.
3. We must have revival in our existing churches.
4. We must have a loyalty to, and a burden for, Texas Free Will Baptists.
5. We must start taking an interest in what everyone else is doing in our state.

---

[334] In 1940 there weren't any boards, just committees.

6. We must find the money for starting new works in the state of Texas, and we must put financial support for new churches in our church budgets.
7. We must find a way to embrace new methods without losing our Free Will Baptist distinctives.
8. We must recruit quality workers to come to Texas to plant new churches and work in our ministries.
9. We must seek God's direction on our future efforts.
10. We must organize our work for the Lord.[335]

Denominational Distinctives

One of the things which contributed to the rapid growth of the Free Will Baptist denomination back in the late 1700s and early 1800s was our denominational distinctives. Dictionary.com[336] defines the word *distinctive* as meaning: 1. serving to distinguish, 2. having a special quality, style, attractiveness, etc.; notable. In the church world in North America at the time there were several beliefs and practices of Free Will Baptists which made them especially attractive, resulting in large numbers of people coming to the fledgling denomination's churches. The two primary distinctives were open communion and general atonement. Open communion was such a big issue that Free Will Baptists were referred to as, and often referred to themselves as, Free Communion Baptists. Why was this such a big issue? It was because most of the established denominations in North America practiced close communion, that is, one had to be a member of the church observing communion to observe it with them. Communion was closed to everyone present except for the members of that particular congregation. Visitors, even though they were born-again Christians, were not allowed to partake. News that Free Will Baptists practiced open communion was heartily received and accepted by the general populace, and they came to the Free Will Baptist churches in large numbers. The Lord's Supper, or communion, was very important to our Free Will Baptist ancestors. Not only did they practice it often in their churches, they practiced it in the Quarterly Meetings, the Yearly Meetings, and at the General Conference, what would be equivalent to our National Association.[337]

The second distinctive that made Free Will Baptists so attractive to people was the doctrine of general atonement. The dominant view among the various denominations was the Calvinistic view of limited atonement that Jesus died for and provided salvation only for the elect, those supposedly chosen to be saved, before God created the world. The gospel that Jesus died for everyone and that "whosoever will" may come and be saved was readily accepted and received by the people. The gospel that made salvation available to everyone, if they would accept Christ, brought large numbers of converts into the Free Will Baptist churches.

As to whether feet washing was then considered a distinctive, as it is now by some, two things could be said. One is that feet washing was not generally practiced by Free Will Baptists in the Randall movement, even though a few did. The denomination stated repeatedly that feet

---

[335] Pages 15-16, 2010 Yearbook
[336] Accessed April 14, 2014.
[337] *Minutes of the General Conference of the Freewill Baptist Connection*, page 2 ; *Minutes of General Conference of the Freewill Baptist Connection, Volume 2*, page 216. Minutes of the Twentieth General Conference state in the aforementioned book of minutes: "At the close of Conference, on the evening of the eighth day, business was suspended, the moderator vacated the chair, and the table was spread for communion service. Revs. S. Curtis and D. Waterman, two of the most aged ministers, presided at the table, and a very precious season was enjoyed."

washing was not to be an issue.[338] At any rate feet washing was not a belief or practice that found a wide acceptance among the general population and did not motivate people to start coming to Free Will Baptist churches in large numbers, as did open communion and a general atonement. It was not something which attracted people to Free Will Baptists. It could be said that just the opposite was true, that the practice of washing feet was not popular among the general population and was a reason some stayed away from Free Will Baptist churches.

Now, in the Twenty-first Century, other than feet washing, which isn't a big draw, Free Will Baptists have, in a sense, lost the two distinctives which in former years brought large numbers of people into the denomination. It isn't that we gave them up, that we stopped believing in open communion and the general atonement of Christ. It is that so many other denominations have adopted those two positions. Today it is not rare at all to attend churches of many denominations and hear them preach that Jesus died for all men, that whosoever will may come and be saved. That doctrine, though still believed by Free Will Baptists, is no longer a distinctive, not something which distinguishes us from other denominations and attracts people to our churches. People can get that doctrine all over town. Likewise, the doctrine of open communion no longer distinguishes Free Will Baptists and attracts people to us, even though we still practice it. The thing is, so do so many other denominations. This loss of distinctiveness was already being recognized by Free Will Baptists as early as 1871, when the Twenty-First General Conference of Free Will Baptists met at Hillsdale, Michigan. The Committee on Doctrine gave a report, signed by A. K. Moulton, which included this information:

> 4. We would, with gratitude and humility, record the cheering fact that nearly all the religious denominations are rapidly converging toward the doctrinal stand-point which we occupy, by advocating a larger liberty of thought and investigation, consistent with proper church order and discipline; no ecclesiastical hierarchy, no apostolic succession, no unsectarian bigotry, the Church spiritual and universal, unity with diversity, free will, free communion, free salvation, and free men.[339]

In 1877, the year after the first white Free Will Baptist Church was established in Texas, the General Conference again includes a reference to the denominational distinctives in its Report on the State of the Denomination. The report states:

> 9. We think it proper that we kindly but firmly declare loyalty to our distinguishing principles, -- the freedom of the will, full salvation, the immersion of all regenerated and forgiven persons, and freedom to the communion table of all who love our Lord Jesus Christ; that there is yet a demand for the proclamation and propagation of these sentiments, and that, therefore, there is reason abundant for the maintenance of our denominational identity, and the vigorous prosecution of the work our Master has evidently called us to perform.[340]

The above report does not give us the setting of the report, the mood of the delegates, nor what was happening on a larger scale. Free Will Baptists were already of the mind to promote unity with other denominations, believing strongly that the body of Christ should not be divided.

---

[338] This position was made clear as stated in the Free Will Baptist Treatises of 1834, 1839, 1941, 1850, and 1854,
[339] *Minutes of General Conference of the Freewill Baptist Connection, Volume 2*, page 252.
[340] *Minutes of General Conference of the Freewill Baptist Connection, Volume 2*, page 350.

From this attitude came several mergers with other denominations, which mostly consisted of the General Conference of Free Will Baptists absorbing some smaller denominations. Eventually the move toward unity, as they saw it, resulted in the General Conference of Free Will Baptists itself being absorbed by the Northern Baptist Convention, what we now refer to as the merger of 1910-1911. One thing that made many of these mergers possible was, as observed above, so many of the other denominations had accepted what were previously Free Will Baptist distinctives. The Twenty-Fourth General Conference of Free Will Baptists again refers to this subject in 1880:

> We recognize the encouraging fact that our principles, doctrines, and usages are commending themselves to others, and gaining favor wherever known, that what was once "heresy" is now orthodoxy.[341]

Please allow me one more quote, lest I bore you too long, but this is important. At the Twenty-Fifth General Conference of Free Will Baptists, held in 1883, in Minneapolis, Minnesota, the report on Doctrine included this observation:

> We rejoice to know that our people are still a unit in doctrinal belief, being sound and Scriptural.
> We take pleasure in noting the fact that the drift of the Christian world is towards our position, as held substantially the same for a hundred years.
> We recommend that our ministers give due prominence to our distinctive doctrines, in their pulpits, as "the faith once delivered to the saints."[342]

Before moving on, let me add that there is one distinctive which we must continue to preach. I refer to the doctrine of the possibility of apostasy, the possibility that a true believer in Christ can, through any number of contributing factors, come to completely deny his faith in Christ and be lost. There are a few small denominations which also preach this doctrine, but we believe it to be the truth and we believe this doctrine should be taught. This is our one great distinctive today, the one thing which separates us and distinguishes us from most other denominations. It is not a popular doctrine and it does not necessarily attract people to our churches, but it needs to be preached because it is the truth.

Free Will Baptist churches can be built in Texas. The past twenty-five years have clearly shown this to be true. There are several examples, such as the Lakehills Free Will Baptist Church in the Austin suburb of Cedar Park, started by Keith Woody; the Eagle Heights Free Will Baptist Church in the Houston suburb of Richmond, started by Randy Puckett; the Collin Creek Free Will Baptist Church in Plano, started by the late Don Guthrie and now pastored by Robert Posner; and the Canyon Country Free Will Baptist Church in Canyon, Texas, pastored by Jeff Cates. Randall Wright is leading in starting the Clearview Free Will Baptist Mission in McKinney and Freddy Gillentine leads the effort in Abilene at the Heritage Parks Free Will Baptist Church. Most of the efforts to start new churches are centered in the Central Texas District: Jeremy Lightsey is leading the CrossLife Free Will Baptist Mission in San Antonio, David Holguin is the pastor of the Magnolia Free Will Baptist Church, Don Bailey leads the North Oaks Free Will Baptist Mission in San Antonio, Heath Ferguson leads the Woodforest Free Will Baptist Mission in Woodforest, and Dr. Eugene Richards pastors the Wildwood Free Will Baptist Church in Porter, Texas. Though there have been some failures, new Free Will Baptist churches can be started in Texas and this

---

[341] *Minutes of General Conference of the Freewill Baptist Connection, Volume 2,* page 404.
[342] *Minutes of General Conference of the Freewill Baptist Connection, Volume 2,* page 458..

great mission field should be prayerfully considered by committed men looking for a place to start new churches.

A Recommendation to Pastors

One very simple recommendation I would like to pass along to all of the Free Will Baptist pastors of Texas: make it your regular practice to attend the quarterly meetings of your district association and the annual session of the Texas State Association. Consider it your duty, part of your job description. We all realize that there is a move away from denominationalism. One feature of this trend is that increasing numbers of churches of all denominations are becoming more and more independent, having little connection to other churches of like faith. They prefer to stand alone as isolated islands in their communities. The pastor's only concern becomes his local church. However, there is much to be said for being an active part of the Free Will Baptist denomination and I have commented on that earlier in this book. Here, let me list ten reasons why all pastors should be actively involved in both the quarterly meetings of their district associations and the annual meetings **of the** Texas State Association:

1. It develops responsibility.
2. It fosters brotherhood.
3. It promotes enthusiasm.
4. It inspires dedication.
5. It enriches total spiritual growth.
6. It strengthens accountability.
7. It establishes and maintains denominational identity.
8. It enables cooperative effort.
9. It provides opportunities to serve beyond your local community.
10. It spreads much needed fellowship and encouragement among the pastors and churches.

One big lesson every pastor needs to learn: we are not just members of a local congregation, we are members of the Church, the worldwide body of Christ. We are part of something much greater than ourselves, greater than our local congregation. We have been gifted to minister in the Great Commission. Standing alone and independent, with concern only for our local parish is not the biblical model. The biblical model has us meeting together and working together to accomplish common goals.

ADDENDUM 1

Closed Churches

It has not been possible to name all of the Free Will Baptist churches in Texas which have closed. The churches listed here are the ones which have been gleaned from various minutes, *The Morning Star*, *The New Morning Star*, minutes of the old Southwestern Freewill Baptist Convention, etc. We have not, therefore, been able to get an accurate count of the number of churches which have closed. Please forgive any duplications and/or omissions from the list.

It should be noted that some of the churches listed were small churches which never really got off the ground, so to speak. On the other hand some of them were leading churches in the state, such as the First Free Will Baptist Church of Denison, the Trinity Free Will Baptist Church of Fort Worth, and the influential and historic First Free Will Baptist Church in Bryan. We should be vigilant because any Free Will Baptist church in Texas is subject to closure, given the rights set of circumstances.

There are reasons why these churches closed and their gospel proclamation was silenced. The reasons are many, as what killed one church was not necessarily the cause of the death of another church. There is usually some shame associated with the death of a church. However, we should realize that any Free Will Baptist minister who has served for very long in Texas has pastored a Free Will Baptist church which closed.

This is perhaps the saddest chapter in this book, but we should take some time to look the list over carefully and give some thought to what can be done to prevent the death of our own churches.

Denton Creek Association

Bethel Free Will Baptist Church
Big Spring Free Will Baptist Church
Corinth Free Will Baptist Church
DeSoto Free Will Baptist Church

Central Texas

Bayshore Free Will Baptist Church, Grand Avenue, Bacliff
Blue Lake Free Will Baptist Church, Piedmont
Calvary Free Will Baptist Church, 815 Count Street, Houston
Calvary Free Will Baptist Church, Lake Charles, Louisiana[343]
Cedros Del Libano Free Will Baptist Church, 1220 Beck, Bryan

---

[343] This church in Louisiana was started by Malcolm Fry, who worked for many years with the Church Training Service Department and the Sunday School Department of the National Association of Free Will Baptists. One of the early pastors was a young Dale Burden, son-in-law of Asa and H. Ray Berry. This information is from Ned Graham.

Christian Home Free Will Baptist Church, Kurtin
Concord, Brazos County
Conroe Free Will Baptist Church, S. 7th Street, Conroe
Cornerstone Free Will Baptist Church, College Station
Cross Free Will Baptist Church, also known as the Spring Hill Free Will Baptist Church, Grimes County. This church hasn't closed but it became a Baptist church
Free Will Baptist Church, 2232 Strawberry, Pasadena
First Free Will Baptist Church, 405 Eberhart Lane, Austin
First Free Will Baptist Church, Bryan
First Free Will Baptist Church, Huntsville
First Free Will Baptist Church, Pasadena
Friendship, Madison County
High Prairie, Madison County
Hollis Free Will Baptist Church, Normangee
Hopewell Free Will Baptist Church
Independence Free Will Baptist Church, RFD 6, Bryan
Liberty Free Will Baptist Church, Edge
Lighthouse Free Will Baptist Church, Temple
Living Hope Free Will Baptist Mission, Missouri City (listed in the 2004 directory)
Macy Free Will Baptist Church, Macy, Texas
New Hope Free Will Baptist Church, 701 Avenue M #1, Huntsville
Northpointe Free Will Baptist Church, The Woodlands
Northwest Free Will Baptist Church, Houston
Plainview Free Will Baptist Church, George
Pine Grove, Falba (pastored by H. M. McAdams in 1943), 1943 Central TX minutes
Reform Free Will Baptist Church, Grimes County
Richard Free Will Baptist Church
Trinity Free Will Baptist Church, Arcadia
Union Hill Free Will Baptist Church, College Station
Wellborn Free Will Baptist Church (merged with the First FWB Church, Bryan)
Westfield Free Will Baptist Church, Katy (left the denomination)
Willow Hole Free Will Baptist Church, Zulch
Zion Free Will Baptist Church, George, Madison County

Central Brazos Association

Alvarado
Eldorado
Fall Creek
Ft. Spunkey
Ham
Mt. View
Oak Grove
Odom Chapel
Post Oak
Union Grove

Midessa District

    Bible Free Will Baptist Church, 4700 Bryan Road, Odessa
    Faith Free Will Baptist Church, 409 SE Avenue C, Andrews
    First Free Will Baptist Church, Abilene
    First Free Will Baptist Church, Lubbock
    First Free Will Baptist Church, San Angelo
    First Free Will Baptist Church, 504 NW Avenue F, Seminole
    Lubbock Free Will Baptist Church, Lubbock
    First Free Will Baptist Church, 7th and Vine, Odessa
    First Free Will Baptist Church, Midland
    Fellowship Free Will Baptist Church, Midland
    Forest Park Free Will Baptist Church, San Angelo
    Free Will Baptist Mission, Big Spring
    Landmark Free Will Baptist Church, 5210 N. Dixie, Odessa
    Seventh Street Free Will Baptist Church, Abilene
    Monahans Free Will Baptist Church, Monahans
    Truth Free Will Baptist Church, Levelland
    Westside Free Will Baptist Church, 4031 W. Illinois, Midland

Mission District

    Christ's Free Will Baptist Church, 3126 Gollihar Road, Corpus Christi
    Faith Free Will Baptist Church, 704 W. Gerald Street, San Antonio
    Northcrest Free Will Baptist Church, 502 Rhodes Road, Victoria
    Zion Free Will Baptist Church, 1126 Stone Street, Flour Bluff

Northwest Brazos

    First Free Will Baptist Church, 900 N. Johnson, Amarillo
    First and Oakdale merged to form Oakdale First Free Will Baptist Church, now closed, 2501 S. Vernon, Amarillo
    First Free Will Baptist Church, Avenue D, Crowell
    First Free Will Baptist Church, Lamesa
    First Free Will Baptist Church, Memphis
    First Free Will Baptist Church, 800 Mansard, Vernon
    Free Will Baptist Church, Seagraves
    Free Will Baptist Church, Wink
    Friendship Free Will Baptist Church, Benjamin
    Goodcreek Free Will Baptist Church
    North Amarillo Free Will Baptist Church, 2502 N. Mirror Street, Amarillo
    Salt Creek Free Will Baptist Church, Cottle County
    Second Free Will Baptist Church, Amarillo

Rio Grande Valley

    First Free Will Baptist Church, 3801 N. Second Street, McAllen. This church didn't close, it left the denomination and became the McAllen Community Church.

Southeast Texas

    Bonami Free Will Baptist Church, Bonami
    Cairo Springs Free Will Baptist Church
    China Grove Free Will Baptist Church
    Friendship Free Will Baptist Church

Northeast Texas Association See the 1918 *New Morning Star*

    Friendship
    Union Hill
    Pleasant Grove
    Cedar Grove

West Fork

    Bedford Free Will Baptist Church, Bedford[344]
    Bethel Free Will Baptist Church, Coppell[345]
    Bethel Free Will Baptist Church, 4225 Avenue G, Fort Worth
    Bluff Spring, Azle, Parker County, joined the West Fork in 1901
    Bonnie View Free Will Baptist Church, 3351 Springview, Dallas
    Canaan (1979 & 1980 state minutes)
    Canton (1979 state minutes)
    Catlett Creek, 10 miles east of Decatur, Wise County, Texas. Organized July 7, 1901
    Chapel Hill Free Will Baptist Church, Brownwood (FM 45 & Country Club Road)
    Community Free Will Baptist Church, NE 33 and N. Hampton, Fort Worth (Org. 1952)
    Concord Free Will Baptist Church, 829 W. Danieldale Road, Dallas
    Faith Free Will Baptist Church, 3301 Townsend Drive, Fort Worth
        (The 45th annual session met there)
    First Free Will Baptist Church, 421 Truman Street, Arlington
    First Free Will Baptist Church, Azle
    First Free Will Baptist Church, 208 E. Oak, Comanche
    First Free Will Baptist Church, Field City, Dallas, (admitted 1934)
    First Free Will Baptist Church, 416 W. Hull, Denison, relocated and renamed
        Cornerstone
    Free Will Baptist Church, relocated again, then closed
    First Free Will Baptist Church, Fort Worth
    First Free Will Baptist Church, 1917 Rice Avenue, 937 Rice (1970) Gainsville
    First Free Will Baptist Church, 822 SW 3rd, Grand Prairie

---

[344] Mentioned in the *New Morning Star*, May 1, 1915.
[345] Minutes of the 1914 session of the Southwestern Convention of Freewill Baptists, page 32.

First Free Will Baptist Church, Grapevine
First Free Will Baptist Church, 3304 Herring, Irving
First Free Will Baptist Church, Jacksboro, organized May 25, 1957, admitted 1958
First Free Will Baptist Church, Lewisville
First Free Will Baptist Church, 1510 Pioneer Road, Mesquite
First Free Will Baptist Church, Oak Cliff (admitted 1934)
First Free Will Baptist Church, 13th at Houston, Paris
First Free Will Baptist Church, 1901 S. 12th Street, Waco
First Free Will Baptist Church 3615 Arthur, Wichita Falls
Free Will Baptist Mission, Arlington
Free Will Baptist Church, Boyd
Free Will Baptist Church, Mineral Wells (may not have been in the West Fork)
Free Will Baptist Church, Richardson
Free Will Baptist Mission, Sherman
Garland Free Will Baptist Church, 2317 W. Kingsley, Garland
Glendale Free Will Baptist Church, Sunset, Montague County
Grace Free Will Baptist Church, Weatherford (admitted 1934)
Grace Free Will Baptist Church, 7800 Corina Drive, White Settlement
Liberty Free Will Baptist Church, 504 E. College, Comanche
Liberty Free Will Baptist Church, Dott
Love Temple Free Will Baptist Church, Fort Worth
Macedonia, Booneville, Wise County
Mount Olive, two miles west of Willow Point, Jack County
New Hope Free Will Baptist Church, Fort Worth
New Hope Free Will Baptist Church, Parker County, Joined the West Fork in 1901
Philadelphia Free Will Baptist Church, 1408 Lexington, Weatherford
Raynelle Free Will Baptist Church, 608 Raynelle, Dallas
Rock Hill, Reno, Parker County
Rock of Ages Free Will Baptist Church, 7413 Calmont, Fort Worth, renamed
    Western Hills Free Will Baptist Church, relocated and renamed City View
    Fellowship, then closed
Salt Springs Free Will Baptist Church, seven miles east of Comanche
Southside Free Will Baptist Church, Comanche
SouthPointe Church, Arlington
Springtown Free Will Baptist Church (?)
Trinity Free Will Baptist Church, 2320 Azle Avenue, Fort Worth (admitted 1934)
    Later at 3715 Flory Street
Union Chapel[346]
Union Grove, Briar, Parker County
Unity Free Will Baptist Church (same as Silver Creek?),[347] Weatherford, admitted 1934
Walnut Creek, Reno, Parker County (May have been the same as Rock Hill)
Westside Free Will Baptist Church, Irving 1962 minutes
Westside Free Will Baptist Mission, Weatherford

---

[346] A 1924 edition of the *New Morning Star* announced that the West Fork Association would meet with the Union Chapel Church, 16 miles northwest of Fort Worth on the fourth Sunday of October, 1924.
[347] Listed as being located in Azle by the 1935 West Fork minutes.

The Southwestern Freewill Baptist Convention operated a Free Will Baptist Mission, a rescue mission, at 1123 North Main Street, Fort Worth. It was directed by G. C. and Annie Morris.[348]

West Texas Association, the old one

>   Liberty Hill
>   Salt Springs, Comanche

West Texas District Association (the new one)

>   Crossroads Free Will Baptist Church, Lubbock

Other Churches in West Texas

>   Faith Fellowship Free Will Baptist Church, 10369 Preston, El Paso
>   First Free Will Baptist Church, 5606 Threadgill Avenue, El Paso
>   First Free Will Baptist Church, Scurry County
>   Free Will Baptist Church, Monahans
>   Grace Free Will Baptist Church, El Paso

East Texas

>   Alto Free Will Baptist Mission, Alto
>   Bethel Free Will Baptist Church, Rusk County (listed in the FWB Register, 1880)
>   Broome Chapel Free Will Baptist Church
>   Campbell Hill Free Will Baptist Church, Rusk County
>   Center Point Church, Beckville
>   Chalk Hill Free Will Baptist Church, Chalk Hill Community, near Tatum
>   Center Point Free Will Baptist Church, four miles east of Tatum
>   Christian Chapel
>   Christian Form Free Will Baptist Church (accepted in 1940)
>   Cross Road Free Will Baptist Church, Harrison County (listed in the FWB Register, 1880)
>   Crystal Farms Free Will Baptist Church, admitted October, 1914
>   Darco Church, Harrison County
>   Dirgin Free Will Baptist Church
>   Dunn's Chapel
>   Fellowship Free Will Baptist Church, out of Henderson
>   First Free Will Baptist Church, Canton
>   First Free Will Baptist Church, Kilgore
>   First Free Will Baptist Church, Nacogdoches
>   Friendship Free Will Baptist Church, Panola County, two miles north of Clayton

---

[348] Minutes of the fourteenth annual session of the Southwestern Convention of Freewill Baptists, 1914, page 13.

Harper's Union Free Will Baptist Church, eight miles south of Henderson. Was this the Harper's Grove Church mentioned in the 1913, 1914, and 1955 minutes?
Isabel's Chapel, Rusk County
Liberty Free Will Baptist Church, Clayton, first white Free Will Baptist church in Texas
Lone Star Free Will Baptist Church, Cherokee County
Longview Free Will Baptist Mission, Longview
New Prospect, Cherokee County
Old Time Gospel Free Will Baptist Church, Texarkana (3402 Ash Street)
Rape's Chapel Free Will Baptist Church
Rose Hill Free Will Baptist Church
Russell Road Free Will Baptist Church, Whitehouse
Sharron, Rusk County
Tatum Free Will Baptist Church, Panola County
Troup Free Will Baptist Church, Smith County
Turner's Chapel
Union Springs Free Will Baptist Church, Rusk County
Union Chapel Free Will Baptist Church (became Union Arbor and still exists)
Venice Church[349]

Woodlawn Association of Free Will Baptists

Eliga Free Will Baptist Church, Eliga, Texas
Liberty Free Will Baptist Church, Dott (also listed in the West Fork)
Long Branch Free Will Baptist Church, Eddy
Long Prairie Free Will Baptist Church, Long Prairie, Texas
Woodlawn Free Will Baptist Church, Bruceville, Texas

Miscellaneous Churches

Cottle Hill Free Will Baptist Church[350]
Free Will Baptist Church, Bradley, Texas[351]
Free Will Baptist Church, Mineola, Texas[352]
Free Will Baptist Church, Tama, Texas[353]
Lake City Free Will Baptist Church[354]
Levelland Free Will Baptist Church, several small churches over the years
Mineral Wells Free Will Baptist Church[355]

---

[349] 1930 and 1932 Minutes of the Texas Association
[350] Minutes of the 1914 session of the Southwestern Convention, page 10. There doesn't seem to be a Cottle Hill, Texas, but there is a Cottle County which had several Free Will Baptist churches. The county seat is Paducah.
[351] The meeting place of the first annual session of the Texas State Association of Free Will Baptists in 1915.
[352] Mineola, Texas, is a city in Wood County. It lies at the junction of U.S. highways 69 and 80, eighty miles east of Dallas in southwestern Wood County in East Texas.
[353] Tama, Texas, was fifteen miles south of Gatesville in south central Coryell County.
[354] Minutes of the 1914 session of the Southwestern Convention, page 8. There is a Lake City in San Patricio County, inland from Corpus Christi, which may or may not be the Lake City where this church was located.
[355] Mentioned in the 1914 minutes of the Southwestern Freewill Baptist Convention, page 23.

New Harmony Free Will Baptist Church[356]
North Prairie Free Will Baptist Church[357]
Rose Wood Free Will Baptist Church[358]
Seymour Free Will Baptist Church[359]
Calvary Free Will Baptist Church, Vernon (not in the Northwest Brazos)

---

[356] Mentioned in the 1914 minutes of the Southwestern Freewill Baptist Convention, page 13.
[357] Mentioned in the 1914 minutes of the Southwestern Freewill Baptist Convention, page 13.
[358] Mentioned on page 14 of the 1952 minutes.
[359] Mentioned in the 1914 minutes of the Southwestern Freewill Baptist Convention, page 23.

ADDENDUM 2

Denominational Distinctives

Each denomination has a belief or set of beliefs that distinguish them from other denominations. That's why there are denominations and why there is a Free Will Baptist denomination. Free Will Baptists came into existence because of certain doctrinal positions that distinguished them from denominations which were already present in the American colonies in the 1700's. They also distinguish us from denominations which have arisen since. We list here the doctrines, beliefs, and practices which are commonly listed as Free Will Baptist distinctives. It is recognized, however, that since the early days of Free Will Baptists other groups have adopted some of the beliefs and practices of Free Will Baptists. Free Will Baptist usually list six distinctives, which are:

1. Free Will Baptists got their name because they believed in the freedom of the will. This was a big issue in the 1700's when Calvinism was dominant in the American colonies and the early United States. Free Will Baptists rejected the Calvinistic view that God had unconditionally chosen who would be saved and go to heaven, leaving all others to reprobation. We believed that each individual was free to choose to accept or reject Christ's offer of salvation, an offer extended to all people, something that a great many denominations have come to believe today.

2. Free Will Baptists believe in the universal atonement of Christ. By this we mean that Christ died for all, electing to save everyone who repents of sin and trusts Christ and His atoning death on the cross for salvation. This distinguishes us from those who believe that the benefits of Christ's death were limited to those whom God had preselected, before he ever made the world, to be saved. The message "whosoever will may come" found a ready acceptance among the people of the 1700's when most denominations were preaching a limited atonement and was one of the primary reasons for the rapid early growth of Free Will Baptists.

3. Free Will Baptists accept baptism by other evangelical denominations, if such baptism is by immersion and administered in the name of the Trinity.

4. Free Will Baptists believe in open communion. When we observe the Lord's Supper we invite all Christian believers present to participate with us, including those not members of our church or denomination. This distinguishes us from those who practice close communion, that is, those who limit the observance of the Lord's Supper to members of that particular church when communion is observed.

5. Some Free Will Baptists practice a third ordinance in addition to baptism and the Lord's Supper, feet washing. There has always been a question among Free Will Baptists about whether Jesus meant for us to literally wash each other's feet. The long held Free Will Baptist heritage and

position on this point is that it is up to the individual person and each local church as to whether they will practice it or not, a position taken at the first general conference in 1831 and maintained ever since.

6   The most significant and most important distinctive now is that Free Will Baptists believe it is possible, though not probable, that a genuine Christian believer can make shipwreck of his faith and be lost. This distinguishes us from those who believe in Calvinism's perseverance of the saints in holiness, a modified version of which is now called eternal security or "once saved, always saved."

ADDENDUM 3

Free Baptists, Freewill Baptists, or Free Will Baptists?

Written by William F. Davidson at the request of clerk Thurmon Murphy for
inclusion in the Digest of Reports of the 1988 Texas State Association of Free Will Baptists

The Free Will Baptist denomination enjoys a long and memorable heritage that can be traced back to England through the old General Baptists, to Kentucky and other states through the Separate Baptists, and to New England through the Congregationalists. With such a varied background, it is not unusual that the name of the denomination has experienced a number of revisions and changes during a history that spans more than 375 years.

Three 17th Century documents indicate that the General Baptists in England were known as "Free-Willers" and "Free-Will Anabaptists as early as 1612.

In America, the name did not gain popular acceptance until the late 19th Century. Benjamin Randall, a Congregationalist, adopted believer's baptism as opposed to his denomination's doctrine of infant baptism and soon found himself unwelcome among his own people. On June 30, 1780, Randall founded a new church and a new denomination. The new church at New Durham, New Hampshire, holds the distinction of being the first Freewill Baptist church in New England. For the first number of years, the church bore many names --- Church of Christ, General Provisioners, Free Willers. The name "Freewill Baptist" first appeared as an official title in the minutes in 1799 and, in 1804, the state of New Hampshire made the name legal by legislative act.[360]

In Tennessee, the present day Free Will Baptists must be traced back to the old Separate Baptists of Kentucky. By 1825, some of the Tennessee segment of Separates had begun to use the name. After that time, the two titles must have been used interchangeably. When the Cumberland Association was formally organized in 1842/43, only the older name was used, but by 1854, both names appeared in the minutes of the conference and its churches.

In North Carolina, by the end of the 18th Century, the General Baptists also were known as "Free-Willers". Tradition suggests that the new name was given in derision by opponents who rejected this group's preaching of a general atonement. In any case, by 1803, they were referred to as "Free-will Baptists" by their enemies. When the group published its first minutes in 1829, they retained the hyphen, but capitalized the first letter of the second word and the new name was now "Free-Will Baptist". Finally, when the first official history was written in 1833, R. K. Hearn dropped the hyphen and "Free Will Baptist" became popular.[361]

In light of the varied backgrounds from which the denomination came, it becomes quite impossible to determine precisely why some segments of the contemporary denomination are known as "Freewill Baptists" while the larger majority prefer "Free Will Baptist". It could be assumed, however, that each segment continues to be influenced by its own heritage. Most of the

---

[360] William F. Davidson, *The Free Will Baptists in America: 1717-1984*, (Nashville: Randall House Publishing Co., 1985), pp. 165-183. Used by permission.
[361] Davidson, *The Free Will Baptists*, p. 198.

churches in the West, including Texas, are directly related to the New England Freewill Baptists and it is not unusual that some churches use the New England spelling. The old Cooperative General Association, founded in 1917, and including churches from the western states (New England heritage), used the Freewill title in their official documents.

On the other hand, in the East, both the old Triennial General Conference and the General Conference adopted the North Carolina spelling, Free Will Baptist. The use of both names in Texas could be explained by the New England heritage mentioned earlier and by the fact that some churches in the state joined the General Conference in the East sometime after 1931. The Eastern General Conference met in Bryan in 1932, and the Texas State Association was included in the minutes of the group in later years.

At last, in 1935, all of the churches and conferences of like persuasion came together in the new National Association of Free Will Baptists. The first constitution reveals that this name [Free Will Baptist] was adopted officially by the new denomination.[362]

---

[362] *Minutes of the First Session of the National Association of the Original Free Will Baptists of the United States*, p. 3

ADDENDUM 4

The Free Will Baptist Logo

Since so many people have enquired about the symbolism of the Free Will Baptist logo, the following explanation is included for your information. The emblem incorporates both historic and contemporary Christian designs to convey the central doctrines and practices of our thriving evangelical faith.

First, the entire symbol incorporates four visual symbols used by the earliest communities in Christendom: the *ship*, the *fish*, the *anchor*, and the *cross*.

These four symbols have been discovered frequently in the catacombs and other Christian ruins.

The *ship* has always been recognized as a symbol of the Church, representing all the members pulling together in one direction, guided and empowered by Christ and the Holy Spirit.

The *fish* represented in the symbol by the space between the bottom of the sail and the top of the ship's body, is one of the most popular symbols for Jesus Christ. It is widely believed to have been a secret symbol used for identification by Christians living during periods of persecution. The word "fish" (*ichthus*) in first century Greek is an acrostic for Jesus Christ, Son of God, Savior. In modern times the fishhook has also come to symbolize witnessing and evangelism.

The *anchor* on the bow of the ship was an early symbol for the Christian hope of salvation, "the sure and stedfast anchor of the soul." Of course, the mast of the ship in the symbol forms the most familiar symbol in the history of the world, the *cross* -- an instrument of execution and death turned into a worldwide emblem of hope and love by the death and resurrection of Jesus Christ. Because of their similarity, the *anchor* and the *cross* were often combined in early Christian art.

In the four corners of the ship's sail, the symbols of earliest Christianity are enhanced by modern emblems of a vital, living faith --- the *Holy Bible*, the *loaf and cup*, the *basin and towel*, and the *clasped hands* --- the symbols of Free Will Baptists.

The *Holy Bible* has always been at the heart of our life as Free Will Baptists, and no emblem for us could be without some representation of the centrality of Scripture. The *cup and loaf* represent the Lord's Supper and the importance of this ordinance to our faith. The *basin and towel* is an historic symbol of the service and outreach of the church, but for many Free Will Baptists it has the added significance of representing the practice of feet washing. Finally, the *clasped hands* have many meanings for us. They stand for fellowship, brotherhood, the warmth of our faith, and the necessity of prayer. But most importantly they stand for our zeal for evangelism, our commitment to reach out to persons around the world with the saving message of God's action in Jesus Christ.

From page 3 of the 1988 state minutes,
Adapted from the explanation of the logo by
The Executive Office of the National Association of Free Will Baptists

www.ingramcontent.com/pod-product-compliance
Lightning Source LLC
Chambersburg PA
CBHW080453110426
42742CB00017B/2876